Data Access, Consumer Interests and Public Welfare

Edited by
German Federal Ministry of Justice and Consumer Protection
Max Planck Institute for Innovation and Competition
(Bundesministerium der Justiz und für Verbraucherschutz
Max-Planck-Institut für Innovation und Wettbewerb)

Nomos

The publication of the printed version and the Open Access-publication of the electronic version of this work were supported by the German Federal Ministry of Justice and Consumer Protection.

The Deutsche Nationalbibliothek lists this publication in the Deutsche Nationalbibliografie; detailed bibliographic data are available on the Internet at http://dnb.d-nb.de

ISBN 978-3-8487-8081-5 (Print)
978-3-7489-2499-9 (ePDF)

British Library Cataloguing-in-Publication Data
A catalogue record for this book is available from the British Library.

ISBN 978-3-8487-8081-5 (Print)
978-3-7489-2499-9 (ePDF)

Library of Congress Cataloging-in-Publication Data
German Federal Ministry of Justice and Consumer Protection | Max Planck Institute for Innovation and Competition
Data Access, Consumer Interests and Public Welfare
German Federal Ministry of Justice and Consumer Protection | Max Planck Institute for Innovation and Competition (eds.)
574 pp.
Includes bibliographic references.

ISBN 978-3-8487-8081-5 (Print)
978-3-7489-2499-9 (ePDF)

1st Edition 2021

Published by
Nomos Verlagsgesellschaft mbH & Co. KG
Waldseestraße 3–5 | 76530 Baden-Baden
www.nomos.de

Production of the printed version:
Nomos Verlagsgesellschaft mbH & Co. KG
Waldseestraße 3–5 | 76530 Baden-Baden

ISBN 978-3-8487-8081-5 (Print)
ISBN 978-3-7489-2499-9 (ePDF)
DOI https://doi.org/10.5771/9783748924999

Onlineversion
Nomos eLibrary

Foreword

Consumers play a key role in the digital economy. They increasingly shop on the Internet. They use multiple digital services offered 'for free' and simultaneously grant access to their personal data to the providers of these services. Consumers increasingly use other connected ('smart') devices that collect and further process data in IoT (Internet of Things) environments.

Thus, the focus of the consumer law debate is shifting to the digital economy and data protection issues. Yet this book does not just add another contribution to the debate. It seeks to push the discussion and the reform process further by addressing the need for and the design of new data access rules both in the interests of consumers and as legal regimes that can promote multiple other public interest objectives.

Thereby, this book builds on the discussions at the 2019 Consumer Law Conference (*Verbraucherrechtstage*) of the German Federal Ministry of Justice and Consumer Protection, which were held in Berlin on 12–13 December 2019 in cooperation with the Max Planck Institute for Innovation and Competition in Munich. This Institute, with its Director Josef Drexl, was chosen to prepare the scientific concept of the conference under the title '*Datenzugang, Verbraucherinteressen und Gemeinwohl*' and to prepare the publication of the proceedings. A report in German language documents the oral presentations and the discussions of the conference. This report is freely accessible on the Internet.[1] To enhance the discussion on the European level, the Ministry decided to support a publication in English and to make this publication publicly available in an open access format.

Both the Ministry and the Max Planck Institute, as the official editors of this book, are enormously grateful to the authors of the contributions for further developing their ideas, taking into account the discussions at the conference, and for agreeing to this English-language publication. The individual chapters take into account the legal development until the summer of 2020. Thus, in principle, the most recent proposals of the European

1 Jure Globocnik and Stefan Scheuerer, 'Datenzugang, Verbraucherinteressen und Gemeinwohl – Bericht über die Verbraucherrechtstage 2019 des Bundesministeriums der Justiz und für Verbraucherschutz in Berlin, 12. und 13. Dezember 2019' (2020) 11 Journal of Intellectual Property, Information Technology and E-Commerce Law 228, <www.jipitec.eu/issues/jipitec-11-2-2020/5100/tagungsbericht_pd.pdf> accessed 31 August 2020.

Commission of November and December 2020 on a Data Governance Act, a Digital Services Act and a Digital Markets Act are not covered.

The editors would also like to thank Allison Felmy and Delia Zirilli from the Max Planck Institute who worked on the language editing and the preparation of the manuscript. Equally, the editors want to express their gratitude to Nomos for acting as the publisher of this book and for supporting an open access publication.

Berlin and Munich, 30 September 2020

Federal Ministry of Justice and Consumer Protection

Max Planck Institute for Innovation and Competition

Special Address of the Federal Minister of Justice and Consumer Protection

Christine Lambrecht

The topic of the 2019 Consumer Law Conference – 'Data access, consumer interests and public welfare' – is a topic that is both current and forward-looking at the same time. One could spend a long time debating which image best illustrates the current significance of data. Is data the new 'oil', the new 'raw material', the new 'currency' or, as it has recently been called, the new 'groundwater'? Whatever the answer, one thing is clear: In our digital world, data play a crucial role – for the state, academia, business, and for all citizens. If used wisely, data has great potential to benefit the public good. For example, it can be used for innovative methods of diagnosis for types of cancer that are difficult to identify, for intelligent traffic management systems in congested city centres, or for search engines that help us to navigate the vast amounts of information available on the Internet.

In order for data to be used for the public good, they must be available in a sufficient quantity and in a suitable quality. This means that rules are needed to ensure that the various stakeholders – whether civil society, research institutions, businesses or the state – have adequate access to data. Allowing 'data ownership' or creating exclusivity rights to data would not be the right approach.

When creating adequate access to data, it is essential that the focus is on people and on the public good. The needs of consumers are of major importance. This broadening of perspective was one of the main goals of the 2019 Consumer Law Conference. But of course, economic interests must also be taken into account. One important example is the need to protect business and trade secrets. By improving access to data, we must not remove the incentive for companies to develop data-based innovations. This applies especially to artificial intelligence.

Privacy protection is of paramount importance to consumers. Personal data can reveal our innermost being, externalising that which we want to keep private. We must not let our personality fall victim to a culture of exploitation. Companies cannot be allowed to boundlessly use or exploit our personality for commercial purposes. We must be able to decide for ourselves what happens to our personal data. This is guaranteed by our constitution, and it is implemented throughout Europe by the General Data Protection Regulation, which contains extensive safeguards.

We must ensure that, for consumers, the right to privacy protection exists not only on paper. Consumers must be able to maintain real control over their data. They must have the power to decide which data are shared and with whom. And they must have the power to decide what happens to the shared data – and for how long. Data trust models, such as those recently proposed by the German Data Ethics Commission, could be a way to help consumers protect their interests and rights.

We need to make sure that the handling of data is more strongly geared towards the public good. Those who have large amounts of data at their disposal, and are in a position to statistically analyse this data with increasing precision, have considerable social power in our digital world. It is the task of the legal system to limit this power for the common good.

Quite understandably, those who help generate data also want to be able to use this data themselves. Consumers who collect data on their health via fitness apps want to be able to give this data to their doctors. Machine manufacturers require access to operational data so that they can make technical improvements to their machines. Start-ups and innovative companies are often also interested in data. And, last but not least, civil society actors and government institutions need data in order to promote the common good and to serve public purposes.

Our task is to find a suitable and fair way of balancing the various interests of these stakeholders – and to do so beyond the relatively narrow field of competition law. It is only fair that the stakeholders who have helped generate data should be able to participate in the use of this data. We must therefore also consider creating an obligation to share data where necessary.

Many of the questions surrounding the topic of data access will not have a single, uniform answer. Instead, specific solutions will need to be found for the various social and economic sectors. However, introducing a 'general part' (*Allgemeiner Teil*) into data access law could also be worth discussing. This could provide an overarching regulation for the fundamental issues, including, for example the way in which data is accessed or how its access is remunerated.

Professor Josef Drexl, Director of the Max Planck Institute for Innovation and Competition in Munich, kindly took on the preparation of the scientific concept of the 2019 Consumer Law Conference, and also provided his professional expertise for the production of the conference proceedings. I would like to sincerely thank him and his team for their work. The 2019 Consumer Law Conference provides important impetus for further discussion – in Germany as well as in Europe.

Contents

Data access as a means to promote consumer interests and public welfare – An introduction 11
Josef Drexl

On the need for additional access rights

Enhancing access to and sharing of data: Striking the balance between openness and control over data 27
Christian Reimsbach-Kounatze

Data access, consumer interests and social welfare – An economic perspective on data 69
Bertin Martens

A legal framework for access to data – A competition policy perspective 103
Heike Schweitzer and Robert Welker

The larger legal framework

The constitutional framework for data access rights 157
Thomas Fetzer

The legal framework for access to data from a data protection viewpoint – especially under the GDPR 175
Indra Spiecker genannt Döhmann

The existing European IP rights system and the data economy – An overview with particular focus on data access and portability 209
Matthias Leistner

Taking stock of existing data access regimes

Data access rules: The role of contractual unfairness control of (consumer) contracts 255
Michael Grünberger

Access to and porting of data under contract law: Consumer protection rules and market-based principles 287
Axel Metzger

Data portability under the GDPR: A blueprint for access rights? 319
Ruth Janal

Safeguarding innovation in the framework of sector-specific data access regimes: The case of digital payment services 343
Jörg Hoffmann

Data access rights – A comparative perspective 401
Louisa Specht-Riemenschneider

Paving the way for future reforms

From (horizontal and sectoral) data access solutions towards data governance systems 441
Wolfgang Kerber

Connected devices – An unfair competition law approach to data access rights of users 477
Josef Drexl

The law and policy of government access to private sector data ('B2G data sharing') 529
Heiko Richter

Contributors 573

Data access as a means to promote consumer interests and public welfare – An introduction

Josef Drexl

A. *Introduction*

Digital technologies transform the economy and society. They are the basis of new products and services. Digital technologies are developed by using data, such as for the training of artificial intelligence systems, and their application generates myriads of new data. Making best use of these technologies and the data they generate, in full compliance with the fundamental values of our diverse and democratic society, is key for economic, social and public welfare.

To achieve this goal, policy makers have to identify and develop the appropriate legal framework for the digital economy. There is growing consensus that promoting data access will have to play a central role in this regard.[1] Yet what the overall legal framework should be and how to implement data access regimes in different fields of the law have so far remained rather unexplored.

The following contributions to this book seek to fill this gap. The book in its entirety aims at clarifying how data access rules can promote consumer interests and public welfare. From the perspective of legal research and policy, this is rather uncharted land. Current law only sporadically provides for data access as a means to regulate private business. This includes the right to portability of personal data as enacted in the General Data Protection Regulation[2] and data access rights of competitors as part

1 See, in particular, the Communication from the Commission of 19 February 2020 to the European Parliament, the Council, the European Economic and Social Committee and the Committee of the Regions, 'A European strategy for data' COM(2020) 66 final 13, announcing the proposal of a 'Data Act' for 2021 that seeks to promote data sharing and could include, among other things, obligations of private actors to grant access to data.

2 Art. 20 Regulation (EU) 2016/679 of the European Parliament and of the Council of 27 April 2016 on the protection of natural persons with regard to the processing of personal data and on the free movement of such data, and repealing Directive 95/46/EC [2016] OJ L119/1.

of sector-specific legislation.[3] The EU has already acquired considerable experience as regards access of private businesses to publicly held data ever since the adoption of the original Public Sector Information (PSI) Directive in 2003.[4] But, given the fact that today private players are among the most important generators of data, the policy debate now also addresses the question of how diverse public interests can be promoted through access of the state to privately held data.[5]

To introduce the following contributions, this chapter first links consumer interest and public interest grounds, on the one hand, and sketches the general policy considerations that matter for data access regimes, on the other (at B. below). Then, it will specify the legal challenges of using data access regimes for the purpose of promoting consumer interests and public interest grounds (at C. below) and identify overarching questions to which the following contributions seek to provide answers (at D. below). Finally, this chapter sketches the structure of the book (at E. below).

---

3 See, in particular, the access regime for motor vehicle repair and maintenance information: Arts 6–9 Regulation 715/2007 of 20 June 2007 on type approval of motor vehicles with respect to emissions from light passenger and commercial vehicles (Euro 5 and Euro 6) and on access to vehicle repair and maintenance information [2007] OJ L171/1, as last amended by Regulation (EU) No 459/2012 of 29 May 2012 [2012] OJ L142/16. Equally, European law provides for a right of the providers of digital payment services to seek access to the bank account data of customers: Art. 36 Second Digital Payment Services Directive (PSD2) (EU) 2015/2366 of the European Parliament and of the Council of 25 November 2015 on payment services in the internal market, Directives 2002/65/EC, 2009/110/EC and 2013/36/EU and Regulation (EU) No 1093/2010, and repealing Directive 2007/64/EC [2015] OJ L337/35.

4 Directive 2003/98/EC of the European Parliament and of the Council of 17 November 2003 on the re-use of public sector information [2003] OJ L345/90, which has meanwhile been reformed and replaced by Directive (EU) 2019/1024 of the European Parliament and of the Council of 20 June 2019 on open data and the re-use of public sector information [2019] OJ L172/56.

5 See Communication from the Commission of 25 April 2018 to the European Parliament, the Council, the European Economic and Social Committee and the Committee of the Regions, 'Towards a common European data space' COM(2018) 232 final, 12–14 (on 'business-to-government data sharing'); Commission Staff Working Document of 25 April 2018, 'Guidance on sharing private sector data in the European data economy' SWD(2018) 125 final.

B. Connecting data access with consumer interests and public welfare

The legal and economic discourse of the last decades has largely been dominated by the economics-based claim that market regulation should strive to increase economic welfare and efficiency. Safeguarding efficient and competitive markets that also promote innovation (in terms of 'dynamic efficiency') certainly remains a fundamental objective of the future legal framework for the digital economy. However, as regards the digital economy, there are good arguments for extending the spectrum of objectives and including broader public interest goals (see at I. below). The underlying assumption of this book is that data access regimes could promote such goals, while the existing law is not well prepared to provide such access (see at II. below). Therein lies both the challenge for policy makers and the legislature as well as the opportunity for the scholars contributing to this book to reflect about innovative legal solutions.

I. The impact of the digital economy on consumer interests and public interest grounds

Digital technologies do not only change how manufacturers produce ('industry 4.0'). They also change how we consume, how we communicate and think, and how we make decisions. As consumers, we nowadays have access to many digital services that are offered 'for free'; but we are only able to get access to such services because we are ready to provide personal data. The digital economy also provides us with new possibilities for social exchange, communication and social organisation in groups of 'friends', which has an impact on what we think, what we believe and how we decide as political beings. Big data analysis and artificial intelligence even enables us to delegate our decisions to autonomous agents, whether it is about business or consumer decisions. Hence, the digital economy impacts society – and the life of individuals – in a much broader way with manifold anthropological, ethical and political implications. Far from only challenging modern societies, digital technologies are enormously promising. They even promise to solve most pressing problems of humanity, whether it is about climate change, still untreatable diseases and current and future pandemics, food security and sustainable development of all regions of the world.[6] These benefits do not at all argue against economic reasoning as a basis for regulation of the digital economy. Yet they support a more holistic approach that takes the larger spectrum of implications and potential benefits as well as the diverse interests of stakeholders and the public into account.

As regards the group of stakeholders, legislation also has to widen the perspective. Therefore, this book is not exclusively on regulating business. Given the impact on the private life of all of us, consumer interests deserve particular attention. And, finally, the state does not only appear as a regulator, but also as an additional stakeholder with a public interest in access to data.

There is of course the question whether it makes sense to distinguish consumer interests from public interest grounds. Indeed, such distinction hardly makes sense against the backdrop of central laws of economic legislation. In particular, competition law safeguards competitive markets both in the public interest in promoting growth, saving resources and enhancing innovation, and in the collective interest of consumers. This explains why it is commonly argued that competition law aims at promoting 'consumer welfare', which is often understood, especially by neoclassical economics, to indicate 'economic efficiency'. Equally, the unfair trading law of the EU in B2C relations protects the 'collective' interests of consumers[7] and, simultaneously, it constitutes a major part of general market regulation that seeks to enhance transparency and, thereby, contributes to economic welfare in the broader sense. In the context of these laws, characterising collective consumer interests as a particular public interest is also supported by the fact that all citizens are consumers. Even more, other public interest grounds may coincide with particular consumer interests. Guaranteeing the safety of food products and pharmaceuticals is both a collective consumer interest and an aspect of the interest in public health. As regards digital mobility, the goal of guaranteeing safety as regards automated and autonomous driving is both a public interest concern and, as regards the safety of concrete devices, a particular consumer interest.

---

6 It was the OECD that some years ago highlighted potential benefits of digital innovation in terms of multiple public interest goals from a global perspective. See OECD, 'Data-Driven Innovation: Big Data for Growth and Well-Being' (OECD 2015).

7 Directive 2005/29/EC of the European Parliament and of the Council of 11 May 2005 concerning unfair business-to-consumer commercial practices in the internal market [2005] OJ L149/22.

Still this equation of consumer interests with a public interest deserves a more nuanced consideration in the context of the digital economy. Traditionally, consumer interests have been understood in terms of economic interests and the interest in protecting the physical integrity and well-being of consumers. In the digital economy, where consumers provide access to their personal data and where access to personal (customer) data drives many digital business models, data protection concerns also have to be integrated in this equation.[8] In this regard, the role of the fundamental right to data protection and its implementation in the form of the GDPR is rather complex. On the one hand, data protection rules may reduce effective market solutions because they prevent firms of the digital sector from making the best commercial use of personal data. However, data protection also has to be considered a precondition for the development of digital markets and business models to the extent that data protection is needed to build consumer trust in the sense that their privacy interests will be respected especially on the Internet ('trustworthy Internet'). The same applies with regard to anti-discrimination rules. In times of big data analytics and AI-based decision-making, it is important that such automated decisions not be based on biased data and that these decisions not discriminate against certain groups of society ('ethical AI'). In certain instances, data protection interests and the interest in non-discrimination may also collide with the interest of the state in data access. How to balance data protection rules with public interest grounds regarding access to personal data has to be decided through a balancing of the fundamental rights concerned and may lead to very different outcomes for different public interest concerns, such as public health, on the one hand, and preventive crime prevention, on the other hand.

Digitisation influences how consumer interests need to be understood and how they relate to public interests in an even more fundamental manner. Especially the business models of the digital platform economy are designed to collect and generate as much data about the personal preferences of individual customers, and as many customers as possible, to provide them with more targeted offers. Automated AI-based decisions may even replace individual consumer decisions in the consumers' best interest. This may serve individual consumers well, namely, those who appreciate the

8 There is therefore growing literature on the relationship between data protection law and consumer law on the EU level in particular. See, for instance, Natali Helberger, Frederik Zuiderveen Borgesius and Agustin Reyna, 'The perfect match? A closer look at the relationship between EU consumer law and data protection law' (2017) 54 Common Market Law Review 1427.

convenience and ease these business models provide. However, this challenges modern competition policy, since these consumers are drawn into closed 'digital ecosystems' where consumers increasingly are supplied with diverse goods and services by a single firm without feeling the need to shop elsewhere.[9] This may lead to a digital economy where the market structure tends to foreclose market access to newcomers, which may be highly innovative but lack sufficient knowledge about customer preferences as a precondition for market success. This shows that individual consumer interests tend to get disconnected from the public interest in an open, procompetitive and innovative digital economy.

Beyond these more economics-based considerations, digitisation also affects the political process and the functioning of democracy. Foremost, this is so because digital business models are based on data as carriers of information and thereby have the potential of fundamentally transforming the markets for ideas. When justifying and exploring the need for regulation of social platforms, which are today among the major providers of political information and ideas, we can of course rely on known economics-based theories. We can argue that those platforms are characterised by a market failure of adverse selection since exclusively business-driven, unregulated social platforms will not guarantee the quality (especially the 'truthfulness') of news. To reject the argument that in digital echo-chambers consumers receive exactly the kind of information and opinions they prefer, we find support in behavioural economics, informing us that users of social media are affected by a confirmation bias when they choose their preferred source of information. Yet all of these economics arguments also express a paternalistic attitude vis-à-vis the individual consumer. Although these arguments may provide rational explanations for the problem, they do not give an answer to the question on how paternalistic regulation can get with a view to guaranteeing the functioning of the democratic process and against the backdrop of the fundamental rights of these consumers to freedom of expression and information. This shows that the digital economy raises fundamental constitutional questions and the need to make decisions on the fundamental rules of both commercial and political interactions of modern society.

---

9 On competition among digital ecosystems, see, among others, the report of the Special Advisors to the EU Commissioner for Competition: Jacques Crémer, Yves-Alexandre de Montjoye and Heike Schweitzer, 'Competition policy for the digital era – Final report (2019) 3–4, 11, 13–14, 30–38 <https://ec.europa.eu/competition/publications/reports/kd0419345enn.pdf> accessed 31 August 2020.

The advent of 'digital consumption' marks another feature of the digital economy that displays a truly anthropological dimension. As 'digital consumers' we receive preselected and more targeted offers based on our past personal decisions as well as empirically inferred preferences based on the consumption habits of 'people like us'. Building on such 'past and inferred' preferences, AI-based automated decision making can replace real consumer decisions. Of course, everybody has a choice whether and to what extent one wants to become such a 'digital consumer'. However, it is another question what 'digital consumerism' does to a democratic society where a constantly increasing number of people delegate daily decisions to anonymous digital agents. This raises the anthropological question of whether and how the delegation of daily economic decisions and the assessment of the pros and cons of such decisions will affect the ability of citizens to take into account the negative consequences of their political decisions.

Indeed, a democratic society has to build on free and responsible citizens. Where, as a consequence of digital business models, consumers lose their data autonomy and sovereignty, they risk losing their ability to act as free citizens when they make political decisions. Therefore, data protection in the digital economy should also be considered a public interest concern.

In sum, this shows that the legislature is confronted with a most complex field of economic regulation with very diverse concerns that often have both a private and a public interest dimension. Data access rights will typically address particular market failures in economic terms or serve a particular individual or public interest. But because of the broader political and societal implications, data access regimes also need to respect the fundamental values and rights of the democratic society and should be based on, or allow for, appropriate balancing with conflicting, potentially very diverse interests.

II. Data as the object of access rights

Legal rules on the data economy have to take into account that data are economic assets with very peculiar features. Indeed, they are often of enormous competitive and monetary value. However, this does not justify metaphors such as the 'oil of the twenty-first century'. In contrast to exhaustible natural resources, data as informational goods are non-rival in nature. Hence, economic welfare will typically increase by data sharing. This is what drives the conviction that society will in principle benefit from the free flow of data, even more where access to data can help address fundamental public interest concerns and modern challenges for humanity, such as public health and pandemics, environmental protection and climate change, food security and poverty.

Yet data access may also come with a price. Investment in data collection and generation as well as control over data are major drivers of competition. Therefore, from an economic perspective, data access should in principle only be ordered where such access addresses a specific market failure, serves to solve a problem of competition, such as market foreclosure, or enables innovation of the data access claimant. Conversely, the legislature should refrain from adopting data access regimes that allow for free-riding on the investment of competitors and reduce incentives for innovation.

Moreover, the existence of sensitive data – personal data and trade secrets – needs to be taken into account. These data deserve special protection against dissemination. Yet the sensitivity of data does not need to exclude data access as such. Anonymisation and confidentiality obligations as part of the terms and conditions of access can often enable sufficient access while respecting the legitimate interest in keeping the information secret.

C. *Data access and the law*

In the current situation, the law does not seem well prepared for enhancing data access. Competition law as the fundamental law of the free market economy that applies across sectors of the economy could in principle work as a basis for a duty to grant access to data. This is possible in the framework of the prohibition of abuse of market dominance, where a refusal to grant data access appears as a sub-category of general refusals to deal.[10] Yet, even if dominance can be shown, enforcers may be rather reluctant to argue a duty to deal, since such duty conflicts with freedom of contract as a paramount principle of the free market economy. In addition, competition law cannot serve as a basis for rules on access of the state to

10 EU competition law has some, albeit limited, experience in this regard. See, in particular, Joined Cases C-241/91 and C-242/91 RTE and ITP v. Commission ('Magill') [1995] ECR I-743 = ECLI:EU:C:1995:98 (on the duty of TV broadcasters to license the copyright protecting the programming information to independent TV guide publishers); Case T-201/04 Microsoft v. Commission [2007] ECR II-3601 = ECLI:EU:T:2007:367 (on the duty of Microsoft to grant access to interoperability information to allow competitors to program competing work-group server operating systems that are compatible with Windows).

privately held data, even less where access would promote other public interest concerns than safeguarding competition.

Of course, data access could also be promoted by general private law. However, the very idea of data access seems opposed to the fundamental exclusivity paradigm of property law regarding physical assets. There is a real danger that the identification of data as an economic asset and as a tradable good will tempt policy makers and scholars alike to rely on ownership concepts when framing the private law of data. The need to protect the integrity of data through general tort law may equally support the view that the exclusivity (property) paradigm should also be applied to data, especially in jurisdictions such as the German one where tort law in principle requires an infringement of absolute rights. Yet these attempts would fundamentally ignore the very nature of data as non-rival informational assets. In sum, this may support protection of the integrity of data in favour of the data holder under tort law, but still argue against the recognition of an exclusive right with *erga omnes* effects to use data in follow-on markets.

In addition, there is a need to develop contract law for the digital economy. In B2B relations in the digital economy data have already become an object of transactions. Since the digital economy often builds on cooperation between firms, and firms frequently generate data within networks (so-called 'co-generated data'), there is of course a need for the interested parties to be able to decide on the rules that are supposed to govern the generation of data as well as access to and use of data. De facto data holding and the possibility to protect against access through technical protection measures already seem to provide enough factual exclusivity to enable transactions on data access and sharing, without additional legislation being needed. Still, recognition of data access rights remains an absolute innovation within the realm of statutory contract law.[11]

Moreover, the question of how to design the legal framework for the digital economy currently challenges all jurisdictions. Given the very different constitutional background and, even more, different attitudes of jurisdictions regarding the right to data protection, it is clear that the answers will differ. Yet the challenges extend beyond borders. Many digital business models, especially those of the Internet platform economy, are designed for global markets. Connected devices are sold in international mar-

11 See, however, the new data access right of consumers under Art. 16(4) Directive (EU) 2019/770 of the European Parliament and of the Council of 20 May 2019 on certain aspects concerning contracts for the supply of digital content and digital services [2019] OJ L136/1.

kets. Therefore, this book discusses the future legal framework for access rights primarily for legislation on the level of the EU as a Union of shared values and with the establishment of an internal market as the centrepiece of its economic objectives.

From a perspective of research, the topic of this book provides significant scope for legal innovation. Data access is an issue that regards multiple fields of the law, including in particular contract law, competition law, intellectual property and data protection law. Similarly, given the constitutional implications and the data protection dimension, as well as the involvement of the state as both a big data holder and a stakeholder that increasingly seeks data access, research on future access rights has to overcome the traditional separation of private law and public law. Furthermore, the future legal framework requires a balancing of most diverse individual and public interests in different parts of the law. The different fields of the law all have their own traditions, and all were framed in the era of the analogue economy. This means that all fields of the law also individually have to adapt to the digital economy. Yet the traditional objectives of the different fields of the law will remain relevant and set limitations to their potential of enhancing data access. This may result in the need of parallel and partially overlapping access regimes of different laws to reach optimal results. In sum, research on the future legal framework of the 'network' economy is best advised to take a holistic 'network' approach that simultaneously looks at different fields of the law and the interactions between them.

Of course, legal research also has to take account of extralegal disciplines to get a proper understanding of the factual issues and context. Even more, to enhance data access, it is not sufficient to concentrate on legislative measures regarding the legal relationship between the different players of the data economy. Data access also depends on the availability of multiple technologies and institutional arrangements, such as standard-setting bodies and procedures, platforms for data sharing and data trustees, which again may be in need of regulation. Of course, legal research on market regulation has to rely on economic insights to identify market failures that data access rights are supposed to address and to predict the effects of regulatory measures. Since consumers play a major role, insights from other social sciences and psychology may also advance better legislation. In sum, this shows that the appropriate policy approach to promote the data economy has to be based on insights from different research disciplines, and the necessary legal measures should be embedded in a broader 'data governance approach' that also promotes the necessary technologies and institutional arrangements.

D. *Towards the future of data access rights*

This book is about the need for future rules on data access. Advocating new rules to regulate the economy always requires caution. Rules are not needed where the market provides appropriate solutions. Based on this, key questions arise that will in principle be relevant for all contributions in this book.

The very first question regards the default rule. Should this rule be 'access by default' or 'exclusivity by default'? At this stage of development, the rule tends towards the latter. Firms are allowed to control 'their' data. Even where they cannot rely on intellectual property rights to control access to data, they can use technical protection measures to exclude others. Legal recognition of de facto data exclusivity is far from economically unsound, since such exclusivity will often be a prerequisite for data transactions based on contract law that ultimately leads to data access and data sharing. Therefore, unrestricted data access should not be the rule since optimal access and optimal use is not without costs. Data access frequently requires investment in data quality and technical arrangements to enable access. Therefore, de facto data holders should in principle be allowed to deny access with the objective of securing remuneration for providing access. In a market economy, contract law and the principle of freedom of contract is in principle the most efficient means to allocate costs among different parties.

As regards data access regimes, the question will therefore be what market failures and what interests will justify a deviation from exclusivity. This question will answer the question where and to what extent 'exclusivity by default' should shift to 'access by default'. It is here that especially consumer interests, data protection interests and public interest grounds will need to be balanced to define the scope and design of data access regimes.

Many follow-on questions will relate to the design of access regimes: What are the data that should be covered? Only personal data or also non-personal data? What about 'derived' data, such as anonymised aggregated data, or 'inferred' data, meaning data generated through empirical assessment of correlations between pre-existing data? Who should be vested with access rights, competitors, consumers or the state? What does a duty to grant access actually mean, only an obligation to provide access to the informational content, transfer of digitally encoded data at a given time or permanent sharing of data, including real-time data?

Granting access rights raises follow-on questions regarding the terms and conditions of access. A duty to grant access to data can be seen as a kind of compulsory licensing system under which a data holder is required to enter into an agreement that allows the other party to use the data at certain terms. Follow-on questions especially regard whether the data holder should be allowed to charge a price or at least claim compensation for the costs of providing data access. What should be the principles for calculating such remuneration or compensation? Another question regards liability of the data holder for the quality of the data. Additional institutional arrangements may be needed to enhance voluntary contracting against the backdrop of legal access regimes, such as collective agreements of business entities, standardisation of data formats and application programming interfaces (APIs), data trustees and institutions for mediation and arbitration.

In the EU context, another question will be to what extent solutions should be transferred to the European level and how much flexibility Member States should be granted to follow national approaches.

E. Structure of the book

The first group of contributions seeks to answer the question whether there is a need for additional access regimes or what justifies new data access rules. The first two contributions do so in the light of general public policy arguments and economics. A contribution on competition law as a basis for data access, and its need for reform in this regard, will prepare the transition to the following contributions.

Then, as part of the second group, several contributions concentrate on the larger legal framework for data access. This includes the constitutional framework and the data protection rules of the General Data Protection Regulation (GDPR). Another contribution analyses the impact of exclusive intellectual property rights as well as trade secrets protection on data access and seeks to accommodate both interests in protection and access in identifying future building blocks for the regulation of the data economy.

The third group of contributions takes stock of existing data protection regimes and their future potentials for the regulation of data access. Two contributions look at the contract law system, one focussing on the fairness control of contract terms, the other one on existing and future data access rights as part of statutory contract law. Within the EU, the most prominent and discussed data access right is the right to portability of personal data under Article 20 GDPR, which another contribution analyses as a potential blueprint for additional data access regimes. Yet another contribution takes a look at data access rights of competitors as part of European sector-specific regulation and its implications for innovation. Finally, against the backdrop of a taxonomy of access rights and based on a comparative approach, the last chapter of this group seeks to investigate what lessons can be learned from data access regimes adopted in various other jurisdictions around the globe.

The final group of contributions looks at new approaches to legislation on data access regimes. This is introduced by a contribution that highlights the need for embedding data access regimes in larger sets of measures as part of more comprehensive data governance regimes. The two remaining contributions focus on more specific new access regimes, namely, regarding data access rights of the users of connected devices for which an unfair competition law approach is discussed, on the one hand, and government access to privately held data ('B2G data sharing') in the public interest, on the other hand.

On the need for additional access rights

Enhancing access to and sharing of data: Striking the balance between openness and control over data

Christian Reimsbach-Kounatze[*]

A. *Introduction*

The effective use of 'big data' and analytics (data and analytics) can help boost productivity and improve or foster new products, processes, organisational methods and markets (data-driven innovation),[1] a phenomenon which is growing in importance with artificial intelligence (AI).[2] As a result, access to data has become a critical factor for the competitiveness and success of businesses.[3] This is reflected in the growing number of mergers and acquisitions (M&As) of data-intensive firms, and most notably the acquisition of smaller, younger data-intensive firms by larger firms. Many of these M&As are motivated by strategic considerations to secure access to data.[4] Between 2013 and 2017, the annual number of acquisitions of data-intensive firms increased by a factor of four, with the average price paid exceeding USD 1 billion in some quarters.[5]

---

* The opinions expressed and arguments employed in this chapter are those of the author and should not be reported as representing the official views of the OECD or of its member countries.

1 See OECD, *Data-Driven Innovation: Big Data for Growth and Well-Being* (OECD 2015).

2 See OECD, *Artificial Intelligence in Society* (OECD 2019) 19–34.

3 Firm-level studies suggest that firms that use data and analytics exhibit faster labour productivity growth than those that do not by approximately 5 % to 10 %. OECD (n. 1) 234. See, for instance, Erik Brynjolfsson and Kristina S. McElheran, 'Data in Action: Data-Driven Decision Making and Predictive Analytics in U.S. Manufacturing' (2019) Rotman School of Management Working Paper No. 3422397 <https://papers.ssrn.com/sol3/papers.cfm?abstract_id=3422397> accessed 31 August 2020.

4 Examples include: Monsanto's acquisition of the Climate Corporation, an agriculture analytic firm, for USD 1.1 billion in 2013; Facebook's acquisition of WhatsApp for USD 14 billion in 2014; and IBM's acquisition of a majority share of the Weather Company, a weather forecasting and analytic company, for over USD 2 billion in 2015.

5 OECD, *Enhancing Access to and Sharing of Data: Reconciling Risks and Benefits for Data Re-Use across Societies* (OECD 2019) 16.

This development in M&As, which points to a tendency towards a concentration of data in favour of larger firms, is in line with trends in the use of data and analytics, where firm size is the most significant determining factor.[6] It is estimated that more than 30 % of all large firms (with 250 or more employees) in the OECD area used data and analytics in 2017 compared to only roughly 12 % of all small and medium-sized enterprises (SMEs) (with 10 to 249 employees) (Figure 1). Adoption has increased in particular among large firms in Germany, France, Finland, Korea and Portugal, although with significant variation by sector. That said, information and communication technology (ICT) firms remain the dominant users of data and analytics: more than 25 % of all ICT firms used data and analytics in the EU 28 in 2018 compared to less than 12 % of all firms (Figure 2).

Figure 1. Business use of data and analytics by country and firm size, 2017
As a proportion of enterprises in each group

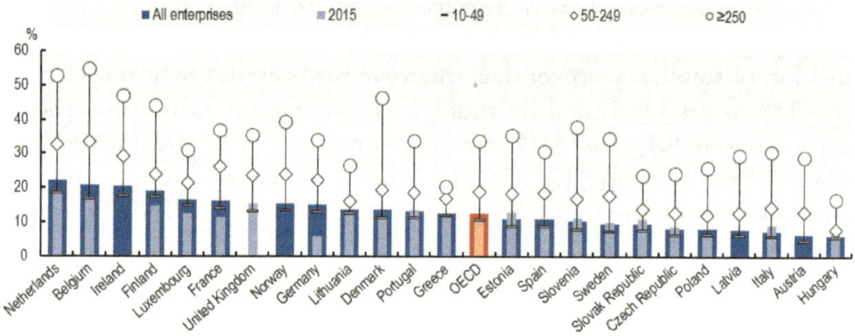

Note: The number of full-time employees defines the firm size. For the United Kingdom, data relate to the year 2015. OECD data figures are based on a simple average of the available OECD countries.

Source: OECD, *Digital Economy Outlook 2020* (OECD, 2020) 108 <https://doi.org/10.1787/888934191825> accessed 20 January 2021.

6 OECD, *Digital Economy Outlook 2020* (OECD 2020) 107-9.

Figure 2. Business use of data and analytics by data type and industry in the EU 28, 2018
As a proportion of enterprises in each group

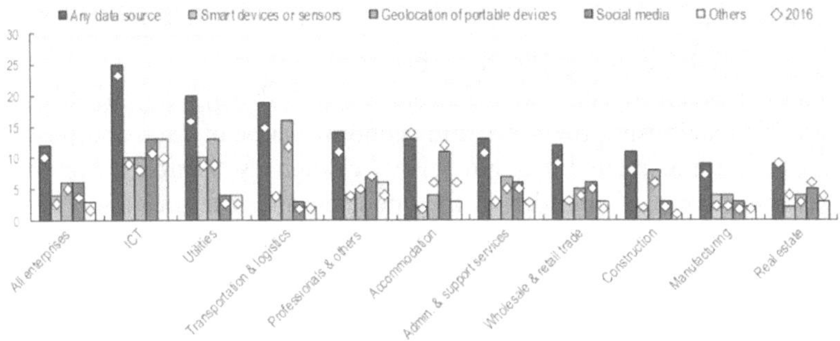

Source: Ibid. 133 <https://doi.org/10.1787/888934192129> accessed 20 January 2021.

The importance of data access goes beyond the positive economic effects on productivity growth as data can also contribute directly to the well-being of citizens. Quantification however remains challenging because many if not most of the social benefits related to the use of data are poorly captured by market transactions.[7]For example, data can be shared and re-used to enhance public service delivery and to address societal needs and emergencies. Data were for instance critical for effective emergency responses during the 2011 Fukushima incident and the 2014–16 Ebola outbreak in West Africa,[8] and recently during the COVID-19 crisis.[9]

Despite the economic and social potential of data, data access and data sharing (data access and sharing), including the commercialisation of data, remain below their potential, even among data-intensive firms. In a survey by Forester Research of almost 1,300 data and analytics businesses across the globe, only a third of the respondents reported commercialising their data.[10] High tech, utilities and financial services rank among the top industries commercialising their data, while pharmaceuticals, government and

7 OECD (n. 1) 29.
8 Ibid. 335.
9 See Section D.III.2.b.
10 Jennifer Belissent, Gene Leganza and Jeremy Vale, 'Top Performers Commercialize Data Through Insights Services' (2017) <https://d3w3ioujxcalzn.cloudfront.net/item_files/206c/attachments/779835/original/forrester_infographic_top_performers_appoint_data_insights_leaders_jennifer_belissent.pdf> accessed 31 August 2020.

healthcare are at the bottom of the list. There are still significant barriers to data sharing and re-use. The risks associated with the revelation of confidential information (e.g. personal data and trade secrets) are often indicated as the main rationale for individuals and organisations not to share their data. This remains true even in cases where commercial and other private interests do not oppose data sharing.[11]

This chapter discusses how data access and sharing can be effective means for maximising the social and economic value of data, and possible venues to address related data governance challenges. Section B first introduces the theoretical foundation for understanding the social and economic potential of data, presenting data as an infrastructural resource, i.e. a general-purpose, non-rivalrous, partially excludable capital good. This functional perspective on data, which is inspired by Frischmann's work on infrastructures,[12] may seem counter-intuitive for some readers at first. However, it is helpful to better understand and explain: (i) how data can support downstream social and economic activities, (ii) why access is a key lever through which data use and value extraction can be controlled (irrespective of the existence of intellectual property rights, IPRs) and (iii) why commons present a promising solution to the collective data governance challenges of data access and sharing. Section C focusses on some of these data governance challenges.[13] Section D then presents a few promising means to address these challenges. It suggests that more differentiated data

11 AIG, 'The Data Sharing Economy: Quantifying Tradeoffs That Power New Business Models' (2016) <www.aig.com/content/dam/aig/america-canada/us/documents/brochure/the-data-sharing-economy-report.pdf> accessed 31 August 2020.

12 See Brett M. Frischmann, *Infrastructure: The Social Value of Shared Resources* (Oxford University Press 2012).

13 Other important data governance challenges had to be omitted due to space constraints, which does not mean that they were considered unimportant. These include: (i) digital security risks, (ii) liability risks in particular in respect to data quality, (iii) the risk of anti-competitive data sharing agreements (collusion), (iv) the role and limitations of data ethical frameworks, (v) the development and adoption of standards for improved interoperability, (vi) the sustainability of open data and last, but certainly not least, (vii) issues related to cross-border data access and sharing, and the interoperability of legal and regulatory frameworks affecting data access and sharing. Furthermore, issues related to IPRs, which are discussed in more detail in other chapters of this publication, are not addressed, although this chapter does discuss issues related to the concept of 'data ownership'. The same applies for issues related to privacy and data protection as well as competition regulation, which are rather superficially addressed to focus on the bigger picture, knowing that these topics are discussed in more detail in other chapters. Readers interested in the work of the Organisation for Economic Co-operation

governance approaches for data access and sharing, as implemented by data commons in combination with technological means for re-establishing control over data and information, are needed to better reflect the various interests of stakeholders and the risks they face. Section E concludes with a few public policy implications.

B. Data as infrastructural resource and the spillover benefits of its shared access

The economic properties of data suggest that data may be considered as an infrastructure or, more correctly, an infrastructural resource. This may sound counter-intuitive, since traditionally infrastructures typically refer to large-scale physical facilities provided for public consumption; the classic examples are transportation systems, communication systems and basic services and facilities such as buildings and sewage and water systems. However, as for example recognised by the US National Research Council, the notion of infrastructure also refers to non-physical facilities, such as education systems and governance systems (including for example the court system).[14] This is in line with Merriam-Webster, which defines infrastructures as 'the resources (such as personnel, buildings, or equipment) required for an activity' and 'the underlying foundation or basic framework (as of a system or organization)'.[15] For Frischmann, infrastructures are 'shared means to many ends'[16] that satisfy the following three criteria:[17]

- the resource may be consumed in a non-rivalrous fashion for some appreciable range of demand (i.e. the non-rivalrous criterion);
- social demand for the resource is driven primarily by downstream productive activities that require the resource as an input (i.e. the capital good criterion); and

---

and Development (OECD) on data governance, and more specifically on data access and sharing, which has informed this work, are advised to consult the website of the OECD Working Party on Data Governance and Privacy in the Digital Economy (http://oe.cd/datagovernance) besides the relevant OECD publications referenced in this chapter.

14 National Research Council, *Infrastructure for the 21st Century: Framework for a Research Agenda* (National Academy Press 1987).

15 Merriam-Webster, 'Infrastructure' (*Merriam-Webster.com Dictionary*) <www.merriam-webster.com/dictionary/infrastructure> accessed 31 August 2020.

16 Frischmann (n. 12) 4.

17 Ibid 62–66.

- the resource may be used as an input into a wide range of goods and services, which may include private goods, public goods and social goods (i.e. the general-purpose criterion).

As discussed in the following three sections, most (though not all) data are indeed 'shared means to many ends' and satisfy these three criteria. Therefore, data can in principle be considered an infrastructural resource.

I. Data as a non-rivalrous although partially excludable good

(Non-)rivalry of consumption describes the degree to which the consumption of a resource affects (or does not affect) the potential of the resource to meet the demands of others. It thus reflects the marginal cost of allowing an additional consumer of the good. A rivalrous good such as oil can only be consumed once. A non-rivalrous good such as knowledge, in contrast, can be consumed in principle an unlimited number of times. This property is the source of significant spillovers and that provides the major theoretical link to total factor productivity growth enabled by data, but it also raises questions about how best to allocate data as a resource.

While it is widely accepted that social welfare is maximised when a rivalrous good is consumed by the person who values it the most, and that the market mechanism is generally the most efficient means for rationing such goods and for allocating resources needed to produce such goods, this is not always true for non-rivalrous goods. The situation is more complex in this case, since non-rivalrous goods come with an additional degree of freedom with respect to resource management: Social welfare is maximised not when the good is consumed solely by the person who values it the most, but when everyone who values it consumes it.[18] Maximising access to the non-rivalrous good will thus in theory maximise social welfare, as every additional private benefit comes at no additional cost.

However, data are not always and in every circumstance non-rivalrous. Some data can lose their value as soon as e.g. illegitimate users have access to them. This would be the case, for instance, when the data contain confidential information, such as trade secrets, and/or could be misused for insider trading. Although the data in these cases are not depleted due to the illegitimate use, the information they contain may lose its economic value, at least for those that wish to protect the information. In other words, in

18 Ibid 28.

these particular cases the consumption of data would affect their potential to meet the demands of (a few) others.[19]

The fact that data may not always be perfectly non-rivalrous does not invalidate the non-rivalrous criterion for data to be considered an infrastructure however. This is because: (i) public goods theory recognises that there are few perfectly non-rivalrous goods[20] and, more specifically, (ii) infrastructures can most of the time be consumed in non-rivalrous fashion only within some appreciable range of demand, for instance, when they are not congested.

It is important to note at this point that non-rivalry of consumption of data does not imply that data are a public good. A public good must satisfy an additional criterion: besides being non-rivalrous, the good must also be non-excludable, i.e. the cost for one person to prevent another from consuming the resource must be significant. While the marginal costs of transmitting, copying and processing data can be close to zero, making it easy for others to reproduce and use them, ICTs including for e.g. user access control and encryption[21] have also dramatically reduced the costs of exclusion. Thus, where data are kept within a controlled environment the cost of exclusion will be typically low enough to prevent others from using them. This is why data can be considered at least partially excludable and not a public good.

II. Data as a capital good with increasing returns to scale and scope

Data are still sometimes described as 'the new oil' of the digital economy. However, besides the non-rivalrous nature of data, data are neither a consumption good such as an apple, nor an intermediate good such as oil. In most cases, data should be classified as a capital good.

---

19 See David W. Opderbeck, 'Socially Rivalrous Information: Of Candles, Code, and Virtue' (2007) Seton Hall Public Law Research Paper No. 1008500, 85 <https://papers.ssrn.com/sol3/papers.cfm?abstract_id=1008500> accessed 31 August 2020, who refers to this particularity as 'social rivalry' with the following argument: 'Because information helps construct communities, those who possess information possess a form of power. Sharing information diminishes the power held by the person who previously restricted access to the information. Information therefore is socially rivalrous.' This argument applies to certain types of information and thus only to certain types of data and this only under certain conditions.

20 See John G. Head, 'Public Goods and Public Policy' in Charles K. Rowley (ed.), *Readings in Industrial Economics*, Vol. II (MacMillan Publishers 1972) 66.

21 See Section D.III.

While consumption goods are consumed to generate direct benefits to the consumer or firm,[22] intermediate goods and capital goods are used as inputs to produce other goods. Intermediate and capital goods are both means rather than ends, and their demand is driven by the demand for the derived outputs. They are thus factors of production.

The difference between intermediate and capital goods is that, while intermediate goods such as raw materials (e.g. oil) are used up, exhausted, or otherwise transformed when used as input to produce other goods, capital goods are not.[23] Furthermore, capital goods 'must have been produced as outputs from processes of production', which explains why 'natural assets such as land, mineral or other deposits, coal, oil, or natural gas, or contracts, leases and licences' are not considered capital goods.[24]

Data, in most cases, are used as an input for goods or services; this is especially true of large volumes of data (i.e. 'big data'), which are means rather than ends in themselves. They are however not an intermediate good, as they are not exhausted when used, given their non-rivalrous nature. This does not mean that data cannot be discarded after they have been used. In many cases, they may be used just once. However, storage costs today have decreased to the point where data can generally be kept for long periods of time, if not indefinitely. This has increased data's capacity to be used as a capital good and production factor.

Furthermore, being a capital good does not mean that data do not depreciate. The value of most capital goods declines 'as a result of physical deterioration, normal obsolescence or normal accidental damage'.[25] In the case of data, depreciation is more complex, however, because it is context-dependent. That is, the value of data depends on the context of their use.[26] Therefore, the relevance, accuracy and timeliness of data will typically af-

---

22 EC and others, 'System of National Accounts 2008' (2008) 179 <http://unstats.un.org/unsd/nationalaccount/docs/SNA2008.pdf> accessed 31 August 2020.

23 Ibid. 120. See also Eurostat, 'NACE Rev. 2 – Introductory Guidelines' (2006) 39 <https://ec.europa.eu/eurostat/documents/1965800/1978839/NACEREV.2INTRODUCTORYGUIDELINESEN.pdf/f48c8a50-feb1-4227-8fe0-935b58a0a332> accessed 31 August 2020.

24 EC and others (n. 22) 123.

25 Ibid.

26 See OECD, 'Exploring the Economics of Personal Data: A Survey of Methodologies for Measuring Monetary Value' (OECD 2013) OECD Ditigal Economy Papers No. 220 <www.oecd-ilibrary.org/docserver/5k486qtxldmq-en.pdf?expires=1604224239&id=id&accname=guest&checksum=90171D5AA0F516519D87E5DD30974A07> accessed 31 August 2020, which shows that assessing the value of data *ex ante* (before use) is almost impossible, because the information derived is context-

fect that value. Data can depreciate, for instance, when they begin to lose their relevance for an intended use. This explains, for example, why there is a temporal premium for 'real-time' data in the financial sector.

The capital-good nature of data has major economic implications. As data are a non-rival capital, multiple users can in theory use them (simultaneously) for multiple purposes (see next section) as an input to produce an unlimited number of goods and services. In addition, increasing returns to scale and scope are possible as the value of data increases when the data can be linked with, and integrated into, a (larger) big data set.[27] In practical terms, these properties find their application in data-enabled multi-sided markets, i.e. economic platforms in which distinct user groups generate benefits (externalities or spillovers) to other groups.[28] In other words, the re-use of data enables multi-sided markets in which huge returns to scale and scope can lead to positive feedback loops on one side of the market in favour of the business, which in turn reinforces success in the other side(s) of the multi-sided market, overall leading to a potential '"winner takes all" outcome in which monopoly is the nearly inevitable outcome of market success'.[29]

III. Data as general-purpose but context-dependent input

Infrastructures are not inputs that have been optimised for a special limited purpose, but 'they provide basic, multipurpose functionality'.[30] In par-

---

dependent: data that are of good quality for certain applications can thus be of poor quality for other applications. Furthermore, the information and thus value that can be extracted from data is not only a function of the data, but also a function of the (analytic) capacity to link data and to extract insights. This capacity is determined by available (meta-)data, analytic techniques and technologies; however, it is also a function of pre-existing knowledge and skills. See also OECD (n. 1).

27 See Bertin Martens, 'Data access, consumer interests and social welfare: An economic perspective on data' (2020) in this publication.

28 See Jean-Charles Rochet and Jean Tirole, 'Two-sided Markets: A Progress Report' (2006) 37 RAND Journal of Economics 645, defining two- or multi-sided markets 'roughly ... as markets in which one or several platforms enable interactions between end users and try to get the two or multiple sides "on board" by appropriately charging each side'.

29 OECD, *Supporting Investment in Knowledge Capital, Growth and Innovation* (OECD 2013) 170.

30 Frischmann (n. 12) 65.

ticular, infrastructures make possible a wide range of private, public and social goods, which users are free to produce according to their capabilities.

How data are used will typically depend on the initial purpose for which they have been collected. For example, at the outset agricultural data will primarily be used for agricultural goods and services. However, in theory, there are no limits with regard to the purposes for which data can be re-used, and many of the benefits stemming from their re-use are based on the fact that data created in one domain can provide further insights when applied in another domain. A clear illustration is provided by open public-sector data, where data sets used originally for administrative purposes are re-used by entrepreneurs to create services unforeseen when the data were originally created. Another example is the use of anonymised mobile call data records (CDRs) of telecommunications services providers that have been re-used to monitor and control the spread of pandemics such as COVID-19.[31]

The general-purpose nature of infrastructure comes with a key policy implication. The production of (*ex ante* unforeseeable) public and social goods via the infrastructure could lead to the market failure of insufficient provision of the infrastructure, which would call for government intervention in some cases. This is because 'users' willingness to pay [for the infrastructure] reflects private demand – the value that they expect to realise – and does not take into account [the social] value that others might realise as a result of their use.'[32] Where this social value is difficult to measure, a 'demand-manifestation problem' can occur, which in turn may lead to an undersupply of the infrastructure and a 'prioritisation of access and use of the infrastructure for a narrower range of uses than would be socially optimal'.[33] This is why, as a consequence, there can be significant (social) opportunity costs in limiting access to infrastructures. In other words: open (closed) access enables (restricts) user opportunities and degrees of freedom in the downstream production of private, public and social goods, many of which by their nature have significant spillover effects. Non-discriminatory access can therefore be an optimal (private and public) strategy for maximising the benefits of an infrastructure, in particular in environments characterised by high uncertainty, complexity and dynamic changes.

31 See Section D.III.2.b.

32 Frischmann (n. 12) 66.

33 Ibid.

This means that markets through which data are commercialised may not be able to fully serve social demand for data where such a demand manifestation problem would occur. Although the data demand manifestation problem remains poorly documented in literature, there are plausible reasons to believe that such a problem may occur in praxis, in particular, when data are used for the production of social or public goods such as to increase transparency in government or to combat poverty and pandemics. In addition, the context dependency of data and the highly uncertain, complex and dynamic environment in which some data are used (e.g. research) make it almost impossible to fully evaluate ex ante the potential of data, which further exacerbates the demand manifestation problem.

The next section briefly summarises the finding of available empirical studies that assess to what extent non-discriminatory access, and open access to data (open data) particularly, in the public[34] and private[35] sector can create social and economic spillover benefits.

---

34 See Office of Fair Trading, 'The Commercial Use of Public Information' (2006); ACIL Tasman, 'The Value of Spatial Information: The Impact of Modern Spatial Information Technologies on the Australian Economy' (2008); ACIL Tasman, 'Spatial Information in the New Zealand Economy: Realising Productivity Gains' (2009); Graham Vickery, 'Review of Recent Studies on PSI Reuse and Related Market Developments' (2011); Graham Vickery, 'Review of Recent Studies on PSI Reuse and Related Market Developments' (2012); Deloitte, 'Market Assessment of Public Sector Information: A Report to the Department for Business, Innovation and Skills' (2013); Deloitte, 'Assessing the Value of TfL's Open Data and Digital Partnerships' (2017).

35 See McKinsey Global Institute, 'Open Data: Unlocking Innovation and Performance with Liquid Information' (2013) <www.mckinsey.com/business-functions/mckinsey-digital/our-insights/open-data-unlocking-innovation-and-performance-with-liquid-information#> accessed 31 August 2020; Nicholas Gruen, John Houghton and Richart Tooth, 'Open for Business: How Open Data Can Help Achieve the G20 Growth Target' (2014) <www.academia.edu/attachments/55569779/download_file?st=MTYwNDIyNDM1OSwxOTMuMTc0LjEzMi42NA%3D%3D&s=swp-splash-paper-cover> accessed 31 August 2020; Nomura Research Institute, 'Research on Spillover Effects of Evolution in Operation and Services by Data Use on the Economy and Society' (2014); Mitsubishi Research Institute, 'De-Ta Ryutuu Purattofo-Mu Ni Kannsuru Tyo-Sajigyo [Study on Platforms for Data Sharing]' (2017); IDC and Lisbon Council, 'The European Data Market Monitoring Tool' (2019).

IV. Empirical evidence of the spillover social and economic benefits of data access and sharing

Although the quantification of the overall benefits remains challenging, available evidence strongly suggests that non-discriminatory access, including in particular open data, generates positive social and economic benefits for data providers (direct impact), their suppliers and data users (indirect impact), and for the wider economy (induced impact). This is thanks to: (i) greater transparency, accountability and empowerment of users, for instance when open data are used for (cross-subsidising) the production of public and social goods; (ii) new business opportunities, including for the creation of start-ups and in particular for data intermediaries and mobile application (app) developers; (iii) competition and co-operation within and across sectors and nations, and including the integration of value chains, (iv) crowdsourcing and user-driven innovation and (v) increasing efficiency thanks to linkages of data across multiple sources.[36]

The magnitude of the relative effects will vary however depending on the sector (public vs. private sector) and the type of effect. Studies show that, while non-discriminatory access to data can increase the value of data to holders (direct impact), it can help create 10 to 20 times more value to data users (indirect impact), and 20 to 50 times more value for the wider economy (induced impact). In some cases, however, non-discriminatory data access and sharing, and in particular open data, may also reduce the producer surplus of data holders, which is the cause of the incentive problem discussed in Section C.II.[37] Overall, these studies suggest that non-discriminatory data access and sharing can help generate social and economic benefits worth between 0.1 % and 1.5 % of GDP in the case of public sector data, and between 1 % and 2.5 % of GDP when also including private sector data.[38]

---

36 OECD (n. 5) 64–71.

37 See for instance Office of Fair Trading, which surveyed more than 400 public sector information holders (PSIHs) and 300 businesses buying or licencing data from PSIHs. It estimates that the producer surplus of the PSIHs (of around GBP 66 million p.a.) would have vanished with open access in favour of an increase of the indirect impact (including the consumer surplus of PSI re-use) by GBP 585 million p.a.

38 OECD (n. 5) 59–64.

C. *Major data governance challenges of data access and sharing*

Data access and sharing through non-discriminatory regimes not only come with social and economic benefits. They also come with risks to individuals and organisations. These may include the risks of confidentiality and privacy breaches, but also the violation of other legitimate private interests such as commercial interests. The pursuit of the benefits of data access and sharing therefore needs to be balanced against the costs and the legitimate national, public and private interests, in compliance with legislations concerning relevant rights and obligations of the stakeholders involved (such as on the protection of privacy and IPRs). This is in particular the case where sensitive data are involved. Otherwise incentives to contribute data and to invest in data-driven innovation may be undermined, in addition to the risks of direct and indirect harm to right holders (including data subjects).

Evidence confirms that risks of confidentiality breach, for instance, have led users to be more reluctant to share their data, including providing personal data and in some cases even in using digital services such as cloud computing.[39] Furthermore, inappropriate sharing of data can lead to significant costs to the organisation, including fines due to privacy violations as well as opportunity costs due to a lower ability to innovate. For example, it has been noted that sharing data prematurely can undermine the ability to obtain IPRs (e.g. on patents and trade secrets).[40]

This section discusses some major data governance challenges that need to be considered to facilitate data access and sharing. These include: (i) risks of violating private (commercial) interests including the interest in the protection of privacy and IPRs, which go hand in hand with the increasing loss of control of individuals and organisations over their data, which in turn is rooted in the partial excludability of data highlighted in Section B.I; (ii) the need to incentivise data sharing and data-related investment in light of the externalities associated with data sharing and the risk of 'free riding'; and (iii) the need to address uncertainties related to 'data ownership', a concept used to re-establish control over data.

---

39 OECD, *OECD Digital Economy Outlook 2017* (OECD 2017) 252–54.

40 Jorge L, Contreras, 'Data Sharing, Latency Variables, and Science Commons' (2010) 25 Berkeley Technology Law Journal 1601; Michael W. Carroll, 'Sharing Research Data and Intellectual Property Law: A Primer' (2015) 13 PLOS Biology e1002235 <https://journals.plos.org/plosbiology/article?id=10.1371/journal.pbio.1002235> accessed 31 August 2020.

I. The loss of control over data, and the risk of violation of privacy and intellectual property rights

Violations of privacy and to some extent of IPRs are often considered as the biggest risks associated with data access and sharing. These include most notably risks of violating (contractual and socially agreed) terms of data re-use, and thus risks of acting against the (reasonable) expectations of users and the law. This is true with respect to individuals (data subjects), their consent and their privacy expectations, but also with respect to organisations and their contractual agreements with third parties and the protection of their commercial interests.

1. Violations of agreed terms and of expectations in data re-use

Even where individuals and organisations agree on (and consent to) specific terms for data sharing and data re-use, including on the purposes for which the data should be re-used, there remains a significant level of risk that the data may end up being used differently by a third party.[41] The violation of these terms may not be always the result of malicious intentions. The contextual change that results from transferring data from one context to another will always make it challenging to ensure that existing rights and obligations are not undermined. This is because assumptions and expectations that were implicit in the initial usage (and context) may no longer apply in subsequent uses, an observation that is coherent with the fact that information derived from data is context-dependent, as highlighted in Section B.III., and so are the risks associated with data sharing.[42]

---

41 The case of Cambridge Analytica illustrates this risk: personal data of Facebook users ended up being used, not for academic purposes as some users had consented to, but for a commercially motivated political campaign, and this although Facebook explicitly prohibits data from being sold or transferred 'to any ad network, data broker or other advertising or monetisation-related service'. Kevin Granville, 'Facebook and Cambridge Analytica: What You Need to Know as Fallout Widens' *The New York Times* (19 March 2018) <www.nytimes.com/2018/03/19/technology/facebook-cambridge-analytica-explained.html> accessed 31 August 2020.

42 This is also in line with Nissenbaum's theory of privacy as 'contextual integrity', according to which adequate privacy protection is tied to the norms of the specific context in which data are used, 'demanding that information gathering and dissemination be appropriate to that context and obey the governing norms of distri-

Some of these concerns and risks have been framed as ethical, to underscore the need to recognise the importance of issues such as fairness, respect for human dignity, autonomy, self-determination, the risk of bias and discrimination as complementary to regulatory actions. Data ethics is highlighted in particular in cases where the collection, processing and sharing of data will be legal under existing law, but may generate moral, cultural and social concerns with potential direct or indirect adverse impacts on individuals or social groups. There are expectations that ethics may thus provide an additional promising venue in particular in light of the loss of control over data and, in particular, the role of consent as discussed below. This, however, raises additional issues such as the risks that some approaches to data ethics might be perceived or (mis-)used as a substitute (i) for full compliance with regulations, or (ii) for a thorough assessment and mitigation of ethical concerns ('ethic washing').

2. *Loss of control over data and the role of consent*

As highlighted in Section B.I., the cost of excluding others from using data will typically be low enough for the original data holder if the data are kept within a controlled environment. However, once the data are shared, unless specific data stewardship and processing provisions are in place, those data move out of the control of the original data holder.[43] The same can be said to be true for individuals, who provide their data and give their consent for their re-use and sharing. In both situations, data holders and individuals lose their capabilities to control how their data are re-used and to object to or (technically) oppose such uses, and can rely solely on law enforcement and redress. The risks of loss of control are multiplied where the data are further shared downstream across multiple tiers, in particular when these tiers are located across multiple jurisdictions.

Consent has been highlighted as a major, although not always effective, mechanism to allow individuals control the collection and (re-)use of their

---

bution within it'. Helen Nissenbaum, 'Privacy as Contextual Integrity' (2004) 79 Washington Law Review 119.

43 See Smitha Sundareswaran, Anna Squicciarini and Dan Lin, 'Ensuring Distributed Accountability for Data Sharing in the Cloud' (2012) 9 IEEE Transactions on Dependable and Secure Computing 556; Martin Henze, René Hummen, Roman Matzutt and Daniel Catrein, 'Maintaining User Control While Storing and Processing Sensor Data in the Cloud' (2013) 5 International Journal of Grid and High Performance Computing 97.

personal data. It requires clear provision of information to individuals about what personal data are being collected and used, and for what purpose – as specified in the data protection and privacy laws of most countries and in the OECD Privacy Guidelines.[44] To assure the maximum level of flexibility in compliance with privacy legislations, some organisations have come to rely, however, on one-time general or broad consent as the basis for data collection, use and sharing. One-time general consent can be used to achieve an appropriate balance between participant rights to determine the future use of their personal data, but only under the condition that data subjects are given reasonable means to extend or withdraw their consent over time. In addition, general consent models have been criticised for posing ethical challenges as data subjects may not realise the full implications of giving a broad consent, particularly in the context of AI and big data.[45]

II. Incentivising data sharing in light of positive externalities and the risk of 'free riding'

While the marginal costs of transmitting, copying and processing data can be close to zero, substantial investments will often be required to collect data and to enable data sharing and re-use. As highlighted in the introduction (Section A), firms are investing a significant share of their capital in the acquisition of start-ups to secure access to data potentially critical for their business. Investments may also be needed for data cleaning as well as data curation,[46] which is often beyond the scope and time frame of the ac-

44 OECD, 'Recommendation of the Council concerning Guidelines Governing the Protection of Privacy and Transborder Flows of Personal Data' (1980) OECD/LEGAL/0188 (OECD Privacy Guidelines).

45 New consent models have been proposed in the scientific literature, including 'adaptive' or 'dynamic' forms of consent to address these concerns. These also include time-restricted consent models, where individuals consent to the use of their personal data only for a limited period. These models typically enable participants to consent to new projects or to alter their consent choices in real time as their circumstances change and to have confidence that these changed choices will take effect. See Jane Kaye, Edgar A. Whitley and others, 'Dynamic Consent: A Patient Interface for Twenty-First Century Research Networks' (2015) 23 European Journal of Human Genetics 141.

46 Data curation embodies data management activities necessary to assure long-term data quality across the data life cycle.

tivities for which the data were initially collected and used.[47] Furthermore, the investments required for effective data access and sharing are not limited to data themselves. In many cases, complementary investments are needed in meta-data, data models and algorithms for data storage and processing, and to secure ICT infrastructures needed for (shared) data storage, processing and access. The overall total upfront costs can therefore be very high.

Given these significant investment requirements, data holders may not necessarily have the incentives to share their data, in particular if the costs (risks) of data access and sharing are perceived to be higher than the expected (private) benefits. In other words, where organisations and individuals cannot recuperate a sufficient level of the return on their data-related investments, for instance through revenues arising from granting data access against licence fees, there is a high risk that data sharing will not occur at a sufficient level.

The root cause of this incentive problem can be attributed to a positive externality and the risk of 'free riding': data access and sharing may benefit others more than it may benefit the data holder, who may not be able to privatise all the benefits of data re-use. Empirical evidence of the spillover social and economic benefits of data access and sharing presented in Section B.IV. suggests indeed that non-discriminatory access to data, even though it can help increase the value of data to data holders (direct impact), will tend to create 10 to 20 times more value to data users (indirect impact), and 20 to 50 times more value for the wider economy (induced impact). In some cases, however, it may even reduce the producer surplus of data holders, as in the case of open data.

Since data are only partially excludable goods for which the costs of exclusion will tend to be high *once* the data move out of the control sphere of the original data holders, there is the possibility that some may 'free ride' on the data holders' investments. The argument that follows is that if data are shared, free-riding users can 'consume the resources without paying an adequate contribution to investors, who in turn are unable to recoup their investments'.[48] This would then lead to a disincentive to share and, where

47 OECD, 'Research Ethics and New Forms of Data for Social and Economic Research' (2016) OECD Science, Technology and Industry Policy Papers No. 34 <www.oecd-ilibrary.org/docserver/5jln7vnpxs32-en.pdf?expires=1604226871&id=id&accname=guest&checksum=8CD30C2A2939BD7217A6AA3693115FC> accessed 31 August 2020.

48 Frischmann (n. 12) 9.

data access and sharing would be made mandatory, to a disincentive to invest in data in the first place.

However, the assumption that positive externalities and free riding always diminish incentives to invest cannot be generalised, and needs careful case-by-case scrutiny. In this regard, Frischmann notes:

> There is a mistaken tendency to believe that any grain or loss in profits corresponds to an equal or proportional gain or loss in investment incentives, but this belief greatly oversimplifies the decision-making process and underlying economics and ignores the relevance of alternative opportunities for investment.[49]

In addition, free riding is sometimes the economic and social rationale for providing access to data. Open data initiatives, for example, are motivated by the recognition that users *will* free ride on the data, and in so doing will be able to create a wide range of new goods and services that were not anticipated and would not otherwise be produced. In this sense, 'free riding is ... a feature, rather than a bug of our economic, cultural, and social systems'.[50] However, even though the externality and the risk of 'free riding' associated with data access and sharing may not necessarily lead to a loss in investment incentives, it may still lead to a loss in incentives to share data and thus to a dysfunctional 'data sharing economy', where only a few market participants are willing to share their data.

III. 'Data ownership' as an attempt to regain control over data

Granting private property rights is often suggested as a solution to the incentive problems related to free riding and, in the case of intangible assets, to address the risk of loss of control that comes with their non-excludability. The often raised question about who 'owns the data' is therefore essentially motivated by the recognition that ownership rights provide a 'powerful basis for control'[51] as 'to have legal title and full property rights to

---

49 Ibid 161.

50 Ibid.

51 Teresa Scassa, 'Data Ownership' (2018) CIGI Paper No. 187 <www.cigionline.org/sites/default/files/documents/Paper%20no.187_2.pdf> accessed 31 August 2020.

something'[52] implies 'the right to exclusive use of an asset'[53] and the 'full right to dispose of a thing at will'.[54]

In contrast to the concept of ownership of physical goods, where the owner typically has exclusive rights and control over the good – including for instance the freedom to destroy the good – this is not the case for intangibles such as data. For these types of goods, IPRs are typically suggested as the legal means to establish clear ownership. While some have expressed the opinion that, in principal, data cannot be owned,[55] 'the ability to access, create, modify, package, derive benefit from, sell or remove data, but also the right to assign these access privileges to [and retrieve them from] others'[56] – what could be defined as the main rights associated with 'data ownership' – are affected by different legal frameworks differently. IPRs, in particular copyright and trade secrets, can be applicable under certain conditions. In certain jurisdictions, cyber-criminal law may have the effects of conferring ownership-like rights to data holders, while 'data ownership' related questions emerging between firms can also be regulated by competition law.[57] And in the case of personal data, privacy protection frameworks will be relevant for the question of 'data ownership' as well. Thus, in contrast to other intangibles, data typically involve complex assignments of different rights across different stakeholders and are governed by multiple overlapping legal and regulatory frameworks.

1. *'Ownership' of personal data*

The complexity of the overlapping legal and regulatory frameworks is particularly apparent when it comes to personal data, which is also the topic where the debate on 'data ownership' seems the most controversial. There seems to be a general belief among many individuals that they 'own' or should 'own' their personal data. The reality, in many, if not most, juris-

52 Malcolm Chisholm, 'What Is Data Ownership?' (*BeyeNetwork* May 2011) <www.b-eye-network.com/view/15697>.

53 Lothar Determann, 'No One Owns Data' (2018) UC Hastings Research Paper No. 265 <https://ssrn.com/abstract=3123957> accessed 31 August 2020.

54 Ibid.

55 Ibid.

56 See David Loshin, 'Who Owns Data?' (*DM Review* March 2003) <http://knowledge-integrity.com/columns/dmr200303.htm>.

57 Osborne Clarke LLP, *Legal Study on Ownership and Access to Data* (European Commission 2016) <https://publications.europa.eu/en/publication-detail/-/publication/d0bec895-b603-11e6-9e3c-01aa75ed71a1> accessed 31 August 2020.

dictions, is that they do *not* legally 'own' their personal data. Data (including personal data) collected by an organisation will typically be considered the property of that organisation. For example, in Canadian case of *McInerney v. McDonald*,[58] 'one of the theories considered, and ultimately rejected, by the court was that a patient owned their personal medical information'.[59] Instead, the court found that the 'physician, institution or clinic compiling the medical records owns the physical records'.[60]

However, in the case of personal data, the 'ownership' rights of the organisation will hardly be comparable to other (intellectual) property rights. As Scassa concludes in regard to *McInerney v. McDonald*, 'the court also recognised an "interest" on the part of the patient amounting to a degree of control over the information.'[61] In fact, most privacy regulatory frameworks give data subjects particular control rights over their personal data, which may interfere with 'the full right to dispose of a thing at will'[62] typically associated with ownership. So in the particular case of personal data, no single stakeholder will have exclusive access and use rights. Different stakeholders will typically have different powers depending on their role.[63] Some authors have therefore stressed that privacy protection frameworks may have some characteristics like those of a property right.[64] As the EU General Data Protection Regulation (GDPR) has extended the control

58 *McInerney v. MacDonald*, 1992 CanLII 57 (SCC), [1992] 2 SCR 138, <http://canlii.ca/t/1fsbl> accessed 10 May 2020.

59 Scassa (n. 51).

60 Ibid.

61 Ibid.

62 Determann (n. 53).

63 See Fred Trotter, 'Who Owns Patient Data? Look inside Health Data Access and You'll See Why "Ownership" Is Inadequate for Patient Information' (*O'Reilly Radar* 2012) <http://radar.oreilly.com/2012/06/patient-data-ownership-access.html> accessed 31 August 2020. The author highlights that in the case of health patient data all stakeholders (including patient, doctor and programmer) 'have a unique set of privileges that do not line up exactly with any traditional notion of 'ownership'. Ironically, it is neither the patient nor the [doctor] who is closest to 'owning' the data. The programmer [or platform] has the most complete access and the only role with the ability to avoid rules that are enforced automatically by electronic health record (EHR) software.'.

64 See Nadezhda Purtova, 'Do Property Rights in Personal Data Make Sense after the Big Data Turn? Individual Control and Transparency' (2017) 10(2) Journal of Law and Economic Regulation 64; Josef Drexl, 'Legal Challenges of the Changing Role of Personal and Non-Personal Data in the Data Economy' in Alberto Di Franceschi and Reiner Schulze (eds), *Digital Revolution – New Challenges for Law* (2019) 19; Francesco Banterle, 'The Interface Between Data Protection and IP Law: The Case of Trade Secrets and the Database Sui Generis Right in Marketing

rights of individual to the right of data portability (Article 20), the similarities have become even stronger.

2. *Contractual arrangements and the role of contract guidelines and model contracts for data sharing*

The discussion above could suggest, and some have suggested, that multiple 'owners' (with co-ownership rights) will have to be assumed, 'as neither the "data producer" nor the "data gatherer" can claim an exclusive right over the data'.[65] As will be further discussed in Section D.II., multiple stakeholders are often involved in the contribution, collection and control of data, including in particular the data subject himself or herself when it comes to personal data. These stakeholders therefore typically have some interests in the data, and the challenge is how to disentangle and address the multiple (potential) interests of the various stakeholders – including the public interest in data – in a way that is compliant with law and aligned with societal values and objectives (see Section D.II.1.). This, combined with the 'intricate net of existing legal frameworks',[66] may explain current controversies and uncertainties related to 'data ownership', a challenge which is exacerbated where data are created, accessed and shared across jurisdictions.

As a response to this situation, businesses have come to rely on contract law as the primary legal vehicle for determining rights related to data control, access and re-use, in particular in business-to-business (B2B) contexts. These contractual arrangements often can better suit the individual context of data access, sharing and use (freedom of contract). While freedom of contract may give stakeholders the ability to construct well-suited contractual arrangements, existing uncertainties may also increase transaction costs, and expose particularly those that are in a weaker position to negotiate fair terms and conditions. These are typically individuals (consumers)

Operations, and the Ownership of Raw Data in Big Data Analysis' in Mor Bakhoum and others (eds), *Personal Data in Competition, Consumer Protection and Intellectual Property Law* (2018) 411.

65 Paul Hofheinz and David Osimo, 'Making Europe a Data Economy: A New Framework for Free Movement of Data in the Digital Age' (Lisbon Council Policy Brief 2017) <https://lisboncouncil.net/wp-content/uploads/2020/08/LISBON-COUNCIL-Making-Europe-A-Data-Economy.pdf> accessed 31 August 2020.

66 Determann (n. 53).

and SMEs.[67] As a result, incentives to share data, including with third parties, remain low and, where data-sharing arrangements are negotiated, they may be perceived as potentially unfair. In addition, the high transaction costs of negotiating fair terms and conditions may prevent the commercialisation of data as a commodity (via data marketplaces).

To address the issues highlighted above, some governments[68] and private sector actors[69] are providing guidance and/or model contracts for data-sharing agreements, including contractual clauses that are based on commonly agreed principles. These clauses constitute the default position that parties can consider when negotiating their data-sharing agreements.[70] Because they are voluntary, parties are free to deviate from the proposed contractual clauses at their will.[71] However, such deviation would have to be justifiable, which is why contract guidelines and model contracts are seen as promising means to assure fair terms and conditions for data access, sharing and re-use, in particular where there are significant power and in-

67 See the conflict between farmers and agriculture technology providers that led in the United States to AG Data Transparent, 'Ag Data's Core Principles: The Privacy and Security Principles for Farm Data' (2016) <www.agdatatransparent.com/principles/> accessed 31 August 2020. Similarly in Europe: COPA-COGECA and CEMA, 'EU Code of Conduct on Agricultural Data Sharing by Contractual Agreement' (2018) <https://copa-cogeca.eu/img/user/files/EU%20CODE/EU_Code_2018_web_version.pdf> accessed 31 August 2020.

68 For example, Japan's Ministry of Economy, Trade and Industry has formulated the 'Contract Guidance on Utilisation of AI and Data', which summarises the issues and factors to be considered when drafting a contract on the utilisation of AI or data. It is intended to be used as a reference when private businesses conclude contracts related to data re-use or development and use of AI-based software. See METI, 'METI Formulates "Contract Guidance on Utilization of AI and Data"' (2018) <www.meti.go.jp/english/press/2018/0615_002.html> accessed 10 August 2020.

69 In July 2019, Microsoft published three data-sharing agreements to be used as a template: (i) the Open Use of Data Agreement (O-UDA), (ii) the Computational Use of Data Agreement (C-UDA) and (iii) the Data Use Agreement for Open AI Model Development (DUA-OAI). These were complemented by a fourth one in November 2019: (iv) the Data Use Agreement for Data Commons (DUA-DC). See Microsoft, 'Removing Barriers to Data Innovation: Empowering People and Organizations to Share and Use Data More Effectively' (2019) <https://3er1viui9wo30pkxh1v2nh4w-wpengine.netdna-ssl.com/wp-content/uploads/prod/sites/560/2019/12/Backgrounder-FAQ-Sheet_FINAL.pdf> accessed 31 August 2020.

70 See European Commission, 'Guidance on Sharing Private Sector Data in the European data economy' SWD(2018) 125 final.

71 It is expected that parties would do so if such deviation better reflected their common interests and the specific context of their data-sharing agreements.

formation asymmetries between parties. Because they are based on agreed principles and refer to applicable national and international laws, contract guidelines and model contracts are expected also to reduce (legal) transaction costs.

However, while these guiding documents can help address the legal uncertainties and also to some extent the power and information asymmetries that may exist between business partners, they may fall short in addressing other important data governance issues where data access and use rights are concerned. This is most notably the case in respect to third parties with an interest in the data but who do not take part in the negotiations of the data-sharing agreements (e.g. consumers, social groups and the public). Therefore, guidelines and model contracts are not a silver bullet solution to maximise the economic and social benefit of data, although they are a promising additional tool in the data governance toolbox to facilitate data sharing.

D. Towards a more differentiated data governance approach for data access and sharing

This section presents possible solutions to the data governance challenges highlighted in Section C., or at least contributions to such solutions. A common cause of these challenges is the loss of control over data, which is rooted in the partial excludability of data, as mentioned several times already. The following section therefore looks at (i) technological means for re-establishing control over data and information, which are promising complementary solutions to legal measures (including IPRs) to help address the risks and challenges discussed in Sections C.I. and C.II. The next section then presents (ii) a data taxonomy for disentangling the various interests in data that can help address some of the challenges related to 'data ownership' discussed in Section C.III. This includes in particular the need to clarify the respective contributions of the potential 'multiple owners' in the data-enabled value creation process, as well as the potential interests of all relevant stakeholders, including the public. The last section briefly looks at (iii) data commons as data-sharing arrangements with variable degrees of openness and control and as a framework solution through which the other solutions discussed before could be implemented.

I. Technological means for re-establishing control over access to data and information

The following sections provide an overview of technological means for re-establishing control over data, many of which are known as privacy-enhancing technologies (PETs). PETs are typically used to prevent and mitigate the risk of privacy and confidentiality breaches and to enable organisations to better manage data responsibly. These technologies thus make it possible to balance the respective interests of stakeholders, namely by enabling data access and use, while protecting the respective rights of stakeholders, including the privacy rights of data subjects.[72] They are also promising means to deliberately adjust the level of data quality (e.g. level of aggregation and timeliness) and thus to control the information and value of data that are shared. These technological means are clustered in two groups: (i) technologies used for data access control and (ii) those traditionally known as PETs, used to protect privacy and confidentiality, and thus to control access to the information. The latter are referred to as 'confidentiality-enhancing technologies'.

1. Data access control mechanisms

There are a wide range of different mechanisms for accessing and sharing data within and across organisational borders. The following three can be considered the most commonly used:[73] data access via (i) (ad hoc) downloads, (ii) application programming interfaces (APIs) and (iii) data sandboxes. These mechanisms are typically implemented in cloud-based solutions, which give data holders an additional level of control, to the extent that the data remain within the same cloud service platform.

a) (Ad hoc) downloads

In the case of data access via downloads, the data are stored, ideally in a commonly used format, and made available online (e.g. via a web site). Da-

---

72 Alessandro Acquisti, 'The Economics of Personal Data and the Economics of Privacy' (2010) <www.oecd.org/sti/ieconomy/46968784.pdf> accessed 31 August 2020.

73 OECD (n. 5) 32–34.

ta access via downloads however raises several issues: Interoperability, for instance, is a major one when it comes to data re-use across applications (e.g. data portability), and one which is not guaranteed even when commonly used machine-readable formats are used.[74] Furthermore, ad hoc downloads fail to address the risk of loss of control over data. Therefore, the provision of data via ad hoc downloads typically comes with significant digital security and privacy risks, as data holders lose their capabilities to enforce any data policies including in respect to the protection of privacy and IPRs.

b) Application programming interfaces (APIs)

APIs enable service providers to make their digital resources (e.g. data and software) available over the Internet. They facilitate the interoperability of the different actors and their technologies and services. A key advantage of APIs (compared to an ad hoc data download) is that APIs enable a software application to directly use the data it needs. Data holders can also implement several restrictions via APIs to better control the use of their data including means to assure data syntactic and synthetic portability.[75] Furthermore, they can help control the identity of API users, the scale and scope of the data used (including over time), and even the extent to which the information derived from the data could reveal sensitive or personal information. APIs thus provide moderate, although in many cases sufficient, control over data.

c) Data sandboxes for trusted access and re-use of sensitive and proprietary data

The term 'data sandbox' is used to describe any isolated environment through which data are accessed and analysed, and analytic results are only

74 These formats may enable *data syntactic portability*, i.e. the transfer of 'data from a source system to a target system using data formats that can be decoded on the target system'. But they do not guarantee *data semantic interoperability*, 'defined as transferring data to a target such that the meaning of the data model is understood within the context of a subject area by the target', ibid. 32.

75 See text at n. 74.

exported, if at all, when they are non-sensitive.[76] These sandboxes can be realised through technical means (e.g. isolated virtual machines that cannot be connected to an external network) and/or through physical on-site presence within the facilities of the data holder (where the data can be accessed). Data sandboxes would typically require that the data processing code is executed at the same location as where the data are stored. Compared to the other data access mechanisms presented above, data sandboxes offer the strongest level of control. Data sandboxes are therefore promising for providing access to very sensitive/personal and proprietary data including across borders.[77]

2. *Confidentiality-enhancing technologies for information access control*

a) Cryptography

Cryptography is a practice that 'embodies principles, means, and methods for the transformation of data in order to hide its information content, establish its authenticity, prevent its undetected modification, prevent its repudiation, and/or prevent its unauthorised use'.[78] It is increasingly used by businesses and for consumer goods and services to protect the confidentiality of data, such as financial or personal data, whether those data are in storage or in transit.[79] A number of innovative cryptography-based applications for data access and sharing are emerging. These include for instance:

- *Homomorphic encryption*, which makes it possible to run computations on encrypted data whilst protecting privacy and confidentiality. As a re-

---

76 See Royal Society, 'Privacy Enhancing Technologies: The Current Use, Development and Limits of Privacy Enhancing Technologies in Data Analysis' (2019) 25–28 <https://royalsociety.org/-/media/policy/projects/privacy-enhancing-technologies/privacy-enhancing-technologies-report.pdf> accessed 31 August 2020, where they are referred to as 'trusted execution environments.'.

77 See for example the Virtual Research Data Center (VRDC) of the the Centers for Medicare and Medicaid Services (CMS). ResDAC, 'CMS Virtual Research Data Center (VRDC)' <www.resdac.org/cms-virtual-research-data-center-vrdc> accessed 12 August 2020. See also Henze and others (n. 43); Yves-Alexandre de Montjoye, Sébastien Gambs, Vincent Blondel and others, 'On the Privacy-Conscientious Use of Mobile Phone Data' (2018) 5 Scientific Data No. 180886 <www.nature.com/articles/sdata2018286> accessed 31 August 2020.

78 OECD, 'Recommendation of the Council concerning Guidelines for Cryptography Policy' (1997) OECD/LEGAL/0289 (OECD Crypto Guidelines).

79 OECD (n. 39) 270–73.

sult, a user can for example encrypt data, send it to the cloud for processing and have the results of the computation sent back to him or her or to third parties, all the while maintaining the privacy of the individual concerned and confidentiality of the data.[80]

- *Blockchain or distributed ledger technologies (DLTs)*, which enable decentralised solutions for the storage and management of data to address some of the challenges related to data control and trust. Instead of relying on a centralised operator, a blockchain relies on a distributed network of peers to maintain and secure a decentralised database. What is significant for trust in data access and sharing is not only the fact that blockchains are highly resilient and tamper-resistant,[81] which enables, for instance, robust auditing of the actual usage of data.[82] In addition, blockchains, via e.g. 'smart contracts',[83] can facilitate the management of access control permissions, including for the licensing of data access and use rights.[84]

b) De-identification: from anonymisation to pseudonymisation and aggregation

De-identification covers a range of practices ranging from anonymisation to pseudonymisation and aggregation. These practices share a common aim of preventing the extraction of identifying attributes (i.e. re-identification), or at least significantly increasing the costs of re-identification. Anonymisation is a process in which an individual's identifying information is excluded or masked so that the individual's identity cannot be, or

---

80 See Royal Society (n. 76) 21–25.

81 Once data have been recorded on the decentralised data store, they cannot be deleted subsequently or modified by any single party.

82 See Sundareswaran, Squicciarini and Lin (n. 43).

83 'Smart contracts' are self-executing decentralised applications based on blockchain that can initiate trackable and irreversible transactions based on predefined conditions. See Mayukh Mukhopadhyay, *Ethereum Smart Contract Development: Build Blockchain-Based Decentralized Applications Using Solidity* (Packt Publishing 2018).

84 See Andreas Muelder, 'Model-Driven Smart Contract Development for Everyone' (*Hacker Noon* 2019) <https://hackernoon.com/model-driven-smart-contract-development-for-everyone-jiu32p0> accessed 31 August 2020; Yongkai Fan, Jinghan Wang, Zhenting Hong and others, 'A Blockchain-Based Data-Sharing Architecture' in Zibin Zheng and others (eds), *Blockchain and Trustworthy Systems* (Springer Singapore 2020) 636.

becomes too costly to be, reconstructed.[85] Some research has shown however that when linked with other data, most anonymised data can be de-anonymised – that is, the identifying information can be reconstructed.[86]

Where stronger protection is required or desired, additional means – including 'noise' addition, functional separation and distribution (decentralisation) and administrative and legal safeguards – are needed. The addition of 'noise' to a data set, for instance, allows analysis based on the complete data set to remain significant while masking sensitive data attributes.[87] Work on 'differential privacy' is one prominent example in which noise is added to the data so that when a statistic is released, information about an individual is not revealed with it.[88] For many applications, however, identifiers are needed because complete anonymity would be useless, preventing for instance two-way communication and transactions. In these cases, pseudonymisation offers a solution whereby the most identifying attributes (i.e. identifiers) within a data record are replaced by unique artificial identifiers (i.e. pseudonyms). Finding the right balance that protects privacy and confidentiality, while minimising the costs to data utility, thus remains a challenge for all these means.

II. A data taxonomy for disentangling the various interests in data

Data are often treated as a monolithic entity, although evidence shows that data are heterogeneous goods whose value depends on the context of their use. A more differentiated approach to the governance of data is therefore needed, and this requires identifying the different types of data and their characteristics.

The following sections present two major dimensions that are considered critical for the governance of data access and sharing. These include:

---

85 Andreas Pfitzmann and Marit Hansen, 'A Terminology for Talking about Privacy by Data Minimization: Anonymity, Unlinkability, Undetectability, Unobservability, Pseudonymity, and Identity Management' (2010) <https://dud.inf.tu-dresden.de/literatur/Anon_Terminology_v0.34.pdf> accessed 31 August 2020; Kato Mivule, 'Utilizing Noise Addition for Data Privacy, an Overview' (2013) <https://arxiv.org/ftp/arxiv/papers/1309/1309.3958.pdf> accessed 31 August 2020.

86 See de Montjoye and others (n. 77). See also Arvind Narayanan and Vitaly. Shmatikov, 'How to Break Anonymity of the Netflix Prize Dataset' (2006) <https://arxiv.org/pdf/cs/0610105.pdf> accessed 31 August 2020.

87 See Mivule (n. 85).

88 Cynthia Dwork and Aaron Roth, 'The Algorythmic Foundations of Differential Privacy' (2014) 9 Foundations and Trends in Theoretical Computer Science 211.

(i) the *domain of the data*, which describes whether there are potentially personal (individual), private (business) and/or public (societal) interests associated with a particular dataset, and the relevant legal and regulatory regimes; and (ii) *the manner in which data originate*, which reflects the level of awareness and control that various data stakeholders, including data subjects, data holders and data users, can have, and therefore, most importantly, the type of contribution of the various potential 'multiple owners' in the data-enabled value creation process.

1. *The overlapping domains of data – reflecting the various stakeholder interests*

Besides the dichotomy between personal and non-personal data, the most frequent distinction made in policy debates is between private and public sector data. It is generally accepted and expected, for example, that public sector data in contrast to private sector data should be made available through open data, free of charge and free of any restrictions from IPRs – where there are no conflicting national security or private interests. However, the private–public data distinction often made is not only blurred since public and private sector data cannot always be distinguished,[89] but more importantly, because it risks distracting attention from the related contentious issues highlighted in Section C and further explained below. A differentiation between the following three domains of data is suggested therefore instead (Figure 3):

- *the personal domain*, which covers all data 'relating to an identified or identifiable individual'[90] (personal data) for which data subjects have an interest in privacy,
- *the private domain*, which covers all proprietary data that are typically protected by IPRs or by other access and control rights (provided by

89 Data can often qualify as both public sector *and* private sector data, and this irrespective of any joint activities between public and private sector entities (e.g. public-private partnerships). For instance, data generated, created, collected, processed, preserved, maintained or disseminated by the private sector that are however funded by or for the public sector would qualify as both public sector *and* private sector data. Compare this with the definition of public sector information in OECD, 'Recommendation of the Council for Enhanced Access and More Effective Use of Public Sector Information' (2008) OECD/LEGAL/0362 (OECD PSI Recommendation).

90 OECD Privacy Guidelines (n. 44).

e.g. contract, cyber-criminal or competition law), and for which there is typically an economic interest to exclude others, and

- *the public domain*, which covers all data that are not protected by IPRs or any other rights with similar effects, and therefore lie in the 'public domain' (understood more broadly than to be free from copyright protection), thus free to access and re-use, as well as data for which there is a public interest.

Figure 3. The personal, private and public domain of data

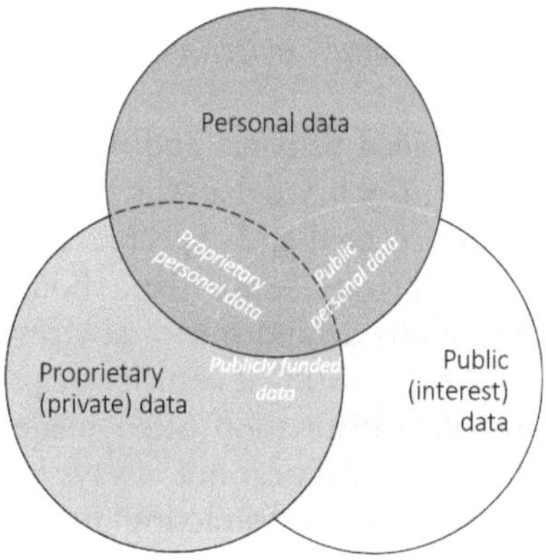

Source: OECD, *Enhancing Access to and Sharing of Data: Reconciling Risks and Benefits for Data Re-use across Societies* (OECD 2019) 29.

These three domains not only overlap as illustrated in Figure 3, but they are also typically subject to different data governance and legal frameworks that can affect each domain differently. For instance, privacy regulatory frameworks typically govern the personal domain, while the private domain is typically governed through e.g. contractual, IPR and/or competition regulatory frameworks. The overlaps may partly explain the potential conflicting views and interests of some stakeholder groups, as reflected for instance in issues related to 'personal data ownership' discussed in Section C.III.[91]

Furthermore, these overlaps can explain why data governance is often perceived as complex from a legal and regulatory perspective, in particular when cross-border data flows are concerned. Depending on the jurisdic-

91 See also the call for collaboration between competition, privacy and consumer protection authorities as discussed, for instance, in OECD (n. 1) 109.

tion, some domains may be prioritised differently over others, and this difference in prioritisation seem to reflect differences in culture and legal systems. This is for example reflected in current privacy and data portability rights, which vary significantly across countries, reflecting various approaches to balancing the conflicting interests of individuals and organisations over 'proprietary personal data' (Figure 3). In the case of data portability, which aims to empower individuals and give them more control rights over their personal data, what type of data falls within the scope of data portability varies across initiatives, partly reflecting the (implicit) priorities of the personal v the proprietary domain.[92]

Another area where data governance has proven to be particularly challenging, and where the 'domains of data' could help make more explicit some of the prevailing tensions, is when public interest in data is concerned, in particular when such interest 'overlaps' with the interests in proprietary and personal data (the centre of the Venn diagram in Figure 3). A few countries have started to specify a new class of data, which is often referred to as *data of public or general interest*.[93] The scope of this class varies significantly across countries however. In some countries, data of public interest explicitly refers to private sector data (of public interest), while in others it refers to public sector data. Sometimes both private and public sector data, as well as personal and non-personal data, are included. What they have in common though is that they seem to refer to data needed to fulfil more or less well-defined societal objectives that otherwise would be impossible or too costly to fulfil. These objectives can include the development of national statistics, the development and monitoring of public policies, the tackling of health care and scientific challenges of societal importance and in some cases the provision of public services.[94]

---

92 See Louisa Specht-Riemenschneider, 'Data access rights – A comparative perspective', in this volume.

93 See Loi n° 2016–1321 du 07 octobre 2016 pour une République numérique 2016 (Law for a digital Republic). It defines 'data of general interest' (données d'intérêt général) as including: (i) private sector data from delegated public services such as utility or transportation services, (ii) private sector data that are essential for granting subsidies and (iii) private sector data needed for national statistics.

94 See Heiko Richter, 'The law and policy of government access to private sector data ("B2G data sharing")', in this volume.

2. *The manner data originate – reflecting the contribution to data creation*

Multiple stakeholders are often involved in the contribution, collection and control of data, including the data subject in the case of personal data. The data categories discussed above – in particular the distinction between the personal domain and the proprietary domain – however do not help differentiate how different stakeholders contribute to data co-creation. The following data categories that differentiate according to the way data are collected or created can provide further clarity in this respect.[95]

- *Volunteered (or surrendered or contributed or provided) data* are data provided by individuals when they explicitly share information about themselves or others. Examples include creating a social network profile and entering credit card information for online purchases.
- *Observed data* are created where activities are captured and recorded. In contrast to volunteered data, where the data subject is actively and purposefully sharing its data, the role of the data subject in the case of observed data is rather passive and it is the data controller that plays the active role. Examples of observed data include location data of cellular mobile phones and data on web usage behaviour.
- *Derived (or inferred or imputed) data* are created based on data analytics, including data 'created in a fairly "mechanical" fashion using simple reasoning and basic mathematics to detect patterns'.[96] In this case, it is (only) the data processor that plays the active role in the creation of data. The data subject typically has little awareness of what is inferred about her or him, given in particular that personal information can be derived from several pieces of seemingly anonymous or non-personal

---

95 They are based on Bruce Schneier, 'A Taxonomy of Social Networking Data' (*Schneier on Security*, 2009) <www.schneier.com/blog/archives/2009/11/a_taxonomy_of_s.html> accessed 31 August 2020; Martin Abrams, 'The Origins of Personal Data and Its Implications for Governance' (2014) <https://ssrn.com/abstract=2510927> accessed 31 August 2020; Productivity Commission of Australia, 'Productivity Commission Inquiry Report: Data Availability and Use' (2017) <www.pc.gov.au/inquiries/completed/data-access/report/data-access.pdf> accessed 31 August 2020.

96 OECD, 'Summary of OECD Expert Roundtable Discussion on "Protecting Privacy in a Data-Driven Economy: Taking Stock of Current Thinking"' (2014) DSTI/ICCP/REG(2014)3, 5 <www.oecd.org/officialdocuments/publicdisplaydocumentpdf/?cote=dsti/iccp/reg(2014)3&doclanguage=en> accessed 31 August 2020.

data.[97] Examples of derived data include credit scores calculated based on an individual's financial history.

- *Acquired (purchased or licenced) data* are obtained from third parties based on commercial (licencing) contracts (e.g. when data are acquired from data brokers) or other non-commercial means (e.g. when acquired via open government initiatives). As a result, contractual and other legal obligations may affect the re-use and sharing of these data.

To illustrate the moment of creation of the different types of data, Figure 4 presents a stylised process in which a product user (e.g. a consumer) would interact with a data product (e.g. an online service or portable smart device) that is provided by a product provider (e.g. a business). The data product would typically (i) observe the activities of its users, in which case *observed data* are created; and/or (ii) be used to input data volunteered by its users (*volunteered data*). The data could then be accessed for further processing (and the creation of *derived data*) by the product provider as well as by any third parties who may have been granted direct or indirect access to the original (volunteered and observed) data – or in a less identifiable form. The creation of derived data can also be enriched when combined with *acquired data* from (other) third parties.

Figure 4. Data products and the different manners data originate

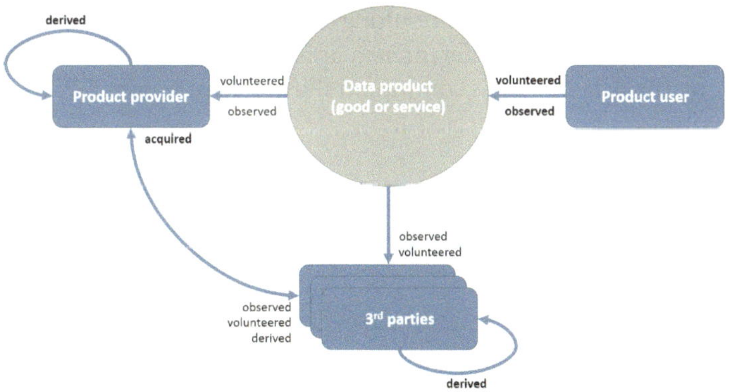

Note: Arrows represent potential data flows between the different actors and a data product (good or service). The type of data is highlighted in bold to indicate the moment at which the data are created.

Source: Ibid. 31.

97 See Narayanan and Shmatikov (n. 86).

This differentiation is relevant for the governance of data for several reasons: (i) it helps determine the level of awareness that product users (including data subjects) can have about the scale and impact of data collection, which is critical, for example, when assessing the privacy risks associated with data collection and the level of control product users can be expected to have. (ii) It also reflects the contribution of various stakeholders to data creation and therefore their potential rights and interests in accessing and re-using the data. (iii) Last, but not least, this differentiation can help identify the geographic location and jurisdiction based on data generation and collection, and it can therefore help determine the applicable legal and regulatory frameworks.

III. Data commons as arrangements with variable degrees of openness and control

The infrastructural nature of data as non-rivalrous, general-purpose productive capital, combined with the spillover benefits of data re-use and the demand manifestation problem, suggest that maximising access to data, for instance through open data, will in theory maximise social welfare if every additional private benefit comes at no additional cost. The latter condition is not always true, however, given the risks and challenges highlighted in Section C and the resulting need for more controlled data access. This calls for more differentiated approaches to data access and sharing along the data openness continuum illustrated in Figure 5.[98]

98 This continuum suggests that data access and sharing should not be seen as a 'binary concept' (opposing closed to open data), but rather a continuum of different degrees of data openness, ranging from internal access and re-use (only by the data holder), to restricted (unilateral and multilateral) external access and sharing, and open data as the most extreme form of data openness.

Figure 5. The degrees of data openness and access

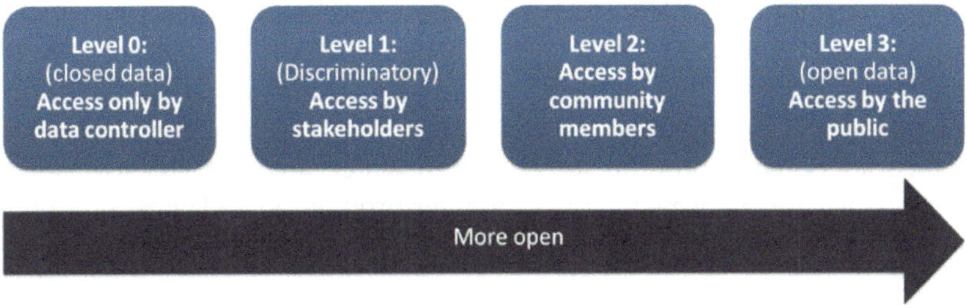

Source: OECD, *Data-Driven Innovation: Big Data for Growth and Well-Being* (OECD 2015) 185.

The most prominent approach to non-discriminatory data access and sharing discussed in the literature and by policy makers is still *open data*. Besides open data, a wide range of other approaches exist, with different degrees of data openness that respond to the various interests of stakeholders and the risks they face in data sharing. Many of these approaches are based on voluntary and mutually agreed terms between organisations, while others are mandatory such as the right to data portability under Article 20 GDPR or Australia's recently proposed Consumer Data Right (CDR),[99] which are both non-discriminatory in respect of the data subject's intent of data re-use.

This section first introduces the concept of 'data commons' and argues that many of the approaches to data access and sharing highlighted above can be seen as a special form of data commons, whereby the relevant community varies, ranging from the public at large such as in the case of open data (level 3 in Figure 5), to the members of a community such as in the case of data partnerships (level 2), or the data subject and data controller such as in the case of data portability (level 1). Due to space constraints, the section then only focusses on restricted data-sharing arrangements (level 2), given that the other approaches to data sharing are well documented in the literature, if not in this publication.

99 See ACCC, 'Consumer Data Right (CDR)' <www.accc.gov.au/focus-areas/consumer-data-right-cdr-0> accessed 31 August 2020.

1. *Data commons for the governance of shared resources of common interests*

The concept of 'commons' has been used to describe natural resources that are managed and used for collective benefits, as well as the governance mechanisms (including informal norms and values) affecting their consumption.[100] Commons are therefore defined as collective goods in which stakeholders have common interests, and which are characterised by the governance mechanisms surrounding their production and consumption.

Applied to data, commons imply formal or informal governance institutions to enable the sustainable shared production and/or use of data. Data commons can therefore be defined as the institutionalised sharing of data among members of a community. Although the concept of data commons has been used most prominently for public sector open data – which may explain why data commons sometimes is misunderstood, and used as a synonym for 'open data' – the community within which data sharing is institutionalised may, but does not necessarily need to, include the public at large (as in the case of open data). Commons will for instance emerge where data are not, or no longer, privately 'owned' by a single entity, but rather considered a collective resource of common interest within a community that requires common management and governance institutions, such as in data partnerships discussed below.

In data commons, data access by community members is often granted, independent of their identity and their intent of use (non-discriminatory access). This does not imply that access must be free, unregulated or without any terms and conditions. The important point here is that non-discriminatory access can maximise the value of data, while the scope of access is essentially defined by the scope of the community. The positive spillovers in combination with non-discriminatory access can lead to Rose's 'comedy of the commons',[101] where greater social value is created with greater use of data, in contrast to Hardin's 'tragedy of the commons',[102] where free riding on common (natural) resources leads to the degradation and the depletion of the resources.

---

100 See Charlotte Hess and Elinor Ostrom (eds), *Understanding Knowledge as a Commons: From Theory to Practice* (MIT Press 2007); Michael J. Madison, 'Commons at the Intersection of Peer Production, Citizen Science, and Big Data: Galaxy Zoo' in Brett M. Frischmann, Michael J. Madison and Kathrine J. Strandburg (eds), *Governing Knowledge Commons* (Oxford University Press 2014) 209.

101 Carole Rose, 'The Comedy of the Commons: Custom, Commerce, and Inherently Public Property' (1986) 53 University of Chicago Law Review 711.

102 Garret Hardin, 'The Tragedy of the Commons' (1968) 162 Science 1243.

That said, the establishment of data commons can be quite complex as it involves a number of considerations such as on community definition, institutional design, the relevant regulatory framework, boundaries and exclusion of non-members, pricing and congestion management to assure the sustainability of the commons, and in some cases even considerations on exceptions from the non-discrimination rule.[103] The complexity of the governance is exacerbated by the fact that commons, and knowledge commons in particular, are often clustered in multiple ways as well as nested within each other.[104] Many knowledge communities (e.g. scientific communities) define, and in turn are defined by, the knowledge commons. Patient-related commons, for instance, are often nested together with scientific knowledge commons, and infrastructure and digital-tools-related commons (e.g. software and data). The understanding, establishment and support of commons therefore require systematic analysis of all relevant contextual factors.[105]

2. *Restricted data-sharing arrangements*

In cases where data are considered too confidential to be shared openly with the public (as open data) or where there are legitimate (commercial and non-commercial) interests opposing such open sharing, restricted data-sharing arrangements can be more appropriate. This is for instance the case when there may be privacy, IPR (e.g. copyright and trade secrets) and organisational or national security concerns legitimately preventing open

---

103 See Frischmann (n. 12) 92, who highlights that 'exceptions [to non-discrimination] arise in many contexts – for reasons of emergency [...] or securing the commons itself. In some cases, sustaining a resource as a commons requires narrowly tailored exceptions to address specific, identifiable uses that degrade, deplete, or otherwise harm the resource itself or risk harm to the community of users. That such exceptions exist in some contexts for certain types of infrastructure resources does not undermine the basic nondiscrimination rule, as long as the exceptions do not swallow the rule.'.

104 See Brett M. Frischmann, Michael J. Madison and Kathrine J. Strandburg (eds), *Governing Knowledge Commons* (Oxford University Press 2014).

105 See Elinor Ostrom and Charlotte Hess, 'A Framework for Analyzing the Knowledge Commons' in Charlotte Hess and Elinor Ostrom (eds) *Understanding Knowledge as a Commons: From Theory to Practice* (MIT Press 2007) 41. The institutional analysis and development (IAD) framework has been used for the systematic analysis of knowledge commons. See also Frischmann, Madison and Strandburg (n. 104).

sharing of data. In these cases, however, there can still be a strong economic and/or social rationale for sharing data among data users within a restricted community, under voluntary and mutually agreed non-discriminatory terms.

It is, for example, common to find restricted data-sharing agreements in areas such as digital security (e.g. for vulnerability disclosure), science and research (e.g. for health care research) and as part of business arrangements for shared resources (e.g. within joint ventures). These voluntary data-sharing arrangements can be based on commercial or non-commercial terms depending on the context. Two types of data-sharing arrangements are highlighted in the following sections in more detail: (i) *data partnerships*, which are based on the recognition that data sharing can provide not only significant economic benefit to data users, but also to data holders; and (ii) *data for societal objectives* initiatives, where data are shared to support societal objectives.

a) Data partnerships

In data partnerships, organisations agree to share and mutually enrich their data sets, including through cross-licensing agreements. One big advantage is the facilitation of joint production or co-operation with suppliers, customers (consumers) or even potential competitors (co-opetition).[106] This also enables data holders to create additional value that a single organisation would not be able to create and provides opportunities 'to join forces *without* merging'.[107] Examples include:[108]

106 It is worth noting that the concept of data partnerships offers some similarities with other concepts known in the world of IPRs, most notably patent pools, which are essentially agreements between two or more patent holders to license one or more of their patents to one another or third parties. See WIPO, 'Patent Pools and Antitrust – a Comparative Analysis' (2014) <www.wipo.int/export/sites/www/ip-competition/en/studies/patent_pools_report.pdf> accessed 31 August 2020.

107 Benn R. Konsynski and Warren F McFarlan, 'Information Partnerships – Shared Data, Shared Scale' (1990) 68 Harvard Business Review 114.

108 Other benefits include the ability to: (i) maximise the *option value* of data (i.e. value of keeping the options for irreversible investments open); and (ii) (cross-)subsidise public and social goods, which otherwise would require picking winners (users or applications). See OECD (n. 1) 177.

- The pooling of aggregated data between Take Nectar, a UK-based programme for loyalty cards, and collaborating firms such as Sainsbury (groceries), BP (gasoline) and Hertz (car rentals) to 'allow ... the three companies to gain a broader, more complete perspective on consumer behaviour, while safeguarding their competitive positions'.[109]
- The joint venture between DuPont Pioneer and John Deere, which was initiated in 2014 with the aim to develop a joint agricultural data tool.[110]

Similar partnerships also exist in the form of public and private partnerships (data PPPs). For example, the sharing of data (including through open data) with major Internet platform providers such as Google, Waze, Twitter and Apple enabled Transport for London (TfL), a local government body responsible for the transport system in Greater London (United Kingdom), to gain access to new data and that was used to improve its business operation and services.[111]

Data partnerships (including data PPPs) however raise several challenges, some of which are similar to those highlighted in Section C.III. For instance, ensuring a fair data-sharing agreement between the partners can sometimes be challenging, in particular where partners have different levels of market power. Privacy and IPR considerations may also limit the potential of data partnerships by making it harder to sustain data sharing in some cases. Where data partnerships involve competing businesses, data sharing may increase the risk of (implicit) collusion including the formation of cartels and fixing of price. In the case of data PPPs, there may also be some challenges due to the double role of governments, namely as an authority on one hand and service (data) provider on the other.

---

109 Michael Chui, James Manyika and Steve Van Kuiken, 'What Executives Should Know about Open Data' (*McKinsey&Company* 2014) <www.mckinsey.com/industries/high-tech/our-insights/what-executives-should-know-about-open-data> accessed 31 August 2020.

110 See Russ Banham, 'Who Owns Farmers' Big Data?' Forbes (*Forbes*, 8 July 2014) <www.forbes.com/sites/emc/2014/07/08/who-owns-farmers-big-data/> accessed 31 August 2020.

111 See Deloitte, 'Assessing the Value of TfL's Open Data and Digital Partnerships' (2017) <http://content.tfl.gov.uk/deloitte-report-tfl-open-data.pdf> accessed 31 August 2020.

b) Data for societal objectives

Data-sharing arrangements can also be found where private sector data are provided (donated) to support societal objectives, ranging from science and health care research to policy making. For instance, in an era of declining responses to national surveys, the re-use of private sector data can significantly improve the power and quality of statistics, in particular in developing economies.[112] The re-use of private sector data also provides new opportunities to better inform public policy making, for instance, when close to real-time evidence is made available to 'nowcast' policy-relevant trends.[113] In some initiatives, private sector data have been provided, for instance, to address urgent societal objective including during disasters and health crises including pandemics such as COVID-19.[114]

For example, mobile telecommunications services providers in a few countries have started to share geolocation data based on CDRs with governments in an aggregated, anonymised format. As these network operators serve substantial portions of the population across entire nations, they can measure movements of millions of people at fine spatial and temporal scales in near-real time. The resulting information is used by governments seeking to track the COVID-19 outbreak, warn vulnerable communities and understand the impact of policies such as social distancing and confinement. The European Commission, for instance, has been liaising with

---

112 See Christian Reimsbach-Kounatze, 'The Proliferation of "Big Data" and Implications for Official Statistics and Statistical Agencies: A Preliminary Analysis' (2015) OECD Digital Economy Paper No. 245 <https://www.oecd-ilibrary.org/science-and-technology/oecd-digital-economy-papers_20716826> accessed 31 August 2020.

113 See Hyonyoung Choi and Hal Varian, 'Predicting the Present with Google Trends' (2009) <https://static.googleusercontent.com/media/www.google.com/de//googleblogs/pdfs/google_predicting_the_present.pdf> accessed 31 August 2020; Derrick Harris, 'Hadoop Kills Zombies Too! Is There Anything It Can't Solve?' (*Gigaom* 18 April 2011) <https://gigaom.com/2011/04/18/hadoop-kills-zombies-too-is-there-anything-it-cant-solve/> accessed 31 August 2020; Yan Carrière-Swallow and Felipe Labbé, 'Nowcasting with Google Trends in an Emerging Market' (2013) 32 Journal of Forecasting 289.

114 OECD, 'Ensuring Data Privacy as We Battle COVID-19' (14 April 2020) <www.oecd.org/coronavirus/policy-responses/ensuring-data-privacy-as-we-battle-covid-19-36c2f31e/> accessed 31 August 2020; OECD, 'Tracking and Tracing COVID: Protecting Privacy and Data While Using Apps and Biometrics' (23 April 2020) <www.oecd.org/coronavirus/policy-responses/tracking-and-tracing-covid-protecting-privacy-and-data-while-using-apps-and-biometrics-8f394636/> accessed 31 August 2020.

European telecommunications operators to obtain from them anonymised aggregate mobile geolocation data, and to coordinate measures tracking the spread of COVID-19 at EU level.[115]

E. Conclusion

This chapter highlighted one of the major tensions that policy makers and practitioners face when dealing with data governance issues, namely the tension between the social benefits of 'data openness' on one hand, and individuals' and organisations' risks and legitimate concerns over such openness on the other hand. This tension is rooted in the economic properties of data presented in Section B, most notably (i) their non-rivalrous nature, which calls for maximum openness (data sharing) to leverage the potential spillover benefits of data as a productive capital (Section B.IV) and (ii) their partial excludability, which comes with the risk of loss of control (Section C.I), which in turn can disincentivise data sharing (Section C.II). The discussion in this chapter suggested that granting private 'data ownership' rights was *not* the silver bullet solution. The fact that data are partly excludable however opens the possibility for a wide range of alternative or complementary solutions presented in Section D. Their combination through data commons arrangements, such as for instance data partnerships, promises to address many, if not most, of the challenges highlighted in Section C.

Besides the need for more research and development (R&D) in technological means for enhancing controlled data sharing (including PETs), a major policy recommendation that results from this chapter is the need for guidance on data commons. As highlighted in Section D.III.1., the establishment of data commons can be quite complex as it requires a careful analysis of all the contextual factors relevant for data sharing. While the institutional analysis and development (IAD) framework developed by Nobel Prize laureate Elinor Ostrom is promising from a research perspective, practitioners, in particular SMEs, may require practical guidelines to be able to establish and take advantage of data commons. In view of countries' experiences on contract guidelines and model contracts for data shar-

115 See Commission Recommendation (EU) 2020/518 of 8 April 2020 on a common Union toolbox for the use of technology and data to combat and exit from the COVID-19 crisis, in particular concerning mobile applications and the use of anonymised mobility data [2020] OJ L114/7.

ing, it would seem desirable that similar guiding documents with a focus on data commons be provided. That the private sector, most notably Microsoft,[116] is moving in this direction is therefore a promising development.

116 See the Data Use Agreement for Data Commons (DUA-DC) (n. 69).

Data access, consumer interests and social welfare – An economic perspective on data

Bertin Martens

A. Introduction

This chapter presents an economic introduction to digital data, data access and the well-being of consumers and society at large. 'Data access' may cover a variety of modalities of data exchange between two or more parties, from monetised trade to free access or exchange of data in return for a service. Any voluntary data exchange is a market-based transaction. A key question for data policy makers is whether private voluntary data access decisions maximise the welfare of society as a whole. Economists define market failures as situations where the aggregate private welfare of firms and consumers remains below the total welfare that society as a whole could achieve. This occurs when the incentives of private firms and/or consumers make them behave in ways that diminish overall social welfare. This may justify regulatory intervention in data markets and the imposition of mandatory access conditions that overrule private decisions. The focus of this chapter is therefore on data market failures.

Following the European Commission's 'Better Regulation Guidelines'[1] we take a broad approach to possible regulatory intervention in data markets and data-driven services markets. It includes monopolistic market failures that are usually handled by competition law and extends to other sources of market failures such as externalities, asymmetric information and missing markets because of high transaction costs and risks. We also point out potential regulatory failures and social concerns, such as welfare distribution and discrimination that could motivate regulatory interven-

1 In European Commission 'Better Regulation Guidelines' (2017) <https://ec.europa.eu/info/law/law-making-process/planning-and-proposing-law/better-regulation-why-and-how/better-regulation-guidelines-and-toolbox_en> accessed on 31 August 2020 and Communication from the Commission to the European Parliament, the Council, the European Economic and Social Committee and the Committee of the Regions – 'A European strategy for data' COM (2020) 66 final, 13 note 39, where the Commission also advocates a market-failure based approach to regulatory intervention in data markets.

tion. While mainstream competition law takes consumer welfare as the policy objective,[2] this chapter takes a wider public policy economics view and focuses on the overall social welfare of society as a policy objective, the combined welfare of firms and consumers. This distinction may become important for example in data-driven online platforms where an exclusive focus on the consumer side may have unintended negative effects on the supply side, and vice versa.

Furthermore, this chapter goes beyond markets and looks at the impact of data on institutions and organisational arrangements in the economy. Digital technology helped to overcome pre-digital information constraints that prevented the realisation of higher levels of social welfare. Digital data contributed to the emergence of new markets for goods and services. These markets often require new ways of organising economic exchange and new types of firms to do this, which are generically labelled as 'platforms', and they give rise to new sources of market failures that need new regulatory interventions.

This chapter is structured as follows. Section B discusses the specific economic characteristics of data that are in several respects different from ordinary goods and services. We explore how these characteristics affect data collection and data use markets. Section C brings digital platforms into the picture, a new type of firms that leverage some of the economic characteristics of data to create new markets. Section D broadens the perspective on data market failures and possible regulatory solutions. Section E adds some concluding observations.

B. The economic characteristics of data

I. Data as intermediary input

Data are usually an intermediary input, not a final consumer good. For example, unless they are aviation aficionados, consumers do not search for flight schedules on Google or Skyscanner because they enjoy looking at these schedules but because they want to buy an air transport service. Data

2 See Jason Furman, Diane Coyle, Amelia Fletcher, Derek McAuley and Philip Marsden, 'Unlocking Digital Competition – Report of the Digital Competition Expert Panel' (UK Government 2019) <https://assets.publishing.service.gov.uk/government/uploads/system/uploads/attachment_data/file/785547/unlocking_digital_competition_furman_review_web.pdf> accessed 31 August 2020 (so-called 'Furman Report').

are not created ex nihilo. They are collected by firms from observing the behaviour of people, machines and nature – the data originators. Data exchange involves at least two markets, an upstream data collection market and a downstream data use market for the production of goods and services. These two markets can be vertically integrated in a single firm or they can be carried out by different firms that trade data between them. Data collection can happen prior to their use in services, or it can be a by-product of services. For example, the Google Search ranking depends on data collected from users of the search engine. There are many data exchange modalities. They can be traded for a monetary compensation or in exchange for a service, sharing can be for free or subject to conditions in other markets, etc. Data can be traded directly – when they are effectively transmitted between parties – or indirectly – when parties do not transmit data but only a data-driven service. For example, Google online advertising services do not transmit consumer data to advertisers. They sell a targeted advertising service based on consumer data which they keep in-house.

II. Data collection has an economic cost

The data collector needs a financial incentive to invest in data infrastructure, for example because it offers the prospect of monetising data. Data originators also need incentives to share their data with a collecting firm. A frequently observed business model in data collection markets is to offer originators a free service in return for sharing their personal or industrial data. The willingness of data sources to share data with collectors will not only depend on conditions in the data market but also on subsequent use of the data in services markets. For example, the willingness of consumers to share their data with a website will depend on the quality of services offered by that website as well as subsequent use of the data by the website, for instance for online advertising. Firms that offer free services need to find a way to cover the cost of producing these services. Google and Facebook offer free services in return for the ability to monetise user data in online targeted advertising. There are no free lunches in the data economy, though the party that pays for the lunch may be different from the party that enjoys the lunch. Any change in the cost of data collection and in benefits for data users will affect the volume and possibly the quality of data collected.

III. The value of data depends on their use

Data have no value on their own; they become valuable only to the extent that consumers and firms can use them to improve their position in data-driven services markets. Economists have tried to get a better understanding of these services markets' effects and the impact on stakeholders. There is no coherent framework yet for the economic analysis of data, though research focuses on the welfare and revenue-shifting potential of data.[3] Pro-competitive data uses imply that both firm revenue and user benefits from a data-driven service increase with additional data. For example, more data collection and more efficient use of the data in hotel booking platforms can simultaneously improve the user experience, revenue for hotels and platform revenue. Competitive use may still cause welfare shifts between firms and their customers and trigger equity and welfare distribution concerns. For example, firms can use data for price discrimination or other forms of discrimination strategies that increase the welfare of the firm but not of all users. All these generic statements on data impact are subject to empirical evidence. This may be easy to obtain for firms that collect large amounts of user data and run behavioural experiments with their online users to decide on their profit-maximising commercial strategies. A wide data-access gap between firms and policy makers often inhibits the design of policies to improve social welfare.[4]

IV. Excludability and monopolistic data trade

In contrast to physical goods, data are not excludable by nature. They can easily be copied and disseminated. The law can assign exclusive rights to

---

3 Alexandre de Cornière and Greg Taylor, 'Data and Competition: A General Framework with Applications to Mergers, Market Structure and Privacy Policy' (2020) CEPR Discussion Paper No. DP14446, <https://ssrn.com/abstract=3547379> accessed on 31 August 2020.

4 Business-to-government data sharing initiatives in several EU Member States and by the European Commission seek to bridge this gap. See for example European Commission, 'Towards a European Strategy on Business-to-Government Data Sharing for the Public Interest: Final Report prepared by the High-Level Expert Group on Business-to-Government Data Sharing' (2020) <www.euractiv.com/wp-content/uploads/sites/2/2020/02/B2GDataSharingExpertGroupReport-1.pdf> accessed 31 August 2020. This subject is discussed in detail by Heiko Richter, 'The law and policy of government access to private sector data ('B2G data sharing')', in this volume.

data originators and/or collectors. So far, there are no general data ownership rights in the EU or elsewhere.[5] In a few cases, the law grants erga omnes exclusive rights. For example, the EU Database Directive[6] grants, under restrictive conditions, sui generis ownership rights to producers of databases. The EU General Data Protection Regulation (GDPR)[7] grants some exclusive and inalienable control rights to natural persons as data subjects, including the right to give consent to access to personal data, and rights to data access, portability and deletion. The data subject is unambiguously defined as the rights holder over personal data. This is not necessarily the case for non-personal machine-generated data that may be co-generated by several parties. Assigning exclusive rights to one party may affect the entire industry value chain.[8] Attempts at assigning exclusive private rights over data are inspired by the Coase Theorem, which hypothesises that markets will work efficiently when ownership rights are well-defined and transaction costs are low or zero. However, the intrinsic social value of many data generates externalities.[9] In these circumstances, private rights cannot bridge the gap between the private and the social value of data.

In the absence of legal private ownership rights, a data-holding firm can apply technical protection measures to protect its de facto exclusive control and access to the data. This enables the firm to raise revenue from selling the data or data-driven services to users, with bilateral contracts that benefit from legal protection under commercial law. However, they can-

5 Néstor Duch-Brown, Bertin Martens and Frank Mueller-Langer, 'The Economics of Ownership, Access and Trade in Digital Data' (2017) Joint Research Centre Working Papers on Digital Economy <https://ssrn.com/abstract=2914144> accessed 31 August 2020.

6 Directive 96/9/EC of the European Parliament and of the Council of 11 March 1996 on the legal protection of databases [1996] OJ L77/20. See also Matthias Leistner 'The existing european IP rights system and the data economy: An overview with particular focus on data access and portability', in this volume.

7 Regulation (EU) 2016/679 of the European Parliament and of the Council of 27 April 2016 on the protection of natural persons with regard to the processing of personal data and on the free movement of such data, and repealing Directive 95/46/EC (General Data Protection Regulation) [2018] OJ L127/2.

8 For an example from the agricultural sector, see Can Atik and Bertin Martens, 'Governing Agricultural Data and Competition in Data-driven Agricultural Services: A Farmer's Perspective', (2020), <www.researchgate.net/publication/342105835_Governing_Agricultural_Data_and_Competition_in_Data-driven_Agricultural_Services_A_Farmer%27s_Perspective> accessed on 31 August 2020.

9 See section B.VIII. below.

not be enforced against third parties. In case of data leaks, firms have no recourse against third parties that benefit from these leaks.

Data use markets require monopolistic conditions to generate revenue. If more parties have access to the same dataset, or to close substitutes, competition will drive prices down to the marginal cost of reproduction, which is usually close to zero for digital data. That eliminates opportunities to generate revenue and incentives to invest in data collection and processing. Monopolistic data pricing above marginal cost requires rationing or reducing the quantity (and possibly the quality) of data that can be accessed. Not all demand will be satisfied, unless perfect price discrimination is feasible. Monopolistic trade does not maximise social welfare. It increases the welfare of the data holding firm at the expense of data users. Data access policies require careful balancing between monopolistic and open data markets.

V. Data are not a homogeneous product

Data are subject to quality differentiation and can be traded in various levels of fine graining and information content. Quality differentiation may be necessary to avoid falling into the Arrow Paradox: once data are revealed to a potential buyer there is no point in trading them anymore because the buyer already has the information he wanted to buy. There are many strategies that a potential data seller can apply to reduce the information content of a 'demonstration' dataset to entice a potential buyer while avoiding this paradox.[10] The seller can offer a reduced sample of the data, or a coarse-grained or aggregated version that does not reveal details, or an anonymised version etc. The seller can also refrain from sharing data directly with a buyer and deliver an indirect data-based service only, as in the Google advertising example. Data quality differentiation may facilitate price discrimination between buyers. Trading detailed consumer data with data users may reduce the willingness of consumers to share data with the collecting firm. Data buyers on the other hand will prefer more detailed data because it enables them to price discriminate in services sales. The data intermediary will adjust the quality of the data that he collects from consumers and sells to users in order to maximise his profits.

10 For an overview, see Dirk Bergemann and Alessandro Bonatti, 'Markets for Information: An Introduction' (2019) 11 Annual Review of Economics 85.

VI. Non-rivalry and economies of scope in data re-use

Data are non-rival. Many parties can use the same dataset at the same time for a variety of purposes without functional loss to the original data collector. Rival goods can only be used by one party at a time. For example, a car is a rival physical good and can only be used by one driver at the time. If a car were non-rival, all drivers could use the same car at the same time to drive to different destinations. The economic welfare gains would be enormous: it would suffice to invest in the production of a single car to cater to the needs of all drivers. This promise of substantial welfare gains from exploiting non-rivalry in data re-use constitutes the foundation stone of the data access and sharing debates.[11] Data collected by one firm can be re-used for other purposes, either by the same firm or by other firms provided they can access the data. The primary data collection effort is a sunk cost that can be amortised across many uses, rather than remaining confined to a single user. It can boost innovation and enable the production of new and innovative data services that the original data collector did not envisage.

Economies of scope in re-use were originally defined in the context of joint production and (re-)use of the same product or asset to produce other outputs.[12] For example, a car manufacturer can re-use the same engines in different car models. Re-use of the same non-rival engine design entails zero marginal re-design costs. However, there is a positive marginal cost for physical re-production of additional engines. Non-rival digital data have quasi-zero marginal reproduction costs because it involves only copying an electronic data file. Still, data re-use by other firms may create interoperability problems and important fixed costs for the design of a data transmission interface.

Data re-use and access by other parties also has a cost side. All digital data can, in principle, be made interoperable and shared for the benefit of so-

11 OECD Directorate for Science and Technology, 'Maximizing the Economic and Social Value of Data – Understanding the Benefits and Challenges of Enhanced Data Access' (OECD 2016) DSTI/CDEP(2016)4 <https://one.oecd.org/document/DSTI/CDEP(2016)4/en/pdf> accessed 31 August 2020; Charles I. Jones and Christopher Tonetti, 'Nonrivalry and the Economics of Data' (2020) 110 American Economic Review 2819.

12 David J. Teece, 'Economies of Scope and the Scope of the Enterprise' (1980) 1 Journal of Economic Behavior and Organization 223; David J. Teece, 'Towards an Economic Theory of the Multiproduct Firm' (1982) 3 Journal of Economic Behavior and Organization 39; John C. Panzar and Robert. D. Willig, 'Economies of Scope' (1981) 71 The American Economic Review 268.

ciety.[13] However, neither firms nor individuals want their private data to be widely available. Privacy and commercial confidentiality are important for the autonomy of private decision-making and for extracting private value from these decisions. While non-rival data can be shared by firms and individuals without functional losses, sharing may entail an economic opportunity cost and losses for the original data holder. Other firms may re-use the data in service applications that compete with those of the original data holding firm and undermine the latter's market position.[14] The data holder may also want to produce these alternative services in-house and appropriate the benefits, rather than leaving it to another firm.

Firms and persons will trade off the expected benefits from data sharing against the expected costs and risks that they might incur from doing so. These private cost-benefit perceptions may limit the extent of data exchange, sharing and re-use. The question for policy makers is whether private data decisions by consumers and firms maximise the welfare that society as whole could derive from the data. If not, there is a market failure that may require policy intervention. Data sharing is not an objective in its own right but a means to achieve higher social welfare for society.

VII. Economies of scope in data aggregation

A second, and often neglected, source of economies of scope in data comes from data aggregation. Merging two complementary datasets can generate more insights and economic value compared to keeping them in separate data silos. This insight can be traced back to the economics of learning and division of labour.[15] When two datasets are complementary and not entirely separable, applying data analytics – the equivalent of learning – to the merged set will yield more insights and be more productive than applying it to each set separately, especially when the marginal cost of applying analytics to a more complex dataset is relatively small.

Economies of scope in data are controversial in economics, in part because they are misunderstood. Authors usually do not distinguish between

13 John Palfrey and Urs Gasser, *Interop: The Promise and Perils of Highly Interconnected Systems* (Basic Books 2012).

14 Hongwei Zhu, Stuart E. Madnick and Michael D. Siegel, 'An Economic Analysis of Policies for the Protection and Reuse of Noncopyrightable Database Contents' (2008) 25 Journal of Management Information Systems 199.

15 Sherwin Rosen, 'Specialization and Human Capital' (1983) 1 Journal of Labour Economics 43.

economies of scale and scope, especially not scope in data aggregation. For example, one author defines economies of scope somewhat ambiguously as cost savings relative to an 'increased level of production of multiple products'.[16] 'Increased level of production' implies economies of scale; 'multiple products' refers to economies of scope in re-use, not in aggregation. A useful way to distinguish economies of scale and scope is to consider a dataset as a two-dimensional spreadsheet, with the number of columns representing the number of variables and the number of rows the number of observations on these variables. Economies of scale refer to increased prediction accuracy due to an increase in the number of rows. Economies of scope refer to increased prediction accuracy due to an increase in the number of columns or explanatory variables. Adding more columns (variables) is not helpful when they are highly correlated or when they are not related at all. A number of empirical studies claim that economies of scope in data are weak or non-existent.[17] All these studies are more about economies of scale rather than scope. Bajari and others[18] come closest to economies of scope in aggregation. They find that product sales forecasts do not become more accurate when historical data from several products markets are aggregated. However, this is explained by weak complementarity among product markets that result in separable datasets and thus in weak economies of scope. The absence of empirical studies on economies

---

16 Catherine Tucker, 'Digital Data, Platforms and the Usual [Antitrust] Suspects: Network Effects, Switching Costs, Essential Facility' (2019) 54 Review of Industrial Organization 683.

17 Lesley Chiou and Catherine Tucker find no decrease in search engine accuracy when time series of consumers' historical searches are shortened because of EU privacy regulation. Nico Neumann, Catherine E. Tucker, Timothy Whitfield, (2019) 'Frontiers: How Effective Is Third-Party Consumer Profiling? Evidence from Field Studies' (2019) 38 Marketing Science 918 show that large data brokers do not necessarily perform better in consumer profiling than data brokers with fewer consumer profile data. Jörg Claussen, Christian Peukert and Ananya Sen, 'The Editor vs. the Algorithm: Targeting, Data and Externalities in Online News' (2019) <https://ssrn.com/abstract=3399947> accessed 31 August 2020, find that more individual user data help algorithms to outperform human news editors but decreasing returns to user engagement set in rapidly. Preston McAfee, 'Measuring Scale Economies in Search' (Lear conference, Rome, 2015) slides available <www.learconference2015.com/wp-content/uploads/2014/11/McAfee-slides.pdf> accessed 31 August 2020, finds that Google Search outperforms Microsoft Bing in long-tail searches because of a higher number of users.

18 Patrick Bajari, Victor Chernozhukov, Ali Hortaçsu and Junichi Suzuki, 'The Impact of Big Data on Firm Performance: An Empirical Investigation' (2019) 109 AEA Papers and Proceedings 33.

of scope in data aggregation is a major gap in data economics. There is some supportive anecdotal evidence. Google gradually improved its targeted advertising by combining personal data from several sources, starting from web searches and adding email and maps (location) data.[19] Navigation apps like Waze and Tom-Tom combine real time GPS location data with maps that are populated with data from a wide range of public and private sources including road and traffic authorities, municipalities, firms and in-map advertisers. These public sector data may have little commercial value on their own but contribute to a valuable service when aggregated with private data.

Economies of scale and scope in data aggregation are a source of positive externalities. In the age of artificial intelligence and machine learning, personal data collected on the behaviour of one set of consumers has predictive value for the behaviour of other consumers.[20] Once a firm has accumulated a critical mass of consumer data, the additional insights obtained from adding another consumer's personal data are small. Acemoglu and others[21] argue that this diminishes the value of individual personal data. Consumers cannot prevent this negative externality and market failure for their personal data. Their best deal is to harvest some consumer surplus by trading their data for an online service that has a higher marginal use value than the depressed market value of their personal data. This could explain the privacy paradox:[22] consumers value their privacy but do not invest in protecting it. They understand the low value of their personal data and the futility of investing in privacy protection in the presence of negative externalities from other consumers' data.

The re-use and aggregation interpretations of economies of scope in data may lead to very different policy implications. Economies of scope in re-use are an argument in favour of data dissemination and de-concentration. Economies of scope in aggregation, by contrast, favour data concentration in large pools. They are not mutually exclusive. Non-rival data can be stored at the same time in concentrated pools and in distributed settings.

---

19 Roger McNamee, *Zucked: Waking Up to the Facebook Catastrophe* (Penguin Random House 2019).

20 Ajay Agrawal, Joshua Gans and Avi Goldfarb, *Prediction Machines: The Simple Economics of Artificial Intelligence* (Harvard Business Review Press 2018).

21 Daron Acemoglu, Ali Makhdoumi, Azarakhsh Malekian and Asuman Ozdaglar, 'Too Much Data: Prices and Inefficiencies in Data Markets' (2019) NBER Working Paper No. 26296 <www.nber.org/papers/w26296> accessed 31 August 2020.

22 Alessandro Acquisti, Curtis Taylor and Liad Wagman, 'The Economics of Privacy' (2016) 54 Journal of Economic Literature 442.

Both concentration and de-concentration can result in market failures that undermine social welfare.[23]

VIII. The social value of data

A peculiar characteristic of many[24] data is their social value. Economies of scope in aggregation add a first social dimension to the value of data. Two owners of separate but complementary datasets can only achieve a higher value from their data if they collaborate and pool the two sets. A second source of social value comes from economies of scale. Once a sufficiently large sample of behavioural observations has been compiled to produce robust predictions, those data can be used to predict the behaviour of agents outside the sample.[25] This implies that collecting more data about other agents with similar characteristics has zero marginal value because the existing dataset is sufficiently representative.

These externalities imply an inherent market failure in exclusive private control over data. The party that does (not) provide the data to a collector is not necessarily (may still be) the party that is affected by their use. The de facto exclusive data holder is not necessarily the party that maximises benefits from the data. Pooling data can generate the full social value. However, coordination costs and risks may undermine spontaneous pooling. An intermediary agent may be required in order to realise the social externalities from data pooling and turn them into benefits that pay for the coordination costs and incentivise individuals to participate in the pool. With this, we reach the world of data platforms in the next section.

---

23 Economies of scope in aggregation and re-use exist in intellectual property rights. The market value of a set of complementary patents may be higher than the sum of their separate values. Hence the practice of patent bundling and thickets, and the bundling of standard-essential patents (SEPs) to facilitate re-use of technical standards. Bundling strengthens the monopolistic position of patent holders. Fair, reasonable and non-discriminatory (FRAND) licensing seeks to avoid abusive behaviour.

24 Some types of data may have little or no social value as it remains situation, person or firm-specific and cannot be used to infer something about other agents or situations, or has no complementarity with other datasets.

25 Dirk Bergemann, Alessandro Bonatti, and Tan Gan, 'The Economics of Social Data' (2020) Cowles Foundation Discussion Paper No. 2203R, revised version March 2020 <https://cowles.yale.edu/sites/default/files/files/pub/d22/d2203-r.pdf> accessed 31 August 2020.; Acemoglu and others (n. 21).

C. Platforms and data-driven network effects

Much of the contemporary policy debate on data access is still set in the context of data trade between traditional firms, consumers and data re-users. However, a substantial volume of data exchanges and data-driven services trade takes place in a new type of firms that are usually classified under the generic label of 'platforms'. In this section we explore the crucial role of platforms in the data economy and the benefits and problems that they generate. We start with network effects and then explain the positive and negative roles that they play in platforms.

I. Data-driven network effects

Network effects occur when bringing more users into a group increases the value of the group for all users. For example, when more users join a telephone or social media network, it becomes more valuable to all users and thereby attracts even more users. Data play a role in generating network effects. In some cases that role is very minimal and static. For example, users in a telephone network differ only by their telephone number, a unique lexicographic address. Users can be unambiguously matched by combining two lexicographic addresses. The only dataset required to make the telephone network operate optimally is a telephone directory. Matching between telephone users cannot be improved by observing the behaviour of the users. Similarly, in simple online e-commerce stores, a targeted search for a well-defined product may just require a catalogue of unambiguously defined products. For example, search for a book title in the Amazon book store. In these cases, network effects are mainly driven by the variety of products and users and their unique identification. Data on user behaviour or product quality play no role in networks with an unambiguous matching process. However, in more complex networks matching is not unambiguous and becomes probabilistic. This requires more data than a simple catalogue of lexicographic addresses. For example, matching in search engines and targeted advertising markets requires more data on the characteristics of users and products, beyond a lexicographic identifier, in order to select the most likely and optimal matches. It collects contents of webpages and tallies user clicks on pages in the search ranking in order to better understand the relevance of pages for a specific search term. It will then carry out a probabilistic matching between users and pages, with a ranking of the most likely matches. More precise data on user preferences will increase the efficiency of probabilistic matching and generate data-driven network effects.[26]

When the quantity and quality of data play an essential role in probabilistic matching we come back to economies of scale and scope in data aggregation.[27] For example, it has been shown that the larger number of users in Google Search make it more efficient in rare search terms than Microsoft Bing, which has a much smaller number of users.[28] That difference in efficiency, in turn, motivates users to shift to Google. Economies of scale mean more observations on similar search terms while economies of scope in aggregation imply collecting search results from a wider variety of search terms. The two may reinforce each other. The rise of artificial intelligence and machine learning has further amplified economies of scale and scope in data aggregation. While human learners can learn a behavioural response from a few observations, machine learning algorithms often require huge numbers of observations to learn an appropriate response.

II. The role of platforms in the data economy

Platforms are well-placed to realise the benefits from economies of scale and scope in data aggregation. There are many definitions of platforms, or multi-sided markets in economic jargon, in the economics literature, and there is no consensus among economists on these definitions.[29] Data played no role in the first generation of multi-sided market models,[30] which were an extension of the economics of infrastructure networks.

26 Data-driven network effects were first analysed by Jens Prüfer and Christoph Schottmüller, 'Competing with Big Data' (2017) TILEC Discussion Paper No. 2017–006 <https://ssrn.com/abstract=2918726> accessed 31 August 2020.

27 Maurice E. Stucke and Allen P. Grunes, *Big data and competition policy* (Oxford University Press 2016) already speculated that there is a link between economies of scope and network effects or network externalities. Tucker is not convinced. See Tucker (n. 16).

28 McAfee (n. 17).

29 For an overview of the (fairly recent) history of economic thinking on platforms, see for example Bertin Martens, 'An Economic Policy Perspective on Online Platforms' (2016) Institute for Prospective Technological Studies Digital Economy Working Paper 2016/05 JRC101501 <https://ssrn.com/abstract=2783656> accessed 31 August 2020.

30 Bernard Caillaud and Bruno Jullien, 'Chicken & Egg: Competition among Intermediation Service Providers' (2003) 34 RAND Journal of Economics 309; Geoffrey Parker and Marshall W. Van Alstyne, 'Two-Sided Network Effects: A Theory

They focused on markets with at least two types of users, for instance buyers and sellers. Platforms are faced with a 'chicken and egg' problem: they need many users in order to attract many users. They can solve this problem by charging a very low or zero price to attract many users on one side of the market and charging a higher price to the other side to pay for the cost of the platform. Users with a high price elasticity of demand pay low or zero entry costs while users with low price elasticity pay a higher price. This explains why advertisers pay for ads while users get free access to search and social media services: advertisers have no choice but to advertise in the platform where users with specific profiles are looking for goods or services that the advertiser sells. Users can however multi-home between many platforms to find what they are looking for. These first-generation models ran into problems distinguishing between intermediary platform and ordinary retailers and defining the type of interaction between two sides.[31] To overcome these problems, recent models have broadened the definition of platforms to firms that bring economic agents together and actively promote network externalities between them.[32] In other words, platforms are firms that seek to maximise the social value of data. Economies of scale and scope in data aggregation in a platform ensure that the collective social value of data exceeds the sum of their individual private values.[33] Individuals cannot realise this social value on their own; only platforms can do this through their data aggregation role. Creating a searchable catalogue of products or a directory of users is a first step in generating that social value. For more efficient matching in ambiguous search settings, the platform operator collects more detailed data on buyer preferences and product characteristics. For example, Netflix can improve its

of Information Product Design'(2005) 51 Management Science 1494; Jean-Charles Rochet and Jean Tirole, 'Platform Competition in Two-Sided Markets' (2003) 1 Journal of the European Economic Association 990; Jean-Charles Rochet and Jean Tirole, 'Two-Sided Markets: A Progress Report' (2006) 37 RAND Journal of Economics 645.

31 Andrei Hagiu and Julian Wright, 'Marketplace or Reseller?' (2015) 61 Management Science 184.

32 Jens-Uwe Franck and Martin Peitz, 'Market Definition and Market Power in the Platform Economy' (2019) Center on Regulation in Europe Report <https://cerre.net/publications/market-definition-and-market-power-platform-economy/> accessed 31 August 2020. This definition does avoid the problem of setting a minimum number of market sides; one is enough.

33 Bergemann, Bonatti and Gan (n. 25).

film title search engine when it learns more about user preferences and film characteristics.[34]

A comparison with traditional offline markets illustrates the importance of online platforms as data collectors and producers of data-driven externalities. In a traditional town market, buyers walk around and collect information on what is on sale, and sales conditions, and make their choices. The town authority as market organiser has hardly any information on sellers' offers, buyer preferences and actual transactions. Each user has to collect this information separately; there is no common information pool. This is costly for users and socially inefficient. Costs increase with market size. In online markets, the platform operator collects an aggregated view of supply and demand and actual transactions. Users can benefit from this aggregated information. It would be impossible for users in large online platforms with millions of product entries to collect all the information on their own. Platforms are in a unique position as third-party data aggregators to realise economies of scale and scope in data aggregation across many users. Individual users cannot realise these benefits.[35]

Platforms are new types of firms that emerged in the wake of digital data. The traditional view of the firm goes back to Ronald Coase.[36] Coase wondered what makes firms an efficient arrangement between workers who divide tasks and exchange intermediate goods between each other within a firm rather than going through the market for these exchanges. He argued that firms reduce transaction costs compared to going through the market. By implication, the borderline of the firm, between in-house production and external trade, depends on transaction costs. Digital data and online platforms have dramatically reduced transaction costs to quasi-zero in many cases. As a result, some firms stop in-house production altogether, delegate production to external agents and transform themselves into market places. In contrast to traditional firms that keep the market

34 Marco Iansiti and Karim R. Lakhani, *Competing in the Age of AI: Strategy and Leadership When Algorithms and Networks Run the World* (Harvard Business Review Press 2020) Ch. 6.

35 For example, Imke C. Reimers and Joel Waldfogel estimate that the welfare effect of aggregated consumer book review data on the Amazon book sales platform is about 15 times larger than the welfare effects from a single-authored book review in a newspaper. Imke C. Reimers and Joel Waldfogel, 'Digitization and Pre-Purchase Information: The Causal and Welfare Impacts of Reviews and Crowd Ratings' (2020) NBER Working Paper No. 26776 <www.nber.org/papers/w26776> accessed 31 August 2020. This informational advantage puts platforms in a strong bargaining position vis-à-vis individual user data.

36 Ronald H. Coase, 'The Nature of the Firm' (1937) 4 Economica 386.

outside, these 'inverted' firms[37] become market organisers rather than production organisers. They organise a market platform where different types of users, for instance buyers and sellers, can trade goods and services. Iansiti and Lakhani[38] show that data-driven platforms are not subject to diminishing returns to scale. Human labour is replaced by data-driven algorithmic procedures with high fixed set-up costs but nearly zero marginal costs. Non-rival data and algorithms make these platforms infinitely scalable. This leads to huge productivity and efficiency gains but also to increased market power and monopolisation.

Many of today's largest online platforms are probabilistic data-driven matching services: Google Search, Facebook, Amazon, Netflix, Uber, e-scooter platforms, etc. They put data at the core of their business model and specialise in transactions that require substantial datasets for efficient matching between users. They compete on increasing matching efficiency. Platforms help to create new markets that were missing in the pre-digital economy because information-related transaction costs were too high. For example, finding a hotel was costly in the analogue economy and required intermediation from travel agencies that offered a limited choice to consumers. Finding 'information' in general was costly. These missing information markets were not a market failure because the technology to overcome them was not available at the time, or remained very imperfect. Digital data technology has dramatically reduced information cost and thereby expanded user choices. However, users require third-party intermediary platforms to collect and classify the avalanche of digital information in order to make efficient use of it.

III. Monopolistic market failures in platforms

In the traditional platform economics model, network effects incentivise users to congregate together on the largest platforms. This strengthens the position of the incumbent platform at the expense of potential new entrants into the market. The latter will have to overcome network effects to compete with incumbent platforms. Ordinary network effects require only simple data, a lexicographic directory of addresses of users. More complex networks require more elaborate data for efficient matching between

37 See Geoffrey Parker, Marshall Van Alstyne and Xiaoyue Jiang, 'Platform Ecosystems: How Developers Invert the Firm' (2017) 41 MIS Quarterly 255.

38 Iansiti and Lakhani (n. 34).

users. Large platforms can compile aggregated datasets on user behaviour and product characteristics. They achieve positive network externalities that enable them to provide more efficient matching services and further amplify network effects. The downside of these positive network externalities is that it reinforces platforms' monopolistic market position and may lead to abuse of dominant market positions.

The strength of data-driven network effects plays a key role in tipping[39] and varies by type of platforms and the relevant data in these platforms. For example, in ride-hailing and e-mobility platforms, network effects are very local. The platform may be organised on a global basis but network effects depend on local supply and users in cities. Expanding the supply in city A has no benefits for users located in city B, unless they happen to travel frequently between the two cities. This makes it easier for smaller local platforms to compete in local markets with global platforms. Hotel booking platforms are global however. Users search for hotels in many cities and platforms have to ensure a wide geographical variety of offers. This makes competition more difficult. Platforms can pursue deliberate strategies to tip the market in their favour, for example by increasing the costs of multi-homing or switching to other platforms. For example, drivers can easily switch between ride-hailing platforms with little costs. To discourage drivers from switching, platforms may offer them an uninterrupted sequence of rides, with advance notice of the next ride before the on-going ride is completed.

Hagiu and Wright[40] illustrate how the value that platforms can extract from data is conditional on several factors. Improving the quality of insights and the matching efficiency of data can be subject to economies of scale. In some cases, a few observations are sufficient to make an accurate prediction, while in other cases millions of observations are required to reach a reasonably accurate prediction. For example, automated driving algorithms are still far from perfect despite millions of miles of accumulated driving data by leading firms such as Google for its Waymo project. This is often true for artificial intelligence-based applications in platforms that depend on large numbers of observations. Insights that can be extrapolated to a wide number of users have high value. For example, personalised music recommendations in Pandora, based on cumulative learning from individual users, cannot easily be applied to other users. Spotify's shared music

39 See Iansiti and Lakhani (n. 34) sec. 6.

40 Andrei Hagiu and Julian Wright, 'When Data Creates Competitive Advantage' (2020) 1 (Jan.-Feb.) Harvard Business Review 94.

recommendations by contrast benefit from strong network externalities because they are useful to many users.

Several competition policy reports investigate the link between data and platform market power.[41] They suggest some re-thinking of competition policy tools to take into account that data-driven network effects are often the cause of competition problems. The reports pay attention to data policy tools as a means to attenuate data-driven monopolistic behaviour, for example by opening access to exclusive datasets, or a variety of data pooling and data sharing modalities. Data sharing with competitors may prevent an upstream monopolistic data collector from foreclosing downstream services markets. For example, car manufacturers design the car data architecture to retain exclusive access to car data, which they can leverage to increase their share in aftersales services markets. Mandatory data access for other aftersales service providers can prevent this competition problem.[42] Opening data access may backfire however. It may reduce rather than increase competition when data from small competitors are aggregated by large platforms that can offer users additional advantages, based on economies of scope in re-use and aggregation with other data sources. For example, payment services offered by Apple and Google, or payment services on the WeChat social media app in China and perhaps in future on Facebook, compete with local banks. Google Android and Apple iOS are increasingly present in cars and may offer a wide variety of aftermarket services that compete with smaller service providers. Since data are not a homogeneous product, data access and sharing can be restricted to a degree of coarseness that preserves some incentives and advantages for the original data collector while still broadening competition in the market

41 Jacques Crémer, Yves-Alexandre de Montjoye and Heike Schweitzer, 'Competition Policy for the Digital Era – Final Report' (European Union 2019) <https://ec.europa.eu/competition/publications/reports/kd0419345enn.pdf> accessed 31 August 2020; Furman and others (n.2); Fiona Scott Morton and others, 'Committee for the Study of Digital Platforms – Market Structure and Antitrust Subcommittee Report' (2019) George J. Stigler Center for the Study of the Economy and the State and the University of Chicago Booth School of Business <www.chicagobooth.edu/research/stigler/events/antitrust-competition-conference> accessed 31 August 2020.

42 Bertin Martens and Frank Mueller-Langer, 'Access to Digital Car Data and Competition in Aftermarket Maintenance Market' (2020) 16 Journal of Competition Law and Economics 116; Wolfgang Kerber, 'Data Governance in Connected Cars: The Problem of Access to In-Vehicle Data' (2018) 9 Journal of Intellectual Property and Information Technology and Electronic Commerce 310, para 1.

for data-driven services. That would require a careful balancing act and constant market and technology monitoring by regulators.

Data sharing with potential competitors will erode firms' data aggregation monopoly,[43] lower the value of the data and undermine their ability to monetise the data and invest in data collection. In a multi-sided market, modifying access conditions on one side of the market will have implications for other sides. For example, forcing a search or social media platform to share consumer data with competitors may not only affect consumer privacy. It lowers entry costs into advertising and will force platforms to increase entry costs on the consumer side, or integrate new money-raising sides into the platform to compensate the lost revenue.

Platforms are both a blessing and a curse in the digital data economy. They are necessary intermediaries to generate benefits from data aggregation, realise data-driven positive network externalities and enable the emergence of new markets that were not feasible prior to the arrival of digital data. At the same time, data aggregation generates new sources of market failures that did not exist in the pre-digital economy. In the next section we discuss non-monopolistic market failures induced by data-driven platforms.

D. *Other data-driven market failures*

The European Commission's 'Better Regulation Guidelines' distinguish between several types of market failures that may require regulatory intervention to maximise welfare for society. Besides monopolistic market failures, other sources of failure include externalities, information asymmetries and missing markets because of high transaction costs and risks. Regulators may also intervene in the case of social concerns such as discrimination and unequal distribution of welfare. In this section we discuss three types of data-driven non-monopolistic market failures: negative externalities from data aggregation, asymmetric information problems that distort decision making by data users, and newly missing markets that emerge in the wake of the data economy because of high data transaction costs and new sources of data-related risks.

43 Competition policy issues in data-driven platforms are discussed by Heike Schweitzer and Robert Welker, 'A legal framework for access to data: A competition policy perspective', in this volume.

I. *Information externalities*

In Section C we discussed the crucial role that platforms play in capturing data-driven positive network externalities, turning them into benefits for users and monetising them to their own benefit. In this section we turn to negative data-driven externalities caused by data aggregation in platforms, with examples on the consumer side in personal data markets, and on the producer side in commercial data markets. While positive externalities increase social welfare, negative externalities should be avoided or internalised by the party that causes them.

A first example of the negative impact of consumer platforms on the value of personal data is mentioned above[44] on economies of scope in data aggregation. Data collected on the behaviour of one set of users has predictive value for the behaviour of other users.[45] Once a firm has accumulated a critical mass of consumer data, the marginal return in terms of improved insights and additional value in the secondary re-use market – for example for advertising purposes – from adding another consumer's personal data is close to zero. This reduces the marginal value of a single person's dataset. It also reduces incentives for consumers to protect their privacy since their profile can be assembled from data collected from other persons. Consumers may not understand the low market value of their personal data and continue to invest in privacy protection. That in itself may have signal value that can be exploited against consumer interests.[46] An empirical study on the use of personal data for advertising in the travel industry[47] finds that, since the entry of the EU GDPR, 12 percent of consumers withhold consent to collect their personal data. The study also finds that the reduction in the supply of available data increases the value of the remaining advertising data and, because of externalities, does not negatively affect the predictability of consumer responses to advertising.

Is this negative externality a market failure that requires regulatory intervention to be corrected? Individuals have no better alternative option to

---

44 See section B.VII.

45 Bergemann, Bonatti and Gan, (n. 25).

46 Sebastian Dengler and Jens Prüfer, 'Consumers' Privacy Choices in the Era of Big Data' (2018) TILEC Discussion Paper No. 2018–014 <https://ssrn.com/abstract=3159028> accessed 31 August 2020.

47 Guy Aridor, Yeon-Koo Che and Tobias Salz, 'The Economic Consequences of Data Privacy Regulation: Empirical Evidence from GDPR' (2020) NBER Working Paper No. 26900 <www.nber.org/papers/w26900> accessed 31 August 2020.

realise a higher value for their personal data. Brynjolfsson and others[48] present empirical evidence that at least some 'free' services platforms actually compensate the negative externality and generate a large consumer surplus. Consumers trade personal data at nearly zero value for valuable online services. That suggests that the positive network externalities produced by platforms outstrip the negative externality on personal data. Consumers get more value out of the trade than they put into it. Zero prices are often seen as a market distortion from a traditional competition policy perspective.[49] However, trying to correct this may reduce overall social welfare because it would reduce the number of consumers and the volume of data and make the platform less attractive for advertisers and for other consumers. Public opinion often goes in the other direction, as the quip 'if you are not paying you are the product' suggests. Some authors suggest that consumers should be paid for the 'data labour' that they contribute to platforms.[50]

A similar phenomenon of data value depreciation because of externalities takes place on the firm or supply side of platforms. Suppliers sell their goods and services through online platforms like Amazon, eBay or Netflix. Platform operators collect and aggregate data on product characteristics, sales and consumer choices across many users. Once sufficient data are collected, the operators can predict market responses to changes in product characteristics and prices. This reduces the marginal prediction value of individual supplier data.

Newspapers are an example of negative externalities between two types of service suppliers on a platform. In the pre-digital era, printed newspapers had a strong market position in advertising, both commercial ads and classifieds. That revenue cross-subsidised news production and kept printed newspaper prices low to maximise consumption. In the digital era, consumers moved online to search engines and social media platforms, and so did advertising, which followed consumers to Google and Facebook. This blew a big hole in newspaper revenue. The revenue from remaining online

48 Erik Brynjolfsson, Avinash Collis, W. Erwin Diewert, Felix Eggers and Kevin J. Fox, 'GDP-B: Accounting for the Value of New and Free Goods in the Digital Economy' (2019) NBER Working Paper No. 25695 <www.nber.org/papers/w25695> accessed 31 August 2020.

49 Joshua S. Gans, 'The Specialness of Zero' (2020): <https://ssrn.com/abstract=3486964> accessed on 03/11/2020.

50 Eric A. Posner and E. Glen Weyl, *Radical Markets: Uprooting Capitalism and Democracy for a Just Society* (Princeton University Press 2018).

ads on newspaper webpages does not compensate the losses from print advertising.

Data-driven market failures may also occur in the presence of positive data externalities when these externalities cannot be captured or monetised by a party, or when contributing parties cannot agree on the distribution of the benefits from these positive externalities. A typical case is the private production of public goods, for example public health. Public goods are non-rival and non-excludable. Their use value cannot be captured and monetised by an agent. As a result, private agents have no incentive to invest in the production of these goods and the production is sub-optimal. This occurs for example when pooling of personal health data would create a dataset that can be used to discover innovative medicines, treatments and therapies or combat viral diseases. However, individuals and medical service providers have no incentive to contribute their data to the pool, unless they could expect direct benefits from new treatments. In some cases, innovative firms can grant direct benefits to individuals. But this is not always feasible and may be costly to achieve. Alternatively, governments can make data pooling mandatory and facilitate open access to the data for health researchers.[51] This imposes costs on contributors and leaves all the benefits to innovators and consumers who benefit from the innovations.

II. Asymmetric information

Asymmetric information between individual users and data-collecting platforms is an almost natural state in a data-abundant digital world. Platforms as data aggregators will always have more and better information on the data collection and use markets that they cover than do individual platform users (persons and firms). Users' willingness to share information with the platform depends on the level of detail and the use of the data.[52] Conversely, platforms will manipulate and may degrade the information that they share with users in order to segment markets and maximise rev-

51 For example, in Finland the government adopted an act that makes health data pooling on a government server mandatory for all private and public health service providers. See Finland Ministry of Social Affairs and Health 'Secondary Use of Health and Social Data' <https://stm.fi/en/secondary-use-of-health-and-social-data> accessed 31 August 2020.

52 Bergemann, Bonatti and Gan (n. 25); In this model, data collection for advertising has a negative effect on the welfare of data originators because there is no compensatory service offered in return for the data.

enue from their data intermediation role. Users may take sub-optimal decisions because of imperfect information signals received from platforms.

An extreme form of information manipulation by platforms is 'self-referencing'. For example, in July 2019 the European Commission opened an investigation into Amazon.[53] Amazon combines the roles of online retailer on its own account and market place for independent sellers. The platform allegedly used data that it collects about the activities of independent sellers to engage in anticompetitive practices and degrade the quality of information signals to consumer search results to favour Amazon sales and reduce the prominence of sales by independent sellers.

The market-distorting effects of asymmetric information in favour of the platform operator is well-documented in empirical studies on all kinds of search engines.[54] Platforms apply business models that may be based on sales margins (for retailers), commissions on sales (for market places) or advertising revenue (pure information matchmakers). The incentives embedded in the business models affect search rankings and drive a wedge between user preferences and the financial interests of platforms. For example, hotel booking platforms can manipulate search rankings towards price offers that increase their fee revenue. Another example of self-referencing occurs in the automotive industry, where car manufacturers have exclusive access to all data collected by connected cars.[55] Manufacturers can give preferential access to their own network of accredited dealers and aftermarket service providers. That distorts competition with independent service providers. Competition policy tools, such as the pre-digital EU Block Exemption on Vertical Restraints and the EU Motor Vehicle Type Approval Regulation, can force manufacturers to share maintenance information with independent repair shops. Industry self-regulation has failed because of weak incentives for industry players to come to an agreement.

53 See European Commission, 'Antitrust: Commission Opens Investigation into Possible Anti-Competitive Conduct of Amazon (Press Release, 17 July 2019) <https://ec.europa.eu/commission/presscorner/detail/en/IP_19_4291> accessed 31 August 2020.

54 See for example Babur de los Santos and Sergei Koulayev, 'Optimizing Click-Through in Online Rankings with Endogenous Search Refinement' (2017) 36 Marketing Science 542.

55 See Martens and Mueller-Langer (n. 42).

There is considerable debate on what an unbiased 'neutral' search engine in an inherently information-asymmetric world would look like.[56] The 'conduit' theory sees search engines as passive intermediaries that make an 'objective' selection of relevant search results in response to a user's search query. The ideal consumer-focused search engine would be a 'trusted advisor' that presents results that match consumer preferences. That search engine is not achievable, but would frustrate the preferences of service suppliers as well as the platform's own profit-maximising objective. At the other extreme, the 'editor' theory sees the search outcome as a subjectively curated ranking of results in response to a query, with the search engine as an active editor. Any ranking would represent the search engine operator's profit-maximising view. In reality, search results are necessarily a combination of objective conduit and subjective editing. Search operators are squeezed between the wishes of different types of platform users and carve out a profit margin while keeping all parties reasonably but not entirely satisfied.[57] The stronger their market position, the more they may distort the information picture. Locked-in users have no choice to go elsewhere for their services. Competitive pressure may sometimes limit platforms' margin for manoeuvre.[58] These models show how ranking bias is inherent to the platform's use of asymmetric information. Platforms need to drive a wedge between the preferences of users on different sides of the market in order to extract a profit margin to ensure the sustainability of their business model. More recent information theory models expand this insight from rankings to the quality of information collected and shared by platforms.[59]

Note that not-for-profit platforms would not perform better in this respect. They have no profit motive and could limit their financial needs to cost recovery by charging users a fixed fee, possibly as a function of their intensity of use. The market side that pays the fee would receive the most optimal information to match their preferences. Other sides may still suffer from bias in the collection and use of information. A platform cannot use its data to simultaneously maximise the welfare of all users on all sides

56 James Grimmelmann, 'Some Skepticism About Search Neutrality' in Berin Szoka and Adam Marcus (eds) *The Next Digital Decade: Essays on the Future of the Internet* (Tech Freedom 2010) 435; James Grimmelmann, 'Speech Engines' (2014) 98 Minnesota Law Review 868.

57 De los Santos and Koulayev (n. 54).

58 Maurice E. Stucke and Ariel Ezrachi, 'When Competition Fails to Optimize Quality: A Look at Search Engines' (2017) 18 Yale Journal of Law and Technology 70.

59 Bergemann, Bonatti and Gan (n. 25).

of the market, unless their preferences are perfectly aligned. Information asymmetry is a fact of life in digital platform economies.

Data sharing is often touted as a means to overcome information asymmetry and maximise social welfare benefits for society[60] because it generates economies of scope in re-use. Data sharing markets may fail however when the data originator or collector perceives a risk of negative repercussions on his private welfare. Data-driven platforms may offer compensation for this perceived risk, for instance by offering consumers a free service in return for sharing their data, or offering firms enhanced market access in return for sharing their data. Alternatively, platforms can modulate the degree of fine-graining and segmentation of the data they collect and share. Mandatory data-sharing obligations upset these platform strategies, both on the data collection and on the data use side of the platform. This may result in less data collection and undermine the positive externalities from data aggregation. Data policy makers need to carefully balance these positive and negative aspects of data-driven platforms.

III. Missing markets because of high transaction costs and risks

High transaction costs in the analogue economy prevented the emergence of many types of markets. Digital data massively reduce information costs and thereby facilitate market entry for consumers and small suppliers, from small hotels and bed & breakfasts that can now compete with large hotel chains on accommodation booking platforms, to independent taxi drivers who can offer their services on Uber and Lyft, and workers entering the online labour market, or staying in touch with a large number of family, friends and professional contacts on social media. All this is made possible by intermediary online data-aggregating platforms. Markets that were 'missing' in the pre-digital era suddenly emerge as a result of the drop in market-entry and transaction costs. However, even in the digital data economy some markets still remain blocked due to high transaction costs. Moreover, new services are required in order to keep digital markets running but they may not appear autonomously because of high transaction costs and risks. In this section we present a few examples of such missing

60 OECD Directorate for Science and Technology (n. 11); OECD, *Enhancing Access to and Sharing of Data: Reconciling Risks and Benefits for Data Re-Use across Societies* (OECD 2019).

markets and explore how these market failures may be addressed by a mixture of regulatory intervention and private third-party intermediation.

1. *Transaction costs in personal data markets*

Under the EU GDPR, data subjects have the right to consent to the use of their personal data before a firm can collect it. Consent notices pop up when consumers browse the internet. Consumers rarely read these notices. Even when they do, personal data consent notices are difficult to read and uninformative about possible data re-use.[61] The cost of time invested in reading these notices is too high compared to their informative value. A consumer survey confirms consumers' ambiguous attitudes towards privacy notices.[62] Another recent consumer survey[63] illustrates how risk assessments about sharing personal data on the internet vary widely according to type of data. Financial and biometric information commands high subjective opportunity costs. Data use for advertising is not perceived as entailing a significant privacy cost. Location and social network data are somewhere in the middle. The use of personal data has ambiguous welfare effects.[64] It can increase personal welfare when the data are used in an informative way, for example by search engines to reduce search costs and provide better search results that are more in line with consumer preferences. It may reduce welfare when data are used for targeted advertising that is more persuasive than informative and drives consumers away from their original preferences.

High transaction costs make the current system of consent notices dysfunctional. Many private start-ups have tried to enter the market for per-

61 See for example Fred H. Cate, Viktor Mayer-Schönberger, 'Notice and Consent in a World of Big Data' (2013) 3 International Data Privacy Law 67.

62 The survey confirms that nearly two-thirds of consumers would appreciate government intervention in setting privacy rules but only about 20 % of consumers bother to regularly read privacy notices. Results from the Brookings survey can be found here: Darrell M. West 'Brookings Survey finds Three-Quarters of Online Users Rarely Read Business Terms of Service (TechTank, 21 May 2019) <www.brookings.edu/blog/techtank/2019/05/21/brookings-survey-finds-three-quarters-of-online-users-rarely-read-business-terms-of-service/> accessed 31 August2020.

63 Jeffrey Prince and Scott Wallsten, 'How Much is Privacy Worth Around the World and Across Platforms?' (2020) <https://ssrn.com/abstract=3528386> accessed 31 August 2020.

64 Alessandro Acquisti, Curtis Taylor and Liad Wagman,'The Economics of Privacy' (2016) 54 Journal of Economic Literature 442.

sonal information management services (PIMS).[65] They offer an intermediary platform to handle personal data exchanges with commercial platforms. However, none of these have scaled up to become significant market players in personal data markets. The reason is clear: they do not really reduce high individual transaction costs. Management costs are still relatively high, at least in time spent on the platform, compared to the depressed value of individual personal data. Economically feasible personal data management would require technology that substantially lowers transaction costs. This could happen for example when consent notices become standardised and machine-readable so that they can be processed by AI-driven machines. Standardisation could include the identity of the data collector, the purpose for which it is collected, the level of fine-graining in use of the data and third-party commercial partners that may access the data. A privacy service provider could machine-read the consent notices, estimate possible risks for the data subject as a function of his or her pre-set preferences and use of the internet, and machine-grant or -deny consent. Machine learning could gradually become more efficient by learning from individual consumer behaviour as well as aggregated data across individuals and websites and collecting evidence on data sharing practices between firms and websites. It could suggest alternative service providers with lower privacy costs. Automation of the consent process would complete it in milliseconds, saving data subjects a substantial amount of time. The bottleneck lies in the standardisation process however. Platforms can produce their own standardised consent notice but without interoperability the system would run into high obstacles. Collective action seems to be required and that requires regulatory intervention.[66]

---

65 Mydata.org <https://mydata.org/> is one example among many initiatives to help individuals manage their personal data. The European Data Protection Supervisor has advocated the use of Personal Information Management Systems (PIMS). For a detailed economic discussion of PIMS, see Jan Krämer, Pierre Senellart and Alexandre de Streel, 'Making Data Portability More Effective for the Digital Economy: Economic Implications and Regulatory Challenges – Report' (Centre of Regulation in Europe 2020) <https://cerre.eu/publications/report-making-data-portability-more-effective-digital-economy/> accessed 31 August 2020.

66 Posner and Weyl (n. 50) propose a particular variant on this theme. They suggest that data subjects should unite in unions to negotiate a higher value for their data with data collecting platforms. Automated data consent notices would reduce coordination and market entry costs for such unions. These unions would still face the problem of allocating the social value of the data between private members. See also the conclusions section in Bergemann, Bonatti and Gan (n. 25).

2. Transaction costs and lack of transparency in commercial services markets

A similar lack of transparency in management services occurs in online advertising markets. Online advertising can be split between 'walled gardens' in Search (Google) and social media (Facebook), and open-display advertising where Google holds a strong position. Advertising is a two-sided market between publishers and advertisers, with several layers of intermediary platforms that do intermediate matching and price auctions for the supply of ad publishing windows and the stock of ads produced by advertisers. For every euro spent on ads by the advertiser, only 62 cents reach the publisher; the rest remains in intermediate steps, largely dominated by Google.[67] It is challenging for advertisers to verify publishing and views of ads because of the lack of transparency in intermediate stages. Price auctions in these markets are problematic[68] because Google itself participates in the bidding while it has privileged information on the offers of its competitors. Self-(p)referencing is an issue. Data transparency and sharing through open standards and automated market tracking tools could be a solution. It could improve transparency and oversight for advertisers, publishers and content providers, increase competition and enable all participants to get a better overview of what they pay for and what they achieve.

Filling missing market gaps does not always require regulatory intervention. Entrepreneurs may propose innovative services to fill the information gap between platform operators and users. For example, data providers like AMZScout and JungleScout[69] collect and analyse data from e-commerce platforms like Amazon, eBay and Zalando and sell findings to independent sellers to help them improve their commercial strategies on the platform. The e-commerce platforms only provide data related to the seller's market.[70] The intermediary service provider aggregates data across

67 Damien Geradin and Dimitrios Katsifis, 'Google's (Forgotten) Monopoly: Ad Technology Services on the Open Web' (2019) 2019–3 Concurrences 1.

68 Ibid. Several EU competition authorities have launched investigations in online advertising, including those in the UK, France and Germany. A UK Competition Market Authority study is exploring potential remedies for ads markets that could be part of an ex-ante regulatory regime.

69 See <https://amzscout.net/> and <https://www.junglescout.com/> accessed 31 August2020.

70 The EU Platform-to-Business Regulation specifies the type of information that platforms have to provide to their business suppliers. See Regulation (EU) 2019/1150 of the European Parliament and of the Council of 20 June 2019 on promoting fairness and transparency for business users of online intermediation services [2019] OJ L186/57.

products on the platform and sells the joint analysis. Adjacent data services may be tolerated by platform operators, or they can be blocked.

3. Risks

There are circumstances in which potential data suppliers refrain from participating in the production of services markets because it may be costly for them. An example is pooling mobility data between transport service providers in a city. This can have positive social welfare effects by improving traffic management and reducing congestion and pollution. However, commercial transport service providers (buses, metros, taxis, e-scooter platforms etc.) may gain or lose market shares from sharing data on a common platform.[71] Competitors may use the data to improve their offers and increase their market share. Alternatively, being on the common platform may attract more users to a particular provider. The net impact is an empirical question. These risks may motivate transport providers to stay away from the platform, unless the platform is in a position to compensate losers by re-allocating part of the overall social welfare surplus to them. For example, if drivers are willing to pay a positive price for improved congestion management, some of that revenue could be re-allocated to transport service providers that lose from participation. Alternatively, regulators can intervene to make data sharing mandatory in the interest of public welfare.[72]

Another dimension of transaction costs is ex-post risk in the execution of contracts. According to incomplete contract theory, contracts of finite length inevitably come with residual uncertainties that can give rise to ex-post costs during monitoring and execution of a contract. This is especially the case for trade in non-rival and hard-to-exclude data. Some contractual provisions may be unenforceable, non-monitorable or lack a commitment device.[73] They are subject to the hold-up problem: parties will try to re-negotiate the contract when an unforeseen or non-committable event occurs.

---

71 Bruno Carballa Smichowski, 'Determinants of Coopetition through Data Sharing in MaaS (Mobility-as-a-Service)' (2018) 2 Management & Data Science <https://doi.org/10.36863/mds.a.4160> accessed 31 August 2020.

72 The European Commission's initiative to promote business-to-government data sharing 'in the public interest' should be seen in this context. See European Commission (n. 4). See also Richter (n. 4).

73 Anastasios Dosis and Wilfried Sand-Zantman, 'The Ownership of Data' (2019) <https://ssrn.com/abstract=3420680> accessed 28 August 2020.

This includes risks from data leaks, unexpected data quality problems or processing errors. In traditional contracts, unexpected costs and benefits are assigned to the owner of the traded good or service. In the absence of legal data ownership rights[74] that is more problematic and may reduce incentives to make data available for re-use. The risks of contractual hold-up may be too big for holders of valuable or commercially sensitive datasets, as the Facebook/Cambridge Analytica case demonstrated. Some authors have suggested assigning data ownership rights to overcome this problem.[75] Debates on the possible introduction of such rights[76] have diminished and attention has now shifted to introducing data access rights.[77] Ownership and access rights are complements. Who should get such rights, if any, is not an easy question. For personal data, there is a 'natural' rights holder, the data subject. For non-personal machine-generated data that may involve several parties for the co-generation of the data, it is often hard to unambiguously identify a 'natural' rights holder. For example, in agriculture land owners, land operators, machine manufacturers, machine operators, sensor owners, data analytics providers, etc. may all claim rights over the data.[78]

A more pragmatic solution may be to appoint a neutral third-party intermediary who is tasked with managing the data exchange in accordance with an agreed protocol. For example, a city mobility service provider may require pooled data from all mobile phone operators in that city to create detailed insights on citizen mobility patterns. None of the data suppliers trust the other to handle the data pool that has strategic commercial value for competitors. Solving this coordination problem requires a trusted

74 Duch-Brown, Martens and Mueller-Langer (n. 5).

75 See Herbert Zech, 'Data as a Tradeable Commodity' in Alberto De Franceshi (ed.), *European Contract Law and the Digital Single Market: The Implications of the Digital Revolution* (Intersentia 2016) 51; and Andreas Wiebe, 'Protection of Industrial Data: A New Property Right for the Digital Economy?' (2017) 12 Journal of Intellectual Property Law & Practice 62.

76 Communication from the European Commission of 10 January 2017 – 'Building a European data economy', COM(2017) 2 final and An Commission Staff Working Document, 'The free flow of data and emerging issues of the European data economy' SWD (2017) 2 final.

77 Communication from the European Commission of 25 April 2018 – 'Towards a common European dataspace' COM(2018) 232 final; Josef Drexl, 'Data Access and Control in the Era of Connected Devices: Study on Behalf of the European Consumer Organisation BEUC' (BEUC 2018) <www.beuc.eu/publications/beuc-x-2018-121_data_access_and_control_in_the_area_of_connected_devices.pdf> accessed 31 August 2020.

78 Atik and Martens (n. 8).

third-party intermediary that collects the data, performs the analysis and ensures that only the processed results are shared with agreed users. This is the domain of semi-commons or governance agreements that seek to overcome the pitfalls of the commons – which lead to overutilisation and underinvestment and facilitate free-riding – and of the anti-commons – exclusive private use that leads to underutilisation and keeps data locked in silos.[79] Semi-commons are often costly to manage. They are economically feasible when the value of the agreement for the participants exceeds the costs.

Data trusts and industrial data platforms fit the neutral intermediary profile. In order to guarantee enforcement, the intermediary should have no stake in the data or the outcomes of the analysis. That avoids strategic behaviour at the expense of the participants. The intermediary should only receive a fixed remuneration to produce the desired outcome. It can enforce the commitment because it has full control over the data and access to the server. That reduces post-contractual risks and monitoring costs for participants. Commercial for-profit data platforms may also provide guarantees against data leaks but they will exploit the data in their own interest, and sometimes against the interests of the data providers. They create new sources of ex-post risks.

E. Concluding remarks

The data economics issues that we have discussed here have much in common with the law and economics of intellectual property rights (IPRs), such as patents and copyrights.[80] The economic characteristics of data, non-rivalry and no natural excludability, are similar to those of innovation. IPRs give exclusive ownership rights to innovators in order to yield a return on investment and an incentive for innovation. IPR policies struggle with the same balancing act as data policies, between the social welfare costs of monopolistic exclusive rights and the social welfare gains from the innovation incentive effects. Monopolistic IPR licence pricing, above the marginal cost of reproduction, reduces access to innovation. This is an unavoidable social harm accepted as the cost of generating dynamic innova-

79 Henry E. Smith, 'Governing the Tele-Semicommons' (2005) 22 Yale Journal of Regulation 289. Exclusive private property rights are cheaper to manage – the exclusive owner sets the price – and so are full commons because the price falls to zero.

80 See Leistner (n. 6).

tion benefits. IPRs compensate this by limiting the scope of exclusive rights. Similar considerations apply to data collection, access and use, including in online platforms. It took several centuries for society to develop a coherent system of IPR rights, and this system is still evolving, driven by technology that affects the cost of innovation production and dissemination and therefore the balance between protection and access. Digital data are a very new product in society. There are lively discussions between proponents of exclusive ownership rights and defendants of more open access rights.[81] A major difficulty with data is the attribution of such rights. Innovations are usually produced by a well-defined innovator or group of innovators with common interests. Data, by contrast, usually originate from a large and poorly defined group of providers, often with diverging interests. While personal data rights may be 'naturally' attributed to a data subject, attribution is more difficult for non-personal data, where many parties may be involved in origination, collection, aggregation and analysis of the data. Changes in attribution of rights may affect entire data value chains and downstream services markets. They will affect the pace of innovation that data can bring to society.

More importantly, both ownership and access rights overlook the inherent social value of data and the externalities that they entail. A single data originator or collector is usually not in a position to internalise these externalities. Market failures will remain. The discussions sometimes give the impression that the attribution of exclusive ownership, access and sharing rights are policy objectives in themselves. This data economics chapter has emphasised that such rights are only policy instruments that should be used to maximise the social welfare that society as a whole can derive from the use of data.

The title of this volume reflects the dichotomy between consumer and social welfare. In line with public policy economics, this chapter has focused mainly on social welfare as a benchmark for identifying market failures and policy intervention. Public policy economics defines the measure of social welfare as the combined welfare of all stakeholder groups in society, including consumers and producers. Mainstream competition law focuses on a narrower consumer welfare benchmark, even in the digital data economy setting with interactions between multi-sided markets.[82] These

81 The European Commission's Communications (n. 4, n. 76 and n. 77) on data issues over the last years reflect this societal debate. See also Wiebe (n. 75) and Zech (n. 75).

82 Furman and others (n. 2).

two measures can easily lead to contradictory conclusions. For example, regulatory intervention to open market access on one side of a platform may reduce welfare on other sides of the platform market. Classic economics rejects the comparison of welfare gains and losses between groups or individuals because consumer welfare is assumed not to be quantifiable. Alternative approaches accept quantification but open the door to measures of social welfare improvement whereby some parties gain at the expense of others. Economics distinguishes between strictly Pareto-improving welfare measures whereby no agent loses welfare and a less stringent Kaldor-Hicks[83] welfare measure whereby some agents may lose but could, in principle, be compensated by the gains that other agents make in order to avoid equity concerns. Western societies have historically put emphasis on individual wellbeing and are reluctant to impose private costs on individuals in order to achieve wider social welfare gains, unless they are compensated by transfers to ensure some degree of equity. Other societies have a more collective view of social welfare and attach less importance to individual welfare. They would find it easier to accept private costs as long as overall welfare increases. This underscores the borderline between the economics of data and cultural, social and political value judgements in society on how to maximise societal welfare from data.

Another dimension of data economics that was not discussed in this chapter is the emergence of ecosystems of bundled platforms. Our focus on individual market failures and multi-sided platforms may have given an excessively static picture of the data economy. Over the last decade, new data- and technology-driven business strategies have resulted in more complex and rapidly evolving ecosystems of interlinked platforms[84] and strong competition between major players. Data can be re-used to build service production conglomerates around a single data source or platform.[85] Platform 'envelopment' strategies[86] seek to re-bundle data-driven services in new ways in order to invade the markets of other platforms. Data-driven

83 For more details on Kaldor-Hicks measures, see for example <https://en.wikipedia.org/wiki/Kaldor–Hicks_efficiency> accessed 31 August 2020.

84 For a definition of ecosystems, see for example Michael G. Jacobides, Carmelo Cennamo and Annabelle Gawer, 'Towards a Theory of Ecosystems' (2018) 39 Strategic Management Journal 2255.

85 Marc Bourreau and Alexandre de Streel, 'Digital Conglomerates and EU Competition Policy' (2019) <https://ssrn.com/abstract=3350512> accessed 31 August 2020.

86 Thomas Eisenmann, Geoffrey Parker and Marshall Van Alstyne, 'Platform Envelopment' (2011) 32 Strategic Management Journal 1270.

bundling of products underpins similar competition strategies.[87] Data-based artificial intelligence technologies have greatly contributed to these market dynamics. Policy makers and regulators appear to be running behind the technology curve, among other reasons because regulatory interventions are slow political processes. The slowness of regulators compared to technological innovators has been underlined in some of the recent data and competition policy reports. Regulatory solutions often engage when the harm is already done. Catching up with the speed of technological innovation may require permanent intensive monitoring of the data economy, as proposed by some regulatory authorities.[88]

87 Yannis Bakos and Erik Brynjolfsson, 'Bundling and Competition on the Internet' (2000) 19 Marketing Science 63, 68.

88 Furman and others (n. 2) suggest that the UK competition authority should set up a digital markets monitoring unit, which it has since done. Scott Morton and others (n. 41) suggest likewise for the US.

A legal framework for access to data – A competition policy perspective

Heike Schweitzer and Robert Welker[*]

A. Data access in the digital economy

The transition of the economy to the new conditions of the digital economy is underway. The new role of data is at its core. There is a broad consensus that data have become a key input for and element of competing in vast areas of the economy and for the development of the European economy at large: Data are at the heart of new and increasingly sophisticated forecasting techniques – often based on machine learning or other artificial intelligence (AI) technologies – that can lead to better decisions in a multitude of economic and societal areas.[1] A key driver of these technologies is the ever-increasing ability to automatically analyse vast amounts of unstructured data that often are generated as a 'by-product' of the use of machines or services or of other business activities without incurring much additional cost.[2] The new, data-driven prediction machinery[3] can help to realise efficiency gains and improve productivity throughout the value chain. Furthermore, it allows for the development of new and more personalised products and services in many areas of the economy, both in business-to-consumers (B2C) and in business-to-business dealings (B2B). By combining usage data generated in the course of the use of different products and services on a multitude of markets concerning different areas of life, digital conglomerates can create increasingly detailed, complex and comprehensive user profiles, rendering the personalisation of products and

* We are grateful to Frederik Gutmann for his valuable research support. Also, we thank Axel Metzger for a greatly stimulating discussion.

1 Communication from the Commission of 19 February 2020 to the European Parliament, the Council, the European Economic and Social Committee and the Committee of Regions – A European strategy for data COM(2020) 66 final, 2–3.

2 Heike Schweitzer and Martin Peitz, 'Ein neuer europäischer Ordnungsrahmen für Datenmärkte?' (2018) Neue Juristische Wochenschrift 275, 275.

3 See Ajay K. Agrawal, Avi Goldfarb and Joshua Gans, *Prediction Machines: The Simple Economics of Artificial Intelligence* (Ingram Publisher Services 2018).

the targeting of marketing activities ever more sophisticated.[4] With the rise of the Internet of Things ('IoT'), business strategies are about to change fundamentally, shifting from the provision of products to the provision of data- and software-based internet services.[5] Data and the ability to draw value from it will drive innovation and growth for decades to come.

Against this background, a debate started some time ago on how to adapt the legal framework to the new reality of the data economy. This endeavour has many facets, ranging from data protection[6] to cybersecurity[7]. One of the main problems identified is a lack of data available for innovative re-use, including for innovating in the area of AI.[8] The European Commission has announced a 'comprehensive approach' that aims to increase the availability, use of and demand for data and data-enabled products and services.[9] Apart from the opening up of public sector information for business use (government-to-business (G2B) data sharing),[10] data sharing between companies (B2B data sharing) shall be promoted.[11] The goal is to create an environment where businesses 'have easy access to an almost infinite amount of high-quality industrial data'[12] as well as the necessary tools, infrastructures and competences for handling data. The new data innovators shall be able to build on the scale of the Single Market, thereby boosting growth and European competitiveness.[13]

To allow companies to take off at sufficient scale within the European Single Market, the Commission has set out to overcome the persisting

4 Heike Schweitzer, Justus Haucap, Wolfgang Kerber and Robert Welker, *Modernisierung der Missbrauchsaufsicht für marktmächtige Unternehmen* (Nomos 2018) 26.

5 Alexander Ziegler, *Der Aufstieg des Internet der Dinge: Wie sich Industrieunternehmen zu Tech-Unternehmen entwickeln* (Campus Verlag 2020).

6 With the GDPR as the main legal pillar.

7 See Regulation (EU) 2019/881 of the European Parliament and of the Council of 17 April 2019 on ENISA (the European Union Agency for Cybersecurity) and on information and communications technology cybersecurity certification and repealing Regulation (EU) No. 526/2013 (Cybersecurity Act) [2019] OJ L151/15.

8 European Commission, 'A European strategy for data' (n. 1) 6.

9 Ibid 1.

10 Ibid 7, 13. See also Directive (EU) 2019/1024 of the European Parliament and of the Council of 20 June 2019 on open data and the re-use of public sector information [2019] OJ L172/56.

11 European Commission, 'A European strategy for data' (n. 1) 7.

12 Ibid. 4–5.

13 Ibid. 3, 5.

market fragmentation and establish a 'European data space' where data can flow within the EU and across sectors.[14]

The principles and rules that can help overcome the persistence of 'data monopolies' and 'data silos' in the market are currently under debate.[15] Markets for specific types of data exist.[16] But in many contexts, relevant data resources will be under the exclusive control of a firm that is not willing to grant access. This is particularly true for the rich data troves controlled by the big online platforms. But it is also true when it comes to the data produced within the evolving IoT.

From a bird's-eye view, the possible approaches to data access can be placed on a scale between two fundamentally different philosophies. On the one end of this scale, data remain under private control. Access is granted, if at all, on the basis of freely negotiated contracts (private control framework). On the other end of this scale, data are regarded as a common good, and access is guaranteed based on broad legal access obligations (open access framework).

In its recent communication on a European data strategy, the Commission has argued for a differentiated, but generally cautious approach. In the G2B sphere, the Commission generally supports an open access approach.[17] In the business-to-government (B2G) sphere, it means to encourage voluntary data sharing, but to complement it with an EU regulatory framework – potentially including data access obligations – to govern the

14 Communication of the Commission, to the European Parliament, the Council, the European Economic and Social Committee and the Committee of Regions – 'Towards a common European data space' COM(2018) 232 final. See also Regulation (EU) Nr. 2018/1807 of the European Parliament and of the Council of 14 November 2018 on a framework for the free flow of non-personal data in the European Union [2018] OJ L303/59; and Directive (EU) 2019/1024 (n. 10).

15 See, for example, Bertin Martens, Alexandre de Streel, Inge Graef and others, 'Business-to-Business Data Sharing: An Economic and Legal Analysis' (2020) JRC Working Papers on Digital Economy 2020–05 <https://ssrn.com/abstract=3658100> accessed 15 September 2020.

16 Cf. Christian Santesteban and Shayne Longpre, 'How Big Data Confers Market Power to Big Tech: Leveraging the Perspective of Data Science' (2020) 65 The Antitrust Bulletin 459, 481–483.

17 See Section B., below, for a description of the fundamental policy approaches. The Commission expressly bases its strategy on the non-rivalrous nature of data and the possibility to replicate it without cost, concluding that there is a need for a broad data access regime: European Commission, 'A European strategy for data' (n. 1) 4.

public sector's re-use of privately-held data for public policy goals.[18] In the B2B sphere, on the other hand, *voluntary* data sharing is to remain the rule. Public interventions should generally be of a facilitative, enabling nature: Since a lack of data interoperability has been identified as one of the hurdles for an increased flow of data in the B2B and G2B context,[19] a 'rolling plan for ICT standardisation'[20] is to encourage the application of shared compatible formats and protocols for gathering and processing data from different sources, such that data become interoperable across sectors and vertically within the supply chain.[21] The development of clear and trustworthy data governance mechanisms is to be supported;[22] and the legal framework for data markets is to be clarified in a future 'Data Act'.[23] Competition law will address power imbalances.[24] Particularly entrenched types of power may justify ex-ante regulation in specific sectors.

This paper broadly supports this approach but strives to further explore and develop its conceptual basis. To this end, the second part of the paper sets out general policy approaches in determining the 'right' amount of data openness and argues for a market-driven system of data allocation (B.). The third part will explore the market failures that call for corrective measures to complement a 'freedom of contract' regime. It is structured around three scenarios: access to individual-level usage data by data co-generators, access to bundled individual-level data or aggregated data by third parties in an aftermarket setting and data access based on general innovation policy aims. Existing sectoral regimes[25] will be scanned for their underlying policy rationale (C.). The paper concludes with some general recommendations (D.).

---

18 European Commission, 'A European strategy for data' (n. 1) 7: The Commission refers to the recommendations of its Expert Group, consisting of 'the creation of national structures for B2G data sharing, the development of appropriate incentives to create a data-sharing culture, and the suggestion to explore an EU regulatory framework to govern the public sector's re-use for the public interest of privately-held data'.

19 Ibid 8.

20 European Commission, 'Rolling Plan for ICT Standardisation 2020' (2020) <https://ec.europa.eu/docsroom/documents/41541> accessed 15 September 2020.

21 European Commission, 'A European strategy for data' (n. 1) 8, 12.

22 Ibid. 5.

23 Ibid. 13.

24 Ibid. 8.

25 See Sections C.I.3. and C.II.3. below. Not all relevant sectoral regimes can be covered, however. In particular, access rules in the transport and mobility sector are outside of the scope of this paper.

Before diving into the debate on data access, one note of caution is in order: data come in many forms and varieties. They can be personal or non-personal,[26] they can be individual-level, bundled-individual-level or aggregated data,[27] structured or unstructured;[28] annotated[29] or non-annotated; content data or metadata; they can refer to environmental information, or to usage patterns; and they can be primary data or processed data at different stages of the value chain.[30] Whenever access to data is agreed on or mandated, the specificities of the relevant type of dataset must be taken into account. The focus of this paper is on usage data – whether individual-level, bundled-individual-level or aggregated, and whether personal or non-personal.

B. *Private data control versus open access – fundamental choices for the data economy*

The public debate on data access frequently circles around two poles: Should data be regarded as just another type of privately controlled resource? The legal recognition of private rights of control and exclusion might – but need not necessarily – result in the creation of a new type of

---

26 For the definition of personal data see Art. 4(1) GDPR.

27 Jacques Crémer, Yves-Alexandre de Montjoye and Heike Schweitzer, 'Competition policy for the digital era', Special Advisers' Report (2019) 25–26 <https://ec.europa.eu/competition/publications/reports/kd0419345enn.pdf> accessed 15 September 2020.

28 Structured data are highly organised and formatted in a way that makes them easily searchable.

29 Annotated data are made usable for the training of machine-learning algorithms through labelling.

30 For a brief description of the data value chain see Schweitzer and Peitz (n. 2) 275–76; Inge Graef, Thomas Tombas and Alexandre de Streel, 'Limits and Enablers of Data Sharing. An Analytical Framework for EU Competition, Data Protection and Consumer Law' (2019) TILEC Discussion Paper No. DP 2019–024, 4–5 <https://ssrn.com/abstract=3494212> accessed 15 September 2020: First, raw personal and non-personal data are collected directly or bought on a secondary data market; second, data are structured and turned into information; third, those structured data are analysed by algorithms and information is turned into knowledge, such as a prediction; and finally the analysis of the structured data leads to an action such as improving products or offerings.

intellectual property right in data.[31] Or should data be a new type of commons in the evolving data economy? Along this line, some propose that data should be considered a new type of infrastructure for the data economy, which could argue for an open access approach. The OECD's 2015 report on data-driven innovation is representative: 'The economic properties of data suggest that data may be considered as an infrastructure or infrastructural resource [...] from a functional perspective'[32] – they are non-rivalrous in consumption, meaning they can be used infinite times without depreciation;[33] the demand for data is, as with physical infrastructure, driven 'primarily by downstream productive activities that require the resource as an input';[34] and they are a general-purpose input, i.e. they can be used and re-used to develop different products and services.[35] Given these features, a general open access regime could seemingly maximise efficiency and innovation.

I. Private control vs. open access: The basic trade-off

The discussion partly repeats debates that are well-known from the area of intellectual property law: there is a trade-off between a free flow of information and exclusive control.[36] Where data are an important input for many promising economic activities, an open access regime would lower barriers to entry and promote competition and innovation in adjacent and novel markets. On the other hand, exclusive control over data facilitates

31 For this debate see: Alain Schmid, Kirsten Johanna Schmidt and Herbert Zech, 'Rechte an Daten – zum Stand der Diskussion' (2018) 11 sic! Zeitschrift für Immaterialgüter-, Informations- und Wettbewerbsrecht 627; Josef Drexl, 'Designing Competitive Markets for Industrial Data Between Propertisation and Access' (2017) 8 Journal of Intellectual Property, Information Technology and E-Commerce Law 257; Wolfgang Kerber, 'Digital Markets, Data and Privacy: Competition Law, Consumer Law and Data Protection' (2016) Gewerblicher Rechtsschutz und Urheberrecht Internationaler Teil 639 – all with further references.

32 OECD, *Data-Driven Innovation: Big Data for Growth and Well-Being* (OECD 2015) 179.

33 Ibid 179–80.

34 Ibid 179–81.

35 Ibid 179, 181–83.

36 Axel Metzger, 'Innovation in der Open Source Community – Herausforderungen für Theorie und Praxis des Immaterialgüterrechts' in Martin Eifert and Wolfgang Hoffmann-Riem (eds), *Geistiges Eigentum und Innovation* (Duncker & Humboldt 2008) 188.

their monetisation and thereby incentivises the collection and processing of the data in the first place. While a consistently proprietary approach would bear the risk of an inefficient under-use of data, a radical open access approach could lead to a 'tragedy of the commons',[37] resulting in under-investment in the creation of data.[38]

II. The benefits of open access to public sector data

In some areas – in particular with regard to large portions of public sector information – negative incentive effects appear to be less relevant, and an open access approach is broadly pursued.[39]

Ensuring better access to public sector data is widely believed to be a key factor to enhance the possibilities to innovate in the emerging European data economy – also because it will open new ways to combine public sector data with private sector data.[40] However, public sector data and the Open Data Directive will not be dealt with in this paper.

III. Private control as the basic paradigm for private sector data

When it comes to private sector data, the debate on data access is not limited to solving the puzzle of how to optimise innovation. The data – in particular usage data – that have become so valuable in the data economy carry a type of information that differs from the information that intellectual property rights have protected so far. For good reason, a relevant part of this information is protected by other legal regimes, e.g. the protection of

---

37 Jane Yakowitz, 'Tragedy of the Data Commons' (2011) 25 Harvard Journal of Law and Technology 1.

38 Heike Schweitzer and Martin Peitz, 'Datenmärkte in der digitalisierten Wirtschaft: Funktionsdefizite und Regelungsbedarf?' (2017) ZEW Discussion Paper No. 17–043, 60 <http://ftp.zew.de/pub/zew-docs/dp/dp17043.pdf> accessed 15 September 2020.

39 Directive (EU) 2019/1024 (n. 10); see also Heiko Richter, 'Open Science and Public Sector Information – Reconsidering the exemption for educational and research establishments under the Directive on re-use of public sector information' (2018) 9 Journal of Intellectual Property, Information Technology and E-Commerce Law 51.

40 Recital 16 Directive (EU) 2019/1024 (n. 10).

trade secrets[41] when it comes to confidential business information or the GDPR when it comes to personal data. Furthermore, an open exchange of competitively sensitive information is prohibited by competition law.[42]

1. *The status quo: Private control through de-facto possession*

The current legal regime for private sector data allocation is built on a private control approach. This is irrespective of the fact that data as such are so far not protected by intellectual property rights: private data control is based on a de-facto possession of data and on the ability of data controllers to regulate other parties' access by technological measures.[43] If in the interest of the data controller, data access is granted selectively based on contractual agreements.

In principle, a regime of private control can lead to the emergence of more or less open and transparent data markets, where companies sell access to their data if the price exceeds the potential gains of an exclusive 'inhouse' monetisation. A system of decentral coordination can ensue that ideally leads to an efficient allocation of data. Where usage data is generated in a co-operative bilateral relationship – e.g. between a service provider and the user of a service, or a producer of industrial machinery and its user – effective competition in the services or machinery market can lead to a coexistence of competing models, where the service or machine user could either get access to 'his' or 'her' data in exchange for a higher product price or forgo data access in exchange for a lower price.[44]

41 Directive (EU) 2016/943 of the European Parliament and of the Council of 8 June 2016 on the protection of undisclosed know-how and business information (trade secrets) against their unlawful acquisition, use and disclosure [2016] OJ L157/1; implemented in Germany through the *Gesetz zum Schutz von Geschäftsgeheimnissen* (GeschGehG).

42 See European Commission, Guidelines on the applicability of Art. 101 of the Treaty on the Functioning of the European Union to horizontal co-operation agreements [2011] OJ C11/1, paras 55 et seq.

43 Schweitzer and Peitz, 'Datenmärkte in der digitalisierten Wirtschaft: Funktionsdefizite und Regelungsbedarf?' (n. 38) 66.

44 See Section C.I.2. below.

2. Limits of the private control approach

In reality, while markets for some types of data indeed exist and have existed for some time,[45] markets for usage data in respect of services and machinery are rare and, where they exist, typically non-transparent.

This may be due to various reasons: For one, private data controllers have to consider the legal constraints to data sharing (following from the GDPR, trade secrets protection, competition law etc.) as described above. As of now, firms have to grapple with a high degree of legal uncertainty, which raises the cost of sharing data.[46] Secondly, the uncertainty extends to the value of data. Methods for assessing the value of data are currently much debated.[47] The value will crucially depend on how the data are used, and it may depend on who has access to the relevant data and which other datasets the data are combined with. Given the dynamic development of the digital economy, it is easily conceivable that a private data controller or a potential data user will under- or overvalue the relevant data,[48] or that the private data controller will fear undervaluing them or missing out on important competitive opportunities, and will therefore be reluctant to cede control. Thirdly, where the exclusive use of data allows the data controller to monopolise adjacent data-driven markets, the expected monopoly rent may exceed the expected value from marketing that data. This may be true with regard to markets like online advertising markets, which currently offer the most obvious opportunities to monetise data on a large scale. It may also be true where exclusive access to usage data leads to a lock-in of users – both with regard to the primary product or service, which becomes more valuable as the product or service is personalised, and with regard to complementary markets.

45 Cf. Santesteban and Longpre (n. 16) 481–83.

46 Cf. German Federal Ministry of Economic Affairs and Energy, 'A new competition framework for the digital economy – Report by the Commission "Competition Law 4.0"' (2019) 56–59 <https://www.bmwi.de/Redaktion/EN/Publikationen/Wirtschaft/a-new-competition-framework-for-the-digital-economy.html> accessed 15 September 2020.

47 Jordi Casanova Tormo, 'Estimating Reasonable Prices for Access to Digital Platforms' Data: What Are the Challenges?' (2020) 4 European Competition and Regulatory Law Review 172; David Nguyen and Marta Paczos, 'Measuring the Economic Value of Data and Cross-Border Data Flows: A Business Perspective' (2020) OECD Digital Economy Papers No. 297, 31–38 <https://www.oecd-ilibrary.org/docserver/6345995e-en.pdf> accessed 15 September 2020.

48 On market failures due to imperfect information in data markets see Martens and others (n. 15) 27.

Fourthly, in some settings, monopolisation tendencies, and sometimes strategies, may extend to the primary services or product market. This is true, in particular, for some online platform markets characterised by strong network effects and efficiencies of scale and scope.[49] The concentration of the primary market will then be accompanied by private control over particularly large and valuable usage data, which in turn further increases the barriers to entering the primary market and thus entrenches the incumbent's pre-existing position of market power.

3. *The gaps of a private control approach do not justify its renunciation*

The first question to be answered is whether these shortcomings of data markets or outright market failures argue against a private data control approach and in favour of an open access approach in a principled way. Broad and general compulsory data access obligations would, however, not make the problems disappear. The legal constraints on data sharing – whether resulting from the GDPR, from competition law or trade secret protection – would remain under an open access approach and would need to be framed as legal exceptions. Their specification case by case would leave much room for legal disputes and require a sophisticated dispute resolution mechanism or regulatory oversight. The same would be true with regard to pricing. Difficult issues would need to be resolved with regard to access conditions and whether access would be limited to primary data or extend to other stages of the data value chain. The regulatory regime required would need to be agile enough to address the many different settings in which data access requests can come up and develop solutions that are sufficiently sensitive to the potentially negative incentive effects that data access obligations would imply. It would need to do so in a setting where the evolution of the data economy – and data markets in particular – are still in flux. It would miss out on the many fine-grained insights that a decentralised search process for context-sensitive data access regimes will arguably produce.

In line with the European Commission's 'agile' approach, there is therefore a strong case for letting markets evolve based on a regime of private control. Firms are currently in the process of experimenting with the po-

49 Stigler Committee on Digital Platforms, 'Final Report' (2019) 8 <https://www.chicagobooth.edu/-/media/research/stigler/pdfs/digital-platforms---committee-report---stigler-center.pdf> accessed 15 September 2020.

tential uses of their data and exploring their value. Novel strategies of and governance regimes for data sharing and data pooling are likely to evolve in different areas of the IoT. While its outcome is unpredictable, this process can be expected to produce a greater variety of more differentiated solutions than any attempt of a centralised rights allocation could.

4. *Addressing the market failures in a private control context: The role of competition law*

Given the societal and economic importance of data access, a private data control regime must, however, be embedded in a legal framework that stands ready to address significant market failures in a forceful and consistent manner. Information asymmetries and monopoly power must be tackled, and positive as well as negative externalities of data access or data exclusivity must be considered. The legal framework to take up these tasks ranges from, *inter alia*, contract law, including, where applicable, consumer protection law, to competition law and, as a measure of last resort, sector-specific regulation. Importantly, the legislator should consider the introduction of access and usage rights to usage data for all co-generators of such data so as to improve the preconditions for competition.[50]

Within the overall legal framework, competition law functions as a background regime and as a benchmark for developing best principles for data access. To live up to this role, competition law must clarify when data sharing and data pooling will constitute an infringement of Article 101 TFEU.[51] As to Article 102 TFEU, the aftermarket doctrine needs to be clarified with regard to data-driven lock-in,[52] so as to provide guidance on when a customer lock-in can lead to data access requirements. Moreover, the concept of data-related abuses must be further explored – where recent case law, such as the German *Facebook* case,[53] has demonstrated that it is not always and not necessarily a refusal to grant access that constitutes an

50 See Section C.I.5.b) below.

51 See Crémer, Montjoye and Schweitzer (n. 27) 94–98, 109. The Commission has already announced an update of the Guidelines on horizontal cooperation agreements with respect to data-sharing and pooling arrangements: see European Commission, 'A European strategy for data' (n. 1) 14. A public consultation process has already begun; see <https://ec.europa.eu/competition/consultations/2019_hbers/index_en.html> accessed 15 September 2020.

52 See Crémer, Montjoye and Schweitzer (n. 27) 87–91, 101–06, 125.

53 See German Federal Supreme Court (BGH), Case KVR 69/19 – *Facebook*.

abuse, but an abuse may also lie in the combination of different sets of usage data by a dominant firm. Finally, Article 102 TFEU should guide the discussion on when data access is an adequate remedy for a data-related abuse.

Where data access is indeed the appropriate remedy, competition law as such will frequently need to give way to sector-specific legislation to ensure that data access is granted on fair, reasonable and non-discriminatory (FRAND) conditions. While the relevant case law on rights to a licence to a standard-essential patent (SEP)[54] may appear to provide a rough role model for the process by which contractual negotiations on data access should take place, data access regimes may turn out to be even more complex and diverse in practice: the proposed use cases for data may differ widely and affect the conditions under which data access should be granted as well as the access pricing. Different datasets may be needed; data access may be requested at different levels of the value chain, and in each case, an inquiry into the indispensability of the access may be required. The requisite timing of data access may differ: in some settings, the provision of historical data will suffice, in other settings, near-time or real-time access may prove necessary for firms to compete effectively. Similar issues may arise regarding the necessary degree of interoperability,[55] the formats in which data access must be granted and the design of the access interfaces. Conflicts will likely be frequent and – in a competition law framework – highly case-specific. Fast-track procedures for resolving such disputes will be needed if data access is to be effective.

In some areas, these challenges will be overcome by setting up a highly standardised data access regime. In particular, access to individual-level usage data with the consent of the relevant individual can be – and has been – organised at reasonable cost.[56] In other areas, the complexity of the challenge may caution against the attempt to set up a compulsory data access regime, and may guide a search for structural solutions that incentivise the

---

54 See in particular Case C-170/13 *Huawei* ECLI:EU:C:2015:477.

55 For the different forms of interoperability see Crémer, Montjoye and Schweitzer (n. 27) 83 et seq. A lack of data interoperability has been identified as one of the hurdles for an increased flow of data B2B and G2B – see European Commission, 'A European strategy for data' (n. 1) 8. On data interoperability see also: Michal S. Gal and Daniel L. Rubinfeld, 'Data Standardization' (2019) 94 New Your University Law Rev. 737.

56 See Section C.I.3. below.

entity mandated with organising access to establish a well-functioning market.[57]

C. Access to usage data in three different baseline settings – Variations in the legal framework and in the role of competition policy

Where the private data control approach is the starting point, the need for market interventions in general and for a competition law intervention in particular turns into a discussion about the existence of a pertinent market failure.

This paper strives to discuss this question against the background of three recurring data access scenarios:[58] Firstly, access to individual level data by a co-generator of usage data in a bilateral scenario (1); secondly, requests for access to bundled individual-level data or aggregated datasets by a third party vis-à-vis a service or product provider who controls broad usage datasets, with the third party claiming that access to the relevant data is needed to effectively compete in complementary markets (2); thirdly, requests by firms to access the large usage data troves of Big Tech companies to compete and innovate in the field of AI (3).

I. Scenario 1: Access to individual level data by data co-generators

1. The data access scenario

A significant part of the debate on data allocation relates to settings where data are co-generated by two or more parties and the exclusive control over this data is in the hand of one party. Examples of co-generated data include the usage data of an IoT device, e.g. a connected car or a piece of connected industrial machinery, or of an online service, including a social network or a search engine.

57 See, in particular, C.II.5. and C.III.4. below.

58 Also see Crémer, Montjoye and Schweitzer (n. 27) 75 et seq.; Heike Schweitzer, 'Datenzugang in der Datenökonomie: Eckpfeiler einer neuen Informationsordnung' (2019) Gewerblicher Rechtsschutz und Urheberrecht 569, 572–73.

2. *Possible market failures*

Where usage data are transmitted automatically to the producer of the machine or the service provider and processed to improve or personalise the service, to predict needs for maintenance of a machine, to learn about typical usage patterns or to develop complementary services, the user may find it difficult to switch the product or service after some time: a competing producer or service provider would need to compensate for the loss in personalisation through an additional advantage in quality or price, making the market entry of newcomers significantly more difficult.

Moreover, the user may be locked into data-driven complementary services of the product or service provider, whereby third parties may find it difficult to compete effectively without (possibly real-time) access to the usage data. Examples of complementary services that depend on access to usage data include predictive diagnostic services for machinery, complementary services for drivers of connected cars that rely on in-car data or smartphone apps that need access to the GPS data stored in the device.

With effective competition on the primary product or services market and optimally informed users, competitive pressure would force producers and service providers to offer customer-friendly contract terms and technical data access solutions.[59] Generally, data access and data portability would be valued by customers because it would allow them to avoid a data-induced lock-in, both on the primary market and on complementary markets. On the other hand, a 'closed' model may allow a producer or service provider to engage in long-term planning and investment, and to pass on part of this advantage to the customer in the form of a better price or quality.[60] Consequently, a multitude of competing systems with varying

---

59 The debate over welfare effects of competition on aftermarkets versus competition between systems with different levels of openness became very extensive following the US Supreme Court's *Kodak* decision: see, *inter alia*, Carl Shapiro, 'Aftermarkets and Consumer Welfare: Making Sense of Kodak' (1995) 63 The Antitrust Bulletin 483. For a discussion of the consequences of the Kodak case in Europe see Robert Bell, Jacob Kramer and Brian Cave, 'Competition/Antitrust Challenges in Technology Aftermarkets' (2015) <http://eu-competitionlaw.com/competitionantitrust-challenges-in-technology-aftermarkets/> accessed 15 September 2020.

60 The possibility to monopolise aftermarkets also enables the producer of the primary product or the provider of the primary service to cross-subsidise the product or service price through the monopoly rents achieved on the secondary market. This pricing model became famous with Gillette razors (free razor, expensive blades; see Joseph Farrell and Paul Klemperer, 'Coordination and Lock-In: Com-

degrees of data openness could coexist, catering to the varying preferences of different groups of customers.[61] This mechanism is well known from markets for operating systems, for example: a more proprietary operating system in which apps have to pass a quality review process in order to gain access to the device's data may have advantages with respect to a more uniform user experience, better app quality standards and better cyber security – while, on the other hand, making apps potentially more expensive and reducing the range of apps to choose from. Based on these trade-offs, different approaches to openness coexist, with Microsoft Windows arguably being more open than Apple's MacOS and Google Android arguably being more open than Apple's iOS.

The competitive mechanism can fail, however. Frequently, the source of such a market failure will be information asymmetries: in B2C markets, consumers will often not be able to calculate the trade-off correctly at the time when they choose the product or service. This is true in particular where long-lasting products or services are chosen. Similarly, it may be very difficult for consumers to evaluate their demand for certain aftermarket services *ex ante* – especially considering that new and innovative aftermarket services may not even have been available at the time of purchase. Consequently, customers will frequently pay less attention to data accessibility than would be appropriate and will not accurately discount the loss of choice on aftermarkets and/or the loss of the possibility to switch. An

---

petition with Switching Costs and Network Effects' in Mark Armstrong and Robert Porter (eds), *Handbook of Industrial Organization*, Vol. 3 (North Holland 2007) 2037; Randal C. Picker, 'The Razors-and-Blades Myth(s)' (2011) 78 University of Chicago Law Rev. 225) but is, for example, also well-known with printers (cheap devices, expensive branded ink; see Lother Determann and Bruce Perens, 'Open Cars' (2017) 23 Berkeley Technology Law Journal 915, 928–29) or machines for the then-patented Nespresso capsules (cheap coffee machines, expensive coffee capsules). This kind of business model may be individually favourable for consumers with a low level of usage. The efficiency effects should be ambiguous, as such a business model leads to an increase in output on the primary market vs. a decrease in output on the secondary market. For an in-depth analysis of business models and lock-in strategies see Carl Shapiro and Hal Varian, *Information Rules: A Strategic Guide to the Network Economy* (Harvard Business Review Press 1998) 103–72.

61 A buyer of industrial machinery who plans to seldom make use of it could, for instance, prefer a cheaper purchase price in return for being locked in with the expensive predictive maintenance services of the OEM. A buyer who plans to make frequent use of the same equipment might prefer a higher purchase price in return for free data access that allows her to choose from a broader option of aftermarket services.

adverse selection may follow, and products and services that restrict access to usage data may prevail.

In B2B settings, market actors can be expected to be more sensitive to lock-in-situations. But in dynamic, fast-changing markets, even they may be unable to predict the future potential uses of the data sets and therefore undervalue choice and the option to switch.

In other settings, competition will fail to produce a customer-friendly market outcome because one product or service provider is dominant or because all product or service providers have opted for the same model of denying data access – either due to (tacit) collusion or because a closed model is the best option for each of them individually. Bilateral bargaining power may provide another explanation.

3. *Legislative reactions*

Most of the data access legislation that currently exists can, in one way or another, be interpreted as a reaction to data access situations of the scenario 1 type. Essentially all of this legislation refers to perceived market failures of the kinds described above. While sectoral regulation (Electricity Directive, PSD2 Directive; see c) below) is, as of yet, usually equally applicable in B2C and B2B settings, a 'horizontal' right to access usage data is only implemented with respect to personal data within the meaning of Article 4(1) GDPR, not with respect to industrial usage data.[62]

a) Article 20 GDPR: A mandatory portability right regarding personal data

The data access rules with the broadest scope of application are enshrined in the GDPR. Wherever personal data within the meaning of Article 4(1) GDPR are at issue, Article 15 GDPR provides any data subject concerned with a non-waivable, general right to access his or her data. Of greater economic importance is the right to data portability as set out in Article 20

62 While usage data in B2B settings will also frequently entail personal data within the meaning of Art. 4(1) GDPR (location data of a person driving a car will, if it can be linked to the driver, be personal data irrespective of whether the journey was undertaken for private or business reasons), a large part of a business's usage data will typically not qualify as personal data (for example: data on its energy use; data on the wear and tear of its equipment etc.).

GDPR.[63] While the data remains under the control of the service provider, each data subject has a right to receive the personal data concerning him or her 'in a structured, commonly used and machine-readable format' and to transmit those data – or have them transmitted – to another controller without hindrance from the current controller.

As has frequently been stated, Article 20 GDPR has been introduced primarily with a view to counteracting data-related lock-in effects:[64] It is intended to facilitate the switching of services whose provision can be significantly informed by historic personal data. Article 20 GDPR thereby enhances each individual's freedom of choice and economic scope of action. From a competition law angle, it thereby lowers barriers to entry to the market for primary services and increases the contestability of the market position of any given service provider.

However, Article 20 GDPR does not qualify as a tailored remedy to the market failure described above: In this perspective, it is both too narrow and overbroad. It is too narrow because it is generally considered that, while Article 20 GDPR grants a right to access and transmit historical data, it does not include a right to full and real-time porting or to data interoperability.[65] With this limitation, Article 20 GDPR is designed 'to enable switching of service providers, rather than enabling data reuse in digital ecosystems'.[66] The lock-in into the primary product or service may be addressed – provided there is sufficient competition in the market for primary products or services. The lock-in into a potentially broad range of aftermarkets is not tackled effectively by Article 20 GDPR where real- or near-time access would be needed. To target the latter lock-in, a right to ensure data interoperability with third party service providers would arguably be required. Under Article 20 GDPR, the decision whether to open data-driven aftermarkets for new entrants or not remains at the discretion of the service provider, however.

63 See also Art. 16(2) of the Directive (EU) 2019/770 of the European Parliament and of the Council of 20 May 2019 on certain aspects concerning contracts for the supply of digital content and digital services [2019] OJ L136/1 – with reference to the GDPR.

64 European Parliament, 'Resolution of 6 July 2011 on a comprehensive approach on personal data protection in the European Union' (2011/2025(INI)) [2013] OJ C33E/101, para. 16.

65 Paul De Hert, Vagelis Papakonstantinou, Gianclaudio Malgieri and others, 'The right to data portability in the GDPR: Towards user-centric interoperability of digital services' (2018) 34 Computer Law & Security Review 193, 200–201; Schweitzer (n. 58) 574.

66 European Commission, 'A European strategy for data' (n. 1) 10.

At the same time, if Article 20 GDPR were meant to remedy the market failure problem sketched above, it would be overbroad: The right to data portability is granted to data subjects irrespective of the existence of a relevant information asymmetry, and it cannot be waived even with full information. Furthermore, Article 20 GDPR is blind to whether the service provider possesses any relevant degree of market power or even bilateral bargaining power. Due to the compulsory, non-waivable nature of the right to data portability, a new entrant into the market would be unable to buy off the right to data portability in exchange for a better price and incentives to invest in a long-term relationship. Under Article 20 GDPR, any new entrant must fear that consumers will switch to the incumbent once the latter enters the market and lures the consumer with the greater size of its network, a higher degree of interoperability or, based on the broad scope of his or her data troves, a greater degree of personalisation.

In its current shape, Article 20 GDPR should therefore not be understood as a reaction to a market failure. Rather, it strives to protect the data subject's 'informational autonomy' and continued control over his or her personal data. The fact that the right to data portability is designed as a non-waivable right is proof of the weight that the EU legislator has given to consumers' continued freedom of choice irrespective of the benefits that might result, in the absence of information asymmetries and power, from increased incentives of a service provider to invest in the bilateral relationship on a long-term basis. Paradoxically, the protection of the data subject's informational autonomy thereby comes with a significant limitation of his or her freedom of contract.

b) Electricity Directive: Access to smart meter data

A sector-specific data access regime that clearly reacts to a market failure – namely stable (quasi-)monopolistic positions in the markets for electricity-related infrastructure – has been established in the context of energy consumption and energy input data collected through connected 'smart' meters.[67] Smart meter data can be useful for consumers in various ways.

67 There are also data access obligations with respect to metering data for natural gas; see Art. 3(6)(b) and Annex I(1)(h) of Directive 2009/73/EC of the European Parliament and of the Council of 13 July 2009 concerning common rules for the internal market in natural gas and repealing Directive 2003/55/EC [2009] OJ L211/94. These access obligations, while following a similar logic as the Electricity Directive (facilitating switching between energy suppliers), have not yet been

While there is no specific risk of data-induced lock-in (there is, as of now, no 'personalisation' in electricity markets that would require consumption data to be ported to a new energy supplier), effortless access to energy consumption data facilitates hassle-free switching of energy suppliers, who can offer prices based on precise, historic consumption data. Access to smart meter data is necessary for 'smart' tariffs that change prices depending on the time of consumption, grid load or wholesale prices. Data access is also a requirement for using 'consumer energy management systems'[68] that are integrated, for example, into smart home devices. Energy-intensive processes, like charging an electric car, could be switched on automatically when the price is low, saving electricity costs and simultaneously stabilising the grid. While switching between energy suppliers requires only one-time access to consumption data, smart home devices will usually require real-time or near real-time data access.

Electricity meters have typically been operated and controlled by distribution grid operators, which possess a natural monopoly. Even where markets for meter operation have been liberalised, the market position of former monopolists has often remained extraordinarily strong. In Germany, for instance, energy consumers have had the right to choose an independent electricity meter operator since 2006.[69] The legal relations between independent electricity meter operators, energy suppliers and grid operators are governed by private contracts (subject, however, to regulation). Nonetheless, grid operators still have a market share of over 90 % in the energy metering market.[70] In such a setting, data access cannot be left to privately negotiated contracts and competition.

---

updated with respect to connected 'smart' meters. They will not be dealt with in depth in this paper.

68 An overview of technical details can be found at Rita Pereira and others, 'Consumer energy management system with integration of smart meters' (2015) 1 Energy Reports 22.

69 Now Sec. 5 Federal Law on Metering Point Operation (*Messstellenbetriebsgesetz*), formerly Sec. 21b Energy Industry Act (*Energiewirtschaftsgesetz*). For more (economic) details about the German liberalisation of metering point operations see Stephan Schmitt and Matthias Wissner, 'Die Liberalisierung des Messwesens – Verhindert das Abrechnungsentgelt freien Wettbewerb?' (2015) 39 Zeitschrift für Energiewirtschaft 171.

70 Bundesnetzagentur and Bundeskartellamt, 'Monitoringbericht 2019' (2019) 322–23 <https://www.bundesnetzagentur.de/SharedDocs/Mediathek/Berichte/2019/Monitoringbericht_Energie2019.pdf?__blob=publicationFile&v=6> accessed 15 September 2020.

Instead, the Electricity Directive 2019/944[71] obliges member states to implement the following mandatory access rights into their national law: customers are to be granted access to data on the electricity they feed into the grid and on their electricity consumption 'through a standardised communication interface or through remote access, or to a third party acting on their behalf, in an easily understandable format allowing them to compare offers on a like-for-like basis' (Article 20(e)). This provision is specifically tailored to facilitate switching between electricity suppliers. Data access for complementary services (smart home devices or other consumer energy management systems) can be obtained through Article 23(2) of Directive 2019/944.[72] While Article 23 does not clearly state that data access is to be provided via real-time or near real-time APIs, Article 19(1) shows that the policy goal of such data access is to promote 'smart metering systems that are interoperable, in particular with consumer energy management systems'. Interoperability requirements can be implemented by the European Commission subject to Article 24(2) of Directive 2019/944. Hence, energy consumers can provide a data access point to the providers of complementary services.[73]

By requiring data interoperability with regard to individual-level data relevant for complementary devices and services, the EU has therefore implemented a mandatory data 'portability' approach that reaches beyond Article 20 GDPR.

c) The Payment Service Directive II (PSD2): Access to accounts and account data

Another sector-specific data access regime that goes beyond Article 20 GDPR but is less clearly tailored to a market failure than the Electricity Di-

71 Directive (EU) 2019/944 of the European Parliament and of the Council of 5 June 2019 on common rules for the internal market for electricity and amending Directive 2012/27/EU [2019] OJ L158/125 (Electricity Directive).

72 According to this provision, 'the parties responsible for data management shall provide access to the data of the final customer to any eligible party [...]. Eligible parties shall have the requested data at their disposal in a non-discriminatory manner and simultaneously. Access to data shall be easy and the relevant procedures for obtaining access to data shall be made publicly available'.

73 As they are eligible parties within the meaning of Art. 23(2).

rective's access regime is contained in the PSD2.[74] It obliges member states to implement certain access rights to payment accounts ('access to account', or 'XS2A',[75] in FinTech jargon): account servicing payment service providers, such as banks, are required to grant real-time access to the account and transaction data of an account holder via APIs to 'account information service providers', or AISPs (Article 67 PSD2), and to allow the initiation of payments via APIs through 'payment initiation service providers', or PISPs (Article 66 PSD2), on a non-discriminatory basis. Also, the account must be accessible online. Such access must, however, be explicitly requested by the account holder. Furthermore, the Directive establishes certain data protection, data minimisation and cybersecurity obligations.[76] The European Banking Authority (EBA) is called upon to establish 'common and open standards of communication to be implemented by all account servicing payment service providers that allow for the provision of online payment services'.[77]

The PSD2 Directive thus goes significantly beyond the 'simple' data portability right as laid down by Article 20 GDPR: not only does it grant real-time data access via standardised APIs (regarding AISPs), it even allows for service interoperability (regarding PISPs). It thereby enables account holders to make use of innovative aftermarkets services that rely on access to their payment accounts and facilitates competition on these aftermarkets. With these provisions, the EU reacts to the difficulties 'for payment service providers to launch innovative, safe and easy-to-use digital payment services and to provide consumers and retailers with effective, convenient and secure payment methods in the Union.'[78] PISPs are regarded as a 'bridge between the website of the merchant and the online bank-

74 Directive (EU) 2015/2366 of the European Parliament and of the Council of 25 November 2015 on payment services in the internal market, amending Directives 2002/65/EC, 2009/110/EC and 2013/36/EU and Regulation (EU) No 1093/2010, and repealing Directive 2007/64/EC [2015] OJ L 337/35 (PSD2 Directive). For the debate see, *inter alia*, Oscar Borgogno and Giuseppe Colangelo, 'Consumer Inertia and Competition-sensitive Data Governance: The Case of Open Banking' (2020) Journal of European Consumer and Market Law 143.

75 See Open Banking Europe, 'Third Party Provider User Management for PSD2 Access to Account (XS2A)' (2017) <https://www.openbankingeurope.eu/media/1176/preta-obe-mg-001-002-psd2-xs2a-tpp-user-management-guide.pdf> accessed 15 September 2020.

76 See Arts 66, 67 PSD2 for details.

77 PSD2, Recital 93.

78 PSD2, Recital 4.

ing platform of the payer's' bank[79] and as a 'low-cost solution' for both merchants and consumers to provide for fast shipments in e-commerce and to reduce transaction costs.[80] AISPs provide for attractive solutions to give the account user 'an overall view of its financial situation immediately at any given moment'.[81] Overall, the PSD2 Directive thereby becomes an important building block of a European internal market in digital times.

In a perfectly competitive market setting with fully informed consumers and a lack of transaction (especially: switching) costs, banks would be incentivised to grant access to a broad range of complementary services on their own initiative to attract potential account holders. Banking markets are, however, frequently characterised by exactly the kinds of informational market failures described above: when deciding where to open a banking account, many potential customers will not pay sufficient attention to which complementary services are compatible with each bank. In particular, consumers would, if at all, focus on compatibility with certain incumbents or important newcomers (like ApplePay). What is more, consumer inertia results in a widespread lack of willingness to switch banks.[82] As a result, banks may be strategically incentivised to vertically integrate and monopolise access for their own complementary payment solutions or restrict access to selected partners.

The PSD2 Directive's data access and interoperability rules are generally well-suited to address these information-based market failures and facilitate competition and innovation in complementary services. Implemented sector-wide they may, however, come with an important downside: they eliminate a possibility for service differentiation – and therefore, a possible competitive advantage – for newcomers in the core market (here: the banking market). In several markets, before the entry into force of the PSD2 Directive, new start-up banks had been emerging whose unique selling point was a bundle of innovative complementary services and/or broad account access for third-party service providers.[83] Certain banking 'dinosaurs' had

79 PSD2, Recital 27.

80 PSD2, Recital 29.

81 PSD2, Recital 28.

82 Borgogno and Colangelo (n. 74); CMA, 'Retail banking market investigation final report' (9 August 2016) paras 64–73 <https://assets.publishing.service.gov.uk/media/57ac9667e5274a0f6c00007a/retail-banking-market-investigation-full-final-report.pdf> accessed 15 September 2020.

83 See, for example, the German upstart bank N26.

already begun to grant access through APIs on a voluntary basis.[84] With the PSD2 Directive, innovative banks may have lost an important competitive 'edge'.

d) Contractual rights to port non-personal data B2C

Finally, the European legislator has recently recognised a contractual right of consumers to port non-personal digital content provided or created by him or her in the course of a contract for the supply of digital content or digital services in case of termination of the contract.[85]

4. Competition law

In the absence of sector-specific data access legislation, data access may be mandated under general competition law.

In B2C relationships, the refusal to allow access to a customer's individual-level usage data upon his or her request in real time may constitute an exploitative abuse. If a third-party undertaking were to request access with the consent of the customer concerned, but were denied such access, this could be part of an exclusionary strategy, undertaken with a view to further entrenching the position of dominance in the primary market or leveraging this position to neighbouring markets. For Article 102 TFEU to apply, a position of dominance of the data controller in the primary market, as well as its abuse, would need to be proven case by case.

In Germany, coinciding principles follow from Section 19 of the German Act Against Restraints of Competition (GWB). Section 20(1) GWB goes further: According to this provision, the prohibition of exclusionary abuses of market power applies not only to dominant firms, but also where a small or medium-sized undertaking depends on another undertaking for the supply or demand of specific products or services such that sufficient and reasonable possibilities to switch to other undertakings do not exist ('relative market power'). In other words: bilateral power suffices to

84 See, for example, Deutsche Bank, 'Unlocking opportunities in the API economy' (2018) <https://cib.db.com/docs_new/Whitepaper_Unlocking_opportunities_in_the_API_economy_Aug_2018.pdf> accessed 15 September 2020.

85 See Art. 16(4) of Directive (EU) 2019/770 (n. 63). Generally for a discussion of contractual data access rights see Axel Metzger, 'Access to and Porting of Data under Contract Law', in this volume.

turn an undertaking into an addressee of the prohibition to unreasonably impair competition or to discriminate between firms competing on a neighbouring market without objective justification. Relative market power can also stem from specific, non-recoverable investments in the business relationship with another undertaking ('company-specific dependency'),[86] even where such dependency is the result of a voluntary contractual relationship.[87] In principle, the refusal to grant access to co-generated usage data can therefore constitute an abuse of relative market power.

Currently, a reform act is pending[88] that proposes to amend Section 20 GWB with a new paragraph (1a) that would recognise that bilateral dependency can arise from the fact alone that an undertaking is dependent on access to data controlled by another undertaking. A dependency on the product or service from which the data derives would not be required.[89] Where complementary products or services are based on the usage data generated in the course of the use of a primary product or service, substitutes for that data will be lacking by definition, such that Section 20 GWB may be broadly applicable to data lock-in scenarios. It would, however, not apply where a firm can gain access to individual-level usage data by turning to the user itself for transmission. If a usage right of data co-generators were to be recognised, this would typically be the case. The main scope of application of Section 20(1a) GWB would then be scenario 2 (see II.4. below).

Finally, the aforementioned reform act would also introduce a new Section 19a GWB, addressed to undertakings on multi-sided markets and network markets that are 'of paramount significance for competition across markets'. Section 19a(2) No. 4 GWB would empower the *Bundeskartellamt* (the German Federal Cartel Office) to prohibit any action that would 'make the interoperability of products or services or the portability of data

---

86 German Federal Supreme Court (BGH) of 23 February 1988, Case KZR 20/86 – *Opel Blitz;* German Federal Supreme Court (BGH) of 21 February 1995, Case KZR 33/93 – *Kfz-Vertragshändler; both regarding brand-specific investments of authorised car dealers and repairers.*

87 Jörg Nothdurft, in Hermann-Josef Bunte (ed.), *Langen/Bunte, Kartellrecht: Kommentar*, Vol. I (13th edn Luchterhand 2018) § 20 GWB para. 38.

88 Gesetzentwurf der Bundesregierung – Entwurf eines Gesetzes zur Änderung des Gesetzes gegen Wettbewerbsbeschränkungen für ein fokussiertes, proaktives und digitales Wettbewerbsrecht 4.0 und anderer wettbewerbsrechtlicher Bestimmungen (GWB Digitalisierungsgesetz) (2020) <https://www.bmwi.de/Redaktion/DE/Downloads/Gesetz/gesetzentwurf-gwb-digitalisierungsgesetz.pdf?__blob=publicationFile&v=6> accessed 15 September 2020.

89 Schweitzer and others (n. 4) 192–93.

more difficult and thereby impede competition'. To the extent necessary to make competition on data-driven markets work, it would allow the *Bundeskartellamt* to impose data access requirements on firms of paramount significance for competition across markets *ex ante*.

5. Policy options

a) Access to individual-level data in B2C settings

Stepping back, significant action has already been taken to update the current legal framework as it applies to scenario 1 cases. A broad consensus is emerging that a general transformation of the right to data portability under Article 20 GDPR into a right to data interoperability would be counterproductive: depending on the specific market conditions, it could work in favour of already data-rich firms that, based on a dominant position of a platform of strategic importance,[90] have the potential to expand that position into neighbouring markets. Also, ensuring data interoperability can be a high burden on small and medium-sized firms. A general data interoperability obligation would therefore tend to increase barriers to entry and hamper innovation. Consequently, in B2C markets, a continuation with a more cautious sector-specific legislation appears to be the right approach. Such legislation should be informed by the insights on the complex trade-offs that come with the opening up of narrowly defined primary markets in aftermarket settings.

The implications are currently much debated, in particular with a view to access to in-car data in an emerging 'connected cars' setting. Connected cars collect a multitude of data about the state of the vehicle and its use, as well as environmental data.[91] To a significant degree, these data will be personal data within the meaning of Article 4(1) GDPR. For access to and the processing of in-car data, whether individual level, bundled individual

90 Special conduct requirements for this set of firms (to be precise: undertakings on multi-sided markets and network markets that are 'of paramount significance for competition across markets') are considered by the German legislature in its amendment of Sec. 19a GWB (see above). Sec. 19a(2) No. 3 GWB would allow the Bundeskartellamt to prohibit the bundling of data across markets where it has the potential to impede competition.

91 Cf. Damien Geradin, 'Access to In-Vehicle Data by Third-Party Service Providers: Is there a Market Failure and, if so, How Should it be Addressed?' (2020) 2 <https://ssrn.com/abstract=3545817> accessed 15 September 2020.

level or aggregate, three technological approaches are currently debated: car manufacturers prefer the so-called 'extended vehicle' concept, where all data is transferred to, processed and stored on proprietary servers of the car manufacturers themselves.[92] In defence of this approach, car manufacturers assert cybersecurity and consequently road safety advantages. These advantages are, however, contested by other market actors[93] and independent studies.[94] Alternatives to the 'extended vehicle' approach are, firstly, 'neutral' servers to which access for third parties is granted on the basis of transparent, non-discriminatory terms and, secondly, 'onboard' processing of all in-car data on an open application platform that allows for the installation of third-party applications.[95] Third-party applications that depend on (possibly real-time) access to individual-level or bundled individual-level in-car data may be, for example, predictive maintenance services, complementary on-the-road services like upgraded navigation or 'smart parking' services or insurance tariffs that are usage-dependent or vary with driving style. The 'extended vehicle' would put car manufacturers in a gatekeeper position that would enable them to monopolise aftermarkets and complementary services. The alternatives would not do so, or (in the case of a 'neutral' gatekeeper) to a much lesser extent.[96]

On competitive markets, car manufacturers would be incentivised to choose the technical solution with the level of openness that best suits consumers' preferences. Different solutions and business models with their respective advantages and disadvantages might co-exist (see 2. above). There is, however, reason to assume a significant degree of market failure on this

---

92 European Automobile Manufacturers Association, 'ACEA Strategy Paper on Connectivity' (2016) 10 et seq. <https://www.acea.be/uploads/publications/ACEA_Strategy_Paper_on_Connectivity.pdf> accessed 15 September 2020.

93 See, *inter alia*, 'Manifesto for fair digitalisation opportunities' <https://www.figiefa.eu/wp-content/uploads/Manifesto-For-equal-Digitalisation-chances.pdf> accessed 15 September 2020, signed by several industry associations.

94 See, for example, M. McCarthy and others, 'Access to In-vehicle Data and Resources – Final Report', TLR Report for the European Commission (2017) 75 et seq. <https://ec.europa.eu/transport/sites/transport/files/2017-05-access-to-in-vehicle-data-and-resources.pdf> accessed 15 September 2020. The authors conclude that, while security is more costly to implement within the alternative technological approaches, it is well possible – and that the demands of safety and security need to be balanced with the goal to achieve fair and undistorted competition (ibid. 8–9).

95 McCarthy and others (n. 94) 32–49.

96 Cf. Wolfgang Kerber, 'Data Governance in Connected Cars: The Problem of Access to In-Vehicle Data' (2018) 9 Journal of Intellectual Property, Information Technology and E-Commerce Law 310, 325.

'systems market'. The problem is not one of market dominance on the car market: markets for consumer cars can be characterised as a reasonably concentrated oligopoly, with a number of established firms and a healthy set of 'challenger' firms. However, information asymmetries are likely to be pervasive: cars are durable investment goods. Customers are therefore locked in to their purchase decision for a significant amount of time.[97] It is difficult for consumers to make a reliable estimate about the full life cycle costs of owning a car of a specific brand – a specific brand's performance on aftermarkets may therefore not be adequately disciplined by the risk of diminishing sales on the primary product market. In such a setting, car manufacturers may be incentivised to monopolise aftermarkets or grant access only to selected partners in exchange for a fee (thereby reaping monopoly rents). While one may argue, on the other hand, that second-hand markets provide a sufficiently convenient way out of the lock-in, the protracted legislative battle to open up markets for automotive repair and maintenance services and spare parts appears to provide proof that a relevant market failure persists nonetheless.[98] Also, the range of possible aftermarkets in the emerging mobility sector is arguably huge, as is the innovative potential that an opening of the relevant data markets can unleash.

To address this case of market failure – and to resolve the persisting legal uncertainty concerning in-car data – there appears to be a case for enacting mandatory real-time data access and portability (or rather: interoperability) rights that enable consumers to choose between independent providers of aftermarkets and complementary services. This would need to be accompanied by a system of certification[99] or technological safeguards

97 Ibid. 317.

98 The type approval regulation of 2007 established non-discriminatory rights to access vehicle repair and maintenance information and on-board maintenance data (vehicle on-board diagnostic information, 'OBD data') – see Regulation (EC) No. 715/2007 of the European Parliament and of the Council of 20 June 2007 on type approval of motor vehicles with respect to emissions from light passenger and commercial vehicles (Euro 5 and Euro 6) and on access to vehicle repair and maintenance information [2007] OJ L171/1. For further details see Kerber, 'Data Governance in Connected Cars: The Problem of Access to In-Vehicle Data' (n. 96) 319; Wolfgang Kerber and Jonas Frank, 'Data Governance Regimes in the Digital Economy: The Example of Connected Cars' (2017) 33 et seq. <https://ssrn.com/abstract=3064794> accessed 15 September 2020. Also see scenario 2 at Sub-section II. below.

99 Cf. Geradin (n. 91) 1–2, with an analogy to the review processes by Apple and Google for their app stores.

(separating basic automotive functions from additional functions, like entertainment) to address relevant security risks.

b) Access to individual-level (industrial) data in B2B settings

The European legislator has been significantly less determined to address data access settings of the scenario 1 type in B2B relationships. In some fields – especially in the area of banking and electricity – access rights of businesses have been recognised alongside those of consumers. Also, depending on the facts of the case, usage data may qualify as personal data even in a business setting,[100] such that Article 20 GDPR applies. But unlike for personal data, there is no generally applicable data access and portability right for industrial data. Consequently, in bilateral settings between a product producer or service provider and its business customer, it is currently mostly left to the parties of the relevant contractual relationship to negotiate a consensual data access solution. Following this logic, the Fairness and Transparency Regulation (EU) 2019/1150,[101] which applies to online intermediation services, such as sales platforms, and online search engines (Article 1(2) Transparency Regulation), refrains from establishing rights of business users of the platform to data access. Instead, it sets out a mere requirement of transparency regarding the 'technical and contractual access, or absence thereof, of business users to any personal data or other data'.[102]

In its communication 'Towards a common European data space', the EU Commission has set out general principles on data sharing B2B, in particular the principles of transparency, shared value creation, respect for each other's commercial interests, protection of undistorted competition and the minimisation of data lock-in.[103] Furthermore, it has sketched different models of data sharing.[104] In its recent communication on a Euro-

100 Case C-398/15 *Manni* ECLI:EU:C:2017:197, para. 37.

101 Regulation (EU) 2019/1150 of the European Parliament and of the Council of 20 June 2019 on promoting fairness and transparency for business users of online intermediation services [2019] OJ L186/57.

102 Art. 9 Regulation (EU) 2019/1150.

103 See European Commission, 'Towards a common European data space' (n. 14) 10 and European Commission Staff Working Document, 'Guidance on sharing private sector data in the European data economy' SWD(2018) 125 final, 3.

104 (i) An open data approach; (ii) data monetisation on a data marketplace; (iii) data exchange in a closed platform. See European Commission SWD, 'Guidance on sharing private data' (n. 103) 5.

pean strategy for data, the Commission has announced its intention to get key players from the manufacturing sector to agree on conditions under which they would be willing to share their data generated by smart connected products.[105] A 'Code of Conduct on Agricultural Data Sharing by Contractual Agreement',[106] which was developed in 2018 by a number of agricultural organisations, provides a first impression of what such an agreement could look like. In order to foster trust in agricultural data sharing it emphasises, *inter alia*, the right of the data originator to control the access to and the use of data. Comparatively far-reaching data-sharing obligations exist or are being explored in the transport sector.[107]

Obviously, competition law continues to apply and complements the contractual regime. Data access obligations may, in particular, follow from Article 102 TFEU (see 4. above).

However, a debate has ensued on whether contractual solutions, backed up by competition law, suffice.[108] The data controller and the product or service user will be in a contractual relationship most of the time, but not necessarily so; the product or service user's legitimate interest in accessing and porting the usage data will be the same, regardless of the existence of such a 'direct' contractual relationship. In such a situation, the creation of a – waivable – data access, usage and portability right *in rem* of all those who have actively participated in the generation of the usage data would help. It would recognise that under the conditions of the emerging data economy, where the usage of a product or service constantly generates data, such usage over longer periods of time simultaneously constitutes a valuable investment and contribution of the user to the value of the product or service that should be legally recognised. Also, the legislative acknowledgment of such an access and usage right would provide a baseline for negotiations on the best allocation of rights in a given case.

At the same time, a waivable access, usage and portability right would not protect business users against information asymmetries, market power

---

105 See European Commission, 'A European strategy for data' (n. 1) 26.

106 EU Code of conduct on agricultural data sharing by contractual agreement, <https://www.copa-cogeca.eu/img/user/files/EU%20CODE/EU_Code_2018_web_version.pdf> accessed 15 September 2020.

107 European Commission, 'A European strategy for data' (n. 1) 28.

108 Drexl (n. 31) 287–291; 'Datenethikkommission der Datenethikkommission [Opinion of the Data Ethics Commission] (October 2019) 147. See also the draft ALI-ELI Principles for a Data Economy which suggest the legislative creation of a right to access or to port co-generated data. For details and discussion see Axel Metzger, 'Access to and porting of data under contract law', in this volume.

and bilateral power imbalances that may lead to the market failures described above. In such cases, additional instruments of intervention continue to be needed. For such interventions, a waivable access, usage and portability right would, however, serve as a legal reference point. In those national legal orders that – like German civil law – provide for a control of standard contract law terms in B2B relationships, the recognition of an access, usage and portability right of data co-generators would set a legislative benchmark for what is typically considered to be fair.[109] Where a waiver is requested by a dominant firm, the deviation from the legislative benchmark may indicate an abuse.[110]

Interestingly, the recognition of a waivable access, usage and portability right of data co-generators would also provide a novel reference point for the application of Article 101 TFEU. An agreement between the data controller and the product or service user to waive or limit the data access, usage and portability right would arguably qualify as an agreement restrictive of competition, as it would tend to hamper the entry of competitors both into the primary market for the product or service by which the data is generated and into complementary markets. At least where such waivers were agreed on systematically, they could have an anti-competitive object or effect. Without the definition of a legal data usage right, data controllers would not need to implement contract clauses with respect to data access at all; instead, they would simply retain their 'de-facto data possession' and refuse to deal with the data – a unilateral behaviour that is only restricted by competition law where dominance is present (Article 102 TFEU). Article 101 TFEU would allow agreements on the waiver of data access rights to be addressed significantly below the threshold of dominance.

Obviously, such waivers can also come with important efficiency gains and pro-competitive justifications. In particular, they would incentivise long-term investments by the product or service provider. On this basis, a new data-related Block Exemption Regulation could and arguably should be drafted: Contractual waivers of data access rights should be generally exempted under Article 101(3) TFEU where the market share of the beneficiary of the waiver on the primary product or services market remains relatively small (15–20 %). The exemption should, however, be withdrawn

---

109 According to the German Civil Code, standard contract law terms agreed B2B would only be subjected to a fairness control where they derogate or supplement legal provisions (Sec. 307(3) German Civil Code).

110 Either an exploitative abuse (imposing unfair trading conditions) or an exclusionary abuse of dominance (impeding switching and/or monopolising aftermarkets).

where contractual waivers are requested by a large portion of the market, such that the demand side would essentially be left without a meaningful choice. Furthermore, contractual waivers should not be exempted where they – together with other provisions in the contract – lead to a durable lock-in, both with respect to the primary product and to aftermarket services.

6. *Conclusions on scenario 1*

Overall, sound legal principles appear to be evolving with regard to data access scenario 1. Generally, the private control paradigm applies. In B2C relationships, this paradigm is somewhat disrupted by the non-waivability of the right to data portability under Article 20 GDPR. Nonetheless, the right of consumers to port 'their' data, as recognised by Article 20 GDPR, has the potential to change the competitive landscape. More practical ways to administer one's data, to manage consent and, where desired, to make personal data available for reuse, including with the help of personal data cooperatives or neutral data intermediaries, remain to be explored.[111]

Also, further sector-specific legislation is to be expected – for example in the context of connected cars – that will endow consumers with rights to real- or near-time access to data. The PSD2 Directive and the Electricity Directive provide role models in this regard. Similar regulation appears to be appropriate where power asymmetries or information asymmetries are systemically prevalent on a data-driven market and tend to produce strong and durable consumer lock-in into aftermarkets that is not overcome either by competition on the primary (systems) market or by well-functioning second-hand markets.

For non-personal data, the creation of a data access and usage right *in rem* – although waivable – would make an important difference. With such data access rights, exclusive control of usage data would no longer be the benchmark. Multiple data access points would arise, with the potential to stimulate innovation and competition. Failures in markets for data as well as in markets for data-driven products and services could then be addressed on a flexible basis, combining the strengths of contract law and competition law.

---

111 See, for example, European Commission, 'A European strategy for data' (n. 1) 10, referring to the MyData movement and similar initiatives and tools.

II. *Scenario 2: Third-party access to bundled individual-level data or aggregated data in aftermarket settings*

1. *The data access scenario*

In data access scenario 1, an undertaking may depend on gaining access to the individual-level usage data of its potential customer in order to provide competitive complementary products or services. For such access, the undertaking should however turn to that customer for consent to data access. This is true for both personal data and non-personal data: if a competitor wants to offer products or services that build on individual-level usage patterns of a primary service, it is for that competitor to convince the potential customer to have that usage data transmitted to it. The question of whether that customer will be entitled to have the relevant data transmitted has been dealt with in data access scenario 1.

There are, however, cases in which a firm's ability to offer competitive aftermarket or complementary products or services depends on access to more than just individual-level usage data. In these cases, the potential customer cannot serve as the sole access point for the necessary data. For example, a complementary service provider may need access to large sets of *bundled* individual-level usage data for anonymous use[112] or to *aggregated* usage data[113] to provide complementary products or services that are competitive. Imagine, for example, a predictive maintenance service that requires aggregated data about the 'wear and tear' of a piece of equipment as training data for its prediction algorithm; or a firm that strives to offer road maintenance and needs access to aggregated in-car sensor data on road quality for this purpose. To the extent that bundled individual-level data or aggregated data are not available through, say, a data pool established by a large number of car owners, machine users or an intermediary

---

112 Cf. Crémer, Montjoye and Schweitzer (n. 27) 25–26: sets of anonymously used individual-level data are typically needed to extract (prediction) patterns out of usage data, but the goal is not to directly provide a service to the individual who generated the data in the first place. For example, with individual-level usage data of a significant amount of subscribers to a video streaming platform, one could train a neural network to make good movie recommendations based on the favourite movies of any given user.

113 Crémer, Montjoye and Schweitzer (n. 27) 26: 'Aggregated data, refers to more standardised data that has been irreversibly aggregated. This is the case for eg sales data, national statistics information, and companies' profit and loss statements. Compared to anonymous use of individual-level data, the aggregation is standard enough that access to the individual-level data is not necessary.'.

(on this, see 5. below), the complementary service provider would need to turn directly to the data controller for data access, i.e. the firm active on the primary market.

Scenario 2 also entails cases where the necessary data are not usage data. One of these cases is currently being investigated by the German *Bundeskartellamt*: Mobility platforms request access to real-time data about train departures and delays from the German railway operator Deutsche Bahn in order to tailor their offer to the needs of the users, e.g. to enable them to book all means of transport to their destination from a single source.[114]

In another subset of cases, competitors on up- or downstream markets face a competitive disadvantage due to the self-preferencing of a vertically integrated competitor. For example, independent retailers on Amazon Marketplace complain that Amazon (allegedly) gains a competitive advantage for its own retail activities on the platform by utilising aggregated data regarding user search and click behaviour on the marketplace.[115] While, in principle, retailers operating on the platform could depend on data access to the Marketplace users' aggregated usage data to remain competitive (hence, a 'clear' data access scenario 2 case), the underlying competition problem is one of a lacking level playing field. It could equally be, and arguably should rather be, addressed by prohibiting Amazon from utilising the Marketplace data for its own merchant activities (see below, 3.).

---

114 Bundeskartellamt, Press Release of 28 November 2019, 'Proceeding against Deutsche Bahn AG – Bundeskartellamt examines possible anticompetitive impediment of mobility platforms' <https://www.bundeskartellamt.de/SharedDocs/Meldung/EN/Pressemitteilungen/2019/28_11_2019_DB_Mobilitaet.html> accessed 15.09.2020.

115 The European Commission is currently investigating this conduct: European Commission Press Release of 17 July 2019, 'Antitrust: Commission opens investigation into possible anti-competitive conduct of Amazon' <https://ec.europa.eu/commission/presscorner/detail/en/ip_19_4291> accessed 15 September 2020. On the antitrust hearing before the US Congress, see, *inter alia*, Washington Post Online of 30 July 2020, 'Amazon may have used proprietary data to compete with its merchants, Bezos tells Congress', <https://www.washingtonpost.com/technology/2020/07/29/bezos-testimony-data-antitrust/> accessed 15 September 2020.

2. *Possible market failures*

In well-functioning markets, access to the necessary bundled and aggregated datasets would arguably be made available by the data controller at an efficient market price. Where the market for the primary product or service is fully competitive, firms active on that market should again be expected to develop different approaches to data openness that cater to the different preferences of their customers. Open systems would try to convince their customers by means of their broad range of diverse complementary services offered on competitive aftermarkets. Closed systems would point to the pros of a more controlled aftermarket environment, possibly with higher quality standards and a higher degree of cybersecurity.[116] Also, a higher commitment to privacy standards may be an argument for not passing on customer usage data, even in the aggregate.

But again, the possibilities for market failures are manifold. In principle, they resemble those identified for scenario 1: information asymmetries may result in customer choice being impaired by bounded rationality. Also, dominant data controllers may find it attractive to extract monopoly rents. Consequently, it may be attractive for firms active on primary product or services markets to foreclose access of potential competitors to aftermarkets to a degree that is not in line with customer preferences.

In some instances, the transaction costs associated with the marketing of data will be prohibitively high.[117] This can result from, *inter alia*, difficulties in estimating the commercial value of the data[118] or uncertainty about the legality of data sharing in the light of the GDPR and Article 101 TFEU.[119] When it comes to personal data, the GDPR may indeed constrain the ability of data controllers to provide access to bundled individual or aggregate data.[120] The same is true with regard to constraints following from

---

116 On the comparison of the pros and cons of open vs. closed systems see, *inter alia*, Shapiro and Varian (n. 60); Autorité de la concurrence and CMA, 'The economics of open and closed systems' (2014) <https://assets.publishing.service.gov.uk/government/uploads/system/uploads/attachment_data/file/387718/The_economics_of_open_and_closed_systems.pdf> accessed 15 September 2020.

117 Martens and others (n. 15) 6; Kerber and Frank (n. 98) 16–17.

118 Tormo (n. 47); Nguyen and Paczos (n. 47) 31–38.

119 Cf. German Federal Ministry of Economic Affairs and Energy, Report by the Commission 'Competition Law 4.0' (n. 46) 56–59.

120 These constraints may be avoided through anonymisation. For an overview of anonymisation techniques and the 'differential privacy' approach towards anonymisation, see Julian Hölzel, 'Differential privacy and the GDPR' (2019) 5 European Data Protection Law Review 184.

Article 101 TFEU with regard to commercially sensitive information. Under these circumstances, the emergence of well-working data markets remains a challenge.

3. *Legislative reactions*

The EU legislator has been cautious in mandating data access in scenario 2 settings.[121] Article 6(1) Regulation (EU) 715/2007[122] obliges car manufacturers to provide independent repairers with unrestricted, non-discriminatory[123] and standardised access to vehicle repair and maintenance information – but not with access to in-car data more generally.[124]

With regard to the Electricity Directive, some uncertainty remains whether the right to access energy consumption and energy input data collected through connected 'smart' meters extends to scenario 2 settings. While energy consumers can provide a data access point to the providers of complementary services for their individual-level data (see above), it is not entirely clear whether these providers can gain 'direct' data access on the grounds of Article 23(2) Electricity Directive as an 'eligible party' (in a non-discriminatory way, under 'clear and equal terms'; see Article 34). In an earlier draft of the Electricity Directive, the provision entailed a non-exhaustive enumeration of 'eligible parties', including, *inter alia*, 'other parties which provide energy or other services to customers'.[125] It therefore

121 There has been notable regulatory action in the area of road transport with regard to scenario 2. An exhaustive overview of this legislation is provided by Julien Debussche, Jasmien César and Isis De Moortel, 'Big Data & Issues & Opportunities: Data Sharing Obligations' (2019) <https://www.twobirds.com/en/news/articles/2019/global/big-data-and-issues-and-opportunities-data-sharing-obligations> accessed 15 September 2020; European Commission, 'Intelligent transport systems: Action Plan and Directive' <https://ec.europa.eu/transport/themes/its/road/action_plan_en> accessed 15 September 2020. Data access obligations provided in the various Delegated Regulations are, however, of a rather fragmentary nature. This paper will not address them in more detail.

122 Regulation (EC) No. 715/2007 (n. 98).

123 Compared to the access given to authorised dealers and repairers.

124 For the ongoing debate on whether access to in-car data – including access to bundled individual-level data and/or aggregated usage data – should be mandated, see Section C.I.5.a) above (with regard to scenario 1; the debate extends to scenario 2, however).

125 European Commission, 'Proposal for a Directive of the European Parliament and of the Council on common rules for the internal market in electricity' COM(2016) 864 final, 2.

seems that access rights are also granted to providers of products and services seeking access to aggregated smart meter data. Access to bundled individual-level data will, however, only be covered by the Directive as far as that data can be shared in compliance with the GDPR[126] (through, *inter alia*, anonymisation).

The PSD2 Directive does not cover scenario 2; access to accounts and access to account data is only to be granted by request of the account holder.[127]

4. *Competition law*

In the absence of a sector-specific regime, requests for access to data have to be based on competition rules. The question of whether and when a denial of access constitutes an abuse of dominance under Article 102 TFEU and/or – under German competition law – under Section 19(2) No. 4 GWB continues to be debated.[128]

Firstly, a position of dominance must be established case by case. In some cases, a firm will be dominant on a specific product or services market. This would appear to be the case, for example, for the Deutsche Bahn in the *Bundeskartellamt*'s investigation on access of mobility platforms to real-time schedule data. In other settings, the question arises whether each product or service provider should be considered to hold a dominant position vis-à-vis those customers who are locked into that product or service, i.e. on the relevant 'aftermarkets'. A precise and context-specific analysis will be necessary in this regard, in particular in the typical settings described above: In a data economy, the exclusive control over the usage data of a product or service may automatically lead to significant competitive advantages for all related complementary or aftermarket services, irrespective of a dominant position on a broader market for such products or services. Nonetheless, the efficiencies related to 'closed systems' strategies

126 Any processing of personal data within the framework of the Electricity Directive needs to comply with the GDPR, pursuant to Art. 23(3) Electricity Directive.

127 See Art. 66(2) PSD2 Directive ('When the payer gives its explicit consent') and Art. 67(2)(a) PSD2 Directive ('only where based on the payment service user's explicit consent').

128 See, *inter alia*, Crémer, Montjoye and Schweitzer (n. 27) 98–107; Schweitzer and others (n. 4) 162–71; German Federal Ministry of Economic Affairs and Energy, Report by the Commission 'Competition Law 4.0' (n. 46), 36–37; Graef, Tombal and de Streel (n. 30) 13–17.

should be recognised – also under the novel conditions of the data economy. Not every lock-in should lead to the acknowledgment of a dominant position on a narrowly defined primary market. One of the important tasks for the European Commission will be to re-define the contours of the so-called aftermarket doctrine with regard to the specificities of the data economy.[129]

The German legislator, on the other hand, seems to be committed to expanding the scope of the aftermarket doctrine, albeit not on the basis of Section 19 GWB (concerning dominance),[130] but on the basis of an expansion of the concept of relational power. The new Section 20(1a) GWB proposed in the current draft of a 10th amendment to the GWB would grant an undertaking a right to data access where it is '*dependent on* access to data controlled by another undertaking *for its own activities*' even 'if there is no trade yet in such data', i.e. even if the data controller has not marketed the data before.[131] The provision does not require a showing of dominance; rather, a bilateral power asymmetry that may stem simply from one firm's dependency on the data controlled by the other firm will suffice. Finally, the refusal of access to such data would need to be an abuse of the bilateral power disparity, which is to be established through a comprehensive balancing of interests in the light of the law's objective to provide for freedom of competition.[132] While the proposed Section 20(1a) GWB seems to be tailored to establishing data access rights of the scenario 2 type, this broadening of potential data access obligations is controversial.[133] Its limits – including those resulting from the GDPR, trade secret protection and Article 101 TFEU – will need to be explored by the courts.

129 See European Commission Notice of 9 December 1997 on the definition of relevant market for the purposes of Community competition law [1997] OJ C372/3, para. 56. The Commission is currently revising the Market Definition Notice; see Press Release of 26 June2020, 'Competition: Commission consults stakeholders on the Market Definition Notice' <https://ec.europa.eu/commission/presscorner/detail/en/IP_20_1187> accessed 15 September 2020. For a discussion of the aftermarkets doctrine with regard to data access rights see also Crémer, Montjoye and Schweitzer (n. 27) 87–91, 101–06, 125.

130 The new Sec. 19(2) No. 4 GWB is rather of a declaratory nature.

131 Emphasis added. See Schweitzer and others (n. 4) 192–93.

132 German Federal Supreme Court (BGH) of 26 October 1972, Case KZR 54/71 (1973) Gewerblicher Rechtsschutz und Urheberrecht 277, 278–79 – *Ersatzteile für Registrierkassen*.

133 Torsten Körber, '"Digitalisierung" der Missbrauchsaufsicht durch die 10. GWB-Novelle' (2020) Multimedia und Recht 290, 292; German Federal Ministry of Economic Affairs and Energy, Report by the Commission 'Competition Law 4.0' (n. 46) 24–25, 36, 52.

When it comes to establishing an abuse under Article 102 TFEU (or Section 19(2) No. 4 GWB), on the other hand, the essential facilities doctrine will typically provide the relevant test. Generally, data – like any other resource – can, in a given situation, be an input, access to which is essential in order to compete.[134] However, the preconditions for applying the essential facilities doctrine are generally strict.[135] The immediate improvement of competition on a downstream market must be balanced against the negative incentive effects on the dominant firm that may result from a requirement to share. Also, where access to an input is granted, competitors are relieved from the need to compete on the primary market, such that more competition downstream may come at the cost of durable entrenchment of market power upstream. Furthermore, access remedies frequently require the precise specifications of access conditions and price as well as intense and constant oversight within a framework that can come to resemble a regulatory scheme (see B. above). Against this background, the question whether an input, including data, qualifies as an essential facility in any given case must be analysed with caution. Some have suggested relaxing the standard due to the non-rivalry of the use of data.[136] Others have pointed to the need to precisely examine the incentive effects case by case.[137]

Finally, and obviously, the limits to data sharing that follow from both the GDPR and Article 101 TFEU will remain in place. For example, both the GDPR and Article 101 TFEU may constrain the access of traders on Amazon to aggregated data regarding user search and click behaviour. In

---

134 Crémer, Montjoye and Schweitzer (n. 27) 101–05. The German legislature is about to clarify the essential facilities doctrine in this regard. In the course of the pending 10th amendment to the GWB (n. 88). Sec. 19(2) No. 4 GWB is to be amended to specify that data can qualify as an essential facility. This amendment is generally perceived to be purely declaratory in nature: see, *inter alia*, Torsten Körber, 'Die 10. GWB-Novelle als "GWB-Digitalisierungs-Regulierungs-Gesetz"' (2019) Neue Zeitschrift für Kartellrecht 633, 634.

135 See Ernst-Joachim Mestmäcker and Heike Schweitzer, *Europäisches Wettbewerbsrecht* (3rd edn, CH Beck 2014) § 19 paras 66–80.

136 Inge Graef, 'Rethinking the Essential Facilities Doctrine for the EU Digital Economy' (2019) TILEC Discussion Paper No. DP2019–028, 19–23 <https://papers.ssrn.com/sol3/papers.cfm?abstract_id=3371457> accessed 15 September 2020; Schweitzer and others (n. 4) 171.

137 Alexandre de Streel, 'Essential Facilities Doctrine in the data-driven economy', Presentation for FSR and FCP at the Annual Scientific Seminar in Florence (22 March 2018) <https://www.slideshare.net/FSRCommunicationsand/essential-facilities-doctrine-in-the-datadriven-economy-alexandre-de-streel> accessed 15 September 2020.

such settings, the competition problem may not be one of a denial of access to data, but rather of a self-preferencing of the platform in granting access to its own trading subsidiary.[138] The appropriate remedy would then be the denial of access to all traders, or access to all on a basis compliant with the GDPR and competition law.[139]

Furthermore, a debate has started over whether the essential facilities doctrine should, where it would apply in principle, also benefit data-rich Big Tech platforms. Granting access to an essential facility is intended to allow market entry; while this is generally desirable from a competition policy perspective, the expansion of Big Tech conglomerates into ever more markets raises concerns: it may allow them to expand their position of dominance to ever more neighbouring markets, expanding their ecosystem and further increasing their competitive advantages from network effects and data concentration. Such a development might make it impossible for challenger firms to grow within a niche market until they are in a position to attack an incumbent platform in its core market. Consequently, an argument can be made that data access – in particular access to IoT usage data – should only be granted to the data-rich Big Tech players on the precondition that they reciprocally open their own data troves to competitors, thereby establishing a (more) level playing field.

Overall, the state of debate on how to handle data access in settings belonging to scenario 2 is still in flux. Few cases have been publicised so far (see 1. above). In some settings, contractual data access agreements will likely emerge. In other settings, the GDPR as well as Article 101 TFEU and trade secret protection will significantly constrain the possibility for data access in these settings from the start – apart from access to highly aggregated and possibly historical data. Furthermore, it is, as of now, unclear how strong the foreclosure effects for third parties will tend to be that result from a lack of access to bundled individual and aggregate data and whether third-party service providers will find ways to overcome these hur-

138 Schweitzer and others (n. 4) 124–28.

139 The 10th amendment to the German GWB (n. 88) also envisages the introduction of special conduct requirements with regard to self-preferencing by (vertically integrated) undertakings on multi-sided or network markets with paramount significance for competition across markets. The proposed text of Sec. 19a(2) No. 1 GWB reads: 'The Bundeskartellamt may prohibit such undertakings whose paramount significance for competition across markets it establishes, ... to treat the offers of competitors differently from its own offers when providing access to supply and sales markets.'.

dles without access to data controlled by the primary product or service provider.

As of now, broad-brush solutions to scenario 2 do not seem to be available or desirable. A relevant case law will need to evolve to provide a better idea of the relevant settings. Given this, the case-by-case approach and context sensitivity of competition law is a strength rather than a shortcoming.

5. Policy options: The role of data intermediaries

As competition law appears to be an appropriate instrument to address anti-competitive refusals to provide access in scenario 2 cases, updated guidelines on how to deal with aftermarket settings will be useful.

Further-reaching policy options are less clear. However, the number of competitively problematic scenario 2 settings could significantly decrease if data intermediaries were to establish themselves in the marketplace. In principle, data intermediaries could provide effective solutions both with respect to personal data and with respect to non-personal data. They may be able to significantly alleviate the transaction cost problem identified above (C.II.2.).[140]

With regard to personal data, data trustees have already caught the attention of policy makers. Data trustees could not only facilitate the access by third parties to individual-level personal data. Intermediaries of some size could also serve as data aggregators and significantly alleviate data shortages of third parties in this regard.

Similarly, data intermediaries of some size could aggregate usage data of a non-personal kind and make it available to firms with an interest in developing complementary services. Initiatives of this kind already exist.[141] Data intermediaries that aggregate usage data provided by machine and service users could evolve from sectoral data pooling initiatives.

The best available and most agile, pro-competitive and innovation-friendly policy option to improve data access in scenario 2 settings therefore seems to be to facilitate and support the set-up, experimentation with and growth of data intermediaries. Much work remains to be done in this regard. With a view to data trustees that would administrate access to per-

---

140 Martens and others (n. 15) 6.

141 See, for example, the International Data Space of the Fraunhofer Institute, <https://www.fraunhofer.de/de/forschung/fraunhofer-initiativen/international-data-spaces.html> accessed 15 September 2020.

sonal data, possible conflicts of interests must be investigated and addressed in a governance framework and regulatory scheme that ensures that data access is managed in line with the will and best interests of consumers. At the same time, a viable business model would need to emerge. This is also true with regard to non-personal data. Furthermore, workable governance regimes for data pools would arguably need to be developed. Nonetheless, the establishment of data intermediaries appears to be a promising path to overcome data access bottlenecks that risk becoming a relevant hindrance for the evolution of a competitive data economy.

III. Scenario 3: Access to data for innovation purposes

1. The data access scenario

The third scenario which has attracted much attention and debate starts from the observation that '[c]urrently, a small number of Big Tech firms hold a large part of the world's data', and that this could 'reduce the incentives for data-driven businesses to emerge, grow and innovate in the EU'.[142] The question therefore is whether the vast data troves accumulated by the particularly data-rich digital conglomerates, for instance Google and Facebook, should be made available, in one way or another, as an input for innovation. Prominently, this has been suggested by Mayer-Schönberger and Ramge in their book *Reinventing Capitalism in the Age of Big Data*,[143] in which they propose a general obligation to share a randomly selected percentage of a firm's data that progressively increases with respect to the total size of the firm's data troves (similar to a tax). In Germany, the Social Democratic Party (SPD) has called for 'data for all' legislation.[144]

Obviously, the big online platforms can also be the addressees of access-to-data requests under scenario 1 and/or 2, where data access is needed to compete on a specific complementary market. This is, however, not the logic of scenario 3. In this setting, the question is whether data should be made available to search for new business ideas, or as an input to train AI, which may then be used to compete on completely unrelated markets.

---

142 European Commission, 'A European strategy for data' (n. 1) 3.

143 Viktor Mayer-Schönberger and Thomas Ramge, *Reinventing Capitalism in the Age of Big Data* (Basic Books 2018).

144 SPD, 'Digitaler Fortschritt durch ein Daten-Für-Alle-Gesetz' (2019) <https://www.spd.de/fileadmin/Dokumente/Sonstiges/Daten_fuer_Alle.pdf> accessed 15 September 2020.

Some conceive of the data troves of Big Tech as quasi-infrastructural resources, similar to public sector data. In this perspective, the data should ideally be available to anybody for experimentation and re-use, with no need to specify the relevant business purpose *ex ante*.

2. *Possible market failures*

Scenario 3 refers back to the fundamental choice between a 'private data control' versus an 'open access' approach (see B. above).

From a private data control perspective, there is a possible market failure to be addressed: extreme economies of scale and network effects have made the big online platform markets tip. The resulting quasi-monopolistic positions are accompanied by a persistent access to a huge stream of rich, high-quality user and usage data. This data not only allows the platforms to constantly improve the quality of service, in particular by providing an ever more targeted service, such that access to data is at the heart of a constant feedback loop safeguarding the existing position of dominance. At the same time, it enables Big Tech firms to monetise their service in the market for targeted online advertising, which is, to a significant extent, a competition for access to the best data troves. Given the general-purpose quality of user data, it can simultaneously provide big B2C platforms with a competitive edge when entering other consumer services markets.

The latter aspect, however, falls under scenarios 1 and 2. Whether a general opening up of the Big Tech data troves would help to make their position on the relevant online platform markets contestable is quite unclear.

The more obvious rationale underlying the call to open up the Big Tech data troves therefore is to enable data-driven innovation on a broad scale. Implied is the proposition to revisit our choice of a private data control approach for scenario 3. The Big Tech data troves are found to flow from the new infrastructural monopolies of the digital times. Purportedly, they are so inextricably intertwined with the structure of our societies that they should be opened up for their broader purposes.

However, whether this line of argument justifies a shift to an open access rationale with respect to the Big Tech data troves is not yet settled. Such a rationale would be in an obvious tension with the GDPR. Much of the behavioural data collected by the big online platforms is personal data in its origin. Their anonymisation may prove to be difficult[145] and may

145 For more details on differential privacy see Hölzel (n. 120).

significantly reduce their value. Nor can clashes with Article 101 TFEU and trade secret protection be ruled out. Moreover, a simple opening of access to the mass of data that Big Tech controls may not be what is really needed and can be used in any meaningful way by innovative firms, including start-ups who may lack the technical infrastructure to handle such volumes of data. Rather, the innovative potential of these data may better be realised by some sort of curated access, an access to a selection of datasets relevant for different purposes, and sometimes access to annotated data.

3. *Competition law*

There is, as of now, no legislative action that attempts to open up the data troves of the Big Tech online platforms for general access.

Obviously, competition law is applicable to the Big Tech online platforms, also with regard to data access requests for innovative purposes. In principle, such requests could, again, be based on the essential facilities doctrine. In this setting, the indispensability of data access would not follow from the principled non-replicability of the data set as in the aftermarket setting, but from the scale and scope of the data pool:[146] specific types of data analysis may only be feasible based on data pools of a size and depth that only the big online platforms control. Whether and which data would qualify as essential and indispensable would then, however, depend on the specific business case of any given petitioner. Yet, a requirement for them to lay open their business plans vis-à-vis the incumbent would give the latter the chance to quickly replicate promising projects, and would therefore raise serious competition concerns. Instead, the essentiality check would either need to be done by a neutral intermediary; or a mechanism would be needed that would ensure data access without an essentiality check. Basically, the latter would translate into an open-access approach. In any case, some sort of curated data access would seem to be required. Also, data access would need to be checked for its GDPR and Article 101 TFEU

146 Crémer, Montjoye and Schweitzer (n. 27) 103. The notion of indispensability within the essential facilities doctrine has been intensely discussed, often with strongly varying results. See Thomas Tombal, 'Economic Dependence and Data Access' (2020) 51 International Review of Intellectual Property and Competition Law 70, 81–86; Martens and others (n. 15) 36; Schweitzer and others (n. 4) 164–68; Giuseppe Colangelo and Mariateresa Maggiolini, 'Big data as misleading facilities' (2017) 13 European Competition Journal 249, 270–73; Drexl (n. 31) 282.

conformity. Regulatory oversight would need to ensure that the access conditions and the access price are fair, reasonable and non-discriminatory. All this would risk resulting in a rather heavy-handed regulatory regime. The 'special obligation' imposed on the big online platforms would surpass what is normal under the essential facilities doctrine.

4. *Policy options?*

Prospectively, the data power of the big online platforms may present the greatest challenge in the endeavour to ensure a competitive data economy. While competition on markets for complementary services can arguably be ensured based on the solutions proposed above (see scenario 1 and 2), the control of huge amounts of behavioural data can provide for a competitive edge in the development of data processing technologies like AI that will drive innovation in great parts of the economy in the years to come. At the same time, the existing instruments do not seem to provide an appropriate lever to address the problem underlying scenario 3.

So far, the Commission has been reluctant to move in the direction of an open access approach for the big online platforms' data troves. In its 'European strategy for data', it has announced that it will consider 'how best to address more systemic issues related to platforms and data, including by ex-ante regulation if appropriate, to ensure that markets stay open and fair'.[147]

From a market perspective, however, a voluntary and/or structural solution would seem to be preferable to ex-ante regulation. For example, one may envision the establishment of a data controlling entity that would be separate from the entity that operates the online platform and would have incentives to make the data accessible on a commercial basis in a neutral manner.[148] Such a model could promote data-driven innovation and at the same time neutralise the data-based conglomerate power of the big online platforms. Simultaneously, it would tend to intrude less into the platforms' business decisions in a longer-term perspective and be more likely to establish a level playing field.

In Germany, the proposed Section 19a GWB is specifically addressed to the (usually data-rich) undertakings on multi-sided or network markets

147 Commission, 'A European strategy for data' (n. 1) 14.

148 For another proposition to implement intermediaries to reduce market failures on data markets see Martens and others (n. 15) 28–34.

that are 'of paramount significance for competition across markets'. It may allow for some form of structural data unbundling: Section 19a(2) No. 1 GWB enables the *Bundeskartellamt* to prohibit self-preferencing practices, which could either encompass an obligation to share the same data under the same conditions with external business partners as in-house, or a prohibition to use said data for a firm's own commercial activities on up- or downstream markets. Section 19a(2) No. 3 GWB would allow the *Bundeskartellamt* to prohibit measures that create or raise barriers to market entry or impede other undertakings with other means by using data relevant for competition which has been obtained from the opposite market side on a dominated market, also in combination with other data relevant for competition from sources beyond the dominated market, or demand terms and conditions that permit such use.

The prohibition is specifically tailored to address data-related platform envelopment strategies[149] such as the data bundling of Facebook, Instagram and other Facebook services that was prohibited by the *Bundeskartellamt*'s decision in February 2019.[150] It could serve as a basis to enforce 'horizontal' data unbundling, meaning a prohibition to merge data acquired on different markets within a single, large data pool.

Section 19a GWB, however, will not provide for a structural remedy which mandates the 'unbundling' of the operation of a service and the control over the data generated through this service, thereby creating an independent data controller that would be incentivised to market the data to a multitude of firms.

---

149 See Daniele Condorelli and Jorge Padilla, 'Harnessing Platform Envelopment through Privacy Policy Tying' (2019) <https://ssrn.com/abstract=3504025> accessed 15 September 2020.

150 Bundeskartellamt of 6 February 2019, Case B6–22/16. The Bundeskartellamt prohibited Facebook from requiring their users to consent to a bundling of data collected through Facebook's various digital services and to consent to a bundling of data collected through the Facebook social plugin APIs. For such an integration of different user data within one profile, Facebook would in the future need users' express consent (opt-in), which must not be made a contractual requirement for the use of the social network. The Bundeskartellamt framed the case as an exploitative abuse of dominance, basing the contract conditions' disproportionality on their violation of data protection law. Facebook has appealed the decision before the Higher Regional Court. In a preliminary proceeding, the Federal Supreme Court has indicated that it will ultimately uphold the Bundeskartellamt's decision, albeit based on a different line of reasoning – see German Federal Supreme Court (BGH) of 23 June 2020, Case KVR 69/19.

At the European level, the 'new competition tool'[151] may provide an instrument to require the establishment of a separate data-trading entity – in particular as a remedy to data-driven conglomerate strategies by the big digital platforms by which they try to expand their digital ecosystems and reinforce consumer lock-in.

D. *A brief summary*

Stepping back, data access remains a convoluted topic. Given the broad variety of data and data access scenarios, there cannot be a 'one size fits all' approach towards data access. Quite in line with the European Commission's agenda, the best way to develop solutions that are tailored to the different settings is to continue with and encourage the ongoing process of decentralised experimentation[152] based, in principle, on a private control approach for data and a system of data allocation through freely negotiated contracts on competitive markets. Already, firms are increasingly trying out various forms of data-sharing arrangements. The Commission strives to facilitate such voluntary data sharing and to put in place an 'enabling legislative framework for the governance of common European data spaces'[153] that will address persisting disincentives to pursue such initiatives[154] in non-interventionist ways.[155] Also, it supports data-driven innovation and strives to stimulate demand for data-driven products and services

151 European Commission, 'Proposal for a Regulation by the Council and the European Parliament introducing a new competition tool', Ares (2020) 2877634.

152 See Commission, 'A European strategy for data' (n. 1) 12–13, generally favouring a market-based approach to data access: 'The general principle shall be to facilitate voluntary data sharing'; 'Only where specific circumstances so dictate ... access to data should be made compulsory'.

153 Ibid. 12.

154 See Ibid. 7, where the following reasons for the current reluctance to share data B2B are identified: 'a lack of economic incentives (including the fear of losing a competitive edge), lack of trust between economic operators that the data will be used in line with contractual agreements, imbalances in negotiating power, the fear of misappropriation of the data by third parties, a lack of legal clarity on who can do what with the data'.

155 *Inter alia*, by supporting decisions on what data can be used in which situations, by facilitating cross-border data use, by prioritising interoperability requirements and standards within and across sectors and by codifying usage rights for co-generated data.

by promoting Europe's capabilities and infrastructures for hosting, processing and using data – not by regulating data access.

To support the search for novel and creative forms of cooperation, firms are to be provided with an opportunity to obtain legal certainty regarding the compatibility of such endeavours with competition rules. The Commission has already signalled its readiness to provide informal guidance more frequently.[156] Additionally, the introduction of a voluntary notification procedure for novel forms of cooperation (with a right to receive a decision within a short period of time) has been proposed.[157] The ongoing review of the Commission's Guidelines on Horizontal Cooperation Agreements will provide a welcome opportunity to systematise and clarify the assessment criteria for the new types of B2B data sharing and pooling agreements already observed or to be expected within the novel context of

156 See Commission, 'A European strategy for data' (n. 1) 14: 'The Commission is … prepared to provide additional individual project-related guidance on the compatibility with EU competition rules, if needed'.

157 See the corresponding recommendation of the German Commission Competition Law 4.0: German Federal Ministry of Economic Affairs and Energy, Report by the Commission 'Competition Law 4.0' (n. 46) 59–60, Recommendation 14. The 10th amendment to the GWB includes a provision that would grant undertakings – under certain conditions – a subjective right to a decision of the Bundeskartellamt on whether it sees, on the basis of the information in its possession, no grounds to initiate infringement proceedings. Sec. 32(1), (4) GWB reads:
(1) The competition authority may decide that there are no grounds for it to take any action if, on the basis of the information in its possession, the conditions for a prohibition pursuant to §§ 1, 19 to 21 and 29 [GWB], Article 101 (1) or Article 102 of the Treaty on the Functioning of the European Union are not satisfied. The decision shall state that, subject to new findings, the competition authority will not exercise its powers under §§ 32 and 32a [infringement proceedings and interim measures]. …
(4) Undertakings or associations of undertakings shall be entitled to a decision pursuant to para. 1 from the Bundeskartellamt if they have a substantial legal and economic interest in such a decision with regard to cooperation with competitors. The Bundeskartellamt shall decide on an application pursuant to sentence 1 within six months.

the digital economy.[158] New models of data trusteeship and public support for such business models may help to promote access to consumer data.[159]

However, while competition law will serve as an important – and necessary – background regime, it has its limits. While its case and context sensitivity is among the great strengths of competition law, this strength can become a shortcoming at times: a case-by-case analysis is resource-intensive and slow and comes with a significant degree of legal uncertainty. Where data access requirements are of systemic relevance and no satisfactory structural solution is available that allows for a self-enforcing and incentive-based data access regime, sector-specific data access regulation may be needed.

To ascertain the optimal policy approach in different data access settings, we identified three scenarios that we believe cover a wide area of potential cases:

(1) Access to individual-level data by a co-generator of usage data in a bilateral scenario to facilitate switching and the utilisation of independent aftermarkets products and service providers,
(2) Requests for access to bundled individual-level data or aggregated datasets by a third party vis-à-vis a service or product provider who controls broad usage datasets, with the third party claiming that access to the relevant data is needed to effectively compete in complementary markets;
(3) Requests by firms to access the large usage data troves of Big Tech to compete and innovate in the area of AI.

Taking these scenarios as reference points, we submit the following recommendations:

Scenario 1: With regard to scenario 1, we need to distinguish between access to personal data and access to non-personal industrial data.

When it comes to personal data, Article 20 GDPR already provides for a broadly applicable data portability right, which is however not tailored to

158 See European Commission, 'A European strategy for data' (n. 1) 14. Some insights regarding the current stance of the Commission can be taken from an investigation into the data pooling system of Insurance Ireland opened in May 2019 – see Euoropean Commission Press Release of 14 May 2019, 'Antitrust: Commission opens investigation into Insurance Ireland data pooling system' <https://ec.europa.eu/commission/presscorner/detail/en/IP_19_2509> accessed 15 Septemberv2020.

159 German Federal Ministry of Economic Affairs and Energy, Report by the Commission 'Competition Law 4.0' (n. 46) 42–43, Recommendation 5.

relevant market failures and does not encompass a right to data interoperability. Where real-time access is needed to overcome a market failure, sectoral regulation is currently the best approach, following the example of the PSD2 Directive and of the Electricity Directive. Competition law provides an important background regime. Market-based solutions could emerge if personal data cooperatives or neutral data intermediaries were to evolve.

No right to access, portability or interoperability currently exists for data co-generators with regard to co-generated industrial usage data in B2B settings. A legislative acknowledgment of a right to real-time access and portability could significantly promote competition in a data-driven economy: It would establish multiple access points to usage data in settings that are otherwise prone to lock-in effects, both with regard to the primary product and/or service and with regard to aftermarkets. Generally, these access and usage rights should remain waivable, however, to grant the parties involved the necessary flexibility in finding the best data access approach for their bilateral relation. Although a waivable access, usage and portability right would not protect business users against information asymmetries, market power and bilateral power imbalances, the recognition of the right would serve as an important legal reference point. Contractual waivers could – depending on the setting – be restrictive to competition by object or effect and therefore fall under Article 101 TFEU. A block exemption regulation could regulate the conditions under which they will nonetheless be considered pro-competitive.

Scenario 2: Settings where firms need access to individual-level data to offer complementary or aftermarket services will and should be dealt with under scenario 1. The situation is different where access to bundled individual-level data and aggregated data is required to compete effectively. For these settings, competition law is – and will arguably remain in most cases – the relevant regime. Its case-by-case approach and context sensitivity is a strength rather than a shortcoming here. In cases of frequent and repeated market failures, sectoral regulation may need to emerge.

With respect to competition law, the aftermarket doctrine will need clarification through updated guidelines.

A general easing of the requirements of the essential facilities doctrine should be regarded with caution. A relevant case law will need to evolve to provide a better idea of the relevant settings.

The policy approach most in line with a private control approach and a system of decentral coordination would be the promotion of data intermediaries that lead to the emergence of new data markets. Legislative action should strive to facilitate and support the setting up of, experimentation with and growth of data intermediaries.

Scenario 3 remains the most challenging one. Based on Article 102 TFEU, a convincing and clear legal solution for access to the huge troves of behavioural data currently controlled by the big digital platforms is difficult to find. At the moment, it is not yet clear whether a general opening up of these data resources is appropriate and required to ensure competition – in particular effective competition in the field of AI. The situation will need to be monitored by the Commission.

In principle, data intermediaries (see scenario 2) could also be able to accumulate and offer for sale the vast data troves needed for technological progress in the field of AI.

Additional incentives for marketing the data could come from different forms of data unbundling: if in-house monetisation is limited and/or self-preferencing regarding data access becomes infeasible, firms in control of large data troves could be incentivised to market behavioural data neutrally. Markets for data could receive an important stimulus, and the risk of an ever-increasing data-driven expansion of digital B2C ecosystems may be reduced.

In our paper, we have tried to offer some additional insights regarding the role that the proposed 10th amendment to German competition law may play with regard to data access. For scenario 1, the proposed Section 19a(2) No. 4 GWB[160] will possibly provide an additional instrument to enforce data portability for co-generated individual-level usage data; however, its scope of application will be limited to platform or network operators with paramount significance for competition across markets. However, Section 19a(2) No. 4 GWB is not directly applicable. The existence of such a position will need to be established by the *Bundeskartellamt* first, and the *Bundeskartellamt* will then need to specify the data access obligations.

With regard to scenario 2, the (declaratory) clarification that data can qualify as an essential facility within Section 19(2) No. 4 GWB[161] will arguably not have a large impact, but it improves legal certainty, nonethe-

160 'The *Bundeskartellamt* may prohibit such undertakings whose paramount significance for competition across markets it establishes to make the interoperability of products or services or the portability of data more difficult and thereby impede competition. This shall not apply where the conduct in question is objectively justified. In this respect, the burden of presenting facts and the burden of proof lie with the undertaking in question.'.

161 'An abuse exists in particular if a dominant undertaking as a supplier or purchaser of a certain type of goods or commercial services refuses to supply another un-

less. Section 20(1a) GWB,[162] which expands the prohibition on unreasonably impeding competition to cases of relational power that exclusively stems from one undertaking's dependence on access to data of another undertaking will potentially have far-reaching impact, however. To prevent regulatory overreach, its limits would need to be cautiously explored by the courts.

With regard to scenario 3, the proposed Section 19a(2) No. 1[163] and No. 3[164] GWB could arguably provide for some form of data unbundling (No. 1: vertical unbundling by prohibiting self-preferencing; No. 3: horizontal unbundling by prohibiting the pooling of data across markets). Section 19a GWB will, however, not provide for a structural remedy.

---

dertaking with this product or commercial service against adequate remuneration, *including access to data*, networks or other infrastructure, the supply is objectively necessary in order to operate on an upstream or downstream market and the refusal to supply threatens to eliminate effective competition on that market, unless the refusal to supply is objectively justified.' (emphasis added).

162 'Dependency in the meaning of paragraph 1 may also arise from the fact that an undertaking is dependent on access to data controlled by another undertaking for its own activities. The refusal of access to such data may constitute an unfair impediment even if there is no trade yet in such data.'.

163 'The Bundeskartellamt may prohibit such undertakings whose paramount significance for competition across markets it establishes to treat the offers of competitors differently from its own offers when providing access to supply and sales markets. This shall not apply where the conduct in question is objectively justified. In this respect, the burden of presenting facts and the burden of proof lie with the undertaking in question.'.

164 'The Bundeskartellamt may prohibit such undertakings whose paramount significance for competition across markets it establishes to create or raise barriers to market entry or impede other undertakings with other means by using data relevant for competition which has been obtained from the opposite market side on a dominated market, also in combination with other data relevant for competition from sources beyond the dominated market, or demand terms and conditions that permit such use. This shall not apply where the conduct in question is objectively justified. In this respect, the burden of presenting facts and the burden of proof lie with the undertaking in question.'.

The larger legal framework

The constitutional framework for data access rights

Thomas Fetzer

A. *Introduction*

Looking at data access rights from the perspective of constitutional law, three categories of potential constitutional requirements need to be considered: Firstly, it must be examined whether any data access rights are derived from the constitution itself. Secondly, it should be considered whether the constitution obliges the legislature to regulate data access rights and enact respective statutory provisions. Thirdly and finally, the constitution must be examined regarding the limits it sets for the legislature if it considers the creation of statutory data access rights. Yet, given the inherent possibility that access to data encroaches on the fundamental rights of the individuals whose data is concerned, the latter question on potential limits for statutory data access rights is relevant regardless of whether the legislature is obliged or simply entitled to create data access rights.

When considering these potential constitutional requirements, a further distinction has to be made depending on who the access petitioner is and who the party obliged to grant access to data is. In the case of access to private data, the fundamental rights set the relevant framework. While fundamental rights can also play a role when access is to be granted to public sector data (e.g. insofar as industrial and business secrets or personal rights of third parties are affected) it is primarily state organisation law that will be relevant in these circumstances. It should also be noted that in the case of statutory data access rights under European Union (EU) law, the EU fundamental rights generally set the standard for legality, even though the German Federal Constitutional Court (*Bundesverfassungsgericht*) has just recently decided that the national fundamental rights can still apply as a fallback in these constellations.[1]

1 German Federal Constitutional Court, 5 May 2020, Case 2 BvR 859/15, (2020) Neue Juristische Wochenschrift 1647.

B. The relevant constitutional standard

The substantive standard for all three abovementioned categories – constitutional data access rights, a legislative duty to enact statutory rights of data access and the constitutional limits of such statutory rights of data access – is primarily derived from the fundamental rights. This is true at least as long as the question of data access rights is not shaped by EU law,[2] as the German Federal Constitutional Court has just recently emphasised once again in its decision on the right to be forgotten.[3] From a procedural point of view, it is primarily the legislative competence that is of importance. In cases of private-access petitioners seeking access to data of private individuals, said legislative competence is most likely to be found in Article 74 No. 11 of the German Basic Law ('law relating to economic matters'). In contrast, if access is sought to public sector data, a distinction must be made between access to data held by federal institutions (*Bund*), the Federal States (*Bundesländer*) or municipal bodies (*kommunale Einrichtungen*).

C. Constitutional data access rights?

I. Access to public sector data

When asking whether data access rights can directly be derived from the constitution, it is self-evident that – if at all – this can only be relevant in cases in which private individuals desire access to public sector data. Given that the fundamental rights are primarily designed as rights of defense of the citizens against intrusions of the state,[4] they consequently can only es-

---

2 German Federal Constitutional Court, 6 November 2019, Case 1 BvR 16/13, (2020) Neue Juristische Wochenschrift 300, para. 74 – *Recht auf Vergessen I*.

3 Regarding the relationship between the European Fundamental Rights Charter and the national fundamental rights see German Federal Constitutional Court, 22 October 1986, Case 2 BvR 197/83, (1987) Neue Juristische Wochenschrift 577 – *Solange II*; German Federal Constitutional Court, 6 November 2019, Case 1 BvR 16/13, (2020) Neue Juristische Wochenschrift 300, paras 42–73 – *Recht auf Vergessen I*; German Federal Constitutional Court, 6 November 2019, Case 1 BvR 276/17, (2020) Neue Juristische Wochenschrift 314, paras 42–82 – *Recht auf Vergessen II*; German Federal Constitutional Court, 5 May 2020, Case 2 BvR 859/15, (2020) Neue Juristische Wochenschrift 1647.

4 German Federal Constitutional Court, 15 January 1958, Case 1 BvR 400/51, (1958) 7 Entscheidungen des Bundesverfassungsgerichts 198, 204-205 – *Lüth*; Horst Dreier, in Horst Dreier (ed.), *Grundgesetz-Kommentar* (3rd edn, Mohr Siebeck 2013)

tablish rights of data access for citizens against the state, but not for the government towards citizens or between citizens.

1. *Article 5(1), first sentence, alt. 2 of the Basic Law – freedom of information*

Constitutional data access rights are by no means unknown to the Basic Law. First and foremost, this is apparent from Article 5(1), first sentence of the Basic Law which guarantees the freedom of speech and the freedom of information. The latter gives citizens a right to inform themselves without hindrance from generally accessible sources.[5] Admittedly, at first glance, it may seem surprising to refer to this provision when considering constitutional data access rights. While the primarily terminological divergence between access to 'information' and access to 'data' stipulates no significant substantive difference from a constitutional point of view,[6] the seemingly disparate motivation for data access may be more troublesome: In the current debate on data access rights, the focus is oftentimes on the economic dimension of data and its significance for digital business models. The freedom of information as laid down in Article 5(1), first sentence, alt. 2 of the Basic Law, however, is traditionally associated with access to data as a prerequisite for the formation of opinions, political participation and thus ul-

---

Vor Art. 1 para. 84; Josef Isensee, 'Das Grundrecht als Abwehrrecht und staatliche Schutzpflicht' in Josef Isensee and Paul Kirchhof (eds), *Handbuch des Staatsrechts*, vol. IX (3rd edn, C.F. Müller 2011) § 191 para. 17; Wolfram Höfling, in Michael Sachs (ed.), *Grundgesetz Kommentar* (8th edn, C.H. Beck 2018) Vor Art. 1, paras 42–45. This is referred to as the 'classical' function of the fundamental rights; see also German Federal Constitutional Court, 17 January 1957, Case 1 BvL 4/54, 6 Entscheidungen des Bundesverfassungsgerichts 55, 71; 12 May 1987, Case 2 BvR 1226/83, 76 Entscheidungen des Bundesverfassungsgerichts 1, 41; 1 December 2009, Case 1 BvR 2857/07, 125 Entscheidungen des Bundesverfassungsgerichts 39, 78.

5 German Federal Constitutional Court, 3 October 1969, Case 1 BvR 46/65, 27 Entscheidungen des Bundesverfassungsgerichts 71, 81 – *Leipziger Volkszeitung*; Helmut Schultze-Fielitz, in Horst Dreier (ed.), *Grundgesetz-Kommentar* (3rd edn, Mohr Siebeck 2013) Art. 5 para. 76; Christoph Grabenwarter, in Roman Herzog and others (eds), *Maunz/Dürig Grundgesetz Kommentar* (90th edn, C.H. Beck 2020) Art. 5 paras 1014–1017; Edzard Schmidt-Jortzig, 'Meinungs- und Informationsfreiheit' in Josef Isensee and Paul Kirchhof, *Handbuch des Staatsrechts*, Vol. VII (3rd edn, C.F. Müller 2009) § 162 para. 35.

6 On the general differences between the terms 'information' and 'data' see Friedrich Schoch, *Informationsfreiheitsgesetz-Kommentar* (2nd edn, C.H. Beck 2016) § 2 paras 13, 17–21.

timately democracy.[7] This notwithstanding, in one of its few decisions on the freedom of information the German Federal Constitutional Court held:

> Accordingly, two components are essential for the freedom of information guaranteed in Article 5(1), first sentence, of the Basic Law. One is the relevance for the democratic principle of Article 20(1) of the Basic Law: A democratic state cannot exist without a free and well-informed public opinion. In addition, the freedom of information has a component of an individual right derived from Article 1 and Article 2(1) of the Basic Law. It is one of the elementary needs of human beings to obtain information from as many sources as possible, to expand their own knowledge and thus to develop as a personality. In addition, in modern industrial society, the possession of information is of essential importance for the social position of the individual.[8]

In this context, the economic position of individuals can certainly be understood as an important aspect of their social position. Thus, even though the German Federal Constitutional Court puts a special emphasis on the democratic relevance of the freedom of information, the quoted passage at least supports the conclusion that seeking access to public sector data for purely economic reasons does not fall outside the scope of protection of the freedom of information.

However, while Article 5(1), first sentence, alt. 2 of the Basic Law may therefore, in substance, also cover an individual's access to public sector data where such access is not primarily politically motivated, it is the prevailing opinion of courts but also of academics that the provision does not contain a direct constitutional data access right to public sector data:[9] Article 5(1), first sentence, alt. 2 of the Basic Law is a fundamental right

7 German Federal Constitutional Court, 3 October 1969, Case 1 BvR 46/65, 27 Entscheidungen des Bundesverfassungsgerichts 71, 81 – *Leipziger Volkszeitung*; Franz Schemmer, in Volker Epping and Christian Hillgruber (eds) *Beck-Online-Kommentar Grundgesetz* (43th edn, C.H. Beck 2020) Art. 5 GG para. 23; Christian Starck and Andreas L. Paulus, in Peter M. Huber and Andreas Voßkuhle (eds), *von Mangoldt/Klein/Starck Grundgesetz Kommentar* (7th edn, C.H. Beck 2018) Art. 5 para. 102; Schultze-Fielitz (n. 5)) Art. 5 para. 76; Schmidt-Jortzig (n. 5) § 162 para. 33; Grabenwarter (n. 5) Art. 5 (1), (2) para. 985.

8 German Federal Constitutional Court, 3 October 1969, Case 1 BvR 46/65, 27 Entscheidungen des Bundesverfassungsgerichts 71, 81 – *Leipziger Volkszeitung*.

9 German Federal Constitutional Court, 24 January 2001, Case 1 BvR 2623/95, 103 Entscheidungen des Bundesverfassungsgerichts 44, 59–60 – *Gerichtsfernsehen*; Grabenwarter (n. 5) Art. 5(1), (2) paras 1011, 1023; Schemmer (n. 7) Art. 5 GG

defined and shaped by statutory law.[10] It only protects access to information that is generally accessible. This, however, is only the case where the source in question is suitable and intended to provide information to the general public.[11] The intended use, i.e. the question which public sector information should be accessible to the general public, initially must be determined by the legislature.[12] Accordingly, the substantive scope of protection of the freedom of information is not concerned if the legislature does not provide for a corresponding legal provision declaring a source to be publicly available, e.g. by creating data access rights. Certainly, this does not enable the legislature to completely undermine Article 5(1), first sentence, alt. 2 of the Basic Law by never opening up any information to the public and keeping all public sector information secret.[13] Consequently, the German Federal Constitutional Court has also held that at least subsidiary data access rights may be derived directly from the constitution.[14] Nonetheless, as described above, Article 5(1), first sentence, alt. 2 of the Ba-

---

para. 32; Herbert Bethge, in Michael Sachs (ed.) *Grundgesetz Kommentar* (8th edn, C.H. Beck 2018) Art. 5 para. 59a; Karl-E. Hain, 'Verfassungsrecht' in Gerald Spindler and Fabian Schuster (eds), *Recht der elektronischen Medien* (4th edn, C.H. Beck 2019) Teil 1 C. para. 24.

10 On the necessity of legislative design of some fundamental rights Ingo von Münch and Philip Kunig, in Ingo von Münch and Philip Kunig (eds), *Grundgesetz-Kommentar* (6th edn, C.H. Beck 2012) Vor Art. 1 para. 33; cf. Dreier (n. 4) Vor Art. 1 para. 107. Relating to Art. 5 cf. Schemmer (n. 7) Art. 5 GG para. 26.1; Hain (n. 9) Teil 1 C. para. 20; Dieter Dörr, in Detlef Merten and Hans-J. Papier (eds), *Handbuch der Grundrechte*, Vol. IV (C.F. Müller 2011) § 103 para. 30; see also German Federal Constitutional Court, 24 January 2001, Case 1 BvR 2623/95, 103 Entscheidungen des Bundesverfassungsgerichts 44, 60 – *Gerichtsfernsehen*.

11 German Federal Constitutional Court, 3 October 1969, Case 1 BvR 46/65, 27 Entscheidungen des Bundesverfassungsgerichts 71, 83 – *Leipziger Volkszeitung*; 9 February 1994, Case 1 BvR 1687/92, 90 Entscheidungen des Bundesverfassungsgerichts 27, 32 – *Parabolantenne*; 24 January 2001, Case 1 BvR 2623/95, 103 Entscheidungen des Bundesverfassungsgerichts 44, 60 – *Gerichtsfernsehen*; Bethge (n. 9) Art. 5 para. 55; for further reference see also Rudolf Wendt, in Ingo von Münch and Philip Kunig (eds), *Grundgesetz-Kommentar* (6th edn, C.H. Beck 2012) Art. 5 para. 23; Dörr (n. 10) § 103 para. 27.

12 Schemmer (n. 7) Art. 5 para. 26.1; Hain (n. 9) Teil 1 C. para. 23; Dörr (n. 10) § 103 para. 30. See also German Federal Constitutional Court, 24 January 2001, Case 1 BvR 2623/95, 103 Entscheidungen des Bundesverfassungsgerichts 44, 60–61 – *Gerichtsfernsehen*.

13 Cf. Bethge (n. 9) Art. 5 para. 57.

14 Cf. German Federal Constitutional Court, 20 June 2017, Case 1 BvR 1978/13, (2017) Neue Zeitschrift für Verwaltungsrecht, 1618, para. 20; Bethge (n. 9) Art. 5 paras 56a, 57.

sic Law does not provide for a general right to access all public sector data.[15] If, however, the legislature decides to create general or specific statutory access rights to public sector data, these statutory rights may be subject to the protection of Article 5(1), first sentence, alt. 2 of the Basic Law and therefore no longer be revoked without cause.[16]

2. *Article 2(1) of the Basic Law – general right of personality*

Regarding personal data, on the other hand, the German Federal Constitutional Court has indeed acknowledged constitutional data access rights independent of corresponding statutory rights.[17] Such rights against the state can arise from the general right of personality and accompany the right to informational self-determination or render it more effective, as self-determination requires knowledge of who possesses what information about a specific person.[18] While constitutional law primarily obliges the legislature

---

15 See references in n. 9; contrary Jürgen Kühling, in Hubertus Gersdorf and Boris P. Paal (eds), *Beck-Online-Kommentar Informations- und Medienrecht* (28th edn, C.H. Beck 2020) Art. 5 GG para. 42.

16 Cf. Bethge (n. 9) Art. 5 paras 56a, 57; German Federal Constitutional Court, 20 May 2017, Case 1 BvR 1978/13, (2017) Neue Zeitschrift für Verwaltungsrecht, 1618, para. 20; 24 January 2001, Case 1 BvR 2623/95, 103 Entscheidungen des Bundesverfassungsgerichts 44, 60, 61 – *Gerichtsfernsehen*. Differently, Schemmer (n. 7) Art. 5 para. 27.1; Schultze-Fielitz (n. 5) Art. 5 para. 79.

17 In general, Schoch (n. 6) Einleitung paras. 74–75; Udo Di Fabio, in Roman Herzog and others (eds), *Maunz/Dürig Grundgesetz Kommentar* (90th edn, C.H. Beck 2020) Art. 2 GG para. 178; German Federal Constitutional Court, 9 January 2006, (2006) Neue Juristische Wochenschrift 1116, paras 20–23; 17 July1991, Case 2 BvR 1570/89, (1991) Beck-online Rechtsprechung 06917. On the right to know one's ancestry German Federal Constitutional Court, 31 January 1989, Case 1 BvL 17/87, 79 Entscheidungen des Bundesverfassungsgerichts 256, 269; 6 May 1997, Case 1 BvR 409/90, 96 Entscheidungen des Bundesverfassungsgerichts 56, 63; 12 February 2007, Case 1 BvR 421/05, 117 Entscheidungen des Bundesverfassungsgerichts 202, 225–226; cf. also German Federal Constitutional Court, 9 April 2003, Case 1 BvR 1724/01, 108 Entscheidungen des Bundesverfassungsgerichts 82, 105. On the right to know public information measures German Federal Constitutional Court, 15 January 2008, Case 1 BvR 2/04, 120 Entscheidungen des Bundesverfassungsgerichts 31, 360–361.

18 Schoch (n. 6) Einleitung paras 74–75; Dreier (n. 4) Art. 2(1) para. 95; German Federal Constitutional Court, 15 December 1983, Case 1 BvR 209/83, 65 Entscheidungen des Bundesverfassungsgerichts 1, 43–46 – *Volkszählung*; 15 January 2008, Case 1 BvR 2/04, 120 Entscheidungen des Bundesverfassungsgerichts 31, 360–361; Rhineland-Palatinate Constitutional Court, 4 November 1998, Case

to create statutory data access rights in this regard,[19] citizens can request access to their personal data directly on the basis of Article 2(1) of the Basic Law if the legislature does not fulfil its responsibility.[20] However, this shall not be discussed in further detail, in particular given that the EU has enacted corresponding provisions in the General Data Protection Regulation (GDPR).[21]

II. Interim result

Although the constitution provides for data access rights of citizens against the government, these rights are only rudimentary or conditional: In the case of Article 5(1), first sentence, alt. 2 of the Basic Law, they require an initial legislative decision on data access. The general right of personality, on the other hand, only becomes relevant if the legislature does not fulfil its obligation to enact statutory data access rights, and it only concerns personal data as opposed to machine or other non-personal data.

D. Constitutional duty to create statutory data access rights?

Given that no general data access rights can be derived from the constitution directly, the question arises whether the constitution imposes a duty on the legislature to create statutory data access rights. In this context, a distinction must be made between data access claims of citizens against the

---

B 5–98, (1999) Neue Juristische Wochenschrift 2264; German Federal Constitutional Court, 10 March 2008, Case 1 BvR 2388/03, 120 Entscheidungen des Bundesverfassungsgerichts 351, 360–362.

19 German Federal Constitutional Court, 15 December 1983, Case 1 BvR 209/83, 65 Entscheidungen des Bundesverfassungsgerichts 1, 44 – *Volkszählung*; 10 March 2008, Case 1 BvR 2388/03, 120 Entscheidungen des Bundesverfassungsgerichts 351, 359, 363. See also German Federal Constitutional Court, 19 October 2000, Case 1 BvR 586/90, (2001) Neue Zeitschrift für Verwaltungsrecht 185; 12 April 2005, Case 2 BvR 1027/02, 113 Entscheidungen des Bundesverfassungsgerichts 29, 58.

20 See references in n. 17. Cf. also Hubertus Gersdorf, in Hubertus Gersdorf and Boris P. Paal (eds), *Beck-Online-Kommentar Informations- und Medienrecht* (28th edn, C.H. Beck 2020) Art. 2 GG para. 81.

21 See Art. 15 GDPR, which includes the right to receive a complete copy of the personal data undergoing processing.

government on the one hand and data access claims of private individuals against one another.

I. Right of access to public sector data

As far as a potential citizen's claims of data access against the government are concerned, it should, first, be noted that a number of relevant statutes have been adopted over the past 25 years or so. At the federal level, these include the Freedom of Information Act (*Informationsfreiheitsgesetz*),[22] the Consumer Information Act (*Verbraucherinformationsgesetz*),[23] the Environmental Information Act (*Umweltinformationsgesetz*),[24] the Act on the Re-use of Public Sector Information (*Informationsweiterverwendungsgesetz*)[25] and the Geodata Access Act (*Geodatenzugangsgesetz*).[26] It must be noted, however, that these statutes are not the result of a constitutional obligation. Instead, they are essentially either the consequences of a changed understanding of how transparent the actions of the government should be,[27] or they are determined by EU law, for which the transparency of sovereign actions plays a different role, particularly for legitimising supranational actions.[28] In fact, there is hardly any link in the Basic Law to an obligation of the government to establish rights of access to public sector information.

---

22 Freedom of Information Act (*Informationsfreiheitsgesetz*) of 15 September 2005, (2005) Bundesgesetzblatt I 2722.

23 Consumer Information Act (*Verbraucherinformationsgesetz*) of 5 November 2007, (2007) Bundesgesetzblatt I 2166, 2725.

24 Environmental Information Act (*Umweltinformationsgesetz*) of 6 November 2014, (2014) Bundesgesetzblatt I 1643.

25 Act on the Re-use of Public Sector Information (*Informationsweiterverwendungsgesetz*) of 13 December 2006, (2006) Bundesgesetzblatt I 2913.

26 Geodata Access Act (*Geodatenzugangsgesetz*) of 10 February 2009, (2009) Bundesgesetzblatt I 278.

27 Grabenwarter (n. 5) Art. 5(1), (2) para. 1011; Kühling (n. 15) Art. 5 GG paras 42, 43; Sonja Wirtz and Stefan Brink, 'Die verfassungsrechtliche Verankerung der Informationszugangsfreiheit', (2015) Neue Zeitschrift für Verwaltungsrecht 1166.

28 Directive 2003/4/EC of the European Parliament and the Council of 28 January 2003 on public access to environmental information and repealing Council Directive 90/313/EEC [2003] OJ L41/26; Directive 2003/98/EC of the European Parliament and the Council of 17 November 2003 on the re-use of public sector information [2003] OJ L345/90; Directive 2007/2/EC of the European Parliament and the Council of 14 March 2007 establishing an Infrastructure for Spatial Information in the European Community (INSPIRE) [2007] OJ L108/1; Schultze-Fielitz (n.) Art. 5 para. 21.

Although Article 5(1), first sentence, alt. 2 of the Basic Law could theoretically serve as an indication of such a legislative duty, it already has been demonstrated that this provision neither establishes a direct constitutional right of access nor an obligation for the legislature to create statutory access rights.[29] On the contrary, it is clear from the above that only where the legislature enacts statutory access rights they will be protected by the freedom of information and can thus not be abolished without cause.[30]

II. Right of access to private data

Even if the Basic Law does not provide for a legislative duty to create data access rights for citizens towards the government, the question remains whether the fundamental rights can stipulate a legislative duty to create rights of private individuals against one another. In this context, the article will only deal with access to non-personal data, not only because this volume contains a separate chapter on personal data;[31] but also because it is important to consider non-personal data separately. To put it another way: Regarding the question of access to data exclusively from a protection of personal rights point of view would neglect the fact that non-personal data can also enjoy constitutional protection.[32]

The idea that fundamental rights can also oblige the legislature to create statutory protection measures for the legal relationship between private individuals is well established under constitutional law.[33] Decisions to this

29 German Federal Constitutional Court, 24 January 2001, Case 1 BvR 2623/95, *Entscheidungen des Bundesverfassungsgerichts* 103, 44 – *Gerichtsfernsehen*; Schemmer (n. 7) Art. 5 para. 32; Schultze-Fielitz (n. 5) Art. 5 para. 244; Schoch (n. 6) Einleitung para. 73.

30 See references at n. 16.

31 See Indra Spiecker gen. Döhmann, 'The legal framework for access to data from a data protection viewpoint – especially under GDPR', in this volume.

32 Cf. Thomas Wischmeyer and Eva Herzog, 'Daten für alle? – Grundrechtliche Rahmenbedingungen für Datenzugangsrechte' (2020) Neue Juristische Wochenschrift 288; Peter Axer, in Volker Epping and Christian Hillgrupber (eds), *Beck-Online-Kommentar Grundgesetz* (43th edn, C.H. Beck 2020) Art. 14 para. 50; Joachim Wieland, in Horst Dreier (ed.), *Grundgesetz-Kommentar* (3rd edn, Mohr Siebeck 2013) Art. 14 para. 72.

33 Di Fabio (n. 17) Art. 2 para. 135; Hans-J. Papier and Foroud Shirvani, in Roman Herzog and others (eds), *Maunz/Dürig Grundgesetz Kommentar* (90th edn, C.H. Beck 2020) Art. 14 para. 133; Eckart Klein, 'Grundrechtliche Schutzpflicht des Staates', (1989) Neue Juristische Wochenschrift 1633.

effect can already be found in the very early case law of the German Federal Constitutional Court, particularly in connection with the right of physical integrity under Article 2(2) of the Basic Law (in some cases in conjunction with Article 1(1) of the Basic Law).[34] The extensive statutory data protection regulations for the processing of private individuals' personal data by other private parties can also be understood as the result of a governmental duty to protect said private individuals from intrusions on their right of informational self-determination by other private individuals.[35] Moreover, a legislative duty to enact statutes to protect the secrecy of telecommunications from infringements by private parties is derived from Article 10 of the Basic Law.[36] These constitutional obligations to protect have three requirements in common: Firstly, a constitutionally protected legal interest is at stake. Secondly, this legal interest is threatened by private parties in a way that is equivalent to governmental restrictions in its effects. And thirdly, the endangered individuals are not in a position to protect themselves effectively without further legal protection and are, therefore, in need of legal protection.[37]

Based on this case law, one could try to argue that a legislative duty to enact data access rights for private petitioners towards other private individuals could be justified on the grounds that: Firstly, access to data is of-

---

34 German Federal Constitutional Court, 7 July 1971, Case 1 BvR 765/66, (1971) Neue Juristische Wochenschrift 2163; 30 November 1988, Case 1 BvR 1301/84, 79 Entscheidungen des Bundesverfassungsgerichts 174; 14 January 1981, Case 1 BvR 612/72, 56 Entscheidungen des Bundesverfassungsgerichts 54; 29 October 1987, Case 2 BvR 624/83, 77 Entscheidungen des Bundesverfassungsgerichts 170; 28 January 1992, Case 1 BvR 1025/82, 85 Entscheidungen des Bundesverfassungsgerichts 191.

35 German Federal Constitutional Court, 15 December 1983, Case 1 BvR 209/83, 65 Entscheidungen des Bundesverfassungsgerichts 1 – *Volkszählung*; 9 March 1988, Case 1 BvL 49/86, 78 Entscheidungen des Bundesverfassungsgerichts 77, 84; 8 July 1997, Case 1 BvR 2111/94, 96 Entscheidungen des Bundesverfassungsgerichts 171, 181; 12 December 2000, Case 2 BvR 1741/99, 103 Entscheidungen des Bundesverfassungsgerichts 21, 31; 12 April 2005, Case 2 BvR 1027/02, 113 Entscheidungen des Bundesverfassungsgerichts 29, 46; 17 July 1984, Case 2 BvE 11/83, 67 Entscheidungen des Bundesverfassungsgerichts 100; Dreier (n. 4) Art. 2(1) para. 79.

36 German Federal Constitutional Court, 2 March 2010, Case 1 BvR 256/08, 125 Entscheidungen des Bundesverfassungsgerichts 260.

37 German Federal Constitutional Court, 31 May 2006, Case 2 BvR 1673/04, 116 Entscheidungen des Bundesverfassungsgerichts 116, 69; Christoph Degenhart, in Michael Sachs (ed.), *Grundgesetz Kommentar* (8th edn, C.H. Beck 2018) Art. 70 para. 63.

tentimes essential for an individual's economic activity, i.e. the exercise of private autonomy and the freedom of occupation protected by fundamental rights. Secondly, this freedom is frequently restricted by private individuals in a way that is comparable with governmental restrictions, e.g. if private players accumulate large amounts of data and refuse access to private third parties. Thirdly, such private third parties cannot effectively defend themselves against this intrusion on their fundamental rights and must, therefore, be protected by statutory data access rights that can, ultimately, be enforced in court. In my opinion, the idea of a general data access right based on such a constitutional interpretation must be rejected: An understanding of the constitution such that it provides for a general duty to protect data access in private relationships, and which ultimately would demand the creation of data access rights, would not adequately balance the fact that the owner of the data in question – also being a private individual – enjoys protection by fundamental rights as well.[38] This is true even though there is currently no data property right or comparable ancillary right that would fall within the scope of protection of the property rights under Article 14(1) of the Basic Law.[39] Yet, in many cases, the 'owners' of data to which access is sought have acquired said data as part of their past professional activity and will want to use it for their professional activity in the future. This generally triggers protection by the freedom of occupation under Article 12 of the Basic Law. Even if this were not the case, the data owner would still be protected by the general freedom of personality of Article 2(1) of the Basic Law. This protection might not be particularly strong from a constitutional point of view, but – in my view – it would in any case prohibit a general right of access to data and thus a corresponding state duty to establish and regulate such a right. In this context, it should be borne in mind that the premature creation of data access rights can also have a negative impact on innovation in data-based business models, given

38 Cf. Wischmeyer and Herzog (n. 32).

39 Cf. Josef Drexl, 'Neue Regeln für die Europäische Datenwirtschaft?' (2017) Neue Zeitschrift für Kartellrecht 339; Jutta Stender-Vorwachs and Hans Steege, 'Wem gehören unsere Daten?' (2018) Neue Juristische Online-Zeitschrift 1361; Simon Adam, 'Daten als Rechtsobjekte' (2020) Neue Juristische Wochenschrift 2063; Wibke Werner, 'Schutz durch das Grundgesetz im Zeitalter der Digitalisierung' (2019) Neue Juristische Online-Zeitschrift 1041; Lothar Determann, 'Gegen Eigentumsrechte an Daten' (2018) Zeitschrift für Datenschutz 503; regarding data ownership Karl-Heinz Fezer, 'Dateneigentum – Theorie des immaterialgüterrechtlichen Eigentums an verhaltensgenerierten Personendaten der Nutzer als Datenproduzenten' (2017) Zeitschrift für IT-Recht und Recht der Digitalisierung 3.

the negative influence on the investment incentives of all market participants.[40] This also needs to be considered in the constitutional context.

Even though the legislature, therefore, does not have a general constitutional duty to create statutory data access rights, it still must be considered whether such a duty can arise in extraordinary situations. Such a situation is inter alia conceivable in case of the emergence of private data monopolies which are capable of permanently eliminating competition in markets in which data is an essential input factor. Even if the refusal to give access to data is in principle protected by the monopolist's freedom of occupation,[41] it is obvious that from a constitutional point of view the legislature would be allowed to impose restrictions on that right of the monopolist in order to protect competition.[42] This could possibly also encompass a statutory right to data access. However, it does not seem impossible that the authority to enact statutes to protect competition may convert to a legislative duty to act if competition becomes permanently and effectively impossible without respective data access rights. In this context, it should clearly be noted that such a legislative duty should only be seen as an ultima ratio. It can only manifest where markets are no longer contestable in the long-term without respective data access rights, in such a way that it becomes effectively and structurally impossible for other holders of fundamental rights to exercise their economic freedoms.

III. Interim result

As a further interim result, the fundamental rights do not stipulate any general duty for the legislature to enact data access rights. This is true of the access to public sector data as well as of the data of private individuals. However, a fundamental duty to create data access rights that safeguard competition should be considered when the control over data leads to a

40 Cf. Martin Peitz and Heike Schweitzer, 'Ein neuer europäischer Ordnungsrahmen für Datenmärkte?' (2018) Neue Juristische Wochenschrift 275, 276; Heike Schweitzer, 'Datenzugang in der Datenökonomie: Eckpfeiler einer neuen Informationsordnung' (2019) Gewerblicher Rechtsschutz und Urheberrecht 569, 571. In general see also Thomas Fetzer, *Staat und Wettbewerb in dynamischen Märkten* (Mohr Siebeck 2013) 215.

41 Similar Wischmeyer and Herzog (n. 32) 292.

42 Cf. Rupprecht Podszun and Stefan Kreifels, 'Ministererlaubnis und Verfahrensrecht' in Christian Kersting and Rupprecht Podszun (eds), *Die 9. GWB-Novelle* (C.H. Beck 2017), ch. 14 para. 46.

permanent and far-reaching exclusion of competition, i.e. when markets are not contestable and the exercise of economic freedoms becomes impossible for other market participants.

E. Constitutional limits for data access rights?

If, in summary, there is no legislative duty to create data access rights but – depending on the circumstances – an authority to enact statutory data access rights, the question arises to what extent the Basic Law sets any limits for the establishment of such rights. In this context, it should be noted that from a constitutional point of view the general authority of the legislature to establish these rights is not in doubt. To answer the question regarding the limits of this authority, a distinction must again be made between data access rights for the government in relation to private data on the one hand and data access rights between private individuals on the other.

I. Data access rights of the government

If the government desires access to data of private individuals, this triggers the protection by the fundamental rights in their traditional capacity as defensive rights, requiring a justification for every state attributed restriction of a protected freedom.[43] Again, it should be emphasised that this also applies to non-personal data. Depending on the specific design of data access rights, the economic rights of Articles 12 (freedom of occupation), 14 (freedom of property) and 2(1) (general freedom of action) of the Basic Law will be relevant.

Against the background of the above, rights of access of the state to data are only permissible where they are founded on a statutory legal basis and if they are proportionate. This means they must pursue a legitimate goal

43 Dreier (n. 4) Vor. Art. 1 GG para. 84; Isensee (n. 4) § 191 para. 2; cf. also von Münch and Kunig (n. 10) Vor. Art. 1 GG paras 11–12; cf. German Federal Constitutional Court, 15 January 1958, Case 1 BvR 400/51, 7 Entscheidungen des Bundesverfassungsgerichts 198, 204-205 – Lüth; 6 January 1957, Case 1 BvR 253/56, 6 Entscheidungen des Bundesverfassungsgerichts 32, 41 – Elfes.

and have to be suitable, necessary and appropriate in relation to said goal.[44] The mere fact that private individuals have access to data that is useful for the government or for the general public is not sufficient to establish a proportionate restriction of the fundamental freedoms of the data owner. Although no court decisions have yet been published in this specific context, it can be deduced from the case law of the German Federal Constitutional Court on the involvement of private parties to fulfil public tasks (*Indienstnahme Privater*) that the government cannot demand access to private resources in the fulfilment of its public duties simply by reason that said resources are at the disposal of a private party. On the contrary, it is required that said private party has a special responsibility or ability for achieving the public purpose, which can particularly result from the fact that a private actor has exclusive access to certain input factors.[45] As a result, it is inter alia conceivable that under certain conditions data access rights are justifiable for the improvement of medical care, as is currently being discussed.[46]

When balancing the public or government interest in obtaining access to private data on the one hand and the interests of a private data owner in maintaining secrecy on the other hand, it is certainly also important to consider the extent to which the existence of the data in question is the re-

---

44 German Federal Constitutional Court, 8 April 1987, Case 2 BvR 909/82, 108 Entscheidungen des Bundesverfassungsgerichts 75, 108, 154–158; 6 June 1989, Case 1 921/85, 80 Entscheidungen des Bundesverfassungsgerichts 137, 153, 159–161; 9 March 1994, Case 2 BvL 43/92, 90 Entscheidungen des Bundesverfassungsgerichts 145, 172–173; Christian Hillgruber, 'Grundrechtlicher Schutzbereich, Grundrechtsausgestaltung und Grundrechtseingriff' in Josef Isensee und Paul Kirchhof (eds), *Handbuch des Staatsrechts*, Vol. IX (3rd edn, C.F. Müller 2011) § 201, paras 51–77; Dreier (n. 4) Vor Art. 1 paras 145–149; Höfling (n. 4) Vor Art. 1 para. 135, Art. 20 GG paras 146, 149–157; von Münch and Kunig (n. 10) Vor Art. 1 para. 38.

45 See Andreas Schirra, *Die Indienstnahme Privater im Lichte des Steuerstaatsprinzips* (Peter Lang 2002) 32. In general, concerning the involvement of private parties to fulfil public tasks, cf. German Federal Constitutional Court, 16 March 1971, Case 1 BvR 52/66, 30 Entscheidungen des Bundesverfassungsgerichts 292, 311; 29 November 1967, Case 1 175/66, 22 Entscheidungen des Bundesverfassungsgerichts 380, 385; 22 January 1997, Case 2 1915/91, 95 Entscheidungen des Bundesverfassungsgerichts 173, 187; 17 February 1997, Case 1 33/76, 44 Entscheidungen des Bundesverfassungsgerichts 103, 103–104; 17 October 1984, Case 1 BvL 18/82, 68 Entscheidungen des Bundesverfassungsgerichts 155, 170.

46 Cf. Torsten Körber, '"Digitalisierung" der Missbrauchsaufsicht durch die 10. GWB-Novelle' (2020) Zeitschrift für IT-Recht und Recht der Digitalisierung 290, 292; Josef Drexl, 'Neue Regeln für die Europäische Datenwirtschaft?' (2017) Neue Zeitschrift für Kartellrecht 415, 416.

sult of the exercise of a freedom protected by fundamental rights in the past and to what extent said data will be important for its owners when exercising their fundamental freedoms in the future. Moreover, even if one were to agree that the establishment of data access rights can generally be constitutionally justified under certain circumstances, the actual access may only be permissible in return for financial compensation.[47]

Finally, additional limits on the state's access rights to data of private individuals can result from legally protected interests of third parties when it comes to access to their data which is held by another private individual. This may even be true where such data is not personal, e.g. when it is subject to intellectual property rights or where it contains business and trade secrets, which may exclude a right of access in individual cases.[48] Data access rights of the state must not force a private party obliged to give access to violate the rights of third parties. In case of doubt, the state must seek access to such data from the primary source, meaning the affected third party.

II. Private data access rights

If the legislature wants to establish statutory data access for private individuals against one another, clearly this also encroaches on the fundamental rights of the individuals obliged to grant access. In this respect, the limits applicable to such rights are generally comparable to those applicable to data access rights of the government. Accordingly, they require a legal basis, have to pursue a legitimate goal and must be proportionate in relation to that goal.

The abovementioned protection of competition from 'data market power' can serve as such a legitimate goal. In this respect, the legislature is also authorised to create competition-protecting statutes concerning private le-

---

47 On the concept of compensatory regulations that define the contents and limits of basic rights see Axer (n. 32) Art. 14 para. 104; cf. German Federal Constitutional Court, 14.07.1981, Case 1 24/78, 58 Entscheidungen des Bundesverfassungsgerichts 137, 150–151.

48 Cf. the similiar limitations under Secs 5 and 6 of the Freedom of Information Act. Concerning Sec. 5 Freedom of Information Act see also Federal Administrative Court, 13 December 2018, Case 7 C 19/17, (2019) Neue Zeitschrift für Verwaltungsrecht 807, paras 41–42; Federal Administrative Court, 17 March 2016, Case 7 C 2/15, (2016) Neue Zeitschrift für Verwaltungsrecht 1014, para. 25, and concerning Sec. 6 Freedom of Information Act, Federal Administrative Court, 25 June 2015, Case 7 C 1/14, (2015) Neue Juristische Wochenschrift 3258, para. 29.

gal relationships.[49] Nonetheless, it is still necessary to thoroughly establish the proportionality of said statutes. In this context, the relevant questions are: Firstly, is the data access really suitable for preventing detriments to competition? Secondly, is the data access necessary to prevent such harm or are there less restrictive measures? Thirdly, is the data access appropriate regarding the fact that it may lead to a devaluation of investments in the development of data collections and therefore reduce future business opportunities if said data collection can no longer be used exclusively by the data owner? A distinction will also have to be made as to whether data access should be designed to depend on an abusive refusal to grant access by the data owner or whether it should also be possible without such an abuse. In the latter case, the constitutional requirements for the justification of a statutory data access right are certainly higher, since the party obliged to give access to data on the basis of its having refused access is in principle exercising fundamental legal freedoms. Finally, it must be considered how compensation for data access can be granted, because it seems to be clear that data access to private data by other private parties will generally speaking only be constitutional if the obliged party is compensated for granting access.

III. Interim result

In principle, the legislature is entitled to create statutory data access rights. However, such access needs to be justified, given the fact that it encroaches on the fundamental rights of the party obligated to grant access – largely irrespective of who is supposed to receive access. In this respect, it is also conceivable to enact data access rights in favour of private individuals in order to protect effective competition. However, these rights need to be weighed against the fundamental rights of the parties obliged to grant the access. The requirements for constitutional justification become higher the more the control over data by a private party is a result of the owners exercising their freedoms protected by the fundamental rights and the more

49 See Art. 74(1) no. 16 GG; on this Degenhart (n. 37) Art. 74 para. 65; Christian Seiler, in Volker Epping and Christian Hillgruber (eds), *Beck-Online-Kommentar Grundgesetz* (43th edn, C.H. Beck 2020) Art. 74 para. 57; German Federal Constitutional Court, 14 March1990, Case KVR 4/88 (KG), (1990) Gewerblicher Rechtsschutz und Urheberrecht 702, 703. Referring to market dominance in data, cf. Sec. 18(3a) No. 4 German Act against Restraints of Competition.

the denial to give access to this data serves the future exercise of the freedoms protected by these fundamental rights.

F. Final result

The constitution provides a framework for data access rights that limits the legislature in terms of the chosen motive and its specific design, but also leaves considerable leeway. The legislature has a general authority to establish data access rights if they are proportionate. A general duty to establish such rights, however, does not exist. Only in extraordinary circumstances can the legislative authority be transformed into a legislative duty if data monopolists are able to hinder competition effectively and permanently in such a way that the respective market is no longer contestable.

The legal framework for access to data from a data protection viewpoint – especially under the GDPR

*Indra Spiecker genannt Döhmann**

A. *Introduction to data protection's regulatory impulse*

I. *Free data for all?*

Access to data and information[1] can be paraphrased with a common saying: 'My data is freely available for anyone to access and use, I do not have anything to hide'. This may be true, but it is certainly wrong. Data access cannot be discussed without focusing on the reasons why completely free access to data is not only impossible but also not desirable.

Since their beginnings in the 1960s and 1970s, with the rise of automated decision-making, efforts to protect data and privacy have tried to act on this common misunderstanding of the equality of factual access to data and the normative 'nothing to hide'.[2] This is because the risk that data protection is intended to prevent is easily undervalued.

---

* I would like to thank members of my staff Mona Winau for further research and Charlotte Humpert for additional information and thorough reading. All references were last checked on 7 August 2020.

1 The terms *data* and *information* are treated synonymously for the purposes of this paper although the author is well aware that there is a substantial difference both between them and to the concept of knowledge. This, however, does not play out for the content of this paper.

2 Spiros Simitis, Gerrit Hornung and Indra Spiecker gen. Döhmann, in Spiros Simitis, Gerrit Hornung and Indra Spiecker gen. Döhmann (eds), *Datenschutzrecht. DS-GVO mit BDSG* (Nomos 2019) Einleitung paras 6–13; cf. Alan F. Westin, *Privacy and Freedom* (Atheneum Press1967) 158–168; Jürgen Kühling and Johannes Raab, in Jürgen Kühling and Benedikt Buchner (eds), *Datenschutzgrundverordnung Kommentar* (C.H. Beck 2017) Einführung para. 37; Spiros Simitis, 'Reviewing Privacy in an Information Society' (1987) 135 University of Pennsylvania Law Review 707, 709–710; Alan F. Westin, 'Science, Privacy, and Freedom: Issues and Proposals for the 1970's: Part I-The Current Impact of Surveillance on Privacy' (1966) 66 Columbia Law Review 1003, 1003. Similar to the dictum 'nothing to hide' is the misunderstanding that 'nobody is going to bother'; Jessica Litman, 'Information Privacy/Information Property' (2000) 52 Stanford Law Review 1283, 1285.

The above assessment is based on two assumptions which contradict this seemingly convincing finding: First, freely available information does not mean equal use of the information. Not everyone who has access to data can also use it. So it is the availability of technology that determines the potential threats. Secondly, there are effects of the use of data that the individual does not control: If an individual's data is being used to assess others, then the effect on these others is not something included in the individual's decision to grant access. There is no direct interaction between the person whose data is being used and the entity using the data, and there is certainly no direct return between the use of data and the making accessible of it.

Data protection law is a core regulatory answer to data protection needs. It addresses at its centre the information-based power asymmetry which derives from the inequality of use and accessibility.[3] However, it naturally does not include all types of data. Rather, data protection law concentrates on personal data, where the risk of imbalanced decisions is most prominent, where the rationality of self-protection cannot necessarily be relied upon and where the consequences for the well-being of society are most pressing.

II. Data protection as a regulatory regime to link data and decision-making

The following insights into data access under the current EU legal regime of the General Data Protection Regulation (GDPR)[4] concentrate on these types of data. It should be noted, however, that there are many other data-

3 Cf. Walter Schmidt, 'Die bedrohte Entscheidungsfreiheit' (1974) 29 Juristen-Zeitung 241, 246; Lorna Stefanik, *Controlling Knowledge – Freedom of Information and Privacy Protection in a Networked World* (Athabaska University Press 2011), 29; Orla Lynskey, 'Deconstructing data protection: the "added-value" of a right to data protection in the EU legal order' (2014) 63 International & Comparative Law Quaterly 569, 589–590; See especially on privacy rights of defence against the state, Serge Gutwirth and Paul De Hert, 'Privacy, Data Protection and Law Enforcement: Opactiy of the Individual and Transparency of Power' in Eric Claes and others (eds), *Privacy and the Criminal Law* (Intersentia 2006) 61, 72–74; Herbert Burkert, *Informationszugang und Datenschutz. Ein kanadisches Beispiel* (Nomos 1992) 12. For an overview of the scientific discourse in Germany at the beginning of data protection law, see Klaus Tiedemann and Christoph Sasse, *Delinquenzprophylaxe, Kreditsicherung und Datenschutz in der Wirtschaft* (Carl Heymanns Verlag 1973) 89–100.

4 Regulation (EU) 2016/679 of the European Parliament and of the Council of 27 April 2016 on the protection of natural persons with regard to the processing of

protecting regimes present, such as the frequently discussed copyright law, which is also covered in this volume, but also, much less focused on, the protection of business and trade secrets or whistleblower protection, which are also present in this volume.

Data protection is one important way to look at guidance for an overall legal regime for access of data. The concept is based on the particular perspective on decision-making and the role information plays in it. According to this perspective, including the present difficulties in establishing an information and knowledge society[5] as well as the manifold perspectives and consequences of legal intervention, data protection scholars are capable to deliver their own and integrating answers on pressing questions on access of data. Though the full range of problems cannot be covered here, questions that remain unsettled include: whether data can be the object of services for the public (*Daseinsvorsorge*) and social participation, how concepts of transparency versus secrecy can be evaluated and established, what the consequences of ubiquitous computing and prolific availability of information are on society and numerous levels of decision, how the value, worth and accounting of information can be construed and legally implemented, whether solidarity concepts require a sharing of data, especially in health care provision, how horizontal and vertical integration of data and information technology can be guided, or who shall, in an international data transfer market, have the power to control data.

Most of the many approaches to solving these questions do not take into account that access to data and access to the infrastructure to use and exploit this data are separate from each other. Data protection law, however, offers solutions combining both venues because it is interested not only in the information part but also in the results and purposes of the use of data. Article 5 (1) lit. b GDPR, with the purpose limitation, makes that clear, as does Article 20 GDPR, with the limitation of automated decision-making. In the end, data protection law offers some concepts on how to deal with the new central resource of data as the 'new oil', and how it can be used for the public and private good without overburdening the individual. The core element of data protection, however, that self-restriction and a moderate use of data may be the way towards a sustainable, democracy-and-free-

---

personal data and on the free movement of such data, and repealing Directive 95/46/EC (General Data Protection Regulation) [2018] OJ L127/2.

5 The term 'knowledge society' was coined by Helmut Wilke, *Systemisches Wissensmanagement* (2nd edn, Lucius & Lucius 2001) 289.

dom-driven society and economy, usually encounters a lot of opposition and misconception.

III. *The lack of control*

The GDPR sees data as an important resource and an influencing factor for decision-making. In this decision-oriented framework, data processing has an impact both on the individual itself and on all groups of individuals within society which are being judged on the basis of information. Typically, the most severely infringing types of data processing such as profiling or scoring are achieved by transforming sets of individual data into generalised information that is then re-applied to individuals by decision-making. Therefore, power over information (and the technology to make use of it) may cause structural disparity and imbalance between those who are decided upon and those who decide with the aid of information and information technology.

The latter are typically unable to control for the data reflected within the decision, which strengthens the position of those using the information to use all accessible information without normative barriers.[6] Thus, a decision may seem to be in accordance with accepted values but really is not. Control over the substantive standards of a decision is therefore difficult, and control over the information input even more so. Thus a number of GDPR provisions are intended to establish control and normative standards for the use of data, among them the requirement to use data primarily directly gathered from the individual.

The GDPR also addresses the additional problem that maintaining control over the decision is typically difficult because individuals do not have the resources to control the technological means of using and assessing information.[7] If artificial intelligence is used to reach an administrative deci-

6 Indra Spiecker gen. Döhmann, 'Profiling, Big Data, Artificial Intelligence und Social Media – Gefahren für eine Gesellschaft ohne effektiven Datenschutz' in Walter Hötzendörfer, Christof Tschohl and Franz Kummer (eds), *International Trends in Legal Informatics: Festschrift für Erich Schweighöfer* (bpa media 2020) 345, 351–355.

7 Sebastian Bretthauer, 'Verfassungsrechtliche Grundlagen, Europäisches und nationales Recht' in Louisa Specht and Reto Mantz (eds), *Handbuch Europäisches und deutsches Datenschutzrecht* (C.H. Beck 2019) § 2 para. 2; Specifically on Art. 22 GDPR see Philip Scholz, in Spiros Simitis, Gerrit Hornung and Indra Spiecker gen. Döhmann (eds), *Datenschutzrecht. DSGVO mit BDSG* (Nomos 2019) Art. 22 para. 3. Isak Mendoza and Lee A. Bygrave, 'The Right Not to Be Subject to Automated Decisions Based on Profiling' (University of Oslo Faculty of Law Stud-

sion, hardly any citizen will be able to attack this decision based on a critique of the functioning of the technology applied. Thus, means like the data protection impact assessment procedure of Article 35 GDPR attempt to limit the harm of uncontrolled use of potentially infringing technology.

IV. The general answer of the GDPR regulatory regime

European data protection law offers a number of tools by which to assist the data subject in controlling data flows and intransparent decision-making. Without going into detail and with an eye on the special perspective of this contribution to a data access regime, there should be a few core elements named for a common understanding when looking at exact regulations on the access to data.

First, the GDPR intervenes as early and as long as possible and thus accompanies every aspect of data use. It does so by using a well-known technology-law instrument, the establishment of the principle of precaution (*Vorsorgeprinzip*), thus reversing the burden of reasoning and potentially proof in general: The data controller in many instances has to establish the use and the exact purposes of the data use rather than the data subject having to demonstrate risks and dangers.

The control of the data protection legal regime begins as early as possible and that is the moment when personal data leaves the sphere of the data subject's immediate and sole control. This can be as early as the emergence of data if this takes place in a social setting with others; it can also be at a much later stage e.g. when entries made in a diary on a computer years ago are exploited in the course of an administrative assessment of potential foster parents. On the other side, in the life cycle of data,[8] the GDPR also controls for the decision and its outcome and in many instances takes the potential consequences of the use of data into account when assessing the lawfulness of an act of or a type of data processing.

ies, Research Paper Series No. 2017–20) 7–8 <https://papers.ssrn.com/sol3/papers.cfm?abstract_id=2964855> accessed 22 July 2020.

8 Cf. Indra Spiecker gen. Döhmann, 'Information Management' in Peter Cane and others (eds), *The Oxford Handbook on Comparative Administrative Law* (2020, forthcoming).

Secondly, the GDPR – and in this, it differs greatly from its predecessor, the Data Protection Directive (DPD)[9] – does not only rely on substantive safeguards but establishes effective means of control and sanctions and institutionalises them.[10] This can be seen in the clarified and increased tasks and powers of the supervisory authorities, Articles 56 and 57 GDPR, but also in the extensive set of sanctions now established under Articles 77 et seq. GDPR or the possibility of representation of data subjects under Article 80 GDPR. It also increases the pressure on data controllers by sharpening and furthering procedural safeguards such as a mandatory internal data protection impact assessment for infringing or risky data processing according to Article 35 GDPR, the duty to demonstrate according to Article 24 (1) GDPR or the duty to inform the data subject according to Articles 13 and 14 GDPR.[11]

---

9 Directive 95/46/EC of the European Parliament and of the Council of 24 October 1995 on the protection of individuals with regard to the processing of personal data and on the free movement of such data [1995] OJ L281/31.

10 Jürgen Kühling and Mario Martini, 'Die Datenschutz-Grundverordnung: Revolution oder Evolution im europäischen und deutschen Datenschutzrecht?' (2016) 27 Europäische Zeitschrift für Wirtschaftsrecht 448, 451–454; Benedikt Buchner, 'Grundsätze des Datenschutzrechts, Datenschutzkontrolle' in Marie-Theres Tinnefeld and others (eds), *Einführung in das Datenschutzrecht, Datenschutz und Informationsfreiheit in europäischer Sicht* (7th edn, De Gruyter 2020) 314–332; Quite positively forecasting an effective and consistent authority, Jan P. Albrecht, 'How the GDPR Will Change the World' (2016) 2 European Data Protection Law Review 287, 289; opposing to Albrecht's viewpoint, Sebastian J. Golla, 'Is Data Protection Law Growing Teeth? The Current Lack of Sanctions in Data Protection Law and Administrative Fines under the GDPR' (2017) 8 Journal of Intellectual Property, Information Technology and E-Commerce Law 70, 77–78.

11 For an overview, see Peter Schantz, 'Die Datenschutz-Grundverordnung – Beginn einer neuen Zeitrechnung im Datenschutzrecht?' (2016) 26 Neue Juristische Wochenschrift 1841, 1846–1847. On the data protection authority's extended responsibilities and powers, Alexander Roßnagel, *Datenschutzaufsicht nach der EU-Datenschutz-Grundverordnung* (Springer 2017); and the Europeanisation of supervisory authority, Hielke Hijmans, 'The DPAs and Their Cooperation: How Far Are We in Making Enforcement of Data Protection Law More European?' (2016) 2 European Data Protection Law Review 362. With regard to sanctions, Golla (n. 10) 74–78. Concerning the implications for foreign companies and states, Cedric Ryngaert and Mistale Taylor, 'The GDPR as Global Data Protection Regulation?' (2020) 114 American Journal of International Law Unbound 5, 7. Pointing out the advantage of willingness to cooperate from an entrepreneur's viewpoint, Michael Wenzel and Tim Wybitul, 'Vermeidung hoher Bußgelder und Kooperation mit Datenschutzbehörden' (2019) Zeitschrift für Datenschutz 290; on the increasing pressure on data processors in business, Tal Z. Zarsky, 'Incompati-

On this general understanding of what data protection law aims to achieve, this paper will first develop some core elements of data protection law without which the concept of access to data under the GDPR as the legal regime of data protection in Europe cannot be understood properly (B.). It will then point out the special qualities of data and information that do not allow for regulatory frameworks typically used for market goods and how data protection law implicitly takes these into account (C.). With this general understanding, the different rights to access to data under the GDPR (and partly national law) and their limits will be analysed (D.). Guidelines for a data-protection-compatible regulatory regime are directed towards an impact of these findings to legislators (E.) before the chapter closes with a conclusion and an outlook (F.).

B. Prerequisites on Access under Data Protection Law

I. Personal Data as the Threshold for Application of Data Protection Regimes

As personal data is the core element to open up the wide regulatory regime of data protection law, it is essential to understand what falls under this terminology and what does not. A data-protection-friendly regulatory regime of data access has to accept that a mixture of personal data and non-personal data will lead to the application of the stricter data protection regime. Thus, whenever there are some personal data elements within a pool of data, any access to this pool in general has to follow the rules of the GDPR.[12]

Article 4 (1) GDPR provides for a legal definition of 'any information relating to an identified or identifiable natural person', clarifying that the critical characteristic of identifiability is constituted if a person can directly or indirectly be identified. Thus, additional knowledge and information that needs to be accessed in order to identify a person has to be taken into account in order to determine whether there is in particular a 'reference [...] such as a name, an identification number, location data, an online identifier or to one or more factors specific to the physical, physiological, genetic, mental, economic, cultural or social identity of the natural per-

ble: The GDPR in the Age of Big Data' (2017) 47 Seton Hall Law Review 995, 1005.

12 Cf. Case C-131/12 *Google Spain v AEPD and Mario Costeja González* [2014] ECLI:EU:C:2014:317.

son'. This legal definition makes it clear that the GDPR follows in the footsteps of the Data Protection Directive,[13] creating in general a large scope of applicability of data protection law as additional information has to be taken into account when determining whether data is personal data or not. In other words: Even if data does not immediately refer to an individual, it can still fall under the regime of the GDPR if additional data allows for a connection.

What remains unclear, however, is how much additional information has to be taken into account and whether or not this additional information must be accessible by the data controller. This ongoing feud over whether to take a more objective or more subjective approach[14] has been in parts decided by the ECJ in the *Breyer* case.[15] There, the ECJ ruled that dynamic IP addresses are typically considered to be personal data unless the identification is prohibited by law or access to the combination of data is only possible if totally disproportionate measures have to be taken. This could be redefined as an objective perspective with subjective elements/ restrictions: In general all additional information which can legally and

---

13 There is no difference between the wording of Art. 4 (1) GDPR and Art. 2 lit. a) DPD in the English version. The altered wording in the German version from 'bestimmt/bestimmbar' to 'identifiziert/identifizierbar' does not have any practical implications; Moritz Karg, in Spiros Simitis, Gerrit Hornung and Indra Spiecker gen. Döhmann (eds), *Datenschutzrecht. DSGVO mit BDSG* (Nomos 2019) Art. 4 No. 1 para. 6; Stefan Ernst, in Boris P. Paal and Daniel A. Pauly (eds), *Datenschutz-Grundverordnung, Bundesdatenschutzgesetz* (2nd edn, Beck 2018) Art. 4 No. 1 para. 3; Tina Krügel, 'Das personenbezogene Datum nach der DSGVO' (2017) Zeitschrift für Datenschutz 455, 455–456.

14 Karg (n. 13) Art. 4 No. 1 paras 58–59; supporting the subjective approach, Mark J. Taylor, 'Data Protection: Too Personal to Protect' (2006) 3 SCRIPTed (Journal) 71, 79–80; Worku G. Urgessa, 'The Protective Capacity of the Criterion of Identifiability under EU Data Protection Law' (2016) 2 European Data Protection Law Review Journal 521, 522; concerning the subjective approach in The UK Data Protection Act 1998, Taylor (ibid) 79; about the former version of the German Federal Data Protection Act (BDSG), Paul Voigt, 'Datenschutz bei Google' (2009) Multimedia und Recht 377, 379.

15 Case C-582/14 *Patrick Breyer v Bundesrepublik Deutschland* [2016] ECLI:EU:C:2016:779.
Frederik Zuiderveen Borgesius, 'The Breyer Case of the Court of Justice of the European Union: IP Addresses and the Personal Data Definition' (2017) 3 European Data Protection Law Review Journal 130, 131, 137. With regard to assignability of the *Breyer* jurisprudence to Art. 4 (1) GDPR, Jens Brauneck, 'DSG-VO: Neue Anwendbarkeit durch neue Definition personenbezogener Daten?' (2019) 30 Europäische Zeitschrift für Wirtschaftsrecht 680, 682–688; Krügel (n. 13) 455–456.

not totally against all proportionality be accessed has to be taken into account, and this includes information which the data controller might not actually retrieve. This leaves a wide range of application of the GDPR to many sets of data, although at first sight they might not seem to be personal data. This should be considered when developing a regime for wide data access: Much data processing is thus restricted by the GDPR.

II. Lawfulness of Data Processing and Procedural Requirements in combination

One of the core elements of data protection law is that any type of data processing has to be justified.[16] Article 6 (1) GDPR (and Article 9 GDPR for data with a high potential of discrimination, e.g. health data, racial or political data) provides for legal grounds, among them consent of the data subject but also overriding public interests. Nevertheless, despite wide possibilities for data processing of personal data, the GDPR also provides for a number of additional requirements and restrictions of these data processings. One could describe this process as a continuous pendulum: Requiring justification lets the pendulum swing in one direction, allowing wide justifications then lets it sway in the other direction, the procedural safeguards send it back again, and the possibilities for loosening these safeguards allow it to turn in the other direction, once more.

16 Jan P. Albrecht, in Spiros Simitis, Gerrit Hornung and Indra Spiecker gen. Döhmann (eds), *Datenschutzrecht. DSGVO mit BDSG* (Nomos 2019) Art. 6 para. 1; Eike M. Frenzel, in Boris P. Paal and Daniel A. Pauly (eds), *Datenschutz-Grundverordnung, Bundesdatenschutzgesetz* (2nd edn, C.H. Beck 2018) Art. 6 para. 1; Benedikt Buchner and Thomas Petri, in Jürgen Kühling and Benedikt Buchner (eds), *Datenschutzgrundverordnung Kommentar* (C.H. Beck 2017) Art. 6 para. 1. In this respect, data protection law takes an exceptional position compared to other information obtained regulatory approaches, Spiecker gen. Döhmann (n. 8) sec. 33.6.1. Alexander Roßnagel speaks out against the frequently used term 'ban with an exemption option' in this context: Alexander Roßnagel, 'Kein "Verbotsprinzip" und kein "Verbot mit Erlaubnisvorbehalt" im Datenschutzrecht' (2019) Neue Juristische Wochenschrift 1. About the intrusive character of data processing, see Herke Kranenborg, 'Article 8 – Protection of Personal Data' in Steve Peers and others (eds), *The EU Charter on Fundamental Rights. A Commentary* (Hart Publishing 2014) Nos 08., 08.88 – 08.90; cf. Case C-131/12 *Google Spain v AEPD and Mario Costeja González* [2014] ECLI:EU:C:2014:317, para. 86.

III. Data Protection for both private and public data processing

Considering the broadness of the application of the GDPR and thus the general standards of data protection, the GDPR creates an extensive framework which regulates in an intensive way the processing of data. However, it should be seen that the GDPR differentiates in many regards – in contrast to the previous DPD – between private and public use of data.[17]

The regulation recognises that there are different interests involved. While private data processing is an expression of the freedom and liberties of the individual and thus might happen arbitrarily and completely in the own interest of both the data subject and the data controller, public (state) processing of data is in general bound by the common good and by the duty to serve a public interest. Public data processing is thus under a double requirement for justification, arising firstly from the special dangers and risks associated with the processing of data, but secondly also deriving from the special obligation of the state to serve the interests of the people.

C. Data as a special good and its effect on regulation

Without going into detail in regard to the special topic of this contribution, data protection law also takes into account that personal data has special qualities. Any type of regulation of personal data – be it a restriction or be it wide access to unlimited use of it – has to take this into account. Data and information cannot be treated as any other good, commodity or content of contractual relations.

This is the case, for one thing, because information and privacy are common goods in the economic sense.[18] This means that there exists no rivalry

---

17 Kühling and Raab (n. 2) Einführung para. 78. Art. 6 (1) lit. c and lit. e GDPR specifically address data processing in public responsibility. Emphasising broad flexibility clauses, Julian Wagner and Alexander Benecke, 'National Legislation within the Framework of the GDPR' (2016) 2 European Data Protection Law Review 353, 354–355. Pointing out the lack of a comprehensive data protection administrative law, Philipp Reimer, 'Verwaltungsdatenschutzrecht' (2018) Die Öffentliche Verwaltung 881, 881–882; more generally concerning different regulatory approaches in information law, Spiecker gen. Döhmann (n. 8) Introduction.

18 They are also experience goods, but this aspect shall not be further pursued in the course of this paper.

in consumption, and also no excludability from consumption of the good:[19] Anyone may use it, may use it again and may pass it on without the originator of the information being able to prevent this or control the flow of information. As a common good can be used multiple times by multiple users it is difficult to make such a good marketable: Market failure and enforcement deficits are typical effects in regard to such a good.[20] For regulatory impact, this means that legal protection of common goods has to start at the beginning of any transfer as any later use of information can hardly be traced. This is one of the reasons why data protection law does not only take into account specific risky handling of data but every step of data processing.

Personal information and privacy are special goods for another reason, as well. Information on a person is not something that cannot be separated from the person it is connected to and to the personality of the person. Information is never free of context. The individual traits and characteristics of a person are inseparable from the personal content of information on this person. Of course, some such links are stronger than others: A diary reveals more about a person than the name or the employer of that person. However, as context always matters, even those seemingly unimportant aspects of a person and his or her personality can, together with other infor-

19 See the report of the German Federal Justice Minister's conference, 'Arbeitsgruppe 'Digitaler Neustart' der Konferenz der Justizminister und Justizministerinnen der Länder' (2017) 30 <https://jm.rlp.de/fileadmin/mjv/Jumiko/Fruehjahrskonferenz_neu/Bericht_der_AG_Digitaler_Neustart_vom_15._Mai_2017.pdf> accessed 26 July 2020. Regarding the characters and difference between property rights and personality rights (192–194), giving a review of the discoursive question whether European Data Protection Law under GDPR contains property right aspects (199–204) and depicting the non-absolute character of data protection rights (201–202), Henry Pearce, 'Personality, Property and Other Provocations: Exploring the Conceptual Muddle of Data Protection Rights under EU Law' (2018) 4 European Data Protection Law Review 190. Arguing for a propertisation of data protection law while recognising privacy as a common good, Paul M. Schwartz, 'Property, Privacy, and Personal Data' (2004) 117 Harvard Law Review 2056, 2084–2090. Pointing out the property-derived rights under GDPR, Jacob M. Victor, 'The EU General Data Protection Regulation: Toward a Property Regime for Protecting Data Privacy' (2013) 123 Yale Law Journal 513.

20 See Alan Randall, 'The Problem of Market Failure' (1983) 23 Natural Resources Journal 131; David Bollier, *Silent Theft: The Privat Plunder of Our Common Wealth* (Routledge 2013) 7; Richard J. Sweeney, Robert D. Tollison and Thomas D. Willett, 'Market Failure, the Common-Pool Problem, and Ocean Resource Exploitation' (1974) 17 Journal of Law and Economics 179, 180. Criticising the ideas of property of facts from a US-law viewpoint, Jessica Litman, 'Information Privacy/Information Property' (2000) 52 Stanford Law Review 1283, 1294, 1297.

mation, become very revealing as to individuality. This makes clear why in the German constitutional understanding of data protection rights (ie the right to informational self-determination[21]) there is a direct link to the constitutional guarantee of the person's dignity in Article 1 (1) of the Basic Law (*Grundgesetz*).

The consequences of this special character trait of information and privacy are – in legal terms – manifold. They include, first, that a property-based approach, similar to the US approach based on trespass,[22] is incompatible with this understanding.[23] Thus, the construction of data protection rights and privacy rights as property rights which can be sold and bought does not fit this quality of information. Secondly, further conclusions cannot be drawn from this concept of property-based information rights: A 'data donation' as has been discussed lately[24] is impossible under such conditions as no person is able to disconnect the information from its

21 Cf. German Federal Constitutional Court, 15 September 1983, Case 1 BvR 209/83, (1983) 65 Entscheidungen des Bundesverfassungsgerichts 1 – *Volkszählung*.

22 Cf. Patricia Mell, 'Seeking Shade in a Land of Perpetual Sunlight: Privacy as Property in the Electronic Wilderness' (1996) 11 Berkeley Technology Law Journal 1, 34; James Q. Whitman, 'The Two Western Cultures of Privacy: Dignity versus Liberty' (2004) 113 Yale Law Journal 1151, 1211–1213; Russell L. Weaver and Steven I. Friedland, 'Privacy and the Fourth Amendment' in Dieter Dörr and Russell L. Weaver (eds), *Perspectives on Privacy – Increasing Regulation in the USA, Canada, Australia and European Countries* (De Grutyer 2014) 1, 2–3, 5 (giving an overview about the modified comprehension in jurisprudences reacting to technological progress), 5–17; Indra Spiecker gen. Döhmann, 'Datenschutz in der Globalisierung – Mission Impossible in einer Welt der Technikzukünfte unter Einwirkung einer neuen Datenschutz-Grundverordnung?' in Thomas Dreier and Indra Spiecker gen. Döhmann (eds), *Informationsrecht@KIT – 15 Jahre Zentrum für Angewandte Rechtswissenschaft* (KIT Scientific Publishing 2015) 63, 77; Schantz (n. 11) Art. 45 paras 41–43; about the lack of a comprehensive regulatory approach and the concept of privacy protection in specific areas, Paul M. Schwartz, 'Privacy and Democracy in Cyberspace' (1999) 52 Vanderbilt Law Review 1607, 1632–1634; Vera Bergelson, 'It's Personal but Is It Mine – Toward Property Rights in Personal Information' (2003) 37 UC Davis Law Review 379, 391–393.

23 Differentiating between the perception of data protection as a privacy law and property, the latter originated from USA, Henry Pearce, 'Personality, Property and Other Provocations: Exploring the Conceptual Muddle of Data Protection Rights under EU Law' (2018) 4 European Data Protection Law Review 190, 197–198. From Pearce's point of view the conception of data protection which the GDPR establishes is not incompatible with a property-right approach all together, but can rather be described as quasi-property rights, 204–205.

24 The German public health authority (Robert Koch Institute) provides an app that collects personal data (residence, height, weight) and has vital data transferred

personal connection. The only way to do this is to anonymise – and then data donation will no longer be necessary because there will be no personal data left. On the other hand, in contradiction to the concept of information/data protection as a property right, the present privacy- and personality right-oriented concept also allows for an acceptance of data to be rarely only one person's data. As the German Constitutional Court put it, human beings are social beings,[25] and as such, they continuously distribute data about themselves, and most of this information is connected to others.

Another consequence of this special character trait of information is the duration of this bond between person and information: Typically, there is a lifelong connection to all information acquired during the lifespan of a person. Age of data or the time span between the emergence of an information and its use do not in general diminish the power of data protection or privacy.[26]

Finally, in reference to an earlier observation: Information typically has no value on its own. It is a resource for making decisions: By incorporating the information present, decision-makers can act on it. However, this relationship between decisions and information only works one way, if at all. It is typically impossible to deduct from a decision the information and the sources which went into it. This has two effects: One is that the price for information is highly dependent on the individual preferences and contexts of the decision-maker; the other is that control of the flow of information is highly difficult to obtain as it would require exact knowledge not only of the information present and its sources but also of the normative values of the decision and the evaluation of potentially uncertain information.

---

from smart watches or activity trackers. The authority uses the app user's 'donated' data for research improving the calculation basis for early recognition of Covid-19 infections. See <https://corona-datenspende.de/>; <www.aerzteblatt.de/nachrichten/112636/RKI-Mehr-als-eine-halbe-Million-Teilnehmer-bei-Datenspende-App>; <www.heise.de/ct/artikel/Corona-Datenspende-App-des-RKI-4704898.html>; <www.reuters.com/article/us-health-coronavirus-germany-tech/germany-launches-smartwatch-app-to-monitor-coronavirus-spread-idUSKBN21P1SS> accessed 27 July 2020.

25 Cf. German Federal Constitutional Court, 15 September 1983, Case 1 BvR 209/83, (1983) 65 Entscheidungen des Bundesverfassungsgerichts 1 – *Volkszählung*.

26 This was recognised by the CJEU in the Google Spain decision; Case C-131/12 *Google Spain v AEPD and Mario Costeja González* [2014] ECLI:EU:C:2014:317.

All three specialties of information and privacy lead to one core conclusion: It is impossible for the individual, the so-called data subject,[27] to enact effective control over the use and processing of his or her data. This is the case, first, because of the huge amount of data in connection with his or her person, second, because of the huge amount of data processing involving personal data that goes unnoticed due to the quality of information as non-rival and non-excludable in consumption, and third, because of the decision to not reveal which information went into building the data set.

D. Data Access under the GDPR

I. Access and Data Processing

According to Article 4 (2) GDPR, data processing covers all and any operation or even sets of operations. Examples given of data processing include 'collection, recording', 'retrieval', 'disclosure' and 'dissemination or otherwise making available'. Thus, any access to personal data is covered by data processing under the GDPR. It does not matter whether this access is provided by activities performed on the side of the data subject (e.g. disclosure or submittal) or by activities on the side of the data controller (e.g. by tracing). Similarly, it does not play a role for the categorisation as processing whether the access to the data is granted by free will or whether it is exercised in the course of *force majeur* or vested powers, e.g. by the state.

II. Right to access of data under the GDPR

The GDPR contains a number of rights and obligations which can be categorised as granting access to personal data. They can be clustered according to the claimant: With most rights, the data subject is the one to demand access; with some rights a third party may do so.

27 Art. 4 (1) GDPR.

1. Rights to access by the data subject, Article 15 GDPR

The most prominent right to access of personal data is that regulated in Article 15 GDPR: It is considered to be the backbone of the power of the data subject: Only if it is known what is saved and how personal data has been processed can the data subject claim any further rights. Therefore, transparency is the first step, but it does not suffice to enact control.

Article 15 GDPR also specifies how far the right of access can be extended: According to Article 15 (1) GDPR, certain information typically has to be revealed on request beyond the fact that there is data processing taking place, e.g. the recipients of data transfers, the duration of data storage, the source of the data if it was not collected from the data subject etc.[28]

What is problematic, however, is whether the right to access under Article 15 GDPR also extends to data which has been recombined with other data, e.g. for the purposes of profiling or scoring where the result of the profile or the score may not necessarily be connected to the data subject.[29]

It also remains questionable whether the precise technology used for these analyses may be covered by the right to access. Article 15 (1) lit. h GDPR states, of the right to access in regard to automated decision-making, that the claim also includes 'meaningful information about the logic involved' as well as consequences and significance.[30] Thus, in a first step

---

28 Matthias Bäcker, in Jürgen Kühling and Benedikt Buchner (eds), *Datenschutz-Grundverordnung, Bundesdatenschutzgesetz Kommentar* (2nd edn, Beck 2018) Art. 15 para. 9; Alexander Dix, in Spiros Simitis, Gerrit Hornung and Indra Spiecker gen. Döhmann (eds), *Datenschutzrecht. DSGVO mit BDSG* (Nomos 2019) Art. 15 para. 16. Art. 15 (1) GDPR contains a right to an affirmation of process and a right of access to all processed personal data, supplemented by the right to be provided with a copy in Art. 15 (3) GDPR. It is limited by rights and freedoms of others (Art. 15 (4) GDPR) and in case of a 'manifestly unfounded or excessive' request (Art. 12 (5) GDPR), Dix (n. 28) Art. 15 paras 12–17, 28–35; a controversy arose about the right's scope. See Philipp Zikech and Daniel Sörup, 'Der Auskunftsanspruch nach Art. 15 DSGVO' (2019) Zeitschrift für Datenschutz 239. Reacting to the decision of Regional Labour Court (*Landesarbeitsgericht*) Baden-Württemberg, 20 December 2018, Case 17 Sa 11/18, (2018), Stefan Brink and Daniel Joos, 'Reichweite und Grenzen des Auskunftsanspruchs und des Rechts auf Kopie' (2019) Zeitschrift für Datenschutz 483; Tim Wybitul and Isabelle Brahms, 'Welche Reichweite hat das Recht auf Auskunft und auf Kopie nach Art. 15 DSGVO? – Zugleich eine Analyse des Urteils des LAG Baden-Württemberg vom 20 December 2018' (2019) Neue Zeitschrift für Arbeitsrecht 672.

29 For further references see Dix (n. 28) Art. 15 No. 25 para. 58.

30 Giving an overview on the academic debate on a 'right to explanation' granted by the GDPR, Diana Dimitrova, 'The Right to Explanation under the Right of Ac-

the data subject may indeed claim the information about the applied technology. This does not, however, include an explanation of the precise decision-making method. Also, the phrasing of Article 15 (1) lit. h GDPR shows that the envisaged consequences have to be revealed and thus not the exact use and the exact consequences. While the claim is precise in regard to the technology, it remains fuzzy in regard to the application of the information.

The right to access does not include, however, the requirement that all material be released in which the personal data is present.[31] Right to access is not the same as a right to the inspection of records or files.[32] This is in accordance with the provision of Article 15 (3) GDPR (right to a copy of the personal data), as that provision allows for presentation of the data in

cess to Personal Data: Legal Foundations in and Beyond the GDPR' (2020) 6 European Data Protection Law Review 211, 214–126. Including systematic data and factors of automated decision making, Bäcker (n. 28) Art. 15 para. 27; Dix (n. 28) Art. 15 No. 25 para. 16; similar, Bryce Godman and Seth Flaxman, 'European Union regulations on algorithmic decision-making and a "right to explanation"' (2016) Oxford Internet Institute <https://arxiv.org/pdf/1606.08813.pdf> accessed 29 July 2020. Supporting a wide reading containing logic and systematic data that is not immediately personal counteracting the discriminatory potential of automated decision-making, Johanna Mazur, 'Right to Access Information as a Collective-Based Approach to the GDPR's Right to Explanation in European Law' (2018) 11 Erasmus Law Review 178, 183–184. Recognising a right to explanation rooted in Art. 15 GDPR in conjunction with Art. 22 and Recital 71 GDPR while evincing legal and technical limitations, Maja Brkan and Grégory Bonnet, 'Legal and Technical Feasibility of the GDPR's quest for Explanation on Algorithmic Decisions: Of Black Boxes, White Boxes and Fata Morganas' (2020) 11 European Journal of Risk Regulation 18, 20–22. Arguing that a right to explanation of specific decisions cannot be derived from the right to access, Sandra Wachter, Brent Mittelstadt and Luciano Floridi, 'Why a Right to Explanation of Automated Decision-Making Does Not Exist in the General Data Protection Regulation' (2017) 7 International Data Privacy Law 76, 83–90. Criticising the focus of discussion on a right to explanation as a core solution for opacity of automated decisions and algorithmic faults, Lilian Edwards and Michael Veale, 'Slave to the Algorithm: Why a Right to an Explanation Is Probably Not the Remedy You Are Looking for' (2017–2018) 16 Duke Law & Technology Review 18, 24–61.

31 Dix (n. 28) Art. 15 para. 17. Concerning inspection of records in German taxation procedure, Anna Sophie Poschenrieder, 'Ein Recht auf Auskunft begründet kein Akteneinsichtsrecht. Grenzen von Art. 15 DSGVO im Besteuerungsverfahren' (2020) 1–2 Deutsches Steuerrecht 21, 23.

32 Dix (n. 28) Art. 15 para. 17.

that format in which they are present with the data controller.[33] The right to obtain a copy in Article 15 (3) GDPR allows for additional control by the data subject because the right to access according to Article 15 (1) GDPR by itself would require the data subject to accept the information presented by the data controller while the copy of the data undergoing processing allows for further, including technological, conclusions.[34]

Finally, the result of the right of access is that the data subject may be able to enact a better judgment on further steps of action, e.g. a complaint to the supervisory authority or a request for erasure. The right of access is not originally meant to enable the data subject to make use of this data.[35] It remains questionable, therefore, whether the right to access gives the data subject the right to use the data from the data controller in an unrestricted way,[36] as trade and business secrets or at least trade and business interests of the data controller may be affected if the data subject makes use of the accessed data. It is clear, however, that the data subject may use the right of access and all information received under it in data-breach-related

---

33 Touching upon synchronous extent and difference in presentation format as regards right of access from Art. 15 (1), Malte Engeler and Daniel Quiel, 'Recht auf Kopie und Auskunftsanspruch im Datenschutzrecht' (2019) Zeitschrift für Datenschutz 2201, 2202–2203; with reference to the CJEU's decision relating to Art. 12 lit.a DPD (Joined Cases Case C- 141/12 and C-372/12 *YS v Minister voor Immigratie, Integratie en Asiel, and Minister voor Immigratie, Integratie en Asiel v M, S* [2014] ECLI:EU:C:2014:2081), Tim Wybitul and Isabelle Brahms, 'Welche Reichweite hat das Recht auf Auskunft und das Recht auf eine Kopie nach Art. 15 I DS-GVO?' (2019) Neue Zeitschrift für Arbeitsrecht 672, 674–676. Dissenting, Sascha Kremer, 'Das Auskunftsrecht der betroffenen Person in der DSGVO' (2018) Computer und Recht 560, 564 para. 34.

34 Dissent exists on the basis of the exact nature and scope of the relationship between the right of access and the right of being provided a copy. Outlining that both are autonomous rights, Stefan Brink and Daniel Joos, 'Reichweite und Grenzen des Auskunftsanspruchs und des Rechts auf Kopie' (2019) Zeitschrift für Datenschutz 483, 434; Bäcker (n. 28) Art. 15 para. 39; dissenting, Philipp Zikesch and Thorsten Sörup, 'Der Auskunftsanspruch nach Art. 15 DSGVO' (2019) Zeitschrift für Datenschutz 239, 239–240; Dix (n. 28) Art. 15 para. 28.

35 Rather, it serves as a security for transparency and law enforcement: Boris P. Paal, in Boris P. Paal and Daniel A. Pauly (eds), *Datenschutz-Grundverordnung, Bundesdatenschutzgesetz* (2nd edn, Beck 2018) Art. 15 para. 3; Bäcker (n. 28) Art. 15 para. 5; Margot E. Kaminski, 'Binary Governance: Lessons from the GDPR's Approach to Algorithmic Accountability' (2019) 92 Southern California Law Review 1529, 1587.

36 The GDPR does not put the data subject's legal position in concrete terms, cf. Angela Sobolciakova, 'Right of Access under GDPR and Copyright' (2018) 12 Masaryk University Journal of Law and Technology 221, 226–227.

activities, ie information of the supervisory authority or a request for erasure. This right of use against private parties is derived not only indirectly from the purpose of Article 15 GDPR to enable control that needs to be effective but also from Article 6 (1) lit. f GDPR: The interests of the data controller cannot override the interests of the data subject in the case of a violation.

2. *Right to data portability, Article 20 GDPR*

The GDPR does not include many innovative regulatory tools in comparison to the DPD, but Article 20 GDPR certainly is one. As this provision will be the core of another paper in this volume, this paper will only look at the provision from the standpoint of access to data from the special perspective of data protection.

Article 20 GDPR is a clear sign that data protection is increasingly including a consumer law perspective and also competition law aspects.[37] Article 20 GDPR reacts to the special qualities of many service providers as part of a larger network economy in which the economy of scale and scope prevents functioning competition.[38] Although this creates information asymmetry and a lack of control by actors other than the data subject and thus refers to some of the concerns of data protection law, the regulation

---

37 Cf. Article 29 Data Protection Working Party, WP 242 rev. 01, (2017) 4 <http://ec.europa.eu/newsroom/document.cfm?doc_id=44099> accessed 27 July 2020; Inge Graef, Martin Husovec and Nadezhda Purtova, 'Data Portability and Data Control: Lessons for an Emerging Concept in EU Law' (2018) 19 German Law Journal 1359, 1375; Helena Ursic, 'Unfolding the New-Born Right to Data Portability: Four Gateways to Data Subject Control' (2018) 15 SCRIPTed (Journal) 42, 44.

38 Lucio Scudiero, 'Bringing Your Data Everywhere: A Legal Reading of the Right to Portability' (2017) 3 European Data Protection Law Review 119, 119. See the resolution of the German National Data Protection Conference, stating the role of the data portability right in strengthening consumers' positions and limiting market-dominating positions: 'Entschließung Marktmacht und informationelle Selbstbestimmung, 88. Konferenz der Datenschutzbeaugten des Bundes und der Länder, 08./09. Oktober 2014', <www.bfdi.bund.de/SharedDocs/Publikationen/Entschliessungssammlung/DSBundLaender/88DSK_Marktmacht.html?nn=5217228> accessed 27 July 2020. The right to data portability was originally targeted to counteract so-called 'lock-in effects', especially in the context of social networking platforms; Dix (n. 28) Art. 20 para. 1; Gerrit Hornung, 'Eine Datenschutz-Grundverordnung für Europa? Licht und Schatten im Kommissionsentwurf vom 25. Januar 2012' (2012) Zeitschrift für Datenschutz 99, 103.

of a failing market order are not the prime interests of data protection.[39] Article 20 GDPR now illustrates that data protection law is becoming more and more a tool for other regulatory aspirations, as well, predominant among them consumer protection law and competition law.[40]

Under Article 20 GDPR, the data subject may request personal data present with a data controller to be presented to him or her in such a way that the data subject may transfer this data to another data controller. Article 20 (2) GDPR clarifies that the data subject may also request a direct transfer from the data controller to another party and need not undergo the effort of becoming a mediator of services.

Thus, consumers are enabled to switch to another service provider with minimal outlay and without loss of data. From an economic view obstacles to market access are reduced, hence conditions of competition should be ensured.[41] The right to data portability, which includes access and transfer services, aims to safeguard the data subject's control over transmission between processors and to extend possibilities of self-determined decision-

---

39 Cf. Article 29 Data Protection Working Party, WP 242 rev. 01, (2017) 4 <http://ec.europa.eu/newsroom/document.cfm?doc_id=44099> accessed 27 July 2020.

40 For the latter cf. only the decision of the German antitrust agency (*Bundeskartellamt*) against Facebook of February 2019; Bundeskartellamt, 'Bundeskartellamt prohibits Facebook from combining user data from different sources' (6 February 2019) <www.bundeskartellamt.de/SharedDocs/Meldung/EN/Pressemitteilungen/2019/07_02_2019_Facebook.html> accessed 27 July 2020; as well as the two consecutive court decisions, Düsseldorf Higher Regional Court, 26 August 2019, VI Kart 1/19 (V), (2019) Multimediarecht 742; German Federal Supreme Court, 23 June 2020, KVR-69/19, <https://www.bundesgerichtshof.de/SharedDocs/Pressemitteilungen/DE/2020/2020080.html?nn=10690868> accessed 4 August 2020 (press release), in the end upholding the decision. Thus, data protection violations were used as a shoehorn for competition law impact. See for comments on the antitrust authority's decision in the literature, Christina Etteldorf, 'Data Protection from a Different Perspective: German Competition Authority Targets Facebook's Data Usage' (2019) 5 European Data Protection Law Review 238; Irene Lorenzo-Rego, 'The Perspective of the Bundeskartellamt in the Evaluation of Facebook's Behaviour: Prior Considerations and Possible Impact' (2019) 3 European Competition and Regulatory Law Review 100; Christoph Becher, 'A Closer Look at the FCO's Facebook Decision' (2019) 3 European Competition and Regulatory Law Review 116.

41 Michael Strubel, 'Anwendungsbereich des Rechts auf Datenübertragbarkeit. Auslegung des Art. 20 DS-GVO unter Berücksichtigung der Guidelines der Article 29-Datenschutzgruppe' (2017) Zeitschrift für Datenschutz 355, 355.

making;[42] simultaneously it is geared towards the goal of regulating market monopoly.[43]

It should be noted that access to data under Article 20 GDPR is limited to data which has been processed on the basis of either consent or a contractual relationship (Article 20 (1) lit. a GDPR).

The exact impact of Article 20 GDPR is still unclear in regard to the scope of data that is covered. It can be argued that only data which the data subject has actively submitted to the data controller or knows that is being processed is captured by the provision in order not to have Article 20 GDPR become a super-right for any type of access to any type of data including evaluation or analysis data.[44]

III. Right to access of data by others than the data subject

Data protection law does protect data and it assures controllability, but it does not hinder data processing. Rather, as any technology regulatory law, it aims at avoiding the pitfalls of digitalisation. On the other hand, this means data protection law is not preventing data processing that follows certain procedures, restricts an overarching impact and remains within the boundaries of the GDPR. Similarly, access of data is not something that the GDPR explicitly forbids but rather restricts in the interest of the data subject and common goals.

---

42 Improving the data subject's control of its personal data is mentioned in Recital 68 sentence 1 GDPR. See also Article 29 Data Protection Working Party, WP 242 rev. 01, (2017) 6 <http://ec.europa.eu/newsroom/document.cfm?doc_id=44099> accessed 27 July 2020; Ursic (n. 37) 44, 58–60; Graef, Husovec and Purtova (n. 37) 1365–1366.

43 Cf. Peter Schantz, 'Die Datenschutz-Grundverordnung – Beginn einer neuen Zeitrechnung im Datenschutzrecht?' (2016) Neue Juristische Wochenschrift 1841, 1845; Ursic (n. 37) 58–59; cf. Graef, Husovec and Purtova (n. 37) 1365, 1369.

44 Dix (n. 28) Art. 20 para. 8; Tobias Herbst, in Jürgen Kühling and Benedikt Buchner (eds), *Datenschutzgrundverordnung Kommentar* (C.H. Beck 2017) Art. 20 No. 11; cf. Article 29 Data Protection Working Party, WP 242 rev. 01, (2017) 10–11 <http://ec.europa.eu/newsroom/document.cfm?doc_id=44099> accessed 27 July 2020; Scudiero (n. 38) 123; Heike Schweitzer, 'Datenzugang in der Datenökonomie: Eckpfeiler einer neuen Informationsordnung' (2019) Gewerblicher Rechtsschutz und Urheberrecht 569, 574. Giving an overview on differing views, Kai von Lewinski, in Stefan Brink and Heinrich A. Wolff (eds), *Beck'scher Online-Kommentar Datenschutzrecht* (C.H.Beck 2020) Art. 20 paras 37–48.

Consequently, the GDPR includes a number of provisions under which access to data can be obtained by parties other than the data subject. They shall – in an overview – be the content of this section. It should be noted that some of these provisions within the GDPR are not formulated as a direct right which can be exercised, but are often more subtly included in other provisions that deal with data processing as such. It should not be forgotten that data access is a type of data processing, and as such some of the provisions may yield data access in a much broader sense than typically associated with the data protection legal regime.

1. *Consent or legal ground as basis for data processing, Article 6 (1) GDPR*

Considering this data access as data processing the first and most important way of gaining access to data protected under the GDPR would be to adhere to the standards of the GDPR on data processing.

Most importantly, the GDPR contains a number of legitimate grounds on which any type of data processing and thus also access to data can be enabled. Within the more specific provisions of Article 6 GDPR, a number of interests are weighted on a general level, taking into account special situations and special circumstances of typical data processing such as contractual or legal obligations or also life-threatening situations. Article 6 (1) lit. f GDPR, finally, opens desirable data processing for a more individualised balancing test, at least between private data controllers.

It should be noted that this generalisation of balancing of interests inherent in Article 6 (1) GDPR takes into account interests on the side of the data processor and potential further third parties who would profit from the data processing and also interests on the side of the data subject and potential further third parties which are affected by data processing.[45] This needs mentioning because the wording in Article 6 (1) GDPR is not always precise. For example, Article 6 (1) lit. f GDPR mentions on the one hand 'interests pursued by the controller or by a third party' and on the other hand 'interests […] of the data subject'. Article 1 (1) GDPR, however, and the aforementioned general purpose of the GDPR, make clear

45 Cf. Peter Schantz, in Stefan Brink and Heinrich A. Wolff (eds), *Beck'scher Online-Kommentar Datenschutzrecht* (C.H.Beck 2020) Art. 1 para. 7. Specific to Art. 6 lit. f GDPR, Schantz (n. 11) Art. 6 paras 98–99, 101–102. A number of interests to be included are identified in Indra Spiecker gen. Döhmann, 'A new framework for information markets: Google Spain' (2015) Common Market Law Review 1033, 1046 et seq.

that data processing not only has effects on the data subject but also on third parties, who are judged on the basis of information gathered from individuals.[46] Thus, on both sides of the scale not only the interests of the parties involved directly, but also the effects on the whole, have to be integrated. This explains why the data protection legal regime is not restricted to certain elements within the information cycle but covers all steps and also integrates effects going beyond individual legal interests and rights and thus offers a comprehensive solution.

The GDPR points out manifold reasons, beyond a balancing of interests in the individual case (typical of this is Artice 6 (1) lit. f GDPR), for granting access. Here, some little-regarded interests shall be pointed out, in particular as they are used as an argument why an extensive data access regime is necessary. The GDPR opens personal data to these purposes so the need for additional access rights is not necessarily pressing.

Foremost, one should mention Article 6 (1) lit. d GDPR which allows for processing necessary 'in order to protect the vital interests of the data subject or of another natural person'. This covers a number of catastrophic, pandemic or life-threatening situations in which data processing assists in curing or at least relieving imminent dangers. Even if Article 9 (1) GDPR is considered to be an additional threshold to health-related data,[47] in a number of cases the clause of Article 9 (2) lit. c GDPR covers even the processing of special data and consent will always be possible according to Article 9 (2) lit. c and 9 (2) lit. a GDPR.

Likewise granting very wide access to data are the provisions of Article 6 (1) lit. c and lit. e GDPR when the purpose of the data processing can be subsumed under the goal of furthering the common good. While the meaning of Article 6 (1) lit. c and e GDPR is often confined to the opening

---

46 Cf. Schantz (n. 11) Art. 6 para.102; Joshua A. Fairfield and Christoph Engel, 'Privacy as a Public Good' (2015) 65 Duke Law Journal 385, 396–406.

47 Cf. Recital 51 sentence 5; Thomas Petri, in Spiros Simitis, Gerrit Hornung and Indra Spiecker gen. Döhmann (eds), *Datenschutzrecht. DSGVO mit BDSG* (Nomos 2019) Art. 9 No. 24; Marion Albers and Raoul-Darius Veit, in Stefan Brink and Heinrich A. Wolff (eds), *Beck'scher Online-Kommentar Datenschutzrecht* (C.H.Beck 2020) Art. 20 paras 37–48; Thilo Weichert, in Jürgen Kühling and Benedikt Buchner (eds), *Datenschutzgrundverordnung Kommentar* (C.H. Beck 2017) Art. 9 No. 4; contradicting this, Frenzel (n. 16) Art. 9 No. 18; Alexander Schiff, in Eugen Ehmann and Martin Selmayr (eds), *DS-GVO Kommentar* (C.H. Beck 2017) Art. 9 No. 9.

clause for member state public interest laws it contains,[48] its importance initially rests in making data protection law applicable for all public interest causes. Thus, although data access in the public interest has to keep in mind the principle of proportionality and may not overburden data protection interests, it nevertheless can be an important reason why data processing is possible.

A similarly hidden door opener to wide access of data is the legitimation clause of Article 6 (1) lit. c GDPR, according to which a legal obligation may cause the access to data. As the legal obligation has to be enacted either by member-state or Union law, there has to be an overriding public interest in this data access.[49]

Thus, under this clause, a number of data accesses in the public interest can be legitimised, and considering the special interests in member states or the Union, very specific interests can be served.

It should be stated, however, that public interests cannot be freely construed and enacted without restrictions but are limited themselves. The principle of proportionality[50] has already been mentioned. Also, they need to have a constitutional or other foundation within member state law, and they may not be construed to violate the core principles of EU law, in particular Articles 7 and 8 of the EU Charter protecting the interests of data, communication and privacy. Thus, ethical or other normative standards, which are sometimes voiced to enable free data access, are not sufficient if they do not have a legal foundation. This is especially true for arguments such as a duty under a principle of solidarity which is raised as a reason for

---

48 Art. 6 (6 (2) and (3) GDPR contain opening clauses in regard to data processing covered by lit. c. While there is some debate over the relationship and scope of the opening clause(s) – cf. Alexander Roßnagel, in Spiros Simitis, Gerrit Hornung and Indra Spiecker gen. Döhmann (eds), *Datenschutzrecht. DSGVO mit BDSG* (Nomos 2019) Art. 6 No. 16–21; Albers and Veit (n. 47) Art. 6 No. 35; Julian Wagner and Alexander Benecke, 'National Legislation within the Framework of the GDPR' (2016) 2 European Data Protection Law Review 353, 354–355 –, its function as gateway for European or national legislation concerning data processing by 'public bodies' is emphasised consistently; cf. Roßnagel (ibid.) Art. 6 para. 52; Benedikt Buchner and Jürgen Kühling, in Jürgen Kühling and Benedikt Buchner (eds), *Datenschutzgrundverordnung Kommentar* (C.H. Beck 2017) Art. 6 No. 83; Wagner and Benecke (ibid) 354.

49 Cf. Roßnagel (n. 48) Art. 6 No. 1 para. 53.

50 Art. 6 (6 (3), fourth sentence GDPR. It should be noted that every legal obligation governing the processing of personal data restricts the freedom under Art. 8 of the EU Charter of Fundamental Rights. Art. 52 (1) second sentence of the Charter requires its accordance with the principle of proportionality. See Roßnagel (n. 48) Art. 6 No. 35.

disclosure and access to information, e.g. in discussions on the legality and desirability of data donations. Even in public health care systems, solidarity is restricted to certain legal forms; in Germany, for instance, solidarity can only be an argument in regard to the financial contribution within the health care system but not in regard to the behaviour of patients and citizens.[51]

2. *Limitation of purpose and extension of purpose*

There are a number of general principles within data protection law; some are listed in Article 5 (1) GDPR.

a) The strict binding of data processing to a specific purpose

Under the DPD, the limitation of purpose was a stronghold of data protection principles. Under the GDPR, a similar and even more explicit formulation can be found in Article 5 (1) lit. b GDPR.

The purpose limitation works two ways:[52] It first binds every gathering of personal data to a 'specified, explicit and legitimate' purpose. Thus, the collection (and storage) of data for no specific reason is unlawful under the GDPR.[53] In a second step, the purpose limitation binds every consecutive step following the original gathering of data to this exact same original

---

51 Cf Sec. 1 German Social Code (*Sozialgesetzbuch*) Part V. See in regard to health insurance as a community of solidarity and the incompatibility of a behaviour-based health insurance system with solidarity the German Ethic Board's statement, Deutscher Ethikrat, 'Big Data und Gesundheit – Datensouveränität als informationelle Freiheitsgestaltung' (2018) 11, 230–237, <www.ethikrat.org/fileadmin/Publikationen/Stellungnahmen/deutsch/stellungnahme-big-data-und-gesundheit.pdf> accessed 1 August 2020; Executive Summary: <www.ethikrat.org/fileadmin/Publikationen/Stellungnahmen/englisch/opinion-big-data-and-health-summary.pdf> accessed 27 July 2020.

52 For a more detailed approach cf. Maximilian von Grafenstein, *The Principle of Purpose Limitation in Data Protection Laws* (Nomos 2018) 425 et seq.

53 Roßnagel (n. 48) Art. 5 No. 72; Schantz (n. 45) Art. 5 No. 13; cf. Zarsky (n. 11) 1006. In regard to purpose under the DPD, Article 29 Data Protection Working Party, WP 203 (2013) 15 <https://ec.europa.eu/justice/article-29/documentation/opinion-recommendation/files/2013/wp203en.pdf> accessed 27 July 2020.

purpose.[54] This is important to note, as a common misunderstanding[55] believes a legitimation to be sufficient only for the first step of data processing, which would then justify all further processing of this data, e.g. the transfer of it to other parties.[56] This is, however, not the case under the GDPR.

In consequence, a situation is created by which the data subject may control the flow of his or her data to the first controller and the more precise circumstances of processing. The purpose itself can be broader or more narrow depending on the weight of infringement: The more infringing the data processing potentially is, the more precisely must the purpose be defined in order to allow a proper assessment.[57]

However, the GDPR contains two big exceptions from the strict principle of binding purpose which allow for further accessing of data despite the boundaries from the purpose limitation. Both are integrated into Article 5 (1) lit. b GDPR. The first one allows for secondary purposes for which data can be processed, so-called compatible purposes, and the second one allows for different entities and different purposes and reacts to the inter-

54 Herbst (n. 44) Art. 5 No. 38. Further issues of admissibility arise just in cases of consecutive processing for another purpose (compatible/incompatible): Herbst (ibid.) Art. 5 No. 22–24; Schantz (n. 45) Art. 5 No. 18–19; Roßnagel (n. 48) Art. 5 No. 92–93, 96–102; with respect to the DPD, see Article 29 Data Protection Working Party, WP 203 (2013) 12 <https://ec.europa.eu/justice/article-29/documentation/opinion-recommendation/files/2013/wp203en.pdf> accessed 27 July 2020; cf. von Grafenstein (n. 52) 34.

55 Part of this misunderstanding arises from an unclear distinction between consecutive data processing for the original purpose and consecutive data processing for a different, albeit potentially compatible purpose.

56 On the question of purpose-compatible further processing, Roßnagel (n. 48) Art. 5 No. 97–99; Lukas Feiler, Nikolaus Forgo and Michaela Weigl, *The EU General Data Protection Regulation (GDPR): A Commentary* (Globe Law and Business Ltd 2018) Art. 6 No. 14; Jürgen Kühling and Mario Martini, 'Die Datenschutz-Grundverordnung: Revolution oder Evolution im europäischen und deutschen Datenschutzrecht?' (2016) 27 Europäische Zeitschrift für Wirtschaftsrecht 448, 451. For instance, in US law, the US Federal Information Privacy Law (esp. FRCA) basically legitimises data processing for a wide range of purposes, exempting processing for employment purposes or when medical data is contained, where consent by an opt-in mechanism is required; Paul M. Schwartz and Karl-Nikolaus Peifer, 'Transatlantic Data Privacy Law' (2017) 106 Georgetown Law Journal 115, 153.

57 Schantz (n. 45) Art. 5 No. 15; with respect to the DPD: Article 29 Data Protection Working Party, WP 203 (2013) 15–16 <https://ec.europa.eu/justice/article-29/documentation/opinion-recommendation/files/2013/wp203en.pdf> accessed 27 July 2020.

ests of 'archiving purposes in the public interest, scientific or historical research purposes or statistical purposes' within the meaning and the boundaries of Article 89 GDPR when these are in accordance with the original purpose.

b) Compatible other purposes

The GDPR – as did the DPD – distinguishes in principle two types of purposes: One type is the original purpose, which may allow for a number of consecutive and parallel instances of data processing once data has been legally obtained under this purpose if further steps are necessary to achieve this purpose. The second type contains all other purposes that may occur with the data which has been obtained under another purpose. This other purpose-oriented data processing is not justified under the original legitimation of the data processing. As a consequence, any data processing for such an 'other purpose' would be unlawful if it could not be justified by itself, and this would require a complete new testing.

The GDPR now opens up another venue by a fiction: According to Article 5 (1) lit. b GDPR's difficult terminology, there exists a 'compatible purpose'. This is, in the above typology, a different purpose from the original one.[58] However, the legal fiction declares such compatible purposes to be covered by the original purpose and thus legal under the same legal grounds and adherence to procedural standards.[59] A change of purpose is thus legally harmless.

Article 6 (4) GDPR gives guidelines as to which factors should be taken into account in order to assess whether a new purpose is compatible, ie the context and the relationship between data subject and data controller (Ar-

58 Schantz (n. 45) Art. 5 Nr 18; Herbst (n. 44) Art. 5 No. 24, 42. Dissenting, Roßnagel (n. 48) Art. 5 No. 97.

59 Further processing for a compatible purpose fulfilling GDPR requirements (e.g. Art. 6 (6 (1) GDPR) is lawful, whereas consecutive processing for an incompatible purpose is unlawful per se. See also Schantz (n. 45) Art. 5 No. 23; Herbst (n. 45) Art. 5 No. 24, 28–29, 47–49; Jessica Bell and others, 'Balancing Data Subjects' Rights and Public Interest Research' (2019) 5 European Data Protection Law Review 43, 48; cf. the difference between the final version and the wording of Art. 5 lit. b GDPR in the Commission proposal interpreted by Article 29 Data Protection Working Party, WP 203 (2013) 36 <https://ec.europa.eu/justice/article-29/documentation/opinion-recommendation/files/2013/wp203en.pdf> accessed 31 August 2020. Dissenting, Roßnagel (n. 48) Art. 5 No. 96–99.

ticle 6 (4) lit. b GDPR), or the consequences of the new purpose-oriented data processing in comparison to the original intended consequences.

In the end, the establishment of compatible other purposes enlarges the possibilities under which data can be accessed because a transfer of data to another entity and another data controller may well be in accordance with the new purpose. Once legally obtained, data may then be continuously used for other purposes, as well. The new controller, however, should take care to inform itself about the restrictions of the original data processing, as those restrictions still apply under the new purpose.[60] This also covers the event that the original purpose is fulfilled. In this case, the justification for the compatible purpose also ceases to apply.

c) Archiving, Research and Statistics as privileged purposes

The second exception is also rooted in Article 5 (1) lit. b GDPR itself. It reacts to a special conflict of interests between the privacy interests of a data subject and the interests in continuous use of personal data for archiving, research and statistics.[61]

All three of these purposes are declared to be compatible purposes per se; further limitations are not expressed. In particular, Article 6 (4) GDPR does not apply and thus no individual balancing of interests takes place; the legitimation for the original processing is extended to the processings for these purposes.

The GDPR recognises this flaw and refers to Article 89 GDPR, according to which any processing for these purposes 'shall be subject to appropriate safeguards' (Article 89 (1) GDPR). These include the requirement to anonymise as early as possible (Article 89 (1), last sentence, GDPR).

This provision in Article 5 (1) lit. b GDPR answers concerns from the side of these interests, in particular research interests, which are often raised when claiming that a comprehensive legal regime to free access of

60 Cf. Roßnagel (n. 48) Art. 5 No. 93; Herbst (n. 45) Art. 5 No. 23; Frenzel (n. 16) Art. 5 No. 29.

61 Alexander Roßnagel, 'Datenschutz in der Forschung' (2019) Zeitschrift für Datenschutz 157, 159; Thilo Weichert, 'Die Forschungsprivilegierung in der DSGVO' (2020) Zeitschrift für Datenschutz 18, 18–19. Disagreement remains on whether the ground for privileged status is that these purposes are more highly valued, Weichert (ibid.) 21, or that these purposes are not connected to the data subject, Frenzel (n. 16) Art. 5 No. 32; Roßnagel (n. 48) Art. 5 No. 104. Taking both aspects into account, Herbst (n. 45) Art. 5 para. 52.

data has to be established. Frequently, it is argued in the interest of research and scientific purposes, based on the assumption that data protection in this regard blocks access and processing, that the data protection regime should be abandoned.[62] These assumptions, however, do not show a consideration for the purposes of the GDPR and they do not reflect the GDPR's standing towards research and scientific interests properly. These purposes are privileged under the GDPR already, and this privilege allows for wide access to existing personal data. Thus, a further research exemption or a further regulatory impact on research data is not necessary as such. Rather, one can ask why there seems to be a desire for almost limitless access to personal data.

Any legal regime could make use of the opening clauses in Article 89 (2) GDPR under which the member states (or EU law) may provide for derogations from central rights of the data subject and thus encroach even further on data subjects' rights than the privilege itself does. This is the case because the GDPR does not provide any obvious restriction on the terminology or the exact purposes of research and science.[63] So any type of science – as obscure and controversial as it may be – could claim the privilege of Article 89 GDPR.[64]

Considering the wide impact of statistical and scientific data processing, a completely unlimited privileging would make the GDPR devoid of application in an area where the risks of automated decision-making and of wide use of personal data that it is intended to mitigate are particularly present. The development, and often the application of Big Data, artificial intelligence, ubiquitous computing, direct marketing, profiling, tracking and scoring would all fall under statistical and/or research purposes and

62 E.g. Amy Kristin Sanders, 'The GDPR One Year Later: Protecting Privacy or Preventing Access to Information' (2019) 93 Tulane Law Review 1229. Dissenting, Kim Leonard Smouter-Umans, 'GDPR and Research: Is the GDPR Eventually Going to Be Good or Bad for Research?' (2018) 2 International Journal for the Data Protection Officer, Privacy Officer & Privacy Counsel 29; Mike Hintze, 'Science and Privacy: Data Protection Laws and Their Impact on Research' (2019) 14 Washington Journal of Law, Technology & Arts 103, 121.

63 See Recital 159, sentences 2–3.

64 Cf. Carolyn Eichler, in Stefan Brink and Heinrich A. Wolff (eds), *Beck'scher Online-Kommentar Datenschutzrecht* (C.H.Beck 2020) Art. 89 paras 3, 7; Alexander Roßnagel, 'Datenschutz in der Forschung' (2019) Zeitschrift für Datenschutz 157, 159; Benedikt Buchner and Marie-Theres Tinnefeld, in Kühling and Buchner, *Datenschutz-Grundverordnung* (n. 28) Art. 89 No. 13. Contradicting this, Johannes Caspar, in Simitis, Hornung and Spiecker gen. Döhmann, *Datenschutzrecht* (n. 2) Art. 89 No. 25; Weichert (n. 61) 20–21.

thus be widely exempted from the bindings of the purpose limitation and many other restrictions of the GDPR.[65] Therefore, restrictions of the purposes of research for data access have to be derived from the inherent meaning and structure of the GDPR itself.

The context of the exceptions help in construing a meaningful description of research and of statistics. That this is the goal of the GDPR itself, rather than unlimited access and data processing for these purposes, can be seen in the wording and the recitals. Archiving, the first of the three special purposes, is restricted by the wording 'public interest'. Also, Recital 162, sentence 5, GDPR clarifies that statistical data may only be aggregated data. The existence of Articles 7 and 8 of the EU Charter of Fundamental Rights requires an interpretation which leaves ample room for the general goals of the GDPR.[66]

Without being able to go further into detail in this paper, the seemingly wide research clause has to be read as research in the public interest. This does not prevent private research from profiting from Articles 89 and 5 (1) lit. b GDPR, as Recital 50 clarifies. But it does exclude a completely commercialised research interested only in commercial use and the own interest of the researching institution.[67] Public interest can be demonstrated by other tools than public research, e.g. by being publicly funded, by being made publicly available (e.g. by patents, licences for use) and by being published and transparent. Thus, any research which aims at remaining a trade and business secret is not considered to be a compatible purpose, just as private archiving or individualised statistical evaluation is not covered.

In the end, this interpretation allows access to data for research purposes in the common interest. It also enables data protection interests and research interests to be aligned.

65 Similar, Johannes Caspar, in Simitis, Hornung and Spiecker gen. Döhmann, *Datenschutzrecht* (n. 2) Art. 89, No. 17; Benedikt Buchner and Marie-Theres Tinnefeld, in Stefan Brink and Heinrich A. Wolff (eds), *Beck'scher Online-Kommentar Datenschutzrecht* (C.H.Beck 2020) Art. 89 para. 12; Weichert (n. 61) 20–21. Although arguing that the purpose limitation principle hinders big data uses significantly, Tal Z. Zarsky assumes that commercial big data analyses cannot be included in statistical purposes; Zarsky (n. 11) 1105–1007.

66 Cf. Johannes Caspar, in Simitis, Hornung and Spiecker gen. Döhmann, *Datenschutzrecht.* (n. 2) Art. 15 No. 32 et seq.

67 Ibid. Art. 15 No. 16; Weichert (n. 61) 20–21.

3. *Freedom of expression, media, press and journalistic purposes, Article 85 (1) GDPR*

Similarly, Article 85 (1) GDPR requires member states to establish a regulatory regime which enables freedom of expression as well as the institutionalised human rights of the media from both an institutionalised and a personal ('journalistic purposes') perspective.

4. *Transparency and freedom of information, Article 85 (1) GDPR*

Article 5 (1) lit. b GDPR, with its extension of the purpose limitation, privileges research, archiving and statistics in a particular way. However, in Article 85 (1) GDPR, the explicit necessity to reconcile data protection interests and interests in transparency and freedom of information is mentioned and left to member state law.

E. *Guidelines for a regulatory regime in conformance with data protection*

Having thus sketched the general framework of the GDPR on how personal data can be assessed, it becomes clear that data protection does not exclude access to data. Rather, it aims at creating access to data in a way that is socially and personally desirable and which – as the purpose limitation illustrates – is limited and controllable. Thus, the GDPR restricts access to data and creates an individualised approach without banning it or being unfriendly towards data processing. Rather, this approach is able to take into account some of the background noise of what data can positively and negatively achieve in the decisions being drafted on the basis of these.

The insights on a meta-level should not be forgotten when analysing the data protection regime as a potential starting point for a wide data access regime.

I. Proactive versus reactive regime

Data protection law as such and the GDPR in all its specificity are technology laws,[68] functioning according to the insights on how to regulate technologies whose development and effects are not yet fully known or indeed predictable. This is very much true for digitalisation and information technology: The tremendous speed in which this technology evolves, the huge investments by private and public actors, the new ubiquity of information technology and data processing, the difficulty of assessing the results of data in decisions and the technology's psychological, cognitive and educational effects are just a few very obvious examples of the unknowns in this multi-actor, complex field.

Experiences from technology law and the understanding of state decision-making under conditions of uncertainty teach us in circumstances such as these to use a proactive, preventive concept of regulation combined with close monitoring and high flexibility and with clear models and structures.[69] Risk prevention, and not security management, has to be the guiding principle.

II. Irreversible and uncontrollable consequences versus liability and damages

Data protection law pays close attention to the understanding that data rights violations are not damages that can easily be controlled for and compensated. As any loss of data means uncontrollable access to this data and potential further use and distribution including recombination with other data, the characteristic of information and privacy as common goods[70] have to be reflected in any regulatory regime. Typical regulatory concepts

68 Cf. on the term 'technology law', Milos Vec, *Kurze Geschichte des Technikrechts* (Springer 2011) 3–91, 4–8; in regard to computer law, Thomas Dreier and Oliver Meyer-Brandt, 'Computerrecht' in Martin Schule and Rainer Schröder (eds), *Handbuch des Technikrechts* (2nd edn, Springer 2003) 823; and data security, Hannes Federrath and Andreas Pfitzmann, 'Datensicherheit' in Schule and Schröder (ibid) 857; in regard to the relationship between technology and data protection law, Hornung and Spiecker gen. Döhmann (n. 2) Einleitung paras 244–249; declaring the aspect of information law a technology law, Michael Kloepfer, *Informationsrecht* (C.H. Beck 2002) § 1 para. 4.

69 See Indra Spiecker gen. Döhmann, *Staatliche Entscheidungen unter Unsicherheit* (Mohr Siebeck 2021, forthcoming).

70 See at C. below.

like absolute liability without culpability and easy compensation[71] do not function in conditions of such great uncertainty.

Understanding this already requires a careful defining of meaningful access to data, as the price for any later corrections has to be paid by the data subjects without being able to receive just compensation because data breaches can hardly ever be fully retracted, certainly not under conditions of professional information technology evaluation and exploitation. Data protection rights violations cannot be cancelled, and they cannot be undone.

III. Specific, controlled, anti-discrimination interests versus overall transparency and access

Transparency and free access to information for each and all sound intriguing. However, they leave out of consideration that information technology is not available for all, and that the need for information depends on the decision in which it is to be incorporated. Information can well be used for purposes which violate common understandings in society, such as anti-discrimination, equality before the law, or fair chances. The purpose and the precise interest determine whether or not it is socially, economically, legally, ethically, internationally and normatively desirable to share data, and if so, under which conditions. Thus, unlimited access to personal data and transparency without any requirement as to purpose do not serve the common interest but the interest of a select few.

F. Conclusion and Outlook

We have lived in a knowledge society long enough to understand the importance of data and also the difficulties in detecting data in decisions and controlling the flow of data once it has been started. Surprisingly, our regulatory impetus to prevent negative impact on society overall and to create a fair division of data is not reacting strongly to this: We are generous in sharing data and making available the backbone of productivity –

71 See Spiecker gen. Döhmann (n. 69).

for free. Numerous freedom of information regulatory impulses tell this story forcefully.[72]

Uncontrollability of the input of data in the output of decisions requires a three-step-test: Both the input of data, with its processing e.g. by recombination, and the outcome of the decision have to be controlled.

Data protection law approaches all three steps from a particular, personality and human rights perspective and thus offers answers to pressing questions. It also gives important guidelines for the necessary weighing of interests between the protection of data and access and distribution of data beyond personal data.

The GDPR does not address the pressing issue of the gains and the added value within the data lifecycle. It is not an instrument creating economic or social distributive justice, nor does it attribute economic value. It explicitly refrains from creating property rights, and it explicitly contradicts the notion of data being foremost an economic asset. But it is an instrument to strengthen democratic values such as liberty, freedom of decision and autonomy.

Access to data is always a decision on third parties without their inclusion, their participation or their knowledge. Modern information technology often has little interest in the individual and its individuality, which makes individual control and countermeasures even more difficult. A data-protection-friendly regulatory regime to access of data will take these third-party-effects into account and builds the limitations to data use into it.

In any decision of the legislature on whom to grant access to data the decision on the use of this data is always incorporated. Data protection's interest in binding data processing to a cause and a purpose relies on basic functionalities in situations of power. Insights into the foundations of state control can assist in finding the proper legal standards. Among these standards is the core of all rationality: If there is a legitimate reason which can be openly discussed, there is ground for data access, but data access with-

72 See, for example, Thomas Dreier and others (eds), *Informationen der Öffentlichen Hand – Zugang und Nutzung* (Nomos 2016); Spiecker gen. Döhmann (n. 8); Kloepfer (n. 68), especially § 4 paras 12–14; Jean Nicolas Druey, *Information als Gegenstand des Rechts – Entwurf einer Grundlegung* (Schulthess 1995); Herbert Burkert, 'Public Sector Information: Towards a More Comprehensive Approach in Information Law' (1992) 3 (1) Journal of Law Information and Science 47; Herbert Burkert, *Informationszugang und Datenschutz: ein kanadisches Beispiel* (Nomos 1992). Cf. in regard to consistency of regulatory instruments like the right to data portability, Graef, Husovec and Purtova (n. 37), proposing a comprehensive legal code concerning access to public information.

out clear purpose cannot claim legitimacy. This, due to the special characteristic of data, is a ground to start from.

In the end, all we know about data, about data processing and about decision-making and its control calls for a data-protection-inspired regulatory regime of data access, and that is in dubio pro data protection – including trade and business secrets!

The existing European IP rights system and the data economy – An overview with particular focus on data access and portability

Matthias Leistner[*]

A. Introduction

When the EU Commission launched its 2017 consultation 'Building the European Data Economy'[1] many commentators were rightly concerned that this might lead to the creation of a new data producer's right (or similar exclusive property rights in data) although doctrinal or empirical evidence on the need for any such right was completely lacking. The subsequent discussion has clearly shown that a data producer's exclusive property right does not contribute to the solution of the very specific problems which have to be solved in order to foster the development of functioning data markets in the EU.[2] Since then, literature has increasingly focused on

* The author thanks his research assistants Lucie Antoine and Lukas Kleeberger for valuable help with research for this chapter.

1 See European Commission, 'Public consultation on Building the European Data Economy' (2017) <https://ec.europa.eu/digital-single-market/en/news/public-consultation-building-european-data-economy> all accessed 31 August 2020.

2 Josef Drexl and others, 'Position Statement of the Max Planck Institute for Innovation and Competition of 26 April 2017 on the European Commission's 'Public consultation on Building the European Data Economy'' (2017) Max Planck Institute for Innovation and Competition Research Paper No 17–08 <www.ip.mpg.de/fileadmin/ipmpg/content/stellungnahmen/MPI_Statement_Public_consultation_on_Building_the_EU_Data_Eco_28042017.pdf> accessed 31 August 2020; Wolfgang Kerber, 'A New (Intellectual) Property Right for Non-Personal Data? An Economic Analysis' (2016) Gewerblicher Rechtsschutz und Urheberrecht Internationaler Teil 989; Wolfgang Kerber, 'Governance of Data: Exclusive Property vs. Access' (2016) 47 International Journal of Intellectual Property and Competition Law 759.

contract law,[3] competition law[4] and/or possible regulation of data access including the more recent discussion on users' access rights.[5]

Consequently, and rightly so, the EU after the initial fact finding followed a very limited, targeted approach in the data economy sector by first enacting the Regulation on free flow of non-personal data in the EU,[6] applicable as of 28 May 2019, whose main objective is to remove any remaining national law obstacles to the free movement of non-personal data within the EU, ie an almost complete abolishment of national data localisation requirements in the EU market. Moreover, the Commission has taken the important and useful initiative to formulate best practices for the contractual allocation of data in data related co-operation networks.[7] In the 2020 Communication on 'A European strategy for data'[8], the Commission concentrates (inter alia) on measures to improve access and use through a cross-sectoral data governance framework, infrastructures for hosting, processing and using data (in particular interoperability), and the develop-

3 Cf. briefly section D. below.

4 Heike Schweitzer, 'Datenzugang in der Datenökonomie: Eckpfeiler einer neuen Informationsordnung' (2019) Gewerblicher Rechtsschutz und Urheberrecht 569; Heike Schweitzer and Martin Peitz, 'Ein neuer europäischer Ordnungsrahmen für Datenmärkte?' (2018) Neue Juristische Wochenschrift 275; Jacques Crémer, Yves-Alexandre de Montjoye and Heike Schweitzer, 'Competition Policy for the digital era – Final report' (European Commission 2019) <https://ec.europa.eu/competition/publications/reports/kd0419345enn.pdf> accessed 31 August 2020; Wolfgang Kerber, 'Digital Markets, Data and Privacy: Competition Law, Consumer Law and Data Protection' (2016) Gewerblicher Rechtsschutz und Urheberrecht Internationaler Teil 639, 642–643; Jason Furman, Diane Coyle, Amelia Fletcher, Derek McAuley and Philip Marsden, 'Unlocking Digital Competition – Report of the Digital Competition Expert Panel' (UK Government 2019) <https://assets.publishing.service.gov.uk/government/uploads/system/uploads/attachment_data/file/785547/unlocking_digital_competition_furman_review_web.pdf> accessed 31 August 2020; Heiko Richter and Peter R. Slowinski, 'The Data Sharing Economy: On the Emergence of New Intermediaries' (2019) 50 International Journal of Intellectual Property and Competition Law 4.

5 See section C.IV. below.

6 Regulation (EU) 2018/1807 on a framework for the free flow of non-personal data in the European Union [2018] OJ L303/59.

7 Communication of the European Commission of 25 April 2018 – 'Towards a common European data space' COM(2018) 232 final and detailed accompanying European Commission Staff Working Document, 'Guidance on sharing private sector data in the European data economy' SWD(2018) 125 final. See further Richter and Slowinski (n. 4).

8 Communication from the Commission of 19 January 2020 to the European Parliament, the Council, the European Economic and Social Committee and the Committee of the Regions, COM(2020) 66 final.

ment of European data spaces in strategic sectors and domains of public interest. This distinctive focus on data access and portability has meanwhile led to the Commission's proposals for a Data Governance Act[9] and a Digital Markets Act (DMA).[10] In particular, the DMA, which follows a concept of targeted regulation in order to improve contestability and prevent unfair practices in the sector of so-called gatekeeper-platforms also contains data-related access and portability provisions inter alia in Article 6(1) lit. h), lit. i) and lit. j).

Apart from these targeted and useful European political projects, academic discussion on access rights has intensely continued since 2017 and developed more specific depth.[11] In particular different access scenarios have been considered. These scenarios – very roughly – comprise, first, access of lawful users to their own individual-level data (collected by the producer or service provider, e.g. in the context of IoT) and portability of such data to other operators.[12] Secondly, access of competitors to entire sets of aggregated data is discussed, where such access is necessary to establish workable competition in certain aftermarkets or complementary markets (and also, under stricter conditions, in the primary market). Thirdly, access to data generated by public bodies is a relevant case group because non-discriminatory access to such data for all interested parties can obviously generate significant positive externalities.[13] Fourthly, and specifically in the context of competition law, access to large aggregated data sets of big data

9 Proposal of 25 November 2020 for a Regulation of the European Parliament and of the Council on European data governance (Data Governance Act), COM(2020) 767 final.

10 Proposal of 15 December 2020 for a Regulation of the European Parliament and of the Council on contestable and fair markets in the digital sector (Digital Markets Act), COM(2020) 842 final.

11 See, for example, Crémer, de Montjoye and Schweitzer (n. 4); Josef Drexl, 'Data Access and Control in the Era of Connected Devices – Study on Behalf of the European Consumer Organisation BEUC' (BEUC 2018) <www.ip.mpg.de/fileadmin/ipmpg/content/aktuelles/aus_der_forschung/beuc-x-2018-121_data_access_and_control_in_the_area_of_connected_devices.pdf> accessed 31 August 2020; Data Ethics Commission of the German Federal Government (*Datenethikkommission*), 'Opinion' (2019) 90–92, 124–157 <www.bmjv.de/SharedDocs/Downloads/DE/Themen/Fokusthemen/Gutachten_DEK_EN_lang.pdf?__blob=publicationFile&v=3> accessed 31 August 2020; Schweitzer (n 4); Schweitzer and Peitz (n. 4) 279.

12 See further on this categorisation, which is also followed in this paper, Schweitzer, 'Datenzugang in der Datenökonomie' (n. 4) 572–74. Of course, different systematisations, some more detailed, exist in abundance.

13 See Richter and Slowinski (n. 4); Schweitzer (n. 4) 572; Opinion of the Data Ethics Commission (n. 11) 148; EU Commission, 'Towards a common European

conglomerates in order to develop entirely unrelated products or services has been discussed, resulting in the recent political initiative for the 10th Revision of the German Act against Restraints of Competition (*Gesetz gegen Wettbewerbsbeschränkungen, GWB*).[14]

All these case groups raise intricate problems concerning their relationship with IP protection of certain data-related creations, investments, products or processes.[15] In that regard, EU policy has increasingly focused on the role of the Database Directive[16] in different typical big data and AI use scenarios. Indeed, the Evaluation of the Database Directive by the Commission[17] as well as in particular the underlying academic Evaluation Report[18] have shown that the Database Directive is a case for imminent reform in this context.[19] However, concentration on the database sui generis

---

data space' (n. 7) 4–8; cf. Heiko Richter, '"Open Government Data" für Daten des Bundes' (2017) Neue Zeitschrift für Verwaltungsrecht 1408.

14 See Schweitzer, 'Datenzugang in der Datenökonomie' (n. 4) 576–80. As regards the Revision of the German Act against Restraints of Competition see the Government Bill Gesetzentwurf der Bundesregierung – Entwurf eines Gesetzes zur Änderung des Gesetzes gegen Wettbewerbsbeschränkungen für ein fokussiertes, proaktives und digitales Wettbewerbsrecht 4.0 und anderer wettbewerbsrechtlicher Bestimmungen (GWB-Digitalisierungsgesetz) (9 September 2020) <www.bmwi.de/Redaktion/DE/Downloads/Gesetz/gesetzentwurf-gwb-digitalisierungsgesetz.pdf?__blob=publicationFile&v=6> accessed 15 September 2020. Concerning access contained in this draft see (from an economic perspective) Wolfgang Kerber, 'Datenzugangsansprüche im Referentenentwurf zur 10. GWB-Novelle aus ökonomischer Perspektive' (2020) Wirtschaft und Wettbewerb 249.

15 The same applies in regard to their interface with the protection of personal data under the GDPR; comprehensively on IP and personal data protection with a particular view to the ongoing and future regulation of the data economy see Matthias Leistner, Lucie Antoine and Thomas Sagstetter, *Big Data – Rahmenbedingungen im europäischen Datenschutz- und Immaterialgüterrecht und übergreifende Reformperspektive* (Mohr Siebeck 2021).

16 Directive 96/9/EC of the European Parliament and of the Council of 11 March 1996 on the legal protection of databases [1996] OJ L77/20.

17 European Commission Staff Working Document, 'Executive Summary of the Evaluation of Directive 96/9/EC on the legal protection of databases' SWD(2018) 146 final.

18 Lionel Bently, Estelle Derclaye and others, 'Study in support of the evaluation of Directive 96/9/EC on the legal protection of databases – Final Report' (2018) <https://op.europa.eu/de/publication-detail/-/publication/5e9c7a51-597c-11e8-ab41-01aa75ed71a1> accessed 31 August 2020.

19 See already Matthias Leistner, 'Big Data and the EU Database Directive 96/9/EC: Current Law and Potential for Reform' in Sebastian Lohsse, Reiner Schulze and Dirk Staudenmayer (eds), *Trading Data in the Digital Economy: Legal Concepts and Tools* (Nomos 2018) 27.

right, although it is indeed the most imminent problem in EU IP law, fails to see the whole picture. In fact, the influence of the existing IP-rights system on (1) the possibility and form of possible access rights as well as (2) on the very infrastructure for data portability, ie the practical achievement of the necessary degree of interoperability and – on that basis possibly in the future – real-time exchange and portability of data, should not be underestimated. In this paper I will try to give an initial overview of the main issues which will have to be considered in this respect.

Accordingly, the focus is on selected aspects of the recent data access and portability discussion, where existing EU IP regulation has a particularly influential impact. First, problems concerning the infrastructural framework for data access and portability will be discussed: Namely, general copyright law, patent law and trade secrets protection should ideally not add unnecessary legal barriers to access to certain mainly technical infrastructures, such as data file formats, application programming interfaces (APIs) as well as interfaces in general (see below B). Secondly, the recent access discussion will be analysed from the perspective of current EU IP law, in particular copyright, sui generis protection and trade secrets protection, resulting in several proposals for an immediate revision of the database sui generis right (see below C). Thirdly, I will briefly discuss a couple of elements in the existing IP regime which might prove helpful as building blocks for a future regulation of the data economy (see below D).

B. IP rights and interoperable formats for data portability

I. Copyright law: freedom of interfaces and data formats

Access to data and the development of data markets in general require that there be free and accessible infrastructures for the exchange of data between different market players.[20] In fact, if real-time exchange of data is needed in certain areas beyond the technically rather limited non-real-time instrument in Article 20 General Data Protection Regulation (GDPR)[21] – and from this author's viewpoint even to make the limited solution in Ar-

---

20 See, for example, Crémer, de Montjoye and Schweitzer (n. 4) 83 et seq. On interoperability see generally Furman and others (n. 4) 64 et seq.

21 Regulation (EU) 2016/679 of the European Parliament and the Council of 27 April 2016 on the protection of natural persons with regard to the processing of personal data and on the free movement of such data, and repealing Directive 95/46/EC [2016] OJ L119/1.

ticle 20 GDPR at least work effectively in practice – open and accessible APIs are of the essence. Copyright protection for computer programs can be a potential problem in that regard if protection is extended to interface structures or data file formats (such as in the highly controversial Federal Circuit's *Google/Oracle* case, which will now be ultimately decided by the U.S. Supreme Court).[22]

In Europe, the situation seems less problematic and comparatively stable. The relevant EU Computer Program Directive[23] of 2009 (originally enacted in 1993) expressly acknowledges the need for interoperability inter alia in its Recitals 11, 15 and 19. Accordingly, the Court of Justice of the EU (CJEU) has decided in its *SAS Institute* judgment[24] that programming languages and data file formats as such are not copyright protected under EU protection for computer programs. Although this is still under discussion in Europe, many authors have derived inter alia from that judgment that API infrastructures as such should not be copyrightable under EU copyright law.[25]

Also, Article 6 of the Computer Program Directive contains a specific exception to copyright for decompilation, ie use acts which are indispensable to obtain the information necessary to achieve interoperability. In line with this objective, the provision covers acts of decompilation performed in order to obtain information on the elements and structure of interfaces. This exception cannot be overridden by contractual agreement. Nonethe-

22 See *Oracle Am., Inc. v Google LLC* 886 F.3d 1179 (Fed. Cir. 2018); pending proceedings *Google LLC v Oracle Am., Inc.* before the US Supreme Court under Docket No. 18-956.

23 Directive 2009/24/EC of the European Parliament and the Council of 23 April 2009 on the legal protection of computer programs [2009] OJ L111/16.

24 Case C-406/10 *SAS Institute v World Programming* ECLI:EU:C:2012:259, paras. 29–46.

25 Jochen Marly, 'Der Schutzgegenstand des urheberrechtlichen Softwareschutzes' [2012] Gewerblicher Rechtsschutz und Urheberrecht 773, 779; more open in the prognosis Simonetta Vezzoso, 'Copyright, Interfaces, and a Possible Atlantic Divide' (2012) 3 Journal of Intellectual Property, Information Technology and E-Commerce Law 153, para. 40, who however herself requests freedom of interface structures; with a useful distinction between the interface structures and their specific implementation and programming in code Pamela Samuelson, Thomas C. Vinje and William R. Cornish, 'Does copyright protection under the EU Software Directive extend to computer program behaviour, languages and interfaces?' (2012) 34 European Intellectual Property Review 158–159, 163–164; similarly Christian Heinze, 'Software als Schutzgegenstand des Europäischen Urheberrechts' (2011) 2 Journal of Intellectual Property, Information Technology and E-Commerce Law 97, para. 8.

less, the provision's impact in practice has remained limited, which might be due to the fact that Article 6 Computer Program Directive – like the majority of exceptions to copyright – does not give a subjective right to access but instead only exempts certain use acts from the scope of copyright protection. Therefore, the bigger problem in regard to access to interface information and other information necessary to achieve interoperability might be caused by factual limits on the accessibility of the information as well as by possible trade secret protection.[26]

II. Patent law: from protection of data formats towards protection of formatted data?

1. Patents on data encryption and transfer processes, in particular standard-essential patents

German and European patent law is (and will become) much more relevant to the question of access to data portability infrastructures than might be assumed at first sight. In fact, data encryption and transfer processes can undoubtedly be patented as procedure patents under certain conditions. Where such patents are essential for the implementation of a standard (standard-essential patents, SEPs), typically, the patent holder will have submitted a so-called FRAND declaration[27] in the standardisation process.[28] In the EU, the enforcement of such FRAND-encumbered SEPs is

---

26 See sub-section III. below.

27 I.e. a declaration to license the patent to any interested party under fair reasonable and non-discriminatory conditions. See, for instance, ETSI's FRAND-licensing declaration <www.etsi.org/images/files/IPR/etsi-ipr-form.doc> accessed 31 August 2020, or the ITU's RAND-licensing declaration <www.itu.int/oth/T0404000002/en> accessed 31 August 2020.

28 In particular, with regard to telecommunications standards, but also with regard to standards in the electronics sector and probably in future for many standards in the AI field, formal processes of de iure standardisation apply, where a valid FRAND declaration is a mandatory requirement for being considered for the standard; see, for instance, the respective policies of ETSI <www.etsi.org/images/files/IPR/etsi-ipr-policy.pdf> accessed 31 August 2020, and ISO/IEC/ITU <https://isotc.iso.org/livelink/livelink/fetch/2000/2122/3770791/Common_Policy.htm?nodeid=6344764&vernum=-2> accessed 31 August 2020. For mere de facto standards it is currently under discussion whether the same principles should apply as under the Huawei/ZTE regime or whether a more limited approach, such as under the old judgment of the German Federal Supreme Court (*BGH*), 6 May 2009, Case KZR 39/06 (2009) Gewerblicher Rechtsschutz und Urheberrecht 694 – *Orange*

governed by the CJEU's judgment in *Huawei/ZTE*.[29] As for the original patent holder who submitted the FRAND declaration, this will result in a limited legal position which does not allow the patent holder to file proceedings for an injunction before making a FRAND offer to the implementer and seriously negotiating a FRAND licence. While there is no room to go into the details and considerable practical difficulties in this particular field,[30] at least on principle this enforcement regime seems capable of enabling sufficient access to the essential patents for any seriously interested party.

One more problem of general importance, however, should be briefly mentioned. This concerns the particularly intricate question of whether an inter omnes effect can be derived from the underlying network of FRAND declarations in such areas. Currently, significant problems arise with regard to situations where the patent has been transferred to third parties, in particular so-called non-practicing entities, which are themselves not bound by the FRAND declaration of the original patent holder. In a recent judgment, the Higher Regional Court of Düsseldorf has assumed that in such cases, if the patent is standard essential and vests a dominant market position in the person of the acquirer, the FRAND declaration will have a 'quasi in rem' effect and equally bind the acquirer.[31] While this is a workable, convincing result,[32] the underlying dogmatic construction of the court (i.e. the assumed in rem effect of the FRAND declaration as such) seems not entirely beyond doubt.

Book Standard, should apply. See for a differentiated view on this with further references Matthias Leistner, 'Intermediary Liability in a Global World' in Tatiana E. Synodinou (ed.), *Pluralism or Universalism in International Copyright Law* (Wolters Kluwer 2019) 471.

29 Case C-170/13 *Huawei* ECLI:EU:C:2015:477.

30 See further, for example, Matthias Leistner, 'European Experiences: EU and Germany' in Kung-Chung Liu and Reto M. Hilty (eds), *SEPs, SSOs and FRAND – Asian and global perspectives on fostering innovation in interconnectivity* (Routledge 2019) Ch. 15; Peter G. Picht, 'The ECJ Rules on Standard-Essential Patents: Thoughts and Issues Post-Huawei' (2016) 37 European Competition Law Review 365; Peter G. Picht, 'FRAND Injunctions: an overview on recent EU case law' (2019) Zeitschrift für Geistiges Eigentum 324.

31 Düsseldorf Higher Regional Court (*OLG Düsseldorf*), 22 March 2019, Case 2 U 31/16 (2019) Gewerblicher Rechtsschutz und Urheberrecht Rechtsprechungs-Report 6087 – *Improving Handovers*.

32 See already Hanns Ullrich, 'Patente und technische Normen: Konflikt und Komplementarität in patent- und wettbewerbsrechtlicher Sicht' in Matthias Leistner (ed.), *Europäische Perspektiven des geistigen Eigentums* (Mohr Siebeck 2010) 14.

Instead of this construction, from this author's viewpoint, an essentially competition law-based solution should be considered as follows.[33] As for Article 102 TFEU, the CJEU in *Huawei/ZTE* did not require that it is the current SEP holder who has declared her willingness to license the patent to any third party on FRAND terms.[34] Instead, the judgment can be read to say that the Court only required that the patent as such be subject to a FRAND declaration in order to trigger the duties under Article 102 TFEU for any subsequent market-dominant acquirer of the patent in question. Therefore, the EU competition law-based specific enforcement regime for SEPs should apply to any market-dominant patent holder who has acquired a FRAND-encumbered patent without regard to the question of whether the (new) patent holder herself declared her willingness to license the acquired patent under FRAND conditions.

Moreover, depending on the applicable substantive law,[35] the FRAND declaration can also entail a contract for the benefit of third parties between the declaring patent holder and the standard-setting organisation whereby the third party, ie the implementer, is entitled to assert the claim to FRAND licensing independently (*Vertrag mit Schutzwirkung zugunsten Dritter*; *stipulation pour autrui*). The catalogue of duties arising from this contract should in principle be the same as under the Huawei/ZTE regime established by the CJEU. From this author's viewpoint, the duties from this contract will also, in certain situations, be passed on to subsequent acquirers of the patent under the principle of good faith as an ancillary duty of the acquiring party under Section 241(2) German Civil Code (obligation to have regard to the generally known interest of the seller to pass on

---

33 I first encountered this basic idea in my Munich seminar on German and European intellectual property law, where it was brought to my attention by my student Mark Hillenbrand.

34 Cf. Case C-170/13 *Huawei* ECLI:EU:C:2015:477, para. 49, according to which the case was characterised by the fact 'that the patent at issue is essential to a standard established by a standardisation body, rendering its use indispensable to all competitors which envisage manufacturing products that comply with the standard'. This clearly refers to the *patent as such*, not to the person of the patent holder.

35 As for the hitherto practically important ETSI FRAND declarations (which might become even more important in the future as ETSI is also preparing standards in the AI field), the applicable substantive law will be French law; see Mary-Rose McGuire, 'Die FRAND-Erklärung – Anwendbares Recht, Rechtsnatur und Bindungswirkung am Beispiel eines ETSI-Standards' (2018) Gewerblicher Rechtsschutz und Urheberrecht 128; Matthias Leistner and Lukas Kleeberger, 'FRAND-Erklärungen ohne Rechtswahl am Beispiel der Standardisierungsorganisationen ITU/ISO/IEC: Ein praxisrelevantes dogmatisches Problem im internationalen Privatrecht' (forthcoming 2021).

the FRAND obligation in order to keep the sales contract valid) even if the parties do not expressly stipulate that obligation in the contract underlying the transfer of the patent. This entire approach, which is set out in another paper,[36] cannot be deepened here in detail. Suffice it to say that, in regard to SEPs which are essential for certain existing or possible future data exchange standards or AI applications, competition and contract law-based solutions can be developed which will ultimately at least on principle enable workable access on fair, reasonable and non-discriminating conditions for any seriously interested party. Moreover, under a more general perspective the contract law-based approach under the principle of good faith and Section 241(2) German Civil Code which has been briefly sketched here might also be useful to acquire limited inter omnes effects of certain basic structural elements of contract-based data biotopes (networks) when parts of the data are passed on to outsiders.

2. *Scope of patents concerning formatted data sequences*

Another even more intricate and difficult problem in patent law, which has the potential to significantly hamper the development of free and accessible technical data exchange infrastructures in the EU and Germany, concerns the scope of protection of process patents on certain data encryption or compression processes, specifically in regard to the data sequences which result from the application of the patented process. In two more recent judgments the German Federal Supreme Court has held that such data sequences or information might enjoy patent protection as a product which is produced directly by a patented process (see Section 9 No. 3 Patent Act).[37] Meanwhile, this therefore conceivable protection has been

36 See Matthias Leistner and Lukas Kleeberger 'Die Drittwirkung von FRAND-Erklärungen aus kartellrechtlicher und vertragsrechtlicher Sicht' (2020) Gewerblicher Rechtsschutz und Urheberrecht 1241.

37 German Federal Supreme Court (*BGH*), 21 August 2012, Case X ZR 33/10 (2012) Gewerblicher Rechtsschutz und Urheberrecht 1230 – *MPEG-2-Videosignalkodierung*, in which the Court assumed that a data sequence directly resulting from the operation of the patented MPEG-2 video compression procedure had to be regarded as a direct product of the patented process and that consequently any import, marketing or distribution concerning such sequences could on principle infringe the patent rights of the holder of the underlying process patent; slightly more cautious already German Federal Supreme Court (*BGH*), 27 September 2016, Case X ZR 124/15 (2017) Gewerblicher Rechtsschutz und Urheberrecht 261 – *Rezeptortyrosinkinase II*.

subjected to certain qualifications[38] and, what is more, patent protection for such data sequences as a direct product of a patented process will generally be exhausted upon first sale of the sequence.[39] Nonetheless, such reach-through patent protection for data files seems unnecessary to incentivise innovation in the field of data encryption and compression technology. At the same time, it has obvious dysfunctional potential to block necessary access to the information as such, based on the mere format in which the information is encrypted or compressed. Therefore, from this author's viewpoint, as a more straightforward solution, patent protection should not be granted for mere data sequences on the basis of Section 9 No. 3 Patent Act.

III. Trade secrets

Obviously, trade secret protection can play a large role with regard to secret information on data file formats and interfaces where this is necessary to achieve interoperability and portability.[40] According to European competition law, access to IP-protected information and data structures will be granted if the information in question is indispensable to offer a new product or service in a secondary market in relation to the (hypothetical) licensing market and if the unjustified denial of access would effectively foreclose workable competition on that market.[41] In these cases, access will be generally granted on the condition that the user pays a fair and reasonable licensing fee, ie on the basis of a compulsory licence. Such access on the basis of compulsory licences can also be granted where trade secret protected information on interfaces is necessary to achieve interoperability, if the conditions of Article 102 TFEU are met.[42] In fact, in the *Microsoft* judg-

38 Information as such will not be protected; instead, the information must be structured in a way which still clearly reflects the patented process and gives the resulting data sequence part of its substantial value; moreover, the resulting data sequence as such will have to be capable of being marketed and traded in a way which is typical for an independent product. See further on these qualifications the judgment in *Rezeptortyrosinkinase II* (n. 37).

39 German Federal Supreme Court in *MPEG-2-Videosignalkodierung* (n. 37).

40 See further on the EU framework for trade secrets protection section C.III below.

41 Cf. generally Joined Cases C-241/91 P and C-242/91 P *RTE v Commission* (*'Magill'*) ECLI:EU:C:1995:98; Case C-418/01 *IMS Health* ECLI:EU:C:2004:257.

42 Cf. Case T-201/04 R *Microsoft v Commission* ECLI:EU:T:2004:372 and Case T-201/04 *Microsoft v Commission* ECLI:EU:T:2007:289. See also section C.IV.3.b) (3) below.

ment, which concerned trade secret-protected interface information the General Court has even watered down the new product or service condition to a mere requirement that the emergence of a competing product with innovative elements must be prevented by the denial of access.[43] Also, while this case group is traditionally based in the prevention of leveraging a dominant position between a primary market and a secondary aftermarket or market for complementary products or services, at a closer look, in the field of compulsory licences for the use of IP rights and trade secrets the CJEU's case law has effectively extended these cases to also cover situations where a new product or service in the actual primary (product or service) market is prevented. This is because in the *IMS Health* judgment, the Court regarded a merely hypothetical upstream market for licences in which the rightholder, who was only active in the downstream product market, had a dominant position as sufficient for a finding of leveraging between two markets.[44] Effectively, thus, a competitor who wanted to offer a competing product in the actual downstream product market where the rightholder was active, was granted a compulsory licence in the so-called (hypothetical) upstream market for licences for the essential IP right.[45]

In regard to trade secrets protection this overall competition law framework provides for a structure which seems reasonably balanced between the possible need to protect the secrecy of essential technical information also in the field of interface infrastructures, and the objective to grant access to interface information in order to protect or enable workable competition. In detail, in cases in which real leveraging between two markets takes place and when the rightholder is indeed a market-dominant undertaking in the upstream market, the new product or service criterion should be given up;[46] but this can be achieved in case law and does not require legislative action. From a practical viewpoint, one might also ask whether the competition law instruments, because of their specific rules on burden of proof and their specific enforcement structures, will not often come too late to remedy actual access problems in the field of the data economy. This indeed is a justified concern which will be discussed below (C IV 3 b (3)) in the context of possible 'IP-internal' provisions on compulsory li-

43 Case T-201/04 *Microsoft v Commission* [2007] ECLI:EU:T:2007:289, paras 643–665.; Schweitzer (n. 4) 578.

44 Case C-418/01 *IMS Health* ECLI:EU:C:2004:257, paras 44–45.

45 See further Matthias Leistner, 'Intellectual Property and Competition Law: The European Development from Magill to IMS Health Compared to Recent German and U.S. Case Law' (2005) 3 Zeitschrift für Wettbewerbsrecht 138.

46 Cf. Leistner (n. 45) 150–152; Schweitzer (n. 4) 578.

cences for systematically identifiable situations, where barriers to market entry necessarily and directly follow from IP protection for certain data. Similar specific provisions for compulsory licences concerning access to trade secret-protected interface information should have been considered in the enactment of the Trade Secrets Directive of 2016;[47] however, at the moment, this is not an immediately pressing political need which would require a revision of the Directive in the short term.

As for the specific issue of decompilation of computer programs in order to obtain information necessary to achieve interoperability of computer programs and portability of data (ie information on data file formats and interfaces), however, a remarkable systematic tension between the approach of the Computer Program Directive[48] and the approach of the Trade Secrets Directive can be observed, which has to be solved immediately. The Trade Secrets Directive provides for a general limitation of protection for any act of 'observation, study, disassembly or testing of a product or object that has been made available to the public or that is lawfully in the possession of the acquirer' (ie reverse engineering, see Article 3(1)(b) Trade Secrets Directive). However, this liberty of the acquirer can be limited by contractual agreement. Insofar as the specific case of decompilation of computer programs is concerned, which will typically be the case when an acquirer tries to obtain information on data file formats and interfaces, this is in tension with the more liberal rule in the Computer Program Directive, which provides for an exception for decompilation that can expressly not be overridden by contract.[49] This latter rule reflects the fact that typically interface information will be of particular importance to foster dynamic efficiency through interoperability, while at the same time interfaces will typically be an essential part of the developed software anyway, so that no additional protection to incentivise innovation in the area via the very strong and long-term copyright regime is needed. The same cost-benefit ratio in fact seems to apply to acts of reverse engineering of interfaces in regard to trade secrets protection; what is more, such tinkering (in this specific field as well as generally) has increasingly become a valuable source of innovation in AI and big data.[50] From this author's viewpoint,

47 Directive (EU) 2016/943 of the European Parliament and of the Council of 8 June 2016 on the protection of undisclosed know-how and business information (trade secrets) against their unlawful acquisition, use and disclosure [2016] OJ L157/1.

48 See section I. above.

49 See section I. above.

50 Pamela Samuelson, 'Freedom to Tinker' (2016) <https://ssrn.com/abstract=2800362> accessed 31 August 2020.

therefore, in cases where decompilation is essential to obtain information necessary for interoperability and data portability, the Computer Programs Directive's approach, as a lex specialis, should be applied, thus also exempting the necessary acts from possible trade secrets protection without a possibility for the owner of the trade secret to override this by way of contractual agreement.[51]

C. *The discussion on access to and portability of data and the existing EU IP-rights framework, in particular database sui generis protection and trade secrets*

I. *Overview*

As for the relationship of access and portability regimes to existing IP protection in Europe, an immediate overlap can indeed occur when use of data is concerned that are as such IP-protected or only accessible via an IP-protected database. Direct IP protection of information as such exists neither in patent law nor in copyright law. However, the database sui generis protection right (and partly also copyright protection in database works), although in theory merely protecting substantial investment into databases, in practice comes close to a protection of information as such in certain situations. Therefore, the main problematic area of IP law which will have to be discussed in this part is the sui generis protection right for databases. Besides, the protection of trade secrets could also sit uncomfortably with data access regimes requiring disclosure of confidential data and will therefore also have to be included in the analysis.

51 Thomas Dreier, in Thomas Dreier and Gernot Schulze (eds), *Urheberrechtsgesetz* (6th edn, C.H. Beck 2018) Sec. 69e UrhG para. 5.

II. Access to data, copyright in databases and database sui generis protection – Current problems and the case for immediate reform of the Database Directive

1. Introduction – impact of European database protection on big data and AI use scenarios

The recent discussion of the function and relevance of the Database Directive's[52] sui generis right for the European data economy has been partly characterised by the assumption that in most big data situations the crucial condition of a 'substantial investment' will not be fulfilled.[53] I have shown elsewhere that this assumption might be mistaken.[54] Instead, one should be aware that database sui generis protection (and partly also copyright protection) can potentially come into play in numerous different typical big data and AI use scenarios. Compilations of independent elements such as geographical data, certain kinds of sensor-measured data (although a number of differentiations has to be made in this case group), sales and all kinds of commercial data etc. can potentially qualify for protection depending on the circumstances of the case. This is not to say that investments in the compilation of such data should be protected in all these different case groups. Instead, this analysis should serve as a *warning* that the database sui generis right might be more relevant than generally thought for both the protection and the access aspects of big data use case scenarios.[55]

2. Copyright in database works – limited and balanced approach in the EU

The typical creativity involved in the development of big data-based AI models and applications, i.e. the structuring and weighing of the cost functions, selection and combination of training data etc.[56] seems on principle eligible for protection as a database work under EU copyright law, i.e. it is potentially copyrightable as a structured compilation of independent ele-

52 Database Directive (n. 16).

53 European Commission SWD (n. 17) 2.

54 Leistner (n. 15). With the same conclusion and a rigorous analysis see also Drexl (n. 11) 67–85; more differentiated also Bently and others (n. 18) 29–31.

55 Cf. also Bently and others (n. 18) 29 referring to Leistner.

56 See further Drexl and others (n. 2).

ments.[57] The same might potentially apply to any creative structuring process (selection or arrangement) behind the creation of inferred data.[58]

Given that in particular in the EU the exceptions to copyright are too narrow and rigid to accommodate the dynamic and multipolar use of training data and weighing factors in different contexts and problem-specific combinations (data biotopes), copyright law could therefore be a significant source of additional transaction costs and contribute to lock-in and even holdup potential if it were over-extended to everyday methods of selecting, structuring and combining datasets. However, the CJEU has rightly specified the condition of copyright protection in Europe in a very strict and targeted way in its more recent case law. Hence, according to the CJEU's judgment in *Football Dataco/Yahoo* mere intellectual effort, skill, judgment and labour in the selection and structuring of the elements of a database work will not suffice for copyright protection. In particular, technical or rather abstract mathematical considerations or methods will not qualify if they do not leave room for the expression of personal creativity in an original manner by making free and creative choices and thus stamping the database with a 'personal touch'.[59]

For this reason, database copyright protection in the EU, while on principle being capable of protecting certain outstanding achievements in the area of AI and big data (in particular certain outstanding sets of training data in specific areas), will not protect the typical selection and combination of data in order to compile and combine optimised training data sets and the respective weighing of factors to optimise the cost functions in

57 By contrast, copyright protection for computer programs will typically not play a significant role in these cases because copyright protection of computer programs is limited to the creative coding as such, whereas the development of underlying mathematical structures, algorithms, abstract procedures etc. is not covered. See Art. 1(2) Computer Programs Directive (n. 23).

58 On the category of inferred data see Crémer, de Montjoye and Schweitzer (n. 4) 24–29; Schweitzer, (n. 4) 571; proposing such categorisation already World Economic Forum, 'Personal Data: The Emergence of a New Asset Class' (January 2011) 7 <www3.weforum.org/docs/WEF_ITTC_PersonalDataNewAsset_Report_2011.pdf> accessed 31 August 2020.

59 Case C-604/10 *Football Dataco v Yahoo* ECLI:EU:C:2012:115, paras 31 et seq., in particular paras 38 et seq. Similarly, in the recent *Funke Medien* judgment, the Court has applied strict criteria to potential copyright protection for mere factual reports and their structure when it is guided by the underlying practical purpose, thereby decidedly reducing the potential of copyright law to protect mere practical, AI-aided 'creations' in the area of written works. See Case C-469/17 *Funke Medien NRW* ECLI:EU:C:2019:623.

normal cases. Therefore, in the EU, copyright in computer programs[60] and compilations (database works) is currently not a significant cost factor for the future development of AI and big data and will presumably not pose substantial obstacles to the future technological development either. Instead, it seems that copyright law is comparatively well adjusted, as it might contribute to incentivising certain highly original, free and creative breakthrough developments in specific areas (in particular the development of fundamentally important, highly original data combinations as training data sets), while it does not have the potential to hamper the normal development of the data economy. If there is any problem with the current status of copyright law at all, it might even be a problem of under-incentivisation concerning the development and publication of valuable training data sets. However, if there were a problem in this sector, this would not be a problem copyright itself could solve. This is because copyright with its exclusive property right character and the unreasonably long term of protection is obviously poorly equipped to serve the – at least conceivable – need for tailor-made flexible and short protection in this area.

By contrast, with regard to underlying materials which are *used* for the compilation of training data and which might be protected by copyright law, the situation in European copyright is more problematic. Indeed, the question has to be asked whether the existing exceptions to copyright law in Europe are sufficient in that regard. Since the topic of this chapter is access to and protection of data (and not of the 'raw material' to create certain data), suffice it to say in this context that even the new text and data mining exceptions in Articles 3 and 4 DSM Directive[61] do not seem sufficient in that regard. Further reform seems imminent and it is submitted that the Japanese copyright law exception for text and data mining (as a non-conclusive case example in the larger realm of irrelevant uses which do not allow the enjoyment of the work as such) could form a model in that regard.[62]

---

60 See section B.I. above.

61 Directive (EU) 2019/790 of the European Parliament and the Council of 17 April 2019 on copyright and related rights in the Digital Single Market and amending Directives 96/9/EC and 2001/29/EC [2019] OJ L130/92.

62 Art. 30–4 Japanese Copyright Act. See further Tatsuhiro Ueno, 'A general clause on copyright limitations in civil law countries: Recent discussion toward the Japanese-style "fair use" clause', in Shyamkrishna Balganesh, Ng-Loy Wee Loon and Haochen Sun (eds), *The Cambridge Handbook of Copyright Limitations and Exceptions* (Cambridge University Press 2021) 211.

3. *Database sui generis protection right: current problems and immediate need for reform*

a) Condition of protection and legal uncertainty in the area of volunteered and observed data

The database sui generis protection right – although on the face of it being limited to the protection of certain substantial investments in the obtaining, verification and presentation of the contents of a database – in many cases can practically come close to granting an exclusive property right against the use of certain data as such. The attempt of the CJEU to ameliorate this situation by excluding investments into the mere generation of data, often resulting in so-called sole-source data, in its leading judgment in *British Horseracing Board* and the resulting complex status quo have been comprehensively discussed elsewhere.[63] Only a brief overview shall be given here.

Concerning the condition of protection of a substantial investment in the obtaining, verification or presentation of the contents of a database, the situation is problematic mainly because at the moment it is characterised by undeniable legal uncertainty about the exact impact of database sui generis protection in typical data collection scenarios (namely concerning volunteered and observed data). In future, further specification of the condition of protection will be required – either in the written law or in case law – which should reflect the comparatively advanced discussion on the need to access these categories of data.

Thus, the collection of data, which on principle can be collected by any competitor, can qualify as a potentially substantial investment. Concerning the particularly problematic and uncertain case group of measured or observed data, the necessary distinctions should be guided by the principle that database sui generis protection should never directly raise unsurmountable barriers to market entry, both in the primary market as well as in aftermarkets or complementary markets.[64] Thus, the guiding principle should be that whenever observed or measured data cannot be observed or measured independently, ie data internal to the very application of a certain product or service (e.g. in particular certain real-time operating data concerning the operation of the product or service as such), the respective investments should not qualify for potential sui generis protection. This is

63 Leistner (n. 19).
64 Similarly Drexl (n. 11) 68, 71–73.

because in these cases, necessarily, there will be no other source for these data and therefore IP protection (in addition to factual control) would as such directly lead to a market-dominant position in the (actual or hypothetical) licensing market for this specific kind of data. By contrast, if certain external data are collected or observed only in the wider context of the application of a product or a service (e.g. a car measuring the outside temperature or collecting certain data on the road conditions; certain observed use data in the context of internet services; agricultural data delivered by farming machines; non-real-time motion profiles of a natural person), the respective investments can qualify for sui generis protection. This is because in these cases, at least if there is competition in the product or service market, such data can be acquired from different operators (sometimes even in different markets, such as different motion profiles which might be compiled by a car as well as by a smartphone) or could even be measured, observed or collected independently.

For the moment, these proposed initial guideposts, however, are neither laid down in the Database Directive nor in case law. Instead, the merely grammatical distinction between so-called 'generated' data and so-called 'compiled' data reigns in this sector and creates legal uncertainty. As a consequence, while there are no significant problems in the field of inferred data, in the area of volunteered or observed data[65] the sui generis right causes legal uncertainty and obviously has significant potential to lead to future access problems and to lock-in effects in certain situations depending on future CJEU case law in this area.

b) Scope of protection and problems for access to aggregated data sets

This is aggravated by the fact that the exclusive rights under Article 7(2) Database Directive, i.e. extraction and re-utilisation, have been construed very broadly in the CJEU's case law. In fact, practices such as indirect extraction and even extraction for the compilation of substantially changed, value-added databases of a more or less different nature will be covered by these exclusive rights.[66] Moreover, the activities of typical meta-databases or meta-search websites, i.e. the automated gathering and compiling of da-

65 Crémer, de Montjoye and Schweitzer (n. 4) 24–29; Schweitzer (n. 4) 571.
66 Case C-304/07 *Directmedia Publishing* ECLI:EU:C:2008:552, paras 29–60.

ta from a multitude of different sources, are potentially infringing the sui generis right.[67]

Compared to this rather broad construction of the exclusive rights, the limitation of the protected subject matter, i.e. the limitation to the use of substantial parts of a database or systematic and repeated extraction of insubstantial parts which add up to be a substantial part of the database,[68] is not an efficient means to protect freedom of competition and to prevent leveraging potential with respect to many typical big data uses. This is because in particular in the case group where competitors need access to aggregated data sets, typically, complete datasets, possibly even from different sources, will be needed. Consequently, the limitation of the protected subject matter to substantial parts of databases does not solve potential problems with access to data, which might arise in this case group.[69]

To mirror this against the different discussed data categories and access scenarios: The database sui generis right can raise serious information and transaction cost problems in its current state, which is characterised by substantial legal uncertainty concerning its potential to protect volunteered or observed data. This particularly concerns the use scenario in which competitors need access to complete, aggregated data sets to access the primary market or certain entirely new, complementary or aftermarkets. Moreover, the sui generis right can worsen lock-in problems and even lead to holdup potential in certain situations where large amounts of individual-level use data are concerned.[70]

c) Exceptions to the sui generis right, public sector data and further problems

Considering access to IP-protected subject matter, the exceptions to the concerned IP right come into focus. In the overarching general framework of EU fundamental rights, such exceptions express genuine user rights to freedom of expression and information which have to be fairly balanced with the right to protection of IP.[71] On a more detailed, technical level, the existing exceptions to the sui generis right (Article 9 Database Directive) undoubtedly are too narrowly designed, in particular in comparison to the

---

67 Case C-202/12 *Innoweb* ECLI:EU:C:2013:850, paras 37–38.

68 Case C-203/02 *British Horseracing Board* ECLI:EU:C:2004:695, paras 87–88.

69 Cf. also Matthias Leistner as reported in Bently and others (n. 18) 57.

70 See section C.IV.3.b)(2) below.

71 Case C-469/17 *Funke Medien NRW* ECLI:EU:C:2019:623, paras 57–58.

broader general copyright exceptions.[72] In fact, this critique becomes even more imminent with respect to the challenges of the data economy.

First, it seems to have been ignored in the legislative process that the sui generis right, by virtue of its autonomous nature, would not be subject to certain traditional limitations set out in national laws with regard to works protected under copyright. This leads inter alia to a significant problem in respect of databases established by public authorities, which are covered by exclusive sui generis protection even in countries where official works by public bodies are generally exempted from copyright under certain conditions. For the moment, this issue should be solved by an analogy to the copyright exception for official databases by public bodies.[73] However, the CJEU never explicitly decided on that question, hence this issue remains legally uncertain on the level of Union law. This also results in considerable tensions between the framework for access and use under the PSI Directive[74] and possible sui generis protection for databases created by public bodies (which will worsen when the new Open Data Directive[75] is implemented). For these problems, it seems that the appropriate solution straightforwardly follows from a contextual comparison to general copyright law. In general copyright law, such creations authored by public bodies are exempted from copyright protection, if the very policy or legal purpose of the creation is to be disseminated to the public to the maximum extent. It seems that under that same condition (i.e. legal or policy interest in maximum dissemination of certain data), a fortiori, databases created by public bodies should also be exempted from possible sui generis protection under the Database Directive. Only in the remaining cases where a direct

72 Annette Kur and others, 'First Evaluation of Directive 96/9/EC on the Legal Protection of Databases - Comment by the Max Planck Institute for Intellectual Property, Competition and Tax Law, Munich' (2006) 37 International Review of Intellectual Property and Competition Law 551, 556-557. See also Matthias Leistner as reported in Bently and others (n. 18) 59.

73 Cf. Matthias Leistner, 'Anmerkung zu BGH, Beschluß vom 28 Spetember 2006, I ZR 261/03 – Sächsischer Ausschreibungsdienst' (2007) Zeitschrift für Gemeinschaftsprivatrecht 190, 193-94. With an overview of the current status of the debate on whether the exception of German copyright law for 'official' copyrighted works can be extended by way of analogy: Martin Vogel, in Ulrich Loewenheim, Matthias Leistner and Ansgar Ohly (eds), *Urheberrecht: Kommentar* (6th edn, C.H. Beck 2020) Sec. 87b UrhG paras 67-68.

74 Former Directive 2003/98/EC of the European Parliament and the Council of 17 November 2003 on the re-use of public sector information [2003] OJ L 345/90.

75 Directive (EU) 2019/1024 of the European Parliament and of the Council of 20 June 2019 on open data and the re-use of public sector information [2019] OJ L172/56.

legal or policy interest in maximum dissemination does not exist, but instead access only seems reasonable in order to increase dynamic efficiency, can alternative access regimes, such as FRAND licences, be considered and will then have to fulfil the requirements provided for by the Open Data Directive.[76]

This particularly problematic example points, secondly, to a more general problem. In fact, the narrow exceptions to the sui generis right should at the very least be aligned and dynamically linked with the exceptions to copyright law under the Information Society Directive.[77] It is therefore of considerable practical interest to enable and oblige Member States to extend, mutatis mutandis, the exceptions and limitations applying to works protected under copyright to sui generis protection of non-original databases.[78] The obligation should be phrased so as to establish a dynamic link between both fields, to the effect that limitations set out in new copyright legislation would automatically also become applicable, under suitable terms and circumstances, to the sui generis right. The new copyright provisions for text and data mining and certain other exempted uses in Articles 3–6 and 8 DSM Directive are examples in point: Rightly, they explicitly extend the scope of the newly proposed exceptions to the database maker's sui generis right. However, the problem is of a more general nature and should be solved in a general way when revising the Database Directive by simply mandatorily aligning the exceptions to the sui generis right with the general exceptions to EU copyright law.

In this context, it should also be clarified that permitted use under the exceptions also covers use acts in respect of complete databases. This is because the current wording of Article 9 Database Directive seems to suggest that even exempted acts must be limited to the use of substantial parts. However, a limitation of the exempted uses to the use of only substantial parts of a database could hardly be accommodated with the access needs of competitors and new market entrants in the context of big data activities. Moreover, the limitation of the personal scope of application of the exceptions to 'lawful users of a database' should be abolished. This qualification is inconsistent with the system of general copyright law exceptions which do not contain an additional legitimacy test since the considerations on whether the use is legitimate are already embedded in the very definition

76 See Open Data Directive (n. 75). See Richter (n. 13) in regard to the German E-Government Act of 2017.

77 Kur and others (n. 72) 556-557.

78 Leistner as reported in Bently and others (n. 18) 16; Drexl (n. 11) 81.

of the scope of the exceptions as such. Therefore, an additional condition of lawful use is systematically inconsistent and unnecessarily endangers the practical utility of the rules on exceptions.

Finally, the strict limitation of the exceptions to non-commercial uses certainly has to be put under scrutiny. This is a more general problem of certain exceptions in EU copyright law, which will have to be discussed generally in future, in particular because it is also inherent to the exception for text and data mining under Articles 3 and 4 DSM Directive.[79] Also, as a more general and by no means new proposition, it should also be considered in future to make the optional exceptions and limitations in the Information Society Directive mandatory in nature.[80] Article 17(7) DSM Directive, with its somewhat arbitrary and therefore insufficient selection of certain now mandatory exceptions and its limited sector-specific scope, can only be a beginning in that regard.[81]

4. *Summary*

In sum, existing European copyright protection in the realm of database works and computer programs does not raise any imminent concern with regard to the balanced and efficient development of the data economy and currently does not need to be immediately revised in this context. However, the hitherto insufficient new exception for text and data mining is a case for (another) revision at least in the middle term.

By contrast, depending on the development of future case law in the area, the database sui generis protection right in its current state has the undeniable potential to substantially aggravate the existing and acknowledged access problems which already follow from factual control over different data sources.[82] Even in areas where it is currently unclear whether the right will develop significant dysfunctional impact, the resulting legal uncertainty is problematic in itself as it can have a chilling effect on certain

79 Cf. section C.II.C.2. above.

80 Leistner (n. 19) 47–48; Drexl (n. 11) 81.

81 Matthias Leistner, 'European Copyright Licensing and Infringement Liability Under Art. 17 DSM-Directive Compared to Secondary Liability of Content Platforms in the U.S. – Can We Make the New European System a Global Opportunity Instead of a Local Challenge?' (2020) 12 Zeitschrift für Geistiges Eigentum 121.

82 Cf. Drexl and others (n. 2) 1-2.; Communication of the European Commission of 10 January 2017 – 'Building the European data economy' COM(2017) 9 final, 9–10.

innovative commercial activities (e.g. the different meta-search platforms in the internet[83] and activities based on certain public sector information[84]). At the same time, the right tends to miss the opportunity to address certain very well defined and targeted protection needs, in particular for high-quality training data, if these needs could in fact be validated beyond the realm of (very limited) copyright protection in the area). The existing database sui generis regime is thus in need of rigorous reform.

III. *Trade secrets protection: A defensive, more flexible hybrid regime which is better equipped for the data economy*

Trade Secrets Protection in Europe has recently been harmonised in the Trade Secrets Directive of 2016[85] which has been implemented in Germany in the entirely new Trade Secrets Act.[86] Similarly, the U.S. have recently consolidated legislation on trade secrets protection on the federal level in the Defend Trade Secrets Act of 2016.[87]

Trade secrets protection, as a hybrid regime,[88] does not constitute property rights in rem, but instead only complements and intensifies de facto exclusivity because of secrecy.[89] Accordingly, it does not vest an exclusive right in the person of the trade secret holder but instead only provides for 'defensive' remedies against certain prohibited acts of misappropriation by third parties.[90] Far from being a disadvantage, the flexible hybrid character of trade secrets protection, which establishes a limited inter omnes effect by way of defensive remedies which can be invoked against acquirers of data and other third persons only under certain conditions and will then be

83 See section C.II.3.b) above.

84 See section C.II.3.c) above.

85 Trade Secrets Directive (n. 47).

86 Trade Secrets Act (*Gesetz zum Schutz von Geschäftsgeheimnissen*) [2019] Bundegesetzblatt I 466.

87 Defend Trade Secrets Act of 2016 Publ L 114–153.

88 Cf. Ansgar Ohly, 'Germany: The Trade Secrets Protection Act of 2019' in Jens Schovsbo, Timo Minssen and Thomas Riis (eds), *The Harmonization and Protection of Trade Secrets in the EU – An Appraisal of the EU Directive* (Edward Elgar 2020, forthcoming).

89 Herbert Zech, 'Information as Property' (2015) 6 Journal of Intellectual Property, Information Technology and E-Commerce Law 192, para. 26.

90 Tanya Aplin, 'Trading Data in the Digital Economy: Trade Secrets Perspective' in Sebastian Lohsse, Reiner Schulze and Dirk Staudenmayer (eds), *Trading Data in the Digital Economy: Legal Concepts and Tools* (Nomos 2018) 59, 70.

specified in enforcement in a very flexible and proportional way, seems to be particularly well suited to serve the purposes of the data economy.[91]

On principle, while a single datum will typically not qualify as a trade secret, datasets[92] and data analysis techniques of even mere potential commercial value can qualify for trade secrets protection on condition that they are kept secret, i.e. not generally known in the relevant circles,[93] and that reasonable steps have been taken to maintain secrecy (Article 2(1) Trade Secrets Directive).[94] This latter condition, which is modelled on the comparable requirement in Article 39 TRIPS, should be interpreted in a rather flexible, broad way, because it is in certain tension with the general objective of trade secrets protection to save transaction costs for factual protection measures[95] and it might unnecessarily disincentivise limited disclosure of trade secrets in protected environments, which is important for the optimal development of data pools in the data economy.

An essential problem of the EU Trade Secrets Protection Regime as a tool in the data economy is the comparatively vague definition of the rightholder in regard to trade secrets (Article 2(2) Trade Secrets Directive).[96] In fact, not only in common data pools, but also in the realm of connected devices and all kinds of data-related networks, it will often be very difficult or even impossible to identify the person or persons who lawfully control the respective trade secrets. This is a problem common to any attempt to regulate the data economy on the basis of instruments which entail property-right elements and therefore need a uniform, clear and unambiguous allocation. By contrast, it is characteristic for the input to and use of data in common datapools and data-related networks that a clear allocation of rights to specific parts of the pool will often simply no longer be possible. In that regard, clearly, only contracts and, consequently, best

91 Josef Drexl, 'Designing Competitive Markets for Industrial Data – Between Propertization and Access' (2016) Max Planck Institute for Innovation and Competition Research Paper No. 16–13, 24 <https://papers.ssrn.com/sol3/papers.cfm?abstract_id=2862975>; Aplin (n. 90) 70.

92 See explicitly European Commission Staff Working Document, 'On the free flow of data and emerging issues of the European data economy – Accompanying the document Communication Building a European data economy' SWD(2017) 2 final, 20. See further on the requirements and differentiations in this field Schweitzer (n. 4) 571.

93 Aplin (n. 90) 65–66.

94 Ibid.

95 See already Mark A. Lemley, 'The Surprising Virtues of Treating Trade Secrets as IP Rights' (2008) 61 Stanford Law Review 311, 348–350 (on Art. 39 TRIPS).

96 Aplin (n. 90) 69.

practices guidance or even non-mandatory default rules in contract law will be able to solve the problems related to allocating ownership shares and – since precise ownership allocation will often no longer be possible in a reasonable way, even more importantly – the mutual relations of numerous co-owners to each other and to outsiders. However, the Trade Secrets Directive does not contain any provisions on licensing or other contracts in the field of trade secrets ownership and use, which is – arguably – its main shortcoming for the purposes of the data economy. It is submitted that the ongoing initiative of the Commission to establish best practices with regard to contractual allocation of rights to data in common data pools[97] is of essential importance in that respect and that the efforts in this sector should even be intensified.

As for the scope of protection, the Trade Secrets Directive generally has model character as a modern, balanced and proportional protection regime. First, it establishes certain lawful acts, most importantly for the data economy, comprising independent discovery or creation and, particularly, reverse engineering (Article 3 Trade Secrets Directive).[98] Only secondly does it define the unlawful acts and effectively provide for mere intensified tort remedies against certain specific acts of misappropriation (Article 4). Thirdly, it provides for a number of exceptions including a catch-all clause for any 'legitimate interest recognised by Union or national law' (Article 5). Finally, the Trade Secrets Directive's provisions on enforcement (Articles 6–15), in particular on injunctions, contain numerous qualifications and flexibilities which, if applied correctly and with caution by the courts, will ideally allow enforcement to be flexibly adjusted to the underlying, innovation-oriented goal of the protection regime. Although certain flexibilities in enforcement are clearly necessary and customary in this sector, given the broadly defined, particularly vague character of the protected subject matter, these modern provisions in the Trade Secrets Directive go further – and way beyond the balances and flexibilities in the older, more general Directive on the enforcement of intellectual property rights

97 See generally Communication from the Commission of 19 February 2020 to the European Parliament, the Council, the European Economic and Social Committee and the Committee of Regions – A European strategy for data, COM(2020) 66 final, 14.

98 Cf. also section B.III. above and further European Commission, 'Towards a common European data space' (n. 7) with European Commission SWD, 'Guidance on sharing private sector data' (n. 7).

of 2004.[99] They have genuine model character for a modern and balanced enforcement regime in the data economy.

Only a couple of points should be kept in mind in the current and future application of the new European trade secrets protection regime in order to streamline it for the purposes of the data economy. Thus, the provisions on lawful acts and on exceptions justly pay particular attention to certain public interest issues (in particular whistleblowing activities, protection of workers and employees etc.), while specific exceptions for the purpose of enhancing competition or for particular needs of the data economy are neither expressly stipulated nor considered. Also, the definition of prohibited acts goes particularly far in regard to the definition of infringing goods in Article 2(4) Trade Secrets Directive, which even comprises goods the marketing of which significantly benefits from trade secrets unlawfully acquired, used or disclosed.[100] This goes even further than the protection for direct products of a patented procedure in patent law, which is problematic for the data economy in its own right, and might pose particular problems for some of the currently economically most important big data applications, as it might have chilling effects on certain marketing methods, based on large data pools, whenever the legal situation of all data in the pool cannot be completely cleared. In order to better accommodate these two problematic points with the needs of the data economy, the criterion of 'significant benefit' as well as the catch-all clause in the catalogue of exceptions should generally be interpreted with a particular view to the just objective to enhance competition and innovation – including by newcomers and with regard to follow-up innovation and innovation in unrelated markets.

In sum, it is submitted that the new EU trade secrets protection regime is rather well equipped to contribute a flexible protection instrument to the regulation of the data economy, justly targeted on confidential, non-disclosed information of at least potential commercial value. To fully exploit this potential, the numerous flexible open-ended provisions in the Trade Secrets Directive will have to be consistently interpreted with a view to enhancing competition and innovation, including follow-up innovation, in the concerned markets.

---

99 Directive 2004/48/EC of the European Parliament and of the Council of 29.04.2004 on the enforcement of intellectual property rights [2004] *OJ L 195/16*.

100 Aplin (n. 90) 70.

IV. Access to data, sui generis database protection and trade secrets: The perspective of current and future access regimes

1. Basic consideration: Access to data and use of data

The following part focuses on the more prospective question of how (the occasional current) and possible future access regimes for certain use scenarios can be accommodated to the sui generis right and what IP law can contribute to the specific shaping of such access regimes.

Initially, in the discussion of access rights and IP protection two different levels have to be distinguished. Access rights provide for an individual right to have data disclosed and might then also entail certain regulation of the conditions of further use of these data (protection of authenticity of data, reciprocal disclosure, use for free or against payment, details of portability, certain limitations of use etc.). IP protection, in particular protection under the database maker's sui generis right, mainly concerns the regulation of *use* of data, i.e. has an impact only on the second 'half' of such access regimes. Therefore, IP rights as such can hardly help to answer the question of when secret or other access-restricted data should be disclosed.[101] In that regard, they are all but an additional barrier, such as the sui generis right or trade secrets protection. At best, they will expressly allow such disclosure, but as such (with very minor exceptions) they will never require it. By contrast, as far as the level of regulation of use of the accessed data is concerned, certain elements of IP rights, and even of the sui generis protection right, might be helpful to further structure the specific conditions in that regard.[102]

2. The basic case groups

As for actual or potential access needs, as has been said before, it seems possible to roughly distinguish certain categories of access and use interests[103] where the database sui generis right will likely be affected. First, as has been described above, the limitation of the exclusive rights to use acts in respect of substantial parts of a database cannot effectively accommo-

101 See on that problem Bently and others (n. 18) 41–42.
102 Partly different Drexl (n. 11) 154–155; see further section D below.
103 Similarly Bently and others (n. 18) 39–40; Schweitzer (n. 4) 572 ff.; see also Drexl (n. 11) 81–82.

date the possible need for use of entire aggregated sets of machine- or sensor-generated use or other data which in certain situations might be necessary for third parties in order to develop, produce, market or distribute value-added or entirely new products or services or to compete in the primary market (case group 1). Secondly, even individual-level use data of single users will often add up to a substantial part of a protected database which is owned by the provider of the product or service, who observes and collects these data (case group 2). As has been shown, the sui generis right sits uncomfortably with the possible legitimate use interests in both these areas. Thirdly, sui generis data base protection already raises actual problems in its relationship to the European access regime in the field of public sector information (PSI) (case group 3). Case group 3 has been discussed already and a solution has been proposed.[104]

As regards case group 1, the discussion meanwhile mainly centers on competition law-based compulsory licences[105] as well as on possible specific provisions for 'IP-internal' compulsory licences concerning access to so-called sole-source data in the context of the sui generis protection right.[106] In the case of the sui generis right such 'IP-internal' provisions on compulsory licences in certain well-defined cases should indeed be considered (see further below at D.). Also, Article 6(1) lit. h) and lit. i) of the newly proposed Digital Markets Act on access and data portability for business or end users of gatekeeper-platforms will be helpful in that regard, although the scope of these provisions is limited to certain very large gatekeeper-platforms (as defined in Article 3 of the proposed DMA). Significantly, these provisions do not specifically regulate the relationship with possibly existing IP-protection. This somewhat fits into the general character of the proposed DMA, which as a measure of sector-specific regulation, focuses on further specification and enforcement by the Commission. However, the problems concerning data access and portability go beyond the limited realm of gatekeeper platforms and can probably only be solved on the basis of individual access and portability rights encompassing further specification and remedies in private law. Therefore, the following considerations of the relationship of such future access rights to existing IP protection and of the accommodation of both regulatory systems in the context of private access and portability rights are of particular importance also for a reasonable and workably specification of these new instruments through

104 See section C.II.3c).
105 Schweitzer (n. 4) 576–580.
106 Drexl (n. 11) 81–83.

the Commission (in particular concerning the actual scope and conditions of access, portability and subsequent use).

Concerning case group 2 (see further below at 3.b)(2)), the structural analysis of individual customers' potential needs to access and port their individual-level data to other providers has recently been further developed and generalised for connected devices in a study by Drexl.[107] Drexl's approach is expressly based on future sector-specific access rights. That means that, on the basis of the distinction established in the preceding part, it focuses on both access to/disclosure of data and use of data. In this context, it seems systematically consistent that the study regards such access rights as independent of the legal status of the concerned data, in particular possible IP protection for the concrete form in which these data are collected and stored, and instead proposes sector-specific access regimes which 'should prevail over any sui generis database right'.[108] The details concerning such data access and use should instead be regulated in the context of these sector-specific access regimes themselves, including the question of whether and in which cases such use should be remunerated. In particular, concerning the question of remuneration, the study argues against the background of balanced economic incentives, which should not go beyond what is necessary to sufficiently incentivise the creation of databases in certain situations. Consequently, e.g. in regard to sensor-produced data and in particular concerning smart devices, the study rightly raises the fundamental question of whether remuneration will be needed at all where data access is necessary and justified.[109]

From Drexl's viewpoint, the Database Directive and EU IP instruments in general only need to be complemented with what we would call a passive 'interface provision', i.e. a general exception which clarifies that IP protection 'does not apply where, and to the extent to which' sector-specific regulations require access to data.[110] However, the devil of this approach of course is in the details as it begs the question of how use of such data should be regulated in detail in the different future cases and whether certain basic case groups can already be distinguished in this regard. In fact, while the approach seems systematically consistent and deserves approval as far as access as such is concerned, in regard to subsequent (commercial) use of the accessed and ported data, any such access regime will need fur-

107 Ibid.
108 Ibid 82.
109 Ibid 82.
110 Ibid 83.

ther refinement of the conditions for and scope of such use anyway. And in that regard, its accommodation to existing IP protection from this author's viewpoint can hardly be entirely ignored, since the existing IP protection rights, including the sui generis right for databases, already contain certain (more or less conclusive) assumptions of the legislature on the need and tailoring of incentives for innovation in certain specifically defined fields. On the contrary, from this author's viewpoint, certain elements of the existing EU IP regime can even provide structural guidance for the further regulation of data *use* in the context of different access scenarios (see further below 3 and D). Similarly, with regard to Article 6 (1) lit. (h) and (i) of the proposed DMA, both the specification by the Commission as well as a system of functional private remedies deviced to enforce these duties of gatekeeper platforms should certainly be inspired by and accommodated with certain principles and experiences concerning the regulation of access in the existing IP regime in order to make them work effectively in practice.

Now how should these two very basic cases (individual access to and portability of customer data inter alia to prevent lock-in; general access to complete databases by competitors or businesses to enable workable competition) be treated from the viewpoint of IP and in particular from the viewpoint of the sui generis right concerning the *use* of such data?

3. *Details of the interface with IP protection, in particular sui generis protection*

a) Cases that should be excluded from protection

From the viewpoint of sui generis protection, in certain cases the general incentives rationale behind the sui generis right might indeed be fundamentally flawed from the outset, if at a closer look incentives are typically not at all necessary in order to foster dynamic competition. As for the protection conditions of sui generis protection, the crucial question is whether these cases can be structured and described in a sufficiently abstract and stable way, i.e. in clearly identifiable case groups that are independent of specific market conditions and can therefore be generalised. If this is the case, from a contextual point of view, respective investments should not be covered by the sui generis right in the first place. Instead, investments in such cases should be excluded from the protectable subject matter as such and consequently should not qualify as relevant for sui generis protection. Actually, the *British Horseracing Board* case, which concerned a typical spin-off situation in which the relevant databases resulted from another (main) commercial activity and an additional protection of the investment to create the database was therefore obviously not necessary, is a case in point.[111] This is another reason why generation of data, if it is not based on observation or measurement of available outside factors and if the structuring of the information does not reach the outstanding level of creativity required for copyright protection in Europe, should remain excluded from the protectable subject matter of the sui generis right. This should be expressly clarified and specified in the Directive. Further case groups should and can be developed.[112] Such cases should be carved out in the application of the condition of protection[113] and sui generis protection should be denied from the start.

b) Cases where the incentive rationale of the sui generis protection right has to be taken into account, but has to be balanced with a specific access and use interest

(1) Overriding interest in access and use

By contrast, in cases where relevant investments are protected by the sui generis regime because incentives generally seem necessary and at least on principle justifiable to foster the creation and structured dissemination of databases, as a starting point, the express will of the legislature of the Database Directive, that use of the protected databases should generally not be for free, has to be accepted.

However, this legislative balancing of interests is not necessarily conclusive in regard to recent technological developments and certain specific, newly emerging access and use interests. Therefore, there might be cases in which the basic balancing of rights and interests (and between static efficiency (access) and dynamic efficiency (incentives)), indeed needs to be overridden beyond the limited possibilities of competition law. Generally, these cases will require the most thorough and specific analysis in particular with regard to the question on which conditions use of the data should be granted. In that regard, in an untechnical way, the existing EU IP regime might provide for some structural guideposts.

---

111 Case C-203/02 *British Horseracing Board* ECLI:EU:C:2004:695 (n. 68).

112 See further section C.II.3.c) above and more comprehensively section C.IV.3.b) below.

113 See section C.II.3.a) above.

(2) Access rights for individual 'lawful customers' with regard to sensor-produced data of smart devices

This is because, naturally, not only for the interface of IP and competition law, but also with a view to the 'IP-internal' structures, these are not entirely new questions. Hence, it is not surprising that existing 'anchors' in EU IT-related copyright law and in the provisions on the sui generis right can already be identified for both case groups, which characterise the current access discussion.[114]

Case group 2, concerning individual customer access, use and portability (namely transfer of the received data to different providers) in the realm of smart devices, sensor-produced data etc., is systematically related to the copyright concept of the so-called lawful user in both the Computer Programs[115] and the Database Directive. Accordingly, the Database Directive contains a provision on mandatory core minimum rights of lawful users of databases which cannot be overridden by contract (Arts 8(1) and 15 Database Directive). Under a broader perspective, another example in the wider context of such mandatory minimum rights of customers outside IP law is Article 16(4) Digital Content Directive,[116] which in turn was modelled on Article 20 GDPR.

In fact, this regulatory technique already partly used in European copyright law, i.e. the provision of certain mandatory minimum rights of legitimate users, has the potential to substantially streamline the function of IP rights in online networks. This is because legally, these minimum rights 'travel' with the legitimate user, who may perform certain minimum acts deemed necessary to effectively use the respective databases.[117] It is this very mechanism that could easily be extended to cover access to data and use rights concerning the transfer to other providers for lawful users of smart devices and machinery which produce sensor-generated sui generis

---

114 As for the third relevant case group, data generated by public bodies, see C.II.3.c) above.

115 See Art. 5 Computer Programs Directive (n. 23).

116 Directive (EU) 2019/770 of the European Parliament and of the Council of 20 May 2019 on certain aspects concerning contracts for the supply of digital content and digital services [2019] OJ L136/1.

117 See fundamentally case C-128/11 *UsedSoft* ECLI:EU:C:2012:407. Although, in case C-263/18 *Nederlands Uitgeversverbond v Tom Kabinet* ECLI:EU:C:2019:1111, the CJEU refused to generalise the UsedSoft doctrine for all categories of copyright-protected works under the InfoSoc Directive, it might still be extended to the area of databases where minimum rights of lawful users are expressly provided for in the Database Directive for both copyright and the sui generis right.

protectable data. Typically, for such use no additional remuneration should be set out since the database producer can factor the associated costs into the conditions of the underlying sales or service contract. Accordingly, the EU copyright framework also regards such rights as part of the contractual consideration and does not provide for additional remuneration claims. The provisions on the minimum rights of lawful users therefore offer the ideal functional context to implement possible sector-specific individual customer access and porting rights in the area of smart devices etc. where these are deemed necessary and where they will be possibly provided in sector-specific regulation in the future. Of course, the main challenge for such sector-specific regulation is to make access and use rights of individual customers functional in practice. In that regard, the model of Article 20 GDPR should be closely followed and IP law should contribute to functional, accessible infrastructures by safeguarding free access to APIs, data formats and other comparable infrastructural technical elements in order not to put additional legal trammels on the at least conceivable future development of tools and service providers for possible real-time porting of specific use data.[118]

The most intriguing question in this regard, which has also in the past been the subject of intense debate in copyright law,[119] is to what extent such rights of lawful users should indeed have mandatory character.[120] This question is not easy to answer in a generalised way, as it depends on the degree of connection between the product or service and the data market and the information of the customer on the resulting dangers of lock-in or leveraging in a given product or service market. An initial consideration might be to provide for mandatory access and portability rights of private users, while access and portability rights of commercial users could be designed as mere non-mandatory default rules. But this bright-line distinction might miss the point in future multipolar data markets, as the example of certain small-scale business customers, such as Uber drivers, shows.

118 See also section B. above. See further in regard to open standards, formats etc. Furman and others (n. 4) 64–74.

119 Cf. for the broad discussion on the dogmatic nature of the provision and the scope of the so-called mandatory core of Art. 5 Computer Programs Directive (n. 23) (and its counterpart in Sec. 69d German Copyright Act) the references in Gerald Spindler, in Ulrich Loewenheim, Matthias Leistner and Ansgar Ohly (eds), *Urheberrecht: Kommentar* (6th edn, C.H. Beck 2020) Sec. 69d paras 1 and 13–14.

120 Schweitzer (n. 4) 575: non-mandatory; Drexl (n. 11) 154, 156: mandatory, at least in regard to consumers. Furman and others (n. 4) 10 seems to be generally sceptical about far-reaching mandatory solutions.

Ultimately, the justification to provide for such access and portability rights in a mandatory way will depend on the concrete market structure and empirical proof of information asymmetries on the side of the customers in specific sectors. If these conditions are fulfilled, admittedly, implementing possible access rights as mandatory minimum rights of the lawful user in this context still results in a certain cross-subsidisation of users who rely on these rights and actively use them to switch their providers, at the expense of less active users who do not use this option. This is because such access and portability rights will generally raise the cost of the provider, which no longer has the possibility to contractually bind certain customers on the basis of control over aggregated individual-level customer data in a closer way and therefore loses possibilities for price discrimination. However, in sectors in which such regulation seems necessary and proportionate to prevent existing or likely concrete lock-in problems, this very effect might be desirable. After all, it would enable and enhance competition in the interest of all customers by nuancedly subsidising the more active customers in their switching endeavours.

Future reform of the Database Directive should keep this overall context in mind. Further details, such as a possible definition of the minimum (mandatory or mere default) use rights and their 'portability' should be regulated in future sector-specific access regulation, where and as far as this is reasonable and necessary. At the 'receiving' end, the current sui generis regime is not at all complete, but at least initially prepared in its basic structures: In future, the dogmatic category of the minimum rights of the lawful user could be extended to cover use in such cases referring to the different sector-specific access regulations. For the moment, the limitation of the rights of the lawful user of a database to extract and re-utilise only insubstantial parts of a database should be eliminated; instead, the lawful user should be able to perform the necessary use acts also in regard to substantial parts of or complete databases.

(3) Access and use rights for competitors: compulsory licences in the specific context of the sui generis right and of trade secrets protection

Access and use rights in regard to entire aggregated datasets and corresponding use rights for competitors or other businesses in order to enhance competition in the area of sole-source data follow different principles. Typically, such use should be remunerated as it seems that the incentives rationale behind the sui generis right will generally be intact in such cases, whereas it is only a specific market situation which requires that the property rule be turned into a liability rule.[121]

In fact, specific compulsory licensing provisions have been considered since the very beginning of policy discussions about a possible need for database sui generis protection in the 1990s.[122] In that regard, it is of particular interest that an earlier Proposal for the Database Directive explicitly included provisions on compulsory licences.[123] Article 8 of the Proposal provided for a compulsory licence on 'fair and non-discriminatory' terms for publicly available sole-source databases as well as for publicly available databases compiled by public bodies.

Meanwhile, the existing case law and practice even more clearly suggest that competition law-based compulsory licences will simply often come too late in the typically very dynamic markets for data-based products or services.[124] Therefore, it seems that specific provisions on compulsory licences in the Database Directive can at least be useful in cases in which the mere generation/collection distinction fails to pro-actively prevent *sole-source situations*, e.g. because 'collected' databases develop into an industry standard, independent obtainment becomes impossible because of ex post network effects or subsequent public regulation etc.[125] Hence, at least a compulsory licensing provision for sole-source databases should be added in the Database Directive. Whether additional cases are conceivable in the wake of big data and the multipolar data economy remains to be seen and should be left to sector-specific analysis and regulation.

As regards the sole-source criterion, the definition of indispensability should follow the CJEU's definition in *Bronner* (concerning a physical newspaper distribution scheme). Hence, a successful claim to a compulsory licence should require that the creation of a comparable database not be viable under reasonable economic conditions for a competitor of compara-

121 Cf. also Leistner (n. 19) 42–46.

122 Jane C. Ginsburg, 'Creation and Commercial Value: Copyright Protection of Works of Information' (1990) 90 Columbia Law Review 1865.

123 Art. 8 Proposal for a Council Directive on the legal protection of databases, COM(1992) 24 final. See further Bently and others (n. 18) 36–37, with further references.

124 Drexl (n. 91) 42–44; Josef Drexl and others, 'Position Statement of the Max Planck Institute for Innovation and Competition on exclusive and access rights of 16 August 2016' (2016) 11–13 <www.ip.mpg.de/fileadmin/ipmpg/content/stellungnahmen/MPI-Stellungnahme_Daten_2016_08_16_final.pdf> accessed 31 August 2020.

125 Cf. on possible reasons and case groups for compulsory licences Bently and ohters (n. 18) 39–43 (albeit with a more open conclusion).

ble size and resources as the original database maker.[126] Moreover, access to the data would have to be indispensable for access to a downstream market in relation to the (hypothetical) upstream licensing market for the data. It has to be noted that, according to the CJEU's *IMS Health* judgment, this so-called downstream market can also be the market where the database maker already offers its own products or services to customers, since the (hypothetical) upstream market would be the (hypothetical) licensing market in such cases, regardless of whether the database maker grants licences to third parties in that market at all.[127] By contrast, the additional criteria from general competition law for compulsory licences (in particular, prevention of the offer of a new product or service) should not apply in case of sui generis protection of sole-source databases.[128] The enhancement of competition in the product or service market or in a downstream, complementary or entirely new market as such should suffice to justify the compulsory licence.[129]

Remuneration should be set on fair and non-discriminatory terms.[130] Depending on the circumstances of the case, this might also result in free use of data where parties might reasonably have negotiated a zero licence fee. In the broader context of the discussion to turn the sui generis right into a registered industrial property right,[131] one might consider making the EUIPO responsible for the granting of such compulsory licences for use in the EU market.[132] In that context an arbitration mechanism and, ultimately, an appeal to the General Court should be provided for in order to set the conditions of such compulsory licences.

An intriguing question, and one that has also been recently asked by Schweitzer, is whether such compulsory licences should generally only be granted on the condition of reciprocity, i.e. the granting of a cross-licence by the licence seeker.[133] Patent law has chosen this solution in Article 31(l) (ii) TRIPS (see also Sec. 24(2) German Patent Act). Also, the usual FRAND and RAND declarations in the context of standard-essential patents offer the SEP holder the option of granting a FRAND licence only on the condi-

126 Cf. Case C-7/97 *Bronner* ECLI:EU:C:1998:569, paras 46–47.
127 Cf. Case C-418/01 *IMS Health* ECLI:EU:C:2004:257.
128 Similarly Schweitzer (n. 4) 578.
129 See already Leistner (n. 45) 150–151; critically Drexl (n. 91) 52.
130 Cf. also Drexl (n. 11) 82.
131 Cf. Leistner (n. 19) 49–50, 56; Leistner as reported by Bently and others (n. 18) 65, 84.
132 Cf. Bently and others (n. 18) 42–43.
133 Cf. Schweitzer (n. 4) 579.

tion of reciprocity.[134] Nonetheless, it seems that the specific situation concerning the database sui generis right is of a slightly different nature. Whereas patents vest a genuine exclusive use right in the person of the rightholder, the sui generis protection right only protects the investment in the collection and presentation of the contents of a database and, as such, does not always exclude independent creation of a comparable or better database. Accordingly, there might be cases in which a mandatory condition of cross-licensing would not necessarily yield the efficient result, such as if a very small, innovative market entrant, under the reciprocity condition, had to grant access to data the incumbent could easily acquire independently. All in all, it might be the best solution to expressly state the possibility that FRAND conditions might comprise a cross-licensing duty on the implementer, but should leave it to the competent authority and, ultimately, to the courts to decide whether such a reciprocity condition is a part of reasonable and non-discriminatory licensing conditions on the facts of a given case.

Compulsory licences under the proposed mechanism on principle[135] should also extend to non-published databases, i.e. should take the form of genuine rights to access and disclosure, where this is needed to enable workable competition.[136] Naturally, this raises intricate issues of third-party rights and interests, in particular concerning privacy protection, protection of personal data and confidentiality in regard to natural persons, but also in regard to businesses whose data are stored in such sole-source databases.[137] Remarkably, even the original Proposal of the Commission, which still envisaged compulsory licences only for published databases, already dealt with the relationship to other legislation concerning privacy, protection of personal data and confidentiality. As for protection of personal data, today it follows mandatorily from the GDPR that respective information duties in relation to and a veto right of affected individual persons must be provided for in cases of upstream compulsory licensing when a business that has stored data relating to these natural persons is con-

134 See, for example, ETSI IPR Policy para 6.1 <www.etsi.org/images/files/IPR/etsi-ipr-policy.pdf> accessed 31 August 2020.

135 But see immediately below on necessary differentiation for databases which are additionally protected as a trade secret, which will often be the case.

136 Still differently and limiting compulsory licences to published databases Ginsburg (n. 122) 1929; Art. 8 of the original Commission's Proposal for the Database Directive (n. 123).

137 Cf., for example, Drexl and others (n. 2) 18-19; Bently and others (n. 18) 42 and Drexl (n. 11) 82.

cerned. At first sight, this might seem like a considerable practical trammel on compulsory licensing. On the other hand, customers would probably rather seldom veto such compulsory licences if they allowed for the offer of new or more efficient products or services. Also, if only individual customers vetoed such licensing this would not entirely devaluate the utility of the remaining parts of the database, subject to compulsory licensing.

As for trade secrets it seems that if trade secrets are concerned, compulsory licences should only be granted under the additional circumstances of the CJEU's *IMS Health* decision[138] and the General Court's *Microsoft* ruling.[139] Accordingly, in these cases compulsory licences would require that access to the data in question be indispensable to offer a new product or service[140] in a downstream market in relation to the (hypothetical) licensing market and that the denial of access would effectively foreclose workable competition on that market. However, this qualification would not have to be implemented in the new compulsory licensing provision in the Database Directive, as it self-evidently follows from the independent nature of trade secrets protection, which would as such not be affected by a compulsory licensing provision for the database sui generis protection right.

Whether further conditions or qualifications would be needed should be a matter for future research.[141] This might concern issues such as additional guideposts for the specification of FRAND terms in certain cases as well as procedural backing for the process of specifying FRAND terms, such as possible specific rights to information and other procedural rules.

D. *Selected elements of IP rights as building blocks for the regulation of future data markets*

Finally, apart from the targeted access-oriented perspective, under which IP rights will typically be observed as a 'negative' possible barrier to access, one might also ask which elements of IP rights might indeed be particu-

138 Case C-418/01 *IMS Health* ECLI:EU:C:2004:257.

139 Case T-201/04 R *Microsoft v Commission* ECLI:EU:T:2004:372 and Case T-201/04 *Microsoft v Commission* ECLI:EU:T:2007:289.

140 But see already B.III. above on the meanwhile very low requirements for a 'new' product or service in this sense.

141 See from the more recent literature comprehensively on compulsory licensing Reto M. Hilty and others (eds), *Compulsory Licensing – Practical experiences and ways forward* (Springer 2015).

larly helpful in building the future legal infrastructure for data markets. Under this 'positive' perspective, a couple of general ideas come to mind where elements of existing IP rights might serve as guideposts or building blocks for the solution of certain recurring problems in the discussion on the legal infrastructure for the data economy.

First, as data markets are currently mainly regulated by contracts, even more complex forms of multipolar, multi-purpose data biotopes develop, mainly on the basis of networks of bilateral or multilateral agreements with mere inter partes effects. It is characteristic of the discussion on the future regulation in this sector that at least in regard to certain aspects of regulation (data access, authenticity of data, control over specific data sets, conditions of use by third parties) a significant need for a *flexible inter omnes effect* of such contracts is felt. Recently, the Data Ethics Commission has proposed the provision of a limited inter omnes effect of data-related contractual agreements roughly modelled on Article 4(4) Trade Secrets Directive.[142] The same general idea, albeit in a different context and much more limited way, has recently been followed in Japan, where the revision of the Japanese Unfair Competition Prevention Act provides for new protection of certain non-secret but 'managed' limited-access data against misappropriation (wrongful acquisition or improper disclosure) and extends this to the use of such data with the knowledge that it was wrongfully acquired.[143] These flexible approaches deserve attention. Indeed, if a need for additional inter omnes regulation (beyond contract law and the effects of contract-based networks) could be concretely proven in certain sectors or with regard to certain rights and interests, concepts and elements from trade secrets law with its rather flexible set of substantive and enforcement provisions would be certainly better equipped to accommodate such regulation needs than any property rights-based regime.[144] Nonetheless, whether such regulation is required at all in certain sectors remains to be seen. Any additional layer of regulation inevitably adds transaction costs, including information costs, trade secrets protection itself being an example in point.[145] As for the inter omnes effect of FRAND licensing declarations, patent practice is just in the process of developing appropriate in-

142 Opinion of the Data Ethics Commission (n. 11) 22, 144, 155.

143 See further Art. 2(7) and Art. 2(xi) et seq. Japanese Unfair Competition Prevention Act.

144 Aplin (n. 90) 59.

145 See on the problems concerning the identification of ownership and even the identification of the exact protected subject matter Aplin (n. 90) 59 and section C.III. above.

struments on the basis of the *existing law*. From this author's viewpoint, this latter development in case law should rightly be based on both contract law and competition law, without a current pressing need for new legislation.[146]

Second, protection of personal data under the GDPR puts considerable trammels on the development of data biotopes, based on networks of contracts, whenever personal data of third parties (consumers or customers) are concerned.[147] In fact, the increasing commodification of data and the development of data related contracts are hampered in this field by the very strict requirements for informed consent laid down in the GDPR as well as by the general principle, underlying the GDPR, that such consent can be freely withdrawn anytime (Article 7(3) GDPR). Accordingly, the interface between new data-related approaches in contract law, such as the new Digital Content Directive,[148] and the comparatively strict requirements of the GDPR raises many questions.[149]

In this respect, it has to be noted that German and continental European copyright laws have for decades had to grapple with similar problems concerning the personality-rights core of copyright and have developed contractual and statutory instruments to bridge the gap. Thus, to mention just one example, copyright law (see Section 42 German Copyright Act) does indeed allow the withdrawal of commercial use rights because of a changed personal attitude towards the work, but subjects this right of the licensor to qualifications and a duty to compensate the licensee for her resulting frustrated expenses. Another, similar instrument for the accommodation of contractual obligations on one hand, and the inalienable moral rights of the author on the other, can be found in Section 41 German Copyright Act. In general, it seems that some highly developed ideas on

---

146 See section B.II.B.1. above.

147 Schweitzer (n. 4) 573–574; Crémer, de Montjoye and Schweitzer (n. 4) 73–87; Schweitzer and Peitz (n. 4) 276–278; Kerber (n. 4) 644–646.

148 Digital Content and Digital Services Directive (n. 116).

149 Axel Metzger and others, 'Data-Related Aspects of the Digital Content Directive' (2018) 9 Journal of Intellectual Property, Information Technology and E-Commerce Law 90; Axel Metzger, 'A Market Model for Personal Data: State of the Play under the New Directive on Digital Content and Digital Services' in Sebastian Lohsse, Reiner Schulze and Dirk Staudenmayer (eds), *Data as Counter-Performance – Contract Law 2.0?* (forthcoming); Gerald Spindler and Karin Sein, 'Die Richtlinie über Verträge über digitale Inhalte' (2019) Multimedia und Recht 415 and 488; Andreas Sattler, 'Neues EU-Vertragsrecht für digitale Güter – Die Richtlinie (EU) 2019/770 als Herausforderung für das Schuld-, Urheber- und Datenschutzrecht' (2020) Computer und Recht 145.

contracts concerning personality rights can be found in copyright law.[150] However, to effectively make use of these approaches in the data economy, it seems that changes to the GDPR will hardly be avoidable in future.

E. Conclusion

The existing EU IP rights system is in reasonably good shape as regards its balanced approach to the protection of APIs, data formats and other more technical infrastructure, which should be open and accessible in order to enable and enhance data portability including future real-time data portability. Only details should be adjusted in this respect. In patent law, compressed or formatted data sequences should not be protected as a direct product of patented data compression or other processes. Minor adjustments are also necessary in regard to the relationship of the respective provisions of the Computer Program Directive and the Trade Secrets Directive on decompilation and reverse engineering. Both problems can be solved in case law. An imminent need for legislative activity cannot be identified in this sector.

As regards the accommodation of the different existing and proposed future access and use regimes for the data economy, the picture is slightly different. Again, European copyright law in the strict sense currently poses almost no significant problems for the development of the data economy. Only the hitherto insufficient new exception for text and data mining is a case for (another) revision at least in the middle term. By contrast, the database sui generis right is in immediate need of reform. Concrete reform proposals have been made in this paper, namely clarifications concerning the substantive condition of protection, new compulsory licensing provisions for sole-source databases and many others.

By contrast, EU trade secrets protection, which has been recently harmonised in the Trade Secrets Directive of 2016, is a modern and remarkably balanced protection regime comprising numerous open-ended terms which provide for necessary flexibility on all levels of substantive law and enforcement. With its hybrid character as a mere protection against misappropriation with certain flexible and qualified – in result only very limited – property rights elements, and with its focus on the protection of confi-

150 Axel Metzger, 'Verträge über digitale Inhalte und digitale Dienstleistungen: Neuer BGB-Vertragstypus oder punktuelle Reform?' (2019) JuristenZeitung 577, 578.

dential, non-disclosed information, it seems particularly well equipped to serve the regulation needs of the data economy. Only minor details will have to be adjusted in the future, and this can be achieved by construing the many open-ended terms and concepts in the Directive with a view to reducing unnecessary barriers to market entry and enhancing workable competition.

Finally, the IP system can contribute certain building blocks and experience to the overall discussion on a balanced and workable regulation of the data economy. Namely, existing experience and instruments in copyright law concerning the accommodation of the protection of personality rights on the one hand, and the commodification of such rights through contracts on the other, as well as existing specific remedies in trade secrets law, based in contractual agreements, but with a limited inter omnes effect, could be particularly helpful in drafting a future regulation of the data economy. Such elements, in a generalised form, could be useful parts of a future, balanced regulation which, from this author's viewpoint, should be based mainly on the further development of contract law and competition law.

Taking stock of existing data access regimes

Data access rules: The role of contractual unfairness control of (consumer) contracts

Michael Grünberger[*]

A. *(Responsive) Contract law shall be Queen*

Legal paradigms express the 'implicit images of one's own society, giving a certain perspective to the practice of both legislation and the law's application'.[1] Paradigms shape the construction and the interpretation of legal rules and principles as 'a response to the challenges of a social situation perceived in a certain way'.[2] This applies in particular to the current debates within data and information law. Twenty years ago the movement from ownership to access was heralded.[3] The shift in business models from the single (digital) transfer to continuous accessibility as well as the rise of the 'sharing economy' are two trends that have shaped the (digital) economy and they both appear to vindicate the prominence of the access paradigm. Furthermore, the most recent developments regarding machine-generated data seem to support the prevalence of the access paradigm: The discussion started off with the proposal of an exclusive 'data producer's right' (*Datenerzeugerrecht*)[4] and, eventually, led to the advocacy of a 'data ownership right' (*Dateneigentumsrecht*).[5] However, it quickly took a very

---

* I would like to thank my doctoral student Katharina Wunner for her valuable input and my student assistants Jana Ebersberger and Daniel Neubauer for their support in adjusting the paper to the formal prerequisites.

1 Jürgen Habermas, *Faktizität und Geltung* (4th edn, Suhrkamp 1994) 468.

2 Habermas (n. 1) 468.

3 Jeremy Rifkin, *The Age of Access* (Pinguin Business Library 2000).

4 Herbert Zech, 'Daten als Wirtschaftsgut – Überlegungen zu einem "Recht des Datenerzeugers"' (2015) Computer und Recht 137; Herbert Zech, 'Data as a Tradable Commodity' in Alberto de Franceschi (ed.), *European Contract Law and the Digital Single Market* (Intersentia 2016) 51, 74.

5 Marc Amstutz, 'Dateneigentum', (2018) 218 Archiv für die civilistische Praxis 438; Karl-Heinz Fezer, 'Repräsentatives Dateneigentum – Ein zivilgesellschaftliches Bürgerrecht' (2018) <www.kas.de/c/document_library/get_file?uuid=f828a351-a2f6-11c1-b720-1aa08eaccff9&groupId=252038> accessed 31 August 2020; Karl-Heinz Fezer, 'Data Ownership of the People' (2017) 9 Zeitschrift für Geistiges Eigentum 356.

different turn against the introduction of new intellectual property rights and in favour of introducing access rules.[6] The policy reasons behind this shift are rather simple: Markets can 'develop with relatively little legal exclusivity where access can effectively be controlled by technical means. Factual exclusivity has the potential of forcing parties into negotiations and can trigger transactions in very similar ways as in the case of intellectual property'.[7] This description captures one of the two pillars of the current *status quo* in the data economy: the facticity of control over data access (*Faktizität der Datenzugangskontrolle*). The *de facto* control over data generated and secured by means of technically structured processes does not entail any notion of normative ownership.[8] But 'the recognition of a *de facto* property over industrial dataset is a non-neutral allocative choice'.[9] This recognition rests on a normative foundation. The second pillar upon which the *status quo* of the data economy is built is the contract between the parties. It is precisely this contract that normatively allocates the control, and therefore the use of the data among the parties. Thus, the contract legally secures the *de facto* control of the producer of the data-generating device or a data service provider. For the purpose of this paper I assume that the contract privileges this party. Henceforth I will call this party the 'data holder' or, synonymously, 'data controller'. Granted, contractual language with 'which the data holder claims "ownership" in the data cannot result in ownership rights as rights *in rem* [and] as a matter of privacy of contract, such stipulation can only produce (*inter partes*) effects among the contracting parties'.[10] But the contractual allocation of the data to the data

6 Josef Drexl and others, 'Data Ownership and Access to Data – Position Statement of the Max Planck Institute for Innovation and Competition of 16 August 2016 on the Current European Debate' <https://papers.ssrn.com/sol3/papers.cfm?abstract_id=2833165> accessed 31 August 2020.

7 Josef Drexl, 'Designing Competitive Markets for Industrial Data' (2017) 8 Journal of Intellectual Property, Information Technology and E-Commerce Law 257, para. 69.

8 See Daria Kim, 'No One's Ownership as the Status Quo and a Possible Way Forward: A Note on the Public Consultation on Building a European Data Economy', (2017) Gewerblicher Rechtsschutz und Urheberrecht Internationaler Teil 697, 702.

9 See Francesco Mezzanotte, 'Access to Data: The Role of Consent and the Licensing Scheme' in Sebastian Lohsse, Reiner Schulze and Dirk Staudenmeyer (eds), *Trading Data in the Digital Economy: Legal Concepts and Tools* (Nomos 2017) 159, 167.

10 Josef Drexl, 'Data Access and Control in the Era of Connected Devices. Study on Behalf of the European Consumer Organisation BEUC' (2018) 29–30 <www.beuc

holder carries considerable normative weight, because it is *prima facie* the only legal justification for the facticity of control over data access.

The introduction of an (intellectual) property right would not substantially alter this picture, regardless of the (problematic) issue[11] to whom the right should be granted: If it were attributed to the party which already enjoys *de facto* control over the data, this normative choice would provide a third pillar to the current allocation of the data use, thus further strengthening the data holder's legal position. If, as proposed for example in the model of data ownership, the right were initially vested in the end-user of the data-producing artefact, the introduction of a property right would add nothing but transaction costs: The contract the end-user enters into either with the producer or, as is the case in end-user licence agreements, with the service provider of the artefact, would, in the light of the respective bargaining power and informational and technological asymmetries between the parties, most likely reallocate the data usage rights to the *de facto* data holder. Enabling this mechanism is but the purpose of introducing property rights for immaterial goods in the first place.[12] Furthermore, property rights are (at present) considered too rigid a corset for effectively regulating dynamic markets. Thus, contractually secured *de facto* access currently not only provides an equivalent regulatory tool but may even be superior due to its flexibility. Regardless of the perspective, the *status quo* can be summed up as follows: Contract is King – and freedom of contract the main self-regulatory instrument within the current data economy. Hence the governing paradigm within the data economy appears to be that of (*de facto*) ownership and (contractual) control, regardless of all the talk about access.

In this paper I would like to challenge this paradigm and to dethrone the 'King'. In his place I would like to implement a responsive contract law as the new Queen. The main feature of responsive contract law is that it conceptualises its instruments from a sociological perspective and conceives of the parties' subjective rights regarding their social functions within the law's social environment (infra C.I.1.a). I will propose the argument that the unfairness control of contractual terms in both business-to-con-

.eu/publications/beuc-x-2018-121_data_access_and_control_in_the_area_of_connected_devices.pdf> accessed 31 August 2020.

11 For the problems associated with the ownership of a data IP right, see Drexl (n. 7) 257, para. 106; Herbert Zech, 'Building a European Data Economy' (2017) 9 Zeitschrift für Geistiges Eigentum 317, 324–325.

12 Hanns Ullrich, 'Lizenzkartellrecht auf dem Weg in die Mitte' (1996) Gewerblicher Rechtsschutz und Urheberrecht Internationaler Teil 555, 565–566.

sumer (B2C) and business-to-business (B2B) relations can from the outset be designed to become an adequate access rule in multilateral contract networks to effectively enforce individual access rights of end-users to co-generated data.

My argument is rather simple: Because the data holder justifies her *de facto* exclusivity through contract, it becomes contract law's responsibility to check on the normative foundation of the *de facto* technological standard by applying an unfairness control to the contractual terms at issue. That is why the unfairness control functions as an 'access rule'. The unfairness control is not necessarily dependent on the availability of supplementary provisions in contract law. The benchmark for the unfairness control is the collective knowledge gathered by the private actors. Enhancing the knowledge-gaining process of private ordering through contract law is at the core of my proposal. My model operates on a (rebuttable) presumption that contractual standard terms are *not unfair* if they are an integral part of model contracts, codes of conduct or best practices that in turn are compliant with certain requirements of procedural justice. If the presumption is successfully rebutted, the access-restricting contract clause is unfair and therefore invalid. If the contractual terms and conditions fail to meet the unfairness test, the contract will turn against the data holder: The technological *de facto* standard regarding exclusivity is in violation of contract law's normative standards regarding the usability of the data at issue. Hence, the facticity of the data holder's control of the data not only lacks a normative justification but runs afoul of contract law's principles regarding fair data allocation and access to co-generated data. To remedy the normative deficit of the facticity regarding data control, contract law demands that data access be reallocated to the other party. As a result, responsive contract law provides a contractual claim of the end-user against the data holder to actively enable access to individual-level data co-generated by the end-user or within the end-user's responsibility. Thus, the unfair terms control is an additional regulatory instrument to enhance data access in the data economy and it should be part of the Member States' and, eventually, the European regulator's toolbox.

The paper will focus on machine-generated data. Having said that, it must acknowledge the fact that because of the multitudes of data-generating contexts it is difficult to impossible to sufficiently distinguish purely machine-generated data from personal data within the meaning of Article 4(1) General Data Protection Regulation (GDPR). An environmentally sensitive contract law solution must therefore address the overlap between non-personal and personal data within machine-generated data (infra B.II). The paper will proceed in three steps: First, I will briefly describe the regulatory problem posed by the need of data access in the data economy and argue to consider contract law as an additional regulatory tool (B). Second, I will sketch a proposal based on the established unfairness control and enhance the latter with procedural elements in order to facilitate knowledge gaining (C). Third, I will address two of the most obvious challenges of this model (D). The paper will end with some concluding remarks (E).

B. The regulatory problem: enabling data access under fair terms

I. Negative impacts of the status quo

The European Commission has been aware of the access issue regarding data generated by machines or processes (machine-generated data): 'In order to extract the maximum value from this type of data, market players need to have access to large and diverse datasets. However, this becomes more difficult to achieve if the generators of the data keep it to themselves.'[13] The situation is aggravated if the user is 'prevented by the manufacturer from authorising usage of the data by another party'.[14] The *status quo* is the *de facto* control of data by the data controller, combined with the contractual justification of this data allocation, regularly accompanied by contractual terms governing access to the data and prohibiting the transfer of the data to third parties. This is a regulatory problem from at least two perspectives:[15] From a competition perspective, the *status quo* leads to negative innovation effects, making market access more difficult and increasing lock-in effects. Additionally, the *status quo* also has negative effects on the contractual balance of interests: There is a serious risk of unequal negotiating positions between the manufacturer or service provider on the one hand and the end-user of the products on the other hand. This may result in unfair standard contract terms which, overall, significantly increase the transaction costs for structurally weaker parties – consumers or SMEs.

The Commission has identified one particular constellation where the aforementioned negative impacts on both competition and contractual equity might come into play: '[I]n some cases manufacturers, companies offering services or other market players holding data keep the data generat-

13 Communication of the European Commission, 'Building a European Data Economy' COM(2017) 9 final, 8.

14 European Commission (n. 13) COM(2017) 9 final, 10.

15 See European Commission (n. 13) COM(2017) 9 final, 8–11.

ed by their machines or through their products and services for themselves, thus potentially restricting reuse in downstream markets.'[16] An example might be helpful to illustrate this point:[17] Gämmerler is a southern German engineering company for components and complete systems for the printing industry. They offer a smart monitoring service to their (professional) customers to avoid unplanned downtimes of the machines. Gämmerler has partnered with the operator of a service platform (Siemens) to collect and analyse usage data on their machines, which are distributed worldwide. The data is provided by the buyer or owner of the machines. For this additional service, Gämmerler charges based on a pay-per-use model. We might infer from the publicly available data that Gämmerler, being the producer of the machines, can technically control the flow of data. This *de facto* control of the data 'can be a source of differentiation and competitive advantage for manufacturers'.[18] To further illustrate this point, let us assume a third party would like to offer the monitoring service. This competitor needs (scenario 1) access to at least the data generated by the individual machines or (scenario 2) access to the aggregated usage data of a large number of machine users. Let us further assume a buyer of the machines would like to switch from Gämmerler's service to the competitor's offer and that the general terms in the sales and/or services contract regarding the upkeep and maintenance of the machines (not the additional smart services) prohibit the buyer and eventual owner of the machines from allowing third parties to access the private application programming interfaces implemented by Gämmerler. Thus, the manufacturer cannot only de facto control the flow of data but has contractually allocated itself a legal title to prevent the buyer from accessing the data. That is the competitive advantage of the manufacturer with regard to the downstream services market. This advantage is exacerbated by the fact that user data cannot or only with difficulty be obtained by means other than direct collection from the machine user.

In 2017 the Commission entertained the idea of solving this problem through the implementation of default contract terms: They 'could describe a benchmark balanced solution for contracts relating to data' and 'could be coupled with introducing an unfairness control in B2B contractual relationships which would result in invalidating contractual clauses

16 European Commission (n. 13) COM(2017) 9 final, 9.

17 Acatech (ed), 'Wegweiser Smart Service Welt' (April 2017) 11 <www.acatech.de/wp-content/uploads/2018/03/acatech2017_SSW_Wegweiser_de_bf.pdf> accessed 31 August 2020.

18 European Commission (n. 13) COM(2017) 9 final, 10.

that deviate excessively from the default rules'. Additionally, 'they could also be complemented by a set of recommended standard contract terms designed by stakeholders'.[19]

II. Disadvantages of a purely self-regulatory approach

It appears that this combined approach is no longer pursued by the Commission. Instead, the Commission focuses primarily on self-regulatory instruments 'with freedom of contract as a cornerstone'.[20] The Commission postulated five key principles that should be respected in contractual agreements: (1) transparency, (2) shared value creation, (3) respect for each other's commercial interests, (4) ensuring undistorted competition and (5) minimising data lock-in.[21] One of the centre pillars of this self-regulatory approach is the code of conduct.[22] An example is Article 6 Regulation 2018/1807/EU on a framework for the free flow of non-personal data within the European Union[23] under which the Commission 'shall encourage and facilitate the development of self-regulatory codes of conduct at Union level [...], in order to contribute to a competitive data economy', including 'best practices for facilitating the switching of service providers and the porting of data in a structured, commonly used and machine-readable format'.

I am rather sceptical regarding the effectiveness of a purely self-regulatory approach in the data economy. Especially large companies often rely on as little intervention as possible and can thus – thanks to a much more integral setup – profit from the uncertainties of the individual regulatory regimes. Consequently, it does not surprise me that stakeholders of the data within the data economy share the opinion that it still is too early for horizontal legislation on data sharing in business-to-business relations.[24] At this point in time most stakeholders cannot securely forecast where they would end up in a more regulated framework: on the favoured or on the regulated side. Thus, it is only rational for them to object to an introduction of a broad horizontal regulation at this time. Meanwhile, established

19 European Commission (n. 13) COM(2017) 9 final, 12.
20 Communication of the European Commission, 'Towards a common European data space' COM(2018) 232 final, 9.
21 European Commission (n. 20) COM(2018) 232 final, 10.
22 European Commission (n. 20) COM(2018) 232 final, 10.
23 [2018] OJ L 303/59.
24 European Commission (n. 20) COM(2018) 232 final, 9.

stakeholders may go back to using one-sided general terms, which they will then combine with technical access controls in order to fortify their market position.

The governance models relating to the mobility of data generated and collected by the 'connected car' are a prime example of how non-intervention works, or rather: does not work. The example also shows that the theoretically separated regimes of personal data as laid down in the GDPR[25] and non-personal machine-generated data in practice regularly overlap when information is extracted.[26] Even if the regulatory focus is on machine-generated data, a modern approach to the data economy has to integrate the perspective of privacy-based data protection as well.[27] There are two basic models of data governance regarding smart cars:[28] In the 'external server' solution, all in-vehicle data is transmitted to an external server outside the car. The server provides sole access to the data. The 'extended vehicle' concept of the European automobile industry[29] is a variant of this solution, because the data is stored on a proprietary server of the original equipment manufacturer, who will exercise exclusive control of the data. Another variation of this 'centralisation of in-vehicle data'[30] model is the 'shared server' concept. Here, the server is not under the exclusive control of the automobile manufacturer but is governed by a third party that must grant access to the data stored on the server to other stakeholders on non-discriminatory terms and within the regulatory framework of the GDPR. The competing technological solutions are known as the 'in-vehicle interface' and the 'on-board application platforms'. In both conceptions the data is stored in the car itself; the models can be distinguished solely by where the data analysis is executed, outside the vehicle system or inside the

25 Regulation 2016/679/EU of the European Parliament and the Council of 27 April 2016 on the protection of natural persons with regard to the processing of personal data and on the free movement of such data, and repealing Directive 95/46/EC (General Data Protection Regulation) [2016] OJ L119/1.

26 See Axel Metzger, 'Digitale Mobilität – Verträge über Nutzerdaten' (2019) Gewerblicher Rechtsschutz und Urheberrecht 129, 131.

27 Josef Drexl, 'Legal Challenges of the Changing Role of Personal and Non-Personal Data in the Data Economy' in Alberto de Franceschi and Reiner Schulze (eds), *Digital Revolution – New Challenges for Law* (C.H. Beck and Nomos 2019) 19, 20.

28 For a detailed analysis, see Wolfgang Kerber, 'Data Governance in Connected Cars' (2018) 9 Journal of Intellectual Property, Information Technology and E-Commerce Law 310.

29 See <www.cardatafacts.eu> accessed 31 August 2020.

30 Communication of the European Commission, 'On the road to automated mobility: An EU strategy for mobility of the future' COM(2018) 283 final, 13.

vehicle environment.[31] In both cases it is the car owner's decision to allow access to the data stored within the car, by granting access to the vehicle itself. The car manufacturers' preference for the centralised model is rather unsurprising, as is their 'compromise' solution to grant neutral service providers access to their servers.[32] Once again, 'the technological solution determines the initial allocation of the *de facto* exclusive control of data and thus the initial allocation of the *de facto* "ownership" of data'.[33] To make matters worse from a competition point of view, the manufacturer most likely acquires the end-user's consent in processing the personal data according to Article 6(1)(a) GDPR with the scope of consent potentially being tailored to address the specific needs of the manufacturer while excluding competing parties. The manufacturer is in a monopolistic gatekeeper position because she can determine whether and under what conditions the users of the vehicles and third parties can access the data relevant to them, consequently limiting or eliminating competition on aftermarkets and complementary services.[34] Also, rather unsurprisingly, the Commission in 2018 was still sceptical whether this model would be sufficient to ensure fair and undistorted competition.[35]

III. Putting unfair terms control back on the stage

After all, regulation is required. The discussion mainly revolves around two competing policy approaches:[36] Does general competition law entail the necessary and appropriate regulatory instruments or should the competition authorities be granted new instruments to tackle the complex issues in the data economy rather than pursuing a sector-specific approach with tailored data governance solutions? Most recently, the Commission has advocated for a cross-sectoral governance framework for data access and use

31 Mike McCarthy and others, 'Access to In-vehicle Data and Resources' (TRL Study, May 2017) 32–45 <https://ec.europa.eu/transport/sites/transport/files/2017-05-access-to-in-vehicle-data-and-resources.pdf> accessed 31 August 2020.

32 <www.cardatafacts.eu/vehicle-data-available-service-providers/> accessed 31 August 2020.

33 Kerber (n 28) para. 19.

34 Kerber (n. 28) paras 24–28.

35 European Commission (n. 30) COM(2018) 283 final, 13.

36 See Josef Drexl 'Connected devices – An unfair competition law approach to data access rights of users', in this volume.

by introducing new horizontal measures.[37] In particular, it outlined the possibility of a Data Act in 2021 to provide incentives for horizontal data sharing between (private) actors and across sectors.[38] However, the Commission still adheres to the general principle of freedom of contract and voluntary data sharing.[39] Access to data should be made compulsory only on a sector-specific level and, additionally, 'if a market failure in this sector is identified/can be foreseen, which competition law cannot solve'.[40] Contract law and the unfairness control appears to have slipped out of sight. I would like to put it back in the spotlight.[41] I build on the Commission's suggestion of 2017 to combine standard contract terms with a robust unfairness control. This is a contribution to the 'debate as to how contract law, including unfair contract terms control, can be developed further in order to create the right incentives and support parties in reaching fair and efficient data access regimes'.[42]

37 Communication of the European Commission, 'A European strategy for data' COM(2020) 66 final, 12.

38 European Commission (n. 37) COM(2020) 66 final, 13.

39 European Commission (n. 37) COM(2020) 66 final, 13.

40 European Commission (n. 37) COM(2020) 66 final, 13 note 39.

41 The German Data Ethics Commission argues in the same direction; see Opinion of the Data Ethics Commission, 'Gutachten der Datenethikkommission' (October 2019) 146 <www.bmi.bund.de/SharedDocs/downloads/DE/publikationen/themen/it-digitalpolitik/gutachten-datenethikkommission.pdf?__blob=publicationFile&v=6> accessed 31 August 2020: 'Insofar as a contractual legal relationship already exists, the principles of fair data access can be taken into account above all by way of the (possibly supplementary) interpretation of the contract – for example by accepting corresponding contractual ancillary obligations – as well as by way of the unfairness control regarding the general terms and conditions of business according to Sec. 307 German Civil Code)'.

42 Neil Cohen and Christiane Wendehorst, 'ALI-ELI Principles for a Data Economy, ALI Council Draft No. 1' (8 December 2019), 'Reporter's notes on Principle 16' 70 (on file with author).

C. *An (additional) regulatory instrument: unfairness control in B2C and B2B data contracts*

I. *The proposition*

1. *Unfairness control as a data access rule*

The main argument of this paper is rather simple, maybe too simple. My thesis is that the unfairness control of general terms and conditions is a suitable regulatory instrument for, first, establishing adequate access rules in multilateral contract networks and, second, effectively enforcing individual access rights of end-users.

Access rule (*Zugangsregel*) is an umbrella term of a sociological conception of copyright law to develop legal mechanisms for the system-specific coordination of exclusivity on the one hand and user freedom on the other hand.[43] Access rules 'fix the conditions under which users enjoy the freedom to use protected material without depending on the permission of the right holder'.[44] They 'prevent the exercise of rights to intellectual goods from undermining the necessary conditions for the creation of those goods. In short, access rules decentralize the authority to select the use of an intellectual resource. [...] This way, they preserve the environmental conditions of knowledge-sharing in social systems'.[45] Accordingly, '[t]he search for limitations of IP rights within the legal system itself is thus to be characterized as an "ecological" question, for it is ultimately aimed at the system's relationship with its environment'.[46] The term is, to oversimplify an elaborated argument, a specific counter term (*Gegenbegriff*) to copyright's exclusive (property) rights. By taking into account 'the multilateral social effects of IP rights',[47] access rules provide a framework capable of designing a balanced regulatory system enabling knowledge sharing with various other social systems. The term addresses 'the epistemological dimension of property rights'.[48]

This functional dimension of 'access rules' is not limited to exclusivity created by (legal) property rights, but applies to any exclusivity with regard

43 Dan Wielsch, *Zugangsregeln* (Mohr Siebeck 2008) 31 et seq.
44 Dan Wielsch, 'Private Governance of Knowledge: Societally-Crafted Intellectual Properties Regimes' (2013) 20 Indiana Journal of Global Legal Studies 907, 928.
45 Ibid. 929.
46 Ibid. 930.
47 Ibid. 925.
48 Ibid.

to information,[49] therefore including *de facto* exclusivity through technological means. This is why the term and its underlying legal theory play an important role in the data context, too. As explained above, the regulatory problem is precisely the combination of the technologically generated *de facto* exclusivity backed by the contractual normativity of the data controller's authority over the data.[50] It is important to note that the *de facto* control is a standard employed within a specific societal functional system: the technological subsystem. Moreover, it is the contract that provides a normative foundation to this social standard or practice. Because '[p]rivate law provides the normative instruments to make social standards binding and enforceable' it follows that it is also the responsibility of private law to 'promote, as well as put limits on, the jurisgenerative force of standards'.[51] In our case such responsibility is assigned to contract law, because it is the contract with the data holder that provides the *prima facie* justification of the social standard.

To summarise: By 'access rules' I refer to instruments of contract law exercising normative power over the data holder's *de facto* control over the machine-generated data. Because the data holder secures her *de facto* exclusivity through contract, it becomes the responsibility of contract law to check on the legal force of the technological standard by applying an unfairness control to the terms at issue. That is why the unfairness control functions as an 'access rule'. Access rules can, under certain circumstances, condense into subjective access rights. This is the case if the contractual terms and conditions fail to meet the unfairness test requirements. Then the contract will turn against the data holder: The technological *de facto* standard with respect to exclusivity is in violation of normative standards of contract law regarding the usability of the data at issue. Thus, the contractually assigned allocation is void. As a consequence, the normative pillar of the private data governance system has collapsed. Hence, the facticity of the data holder's control of the data not only lacks a normative justification but runs afoul of contract law's principles regarding fair data allocation and access to co-generated data. To remedy the normative deficit of the facticity regarding data control, contract law demands that data access

---

49 The terms 'information' and 'data' should generally be distinguished; see Zech (n. 4) 51, 53–54. However, de facto control of the raw data includes the control of this particular encoding of information as well and it is very unlikely that exactly the same information is encoded in other raw data. Therefore, de facto control over data obstructs the flow of information.

50 See sections A. and B. I. above.

51 Wielsch (n. 44) 925.

be reallocated to the other party. As a result, contract law has to provide for a contractual claim of the end-user against the other party to actively enable access to individual-level data generated by the end-user or within the end-user's responsibility. Furthermore, the end-user may transfer the exercise of this access right to a third party.[52]

2. *Premises*

This argument is based on three premises.

a) Methodological framework: responsive private law theory

The first premise is my methodological framework. The argument is built upon a consequence-oriented, regulatory[53] or, more accurately: 'responsive'[54] conception of private law. The main methodological idea behind responsive law[55] is to 'translate' social theories of, for example, economic, sociological, or philosophical nature into law. It is important to note that responsiveness informs the law on the multitude of functional systems in its environment, each of which follows its own inner logic and each of which can raise its own normative claims. Furthermore, economic social theories should not enjoy preferential treatment, but the various other different social spheres of autonomy are of equal priority and must be treated with equal respect by the law as well. An exclusively economic focus does not do justice to this task of law.[56] Responsive law, first, requires the legal doctrine to treat the descriptions of its environment provided by social theories as productive irritations. Second, the law must reconstruct the insights gained by those social theories within the legal system and using its own concepts and terms. Finally, it shall 'react' to these irritations by using a

---

52 See section D. I.

53 For an in-depth account see Alexander Hellgardt, *Regulierung durch Privatrecht* (Mohr Siebeck 2016).

54 For a detailed account see Michael Grünberger, 'Responsive Rechtsdogmatik' (2019) 219 Archiv für die civilistische Praxis 924. My conception has been heavily influenced by Gunter Teubner, *Law and Social Theory: Three Problems* (transl. Alison Lewis, Ancilla Iuris 2014) 135.

55 Locus classicus: Philippe Nonet and Philip Selznick, *Law and Society in Transition: Towards responsive law* (Routledge 1978).

56 Teubner (n. 54) 183, 190.

more suitable construction of legal norms and concepts, in order to be able to adequately address the various needs of the different functional systems in its environment. This irritation process is productive in the sense that the law enables itself to adequately react to the social embedding of (private) law. One could also speak of a 'multilateralism of private law institutions'.[57]

I therefore understand law as a specific social practice and consider the conflicts to be resolved by law primarily based on their respective social context. In this sense the responsive law approach is environmentally sensitive.[58] With regard to the specific (power) dynamics in the data economy I plead for a more economic, a more technological and a more sociological approach. In particular, I advocate for abandoning the traditional division of labour within private law, according to which contract law is limited to governing the interests within the bilateral legal relationship, while all the irritations of the functional conditions of this relationship are assigned to competition law.[59] Competition law in the digital age has had a tendency to take effect too late to significantly alter the rules of the game. Contract law has to step up and fill the regulatory void left by an inadequately tailored competition law.[60] Compared to competition law, judicial control of unfair terms might be profitable for SMEs and consumers in order to timely protect their legitimate interests.[61] Also, contract law is much more flexible in balancing conflicting interests in a multitude of applications. Additionally, responsive contract law must integrate two perspectives: the quest for an efficient and data-trading-enhancing market regulation must be balanced with the requirements of a privacy-based data protection regime[62].

---

57 Dan Wielsch, 'Die Vergesellschaftung rechtlicher Grundbegriffe' (2018) 38 Zeitschrift für Rechtssoziologie 304.

58 Groundbreaking Wielsch (n. 43) 31 et seq.

59 Michael Grünberger, 'Verträge über digitale Güter' (2018) 218 Archiv für die civilistische Praxis 213, 245.

60 For further analysis why competition law does not offer sufficient solutions, see Drexl (n. 10) 36–37, but see Heike Schweitzer and Robert Welker 'A legal framework for access to data – A competition policy perspective', in this volume.

61 Gerald Spindler, 'Data and Property Rights' (2017) 9 Zeitschrift für Geistiges Eigentum 399, 402.

62 Drexl (n. 27) 19, 20. One could add a third concern, the data holder's legitimate interest in securing her trade secrets as protected by Directive 2016/943/EC on the protection of undisclosed know-how and business information (trade secrets) against their unlawful acquisition, use and disclosure [2017] OJ L157/1. However, I would argue that this is an element that is crucial for the efficient functioning of data markets and is, therefore, 'built in' in the first prong.

In particular, contract law doctrine must resist the temptation to tame the restrictions provided by data protection law by referring back to traditional contractual means. It shall not, for example, limit or impact the exercise of the data subject's withdrawal right under Article 7(3) GDPR if the data subject has entered into a contract regarding the supply of digital content and digital services by providing data to the trader under Article 3(2) Digital Content Directive.[63]

b) General regulatory framework of the data economy

A regulatory conception of contract law requires a regulatory framework. Josef Drexl has developed a regulatory theory for the data economy, identifying four objectives that should be understood from a perspective of public interest and be considered simultaneously: (1) establishing a functioning and competitive market for the data economy; (2) promoting innovation; (3) protecting consumer interests with a particular focus on protecting the privacy of natural persons; and (4) promoting additional public interests.[64] He argues that this regulatory theory reflects 'the constitutional framework of fundamental rights in its entirety [and] provides a comprehensive theory for assessing regulation of the economic economy from a justice perspective'. Based on this claim he urges scholars and regulators to dismiss recommendations 'based on pure justice arguments without being capable of being explained against the backdrop of this regulatory theory'.[65] Although I hesitate to subscribe to the two latter statements, which are unnecessarily broad, I can agree with the relevance of the four elements outlined above within a responsive law theory.

I will not further elaborate on the first two objectives, because all relevant aspects have been laid out already.[66] Regarding the third objective I would like to clarify that for my analysis the regulatory goal should not be limited to consumer interests, but include (business) interests of non-consumer entities, in particular SMEs, as well. The fourth prong is of particular importance to responsive contract law in view of it raising awareness for the contract's societal functions. I think that both interests highlighted

63 Directive 2019/770/EU of the European Parliament and the Council of 20 May 2019 on certain aspects concerning contracts for the supply of digital content and digital services [2019] OJ L136/1.
64 Drexl (n. 10) 48–59; see also Drexl (n. 27) 19, 20.
65 Drexl (n. 10) 50.
66 For a detailed analysis, see Drexl (n. 10) 51–53.

by Drexl, the freedom of information and the legitimate governmental interest to gain access to privately held data, are important examples of the grounds of public interest.[67] Having expressed my desire to emphasise that there are additional aspects to be considered by a responsive law approach, I will first take notice of the negative social effects of the (aggregated) individual exercise of private autonomy. One example is the 'unraveling effect' occurring when some of the data subjects exercise their subjective right by giving consent to data collection, whereas others refuse to do so.[68] This exercise of private autonomy by a few will eventually pressure others into adjusting their behaviour:

> Everyone may eventually discover, however, that they have little choice. At first, those with positive private information (the 'top' of the pool) will disclose to seek discounts and economic benefit and to defend against the negative effects of the digital dossier. Eventually, even those with the worst private information (the 'bottom' of the pool) may realize that they have little choice but to disclose to avoid the stigma of keeping information secret.[69]

Thus, individual consent, as heralded by both data privacy and contract lawyers does 'not capture the behavioral pressure associated with unraveling'[70] and might not be the best fit for the collective good. This argument has been further developed into a concept of 'data pollution', which 'invites us to expand the focus and examine the ways the collection of personal data affect[s] institutions and groups of people – beyond those whose data is taken'.[71] The law has to be aware of this additional negative externality since the 'participation of people in data-harvesting services affects others, and the entire public'.[72] Therefore, the unfairness control must not limit itself to the interests of the parties involved, but take into consideration negative external effects of data access as well.

---

67 Drexl (n. 10) 56–58 limits his account to these two grounds.

68 Scott Pepper, 'Unraveling Privacy: The Personal Prospectus and the Threat of a Full-Disclosure Future' (2011) 105 Northwestern University Law Review 1153, 1176–1182; Yoan Hermstrüwer, 'Contracting Around Privacy' (2017) 8 Journal of Intellectual Property, Information Technology and E-Commerce Law 9, paras 21–28.

69 Pepper (n. 68) 1176.

70 Hermstrüwer (n. 68) para. 25.

71 Omri Ben-Shahar, 'Data Pollution' (2019) 11 Journal of Legal Analysis 104, 106.

72 Ben-Shahar (n. 71) 106. For an illuminating example see Hermstrüwer (n. 68) para. 12.

c) Specific regulatory framework for contractual data access rules

Designing access rules through contract law requires looking beyond the bidirectional contractual relationship of two parties and understanding the multilateralist nature of data governance structures. 'In complex processes of data generation – understood in a broader sense, including different phases of data production, data enrichment and data refinement – several actors with differing goals often interact with each other and contribute to the generation of data in different roles.'[73] However, the facticity of data co-generation by multiple actors is entangled with the *de facto* allocation of powers to one actor only by virtue of her control over the technical infrastructure.

This is the challenge of implementing data-governance structures: Should a normative order accept the *status quo's* facticity, or should it reign it in, and, if so, how shall this be done? The German Data Ethics Commission has been supportive of a normative order, supplementing the facticity of the current data economy.[74] Based on the co-generation processes it pleads for 'data-specific rights of co-determination and participation, which in turn may lead to corresponding obligations on the part of other parties'.[75] 'From an ethical point of view, therefore, a dynamic special relationship develops between an actor who was involved in the generation of data and an actor who *de facto* controls this data.'[76] It has developed five criteria for the recognition and design of data rights and corresponding data obligations in dynamic environments, among them the data holder's duty to grant access to data: '(1) the nature and scope of [the access-seeking] party's contribution to data generation, (2) the weight of that party's legitimate interest in being granted the data right, (3) the weight of any possibly conflicting interests on the part of the other party or of third parties, taking into account any potential compensation arrangements (e.g. protective measures, remuneration), (4) the interests of the general public, and (5)

---

73 Data Ethics Commission (n. 41) 85.

74 Data Ethics Commission (n. 41) 85–94.

75 Data Ethics Commission (n. 41) 85; quote taken from Data Ethics Commission, 'Opinion of the Data Ethics Commission' (English executive summary) 8–9 <www.bmi.bund.de/SharedDocs/downloads/EN/themen/it-digital-policy/datenethikkommission-abschlussgutachten-kurz.pdf;jsessionid=06B302BE9C6688059CC584A27ED59F0F.2_cid364?__blob=publicationFile&v=2> accessed 31 August 2020.

76 Data Ethics Commission (n. 41) 85.

the balance of power between the parties involved'.[77] If data access will be granted through an unfairness control – and the Data Ethics Commission has approved of this approach – the requirements outlined above will provide an additional framework for designing adequate access rules.

II. The benchmark and the knowledge problems

1. The lack of a statutory default rule

The unfairness control of general terms requires a legal benchmark for what shall be considered a fair term. According to the standard established by Article 3(1) Unfair Terms Directive,[78] a contractual term 'shall be regarded as unfair if, contrary to the requirement of good faith, it causes a significant imbalance in the parties' rights and obligations arising under the contract, to the detriment of the consumer'. 'Article 3 […] merely defines in a general way the factors that render unfair a contractual term that has not been individually negotiated.'[79] The Court of Justice of the EU (CJEU) has established a division of labour in cooperation with national courts, which assigns the competence to determine whether a contractual term is 'unfair' to the national courts.[80] German law has established that a contractual term unreasonably disadvantages the other party and is, thus, to be considered unfair, if it is, inter alia, 'not compatible with essential principles of the statutory provision from which it deviates' (Sec. 307(2)(1) German Civil Code). Supplementary provisions of national law (*dispositives Vertragsrecht*) serve as the main benchmark for the unfairness test. Contractual terms reflecting provisions of national law are generally excluded from the scope of the unfairness control (Article 1(2) Unfair Terms Directive[81]) if it can be presumed that the national legislature struck an ap-

77 Data Ethics Commission (n. 41) 85–86; quote taken from the English executive summary (n. 75) 9.

78 Directive 93/13/EEC [1993] OJ L95/29.

79 CJEU, Case C-243/08 *Pannon GSM Zrt. v. Erzsébet Sustikné Győrfi* ECLI:EU:C:2009:350, para. 37.

80 CJEU, Case C-137/08 *VB Pénzügyi Lízing Zrt. v. Ferenc Schneider* ECLI:EU:C:2010:659, para. 47.

81 CJEU, Case C-92/11 *RWE Vertrieb AG v. Verbraucherzentrale Nordrhein-Westfalen e.V.* ECLI:EU:C:2013:180, paras 27–30.

propriate balance between all rights and obligations of the parties within certain contracts.[82]

At the moment, national law lacks specific supplementary provisions regulating data access. This is a challenge for the unfairness control. It has been argued that it 'is necessarily dependent on the availability of supplementary provisions in contract law (*dispositives Vertragsrecht*) that can be used as a benchmark for an appropriate contractual balance of interests'.[83] Due to the lack of a legal benchmark, courts would be at a loss to determine the fairness of contractual terms. It has been argued that corresponding default contract rules would need to be adopted before extending the unfairness control to data access rights.[84] With the notable exception of personal data governed by the GDPR and the Directive on digital goods, 'the European legislature still has a long and possibly rocky road ahead of it in the development of an optional common European contract law for the data economy in the B2B-sector'.[85] This situation is aggravated by the fact that designing statutory default rules requires knowledge of the data markets as well as their probable evolvements. The task of designing default contract statutes for the data economy faces the same fundamental challenge as any regulatory attempt: the knowledge deficit of state actors. This squaring of the circle is also the main reason for academics to be cautious of premature interventions.[86] To put the argument in a nutshell: The unfairness control should not be part of the regulatory toolbox, due to a lack of supplementary statutory law. This results from a shortcoming of knowledge regarding the data economy. A broad government interference using general contract law would, at this time, most likely fail to adequately address the intricacies of different developing markets and could therefore not be justified.

---

82 CJEU, Case C-260/18 *Kamil Dziubak and Justyna Dziubak v. Raiffeisen Bank International AG*, ECLI:EU:C:2019:819, para. 59.

83 Josef Drexl, 'Neue Regeln für die Europäische Datenwirtschaft? Ein Plädoyer für einen wettbewerbspolitischen Ansatz – Teil 2' (2017) Neue Zeitschrift für Kartellrecht 415, 420 (emphasis added).

84 Drexl (n. 10) 38.

85 Drexl (n. 83) 420.

86 See Axel Metzger, 'Access to and porting of data under contract law: Consumer protection rules and market-based principles', in this volume.

2. *The vocation of our digital age for legal science*

I have a rather different vision 'of the vocation of our age for legislation and legal science'[87]. I think that the cautious 'We-Don't-Know-It-Well-Enough-To-Regulate-It' approach of some voices in legal academia will eventually make matters worse. We should be aware that the *status quo* of the data economy can be compared to the Wild West: If we start regulating after the big stakeholders have secured their claims there is little left to be effectively regulated. However, the lack of knowledge has to be taken seriously. I believe that the procedural model presented in this paper adequately addresses it by relying on both the production and, subsequently, the judicial acquisition of private knowledge in various industry sectors while, at the same time, implementing normative instruments that continuously irritate the private order in a productive way. One size doesn't fit all. The increasing support for a sector-specific regulatory approach and for sector-specific data access rights[88] has evidential value for this statement. Therefore, it does make sense to leave the initial decision regarding the fairness of contractual terms up to the stakeholders involved in the concerned sectors. Normative governance structures must then ensure that the voices of all stakeholders regardless of their market power and, in addition, the viewpoints of agents of public interests, will be heard.

The unfairness control is structurally capable of reflecting the necessary distinctions. First, the established enforcement mechanisms regarding the unfairness control, representative actions for the protection of collective interests and, in Germany, unfair competition law proceedings can be deployed as effective instruments of knowledge acquisition in the data economy. Second, the court procedure provides a forum to the parties who, as agents of the conflicting social functions of data exclusivity vs. data access, shape the discussion of what is to be deemed 'unfair'. Third, for any decision, being but case law, it can – depending on the jurisdiction – rather easily be overruled in new cases after more complex information has been extracted. This is why the unfairness control is a flexible tool that belongs in the regulatory toolbox.

---

87 The reference to Friedrich Carl von Savigny, *Vom Beruf unserer Zeit für Gesetzgebung und Rechtswissenschaft* (Heidelberg, 1814), is intended.

88 See Josef Drexl, 'Connected devices – An unfair competition law approach to data access rights of users', in this volume; Wolfgang Kerber, 'From (horizontal and sectoral) data access solutions – Towards data governance systems', in this volume; Heike Schweitzer and Robert Welker, 'A legal framework for access to data – A competition policy perspective', in this volume.

3. Statutory default rules are not required

The argument against unfair terms control based on the lack of statutory benchmarks is surprisingly unimaginative and state-centered. It starts from the wrong, or at least, an incomplete premise. The unfairness control is not necessarily dependent on the availability of supplementary provisions in contract law. Still, it is true that default contractual rules could constitute benchmarks for a standard contract terms control.[89] They are, however, not the only imaginable benchmarks. Section 307(2)(2) of the German Civil Code provides additional standards: the 'essential rights or duties inherent in the nature of the contract [may not be limited] to such an extent that attainment of the purpose of the contract is jeopardised'. To put it pointedly: A fairly balanced contract law practice within the data economy could deliver the benchmark for individual contracts. It is too shortsighted to focus only on the legislature for establishing benchmarks. The best approach is to incentivise the individual and/or collective actors in the data economy to draft and make use of model contract clauses[90] or codes of conduct.[91] This will be the focus of the next chapter.

The second-best solution for the benchmark problem is to rely on model agreements developed by legal academics with a fairness approach in mind. The ALI-ELI Draft Principles for a Data Economy[92] meet the criteria.[93] They could not only be conducive 'to facilitate the drafting of model agreements [...] by parties in the data economy' (Principle (1)(e)), but also 'be used as a source of inspiration and guidance for the further development of the law by courts' (Principle (1)(b)). The Principles contain 'data rights', that is, 'rights that a party has against a controller of data arising from the nature of the data and its generation' (Principle 15(1)), including 'the right to be provided access to data or port data' (Principle 15(1)(2)(a)).

---

89 European Commission, 'Staff Working Document on the free flow of data and emerging issues of the European data economy' SWD (2017) 2 final, 32.

90 This appears to be the approach of the European Commission, too; see European Commission (n. 13) 12; European Commission (n. 20) 10–11.

91 This is part of the new Commission's sectoral data strategy regarding 'data spaces': see European Commission, 'A European strategy for data' (Communication) COM(2020) 66 final, 30–32.

92 'ALI-ELI Principles for a Data Economy, Preliminary Draft No. 3' (15 October 2019) (on file with author). Henceforth I will cite the most recent Draft available to me: the ALI Council Draft No. 1 version of 08 December 2019 (n. 42).

93 For an introduction, see Christiane Wendehorst, 'The ALI-ELI Principles for a Data Economy' in Alberto de Franceschi and Reiner Schulze (eds), *Digital Revolution – New Challenges for Law* (Munich, 2019) 41.

These rights are justified by fairness considerations (Principle 15(3)), which are based on the fact that the party had a share in the generation of the data at stake.[94] Principles 17 through 19 provide further guidance regarding the factors and criteria for establishing a data access right of one party: Article 17 of the Principles lists three factors that should be taken into account when determining (access) rights to co-generated data:

(1) the extent to which that party is the subject of the information coded in the data, or is the owner of the object of that information;
(2) the extent to which the data was generated by an activity of that party, or by use of a device in which that party had ownership or any similar property rights; or
(3) the extent to which the data was generated by use of a computer program or other relevant component of a device in which that party holds intellectual property rights or in whose development that party has made investment.

Article 19 of the Principles contains an exemplary list of grounds that may give rise to a right to access: (1) the normal, foreseeable use, including resale, by the user of the commodity, (2) for quality monitoring, (3) for establishing facts of the party's own operations, (4) for developing new business models by a party with additional safeguards to protect the legitimate interests of the data holder/controller, and (5) to avoid lock-in effects, such as switching suppliers for a service. Finally, Article 18 of the Principles requires a general balancing exercise between (1) the factors established by Articles 17 and 19, respectively, (2) the legitimate interests of the data holder/controller, (3) the bargaining power between the parties and (4) the public interests.

4. *A procedural model for the unfairness control*

As explained above, I claim that the unfairness control of general terms is a suitable regulatory instrument for, first, establishing adequate access rules in multilateral contract networks and, second, to effectively enforce individual access rights of end-users.[95] As previously discussed, the unfairness control requires a suitable benchmark.[96] The best benchmark for the un-

94 Cohen and Wendehorst (n. 42) 66.
95 See section C. I. 1.
96 See sections. C. II. 1. and 2.

fairness control is the collective knowledge gathered by the private actors. The process of gaining such knowledge with the help of private ordering is at the core of my proposal to create a contract-law-based access rule for the data economy. This benchmark is provided by model contracts. However, not every model contract will suffice. It must meet a certain standard of (procedural) justice as fairness. In the following Section I will propose a both regulated and self-regulatory approach applying the unfairness control to the data economy. This is a solution based on the cooperation between private knowledge production, private standardisation and private rule-making on the one hand ('self-regulation') and governmental (framework) regulation on the other. Governmental regulation reacts to the pressure of making decisions under conditions of uncertainty by tying in with methods and models employed by non-state actors intended to acquire knowledge. This knowledge production occurs within the private law arena, allowing hypotheses to be formulated and tested and regulations to be implemented step by step, anticipating the production of new knowledge by the economic and/or technological systems affected by these regulations.[97]

a) Rebuttable presumption of fairness

At the core of this model is a (rebuttable) presumption that contractual standard terms are not unfair in the sense of Section 307(1)(1) German Civil Code if they are an integral part of model contracts, codes of conduct or best practices that in turn are compliant with certain requirements of procedural justice. If the presumption is successfully rebutted, the access-restricting contract clause is unfair and therefore invalid.[98] The normative pillar justifying the *de facto* control of the data holder has crumbled and the ongoing *de facto* control and the refusal to grant access to the relevant data is no longer tolerable. To remedy the normative deficit of the facticity regarding data control, contract law requires data access to be reallocated to the other party by granting her a right to access the data against the data holder. The latter party must authorise the former party's access to the par-

97 See Karl-Heinz Ladeur, 'Die Regulierung von Selbstregulierung und die Herausbildung einer "Logik der Netzwerke"' in (2001) Regulierte Selbstregulierung als Steuerungskonzept des Gewährleistungsstaates. Die Verwaltung, Beiheft 4, 59, 76.

98 See Art. 6(1) Unfair Terms Directive.

ticular data or a particular data source[99] governed by the unfair contractual term and must, depending on the technological design of her *de facto* control, enable this party to effectively access this data. For example, the data holder must open the private application programming interfaces, thus allowing data transfer to the other party.

b) Role model I: equitable remuneration scheme in copyright law

This model is influenced by standards providing equitable contractual remuneration for copyright licensing contracts.[100] Under Section 32 German Copyright Act, each author has a right to the contractually agreed remuneration in return for exploitation rights. If the contractually agreed remuneration is not equitable, the author is entitled to sue the other party to consent to a modification of the agreement ensuring that the author eventually receives equitable remuneration (Section 32(1)(3) Copyright Act). There are three stages to establish whether the agreed remuneration is equitable.[101] The first stage is to identify whether there are relevant collective bargaining agreements. If this is the case, the author's remuneration is solely determined by this instrument and she does not have a claim to adjust the remuneration set forth in the bargaining agreement (Section 32(4) Copyright Act). However, in most cases we are either lacking such agreements or the exploitation is outside their scope. Second, the contractually agreed remuneration is irrefutably (!) deemed equitable if it is covered by a joint remuneration agreement, established between authors' associations

99 This remedy has been inspired by Art. 10 ALI-ELI Principles for a Data Economy; see Cohen and Wendehorst (n. 42) 60–64.

100 Art. 18 of Directive 2019/790/EU of the European Parliament and the Council of 17 April 2019 on copyright and related rights in the Digital Single Market and amending Directives 96/9/EC and 2001/29/EC [2019] OJ L130/92 has recently harmonised the principle of appropriate and proportionate remuneration of authors and performing artists. Member States remain free to use different implementation mechanisms (Art. 18(2) of the Directive), and Recital 73 clarifies that these instruments may include collective bargaining and other (collective) mechanisms.

101 See BGH (Federal Supreme Court), 21 May 2015 – *GVR Tageszeitungen I* (Joint Remuneration Agreement Daily Newspapers I), (2016) Gewerblicher Rechtsschutz und Urheberrecht 62, para. 13 (sketching out the three steps); BGH (Federal Supreme Court), 15 November 2016 – *GVR Tageszeitungen III* (Joint Remuneration Agreement Daily Newspapers III), (2016) Gewerblicher Rechtsschutz und Urheberrecht 1296 (fine-tuning the prerequisites for each step).

on one and associations of exploiters of works or individual users of works on the other side (Sections 32(2)(1) and 36(1) Copyright Act). The determination of appropriateness of the joint remuneration agreements applies also to non-members of the associations. Third, if neither collective bargaining nor joint remuneration agreements are directly applicable, the courts must determine whether the contractually agreed remuneration corresponds to what is customary and fair in comparable business relations, given the nature of the exploitation of copyright protected subject matter by the licensee and the extent to which exploitation can possibly be granted, particularly in terms of duration of the licensing agreement, the specifics of the exploitation, and considering all remaining circumstances (Section 32(2)(2) Copyright Act). Courts may seek guidance from joint remuneration agreements covering the same forms of exploitation even if they are not directly applicable.[102] The equitable remuneration scheme in German copyright law is purposefully designed to provide incentives for joint remuneration agreements.[103] By establishing an irrefutable presumption, the law privileges a self-regulatory model over an individual judicial decision assessing the equity of the remuneration. The law assumes, first, that the joint agreement bundles the knowledge of a social practice and, second, that it adequately balances the competing interests of authors and exploiters. Consequently, the joint remuneration agreement will most likely yield better results than an individual assessment of a court.

It is precisely this nexus that is at the core of the unfairness model developed in this paper. By introducing a presumption of fairness if the contractual terms are in line with exemplary rules concerning access in the data economy, contract law refers to the knowledge gained within the regulated system and by the relevant actors within this system. However, differing from the Copyright Act's precedent, the presumption in my model shall be rebuttable. There are two reasons for this deviation: First, the Copyright Act has to answer the question of how to establish a fair and equitable remuneration, whereas the unfairness control applies 'neither to the definition of the main subject matter of the contract nor to the adequa-

102 BGH (Federal Supreme Court), 21 May 2015 – *GVR Tageszeitungen I* (Joint Remuneration Agreement Daily Newspapers I), (2016) Gewerblicher Rechtsschutz und Urheberrecht 62, para. 16 (holding that the remuneration criteria set forth in a joint remuneration agreement for newspaper journalists can also be used as a benchmark if the conditions for their application are not (fully) fulfilled and therefore do not have an irrefutable presumption of conformity).

103 Karl-Nikolaus Peifer in Ulrich Loewenheim, Ansgar Ohly and Matthias Leistner (eds), *Schricker – Urheberrecht* (6th edn, C.H.Beck 2020) § 36 UrhG para 46.

cy of the price and remuneration' (Article 4(2) Unfair Terms Directive). Assessing the iustum pretium is notoriously difficult for a court to achieve. Thus, it is advantageous for a court to rely on applicable joint remuneration agreements without having to second-guess its ability to balance the interests appropriately. Following this train of thought, my model has to exempt the core of the contractual agreement from judicial review. Second, unlike the situation in the copyright remuneration issue, we are at the very beginning of designing governance rules for the data economy. Although it is most likely that a privately dominated process of gaining knowledge will yield superior results, it might be wise to design a system with built-in normative checks and balances regarding the fairness of the solutions found. The possibility to rebut the presumption of fairness exerts normative pressure on the private order to continuously re-evaluate and adapt the solutions presented in the model rules. Hence, it is a regulatory tool to further improve the societal knowledge-gaining process.

c) Procedural requirements

The solution presented by the Copyright Act is informative for a second reason. The prevalence of joint remuneration agreements over an individual judicial assessment and its extension to 'outsiders' requires that self-regulatory model of knowledge gaining to meet certain procedural criteria: The associations signing such agreements must be representative, independent and empowered to establish such joint remuneration agreements (Section 36(2) Copyright Act).[104] The law can refer to the results of private ordering only if it can rightfully be assumed that all relevant perspectives, interests and stakeholders are represented in the process of gaining societal knowledge. On a procedural level, this is why the model developed here must ensure that the model contracts, best practices or code of conduct actually reflect a sufficiently widespread, appropriate and fair social practice. That is not a small challenge.

The European Commission has presented normative guidelines[105] that are intended to foster fair and open data markets. The ALI-ELI Principles for a Data Economy[106] and the propositions of the German Data Ethics

104 For a detailed analysis, see Peifer (n. 103) paras 52–62.
105 European Commission (n. 20) 10.
106 Cohen and Wendehorst (n. 42); see section C. II. 3.

Commission[107] provide a normative framework that could be used as a starting point for private ordering instruments. However, the model presented here requires actual model contracts or best practices within the data economy. Those have to be found and evaluated. The Support Centre for Data Sharing (SCDS) could solve this issue.[108] The European Commission has assigned the SCDS the task to 'provide practical advice, best practices and methodologies for data sharing and data analytics. For example, the platform will give access to model contract clauses tested in previous data transactions and backed by public authorities'.[109] The SCDS has so far collected and classified twelve model contract terms used for data-sharing purposes.[110] The effort is laudable, although the licensing contracts analysed by the SCDS are far from helpful for solving my benchmark problem, because the contracts at issue do not cover the relevant industrial sectors. The same holds true for the data-sharing practice examples collected by the SCDS.[111] The examples listed on the website are apparently chosen rather arbitrarily, do not follow a structuring pattern and are not of critical-analytical, but rather affirmative-descriptive nature. To conclude: The SCDS's resources are not suited to deliver the knowledge necessary in order for my unfairness model to work.

d) Role model II: the (German) Corporate Governance Code

I doubt that we could start solving my model's benchmark problem on the European level. Instead, I propose a bottom-up approach. The governments of the Member States should set up commissions consisting of all relevant stakeholders and agents of the public interests. They should assign these commissions the task of identifying and fostering best practices as well as drafting a code of conduct regarding data sharing. Insofar we can learn from a rather successful example displaying a combination of private

107 Data Ethics Commission (n. 41) 85–92; see section C. I. 2. c) above.

108 <https://eudatasharing.eu/about-us> accessed 31 August 2020.

109 European Commission, 'Annex to the Commission Implementing Decision on the adoption of the work programme for 2018 and on the financing of Connecting Europe Facility (CEF) – Telecomunications Sector' C(2018) 568 final, 42.

110 SCDS, B.1 – Report on collected model contract terms (26 July 2019) <https://eudatasharing.eu/sites/default/files/2019-10/EN_Report%20on%20Model%20Contract%20Terms.pdf> accessed 31 August 2020.

111 <https://eudatasharing.eu/data-sharing-practice-examples> accessed 31 August 2020.

knowledge gaining (self-regulation) and proper regulation: the German Corporate Governance Code. It illustrates the mutual irritation between autopoietic societal subsystems.[112]

(1.) The Corporate Governance Code identifies social practices in the economic system and sets them up as an optional (normative) standard of behaviour. It therefore formulates legal rules of a special kind: behavioural appeal and informal recommendations, without any claim of binding force or sanctions, in short: a regulatory offer to the subsystem (= corporation). (2) The individual corporation accepts this recommendation by implementing it within its organisation and setting normative standards regarding legal and economic communications. If the corporation does not integrate the recommendations, the standardised social regulation of the economic system remains ineffective within the corporate subsystem. If the subsystems fail to follow the Code by the dozen, the Code will be forced into new learning processes which improve the communications within the corporate subsystems. The Code perceives this refusal as new, additional knowledge and will subsequently adapt the recommendations to the willingness to accept it, for it does not want to call its overall acceptance into question. (3.) The management board and the supervisory board of a company listed on the stock exchange must annually declare that the Code's recommendations have been and are being complied with, or which of the Code's recommendations have not been applied or are not being applied and the reasons therefore (Section 161(1) German Stock Corporation Act). This is traditional hard law. With the options given to the corporation, hard law facilitates the learning process in the economic system. The corporation has to inform its environment of which of the three explanation variants it has chosen. The hard law does not contain a presumption in favour of the Code's recommendation in the legal system. However, the mutual interference between law and economics is not taken into account if the recommendations are being qualified as non-binding 'food for thought' only. This could also be achieved through an opt-in rule. However, Section 161 Stock Corporation Act is designed as an opt-out rule: It is not the compliance but the deviation that must be justified. The law thus takes on a substantive position. It adopts the view that the Code's recommendations are in fact the best practice of listed companies. Thus, Section 161 recommends compliance with the rule without making it compulsory. Obligations to give reasons and justify the deviation, how-

112 Michael Grünberger, 'Geschlechtergerechtigkeit im Wettbewerb der Regulierungssysteme' (2012) 3(1) Rechtswissenschaft 31–33.

ever, result in encouraging conduct in conformity with the rule. As soft law, this standard thus ensures that the recommendations of the Commission become the default rule.

D. Problems

I. Privity-of-contract problem

The main objection against the use of the unfairness control to secure data access rights is the theory of privity of contract (*Relativität der Schuldverhältnisse*): Following the traditional principle of relative effect of contracts the proposed contract law solution 'only works where the person interested in access and the data holder enter into a direct contractual relationship. However, such direct relationship does not always exist'.[113] There are two prevailing situations in which a lack of direct contractual relationship between the data holder/controller and the party requiring data access becomes apparent: (1) The direct purchaser and owner of the data-gathering device leases or sells it to a third party. 'Under the principle of privity of contract, the contractual right of access to the data will not travel with the property in the used device.'[114] (2) A third party requires data access in order to provide data-related services to the party which has or had a contractual relationship with the data holder. In comparison, a statutory data access right applies without the need for a direct contractual relationship with the producer or supplier of the intelligent product, and, in addition, such statutory regulations generally cannot be waived by the entitled person, thus being more likely to produce adequate results.[115]

This argument is based on the premise that the privity-of-contract doctrine strictly limits contractual rights and duties to the parties of the contract. This is, at least regarding German civil law, not the case: 'The isolation of creditor and debtor in the contractual relationship, the isolation from "the rest of the world", is no longer satisfying. Therefore, the contractual relationship is increasingly extended by third-party effects. A consider-

113 Drexl (n. 9) 38.

114 Josef Drexl and others, 'Position Statement of the Max Planck Institute for Innovation and Competition of 26 April 2017 on the European Commission's "Public consultation on Building the European Data Economy"', 7 <www.ip.mpg.de/fileadmin/ipmpg/content/stellungnahmen/MPI_Statement_Public_consultation_on_Building_the_EU_Data_Eco_28042017.pdf> accessed 31 August 2020.

115 Drexl (n. 83) 420.

able number of them take account of particular social ties which extend beyond the legal microcosm of the contractual obligation.'[116] Whether such third-party effects are possible and desirable and how they should be designed is, following traditional German doctrine, a question that might be answered differently over time and depending on the specific regulatory issues to be addressed.[117] In the digital and networking economy we are faced with the pressing question whether the economic and/or technological connections can also be legally re-constructed by assuming a network effect in the various contractual relationships at issue or at least by establishing a quasi-contractual connection.[118] I would argue that the construction of third-party effects can be a suitable regulatory instrument in contract law. They are building blocks of an environmentally sensitive data contract law.

I will briefly sketch my argument to demonstrate that contract law can effectively be used for tailored access rights responding to the parties' individual needs that can also be exercised by a third party. In reference to the model presented here, the other party has a data access right based in her contract with the data holder if the contractual terms concerning data usage between her and the data holder is unfair.[119] In order to safeguard the effectiveness of this remedy, any contractual waiver of this right that has not been individually negotiated is an unfair term and, therefore, void. The data access right can be transferred to a third party.[120] However, any third party will only get access to the individual-level data generated by the machines and not to the aggregated usage data of a large number of machine users. If the transfer of title should be excluded in the contract with the data holder/controller and if this term has not been individually negotiated, it shall, in general, be deemed unfair as well, because it is a further restriction of the effectiveness of the other party's remedy. If the data-gathering device is transferred to a third party (lessee, buyer or service provider), it shall be assumed through interpretation of the contractual arrangement with this party that she will also be assigned the data access right rooted in the first contract. If the data access right entails access to

116 Dieter Medicus, 'Drittbeziehungen in Schuldverhältnissen' (1974) Juristische Schulung 613.

117 Joachim Gernhuber, *Das Schuldverhältnis* (Mohr Siebeck 1989) 461.

118 For a detailed analysis, see Lukas Firsching, *Vertragsstrukturen des Erwerbs einheitlicher IoT-Produkte* (Duncker & Humblot 2020).

119 See section C. I. 1.

120 Secs 398, 413 German Civil Code allow for the transfer of rights by the right holder to a third party through assignment.

personal data as well, the third party must be able to justify the data processing in accordance with the requisites established in Article 6(1) GDPR.

II. Transnational dimension

The model developed in this paper could be applied to B2C contracts within every EU Member State. With regard to B2B transactions, only a few Member States have enacted a robust unfair terms control, Germany among them. However, the criticism against the wide scope of application of the unfair terms control has recently been increasing. The 'Coalition Agreement' between the three governing parties in Germany declares that the parties 'will review the law on general terms and conditions for contracts between companies with the aim of improving legal certainty for innovative business models'.[121] It will not be surprising that in my learned opinion, the unfair terms control is central to the normative monitoring and effective governance of data-driven business models.

E. Conclusion

The real shortcoming of the model presented here is the fact that it securely applies only to national circumstances, whereas the data access issues are very often transnational issues. The problem can be solved within B2C relations. If the consumer has her habitual residence in Germany, the German unfair terms control will apply (Article 6(1) Rome I Regulation).[122] If the contract has a choice-of-law clause, the German consumer will still enjoy the protection by the mandatory unfair terms control (Article 6(2) Rome I Regulation). This picture significantly shifts in B2B relations. Due to the exercise of party autonomy (Article 3(1) Rome I Regulation), or, in absence of a choice-of-law clause, applying the objective connecting factors set forth in Article 4(1)(a) and (b) Rome I Regulation, foreign law will be applicable in many cases. One possible, and, I must admit, a bit far-fetched solution for saving the unfair terms data access model is to construct it as

121 Koalitionsvertrag zwischen CDU, CSU und SPD für die 19. Legislaturperiode (2018) <www.cdu.de/system/tdf/media/dokumente/koalitionsvertrag_2018.pdf?file=1, line 6186> accessed 31 August 2020.

122 Regulation (EC) 593/2008 of the European Parliament and of the Council of 17 June 2008 on the law applicable to contractual obligations (Rome I) [2008] OJ L177/6.

an overriding mandatory provision in the sense of Article 9 Rome I Regulation. If one does not follow this suggestion, and, in view of the lack of EU harmonisation, the suitability of the unfair terms control as a regulatory instrument is indeed severely limited.

In the ongoing competition – perhaps even battle – for supremacy between the two opposing legal paradigms in the data economy (ownership and control vs. access) this paper pleads for access. I have presented a model to utilise the unfair terms control to design an access rule to effectively govern legitimate access to data in the data economy. The contractual unfairness control functions as an access rule which might develop into an access right. It partially removes the *de facto* allocation of data and its contractual justification by, first, restricting the data holder's (manufacturer's or service provider's) freedom of contract to include respective general terms and conditions and, second, by enabling the other party technological access to the data. The purpose of this paper was to demonstrate that the unfair terms control is, in its initial premises, a suitable regulatory instrument. If it is properly designed, it will foster knowledge gaining and sharing by private ordering, thus providing courts and legislatures with the necessary insights to adequately address the data access issues *now*. This paper does not present a complete account of the model and it does not address all of the possible objections, for example to the assignability of the access right. It serves the sole purpose of sketching out a path for the role of legal science to respond to conditions of uncertainty by designing creative legal tools.

Access to and porting of data under contract law: Consumer protection rules and market-based principles

*Axel Metzger**

A. Introduction

Is a party under a contract obliged to grant the other party access to data it has collected? From a contract law perspective, one is tempted to give the simple answer: 'Yes, if there has been an agreement that the party should have a right of access!' However, such an answer would seem too simplistic. Even though today's contract law is still based on the principle of freedom of contract, consumer protection and other policies (e.g. protection of employees, commercial agents, authors or other weaker parties) have changed its character. The present European contract law is permeated by mandatory provisions, information duties, correction mechanisms, default rules with regulatory objectives, procedural instruments and other kinds of rules which are meant to protect one contracting party from the other in asymmetric relationships. Therefore, the initial question must be raised in a more nuanced version: Is one party under a contract obliged to grant the other party access to the data it has collected even if the contract does not provide for such a right of access? Framed like this, the answer to the question will very much depend on the impact of the mentioned protective policies, especially consumer protection, on possible data access rights. It should be obvious that contract law is of main interest as a legal basis for access to data that has been collected within the contractual relationship. By contrast, any right of access to data collected outside of a contractual arrangement must be based on different legal grounds, e.g. data protection law, competition law, public sector information regulations. Such non-contractual legal grounds will only be taken into account for comparison in this chapter. The term 'access right' will be used in a broad sense, comprising both simple rights to access and also more technically demanding portability rights.

* The author would like to thank Lena Mischau, Heike Schweitzer, Herbert Zech and the participants of the Consumer Law Confernce 2019 for comments and discussions of the issues explored in this chapter.

B. Consumer protection – Data access and porting under the DCSD

I. Current state of the DCSD

The recent EU legislative package on consumer contracts – Directive 2019/770 on digital content and digital services (DCSD),[1] Directive 2019/771 on the sale of goods,[2] and Directive 2019/2161 on the modernisation of Union consumer protective rules ('Omnibus Directive')[3] – serves as a starting point for this chapter because the new Directives strive at reforming the regulatory framework for consumer contracts for the coming years if not decades. Therefore, one should search for contractual data access rights for consumers in this framework.

The DCSD with its focus on data-intensive e-commerce services is of major interest in this regard. The DCSD is applicable to a wide range of contracts for the supply of digital contents and digital services, including many Internet and social media services. It is applicable both to paid services and to services where consumers provide their personal data instead of a money consideration; see Article 3(2):

> This Directive shall also apply where the trader supplies or undertakes to supply digital content or a digital service to the consumer, and the consumer provides or undertakes to provide personal data to the trader, except where the personal data provided by the consumer are exclusively processed by the trader for the purpose of supplying the digital content or digital service in accordance with this Directive or for allowing the trader to comply with legal requirements to which the trader is subject, and the trader does not process those data for any other purpose.

1 Directive (EU) 2019/770 of the European Parliament and of the Council of 20 May 2019 on certain aspects concerning contracts for the supply of digital content and digital services [2019] OJ L136/1.

2 Directive (EU) 2019/771 of the European Parliament and of the Council of 20 May 2019 on certain aspects concerning contracts for the sale of goods, amending Regulation (EU) 2017/2394 and Directive 2009/22/EC, and Repealing Directive 1999/44/EC [2019] OJ L136/28.

3 Directive (EU) 2019/2161 of the European Parliament and of the Council of 27 November 2019 amending Council Directive 93/13/EEC and Directives 98/6/EC and 2011/83/EU of the European Parliament and of the Council as regards the better enforcement and modernisation of Union consumer protection rules [2019] OJ L328/7.

Typical data-driven Internet services do not just process user data for the purpose of supplying the respective content or services or for compliance with legal requirements but also use such data for other purposes, namely for marketing and advertising, for market analysis, as training data for artificial intelligence tools etc. This is the very nature of today's data-driven business models. The rules of the DCSD will therefore apply to many of those contracts (but also to contracts with a money consideration), which raises the question whether consumers should have a right to access data collected in the course of these contractual relationships. The European legislature now has affirmed such a right in Article 16(2) DCSD with a reference to the General Data Protection Regulation (GDPR)[4] for personal data and in Article 16(4) DCSD with regard to non-personal data but only in case of a termination of the contract.

The Directive on the sale of goods does not provide a comparable rule for digital content, especially software, that is embedded in a physical product. Therefore, consumers will not have respective contractual data access rights with regard to devices used in the 'Internet of things'. This disparate approach has been criticised during the legislative process, but the legislature did not resolve the problem.[5] The Omnibus Directive is concerned with different matters and does not provide for additional access rights. The DCSD and the Directive on the sale of goods have to be transposed by the Member States by 1 July 2021. The new national contract law rules based on the two Directives will then apply from 1 January 2022.[6] For the Omnibus Directive, the implementation period runs until 28 November 2021. The new rules will then apply from 28 May 2022.[7] Germany has not yet published a draft proposal for the transposition of the three Directives into German law.

---

4 Regulation (EU) No. 2016/679 of the European Parliament and of the Council of 27 April 2016 on the protection of natural persons with regard to the processing of personal data and on the free movement of such data, and repealing Directive 95/46/EC, [2016] OJ L119/1.

5 See European Law Institute (ELI), 'Statement on the European Commission's proposed directive on the supply of digital content to consumers' (2015) 10–14, <www.europeanlawinstitute.eu/fileadmin/user_upload/p_eli/Publications/ELI_Statement_on_DCD.pdf> accessed 31 August 2020; Axel Metzger, Zohar Efroni, Lena Mischau and Jakob Metzger, 'Data-Related Aspects of the Digital Content Directive' (2018) 9 Journal of Intellectual Property, Information Technology and E-Commerce Law 90, paras 29–40.

6 Art. 24(1) DCSD; Art. 24(1) Directive on the sale of goods.

7 Art. 7(1) Omnibus Directive.

II. Access to non-personal data under Article 16(4) DCSD

The DCSD provides for an access right of the consumer in the case of a termination of the contract. Article 16 DCSD stipulates the obligations of the trader in the event of termination. Paragraph 4 reads:

> Except in the situations referred to in point (a), (b) or (c) of paragraph 3, the trader shall, at the request of the consumer, make available to the consumer any content other than personal data, which was provided or created by the consumer when using the digital content or digital service supplied by the trader.
> The consumer shall be entitled to retrieve that digital content free of charge, without hindrance from the trader, within a reasonable time and in a commonly used and machine-readable format.

The access right of Article 16(4) is bound to a number of conditions which, taken in sum, may reduce its scope of application to a large extent:

First, the access right of Article 16(4) only applies to 'content other than personal data, which was provided or created by the consumer'.[8] For personal data, the provisions of the GDPR take priority over the DCSD (Arts 3(8), 16(2) DCSD). Given the broad definition of personal data in Article 4(1) GDPR and the equally broad approach taken by the CJEU,[9] Article 16(4) has only limited practical value under the current circumstances.[10] As long as the service provider collects and processes data of a specific user who is identifiable by the (dynamic) IP address used during the visit to a website, such data is covered by the GDPR. This also holds true for any content that is created or uploaded by the user, e.g. texts, pictures, music or video files, digital goods in video games etc. Only when the contents or

---

8 The formulation has a tendency to exclude data derived or inferred by the trader; see Inge Graef, Martin Husovec and Nadezhda Purtova, 'Data Portability and Data Control: Lessons for an Emerging Concept in EU Law' (2018) 19 German Law Journal 1359, 1394.

9 See Case C-582/14 *Breyer* ECLI:EU:C:2016:779.

10 The extension to non-personal data is nevertheless supported in the literature; see Josef Drexl, 'Data Access and Control in the Era of Connected Devices – Study on Behalf of the European Consumer Organisation BEUC' (BEUC 2018) 123–126, <https://www.beuc.eu/publications/beuc-x-2018-121_data_access_and_control_in_the_area_of_connected_devices.pdf> accessed 31 August 2020; Ruth Janal, 'Data Portability – A Tale of Two Concepts' 8 (2017) Journal of Intellectual Property, Information Technology and E-Commerce Law 59, para. 35; Gerald Spindler, 'Die Richtlinie über Verträge über digitale Inhalte: Gewährleistung, Haftung und Änderungen' (2019) Multimedia und Recht 488, 492.

data are anonymised (if this is technically possible at all) may one consider applying Article 16(4) instead of the provisions of the GDPR. Also, one may discuss cases of consumers using anonymisation tools like VPN or TOR. However, the question then would be how to make and, if necessary, enforce a claim for access if the consumer wants to stay anonymous until she receives the content. It is therefore not surprising that commentators have difficulties giving concrete examples for the application of Article 16(4) DCSD.[11] But things may change in the future, especially if the principle of data minimisation in Article 5(1)(a) GDPR comes to be taken more seriously.

Second, the trader may refuse to grant access to the contents provided or created by the consumer if one of the situations described in Article 16(3)(a)-(c) is given. Under (a), the trader may deny any access if the 'content has no utility outside the context of the digital content or digital service supplied by the trader'. In this regard, it cannot suffice for the trader to assert that the content is of no such utility; rather, such utility should be assumed if the consumer claims to have an interest to use the content outside the context of the content or service. But even then, the trader may still argue that under (b) the content 'only relates to the consumer's activity when using the digital content or digital service supplied by the trader'. This proviso, if given a broad interpretation, could be used to undermine the access right significantly. All content stored on the trader's product or service 'relates to the consumer's activity'. Given the aim of Article 16(4), which is to not discourage the consumer from exercising the remedies of the DCSD and terminating a contract,[12] the proviso should be narrowed down to mere use data collected by the trader and to personalisation of the content or service made by the user,[13] whereas any content actively created or uploaded by the consumer should be subject to the access right.[14] Finally, according to (c) the trader may also refuse to grant access to content 'that has been aggregated with other data by the trader and cannot be disaggregated or only with disproportionate efforts.' In this regard it has al-

11 But see Recitals 69, 71 DCSD. The former lists images, video and audio files as possible candidates for Art. 16(3), (4) without any discussion of the problem.

12 Recital 70 DCSD.

13 This second aspect is emphasised by Bernhard A. Koch, 'System der Rechtsbehelfe' in Wolfgang Stabentheiner, Christiane Wendehorst and Brigitta Zöchling-Jud (eds), *Das neue europäische Gewährleistungsrecht* (Manz 2019) 157, 178.

14 Interestingly, the proviso does speak of 'content' and not as in Art. 3(1)(2) of 'data'. This may be seen as a further argument that the portability right is not applicable to mere use data collected by the trader.

ready been stated that the proportionality requirement should be understood as explicitly obliging the supplier to configure its service in a way that allows contents to be extracted separately for each consumer. Service providers should apply state-of-the-art technology to protect the consumers' interest in their own contents. If suppliers do not set up their services in such a way as to facilitate the retrieval of consumers' content to the maximum effect possible according to state-of-the-art technology, they should not be heard with the argument of disproportionality.[15]

Third, the right of access under Article 16(4) DCSD is only applicable in case of termination of the contract, which limits its scope of application. Consumers who wish to use their contents on different services in parallel ('multi-homing'), e.g. playlists or search histories of music streaming services or sharing of photos and videos over social media platforms, may not rely on Article 16(4) DCSD. They must choose between the two services, terminate one of the contracts, claim for access under Article 16(4) DCSD and then port their contents to the other service. Moreover, Article 16(4) is only (directly) applicable in case of a termination which is based on a failure to supply by the trader or the lack of conformity or in case of modification of the content or service in accordance with Article 19. All other grounds of termination, especially the right to terminate long-term contracts after a certain period of time,[16] are outside the scope of the DCSD. However, Member States are free to expand the portability right to such situations.[17]

If all conditions are fulfilled, the consumer 'shall be entitled to retrieve that digital content free of charge, without hindrance from the trader, within a reasonable time and in a commonly used and machine-readable format', under Article 16(4)(2). The DCSD thus does not just provide a simple right of access but a more advanced right of portability. If the consumer receives the contents in a commonly used and machine-readable format, it should be possible for competing services to offer the necessary interfaces and to help the consumer to port the contents.

---

15 See Metzger and others (n. 5) para. 54.

16 See Annex 1(h) Unfair Terms Directive (EEC) 93/13 and, as an example, the German implementation in Sec. 309(9)(a) German Civil Code (*Bürgerliches Gesetzbuch*) (preclusion of termination in general terms for more than two years is void). Compare Wolfgang Wurmnest, in *Münchener Kommentar zum Bürgerlichen Gesetzbuch* (8th edn, C.H. Beck 2019) § 309 Nr. 9 paras 2–4.

17 The full harmonisation approach does not cover other grounds of termination; see Art. 3(10), Recitals 11, 12 DCSD.

Like all consumer rights of the DCSD, Article 16(4) is of a mandatory nature; see Article 22(1). However, the trader may specify the conditions of the right of access as long as these conditions do not deviate from Article 16(4) to the detriment of the consumer (Article 22(2)). One may justify this strict regulatory approach by multiple market failures, ranging from the (general) asymmetry between consumers and professionals[18] to the dysfunctional competition on some of the markets for digital services caused by network effects[19] to the threat of lock-in effects.[20] These market failures are amplified by cognitive biases of consumers, who overvalue short-term benefits from services over long-term risks.[21]

III. Comparison of Article 16(4) DCSD and Articles 15, 20 GDPR

Consumer claims for access to personal data can only be based on the provisions of the GDPR, irrespective of whether the controller has concluded a contract on the supply of a digital good or digital service with the consumer or not. Article 16(4) DCSD excludes claims for access to personal data, Article 3(8) clarifies that 'Union law on the protection of personal data shall apply to any personal data processed in connection with contracts referred to in paragraph 1'. The access rights of the GDPR are of a different

---

18 Shmuel I. Becher, 'Asymmetric Information in Consumer Contracts: The Challenge That Is Yet to Be Met' (2008) 45 American Business Law Journal 723, 728, 733–35; Holger Fleischer, *Informationsasymmetrie im Vertragsrecht* (C.H. Beck 2001) 203–08, 570–72; Giesela Rühl, 'Consumer Protection in Choice of Law' (2011) 44 Cornell International Law Journal 570, 571–595.

19 Jacques Crémer, Yves-Alexandre de Montjoye and Heike Schweitzer, 'Competition policy for the digital era – Final report' (2019) 4–5, <https://ec.europa.eu/competition/publications/reports/kd0419345enn.pdf> accessed 31 August 2020.

20 Ibid. 34.

21 The bias has been described for free services offered in exchange for personal data. See OECD, 'Big data: Bringing competition policy to the digital era: Background note by the Secretariat' (November 2016) para. 91, <https://one.oecd.org/document/DAF/COMP(2016)14/en/pdf> accessed 31 August 2020: 'The user is given the immediate benefit of the zero-price service, but is unaware of the short or long-term costs in divulging information, as they do not know how the data will be used and by whom.' See also Cory Hallam and Gianluca Zanella, 'Online self-disclosure: The privacy paradox explained as a temporally discounted balance between concerns and rewards' (2017) 68 Computers in Human Behavior 217; Yoan Hermstrüwer, *Informationelle Selbstgefährdung* (Mohr Siebeck 2016) 93ff. The argument should apply similarly for non-personal data provided by consumers in ignorance of the long-term disadvantages.

nature. Their aim is not to balance the interests of contracting parties but to protect the fundamental rights and freedoms of natural persons, in particular their right to the protection of personal data.[22]

The GDPR recognises a general right of access in Article 15 and a more specific right to data portability in Article 20. The right of access in Article 15 is broader in scope.[23] It covers not just the data processed by the controller but also additional information with regard to the processing, ranging from (a) the purpose of processing to (h) the existence of automated decision-making, including profiling. Article 15 GDPR is not limited to specific legal grounds of the processing. However, the controller has only limited obligations on the format of the information, which must be provided according to paragraph 3 in a 'commonly used electronic form'. Article 20 GDPR is more limited in scope. It is only applicable to data that the data subject 'has provided to a controller'.[24] Also, Article 20 GDPR requires that the 'processing is based on consent pursuant to point (a) of Article 6(1) or point (a) of Article 9(2) or on a contract pursuant to point (b) of Article 6(1).'[25] But the rights of the data subject under Article 20 GDPR are more extensive. Under Article 20 GDPR, the data subject cannot just ask for the disclosure of the processed personal data but for a transmission 'in a structured, commonly used and machine-readable format'. The data subject has the right to 'transmit those data to another controller without hindrance from the controller' and even ask the data controller to transmit the data directly to another controller, 'where technically feasible' (Article 20(2)). The porting of data may be combined with a claim to erase all data stored by the controller (Article 20(3)). However, the rights and freedoms of third parties may not be affected by any access to or porting of data, according to Articles 15(4) and 20(4) GDPR.[26]

---

22 Recital 1 GDPR.

23 Drexl (n. 10) 151.

24 For a broad interpretation see Janal (n. 10) para. 9: Right to portability extends to data provided by the consumer's conduct and use of gadgets or services. See also Drexl (n. 10) 152: Right extends to 'observed' data.

25 For an application of Art. 20 GDPR with regard to illegally processed data Janal (n. 10) para. 11; see also Drexl (n. 9) 153.

26 Art. 20 is lex specialis to Art. 15 if the data subject requests their personal data in a 'structured, commonly used and machine-readable format' or if a transmission to another controller is requested; see Lorenz Franck in Peter Gola, *Datenschutzgrundverordnung* (2nd edn, C.H. Beck 2018) Art. 15 para. 4. However, if the data subject requests the additional information listed at the end of Art. 15(1) GDPR, then this provision is lex specialis to Art. 20 GDPR.

The access rights of the GDPR are broader in scope and more favourable to consumers than Article 16(4) DCSD in many respects. They do not require the conclusion and later termination of a contract. Article 20 (but not Article 15) GDPR provides for more advanced requirements with regard to the format of the data ('structured') and grants the right to transmit the data received or to request a direct transmission from one controller to another controller. Both Articles 15 and 20 GDPR are not bound to restrictive conditions comparable to Article 16(3) DCSD[27] but provide for a reservation for the rights and freedoms of third parties. Article 15 GDPR (but not Article 20) is applicable to any data processed by a controller, plus additional information on the processing, irrespective of the legal basis of such processing.

In sum, one may regret the inconsistencies and unintentional differences between the legal regimes for access and porting of non-personal contents under Article 16(4) DCDS and personal data under Articles 15, 20 GDPR. However, the underlying pattern to leave the rules of the GDPR untouched by the DCSD serves the goal of coherence in this regard.[28] Moreover, it is plausible to grant more far-reaching access rights with regard to personal data: Article 16(4) DCSD is primarily concerned with consumer rights (with a pro-competitive side-effect); by contrast, Articles 15, 20 GDPR protect fundamental rights (also with a pro-competitive side-effect).[29]

IV. Individual and collective enforcement

The remedies for consumers under the DCSD are drafted as individual claims. This is also the case for Article 16(4) DCSD, which obliges the trader to grant access to contents 'at the request of the consumer'. Courts and data protection supervisors are still in an experimental stage with individual rights of access to personal data under the GDPR.[30] Data protection law

27 Critical Janal (n. 10) para. 10: proportionality should also apply with regard to Art. 20 GDPR. See also Drexl, (n. 10) 152.

28 See Metzger and others (n. 5) para. 54.

29 Janal (n. 10) paras 4, 5 with further references.

30 See Stefan Brink and Daniel Joos, 'Reichweite und Grenzen des Auskunftsanspruchs und des Rechts auf Kopie' (2019) Zeitschrift für Datenschutz 483; Niko Härting, 'Was ist eigentlich eine "Kopie?"' (2019) Computer und Recht 219; see also *Dawson-Damer v. Taylor Wessing LLP* [2017] EWCA Civ 74 (16 February 2017) on the Data Protection Act 1998.

in general suffers from private enforcement in legal practice. It is thus for good reasons that Article 21(2) DCSD allows collective enforcement, as determined by national law, by (a) public bodies or their representatives, (b) consumer organisations having a legitimate interest in protecting consumers, (c) professional organisations having a legitimate interest in acting, and (d) not-for-profit bodies, organisations or associations active in the field of the protection of data subjects' rights and freedoms as defined in Article 80 GDPR.[31]

Besides these collective entities, it will be a question of special interest in Germany whether competitors may raise claims based on unfair competition if their competitors do not make available contents provided or created by the consumers in compliance with Article 16(4) DCSD. Germany has a broad practice of private enforcement of public and private law regulations by means of unfair competition law.[32] According to Section 3a Act against Unfair Competition, competitors may bring claims based on the breach of law 'where a person violates a statutory provision which is also intended to regulate market conduct in the interest of market participants and the breach of law is suited to appreciably harming the interests of consumers, other market participants and competitors.' German courts have allowed such claims for a variety of provisions, including provisions of the Consumer Sales Directive (EC) 1999/44,[33] the Unfair Terms Directive (EC) 93/13[34] and some provisions of the pre-GDPR German Federal Data Pro-

31 Art. 21(2)(d) DCSD does not specify whether such organisations may only enforce rights grounded in data protection law or whether they may also enforce claims arising from contract law. One may argue for the latter approach with the position of the rule in the DCSD, which provides only contractual remedies and leaves the data protection issues to the GDPR. Limiting the scope of Art. 21(2)(d) DCSD to claims from the realm of data protection law would reduce its scope of application to zero. Still, the mandate of such organisations may be limited by their own by-laws to data protection law.

32 On the compliance of this practice with Directive (EU) 2005/29 of the European Parliament and of the Council of 11 May 2005 concerning unfair business-to-consumer commercial practices in the internal market [2005] OJ L149/22, see Axel Metzger, 'Die Entwicklung des Rechtsbruchtatbestands nach der Umsetzung der UGP-Richtlinie – ein Zwischenbericht' (2015) Gewerblicher Rechtsschutz und Urheberrecht Internationaler Teil 687.

33 German Federal Supreme Court (*BGH*), 31 March 2010, Case I ZR 34/08 (2010) Gewerblicher Rechtsschutz und Urheberrecht 1117 – *Gewährleistungsausschluss im Internet*.

34 German Federal Supreme Court (*BGH*), 31 May 2012, Case I ZR 45/11 (2012) Gewerblicher Rechtsschutz und Urheberrecht 949 – *Missbräuchliche Vertragsstrafe*.

tection Act[35] and now also of the GDPR.[36] It is thus a realistic scenario that some of the provisions of the DCSD including Article 16(4) will also be characterised as provisions intended to regulate market conduct in the interest of consumers. The consequence would be that competitors could indirectly claim violations of Article 16(4) through the backdoor of unfair competition law. This would also permit them to send cease-and-desist letters and to claim for recovery of their expenses according to Section 12(1)(2) Act against Unfair Competition, an enforcement mechanism which has turned out to be very effective in some areas, but which may also be abused as a (lawyer's) business model.

V. Transfer or fiduciary exercise of rights

A different approach to strengthen the enforcement of portability claims under Article 16(4) DCSD would be to allow for their transfer to other providers of digital contents or services. If such providers were allowed to acquire portability claims of users against their old service providers, they could enforce those rights and claim for a direct transmission of the contents from the old service provider to their database, e.g. Flickr could ask Apple for a direct transmission of pictures stored on a cloud, Soundcloud could claim for playlists and search history to be transmitted by Spotify etc. – based on the premise that these contents would be non-personal data and covered by Article 16(4) DCSD. Such an approach could boost the enforcement of portability claims. The incentive for the new provider to enforce such claims would be higher than for the individual user, since it would permit the provider to win new customers and not, as in the case of

35 On Sec. 28 (pre-GDPR) German Federal Data Protection Act, see Cologne Higher Regional Court (*Oberlandesgericht Köln*), 17 January 2014, Case 6 U 167/13 (2014) Beck-Rechtsprechung 07826 – *Unzulässige Datenverwendung zur Mandatsakquise-Anlegerbrief*; Karlsruhe Higher Regional Court (*Oberlandesgericht Karlsruhe*), 9 May 2012, Case 6 U 38/11 (2012) Gewerblicher Rechtsschutz und Urheberrecht Rechtsprechungs-Report 396 – *Werbung nach Versorgerwechsel*. But see also Munich Higher Regional Court (*Oberlandesgericht München*), 12 January 2012, Case 29 U 3926/11 (2012) Gewerblicher Rechtsschutz und Urheberrecht Rechtsprechungs-Report 395 – *Nutzung von Daten ehemaliger Gaskunden*.

36 See Hamburg Higher Regional Court (*Oberlandesgericht Hamburg*), 25 October 2018, Case 3 U 66/17, (2019) Gewerblicher Rechtsschutz und Urheberrecht 86 – *Allergenbestellbögen*. The question of whether this practice is compatible with the GDPR has just recently been referred to the CJEU: see German Federal Supreme Court (*BGH*), 28 May 2020, Case I ZR 186/17.

the individual user, to port his or her user-generated contents from a poorly performing service to another functionally equivalent and hopefully satisfactory service. Also, transaction costs would be lower; providers would implement standardised claim-enforcement mechanisms and profit from the economy of scales. If the transfer were only allowed as part of a contract on digital contents or services with the new provider, the consumer would profit from such an arrangement. The new provider would release the consumer from enforcing the portability claim against the old provider without the risk of a later transfer of his claims to third parties. As an additional safeguard, one could allow such a transfer strictly on condition that the new provider has a duty to enforce the portability claim.

The DCSD does not preclude such a transfer. A transfer to a new provider would not lead to a derogation from the provisions of the DCSD 'to the detriment of the consumer' in the sense of Article 22(1) DCSD.[37] Rather, it would help to strengthen the impact of the portability rules. Also, a transfer would not conflict with the principle of inalienability of personality rights,[38] since Article 16(4) is only concerned with non-personal contents. Consumers, moreover, would have a mandatory portability right against the new provider under Article 16(4) DCSD once the contents have been transferred. The transfer would therefore not lead to a situation in which the consumer would lose any right against the new provider.

However, if a transfer of the portability claim is still seen as a too far-reaching disposition of mandatory consumer rights, one could instead use instruments like fiduciary entitlements or authorisations that allow the new provider to exercise the portability claim in the name of the con-

37 Art. 22 DCSD restricts contractual arrangements between the consumer and the (old) service provider but does not explicitly restrict such arrangements with third parties. However, such agreement could still be seen as an indirect derogation or variation of the mandatory consumer rights. See on the parallel provision in Art. 7 Consumer Sales Directive (EC) 1999/44 and the German implementation in Sec. 476 German Civil Code Florian Faust, in *Beck Online-Kommentar zum BGB* (53rd edn, C.H. Beck 2020) § 476 para. 11; Stefan Lorenz in *Münchener Kommentar zum Bürgerlichen Gesetzbuch* (8th edn, C.H. Beck 2019) § 476 paras 7, 33.

38 This principle is known, inter alia, in German and French law, though with many nuances and exceptions; see Huw Beverley-Smith, Ansgar Ohly and Agnès Lucas-Schloetter, *Privacy, Property and Personality: Civil Law Perspectives on Commercial Appropriation* (CUP 2005) 129–138, 194–95 with further references.

sumer.[39] Such an entitlement or authorisation could suffice to enable the party with the highest incentive to enforce portability claims directly.

C. Data access and porting under general contract law principles

I. No mandatory access rules in European and German general contract law

1. European contract law

The analysis so far has shown that EU law grants to consumers (and data subjects) access and portability rights both for personal data under Articles 15, 20 GDPR and for other data under Article 16(4) DCSD. Yet it has also become clear that these European consumer (or data subject) rights are not without gaps, especially with regard to embedded contents under Directive (EU) 771/2019 on the sale of goods but also with regard to the portability of data in the case of regular termination of long-term contracts, which is not covered by Article 16(4) DCSD.

A much broader gap, however, exists with regard to business-to-business (B2B) contracts. Access to and portability of data are of major importance in B2B contractual relationships. Professional users of digital services, e.g. cloud services, business platforms and software tools, have a vital interest to obtain access to contents and data they have stored or processed on these services or platforms or which they have produced with these software tools. Such data may have been actively uploaded to or produced with the service, platform or tool. But data may also be based on an observation or profiling of the business customer's activities. Businesses do also have an interest to access data that their contracting parties have derived from original raw data produced by the customer. In addition, data embedded in machines and other (tangible) devices is of enormous economic importance for both contracting parties, including data processed and recorded in airplanes (both for the manufacturer and the airline), in agricultural machines (both for the farmer and the producer of the machine, but also third parties, e.g. for providers of information services on the cli-

39 Such a specific fiduciary entitlement would not replace the more general idea of establishing general data fiduciaries or personal information management systems (PIMS) as neutral entities which administer the personal data in the interest of the provider's customers; see European Data Protection Supervisor, Opinion 9/2016 on Personal Information Management Systems, <https://edps.europa.eu/sites/edp/files/publication/16-10-20_pims_opinion_en.pdf> accessed 31 August 2020.

mate, producers of seed or fertilisers or herbicides) or in wind power stations (both for the owner of the station and the producer).

The few as yet existing mandatory B2B data access or portability rights under EU law are not to be qualified as contract law rules. They are of a different nature, namely general competition law under Article 102 TFEU,[40] or relate to more specific regulatory regimes like the EU rules on access to vehicle repair and maintenance information under Regulation 715/2007,[41] the EU rules in the banking sector under the Payment Services Directive 2015/2366[42] and the EU rules on access to data of 'smart meters' for electricity and natural gas under Directives (EU) 2009/73 and 2019/944.

In the area of contract law, the European Commission by now has published a number of soft law instruments defining principles on data-sharing between businesses (B2B) and between businesses and governmental authorities (B2G) and describing different models of data sharing with a number of examples.[43] The principles explained in the instruments, 'transparency', 'shared value creation', 'respect for each other's commercial interests', 'undistorted competition', and 'minimised data lock-in', should indeed guide every contractual relationship. But one should not be surprised that market actors do not always follow these principles but rather seek to maximise their profit. One may describe these statements of principles either as toothless or as market-oriented and liberal, depending on the observer's perspective.

The – more general – soft law instruments of the European Commission have been complemented with specific duties for 'online mediation ser-

---

40 See Heike Schweitzer and Robert Welker, 'A legal framework for access to data – A competition policy perspective', in this volume.

41 Arts 6–9 Regulation (EC) No. 715/2007 of the European Parliament and of the Council of 20 June 2007 on type approval of motor vehicles with respect to emissions from light passenger and commercial vehicles (Euro 5 and Euro 6) and on access to vehicle repair and maintenance data [2007] OJ L171/1; see on this Wolfgang Kerber and Daniel Gill, 'Access to Data in Connected Cars and the Recent Reform of the Motor Vehicle Type Approval Regulation' (2019) 10 Journal of Intellectual Property, Information Technology and E-Commerce Law 244–257.

42 Arts 38–60 Directive (EU) 2015/2366 of the European Parliament and of the Council of 25 November 2015 on payment services in the internal market, amending Directives 2002/65/EC, 2009/110/EC and 2013/36/EU and Regulation (EU) No. 1093/2010, and repealing Directive 2007/64/EC [2015] OJ L337/35.

43 See Communication of the European Commission to the European Parliament, the Council, the European economic and Social Committee and the Committee of the Regions – 'Towards a common European data space' COM(2018) 232 final and European Commission Staff Working Document, 'Guidance on sharing private sector data in the European data economy' SWD(2018) 125 final.

vices' by the Fairness and Transparency Regulation (EU) 2019/1150.[44] The Fairness and transparency Regulation targets online sales platforms like Amazon. The Regulation does not oblige those platforms to grant their business users access to personal or other data which the users of the platform provide for their use or which is generated by the platform. However, the Regulation puts the platforms under an obligation to provide their business users 'in their terms and conditions a description of the technical and contractual access, or absence thereof, of business users to any personal data or other data',[45] and moreover to provide a description of 'any differentiated treatment which they give, or might give, in relation to goods or services offered to consumers through those online intermediation services by, on the one hand, either that provider itself or any business users which that provider controls and, on the other hand, other business users', including the 'access that the provider, or that the business users or corporate website users which that provider controls, may have to any personal data or other data' and the 'access to, conditions for, or any direct or indirect remuneration charged for the use of services or functionalities, or technical interfaces, that are relevant to the business user or the corporate website user and that are directly connected or ancillary to utilising the online intermediation services or online search engines concerned.'[46] These information duties are supplemented by a specific right of access to data in case of a restriction or termination and later reinstatement of the online mediation service.[47] The Fairness and Transparency Regulation, however, does not introduce any further mandatory or default access rights. As such, it will strengthen transparency with regard to the existence or non-existence of contractual data access rights for the specific case of 'online mediation services' but it is far from establishing a general right of access or portability to data in B2B relationships.

The recently published 'European strategy for data' of the European Commission seems to follow the cautious approach of the last years with

44 The Regulation applies also to online search engines: see Art. 1(1) Regulation (EU) 2019/1150 of the European Parliament and of the Council of 20 June 2019 on promoting fairness and transparency for business users of online intermediation services [2019] OJ L186/57. However, the provisions of interest in this paper are only applicable to online mediation services.

45 Art. 9 Regulation (EU) 2019/1150.

46 Art. 7(1), (3)(a) and (d) Regulation (EU) 2019/1150.

47 Art. 4(3) Regulation (EU) 2019/1150.

regard to B2B contracts.[48] The strategy paper emphasises the vision to create a European data space where data can flow within the EU across sectors and addresses the problem that 'data sharing between companies has not taken off at sufficient scale'. However, the measures announced, especially the 'Data Act (2021)', seem to follow a market-based approach for B2B contracts: 'The general principle shall be to facilitate voluntary data sharing.' And: 'only where specific circumstances so dictate, access to data should be made compulsory'.[49]

In sum, EU contract law legislation so far does not provide for a general right of access or portability of data with regard to B2B relationships. Yet one may ask whether such a right may be inferred from general principles of contract law, such as the Principles of European Contract Law (PECL), the Unidroit Principles or the Draft Common Frame of Reference (DCFR). Starting points for such access rights could be information duties, implied terms or restitution rights in case of termination of contract. However, the collections of principles, at least for the most part, contain principles of a non-mandatory nature.[50] They do not provide for any mandatory access rights.

2. *National contract law – The case of Germany*

On the national level, again one may use different legal doctrines of general contract law to construe access rights. With regard to information duties inferred from the principle of good faith and fair dealing, contract law traditions of EU Member States differ significantly. Some states follow a tradition in which one contracting party, at least to a certain extent, is responsible for the well-being of the other party, whereas other jurisdictions emphasise the principle of self-responsibility. Yet the differences should also not be overemphasised. Comparative analysis of concrete cases shows that

48 Communication of the European Commission to the European Parliament, the Council, the European Economic and Social Committee and the Committee of the Regions – 'A European strategy for data' COM(2020) 66 final.

49 Ibid. 13.

50 See Art. 1:102(2) Principles of European Contract Law (PECL), but see also Art. 1:201 PECL (good faith and fair dealing mandatory); Art. 1.5 Unidroit Principles 2016, Art. II.1:102(2) Draft Common Frame of Reference (DCFR).

apparently divergent traditions come to surprisingly consistent judgments.[51]

German law is well known for its strong emphasis of the principle of good faith.[52] German judiciary and doctrine have developed a variety of information duties and other implied secondary obligations of the parties to a contract.[53] However, any of the so far recognised duties of one party to disclose information to the other party to the contract are highly case-specific. Therefore, one might well expect that German courts would grant access rights in specific cases under the guiding principle of good faith. But this approach would certainly not lead to a general right of access and portability in B2B contracts. Also, information duties are not per se of a mandatory nature. Still, one could consider examples of access rights based on such general information duties. If for example the owner of an industry machine needs certain data for the maintenance of the machine one could consider such a right of access, at least in cases in which the producer does not offer maintenance services. To give a second example: A customer of a cloud service should certainly have a right to access the data and content stored on the cloud server during the contract and after its termination. The Higher Regional Court of Munich derived such a right of access as an implied term from the principle of good faith and obliged the service provider, after termination of the contract, to support the customer in the porting of its data to a different service provider.[54]

Besides information duties and implied terms, courts could also consider other legal doctrines of contract law as legal grounds for access rights. Depending on the concrete nature of the rights and duties of the parties to the contract, provisions from the specific contracts section of the German Civil Code (BGB) could be applicable. According to Section 667 BGB, in the case of a contract of mandate, 'the mandatary is obliged to return to the mandator everything he receives to perform the mandate and what he obtains from carrying out the transaction.' The concept of mandate (in-

---

51 Cf. Reinhard Zimmermann and Simon Whittaker (eds), *Good Faith in European Contract Law* (CUP 2000) 653.

52 See Sec. 242 German Civil Code (performance in good faith): 'An obligor has a duty to perform according to the requirements of good faith, taking customary practice into consideration.'.

53 The concept of implied secondary obligation is today codified in Sec. 241(2) German Civil Code: 'An obligation may also, depending on its contents, oblige each party to take account of the rights, legal interests and other interests of the other party.'.

54 Munich Higher Regional Court (*Oberlandesgericht München*), 22 April 1999, Case 6 U 1657/99, (1999) Computer und Recht 484, paras 179–186.

cluding paid management of the affairs of another, Section 675 German Civil Code) is broad and could also cover, eg, escrow agreements or agreements on the data processing on behalf of a controller in the sense of Article 28(1) GDPR.[55] However, Section 667 German Civil Code can be waived.[56] In the case of a contract on safekeeping, according to Section 695 German Civil Code, 'the depositor may at any time demand that the thing deposited is returned, even if a period for safekeeping has been specified.' It has been suggested that (at least certain) cloud service contracts be characterised as safekeeping contracts.[57] If the provisions on safekeeping contracts were applicable here, it would still be controversial whether the parties were allowed to exclude the right to claim for return according Section 695 German Civil Code.[58]

Finally, rights and duties in case of termination of a contract could provide a basis for access claims. The basis for such claims could be found in the general contract termination rules, especially Section 346(1) German Civil Code: 'If one party to a contract has contractually reserved the right to revoke or if he has a statutory right of revocation, then, in the case of revocation, performance received and emoluments taken are to be returned.' This could justify a claim by one contracting party against the other contracting party to return data or content transmitted or collected during a contract, e.g. if a buyer of a machine revokes the contract after some months because of lack of conformity and requests access and transmission of valuable data collected and stored by the machine.[59] However, Section

55 See for further examples Marc Strittmatter, in Fabian Schuster and Malte Grützmacher (eds), *IT-Recht Kommentar* (Beck 2020) § 675 BGB paras 17–24. See for a client's access claim to data stored by a tax consultant German Federal Supreme Court (*BGH*), 11 March 2004, Case IX ZR 187/03, (2004) Neue Juristische Wochenschrift Rechtsprechungs-Report Zivilrecht 1290.

56 Detlef Fischer in *Beck Online-Kommentar zum BGB* (53rd edn, C.H. Beck 2020) § 667 para. 5.

57 See, for example, Martin Henssler in *Münchener Kommentar zum Bürgerlichen Gesetzbuch* (8th edn, C.H. Beck 2020) § 688 para. 9; Frank A. Koch, 'Application Service Providing als neue IT-Leistung' (2001) Der IT-Rechtsberater 39, 42.

58 See Henssler (n. 57) § 695 para. 2 with further references.

59 This would require characterising the active provision of data by the buyer or the passive acceptance of data collection by the seller as the performance of an explicit or implied secondary obligation of the buyer under the contract, the value of which would then be returned in accordance with Sec. 346(1)(1), (2) German Civil Code, cf. German Federal Supreme Court, 28 November 1997, Case V ZR 178/96, (1998) Neue Juristische Wochenschrift 1079, 1080–81. On the application of Sec. 346(1) German Civil Code in case of provision of data as performance, see

346 BGB can be modified and even excluded by the parties.[60] It does not provide a basis for mandatory access rights. Also, Section 346 is not applicable in case of termination of a long-term contract.[61] In this regard, a claim based on unjust enrichment in accordance with Section 812(1)(1) BGB could be considered.[62]

To sum up, German law of contracts does not provide for a general access right to data transmitted, created or observed by contracting parties, be it during the contractual relationship or after its termination. The existing information, access and return duties are case-specific and for the most part of a non-mandatory nature. This makes it clear that there will be no legal ground for access claims in many cases without explicit contract provision and without the special circumstances of good faith etc. discussed above, e.g. no contractual data access right for airlines or farmers covering data processed and recorded in airplanes or agricultural machines etc.

II. A case for mandatory access rules in B2B contracts?

European and German contract law do not provide for a general mandatory access and portability right that would also be applicable in B2B contracts. Whether it should provide for such access rights is a question of politics, which however should try to back its arguments with findings from law and economics research. From this perspective, the starting point is a market model where perfect competition and freedom of contract lead to an allocation of goods, here the data in question, to the market actor who can maximise welfare out of the use of this good.[63] Unfortunately, markets are not always fully functioning. The allocation mechanisms of markets

---

Axel Metzger, 'Dienst gegen Daten: Ein synallagmatischer Vertrag' (2016) 216 Archiv für die civilistische Praxis 817, 861.

60 See Reinhard Gaier, in *Münchener Kommentar zum Bürgerlichen Gesetzbuch* (8th edn, C.H. Beck 2019) § 346 para. 1.

61 Ibid. para. 17.

62 Sec. 812(1)(1) German Civil Code: 'A person who obtains something as a result of the performance of another person or otherwise at his expense without legal grounds for doing so is under a duty to make restitution to him.' However, such a claim would be of a non-contractual nature.

63 This is a very basic assumption of every welfare economics model since Adam Smith's famous 'invisible hand' theorem; see Adam Smith, *An inquiry into the nature and causes of the wealth of nations* (The Modern Library 1937) 423. See also Robert B. Cooter and Thomas Ulen, *Law and Economics* (6th edn, Pearson 2014) 275–279.

are often distorted. Based on this premise, the research on law and economics refers to different kinds of market failures as justification for state intervention.[64] A first reason to intervene in B2B markets is lack of competition. But other market failures, namely asymmetries of information or negative externalities, may also call for state intervention. Moreover, state regulation may be helpful to safeguard legal certainty and lower transaction costs.

The clearest case for a possible failure of data markets concerns negative externalities caused by data access rights. If the data in question is personal data in the sense of the GDPR, any access granted to third parties causes negative externalities with regard to the data subjects. This risk, however, is ruled out to a large extent by the GDPR. Any granting of access to personal data fulfils the definition of a 'processing of data' in the sense of the GDPR[65] and as such requires a justification in accordance with Article 6 GDPR. Violation of the requirements of the GDPR is sanctioned by severe penalties. It is evident that the current European law is torn between a strong data protection policy and the wish to stimulate the European digital economy by encouraging data sharing.

With regard to lack of competition as a market failure, the situation is less evident. Obviously markets for digital goods and services have a tendency to concentrate on a small number of competitors. In particular, some Internet services function as platforms for their different kinds of users and have as such a natural inclination towards dominance.[66] Network effects push consumers and businesses to become the customers of highly centralised communication or trading platforms. Once services have established a dominant position in one market, they might leverage their market power to closely related markets. These effects may be reinforced by lock-in effects that prevent users from changing from one service to another. Competition law nevertheless so far has difficulties remedying those problems, especially when service providers grow into a dominant

---

64 See Steven Shavell, *Foundations of Economic Analysis of Law* (Harvard University Press 2004) 320–22; Hans-Bernd Schäfer and Claus Ott, *Lehrbuch der ökonomischen Analyse des Zivilrechts* (5th edn, Springer 2012) 78–81; Cooter and Ulen (n. 63) 286–291.

65 Art. 4(2) GDPR: 'disclosure by transmission, dissemination or otherwise making available'.

66 On the following see Crémer, de Montjoye and Schweitzer (n. 19) 19ff.; Lena Mischau, 'Market Power Assessment in Digital Markets – A German Perspective' (2020) GRUR International – Journal of European and International IP Law 233–248.

position.[67] But is it the right answer to intervene in these markets with mandatory contract rules, more specifically with mandatory access and portability rights to overcome, at least, the mentioned lock-in effects? There are good arguments to answer the question in the affirmative, at least for service providers with a dominant market position or in other cases of restraints of competition.[68] But the situation is different if the user has a choice between several services and may compare access and portability rules before entering into a contract. In a market with competition, a professional user should be in a position to choose the service with the preferred access rules. And if, as a consequence of competition, this feature turns out to be of importance for the customer's choice, the service providers should react to this demand.[69] Therefore, prevention of lock-in effects is indicated in markets with dominant actors but less evident for other situations. A mandatory access and portability rule that is applicable to all B2B contracts and does not require such a dominant position would most likely overshoot the mark. General access rules could be used by already dominant companies to gather data stored by other market actors, e.g. aircraft manufacturers could claim for access to data collected by airlines in their own monitoring devices. Access and portability rules could also be used to incentivise customers of smaller competitors to switch to

67 The currently pending Legislative draft for a 10th revision of the German Act against Restraints of Competition tries to introduce new instruments or up-date existing ones, especially Sec. 18(3b): Intermediation power; Sec. 19a: Paramount cross-market importance for competition; Sec. 20(1) and (1a): Relative market power; see the Government Bill for the 10th revision: 'Gesetzentwurf der Bundesregierung – Entwurf eines Gesetzes zur Änderung des Gesetzes gegen Wettbewerbsbeschränkungen für ein fokussiertes, proaktives und digitales Wettbewerbsrecht 4.0 (GWB-Digitalisierungsgesetz)' (9 September 2020) <www.bmwi.de/Redaktion/DE/Downloads/Gesetz/gesetzentwurf-gwb-digitalisierungsgesetz.pdf?__blob=publicationFile&v=6> accessed 15 September 2020. On the whole, see Mischau (n. 66) 246–248. See also the recent decision German Federal Supreme Court (BGH), 23 June 2020, Case KVR 69/19 (2020) 51 International Journal of Intellectual Property and Competition Law (forthcoming) (English translation) – *Bundeskartellamt/Facebook* (not yet published).

68 See Josef Drexl, 'Neue Regeln für die Europäische Datenwirtschaft? Ein Plädoyer für einen wettbewerbspolitischen Ansatz' (2017) Neue Zeitschrift für Kartellrecht 415, 418; Axel Metzger, 'Mehr Freiheit wagen auf dem Markt der Daten: Voraussetzungen und Grenzen eines Marktmodells für "big data"' in Anatol Dutta and Christian Heinze (eds) *Mehr Freiheit wagen – Symposium zur Emeritierung von Jürgen Basedow* (Mohr Siebeck 2018) 131, 144–45.

69 If all competitors exclude access, one should the raise the question if the market is fully functioning or if competition law must intervene.

larger competitors on cloud markets. Moreover, claims for access to data may arise out of contractual relationships, e.g. if an independent flight-tracking service seeks access to data collected by aircrafts. In such a case, no pre-existent contract can be supplemented by mandatory (or implied) duties but a regulatory intervention would have to create a right of access on a direct statutory basis. Therefore, legislatures should only introduce contractual access rights based on lack of competition if competition law requires such rights. In this case, the remedy to cure the competition law issue can be an intervention with mandatory rules for contracts, e.g. access to and porting of data. But such an approach should be justified by a clear indication of competition law. Still, this reluctance towards general access rules for B2B contracts should not preclude court intervention if a lock-in situation is abused by the service provider in a concrete case, e.g. if a denial of access would be against good faith given the concrete contractual arrangement and the circumstances of the case.[70]

Another consideration to justify data access rights in B2B contracts could be found, at least at first glance, in the different theories of asymmetric information in contract negotiations.[71] It may appear as intuitive to discuss the access to data cases along the lines of the different information disclosure doctrines known in many jurisdictions, according to which one party to a contract may have a duty to disclose information during the negotiation of the contract. Economic analysis of law has developed several approaches to explain these doctrines and to identify their limits. However, on closer scrutiny, the cases in which disclosure duties are seen as necessary to remedy asymmetric information concern situations different from the claims for access discussed here, especially if the buyer or seller of a commodity possesses information that is relevant for the contract with regard to the price paid for the commodity, e.g. if the basement of a home leaks or if a property bears minerals or oil. Here it may be socially desirable or not that information be disclosed with regard to factors[72] like who controls the information – the buyer or the seller – and who can make more socially valuable use of the information, which party can provide the information at which costs, whether the incentive to acquire the information would be undesirably reduced by a disclosure obligation or whether the information is socially valuable or has only private use. Those cases and cri-

---

70 Compare Munich Higher Regional Court (*Oberlandesgericht München*), 22 April 1999, Case 6 U 1657/99, (1999) Computer und Recht 484, paras 179–186.

71 See for a comprehensive comparative legal and economic analysis Fleischer (n. 18) passim. See also Cooter and Ulen (n. 63) 289–90; Shavell (n. 64) 331–335.

72 See Fleischer (n. 18) 175–177, 1000–1001; Shavell (n. 64) 332–334.

teria concern disclosure obligations relevant for the determination of the price of a commodity or service during the contract negotiation stage. They do not concern possible access rights with regard to data collected and processed in the course of a contract. Here, the information itself is the asset that should be allocated efficiently by the mechanisms of the market.[73] It would be an oversimplification to infer an information asymmetry to be remedied by state intervention from the fact that one party has an asset, here data, which the other party has not. Interestingly, the recently adopted Fairness and transparency Regulation does not oblige platforms to grant its business users access to personal or other data but mainly provides a duty to disclose whether the platform grants access to data and under which conditions. In the legal literature, additional information duties for B2B contracts have been suggested, in particular in regard of the general information of whether the other contracting party has collected data and what data has been collected and processed.[74]

To sum up, based on the established models of economics analysis of contracts, one can hardly justify general mandatory access and porting rules for data collected and processed by one of the contracting parties during a B2B contract. In situations of restraints of competition, competition law may require certain limits of party autonomy which may come along as mandatory rules for contracts; but such rules must be clearly justified on a competition law basis. With regard to information asymmetries, it may be useful to implement information duties with regard to the data collected and processed and, if applicable, to the conditions of access. However, the economics of information so far have not revealed a clear case for a general right of access to data.

III. Access and porting as default rules for B2B contracts?

1. Concept and functions of default contract rules

Given that most provisions of contract law are of a non-mandatory nature, it may be more intuitive to ask whether European or German contract law should implement default rules on data access and porting for B2B contracts.

73 See Herbert Zech, *Information als Schutzgegenstand* (Mohr Siebeck 2012) 152–57.
74 Drexl (n. 68) 418; Metzger (n. 68) 151–52.

The starting point for such an approach is the theory of incompleteness of contracts.[75] Contracts typically omit arrangements for circumstances and situations that are of potential importance to the parties at a later stage. Drafting complete contracts, if possible at all, would be burdensome and costly. Default rules in contract law legislation help to lower transaction costs. Contracting parties may rely on such default rules without making the effort to negotiate a similar solution. The major sources for default rules are typical contract provisions used in legal practice. Such majoritarian default rules are used as a proxy for the assumption of what parties would have agreed upon if they had foreseen the need for an arrangement for a given situation.[76]

Default rules are nonetheless of a normative nature – even if inspired by neutral majoritarian default.[77] Contracts are negotiated 'in the shadow of default rules'.[78] The party who wishes to deviate from a default has the burden to argue against a statutory rule. Default rules may be used, e.g. in Germany, for challenging standard terms and conditions as deviations from a statutory standard.[79] Therefore, legislatures should not codify default rules which may lead to socially undesirable results. Moreover, default rules can be used proactively to 'nudge' the parties in the direction of what the legislature deems to be an individually or socially desirable choice.[80] With regard to contracts, such biased default rules have the effect

75 See already Friedrich C. von Savigny, *System des heutigen römischen Rechts, Bd. 1* (Veit 1840) 58; for the current law and economics theory of incomplete contracts see Cooter and Ulen (n. 63) 283–86; Shavell (n. 64) 299–301; Schäfer and Ott (n. 64) 431–34.

76 See Ian Ayres and Robert Gertner, 'Filling Gaps in Incomplete Contracts: An Economic Theory of Default Rules' (1989) 99 Yale Law Journal 87, 93; Gerhard Wagner, 'Zwingendes Privatrecht – Eine Analyse anhand des Vorschlags einer Richtlinie über Rechte der Verbraucher' (2010) Zeitschrift für europäisches Privatrecht 243, 256.

77 On the different theories of a normative function of default rules see Johannes Cziupka, *Dispositives Vertragsrecht* (Mohr Siebeck 2010) 90–136: '*gebietende Dimension des dispositiven Rechts*'.

78 Ayres and Gertner (n. 76) 95.

79 See Sec. 307 German Civil Code: '(1) Provisions in standard business terms are ineffective if, contrary to the requirement of good faith, they unreasonably disadvantage the other party to the contract with the user. ... (2) An unreasonable disadvantage is, in case of doubt, to be assumed to exist if a provision (1.) is not compatible with essential principles of the statutory provision from which it deviates ....'.

80 Cass Sunstein and Richard Thaler, *Nudge: Improving Decisions about Health, Wealth, and Happiness* (Yale University Press 2008) passim.

of, though are less intrusive than, means of market regulation. However, as means of market regulation they presuppose a political decision,[81] which in case of contracts and market regulation should be based on evidence of a market failure.[82]

2. *Building blocks from EU instruments, contract law principles and national law*

Based on this two-fold function of default contract rules, the first source for non-mandatory contractual rights of access and portability should be the majoritarian default approach. In which contract scenarios and under which circumstances would the parties to a B2B contract agree on access to and porting of data? Unfortunately, economic research does not provide much empirical evidence on this question.[83] Soft law instruments and the above-cited experience from national contract law may be used to suggest some first building blocks for possible default rules. However, such an approach can only be tentative and subject to further revision in the light of the development of business models and typical contractual arrangements in the market.

Starting with the European Commission's Communication 'Towards a common European data space' and the corresponding Staff working paper ('How to' guide), it is apparent that the Commission is on one side monitoring closely what is happening on the different markets, but on the other side is rather reluctant to come up with concrete suggestions for default rules. The Communication itself explains on a very abstract level what key principles should be respected in B2B contracts.[84] These principles can be used by courts and legislatures to develop more concrete default rules. However, they are far from giving direction for specific cases. The corresponding Staff working paper explores different business models for data-

81 More general Cass Sunstein, 'The ethics of nudging' (2015) 32 Yale Journal on Regulation 413, 415: 'It is true that all government action, including nudges, should face a burden of justification (and sometimes a heavy burden)'.

82 See Horst Eidenmüller, 'Liberaler Paternalismus' (2011) 66(17) JuristenZeitung 814, 819–20, who recommends welfarism as normative concept to justify nudges.

83 Only individual business models have been explored in the literature, e.g. European Commission Staff Working Document (n. 43) 8–18; see also Axel Metzger, 'Digitale Mobilität – Verträge über Nutzerdaten' (2019) Gewerblicher Rechtsschutz und Urheberrecht 129–136 on the automotive industry.

84 See at C.II.1., above, and European Commission, 'Towards a common European data space' (n. 43) 10.

sharing (open-data approach, data monetisation on a data marketplace, data exchange in a closed platform) and explains what parties should consider when agreeing on data access, e.g. what data is to be made available, who can access and (re-)use the data in question, what can the (re-)user do with the data, how to protect data, liability provisions, rights and obligations with regard to audits, duration of the contract, applicable law and dispute resolution mechanisms.[85] Yet the different aspects are drafted in the form of a checklist without concrete recommendations. Moreover, the issues addressed in the checklist are only of interest once the parties have reached consensus that one party should get access to data held by the other party. The key question, in which situations one party should have a (default) right to claim for access if not explicitly provided for in the contract, is not answered by the Staff working paper.

Looking into soft law principles developed by academic projects, two already mentioned general doctrines could be used for deriving access rights. First, it is commonly accepted, at least if one follows the Principles of European Contract Law, the Unidroit Principles or the Draft Common Frame of Reference (DCFR) that the parties to a contract must act in accordance with good faith and fair dealing.[86] One may well consider whether parties may infer from this principle certain information duties and claim for access to data, e.g. if the owner of an industry machine needs certain data for the maintenance of the machine – a case explicitly discussed as an illustration in the Comments to Article 5.1.2 Unidroit Principles.[87] Second, one may construe access rights as restitution claims in case of termination of a contract.[88] Also, one could consider – more specifically – applying the client's claim for the 'return of the thing processed' under the DCFR principles on service contracts.[89] These approaches, though drafted in a more general way, coincide to some degree with the non-mandatory rules of German contract law described above, according to which access rights can be justified in cases (1.) in which access to data is necessary for the stipulated use of the good or service, (2.) in which data has been transmitted to or deposited with a fiduciary or data processor

85 European Commission Staff Working Document (n. 43) 5–11.

86 See Art. 1:201 and 6:102 PECL; Arts 1.7. and 5.1.2. Unidroit Principles 2016; Art. I.1:103, II.9:101 DCFR. See also Arts 2 and 68 Common European Sales Law (CESL).

87 See Unidroit Principles 2016, 152.

88 See Arts 9:305–9:309 PECL; Arts 7.3.5.-7.3.7 UNIDROIT Principles 2016, Art. III.3:506–514 DCFR for the case of termination based on non-performance.

89 Art. IV.C.4:105(2) DCFR.

who processes the data on behalf of the client and (3.) in case of termination of a contract. It could be of main interest to gather experiences from other European jurisdictions to draw a more nuanced picture.

3. *ALI–ELI Principles for a Data Economy*

The American Law Institute and the European Law Institute are currently working on a joint set of 'ALI-ELI Principles for a Data Economy – Data Rights and Transactions'. The project started in 2016.[90] The latest draft of black letter Principles and (tentative) comments is dated 22 May 2020.[91] The Principles contain non-mandatory rules for different kinds of data contracts in Principles 7 to 14. These contract law principles presuppose that the data controller has agreed to transfer or grant access to data or to permit the exploitation of data. The question discussed in this paper, whether a party can claim for access if the contract does not explicitly provide such a right, is not of interest in this part of the Principles.[92]

The ALI-ELI Principles do not stop at this point but also suggest, in Part III 'Rules and Principles Governing Data Rights', including a right to access or to port co-generated data. The access rights drafted so far are restricted to 'co-generated data'. Possible access rights for other data have not yet been drafted.[93] The notion of co-generated data is not defined with a hard and fast rule but depends on a set of factors, including whether the party interested in the data is the subject of the data, whether the data has

---

90 See <www.europeanlawinstitute.eu/projects-publications/current-projects-feasibility-studies-and-other-activities/current-projects/data-economy> accessed 31 August 2020.

91 The author of this contribution serves as a Member of the ELI Advisory Committee but has not been actively involved in the drafting of the Principles or comments. Direct citations from the draft principles are not permitted.

92 One provision resembles the problems discussed above: In a contract for the processing of data, where the processor undertakes to process data on behalf of the controller, the controller may ask for the processor to erase all data after the contract has been performed and the processed data has been provided to the controller. This reminds the reader of Art. IV.C.4:105(2) DCFR.

93 But the Principles already provide a section for 'Data Rights Beyond Co-Generation' in Principles 23–25. An additional special right of portability of reviews is suggested by Art. 7 ELI Model Rules on Online Platforms; see <www.europeanlawinstitute.eu/fileadmin/user_upload/p_eli/Publications/ELI_Model_Rules_on_Online_Platforms.pdf> accessed 31 August 2020, and Busch and others, 'The ELI Model Rules on Online Platforms' (2020) 9(2) Journal of European Consumer and Market Law 61, 68.

been generated by the party's activity or use of a product or service or whether the data has been generated with a software or product produced by that party.[94] For co-generated data in that sense, the Principles suggest taking general factors into account when determining possible data rights, namely the share in the generation of the data, the weight of the legitimate interests of the parties, the imbalance of bargaining power and the public interest.[95] For access and porting rights, the Principles provide a non-exhaustive list of circumstances that may give ground for an access and porting right, especially if the data is necessary for the normal use, maintenance or resale of the product or service, for quality monitoring, for the understanding of the party's own operations, for the development of new products or services or for preventing a lock-in situation.[96]

The 'Rules and Principles Governing Data Rights' in Part III are not characterised as contract law but leave it to the applicable law to implement them in the appropriate legal framework.[97] This has the advantage of giving flexibility to courts, legislatures and other possible users of the principles. However, the mix of factors may also be seen as an impediment to their adoption since it may be difficult to use the suggested tests in a national legal framework which insists on the dividing line between the different areas of contract, competition and public law. The issue is not a merely doctrinal one but raises more fundamental concerns of policy. Is it, for example, reasonable to refer to a vague idea of imbalance of power if the threshold for a dominant position in the sense of Article 102 TFEU (or for one of the more recent concepts of competition law, e.g. from the current German reform projects)[98] is not met? One should keep in mind that the B2B contracts in question are not characterised by a structural imbalance like employer-employee, trader-consumer, landlord-tenant or publisher-author relationships.[99] Therefore courts and legislatures should be cautious to interfere with the freedom of contract in cases in which big and

94 See Principle 17(1) ALI-ELI Principles.

95 See Principle 18(1) ALI-ELI Principles.

96 See Principle 19(1) ALI-ELI Principles.

97 See Principle 15(2) ALI-ELI Principles.

98 See Sec. 18(3a) German Act Against Restraints of Competition; see also the Government Bill for a 10th revision of the German Act against Restraints of Competition (n. 67).

99 The argument of structural imbalance is used in German contract law to justify regulatory intervention in the mentioned areas; in this regard see the contributions of Karl Riesenhuber, 'Private Macht im Vertragsrecht – Langzeitverträge', Gralf-Peter Calliess, 'Private Macht und Verbraucherrecht' and Eva Kocher, 'Private Macht im Arbeitsrecht' and in Florian Möslein (ed.), *Private Macht* (Mohr

small companies conclude contracts, as long as those contracts are concluded on a market with functioning competition. The mere imbalance of power does not per se justify state intervention.[100] All European collections of soft law contract principles provide some sort of emergency exit for extreme cases with doctrines like excessive benefit, gross disparity, unfair exploitation.[101] One should not go beyond these doctrines – at least under contract law principles. The same line of argument may be applied to the criteria of prevention of lock-in situations. Are we sure that a lock-in situation with regard to maintenance services of digital products or services is always inefficient, even if a smaller competitor on the market for the product protects a specifically safe and therefore costly environment for its customers? This may be the unique selling point of such a smaller competitor in a market with other more dominant actors. Or as final point, do we really want courts and legislatures to interfere with the freedom of contract based on a broad notion of public interest? Should courts engage in industry policy or save jobs or the local businesses? For the purpose of this paper, which is focused on contract law, it must suffice to say that any intervention affecting freedom of contract should be based on clear evidence of a market failure. It is admitted that the ALI-ELI Principles give total flexibility to legislatures and courts to pick and choose the factors that may fit into the respective regulatory framework and set aside the other listed criteria. However, one should not be surprised if in the end the factors are also used for the justification of misguided and inefficient interventions.

The critical stance taken here on some of the factors suggested by the ALI-ELI Principles reflects in more specific terms what has been said earlier about the function of default contract rules. Either they codify majori-

---

Siebeck 2016) 193, 213, 241 respectively. From the older literature see Lorenz Fastrich, *Richterliche Inhaltskontrolle im Privatrecht* (C.H. Beck 1992) 159–201, 216–21; Günther Hönn, *Kompensation gestörter Vertragsparität* (C.H. Beck 1982) 153–160.

100 See in this regard the apparent caution of leading law and economics handbooks, e.g. Richard A. Posner, *Economic Analysis of Law*, (9th edn, Wolters Kluwer Law & Business 2014) 127–28; Schäfer and Ott (n. 64) 487–90. See also Roland Kirstein and Matthias Peiss, 'Quantitative Machtkonzepte in der Ökonomik' in Florian Möslein (ed.), *Private Macht* (Mohr Siebeck 2016) 91–117. See also the contributions of Carsten Herresthal, 'Private Macht im Vertragsrecht – Austauschverträge' Friedemann Kainer, 'Private Macht im Kapitalmarktrecht' and Heike Schweitzer, 'Wettbewerbsrecht und das Problem privater Macht' in Möslein (ibid.) 145, 423, 447 respectively.

101 In this regard see Art. 4:109 PECL; Art. 3.2.7 Unidroit Principles; Art. II.7:207 DCFR; see also Art. 51 CESL.

tarian default rules to help parties with incomplete contracts or they pursue enforcement of policy choices through the, compared to mandatory rules, less intrusive mechanism of defaults. Some of the factors listed by the ALI-ELI Principles may help to identify majoritarian defaults, e.g. the share of the contracting parties in the generation of the data, the necessity of the data for the normal use, maintenance or resale of the product or service, or its necessity for quality monitoring or for the understanding of the party's own operations. However, it is apparent that some of the factors suggested by the ALI-ELI Principles belong to this second type of default rules, e.g. the imbalance of bargaining power, the public interest, the necessity of data for the development of new products or services or for preventing a lock-in situation. This begs the question of the justification of policy choices behind those factors and how well they serve the purpose of increasing social welfare.

D. Conclusion

This chapter started with the question whether a party under a contract is obliged to grant the other party access to data it has collected. The answer given in this chapter based on an analysis of European and German contract law depends on whether the claimant is a consumer or a business user.

For consumers, Article 16(4) DCSD now stipulates for a right of access and portability with regard to non-personal data, which was provided or created by the consumer. However, this right is superseded to a large extent by Article 20 GDPR, which takes priority for personal data. Moreover, Article 16(4) DCSD is not applicable to access to data stored in devices with embedded software on which the new Directive on the sale of goods is applicable. Additional limitations of the scope of Article 16(4) DCSD arise from the fact that the provision is only applicable in the case of termination of the contract resulting from the failure to supply or a lack of conformity. The scope of application of Article 16(4) DCSD will therefore be rather limited. It will be of interest in the coming months to see how EU Member States deal with this limited scope and whether they go beyond this minimalist approach – if not in the implementing legislation then by case law in the years to come. Arguments for a careful extension could be taken from the principles of general contract law described in this paper, which are applicable both to B2B and B2C contracts. In this regard, it has been shown that national contract law may grant specific access rights based on the principle of good faith or as implied terms, e.g. with regard to cloud services that store data on behalf of the client, for data necessary for the performance of a purchased good or in cases of termination of contracts. In regard to these general contract law doctrines, Article 16(4) DCSD does not fall into a vacuum. The DCSD could be used as a focal point for further development of contractual access rights for consumers, even though the scope of application of Article 16(4) may remain limited in the near future.

For B2B contracts, it has been shown that neither European nor national contract law provides for mandatory access and porting rights until now. Against this backdrop, the paper has argued that there is no legal basis or economic evidence justifying the introduction of general contractual access or porting rights. Competition law may call for additional access rights effected by contractual means if markets are not functioning well. Information asymmetries may require transparency on the existence or non-existence of collected data and contractual data access rights, as now partially provided for in the Fairness and transparency Regulation. But legislatures should be cautious to adopt broad contractual access rights beyond these sector-specific instruments with reference to concepts like imbalance of bargaining power, prevention of lock-in or the general public interest. Yet, this cautious approach should not prevent European or national legislatures to enact default rules on data access and portability applicable to B2B contracts, which can be derogated from by agreement. Such rules should reflect the majoritarian defaults used – or presumably used – in the market. In this regard, the above-mentioned experience from national contract law could be helpful. Also, the principles developed by the EU Commission in its recent Communications and some of the factors put forward by the ALI-ELI Principles for a Data Economy can play a role. Also, it will be highly interesting to see whether Article 16(4) DCSD triggers a change of the business practice of traders also for professional users or if it changes at least the courts' perceptions of what reasonable parties would have agreed upon if they had foreseen a later claim for access to data. But these default rules should be based on actual or presumed majoritarian defaults. Such an approach could help to facilitate data sharing as envisioned by the recent 'European strategy for data'.[102] Going beyond this line – with default rules as 'nudges' for horizontal B2B access rights – would require evidence for a market failure beyond specific sectors.

102 COM(2020) 66 final, 13.

Data portability under the GDPR: A blueprint for access rights?

Ruth Janal

A. *Introduction*

I. *From ownership to access*

With the rise of industry 4.0 and the advent of Big Data, data markets and data value chains are still evolving. The discussion about an adequate legal framework for the data economy has shifted its focus from an exclusionary right to data (ownership/IP right)[1] to the question of access to data.[2]

Under the EU's General Data Protection Regulation (GDPR), the data subject is granted 'portability', i.e. a right to receive the personal data relating to her or him and to transmit this data to another controller.[3] This paper explores whether the portability right might serve as a model for access rights in the business context. Let me briefly note that the Directive on contracts for the supply of digital content and digital services contains a

1 Herbert Zech, 'Daten als Wirtschaftsgut – Überlegungen zu einem Recht des "Datenerzeugers"' (2015) Computer und Recht 137, 144–46; Louisa Specht, 'Ausschließlichkeitsrechte an Daten – Notwendigkeit, Schutzumfang, Alternativen' (2016) Computer und Recht 288, 294–96; Andreas Wiebe, 'Protection of industrial data – a new property right for the digital economy?' (2016) Gewerblicher Rechtsschutz und Urheberrecht Internationaler Teil 877, 881–84.

2 Josef Drexl and others, 'Data Ownership and Access to Data – Position Statement of the Max Planck Institute for Innovation and Competition of 16 August 2016 on the Current European Debate' (2016) Max Planck Institute for Innovation and Competition Research Paper No. 16–10 <https://ssrn.com/abstract=2833165> accessed 31 August 2020; Lothar Determann, 'Gegen Eigentumsrechte an Daten: Warum Gedanken und andere Informationen frei sind und es bleiben sollten' (2018) Zeitschrift für Datenschutz 503, Jürgen Kühling und Florian Sackmann, 'Irrweg "Dateneigentum" – Neue Großkonzepte als Hemmnis für die Nutzung und Kommerzialisierung von Daten' (2020) Zeitschrift für Datenschutz 24.

3 Art. 20 Regulation (EU) No. 2016/679 of the European Parliament and of the Council of 27 April 2016 on the protection of natural persons with regard to the processing of personal data and on the free movement of such data, and repealing Directive 95/46/EC, [2016] OJ L119/1.

similar provision, which however is limited in scope.[4] I will therefore limit my remarks to Article 20 GDPR.[5]

II. Overview of Article 20 GDPR

Under Article 20 GDPR, data subjects have the right to receive personal data that they have provided to a controller in a structured, commonly used and machine-readable format. Furthermore, data subjects have the right to transmit their personal data to another controller without hindrance. The right to portability constitutes an outlier amongst GDPR data subject rights. While most of the GDPR's rules shield the data subject from unwanted data use by others, Article 20 GDPR acts as a sword (albeit a blunt one): It grants data subjects the right to use (ie transfer) their personal data.[6]

The legislative intent behind Article 20 GDPR is not entirely clear. Its obvious purpose is to empower the data subject. However, this empowerment seems to serve a larger goal, namely, to facilitate competition among data controllers by preventing lock-in effects.[7]

4 Art. 16(4) Directive (EU) 2019/770 of the European Parliament and of the Council of 20 May 2019 on certain aspects concerning contracts for the supply of digital content and digital services [2019] L136/1. This rule only applies to non-personal data in cases of termination of a consumer contract regarding digital content. Even cat videos, sometimes cited as an example of data within the scope of that rule, often relate to a particular, identifiable person. The scope of the rule is further minimised by the fact that contracts relating to smart gadgets are not within the ambit of the regulation; cf. Gerald Spindler und Karin Sein, 'Die endgültige Richtlinie über Verträge über digitale Inhalte und Dienstleistungen: Anwendungsbereich und grundsätzliche Ansätze' (2019) Zeitschrift für IT-Recht und Recht der Digitalisierung 415, 416.

5 For other data access regimes cf. Inge Graf, Martin Husovec and Jasper van den Boom, 'Spill-Overs in Data Governance: The Relationship Between the GDPR's Right to Data Portability and EU Sector-Specific Data Access Regimes' (2019) TILEC Discussion Paper No. DP 2019-005 <https://ssrn.com/abstract=3369509> accessed 31 August 2020.

6 According to Recital 68 GDPR, data portability strengthens the data subject's control over his or her own data; see also Article 29 Data Protection Working Party, 'Guidelines on the right to data portability' (5 April 2017) Working Paper 242, 4 <http://ec.europa.eu/newsroom/document.cfm?doc_id=44099> accessed 31 August 2020; Michael M. Maisch, *Informationelle Selbstbestimmung in Netzwerken* (Duncker & Humblot 2015) 311.

7 European Commission Staff Working Document on the free flow of data and emerging issues of the European data economy of 10 January 2017, SWD(2017) 2

The portability right under Article 20 GDPR applies to personal data 'provided' by the data subject to a controller. As a further qualification, the right to portability only arises where the processing is carried out by automated means and is based upon consent or contract (Article 6(1)(a), (b); Article 9(1)(a) GDPR). The controller must transmit this data to the data subject in a structured, commonly used and machine-readable format, acting without undue delay and generally within one month at the latest (Article 12(3) GDPR). Where technically feasible, the data subject may require the controller to transfer the data directly to another controller. Portability can be required at any point in time and is in principle free of charge.[8] The right to receive the data is subject to three exceptions: First, a transmission of data cannot be requested with respect to data that has already been deleted or anonymised.[9] Second, the portability right may not interfere with a task carried out in the public interest.[10] Third, portability shall not adversely affect the rights and freedoms of others.[11]

---

final, 11. Niko Härting, 'Starke Behörden, schwaches Recht – der neue EU-Datenschutzentwurf' (2012) Betriebs-Berater 459, 465; Dennis-K. Kipker and Friederike Voskamp, 'Datenschutz in sozialen Netzwerken nach der Datenschutzgrundverordnung (2012) Datenschutz und Datensicherheit 737, 740; Jürgen Kühling and Mario Martini, 'Die Datenschutz-Grundverordnung: Revolution oder Evolution im europäischen und deutschen Datenschutzrecht?' (2016) Europäische Zeitschrift für Wirtschaftsrecht 448, 450; Peter Schantz, 'Die Datenschutz-Grundverordnung – Beginn einer neuen Zeitrechnung im Datenschutzrecht' (2016) Neue Juristische Wochenschrift 1841, 1845; Inge Graef, Martin Husovec and Nadezhda Purtova, 'Data Portability and Data Control: Lessons for an Emerging Concept in EU Law' (2018) 19 German Law Journal 1359, 1365; Heike Schweitzer, 'Datenzugang in der Datenökonomie: Eckpfeiler einer neuen Informationsordnung' (2019) Gewerblicher Rechtsschutz und Urheberrecht 569, 574; Alexander Dix, in Alexander Dix, Spiros Simitis, Gerrit Hornung and Indra Spiecker gen. Döhmann (eds), Datenschutzrecht (4th edn, Nomos 2019) Art. 20 DSGVO para. 1; Deutsche Bundesregierung (Federal Government of Germany), 'Antwort der Bundesregierung auf die Kleine Anfrage' (Deutscher Bundestag 10 August 2012) Bundestags-Drucksache 17/10452, 7 <dipbt.bundestag.de/doc/btd/17/104/1710452.pdf> accessed 31 August 2020. For the economic consequences of portability cf. European Commission SWD (ibid) 47 et seq.

8 Art. 12(5) GDPR. This does not apply to manifestly unfounded or excessive (i.e. repetitive) requests. Article 29 Data Protection Working Party (n. 6) 12 argues that '[f]or information society or similar online services that specialise in automated processing of personal data, it is very unlikely that the answering of multiple data portability requests should generally be considered to impose an excessive burden'.

9 Art. 20(3), sentence 1 and Recital 26 GDPR; Article 29 Data Protection Working Party (n. 6) 7.

10 Art. 20(3) sent. 2. On the concept of public interest cf. Recital 73 GDPR.

11 Art. 20(4) GDPR.

III. Structure of Arguments

Any attempt to draw inferences from Article 20 GDPR about the business world must first query the similarities of the two settings. In the following, I will first expound on how a B2B setting differs from the data context of the GDPR. In the light of this analysis, the paper then focuses on several key ambiguities of Article 20 GDPR and how these issues might translate to the business scenario: (1) The data covered by the right to portability, (2) the protection of the rights and freedoms of others and (3) the modus operandi of 'portability'.

B. Distinctions between the GDPR setting and a B2B scenario

When considering whether Article 20 GDPR can function as a blueprint for a business portability right, one needs to keep in mind that a B2B scenario often differs significantly from the scenario regulated by the GDPR. In the following, I will highlight some of the key differences.

I. Personal data and non-personal data

While the GDPR only pertains to personal data, the interest of the business world is not limited to such data. Commercial value may lie in all kinds of data, personal and non-personal data alike.

II. Attribution of data

1. The GDPR setting

More importantly, the GDPR provides for a clear attribution of data. The Regulation addresses personal data concerning an identified or identifiable individual and bestows rights upon data subjects because the data processed relates to their personal identity. If the data relates to several identifiable individuals (such as pictures, chat records and data generated by shared gadgets), the data is attributed to each of these individuals. Admittedly, the regulation does not provide for a clear mechanism on how to resolve a conflict of interest between data subjects. This may be due to the fact that such multi-polar personal data is hardly the norm (the exception being data processed by social networks).

2. *The business setting*

a) Lack of legal attribution

With respect to business data, such a clear legal attribution of data to any one party cannot be identified.[12] In practice, the data is either attributed on the basis of factual barriers to access or on the basis of data-sharing agreements.[13] However, there is no common ground as to which connecting factors are sufficient to deem data as legally related to a particular business. Nor is there generally a right to confidentiality or even a reasonable expectation of confidentiality with respect to data. Furthermore, using Article 4(1) GDPR (the criterion of identifiability) as a model for attribution will not work. In the business context, the possibility of identification is not an adequate criterion for attribution. Data relating to an identifiable natural person is protected because the identity is a core element of a human's existence. In a business context, data is not an element of identity, but rather allows for value creation.[14] Since data is a tradeable commercial commodity,[15] and businesses may purchase data from others, identifiability should not even be used as a minimum criterion.

---

12 Martin Fries and Marc Scheufen, 'Märkte für Maschinendaten: Eine rechtliche und rechtsökonomische Standortbestimmung' (2019) Zeitschrift für IT-Recht und Recht der Digitalisierung 721, 721; Udo Kornmeier and Anne Baranowski, 'Das Eigentum an Daten – Zugang statt Zuordnung' (2019) Betriebs-Berater 1219, 1223; Specht (n. 1) 289.

13 Kornmeier and Baranowksi (n. 12) 1221.

14 Fries and Scheufen (n. 11) 721; Schweitzer (n. 7) 569–70.

15 Jutta Stender-Vorwachs and Hans Steege, 'Wem gehören unsere Daten? Zivilrechtliche Analyse zur Notwendigkeit eines dinglichen Eigentums an Daten, der Datenzuordnung und des Datenzugangs' (2018) Neue Juristische Online-Zeitschrift 1361; Herbert Zech, 'Industrie 4.0 – Rechtsrahmen für eine Datenwirtschaft im digitalen Binnenmarkt' (2015) Gewerblicher Rechtsschutz und Urheberrecht 1151, 1151–52.

b) Multi-relational nature of data

Business data is also typically multi-relational. Personal data which is processed for business purposes will relate to the business' customers or employees as well as the business itself. Furthermore, in interdependent manufacturing chains or service industries, data often relates to the interests of various market players.[16] Consider an enterprise resource planning (ERP) system employed for quality control in industrial production: A machine which manufactures metal sheets is equipped with a camera that examines the sheets for manufacturing defects and determines rejections. The data regarding rejections is finally analysed using applications running on a cloud infrastructure. This data will relate to various businesses: the supplier of both the raw material and the machines, the manufacturer as well as the data processor. Should the data be attributed to all these businesses or is one business 'more worthy' than the other? In its communication 'Towards a common European data space', the European Commission expresses the hope that contracts 'recognise that, where data is generated as a by-product of using a product or service, several parties have contributed to creating the data.'[17] The Commission does not substantiate what kind of contribution it deems significant enough for a business to have contributed to such shared value creation.

c) The Trade Secrets Directive

Arguably, some legal attribution of data is achieved by means of the Trade Secrets Directive,[18] even though the Directive does not create any exclusive

---

16 Wolfgang Kerber, 'Rights on Data: The EU Communication "Building a European Data Economy" from an Economic Perspective' in Sebastian Lohsse, Reiner Schulze and Dirk Staudenmayer (eds), *Trading Data in the Digital Economy: Legal Concepts and Tools* (Hart and Nomos 2017) 109, 127–28; also Herbert Zech, 'Industrie 4.0 – Rechtsrahmen für eine Datenwirtschaft im digitalen Binnenmarkt' (2015) Gewerblicher Rechtsschutz und Urheberrecht 1151, 1156.

17 Communication from the Commission to the European Parliament, the Council, the European Economic and Social Committee and the Committee of the Regions – 'Towards a common European data space' COM(2018) 232 final.

18 Directive (EU) 2016/943 of the European Parliament and of the Council of 8 June 2016 on the protection of undisclosed know-how and business information (trade secrets) against their unlawful acquisition, use and disclosure [2016] OJ L157/1. Legal attribution of data as a consequence of the Directive is discussed by Lukas Staffler, 'Industrie 4.0 und wirtschaftlicher Geheimnisschutz' (2018) Neue

right to know-how or information.[19] Rather, the Directive shields the trade secret holder against unlawful acquisition, use and disclosure of trade secrets (i.e. information that is secret, is of commercial value because it is secret and has been subject to reasonable steps to be kept secret). It is noteworthy that a trade secret holder is defined by the Directive as a person lawfully controlling a trade secret. Whatever the meaning of 'lawful control',[20] any such person would presumably not have to rely on a portability right for a transfer of data, because they would already possess the necessary control.

III. Structural power imbalances

Under the GDPR, the relationship between the data subject and the data controller is characterised by a structural power imbalance. Typically, the data controller is a business or public body, whereas the data subjects are consumers who often have little choice in how their data is processed.

Business scenarios are much more diverse. For example, a machine builder who also processes industrial data may or may not be in a more powerful economic and negotiating position than its customer: The machine builder might be a small start-up that provides autonomous mobile robots to an international logistics company. The machine builder could just a well be a major automaker selling cars to a small courier service. Alternatively, the parties' bargaining position could be equal. In the absence of clear structural power imbalances, an argument may be made that a contractual right to portability should be left to the parties' negotiation

---

Zeitschrift für Wirtschafts-, Steuer- und Unternehmensstrafrecht 269, 273; Andreas Wiebe, 'Protection of industrial data – a new property right for the digital economy?' (2016) Gewerblicher Rechtsschutz und Urheberrecht Internationaler Teil 877, 881–84; Zech (n. 16) 1155–56.

19 Recital 16 Directive (EU) 2016/943.

20 For the discussion of whether 'control' is to be determined purely on a factual or also on a normative basis cf. Staffler (n. 18) 272 et seq. (arguing for the introduction of normative criteria). Arguing for a determination simply upon factual criteria; Michael Goldhammer, 'Geschäftsgeheimnis-Richtlinie und Informationsfreiheit: Zur Neudefinition des Geschäftsgeheimnisses als Chance für das öffentliche Recht' (2017) Neue Zeitschrift für Verwaltungsrecht 1809, 1810 et seq.; Björn Kalbfus, 'Die EU-Geschäftsgeheimnis-Richtlinie: Welcher Umsetzungsbedarf besteht in Deutschland?' (2016) Gewerblicher Rechtsschutz und Urheberrecht 1009, 1011.

and legislation should only concern itself with portability obligations imposed upon dominant undertakings.

IV. *Remuneration for data analysis*

The saying 'You are not the customer, you are the product' illustrates a third major difference between data subjects and businesses seeking portability: Individual data subjects usually do not pay the data controller for an analysis of their data.[21] Rather, data controllers process and analyse the customer data in their own interest, which is sometimes so profitable that they need not charge their customers for the services offered. Again, this may be very different in a B2B context. For example, the Airbus Skywise platform allows participating airlines to deeply analyse the airline fleet's reliability and the passengers' behaviour – for a fee, of course.

V. *Commercial value*

Finally, an individual's personal data is typically of little commercial value.[22] Commercial benefits from the processing of personal data typically arise from the pooling of data across a large customer base. Consequently, there is relatively little outside interest in the transfer of one particular individual's data. In contrast, the data sets generated by an individual company or individual segments of their business are oftentimes already large enough to generate both internal as well as outside interest.

VI. *Summary*

In sum, a portability B2B scenario differs immensely from the scenario addressed by Article 20 GDPR: The data requested may include both personal and non-personal data. The data is not legally attributed to the business making the portability request. A typical structural power imbalance between the party making the request and the addressee of the request can-

21 This may be different with respect to some smart gadgets, such as fitness trackers.
22 Marcel Bisges, 'Personendaten, Wertzuordnung und Ökonomie: Kein Vergütungsanspruch Betroffener für die Nutzung von Personendaten' (2017) Zeitschrift für IT-Recht und Recht der Digitalisierung 301, 302.

not be identified. The controller may have been remunerated for data analytics services, and the commercial value of the data requested may be much higher than in cases of requests under Article 20 GDPR.

C. Transfer of ideas and principles

Keeping those key differences in mind, let us now return to Article 20 GDPR. In the following section, I shall explore whether Article 20 GDPR leads itself to generalisations. In doing so, I will focus on three critical aspects of the provision which are ambiguous: (I) Which data is covered by the right to portability, (II) how can the rights and freedoms of others be protected and (III) what is the adequate modus operandi of 'portability'?

I. The data encompassed

1. Data covered by Article 20 GDPR

Under Article 20(1) GDPR, the data subject shall have the right to receive and transmit data 'which he or she has provided to a controller', where the legal basis for processing is consent or contract. Clearly, the wording of the provision covers personal data explicitly provided by the data subject, such as contact information, comments und uploaded material. It is also undisputed that information which the data controller has inferred from its customers' data does not constitute data 'provided' by the data subject. As a result, data derived by means of aggregation and analysis, such as user profiles and credit scores, are not subject to the portability requirement of Article 20 GDPR.[23]

Other personal data falls between these poles. This is true for data which a third party has provided to the controller based on a relationship with the data subject, in particular all communication sent to the data subject (emails, chat records, comments on posts etc.). The wording of Article 20 GDPR does not seem to encompass such data.[24] On the other hand, the

23 Article 29 Data Protection Working Party (n. 6) 10; Stiftung Datenschutz, 'Practical Implementation of the Right to Data Portability – Summary and Recommendations' (2017) 7 <www.stiftungdatenschutz.org/fileadmin/Redaktion/Datenportabilitaet/kurzversion_studie_datenportabilitaet.pdf> accessed 31 August 2020.

24 Some authors even argue that any data with a third-party relation is not covered by Art. 20 GDPR; cf. Tim Jülicher, Charlotte Röttgen and Max v. Schönfeld, 'Das

ability to transfer this data is important for data subject empowerment and the prevention of lock-in effects. The Article 29 Data Protection Working Party (the predecessor of the European Data Protection Board), considers such data to be covered by Article 20 GDPR (without offering any explanation).[25]

There is also a vigorous debate as to whether Article 20(1) GDPR covers data that the data controller has observed from the data subject's behaviour, specifically data regarding the use of a smart gadget or the use of a digital service. Arguably, such data is 'collected' by the controller, rather than being 'provided' by the data subject.[26] But it is important to stress that Article 20(1) presupposes a lawfulness of processing based upon consent or contract. Consequently, the data subject has willingly allowed the controller to collect this data and thus provided access to it.[27] This broader interpretation is supported by Article 60 sent. 4 GDPR which considers collection as a form of provision of data ('Where the personal data are collected from the data subject, the data subject should also be informed

---

Recht auf Datenübertragbarkeit: Ein datenschutzrechtliches Novum' (2016) Zeitschrift für Datenschutz 358, 361.

25 Article 29 Data Protection Working Party (n. 6) 11; see also Schantz (n. 7) 1845.

26 Carlo Piltz, in Peter Gola, Datenschutz-Grundverordnung DS-GVO, Kommentar (2nd edn, C.H. Beck 2018) Art. 20 para. 14–15; Sebastian Brüggemann, 'Das Recht auf Datenportabilität' in Jürgen Taeger (ed.), *Recht 4.0 – Innovationen aus den rechtswissenschaftlichen Laboren* (Oldenburger Verlag für Wirtschaft, Informatik und Recht 2017) 1, 4; Hans-Georg Kamann and Martin Braun, in Eugen Ehmann und Martin Selmayr (eds), Datenschutz-Grundverordnung: DS-GVO, Kommentar (2nd edn, C.H. Beck 2018) Art. 20 para. 13; Handelsverband Deutschland e.V., 'Antworten des Handelsverbands Deutschland auf die Fragestellungen hinsichtlich des RL-Entwurfs für Verträge über digitale Inhalte' (2016) 2 <www.bmjv.de/SharedDocs/Downloads/DE/Ministerium/AbteilungenReferate/IB6_VA_Digitales_Vertragsrecht_Stellungnahme_HDE_2.pdf?__blob=publicationFile&v=1> accessed 31 August 2020.

27 Article 29 Data Protection Working Party (n. 6) 10: Observed data are 'provided' by the data subject by virtue of the use of the service or the device. The European Commission SWD (n. 7) 46, seems to share this view. See also Lukas Dalby, in Gerald Spindler and Fabian Schuster (eds), *Recht der elektronischen Medien* (4th edn, C.H. Beck 2019) Art. 20 DS-GVO para. 7–8; Moritz Hennemann, 'Datenportabilität' (2017) Privacy in Germany 5, 6–7.; Peter Krause 'Datenportabilität: Anwendungsbereich des Rechts auf Datenübertragbarkeit (Teil 1)' (2018) Privacy in Germany 239, 240–42; Maisch (n. 6) 304; Gerald Spindler, 'Verträge über digitale Inhalte – Haftung, Gewährleistung und Portabilität: Vorschlag der EU-Kommission zu einer Richtlinie über Verträge zur Bereitstellung digitaler Inhalte' (2019) Zeitschrift für IT-Recht und Recht der Digitalisierung 219, 222.

whether he or she is obliged to provide the personal data and of the consequences, where he or she does not provide such data').

Data should thus be considered as 'provided' by the data subject whenever the data subject willingly contributed to the acquisition of such data and the controller did not add any value to the data besides storage. This would encompass both communication to the data subject provided by third parties and observed personal data. Let me point out that much of the data collected on the data subject's behaviour will be helpful neither in empowering the data subject nor in preventing lock-in effects. Consider, for example, the amount of data collected by online shops or online streaming services on individual customers, which includes the entire clickstream up to buying an article or watching a movie, times of purchase and devices used, abandoned searches and so forth.[28] As I have argued elsewhere, it seems prudent to make the right to data portability subject to a proportionality requirement.[29]

2. *Data that might be covered by a business portability right*

While the interpretation of Article 20 GDRP is ambiguous, drawing inferences for a B2B scenario is even more complicated.

a) Beneficiary and addressee

Any new right would need to define a beneficiary and an addressee. The GDPR bestows a right to receive the data on data subjects. But as I have explained above (section B.I.), it is not clear who the beneficiary of a busi-

28 Katharina Nocun, 'Netflix weiß, was ich letzten Sommer geguckt habe' (21 August 2018) Die Zeit <www.zeit.de/digital/datenschutz/2018-08/streaming-dienst-netflix-datenschutz-nocun> accessed 31 August 2020.

29 Ruth Janal, 'Data Portability – A Tale of Two Concepts'(2017) 8 Journal of Intellectual Property, Information Technology and E-Commerce Law 58, 62; cf. Christoph Werkmeister and Elena Brandt, 'Datenschutzrechtliche Herausforderungen für Big Data' (2016) Computer und Recht 233, 237; Stiftung Datenschutz (n. 23) 3; Sebastian Brüggemann, 'Das Recht auf Datenportabilität: Die neue Macht des Datensubjekts und worauf Unternehmen sich einstellen müssen' (2018) Kommunikation & Recht 1, 4. Note also Art. 16(4) Directive (EU) 2019/770 on digital content and digital services (n. 4).

ness portability right should be, as a legal attribution of such data is missing.

The addressees of a new portability right would also have to be defined. Portability under Article 20(1) GDPR may be requested from the controller, ie any person who, 'alone or jointly with others, determines the purposes and means of the processing of personal data' (Article 4 No. 7 GDPR). This definition would not serve well in a business context, as it is equally too broad and too narrow. In a business setting, the business requesting portability might be the person who determines the purposes of the processing, whereas the person from whom the data is requested might only be a 'processor' within the meaning of Article 28 GDPR.

Further, in cases of joint control, Article 26(3) GDPR allows data subjects to exercise their rights against any of several joint controllers. Suppose a business regularly uses a specific airline for company travel and now realises that this airline uses the Airbus Skyways Platform. Suppose that same business delivers components to a manufacturer which has a data-sharing agreement with a machine builder. If the GDPR's model was copied, this business would be allowed to request data from anyone along the contractual chain, as long as the addressee could be considered a 'joint controller'.

b) Data provided because of a contract or consent

In the absence of a clear attribution of business data to an individual business (above at section B.I.), the beneficiary of a business portability right needs to be determined based upon other criteria. These criteria must be set to fit the purpose of the rule. If the prime purpose of an eventual portability right was to minimise data lock-in, the portability right could be made contingent upon the existence of a contractual relationship between the business making the request and the addressee. However, there is also discussion of introducing a business portability right to facilitate data-driven aftermarket and complementary services and enhance competition. This purpose would not be served if the existence of a contract was made a requirement for portability, as contractual relations between competitors are not the norm.[30]

Article 20 GDPR allows for a portability request only if the data is being processed because of consent or based on a contract. Since the processing of non-personal data does not require consent, relying on consent for a

30 Cf. Schweitzer (n. 7) 575.

portability right to arise might lead to random results. While some industry players may ask their suppliers and co-operating businesses to consent to the processing undertaken by a commissioned controller, others may not. Arguably, therefore, the existence of a contractual agreement is a better criterion in the business context. But should any kind of contract suffice? Or is a distinction warranted between data-sharing agreements, contracts pertaining to digital services, confidentiality agreements (required to safeguard trade secrets in accordance with Article 2(1)(c) Trade Secrets Directive) and classic sales contracts? One option might be to exclude contracts which do not entail a digital transfer of data. With this distinction, a portability right would arise (a) from contracts for digital content and services and (b) from sales and rental contracts for IoT machinery and connected means of transportation. A portability right would not arise from sales contracts regarding unconnected goods.

c) Observed and inferred data

Unlike an individual data subject, a business user will ordinarily be very interested in the 'observed' data generated by their company's use of machines or digital services. A private data subject will generally not be able to reuse observed data in a different context. From a business perspective, however, there is tremendous value in observed data.[31] A portability right encompassing observed data will put the business in the position to sell or further process such data. Also, retention of data that was originally provided by others, such as employees and suppliers, may be of vital interest to the business. If a portability right for businesses is to be introduced, it should encompass any data that was originally willingly transferred from the business' sphere to the controller, irrespective of whether the data was actively supplied by the business, collected from machines or supplied by others on the basis of a relationship with the business. Insofar, a parallel may be drawn to the interpretation of Article 20 GDPR suggested above.

There is, however, an important distinction to be drawn between the portability right under Article 20 GDPR and a possible business portability right: In the B2B context, a data controller will often be compensated by businesses for the retention and analysis of their data (fleet analysis, predictive maintenance, heating cost accounting and so forth). If a business has provided remuneration for the creation of 'inferred data', such data should

31 Ibid. 569.

be within the scope of any data portability right. In other instances, data analytics services are provided on a seemingly gratuitous basis. Such 'gratuitous services' may be a calculated choice in the interest of customer retention[32] and may not generate any additional cost for the service provider if the data is analysed anyway. Particularly in the case of predictive maintenance, such services will often be cross-financed through the purchase price or rental cost of the machines sold or rented. Thus, there is a strong case to be made that the portability right should apply to 'inferred data', even if such a service was offered on a seemingly gratuitous basis.

d) Preliminary findings

In short, there is considerable debate about the scope of data within the realm of Article 20(1) GDPR, and no definite inferences can or should be drawn with respect to the scope of a potential data portability right for businesses.[33] Rather, Article 20(1) GDPR demonstrates that any future legislature needs to carefully consider what kind of data is to be subject to an eventual portability right. Moreover, clear wording is needed to cast such intentions in law.

II. Rights and freedoms of others

1. Relevant rights and freedoms of others under the GDPR

Following Article 20(4) GDPR, the right to data portability 'shall not adversely affect the rights and freedoms of others'. This is a rather vague spec-

---

32 Esther Bollhöfer, Daniela Buschak, Christian Lerch and Matthias Gotsch, 'B2B-Dienstleistungen im Kontext von Industrie 4.0 – Neue Formen der Interaktion im Maschinen- und Anlagenbau' in Manfred Bruhn and Karsten Hadwich (eds), *Interaktive Wertschöpfung durch Dienstleistungen – Strategische Ausrichtung von Kundeninteraktionen, Geschäftsmodellen und sozialen Netzwerken* (Springer 2015) 517, 521; cf. Christian van Husen, 'Neue Serviceprodukte in industriellen Wertschöpfungsnetzwerken' in Bruhn and Hadwich (ibid.) 493, 503; Björn Ivens, Stephan Henneberg and Sebastian Forkmann, 'Service Infusion im Industriegütermarketing – Konzept, Wertschöpfung, Wirklichkeit' in Manfred Bruhn and Karsten Hadwich (eds), *Service Value als Werttreiber – Konzepte, Messung und Steuerung* (Springer 2014) 267, 279.

33 Datenethikkomission, 'Gutachten der Datenethikkomission der Bundesregierung' (2019) 137.

ification, to say the least. Let us start with the easy part: What are the rights and freedoms that might stand in the way of portability? The provision seems to mainly address personal data of other data subjects and trade secrets of the data controller and/or other parties.[34] Economic interests of the controller are not to be considered: First, Article 12(5) GDPR provides that the portability request must generally be fulfilled free of charge. Secondly, the entire purpose of Article 20 GDPR is to enable the data subject to change service providers and/or engage in multi-homing, which both may lead to adverse economic effects for the controller.

2. *Balancing of interests under the GDPR*

a) Data rights of third parties

The transfer of data either to the data subject or to another controller under Article 20(1) and (2) GDPR constitutes a processing of data within the meaning of Article 4 No. 2 GDPR. Insofar as the data is only related to the data subject making the request, this processing is covered by consent under Article 6(1)(a) GDPR. However, a picture may show more than one person and communication by its very meaning requires a minimum of two parties communicating. Insofar as the data also relates to other data subjects, the transfer of data must either be covered by their consent or be covered by another lawful basis for transmission.[35]

If the other data subject does not provide consent or cannot be reached for consent, Article 6(1)(f) GDPR may provide a legal basis for the transfer of data.[36] Under this provision, the processing is lawful if it is necessary for the purposes of legitimate interests of third parties (i.e., the data subject requesting portability), except where such interests are overridden by the interests or fundamental rights and freedoms of the data subject. Consequently, the portability of data relating to more than one data subject requires either consent of all the data subjects concerned or depends upon a balancing of interests of the respective individuals' data rights. The balanc-

34 Cf. Recital 63. sentence 5, regarding the right of access (Art. 15 GDPR). See also Kai von Lewinski, in *Beck Online-Kommentar Datenschutz-Grundverordnung* (31st edn, C.H. Beck 2020) Art. 20 para. 99; Judith Klink-Straub and Tobias Straub, 'Vernetzte Fahrzeuge – portable Daten: Das Recht auf Datenübertragbarkeit gem. Article 20 DS-GVO' (2018) Zeitschrift für Datenschutz 459, 462.

35 Piltz (n. 26) Art. 20 para. 23.

36 Article 29 Data Protection Working Party (n. 6) 11.

ing of interests will lead to different results depending on who supplied the respective data and under which expectations such data was provided. If the data was originally supplied by the individual who requests the transmission, the data rights of other parties do not stand in the way, as long as the new controller processes the data for the same purposes as the original controller.[37] Thus, a user who has provided a service provider with a list of their contacts can request a transfer of this contact information to another controller, even though the list includes the personal data of third parties.

As I have argued above, the data 'provided' by the data subject within the meaning of Article 20(1) GDPR may also in fact be supplied by other individuals (i.e. in case of emails and other communication) or may be collected from a gadget or service shared by several data subjects. Where the data was provided by a third party, the transfer request should not be fulfilled if there was a reasonable expectation on the part of the other data subject that the processing of information would be confined to a particular controller.[38] A person who sends an email or sends a credit transfer will generally not expect the addressee to keep the receiving account until the end of time, nor will they care if the addressee switches providers. On the other hand, a person who sends a communication within a closed social media group may very well have a reasonable expectation that this data will only be processed by the particular social networking provider. This is even more true in instances where the data was generated by a shared gadget, as the transfer to another controller may imply a change of gadget and thus possibly a change of users. In those instances, the right to portability will have to be denied, absent the consent of the other data subject.[39]

b) Trade secrets

There is some discussion that a transmission of data under Article 20 GDPR might also be thwarted if it led to the disclosure of the controller's trade secrets. Arguably, the 'rights and freedoms of others' referred to in

37 Von Lewinski (n. 34) Art. 20 para. 97; sceptical Jülicher and others (n. 24) 361–362.
38 Janal (n. 29) 62.
39 Klink-Straub and Straub (n. 34) 462.

Article 20(4) GDPR also include the rights and freedoms of the controller.[40] As Article 4 Trade Secrets Directive only protects the trade secret holder against unlawful acquisition, use and disclosure of a trade secret, the request for portability does not fall within the ambit of the Trade Secrets Directive.[41] Nonetheless, the interest of the controller to protect an existing trade secret may be considered under Article 20(4) GDPR. Such secrets might include the amount of data processed, the structure of the data processed and possibly accompanying metadata. It is hard to see how the interest in keeping this information secret could outweigh the data subject's right to portability. The GDPR certainly does not recognise a controller's right to keep secret the amount of personal data processed; Article 15 GDPR rather provides for the exact opposite. Also, considering the scope for implementation that Article 20 GDPR grants to the controller, it is incumbent upon the controller to organise the transmission in a way that does not reveal structural and metadata information.

3. *Duty of care when complying with a portability request*

Article 20 GDPR does not spell out the degree of care borne by the controller in complying with a portability request. The controller must certainly guarantee that the person requesting portability is the person who has either formed the contract or given the consent that is a prerequisite for the portability right to arise under Article 20(1)(a) or (b) GDPR.[42] Empirical studies show that a lot is left to be desired with respect to such verification procedures.[43] In case the data relates not only to the person making the request, but also to other individuals who have allegedly consented

40 While Recital 68, sentence 6, only refers to third parties when expounding on Art. 20(4) GDPR, Recital 63, sentence 5, clarifies regarding the similarly worded Art. 15(4) GDPR that interests of the controller may be taken into account. Cf. also Piltz (n. 26) Art. 20, para. 36; of a differing opinion Matthias Rudolph, in Rolf Schwartmann, Andreas Jaspers and Gregor Thüsing (eds), *Datenschutz-Grundverordnung/Bundesdatenschutzgesetz, Kommentar* (C.F. Müller 2018) Art. 20 para. 109.

41 Apparently of a different view von Lewinski (n. 34) Art. 20 paras 101 et seq.

42 Recital 64: 'The controller should use all reasonable measures to verify the identity of a data subject' making the request; see also Stiftung Datenschutz (n. 23) 4.

43 Dominik Herrmann and Jens Lindemann, 'Obtaining personal data and asking for erasure: Do app vendors and website owners honour your privacy rights?' in Michael Meier, Delphine Reinhardt and Steffen Wendzel (eds), *Sicherheit 2016 – Sicherheit, Schutz und Zuverlässigkeit* (Gesellschaft für Informatik e.V. 2016) 149.

to the transfer, the identity of those other data subjects must also be verified. The scope of such duties is – as of yet – undefined. I.e., it is unclear whether the controller is obliged to investigate whether an IoT gadget is used by several parties, which might exclude the right to portability.

Finally, some argue that in instances of direct transmission to a new controller, the old controller should provide the data subject with information regarding the usage envisioned by the new controller.[44] In my view, such an obligation should not be imposed: The new controller is also bound by the GDPR's rules, and it is a) upon the data subject to safeguard their rights vis-à-vis a new controller and b) upon the new controller to inform the data subject about its processing intentions in accordance with Article 13 GDPR.

4. *Inferences for a business portability right*

With respect to a possible portability right for businesses, it is possible to identify three groups whose interests may interfere with the portability request: Individuals whose personal data is contained amongst the data sets, third-party businesses with secrecy interests regarding the data sets and the economic interests of the service provider who is asked to transfer the data.

With respect to personal data (ie of customers and employees), the migration of data from one service provider to another constitutes a processing of data under Article 4 No. 2 GDPR and must be covered by a lawful basis in accordance with Article 6 GDPR. The transfer of data will generally not pose a problem if the person requesting the transfer is considered a controller for the purposes of the GDPR and the addressee of the request is a processor (Article 28 GDPR). However, if the parties possess joint control (Article 26 GDPR), the migration of personal data might currently lack a basis in law. The introduction of a portability right for businesses would impose a legal obligation to process data and could thus provide a lawful basis under Article 6(1)(c) GDPR. However, I suggest that the GDPR should generally take precedence over a business portability right and that any such right should clarify that the migration of personal data is subject to the restrictions of the GDPR.

---

44 Article 29 Data Protection Working Party (n. 6) 19; Personal Data Protection Commission of Singapore, 'Discussion Paper on Data Portability' (25 February 2019) 19–20 <www.pdpc.gov.sg/-/media/Files/PDPC/PDF-Files/Resource-for-Organisation/Data-Portability/PDPC-CCCS-Data-Portability-Discussion-Paper--250219.pdf> accessed 31 August 2020.

The data stored may not only contain information regarding third-party data subjects, but also information regarding third-party businesses. In the absence of the legal attribution of data to a specific business (section B.II. above), the law does not require third parties to consent to the transfer of non-personal data. Trade secrets are an exception: Secret information of commercial value which has been subject to reasonable steps to be kept secret may not be divulged to non-authorised parties by any other party than the trade secret holder (Article 4 Trade Secrets Directive). In the case of digital storage of information, data can only be considered a trade secret if the parties involved have formed a confidentiality agreement. Thus, the addressee of any portability request may refuse the transfer of data, unless each trade secret holder has released them from the confidentiality agreement.

Finally, the interests of the addressee of the portability request need to be considered. However, I suggest that the adequate balance of interests between the party requesting portability and the addressee is achieved by defining the scope of the portability right, not through the insertion of an exception à la Article 20(4) GDPR. As has been explained above (section C.I.2.), the adequate balance between the interests of the parties depends upon the legislative objective of any future business portability right: A portability rule to enhance competitive markets should provide less access to data than a rule granting portability after the termination of a remunerated data analytics contract.

III. Modus operandi

1. The implications of portability under the GDPR

Under Article 20 GDPR, the data subject 'shall have the right to receive the personal data [...] in a structured, commonly used and machine-readable format and have the right to transmit those data to another controller'. Figuratively speaking, portability of data is envisioned like a jacket returned from a theatre's cloakroom: All data is handed over either to the data subject or to another controller once the data subject issues their request. This 'download your data' concept is exemplified by Google Takeout – a feature allowing google users to download their user archive.[45] Of course, unlike the jacket in the cloakroom after a return request, the data

45 <http://takeout.google.com/settings/takeout> accessed 31 August 2020.

on the controller's servers will remain there after a portability request, unless the data subject also requests the deletion of data.

In practice, data is probably more often than not transferred to another controller on the basis of co-operation agreements. An app or web service will allow the user to 'sign in with' their Google, Facebook, Microsoft or Apple account. The amount of data which is thereupon shared via the API varies from provider to provider.[46] In my view, such a model does not constitute 'portability' in the meaning of Article 20 GDPR. Rather, the transfer of data in those instances is a case of mutual processing under Article 26 GDPR. Initiatives such as the Data Transfer Project[47] aim to 'allow individuals to transfer their data seamlessly between online service providers'[48] using a platform-model. However, the co-operation of major players such as Google, Facebook, Apple, Microsoft and Twitter may lead to an even greater distribution of personal data and must therefore be observed closely. The platform-model portability envisaged by major data controllers may not necessarily be the scheme that is data protection-friendly. When Mark Zuckerberg announces that '[t]rue data portability should look more like the way people use our platform to sign into an app than the existing ways you can download an archive of your information',[49] this brings back not-so-pleasant memories of the Cambridge Analytica scandal.[50]

46 Antonie Moser-Knierim, '"Facebook-Login" – datenschutzkonformer Einsatz möglich? Einsatz von Social Plug-ins bei Authentifizierungsdiensten' (2013) Zeitschrift für Datenschutz 263; Amanda Schupak, 'What are you sharing when you sign in with Facebook or Google?' (3 November 2015) CBS News <www.cbsnews.com/news/what-are-you-sharing-when-you-sign-in-with-facebook-or-google/> accessed 31 August 2020.

47 <https://datatransferproject.dev> accessed 31 August 2020.

48 For Facebook see its White Paper: Erin Egan, 'Data Portability and Privacy – Charting a Way Forward' (6 September 2019) <https://fbnewsroomus.files.wordpress.com/2019/09/data-portability-privacy-white paper.pdf> accessed 31 August 2020.

49 Marc Zuckerberg, 'The Internet Needs New Rules. Let's Start in These Four Areas' (30 March 2019) Washington Post <www.washingtonpost.com/opinions/mark-zuckerberg-the-internet-needs-new-rules-lets-start-in-these-four-areas/2019/03/29/9e6f0504-521a-11e9-a3f7-78b7525a8d5f_story.html> accessed 31 August 2020.

50 Carole Cadwalladr and Emma Graham-Harrison, 'Revealed: 50 million Facebook profiles harvested for Cambridge Analytica in major data breach' (17 March 2018) The Guardian <www.theguardian.com/news/2018/mar/17/cambridge-analytica-facebook-influence-us-election> accessed 31 August 2020.

It is important to note that Article 20 GDPR does not provide for real-time portability.[51] In principle, the rule envisions a single-time transfer of data. Multiple requests within a reasonably long timeframe will also succeed. If the requests become repetitive, however, they may be deemed excessive and be refused or made subject to a fee under Article 12(5) GDPR. Thus, the right basically guarantees an option to change service providers.[52] It may also facilitate the beginning of multi-homing, but does not allow for a constant cross-use of different services.

2. *Data format*

Data is to be transferred in a 'structured, commonly used and machine-readable format' (Article 20(1) GDPR). The Regulation does not offer any guidance for situations in which a commonly used format does not exist. Further, a direct transmission from one controller to another can be required 'where technically feasible' (Article 20(2) GDPR). The latter requirement is quite curious: It is hard to think of an example where transmission to the data subject is feasible, but transmission to another controller is not. Thus, Article 20(2) seems to address inter-operability. This interpretation is supported by Recital 68: While 'data controllers should be encouraged to develop interoperable formats', the portability right 'should not create an obligation for the controllers to adopt or maintain processing systems which are technically compatible.' The implication is that the right to portability fails in the absence of commonly used data formats.[53] Adding to the lack of clarity, there is no indication whether 'feasibility' is to be determined on the basis of objective standards or subjective criteria tailored to the person of the controller.[54] A suggestion by the Council of

51 Cf. the time period upon which to act under Art. 12(3) GDPR; see also Schweitzer (n. 7) 574.

52 Ibid. 574.

53 This interpretation is shared by Denni-Kenji Kipker and Friederike Voskamp, 'Datenschutz in sozialen Netzwerken nach der Datenschutzgrundverordnung' (2012) Datenschutz und Datensicherheit 737, 740; Peter Bräutigam and Florian Schmidt-Wudy, 'Das geplante Auskunfts- und Herausgaberecht des Betroffenen nach Article 15 der EU-Datenschutzgrundverordnung: Ein Diskussionsbeitrag zum anstehenden Trilog der EU-Gesetzgebungsorgane' (2015) Computer und Recht 56, 60.

54 Stiftung Datenschutz (n. 23) 6.

the European Union to consider the economic capabilities of the controller did not make the final cut of Article 20 GDPR.[55]

Let me add an interesting tidbit here: Google, Facebook, Apple, Microsoft and Twitter are engaged in the Data Transfer Project, which aims to create an open-source, service-to-service data portability platform.[56] The project's mission statement contains the following sentence: 'Companies have (for some reason) [sic!] all started offering their data in structured, commonly used and machine-readable formats, however in most cases those formats are not compatible with one another making it hard for users to re-import data they have exported.' This sentence reveals both the power and the shortcomings of Article 20 GDPR.

3. *Inferences for businesses*

What benefits would an Article 20-style rule bring to the B2B-context? Art. 20 GDRP contains a minimum requirement for the transmission of data that would help businesses switch data services. Apart from that, it is of little use to businesses, as they will regularly depend upon real-time access to the data.[57] Without such real-time access, neither an autonomous analysis nor the creation of aftermarket or complementary data-driven services seem feasible.[58] The transfer obligations under Article 20 GDPR therefore do not suffice for business purposes. Also, while the 'download your data' approach to portability may serve important data protection functions, businesses will most likely prefer a platform-model type of 'portability' which enables real-time data exchanges via APIs. Finally, as business data sets are exponentially greater than personal data sets, imposing a fee for the intermediate storage and/or transfer of the data might be adequate.

A key obstacle to expedient portability is interoperability. Machine-generated data is generally processed in specific proprietary data formats – even more so than personal data. However, it should be noted that several

55 Council of the European Union, 'Proposal for a Regulation of the European Parliament and of the Council on the protection of individuals with regard to the processing of personal data and on the free movement of such data (General Data Protection)'(27 November 2015) Doc. 14481/15, 95.

56 <https://datatransferproject.dev> accessed 31 August 2020.

57 Schweitzer (n. 7) 574.

58 Schweitzer (n. 7) 574.

initiatives aim for inter-operability specifically for the industry 4.0.[59] If the law demands portability only where 'feasible', the law incentivises the development of proprietary data formats. But keep in mind that mandating interoperable standards may not only have beneficial effects on competition. The reverse may also be true: Interoperability may limit product design options and hamper innovation, may allow dominant market players to accrue even more data and may reduce network benefits for smaller players.[60] In trying to find middle ground, the law could require the provision of standardised retrieval software with respect to industry-specific data points.[61]

D. Conclusions and recommendations

I would hope that my conclusion is self-evident, but let me be clear:

Article 20 GDPR cannot serve as a blueprint for a business right to portability. It is rather of use to illustrate the pitfalls that need to be considered when creating any new portability right.

Any plan to introduce a portability right for businesses must be rooted in a clear policy objective. As such, different objectives come to mind: granting distributive justice to companies who contribute to a data value chain, preventing lock-in effects for small and medium enterprises, ensuring market efficiency by restraining dominating undertakings. The scope of the portability right as well as any exceptions and limitations must be

59 <https://opcfoundation.org>; <https://openindustry4.com>; <www.opengroup.org> all accessed 31 August 2020; cf. also Plattform Industrie 4.0, 'Shaping Industrie 4.0. Autonomous, interoperable and sustainable' (2019) 15–20 <www.plattform-i40.de/PI40/Redaktion/EN/Downloads/Publikation/2019-progress-report.pdf?__blob=publicationFile&v=7> accessed 30 August 2020.

60 See the Memorundum on the Bill of the Federal Government for the reform of the German Act against Restraints of Competition: Gesetzentwurf der Bundesregierung – Entwurf eines Gesetzes zur Änderung des Gesetzes gegen Wettbewerbsbeschränkungen für ein fokussiertes, proaktives und digitales Wettbewerbsrecht 4.0 und anderer wettbewerbsrechtlicher Bestimmungen (GWB-Digitalisierungsgesetz) (9 September 2020) 89 <www.bmwi.de/Redaktion/DE/Downloads/Gesetz/gesetzentwurf-gwb-digitalisierungsgesetz.pdf?__blob=publicationFile&v=6> accessed 15 September 2020; Inge Graef, Martin Husovec and Nadezhda Purtova, 'Data Portability and Data Control: Lessons for an Emerging Concept in EU Law' (2018) 19 German Law Journal 1359, 1374.

61 Cf. US National Highway Traffic Safety Administration (NHTSA) rule 49 CFR Part 563 for the retrieval of event data recorders (in cars).

tailored towards this policy objective. Possibly, the solution does not lie in a one-size-fits-all norm, but in various more limited, but adequately tailored rules (that might even be industry-specific).

If the purpose of portability is to guarantee competition in data-driven aftermarket services or complementary products, then Article 20 GDPR does not provide an adequate model. However, Article 20 GDPR may be considered as a starting point for contractual portability rights, particularly regarding post-contractual transfer obligations. The introduction of such a contractual portability right to prevent lock-in effects certainly has its merits. The difficulties in defining such a right, however, are numerous and have been explained above.

In a European Union context, one also needs to be clear-eyed with respect to the possible harmonising gains of a contractual portability right. The harmonising effect of a non-mandatory contractual right may prove to be minimal, as businesses are bound to deviate by agreement from the rule. It is to be expected that repeat players will derogate from the portability rule in their standard terms and conditions. I include a gentle reminder that the approach to unfair contract terms in business contracts differs immensely amongst the Member States.[62]

In conclusion, let me emphasise that portability is an instrument and not a principle. Such an instrument needs a framework in which to flourish. The portability right created by Article 20 GDPR is embedded in the broader system of the GDPR. Whilst not all the provisions of the GDPR are crystal clear, the Regulation does provide a framework for the attribution of data, the legality of processing and the addressees of data subjects' rights. This framework is sorely missing for non-personal data. Any initiative to introduce a portability right for businesses must therefore first prepare the ground upon which the portability right might grow.

62 Cf. Alessio Zaccaria, 'Anmerkungen zur Umsetzung der Richtlinie 93/13/EWG über missbräuchliche Klauseln in Verbraucherverträgen in Europa' (2016) Zeitschrift für Europäisches Privatrecht 159.

Safeguarding innovation in the framework of sector-specific data access regimes: The case of digital payment services

Jörg Hoffmann

A. *Introduction*

The expected economic and social benefits of data access and sharing are enormous.[1] Data-driven innovations have already transformed multiple sectors in the economy and are seen as a new disruptive source of productivity growth. In particular, the advanced use of data analytics and further applications of artificial intelligence (AI) enables undertakings to scale their business at much lower costs than in analogue times.[2] Even beyond productivity growth, a greater availability of data can create beneficial spill-overs, where data can be re-used to open up further benefits and cost savings for society.[3]

In the European strategy for data, the European Commission addresses the need to ensure better availability of data and its responsible and efficient uses, as currently there are not enough data available for innovative re-use. Despite the current ongoing debate of further strengthening consumer data rights, particularly in a B2B context, data sharing of privately

1 According to one of the most recent studies conducted by the OECD, data access and sharing can help generate social and economic benefits worth between 0.1 % and 1.5 % of gross domestic product (GDP) in the case of public-sector data, and between 1 % and 2.5 % of GDP (in few other studies up to 4 % of GDP) when also including private-sector data. See OECD, *Enhancing Access to and Sharing of Data* (OECD 2019) 60.

2 And this goes much beyond 'scaling without mass'. Cf. Erik Brynjolfsson, Andrew McAfee, Michael Sorell and Feng Zhu, 'Scale Without Mass: Business Process Replication and Industry Dynamics' (2008) Harvard Business School Technology & Operations Management Unit Research Paper No. 7/16 <https://papers.ssrn.com/sol3/papers.cfm?abstract_id=980568> accessed 31 August 2020.

3 This ranges from greater transparency, accountability and empowerment of users, the creations of new business opportunities and user-driven innovations to increased efficiency due to a linkage and integration of data across multiple sources, OECD (n. 1) 64.

held data between undertakings has not taken off at an efficient scale.[4] This has already led to claims of lowering the competition law thresholds in data-specific refusal-to-deal cases and to the adoption of sector-specific data access and portability regimes in certain fields.[5] It further drives the debate on how to foster private incentives for data sharing, e.g. by creating European data spaces fostering data interoperability or establishing data infrastructure like GaiaX.[6]

Yet, there might also be hidden costs and challenges of increased data sharing. The reaping of the advantages that come with enhanced data access requires the inclusion of the use of data in the business models of pri-

4 See for the discussion about consumer data rights OECD, 'Consumer Data Rights and Competition – Background note' (2020) DAF/COMP(2020)1 <https://one.oecd.org/document/DAF/COMP(2020)1/en/pdf> accessed 31 August 2020, which was triggered by their introduction through legislation in Australia – see Louisa Specht-Riemenschneider in this volume. Cf. Communication from the Commission of 19 February 2020 to the European Parliament, the Council, the European Economic and Social Committee and the Committee of Regions – A European strategy for data, COM(2020) 66 final, 3, 6, 7.

5 Cf. Jacques Crémer, Yves-Alexandre de Montjoye and Heike Schweitzer, 'Competition Policy for the Digital Era – Final Report' (2019) 91–107 <https://ec.europa.eu/competition/publications/reports/kd0419345enn.pdf> accessed 31 August 2020, and see Heike Schweitzer and Robert Welker, 'A legal framework for access to data – A competition policy perspective', in this volume. Such fields are for instance repair data for vehicles – Regulation (EC) 715/2007 of the European Parliament and of the Council on type approval of motor vehicles with respect to emissions from light passenger and commercial vehicles (Euro 5 and Euro 6) and on access to vehicle repair and maintenance data [2007] OJ L171/1, as amended by Regulation (EU) 595/2009 of the European Parliament and the Council of 18 June 2009 [2009] OJ L188/1, smart metering information – Directive (EU) 2009/73 of the European Parliament and of the Council of 13 July 2009 concerning common rules for the internal market in natural gas and repealing Directive 2003/55/EC [2009] OJ L211/94, electricity network data – Directive (EU) 2019/944 of European Parliament and of the Council of on common rules for the internal market for electricity and amending Directive 2012(27/27/EU [2019] OJ L158/125, or electricity transmission – Commission Regulation (EU) 2017/1485 of 2 August 2017 establishing a guideline on electricity transmission system operation [2017] OJ L220/1, intelligent transport systems – Commission Regulation (EU) 2015/703 of 30 April 2015 establishing a network code on interoperability and data exchange rules [2015] OJ L113/13.

6 Cf. European Commission, 'A European strategy for data' (n. 4) 4; on the joint hybrid endeavour of the French and German Government together with private stakeholders Gaia X see Federal Ministry of Economics Affairs and Energy, 'GAIA X – A Federated Data Infrastructure for Europe' <www.bmwi.de/Redaktion/DE/Dossier/gaia-x.html> accessed 31 August 2020; on the standardisation of web information, i.e. linked data, see World Wide Web Consortium (W3C), 'Linked Data' <www.w3.org/standards/semanticweb/data> accessed 31 August 2020.

vate actors. This makes complementary investments in skills and infrastructures necessary, which may potentially exclude traditional market actors.[7] Moreover, data entail multidimensional regulatory goals. Exclusively held data can offer an enormous competitive advantage and may be one of the innovation incentives for undertakings. On the other side, data lock-ins and excessive aggregation of data can also have negative effects on competition. Data can also consist of personal information that can be used in such ways that might not only create societal change, it might also impact the sovereignty of consumers and their privacy. Another factor that has to be considered is that the freedom of information and the free flow of information are prerequisites for a democratic society.

The design of future data access and governance[8] regulation therefore requires a broad regulatory theory that takes into account all the different implications of a wider data access regime.[9] Only a holistic assessment of the overall regulatory goals may make consistent regulation of data access possible and feasible.

Accordingly, the paper firstly outlines the role factual data exclusivity plays in light of the broad regulatory theory mentioned above and thus will also relate to other market failures that at first sight may be solved within other legal regimes, i.e. data protection law, consumer protection law or (general) competition law. Even under the sole analysis of a market failure with regard to data-driven innovation capacities of a European Single Data Market, such considerations may ultimately also define the ideal legal framework for data access in order to better enable data-driven inno-

7 Peter A. Johnson and others, 'The Cost(s) of Geospatial Open Data' (2017) 21 Transaction in GIS 434, 442.

8 The term 'data governance framework' relates to a complex set of rules (laws and standards) relating to data. In the payments sector for example public laws establish ex ante regulation that require pre-set corporate data management solutions in firms. The regulation on regulatory technical standards set out certain interoperability provisions, which compliance need to be monitored by the competent administrative authorities. The introduction of certain rights of payment service users however are private laws that define the contractual relationship of the parties involved. Both forms of regulation are defining the data access regime for the use of specific payment services. On the term 'data governance' from a corporate governance and IT perspective, see Boris Otto, 'Data Governance' (2011) 3 Business & Information Systems Engineering 241. See also Kerber 'From (horizontal and sectoral) data access solutions – Towards data governance systems', in this volume.

9 Cf. Josef Drexl, 'Legal Challenges of the Changing Role of Personal and Non-Personal Data in the Data Economy' (2018) Max Planck Institute for Innovation and Competition Research Paper No. 18–23, 6 <https://papers.ssrn.com/sol3/papers.cfm?abstract_id=3274519> accessed 31 August 2020.

vation. There are at least four aspects that must be always considered: (1) setting innovation incentives for undertakings; (2) the role of direct market regulation; (3) ensuring consumer sovereignty and choice; (4) hindering data-induced distortions of competition.

In this light, the paper further analyses the sector-specific data access regulation pertaining to payment initiation and account information services enshrined in the Second Payment Services Directive[10] (PSD2) and implemented into German law. It will analyse whether the legal access regimes are well designed for safeguarding (data-driven) innovation and how the different regulatory goals and the public and private interests are addressed and should be better aligned. It will be seen that the implementation of the access rules in both private and public laws cause certain tensions and create legal uncertainty as the legal rights and obligations between third party payment providers and incumbent banks are not well outlined but still influenced by the private statutory right of customers – including consumers and merchants – to make use of certain payment services. Nonetheless it will be shown that the chosen data governance model could serve as regulatory model for safeguarding data driven innovation that can be applied to other already existent and future (sector-specific) data access and portability regimes. The paper concludes by contrasting the findings with the EC's recent data strategy. It does not analyse the data access and governance regime for payment instrument issuing services and only briefly outlines the role of data interoperability that may affect the potential adverse effects of too broad access regimes. Furthermore, it does not analyse the current endeavours for fostering voluntary data sharing.

B. *Defining a holistic framework for data access regimes*

I. *Data-driven innovation capacities of markets and factual data exclusivity*

The availability of data is certainly one of the main driving factors for establishing a functioning and competitive digital single market. The role of factual data exclusivity, however, may also serve as a private innovation incentive for undertakings to invest in data production and analysis. This

10 Directive (EU) 2015/2366 of the European Parliament and of the Council of 25 November 2015 on payment services in the internal market, amending Directives 2002/65/EC, 2009/110EC and 2013/36/EU and Regulation (EU) No 1093/2010 and repealing Directive 2007/64/EC [2015] OJ L337/35 (PSD2).

again could not only spur data-driven innovations, it could also make the regulation of quality standards for data less important. Once markets value higher quality data, there will be demand-side-driven incentives for providing quality data.[11] In this context it is important not to mix up data exclusivity with a need for introducing further exclusive rights. A few economists and legal scholars are already inclined to think that well-defined and easily enforceable data ownership rights were an efficient way to organise the data-driven economy.[12] Exclusive rights in data would reduce uncertainty and the margins for bargaining. This in turn would reduce transaction costs that create deadweight welfare losses for society and ultimately tackle a public good market failure.[13] Despite these potential benefits, one has to negate the need for an ownership right. This is not only because transaction costs would hinder the ideal allocation of rights, but also because factual exclusivity may already create enough incentives for undertakings to invest and therefore no public good market failure exists. However, if factual excludability may now be overridden by regulating too broad access to data, the question of how to balance (factual) exclusivity in order to safeguard innovation incentives for undertakings and ensure adequate access for value-creating data re-use is inevitably arising again. This also becomes relevant from a fundamental rights perspective, as different

---

11 This could also be established via a certain label for specific quality data in order to avoid a typical lemon market scenario.

12 See Daron Acemoglu, Ali Makhdoumi, Azarakhsh Malekian and Asuman Ozdaglar, 'Too Much Data: Prices and Inefficiencies in Data Markets' (2019) NBER Working Paper No. 26296 <www.nber.org/papers/w26296> accessed 31 August 2020; Karl-Heinz Fezer, 'Dateneigentum – Theorie des immaterialgüterrechtlichen Eigentums an verhaltensgenerierten Personendaten der Nutzer als Datenproduzenten' (2017) MultiMedia und Recht 1. On a thorough analysis of why no ownership rights are needed and the creation of an ownership right would have adverse effects Josef Drexl, 'Designing competitive markets for industrial data: Between propertization and access' (2017) 8 Journal of Intellectual Property, Information Technology and E-Commerce Law 257, paras 74, 81, 89, 91, 93, 103 et seq.

13 Yet what has to be noted is that such considerations build on the (wrong) assumption of the Coase Theorem that any a priori given IP right eventually will end up in the hands of the party that attaches the most value to these resources, leading towards an ideal allocation of intellectual property rights. Where transaction costs are rather high with regard to the value of the right, these considerations do not apply. New Institutional Economics already assessed this. However, high transactions in relation to the value of the right would resemble big data scenarios and therefore should not be taken as an economic rationale for the creation of exclusive rights in data. Cf. Ronald H. Coase, 'The Problem of Social Costs' (1960) 3 Journal of Law & Economics 1, 44.

interests are protected under the Charter of Fundamental Rights of the EU (CFR) and thus also need to be reconciled with the goal of fostering data-driven innovation.

1. *Applying IP Economics in data access cases – the innovation incentive of factual data exclusivity*

Factual data exclusivity may serve as innovation incentive for undertakings and thus the considerations of intellectual property rights (IPRs) economics also become relevant.[14] The standard economic model of IPRs is based upon a utilitarian incentive theory.[15] This theory revolves around the trade-off between static social welfare losses from over-protection of exclusivity and dynamic welfare gains achieved through the incentive effect for more investment in production of creative or innovative content.[16] Translated into the data access context this would mean that the incentive effects of factual data exclusivity and exclusive endogenous data-driven innovation need to be reconciled with the spill-over effects of available data for everyone.

The basic economic rationale behind IPRs is that the static short-term welfare loss is compensated by dynamic long-run gains generated by a continuous stream of new creations and innovations. This is only possible as IP rights allow the right owners to recoup their investments without potential free riders being able to sell the same product. The key consideration behind this would be to block others from entering the market unless the rights holder licenses the rights, and thus to reduce intra-brand competition. The same market-specific reasoning of IPRs can only be applied to data once data are essential facilities, and become relevant under market foreclosure considerations. The application of the essential facilities doc-

14 Wolfgang Kerber, 'A New (Intellectual) Property Right for Non-Personal Data? An Economic Analysis' (2016) Gewerblicher Rechtsschutz und Urheberrecht Internationaler Teil 989, 993; Nestor Duch-Brown, Bertin Martens and Frank Müller-Langer, 'The economics of ownership, access and trade in digital data' (2017) JRC Digital Economy Working Paper 2017–01, 25–29 <https://ec.europa.eu/jrc/sites/jrcsh/files/jrc104756.pdf> accessed 31 August 2020.

15 Cf. Richard A. Posner, *Economic Analysis of Law* (7th edn, Wolters Kluwer 2007) 38. Steven Shavell, 'Economic Analysis of Welfare Economic, Morality and the Law' (2003) NBER Working Paper No. 9700, 669 <https://ideas.repec.org/p/nbr/nberwo/9700.html> accessed 31 August 2020.

16 See William D. Nordhaus, *Invention, Growth, Welfare: A Theoretical Treatment of Technological Change* (MIT Press 1969) 71.

trine in these cases however may have to be broader defined and should not be restricted to traditional indispensability considerations of exclusive information. Data specific economies of scope may also lead to such knowledge of firms that constitute a competitive advantage that in the very end has the same market foreclosing effect as indispensable exclusive information. The knowledge inferred from multiple data sets may constitute such an advantage that others may simply not be able to achieve anymore. Yet data can also only be mere by-products that lack certain economic value – particularly in the context of IoT.

The potential excludability that would result from the creation of an ownership right on data would hinder the further use of the data. According to new institutional IPR economics, the welfare-enhancing effects of exclusivity might dwindle if IP rights preclude independent subsequent creation and innovation that build on the protected input.[17] This is also true in light of potential negative externalities that also relate to lower investment incentives for undertakings.[18] Yet the fact that tomorrow's innovators can benefit from 'standing on the shoulders of giants',[19] while potentially not sharing gains with their predecessors, makes a nuanced assessment of the 'free-rider' issue necessary.

Data availability may enable subsequent use of data within the data value chain or network, and thus may create further data-driven innovation.[20] In this context, however, it has to be noted that any innovation requires

17 Jeffrey L. Furman and Scott Stern, 'Climbing atop the Shoulders of Giants: The Impact of Institutions on Cumulative Research' (2011) 101 American Economic Review 1933; Heidi L. Williams, 'Intellectual Property Rights and Innovation: Evidence from the Human Genome' (2014) 121(1) Journal of Political Economy 1; Paul M. Romer, 'Endogenous technological change' (1990) 98(5) Journal of Political Economy 71, 71–75.

18 Kenneth J. Arrow, 'Economic Welfare and the Allocation of Resources for Invention' in National Bureau of Economic Research, 'The Rate and Direction of Inventive Activity: Economic and Social Factors' (Princeton University Press 1962) 609, 620. Different opinions on this: Joseph Schumpeter, *Theorie der wirtschaftlichen Entwicklung* (Duncker & Humblot 1912) 157 and Philippe Aghion and Peter Howitt, 'A model of growth through creative destruction' (1992) 60(2) Econometrica 323.

19 Suzanne Scotchmer, 'Standing on the Shoulders of Giants: Cumulative Research and the Patent Law' (1991) 45(1) Journal of Economic Perspectives 29, 29–30.

20 Most data-driven innovation is enabled by the use of artificial intelligence. In this regard particularly software copyright protection for machine learning models becomes relevant, as it may also block further subsequent data-driven innovation. See on this Reto M. Hilty, Jörg Hoffmann and Stefan Scheuerer, 'Intellectual Property Justification for Artificial Intelligence' (2020) Max Planck Institute for

something new or improved that actually gets implemented.[21] This not only means that data need to be consolidated or aggregated in order to further infer some information, but such information also has to add something new on the knowledge level. Therefore, the mere gathering of data without making proper use may not constitute a data-driven innovation and one needs to be cautious as to whether data-driven innovation is used to an inflationary extent for justifying access to data.

In order to ascertain the right scope of excludability, or in other words the right relationship between factual exclusivity and data access, the economic model build by Zhu et al. can serve as a good starting point. Accordingly, the following factors[22] should be assessed: (1) fixed investment costs in the production, processing and analysis of data; (2) the likelihood of potential free-riders exceeding the marginal benefits of data producers and holders;[23] and (3) functional equivalence between the re-used data and the (factual) exclusive data.[24]

With regard to the investment cost, the empirical facts show that in the data-driven economy much data can be produced or collected at very low

---

Innovation and Competition Research Paper No. 20–02, 25 <https://papers.ssrn.com/sol3/papers.cfm?abstract_id=3539406> accessed 31 August 2020.

21 The 3rd edition of the Oslo Manual defines innovation as the implementation of a new or significantly improved product (good or service), or process, new marketing method, or new organisational method in business practices, workplace organisation or external relations. See OECD, 'Oslo Manual: Guidelines for Collecting and Interpreting Innovation Data' (2005) 1, 45. Data-driven innovation can thereby happen in all the different categories and take place in data value cycles. Therein data are firstly collected, then analysed, knowledge inferred and then applied in the decision-making process. See OECD, 'Data-Driven Innovation: Big Data for Growth and Well-Being' (OECD 2015) 33.

22 These simplified factors resemble the key economic considerations new institutional IPR economics are built on and relate to the economic model Zhu and others developed in their economic analysis pertaining to the functionality of the sui generis database protection regime. See Hongwei Zhu, Stewart E. Madnick and Michael D. Siegel, 'An Economic Analysis of Policies for the Protection and Reuse of Non-copyrightable Database Contents' (2008) 25(1) Journal of Management Information Systems 199. Indeed, even though the database sui generis right only protects the substantial investments made in obtaining or verifying existing data and not in the creation of data, it can still serve as reference for mere investment protection considerations.

23 From an economic point of view, it can be expected that data are produced and analysed as far as the marginal benefits of the data producers and holders exceed their marginal costs. See Kerber (n. 14) 993.

24 Translated into a competition law perspective this would mean complementarity or substitutability under essential facility considerations.

costs, often only as a free by-product of offered services.[25] However, the costs vary depending on the type of data (e.g. unstructured, semi-structured vs. structured data).[26] Particularly extracting information from unstructured data used to be labour-intensive. With growing computing capacities, however, such differentiation is becoming less important, since data analytic tools are increasingly able to automatically extract the information embedded in unstructured data. Nonetheless specifically labelled data is still important, and still labour-intensive and costly.[27] Moreover, data governing and transmitting costs can also be substantial.[28]

With regard to the extent of functional equivalence between the re-used data and the original exclusive data, it may be hard to assess to what extent a data-driven innovation exists and whether this can be considered as a substitute for or complementary to the original data or data-driven service.[29] This holds particularly true in AI applications, where specific machine learning (ML) models may build on multiple data throughout the learning process. The quality of the ML model is commonly claimed to be dependent on multiple data from many different sources in order to better train and optimise the model. In both cases, it seems on first sight that any data would enhance data-driven innovation, as the output of the ML process will never be simply equivalent to the original data. However, only data that are (partly) related to each other can improve ML models.[30]

---

25 Duch-Brown, Martens and Müller-Langer (n. 14) 25–29.

26 Kerber (n. 14) 993.

27 There are high costs for labelling data in the context of supervised learning in deep learning applications. See WIPO, 'Technology Trends 2019: Artificial Intelligence' (WIPO 2019) 89.

28 E.g. secure and common standards of communication require investments in an in-house IT infrastructure or technology developers (with regard to APIs). Other costs relate to cloud services or data standardisation. See on the costs for instance Marc Walterbusch, Benedikt Martens and Frank Teuteberg, 'Evaluating cloud-computing services from a total cost of ownership perspective' (2013) 36 Management Research Review 613. See on an overview of different data quality categories and the already existent standards under the ISO-8000 data standard, Li Cai and Yangyong Zhu 'The Challenges of Data Quality and Data Quality Assessment in the Big Data Era' (2015) Data Science Journal 5–9 <https://datascience.codata.org/articles/10.5334/dsj-2015-002/print/> accessed 31 August 2020.

29 Once the data is used and the coding team creates something of equal or even better value that would be a substitute to the existent data or data-driven service, there will be less incentive for the company to further invest in data.

30 Looking for structures and regularities in data is not enough to understand or acquire knowledge. Knowledge cannot be derived through induction alone; it requires a theory or a prior framework that can be tested. Humans necessarily pre-

2. *Legal Framework of essential facilities – EU competition law, EU utilities market regulation in the telecommunication sector and EU fundamental rights*

Under legal considerations, in cases in which IP rights create legal exclusivity to offer market options for boosting dynamic (inter-brand) competition, the European case law with regard to Article 102 lit. b) TFEU and unilateral exploitation of IP rights has always been restrictive. At first, the CJEU in its *Volvo* decision set out the general principle that the right of the holder of an IPR to make exclusive use of it is precisely the substance of the exclusive right. Therefore, the mere refusal to license the IPR – even if the terms were reasonable – was held to be, in principle, no abuse of dominant position.[31] Yet, the CJEU allowed the European Commission in the judgment of *Magill* to rely on competition law for overcoming non-availability under copyright law. Accordingly, only exceptional circumstances require access on the basis of Article 102 lit. b) TFEU in order to prevent a unilateral restriction of production, sale or technical development to the detriment of consumers once an IP right owner refuses to grant a licence and, *a fortiori*, is bringing an action for infringement. The presence of exceptional circumstances is according to the CJEU in *Magill*[32] subject to the following four requirements: (1) the licensing must be indispensable for access to the downstream market, (2) the refusal to grant a licence must exclude any effective competition in this market, (3) the refusal to grant a licence must prevent appearance of a new (but dependent) product on an adjacent market which it does not supply itself, and (4) the refusal to license must not be objectively satisfied by way of exception. According to the CJEU in *IMS Health* the requirements must be cumulatively satisfied. However, the Court also found that a hypothetical market would suffice to meet the exceptional circumstances threshold.[33]

determine this framework and thus data have to be related – at least to some extent. See Ronaldo Vigo, 'Complexity over uncertainty in generalized representational information theory (GRIT): A structure-sensitive general theory of information' (2013) 4 Information 1.

31 Case 238/87 *Volvo* [1988] ECR 6211 = ECLI:EU:C:477, para. 8.

32 Joined Cases C-241/91 and C-242/91 *RTE and ITP v. Commission* ('*Magill*') [1995] ECR I-743 = ECLI:EU:C:1995:98, paras 39–42.

33 Case C-418/01 *IMS Health* [2004] ECR I-5039 = ECLI:EU:C:2004:257, paras 34, 44.

Particularly by stressing the 'new product rule' the CJEU in *Magill*[34] and – despite the hypothetical market exemption – *IMS Health*[35] correctly followed the role competition law traditionally plays in IP law. In unilateral refusal-to-deal cases, competition law ought to safeguard the goal of inter-brand competition generated by IP rights and therefore abstain from interfering with the terms or the operation of the IP system per se. Only where IP law fails to provide for dynamic inter-brand competition may competition law serve as a complementary tool in order to safeguard the well-functioning of markets that are enabled by IP rights. In other words, Article 102 TFEU is in general not meant to enforce direct market access to allow mere intra-brand competition by imitation and restrict competition on the merits.[36] This would contradict the role competition law plays within a free market economy, where markets typically evolve spontaneously and are only framed by a competitive process that should be safeguarded by competition law rules.

In cases of refusal to disclose trade secrets[37] or supply access to other exclusive facilities,[38] however, the CJEU explicitly abstains from the traditional delineation of intra-brand and inter-brand competition and lowered the threshold of intervention. Yet, it still outlines the role exclusivity plays under innovation incentive considerations and the defendants' rights of freely conducting a business. In *Bronner*, for instance, the Court found no abuse of dominance, as the facility – a home-delivery service for newspapers – was already not indispensable and could be developed by other competitors.[39] There the Court stressed the particular need of maintaining innovation incentives for undertakings in order to safeguard competition in the long term.[40] However, in *Microsoft*, the General Court desisted from

---

34 Joined Cases C-241/91 and C-242/91 *RTE and ITP v. Commission* ('*Magill*') [1995] ECR I-743 = ECLI:EU:C:1995:98, paras 39–42.

35 Case C-418/01 *IMS Health* [2004] ECR I-5039 = ECLI:EU:C:2004:257, para. 48. Therein, the Court underlined 'that, in the balancing of the interest in protection of the intellectual property right and the economic freedom of its owner against the interest in protection of free competition, the latter can prevail only where refusal to grant a licence prevents the development of the secondary market to the detriment of consumers.'.

36 Torsten Körber, *Standardessentielle Patente, FRAND-Verpflichtungen und Kartellrecht; Standard Essential Patents, FRAND Commitments and Competition Law, Kartell-und Regulierungsrecht* (Nomos 2013) 212–14.

37 Case T-201/04 *Microsoft v. Commission* [2007] ECR II-3602 = ECLI:EU:T:2007:289.

38 Case C-7/97 *Bronner* [1988] ECR I-7791 = ECLI:EU:C:1998:569.

39 Opinion of AG Jacobs in Case C-7/97 *Bronner* ECLI:EU:C:1998:264, para. 57.

40 Ibid.

the strict requirement of the new product rule in a secondary market set out in *Magill* and *IMS Health* and allowed access even if it may only create competition within the primary market. Therein, the Court held that the exclusivity of interoperability information is tantamount to an abuse of dominance under Article 102 lit. b) TFEU. The Court stated that the new product rule 'cannot be the only parameter'. The relevant question is rather whether the refusal to grant a licence will limit technical development to the detriment of the consumers.[41] This requirement was considered to have been met because the lacking interoperability of the competitors' software would bind customers to Microsoft and prevent competitors from successfully selling their innovative products and thus from entering a market. This would tantamount to an exclusionary abuse constellation. According to the Court's opinion in *Microsoft*, it indeed seems not to matter anymore whether access to the facility enables innovation on a secondary market (downstream market), but whether innovation *per saldo* is actually increased or not.[42] This applies to both the prospect of incremental innovation within the already existent market and radical innovations on a secondary – even hypothetical – market. By taking *per saldo* innovation into the equation of Article 102 lit. b) TFEU the Court has given up the clear distinction between competition within the market and competition for the market. Applied to the question of how to draw the line between factual data exclusivity and access, such interpretation would constitute an argument in favour of a broader data access regime - if the information needed are indispensable for achieving interoperability.

In the case of de facto standardisation, exclusivity of interoperability information has effects on dynamic competition in the long run. Exclusivity in these cases may eventually lead to a market foreclosure on both the already existent and the adjacent markets. This holds particularly true in systems markets, where product compatibility connects the neighbouring markets in such a way that a decrease in competitive pressure and competitive process on the primary market may eventually cause dynamic competition and its innovation effects to deteriorate.[43] Under this theory of contestability the intervention is justified. However, even in *Microsoft*, it was

41 Case T-201/04 *Microsoft v. Commission* [2007] ECR II-3602 = ECLI:EU:T:2007:289, para. 647.

42 As innovation always requires implementation and is hard to measure, such reasoning creates much legal uncertainty. See Körber (n. 36) 212–14.

43 Heinemann refers to this under the theory of contestability, according to which vertical, but also neighbouring, markets that are anti-competitively foreclosed by a dominant undertaking must remain contestable. Andreas Heinemann, 'The

considered whether the competitors' products included 'substantial elements based upon the [competitors'] own efforts'.[44] This is at least some reference to the need of also limiting imitation (intra-brand) competition in these cases. The General Court also considered Microsoft's argument that the compulsory licensing of data would eliminate its future incentive to further invest in innovation. Yet the Court dismissed it, purportedly, with the reasoning that the particular role of disseminating the de facto technical standard has to prevail over the interests of Microsoft in the case.[45]

The particular role of standardisation and exclusivity in competition law can also be seen in cases concerning standard-essential patents (SEPs) where standards are established by way of open standardisation processes through standard setting organisations (SSOs).[46] Even though this system is one that falls under 'regulatory self-regulation', wherein the scope of the SEP is determined by FRAND (fair, reasonable and non-discriminatory) licensing commitments, the CJEU in *Huawei* outlined the role of Article 102 TFEU for examining the FRAND terms for cases where the proprietor of the SEP brings a legal action against the contracting partner for infringement.

The Court dismissed the right of the SEP owner to exclude the infringer. It ruled that the voluntary act of exploiting a patent via open standardisation justifies the imposition on the proprietor of an obligation to comply with specific requirements when bringing actions against an alleged infringer for a prohibitory injunction or for the recall of products.[47] SEPs in open standardisation processes are per se indispensable to all competitors, which envisage manufacturing products that comply with the

contestability of IP-protected markets' in Josef Drexl (ed.), *Research Handbook on Intellectual Property and Competition Law* (2008) 54. See also Josef Drexl 'Intellectual property and sources of market power' in Inge Govaere and Hanns Ullrich (eds), *Intellectual Property, Market Power and the Public Interest* (2008) 13.

44 Case T-201/04 *Microsoft v. Commission* [2007] ECR II-3602 = ECLI:EU:T:2007:289, para. 631.

45 This also led to criticism of the *Microsoft* case being driven by policy considerations regarding the technological dissemination of certain standards. Gustavo Ghidini, *Rethinking Intellectual Property – Balancing Conflicts of Interest in the Constitutional Pradigm* (Edward Elgar 2018) 339–41.

46 Cf. Hanns Ullrich, 'Technology protection and competition policy for the information economy' (2019) Max Planck Institute for Innovation and Competition Research Paper No. 19–12, 8 <https://papers.ssrn.com/sol3/papers.cfm?abstract_id=3437177> accessed 31 August 2020.

47 Case C-170/13 *Huawei* ECLI:EU:C:2015:477, para. 59.

standard to which it is linked. Accordingly, the Court held that this was already tantamount to an abuse under Article 102 TFEU,[48] as the case was different from *Volvo*, *Magill* or *IMS Health*.[49]

By rejecting the right of exclusivity, however, the Court implicitly establishes markets where competition only between standard-compliant products becomes the prevalent form of competition. Here it becomes obvious that the innovation-incentivising role of IP is again reoriented towards facilitating the dissemination of the open innovative standard in order to establish intra-standard competition.[50] Therefore, *Huawei Technology/ZTE* may indeed be seen as a case in which the Court abandons the traditional role of exclusivity in favour of granting broader access – in this case by denying the proprietor of an SEP in open standardisation processes injunctive relief. Yet what has to be considered in this case is the particular role the voluntary FRAND commitment plays in open standardisation processes and the potential effects of the commitment *in rem*.[51] Accordingly, a voluntary act that led to the indispensability of the SEP justifies a lower threshold for granting access.

Non-economic considerations, namely equity-based universal service, redistributive objectives and political inclusion has compelled the legislature to enact market regulation. This could already be seen in the post service and telecommunication sectors throughout the European integration process in the late 1980s and early 1990s.[52] In the telecommunication sectors, for instance, these factors together with a natural monopoly market failure associated with high levels of monopolisation stemming from traditional state monopolies led to regulatory responses that granted universal access

---

48 Ibid. para. 53.

49 Ibid. para. 49.

50 See Ullrich (n. 46) 8; Ghidini (n. 45) 339. Giuseppe Colangelo and Roberto Pardolesi, 'Intellectual property, standards and antitrust: A new life for the essential facilities doctrine?' (2017) in Gustavo Ghidini, Hanns Ullrich and Peter Drahos (eds), *Kritika – Essays on Intellectual Property* (Vol. II, Edward Elgar 2017) 70.

51 Ullrich therefore argues that the Court's consideration rather builds on the FRAND commitment by the SEP owner and competition law only intervenes in order to observe the FRAND negotiation process and the FRAND conditions. See Ullrich (n. 46) 16. It still has to be considered though which doctrinal basis such considerations are really built on – estoppel, good faith or material agreement with a *pactum di non petendo*.

52 Cf. Jürgen Bast, in Eberhard Grabitz, Meinhard Hilf and Martin Nettesheim (eds), *Das Recht der Europäischen Union* (C.H. Beck 2011) Art. 26 AEUV para. 8, Hans-Wolfgang Arndt, Kristian Fischer and Thomas Fetzer, *Europarecht* (C.F. Müller 2010) 28.

to telecommunication infrastructure below competition law thresholds. Asymmetric ex ante access provisions guaranteed access to telecommunication services to all parts of the country (regardless of low-cost or high-cost customers). The costs were unilaterally borne by the incumbents in the very beginning.[53]

This – asymmetric – universal service obligation left the incumbents with competitive disadvantages, particularly as other competitors could freely choose to only provide services to low-cost customers.[54] This was justified, because there was – similar to the open standardisation cases – already an indispensability of the facility that did not stem entirely from the undertakings' endeavours. The facility was derived from a state monopoly, which is not necessarily the case in a typical B2B data sharing context.[55] Throughout the years, however, technical developments and innovations in the telecommunication markets increased competition and reduced the need for strong market regulation. The open-access regulatory approach transitioned to a strategy of deregulation, which seeks to limit access regulation to abuse-of-dominance cases. It is thus now focused on realigning sector-specific access regimes with the general competition law thresholds, emphasising the need for protecting investment incentives of undertakings.[56]

This analysis shows that the trend over time has been towards granting broader access. Nonetheless the economic criteria outlined above should not be overseen and be well aligned with the prevailing view of the European competition law case law if it comes to data access market regulation.[57] Utilities regulation – under data as infrastructure considerations –

53 On the development of telecommunication regulation in light of privatisation and harmonisation see Thomas Fetzer, *Staat und Wettbewerb in dynamischen Märkten* (Mohr Siebeck 2013) 145.

54 See Peter Alexiadis and Martin Cave, 'Regulation and Competition Law in Telecommunications and Other Network Industries' in Robert Baldwin, Martin Cave and Martin Lodge (eds), *The Oxford Handbook of Regulation* (2010) 500, 504–506.

55 In this context, however, it again depends on the data at stake. The case needs to be differently assessed in Public Sector Information cases for instance.

56 See Art. 8(5) lit. d), Directive 2009/140/EC of the European Parliament and of the Council of 25 November 2009 on a common regulatory framework for electronic communications networks and services [2009] OJ L337/37. On the antinomy of regulation and competition law in natural monopoly cases see Ernst-Joachim Mestmäcker, 'Private Macht – Grundsatzfragen in Recht, Wirtschaft und Gesellschaft' in Florian Möslein (ed.), *Private Macht* (Mohr Siebeck 2016) 25, 42.

57 This was already emphasised by the European Commission in its Communication on Building a European Data Economy. Despite outlining the need for enhanced

typically build on natural monopoly market failures and thus can only serve as a reference point in similar cases.

It should be kept in mind that under specific dynamic competition considerations and the theory of contestability, a broader access regime under which the licensing of data tackles incontestable market dominance of the current undertakings with paramount importance for competition across markets seems justified.[58] This approach should not be mixed up with mere policy considerations of directly spurring other public interests (i.e. interoperability in order to further create intra-standard innovations).[59] In this case, competition law runs the risk of being instrumentalised as a tool of direct market intervention, which eventually marginalises the undertakings' interests to further invest and illegitimately hampers the core function of markets, namely to establish efficient product allocation and dynamic competition that leads to innovation – this applies to data-driven innovation too.[60]

It should be further noted that factual data exclusivity may also become relevant under a fundamental rights perspective, notably with regard to the right of intellectual property, Article 17(2), (1) CFR – where data is protected subject matter of IP rights[61] – and the right to freely conduct a business, Article 16 CFR. This not only refers to the question of granting access or not, but also to the right of exploiting the granting of access.[62] Thus, before defining too heavy-handed access modalities one needs to consider that this further contradicts the principle of contractual freedom, may infringe the undertakings' fundamental rights and may lead to distor-

---

data access, the relevant legitimate interests, as well as the need to protect trade secrets, would need to be taken into account. See Communication from the Commission of 10 January 2017 to the European Parliament, the Council, the European Economic and Social Committee and the Committee of the Regions – 'Building a European data economy' COM(2007) 9 final, 13.

58 Cf. Carsten Herresthal, 'Private Macht im Vertragsrecht – Austauschverträge', in Florian Möslein, *Private Macht* (Mohr Siebeck2016) 146, 157.

59 Cf. Wolfgang Kerber and Heike Schweitzer, 'Interoperability in the Digital Economy' (2017) 8 Journal of Intellectual Property, Information Technology and E-Commerce Law 39, paras 1, 71–75.

60 Walter Eucken, *Die Grundlagen der Nationalökonomie* (1947, 9th edn, Springer 1989) 313; Claus-Wilhelm Canaris, 'Wandlungen des Schuldvertragsrechts – Tendenzen zu seiner "Materialisierung"' (2000) 200 Archiv für civilistische Praxis 273, 293.

61 Cf. Drexl (n. 12) paras 42–61.

62 Rolf H. Weber and Florent Thouvenin, 'Dateneigentum und Datenzugangsrechte – Bausteine der Informationsgesellschaft?' (2018) 137 Revue de Droit Suisse 43, 70–72.

tions of efficient data allocation driven by non-market forces. Therefore, even a FRAND licensing obligation should be considered with due caution as it should only be applied once the competitive process is really at stake and private autonomy jeopardised.[63]

II. Industrial policy-driven market regulation and the principle of free market economy – a call for more market-driven innovation

The abovementioned considerations unveil the underlying issue of which respective roles the EU and states should play in regulating the economy. One of the goals of the EU is to establish an internal market that is based on balanced economic growth and price stability and a highly competitive social market economy that promotes technological advancement and aims for a high level of protection and improvement of the quality of the environment, according to Article 3(3) TEU. Article 119(1) TFEU specifies that the EU and its Member States should achieve this in accordance with the principle of an open market economy with free competition. This – at least under a liberal reading – should guarantee a separation of powers between states and the economy. It should not only reduce the competences of the EU and the correlating abandonment of state sovereignty in the EU integration process but it should also limit the capability of Member States to pursue their own industrial policies by modelling and centrally planning their own economy detached from the requirement of competitive market processes.[64] Indeed, it has to be noted that the principle of an open market system lacks normative strength and according to the CJEU consti-

---

63 In *Microsoft*, the General Court stated that 'the mere fact that the contested decision requires that the conditions to which any licences are subject be reasonable and non-discriminatory does not mean that Microsoft must impose the same conditions on every undertaking seeking such licence.' See Case T-201/04 *Microsoft v. Commission* [2007] ECR II-3602 = ECLI:EU:T:2007:289, para. 811. On the role of competition law as a safeguard of private autonomy and on advocating for an order-principled design of market rules and competition as a social institution see Franz Böhm, 'Freiheit und Ordnung in der Marktwirtschaft' (1971) ORDO 11, 20; Franz Böhm, 'Privatrechtsgesellschaft und Marktwirtschaft' (1966) ORDO 75, 140.

64 On the theory of economic constitution and the functionality of harmonisation in the internal market see Ernst-Joachim Mestmäcker, 'Soziale Marktwirtschaft und Europäisierung des Rechts' in Ernst-Joachim Mestmäcker (ed.), *Wirtschaft und Verfassung in der Europäischen Union* (Nomos 2003) 294. Peter-Christian Müller-Graff, 'Die wettbewerbsverfasste Marktwirtschaft als gemeineuropäisches

tutes neither a justiciable right of individuals nor a general obligation of Member States to comply with that principle.[65] Moreover, the EU treaties particularly with regard to the fundamental freedoms still give Member States a right to national limitations. Therefore, a mere liberal interpretation of this principle which does not take the social aspect of the market economy into account falls short of giving a conclusive answer to the question of what normative findings can be drawn from the open market economy principle.[66] Yet it should be borne in mind that markets are constituted by the consent of economic citizens to individual transactions and typically do not require centralised coordination in the sense of a centrally planned economy. The legal foundation of markets consists in the freedom-of-contract principle, which is safeguarded by competition law.[67] Decentralised decision making between the parties of the contract is to be favoured because individual economic preferences of numerous economic agents would be outvoted in a centralised decision-making process, and this would contradict the principles of individual freedom and self-determination, which are also enshrined in Articles 6, 16 and 17 CFR.[68]

Applying this principle of an open market and competition system to the question of how to regulate access to data one should note that the EU or states should refrain from directly innovation-enabling ex ante regu-

---

Verfassungsprinzip' in Peter-Christian Müller Graff and Eibe Riedel (eds), *Gemeinsames Verfassungsrecht in der Europäischen Union* (Nomos 1998) 53, 58.

65 Case 126/86 *Giménez Zaera* [1987] I-3697 = ECLI:EU:C:1987:395, para 10. The German Federal Constitutional Court further argued that the principle of free competition is only located within the operative part of the EU treaties and thus should not be the prevailing one, but can accordingly be balanced with other welfare goals of Member States. See German Constitutional Court, 30 June 2009, Cases 2 BvE 2/08 and others [2009] Entscheidungen des Bundesverfassungsgerichts 267, para. 396. Yet scholars argue that the economic constitutional dimension of this principle stems from the entrenchment of the market freedoms in the competition rules and the fact that it is clearly stated within Art. 3(2) TEU. See on this Ulrich Immenga and Ernst-Joachim Mestmäcker, 'Die Bedeutung der Wettbewerbsregeln in der Verfassung der EU' in Ulrich Immenga and Ernst-Joachim Mestmäcker (eds), *EU-Wettbewerbsrecht* (C.H. Beck 2012) 1, 20.

66 See on this and competition law as part of the European Constitution, Josef Drexl, 'Competition Law as Part of the European Constitution' in Armin von Bogdandy and Jürgen Bast (eds), *Principles of European Constitutional Law* (Hart, C.H.Beck, Nomos 2010) 633, 642. Alfred Müller-Armack, 'Die Wirtschaftsordnungen sozial gesehen' (1948) ORDO 125.

67 Franz Böhm, *Wirtschaftsverfassung und Staatsverfassung* (Mohr Siebeck 1950) 50–51; Böhm, 'Privatrechtsgesellschaft und Marktwirtschaft' (n. 63) 92.

68 See Drexl (n. 66) 660. It has to be noted that there are also direct market regulatory tools in the EU, e.g. agricultural policy.

lation going beyond merely safeguarding the well-functioning of open competitive markets. Libertarian market considerations build their assumptions on the fact that under conditions of effective competition, rule-based economic freedoms of action lead to results that correspond to positive general welfare effects.[69] One of the prerequisites of a competition system is thereby the primacy of exclusivity and imperfect knowledge that is usually constituted by a property system or factual exclusivity combined with contractual freedoms that are primary enablers of markets and that are again framed by regulation that safeguards the competitive process (freedom of competition) per se.[70] Under these circumstances markets evolve spontaneously and usually regulate themselves.[71] Competition is thereby an incentive for innovation and a means to discover new innovations.[72] This still applies regardless of the introduction of the more economic approach and the new utilitarian and neo-classical welfare economics in the EU competition law framework in the early 2000s. Indeed, the static models that build on different efficiency criteria may define expected welfare outcomes and therefore may better detect individual welfare-reducing behaviour.[73] This does not mean that the more economic approach simply renders the principle of an open market economy with free competition characterised by an evolutionary competitive process obsolete.[74] Therefore, one should be cautious when directly regulating innovation-enabling open data access instead of only safeguarding competitive markets per se. Granting too broad access – similar to the public domain consideration in IP laws – may de facto destroy one of the prerequisites of markets and competition, namely the excludability of others. This in turn may not only en-

69 Ernst-Joachim Mestmäcker, 'Europäische Wirtschaftsverfassung' in (2009) *Handwörterbuch des Europäischen Privatrechts* Part 2 <hwb-eup2009.mpipriv.de/index.php/Europäische_Wirtschaftsverfassung> accessed 31 August 2020.

70 Eucken (n. 60) 256; Böhm, *Wirtschaftsverfassung und Staatsverfassung* (n. 67) 50.

71 Friedrich A. von Hayek, 'Der Wettbewerb als Entdeckungsverfahren' in Friedrich A. von Hayek (ed.) *Freiburger Studien* (Mohr Siebeck 1969) 249.

72 Ibid.

73 Mestmäcker (n. 56) 25, 39.

74 Cf. Viktor Vanberg, 'Consumer Welfare, 'Total Welfare and Economic Freedom – On the Normative Foundations of Competition Policy' (2009) Freiburg Discussion Papers on Constitutional Economics 09/3 <www.econstor.eu/bitstream/10419/36471/1/617387532.pdf> accessed 31 August 2020.

danger the entire competitive process, it also may constitute a shift towards a more industrial policy-driven stance of direct market intervention.[75]

III. Adverse effects of data sharing for consumer sovereignty, privacy and innovation

Digitisation and the increasing use of big data combined with the widespread use of ML have led to new challenges that also affect information-specific power asymmetries between undertakings and consumers. In the privacy discussion of the digital economy regarding personal data, one of the most heatedly debated issues is whether consumers as users of internet-based services are capable of making rational and/or well-informed decisions about their data. This in turn has raised the legal issue of whether the contractual arrangements that are offered to them sufficiently protect consumers or whether markets suffer from a market failure due to information asymmetries and related behavioural issues of consumers, i.e. adverse selection and irrationality (or the so-called privacy paradox).[76] Empirical research has shown that along with advancements that have made technologies more and more privacy intrusive, one can observe a growing number of people willing to reveal personal data.[77] This has already led to

---

75 This is why in the latest phase of de-regulation of the telecommunication sector in 2003 and particularly from 2009 onwards, competition law has been juxtaposed to the EU's regulatory policy; cf. section B.I.2. above.

76 Applying Akerlof's example of market of lemons to data markets, the level of data protection as a value parameter of the offered service can only serve its purpose if the consumer understands what data protection really means. According to most recent empirical findings in relation to the economics of data, most consumers are aware of data protection but they simply do not care about their privacy anymore. This however leads to a market similar to those in Akerlof's example, namely one that does not make a higher quality service – meaning a service which offers a higher level of data protection – economically useful. This eventually leads to a market that only offers the minimum standard of data protection required. George A. Akerlof, 'The market for Lemons: Quality Uncertainty and the Market Mechanism' (1970) 84 Quarterly Journal of Economics 488. On the privacy paradox see Spyros Kokolakis, 'Privacy attitudes and privacy behaviour: A review of current research on the privacy paradox phenomenon' (2015) 64 Computers & Society 122; Laura Brandimarte and Alessandro Acquisti, 'The Economics of Privacy' in Martin Peitz and Joel Waldfogel (eds) *The Oxford Handbook of the Digital Economy* (OUP 2012) 1, 14.

77 Daniel J. Solove, 'A Taxonomy of Privacy' (2006) 154 University of Pennsylvania Law Review 477.

the introduction of the purpose limitation and transparency duties in the GDPR in order to better inform consumers about the purpose and conditions for future use of those data. Nevertheless, individuals may still be subject to bounded rationality and therefore end up not protecting their privacy.[78] This issue of information asymmetries with regard to the use of data may be even more complex in times of AI.

The emergence of widespread use of ML has led to better insights into consumers' behaviours and preferences. Human experience as free raw material for translation into behavioural data thereby not only created enormous product or service improvements but also proprietary behavioural surplus, which, fed into ML applications, enabled predictions about consumers.[79] This information resembles a digital reality, which is first of all detached from the traditional rational understanding of information by society and secondly is also detached from its traditional role within a sphere of social communication. Digital technologies led to a bifurcation and dissociation of information and communication.[80] This has consequences for the role of communication in a digital age. Automated algorithmic information selection on the Internet governs a wide spectrum of individual action and creates statistical knowledge that is detached from a social reality. Entire business models and marketing strategies in e-commerce are now built on the creation of ML algorithms that govern or determine what information is found on the Internet,[81] produced,[82] considered relevant for each individual[83] and chosen and/or consumed.[84] Algorithmic selection essentially co-governs the evolution and use of the Internet by influencing the behaviour of individual producers and users, shaping the formation of preferences and decisions in the production and consumption of goods and services.[85] This leads to a construction of reality, a kind of

78 Alessandro Acquisti, 'Nudging Privacy: The Behavioral Economics of Personal Information' in (2010) 7(6) IEEE Security and Privacy Magazine 82.

79 Shoshana Zuboff, *The Age of Surveillance Capitalism – The Fight for a Human Future at the New Frontier of Power* (Public Affairs 2019) 8.

80 Friedrich Kittler, *Optische Medien* (2nd edn, Merve 2011) 26.

81 Search filtering and aggregation applications, e.g. what is indexed by search engines/crawlers.

82 Content production applications like algorithmic journalism.

83 Search and scoring applications; ranking.

84 Recommendation, scoring and allocation applications; both for economic and social choices – ranging from commercial goods to friends and partners.

85 Natascha Just and Michael Latzer, 'Governance by Algorithms: Reality Construction by Algorithmic Selection on the Internet' (2016) 39 Media, Culture & Society 238.

governance marked by the targeted selection or omission of information, which eventually subconsciously shapes the consumers' behaviour.

This has led to the discussion of further introducing soft-paternalistic forms of data protection laws and direct market regulation of digital services in Europe, as under the current GDPR consent by the data subject makes any exploitative processing of data legally permissible and consumers still fail to value their privacy.[86] Moreover, the role of information intermediaries and their economic power is under particular scrutiny in the current platform regulation debate.[87] Despite these effects, algorithmic governance[88] may also have an impact on the innovation capacities within an algorithmic society. As already outlined above, applying the knowledge inferred from behavioural data of consumers always implies that individuals are categorised in different groups under which attention markets and the respective products and services are then 'individually' modulated. Despite great advantages that come with the use of ML in the Internet and e-commerce, it should also be considered whether it leaves the targeted consumer with enough possibility of alternative choices. Choice is usually safeguarded in efficient, competitive markets, as market forces that are driven by individuals' pursuit of self-interest lead to static and dynamic forms of competition. In this setting, markets typically generate an array of different products and services that reflect the need of the demand side.[89] Yet algorithmic governance (or increasing widespread technological ad-

---

86 This is well-known under the so-called privacy paradox. Cf. Acquisti (n. 78) 82–85; Frederik J. Zuiderveen Borgesius, 'Behavioural Sciences and the Regulation of Privacy in the Internet' in Alberto Alemanno and Anne-Lise Sibony (eds), *Nudge and the Law: A European Perspective* (Hart Publishing2015) 179; Christoph Krönke, 'Datenpaternalismus – Staatliche Interventionen im Online-Datenverkehr zwischen Privaten' (2016) 55 Der Staat 319.

87 Crémer and others (n. 5) 54–60.

88 Cf. Antoinette Rouvroy, 'Technology, virtuality and utopia: Governmentality in an age of autonomic computing' in Mireille Hildebrandt and Antoinette Rouvroy (eds), *Law, Human Agency and Automatic Computing* (Routledge 2011) 119, 135–41; Marc Amstutz, 'Dateneigentum – Funktion und Form' (2018) 218 Archiv für civilistische Praxis 438, 445–551; Wolfgang Hoffmann-Riem, 'Verhaltenssteuerung durch Algorithmen – Eine Herausforderung für das Recht' (2017) Archiv des öffentlichen Rechts 1.

89 On the very notion of free markets and their forces see Adam Smith, *An Inquiry into the Nature and Causes of the Wealth of Nations* (University of Chicago Press 1976, first published 1776): 'By directing that industry in such a manner as its produce may be of greatest value, he intends only his own gain, and he is in this, as in many other cases, led by an invisible hand to promote and end which was no part of his intention.'.

vancements) seems to reduce the various forms of demand in a pluralistic society. Personalisation stems from a mere prediction created by machines that analyse past behaviour. This however means that consumers are already bound by their personal past and potentially cannot simply make a new choice. Indeed, according to the ambiguity aversion and the Ellsberg paradox, humans generally tend to choose the known instead of the unknown.[90] This however, does not mean that humans should be deprived of other non-personalised product and service choices. Another factor to be borne in mind is that personalised services and products only resemble the categorical social stratification established by the ML analysis of the behavioural data and their categorisation. This may in the very end shape the society overall and may deteriorate a pluralistic one. Societal plurality in turn may be one of the sources of innovation. In the final analysis, technological advancement runs the risk of causing negative externalities where too wide access regimes for personal data have the potential to decrease consumer sovereignty and eventually innovation capacities of markets.

IV. Adverse effects of data sharing on competition and innovation

Too broad data access regimes could also distort competition and may even have adverse effects on innovation in the long run. From a competition point of view, information embedded in data becomes relevant under two different considerations. First, data sharing may create too much market transparency, which could lead to anti-competitive (tacitly) collusive practices.[91] Second, the information in data can also provide an advantage for undertakings that distorts competition. The combination of non-exclusively held information from several sources may provide certain already data-rich undertakings with additional knowledge that, due to data-specific economies of scope and scale, other competitors may not be able to reach. This may reduce both static and dynamic competition not only in markets where the digital conglomerates are already present but also across other markets.[92]

90 Jürgen Eichberger, David Kelsey and Burkhard C. Schipper, 'Ambiguity and social interaction' (2009) 61 Oxford Economic Papers 355.

91 See Ariel Ezrachi and Maurice E. Stucke, 'Sustainable and Unchallenged Algorithmic Tacit Collusion' (2020) 17 Northwestern Journal of Technology and Intellectual Property Law 218.

92 It has already been subjected to scrutiny in the EC merger control practice whether the concentration of control over valuable and (non-) replicable data re-

As competition is defined as a discovery process (*'Entdeckungsverfahren'*), which builds on a certain degree of imperfect knowledge, high market transparency may simplify coordinated practices and eventually dismantle competition. The use of AI may enable the companies to gain such knowledge that facilitates coordinated practices. As algorithmic collusion also allows for unconscious parallelism, the coordination of market behaviours may even fall outside the scope of Article 101(1) TFEU.[93] Indeed, the anti-competitive effect of broader data access regimes depends on many factors. In markets with more heterogeneous products and services where competition is not simply defined by price parameters real coordinated practices with anti-competitive effects are less likely.[94] The potential increase in market transparency makes a thorough assessment of potential adverse effects of the respective access regime necessary.

If market-dominant undertakings that are of paramount importance for competition across markets are also granted data access, this may give these dominant players such a competitive advantage that it may even render further data access regulation dysfunctional with regard to their innovation enabling function. AI is still predominantly used and developed by a handful of market-dominant companies. Although technological inclusion is already on the policy agenda of the EU and its Member States, particularly SMEs are lagging behind. Digital transformation requires high investment costs. Together with deterrence effects of the dominant incumbents, SMEs may have lesser incentives for further accessing and using data.[95] Thus even though granting access to data does most likely increase the pos-

---

sources may create a significant impediment of efficient competition by either strengthening market power or leveraging their data advantages to other markets and thus create foreclosure concerns. See for example *Apple/Shazam* (Case M.8788) Commission decision of 6 September 2018 C(2018) 5748 final; *Microsoft/LinkedIn* (Case M.8124) Commission decision of 6 December 2016 C(2016) 8404 final; *Facebook/WhatsApp* (Case M.7217) Commission decision of 3 October 2014 C(2014) 7239 final; *Telefónica UK/Vodafone* (Case M.6314) Commission decision of 4 September 2012 C(2012) 6063 final. Cf. Jörg Hoffmann and German Johannson, 'EU Merger Control and Big Data – On Data-specific Theories of Harm and Remedies' (2019) Max Planck Institute for Innovation and Competition Research Paper No. 19–05 9–29 <https://papers.ssrn.com/sol3/papers.cfm?abstract_id=3364792> accessed 31 August 2020.

93 OECD, 'Algorithms and Collusion: Competition Policy in the Digital Age' (OECD 2017) 51.

94 Cf. *Gencor/Lonrho* (Case IV/M.619) Commission Decision of 24 April 1996 [1997] OJ L11/30, para. 141.

95 In its Communication on AI the European Commission already stated that it will facilitate access to AI of all potential users, especially small and medium-sized en-

sibility for all firms to (theoretically) benefit from new data-driven innovation and AI technologies, the dominant incumbents may benefit disproportionately more. Data is one of the key components of AI applications. Enhanced data access will give them insights in consumer preferences that are relevant for succeeding in other market segments. Data access may thus strengthen the economic power of the dominant incumbents, which could have negative effects on static and dynamic competition in the long run.

Indeed, particularly in the case of digital conglomerates, undertakings often not only hold a dominant position on the individual platform or network market but they also have the resources and the strategic positioning to enable them to exert significant influence on the business activities of third parties or to expand their own business activities into ever new markets and sectors. This is also one of the reasons why markets of the digital economy already show strong and rapidly emerging concentration tendencies. Contrary to the expected market dynamism in digital platform markets,[96] platform-specific network effects together with the data advantages and associated self-reinforcing effects have led to a tipping effect whereby the digital conglomerates seem to win entire markets.[97] These circum-

terprises, companies from non-tech sectors and public administrations, to the latest technologies and encourage them to test AI as they are the ones simply not using it. See Communication from the Commission of 25 April 2018 to the European Parliament, the Council, the European Economic and Social Committee and the Committee of the Regions – 'Artificial Intelligence for Europe' COM(2018) 237 final, 8.

96 The European Commission's merger practice has been built on the traditional error cost framework that favoured false negatives and seemed to be particularly relevant in the consumer communication sector. In the merger of *Facebook/WhatsApp* for instance, the Commission cleared the merger and stated that 'the consumer communications sector is a recent and fast growing sector which is characterised by frequent market entry and short innovation cycles [...]. In this market high market shares are not necessarily indicative of market power and, therefore, of lasting damage to competition.' *Facebook/WhatsApp* (Case COMP/M.7217) Commission decision of 3 October 2014 C(2014) 7239 final; para. 99. Latest studies show, however, that this was a wrong assumption and the predicted market disruptions have not occurred. There has been a general tendency towards less dynamism in platform markets and a higher likelihood of concentration tendencies in digital markets not only leading to static efficiencies but also creating dynamic costs. See Crémer and others (n. 5) 4; Jason Furman and others, 'Unlocking digital competition – Report of the Digital Competition Expert Panel' (2019) 4 <https://assets.publishing.service.gov.uk/government/uploads/system/uploads/attachment_data/file/785547/unlocking_digital_competition_furman_review_web.pdf> accessed 31 August 2021.

97 Ibid.

stances together with additional economies of scale and enormous resources of the incumbents have already led to strong market positions, which seem to cause both static and dynamic costs.[98] The increasing market concentration may also lead to a higher static productive efficiency, which could outweigh losses in both static allocative efficiency and dynamic efficiency, and thus no intervention in increasing concentration tendencies is needed. Yet it seems that high concentration in digital markets causes static costs as it may reduce effective prices for consumers, reduce choice or affect quality.[99] Although most of the services may be free of charge, consumers in more dynamic markets might have given up less in terms of privacy or might have been paid for their data.[100] Even beyond considerations specific to the platform market, it has become apparent that individual companies occupy central strategic positions with their products and services. Moreover, they create a wide range of dependencies on other market participants that allow the companies to distort the competitive process to their own advantage and to leverage their market power to other adjacent markets.[101] Together with the creation of interrelated products and increased consumption synergies, this further increases switching costs for consumers and has led to the creation of so-called digital ecosystems.[102] The digital ecosystem combined with a strategy of early elimination of potential rivals through start-up acquisition is not only consolidating the incumbents' strong market position but may also further increase entry barriers for rivals on the same or adjacent markets and segments – potentially even on market segments where the incumbent is currently not present.[103] This in turn could then impede innovation as larger companies have less to fear from new entrants. Even if companies consider entering markets, many new entrants are not scaling up in the long run, as they simply cannot compete with the dominant market power of digital conglomerates and are thus already deterred from further investing in

98 Ibid.

99 Ibid.

100 Ibid.

101 Cf. Massimo Motta and Martin Peitz, 'Big Tech Mergers' (2020) Collaborative Research Center TR 224 Discussion Paper No. 147, 26–29, 30, 31–33, 34 <www.crctr224.de/en/research-output/discussion-papers/discussion-papers#DP147> accessed 31 August 2020.

102 Ibid. 29, on the negative effects of one-stop-shopping and consumption synergies.

103 Ibid. 4–9. The issue of killer acquisitions or killer zones is the subject of current competition policy discussions. See e.g. Crémer (n. 5) 110.

R&D.[104] This on the other hand leads to a reduction of further innovation incentives for market-dominant incumbents.[105] This may render the role of innovation competition less relevant for succeeding in markets and thus may reduce both static and dynamic competition by non-contestable digital conglomerates.

This issue may be further amplified as the general rules on ex post abuse control under the current competition laws may fall short of adequately dealing with the increased risk of vertical and conglomerate exploitation of economic power. Even though the actual effects of such conduct may lead to market foreclosures (i.e. via platform envelopment[106]) if the changes that create these high market entry are merely structural in nature, they fall outside the scope of control. This led to the current debate about the future competition policy for both the EU and its Member States. Thereby the reconciliation of competition on the merits on the one hand and the goal of competition law to also protect the competition process as such, on the other, needs to be thoroughly assessed. In this context, the demarcation line between direct market regulation of digital conglomerates and a general competition law framework becomes increasingly blurred.

The current European legislative endeavours under the Digital Markets Act and the German legislature have already considered preventing digital

---

104 Carl Shapiro, 'Competition and Innovation: Did Arrow Hit the Bull's Eye?' in Josh Lerner and Scott Stern (eds), *The Rate and Direction of Inventive Activity* (University of Chicago Press 2011) 361, 364.

105 Cf. Arrow (n. 18) 620. Put differently, the secure monopolist's incentive to achieve a process innovation is less than that of a competitive firm because the monopolist with lower costs will merely replace itself, while the competitive firm will (by assumption) take over the market, in which it previously earned no economic profits. See also on the 'replacement effect' Jean Tirole, *The Theory of Industrial Organization* (MIT Press1988) 392–98.

106 Platform envelopment is a common and widespread phenomenon with significant implications for the evolution of platform and intermediation markets. Envelopment entails entry by one platform provider into another's market by bundling its own platform's functionality with that of the target so as to leverage shared user relationships and common components. Dominant firms, which are otherwise sheltered from entry by stand-alone rivals due to network effects and high switching costs, can be vulnerable to an adjacent platform provider's envelopment attack and this can eventually lead to a market tipping for the platform. See on this Thomas Eisenmann, Geoffrey Parker and Marshall Van Alstyne, 'Platform Envelopment' (2011) 32 Strategic Management Journal 1270, 1271. For an example in the retail banking and payments sector see Miguel de la Mano and Jorge Padilla, 'Big Tech Banking' (2018) 14 Journal of Competition Law & Economics 494, 504–506.

conglomerates from using their foreclosing strategies so as to ultimately safeguard other companies' ability to compete for market shares and customers by competitive means.[107] This led to the call for specific restrictions on certain conducts of digital conglomerates that are typically used to further consolidate their ecosystems across markets.[108] Along this line, the 10th amendment of the German Act Against Restraints of Competition (GWB) entails a pro-active preventive control regime for undertakings of paramount importance for competition across markets.

Art. 19a GWB establishes a three-step control regime that first of all gives the German Federal Cartel Office (BKartA) the power to ascertain an undertaking's superior economic power[109] and its particular relevance for competition across markets. Once such a position is ascertained, these undertakings are subject to the special obligations to refrain from certain conduct.[110] Ultimately the laws provide for an efficiency justification where the burden of proof lies with the undertakings. The laws further set out the obligation to refrain from creating or consolidating further entry barriers with regard to data.[111] Here the role of data access rights becomes particularly relevant as the official grounds of the law explicitly refer to 'digital conglomerates' further data access sources as one of the reasons for further foreclosure scenarios.[112]

This is exactly where another tension between data access and exclusivity arises. A too broad access regime could eventually favour dominant in-

---

107 See Crémer and others (n. 5) and Report of the German Wettbewerbskommission 4.0, 'Ein neuer Wettbewerbsrahmen für die Digitalwirtschaft' (2019) paras 9–11 <www.bmwi.de/Redaktion/DE/Publikationen/Wirtschaft/bericht-der-kommission-wettbewerbsrecht-4-0.pdf?__blob=publicationFile&v=12> accessed 31 August 2020.

108 Ibid.

109 Which goes beyond the traditional dominant market power assessment.

110 Sec. 19a(2) GWB-new. Gesetz zur Änderung des Gesetzes gegen Wettbewerbsbeschränkungen für ein fokussiertes, proaktives und digitales Wettbewerbsrecht 4.0 und anderer Bestimmung (GWB-Digitalisierungsgesetz) Gesetz von 01.01.2021 – Bundesgesetzblatt Teil I 2021 Nr. 1 von 18 Januar 2021. Cf. Gesetzentwurf der Bundesregierung – Entwurf eines Gesetzes zur Änderung des Gesetzes gegen Wettbewerbsbeschränkungen für ein fokussiertes, proaktives und digitales Wettbewerbsrecht 4.0 und anderer wettbewerbsrechtlicher Bestimmungen (GWB-Digitalisierungsgesetz) (9 September 2020) 15 <www.bmwi.de/Redaktion/DE/Downloads/Gesetz/gesetzentwurf-gwb-digitalisierungsgesetz.pdf?__blob=publicationFile&v=6> accessed 15 September 2020.

111 Sec. 19a(2) No. 3 (ibid.).

112 Bill of the Federal Government on the 10th amendment of the German Act Against Restraints on Competition (GWB) (n. 111) 84.

cumbents and may fall short of maintaining competition in the long run. It is crucial that the long-term effects of such access regimes are thoroughly considered. Accordingly, one can think of three potential ways forward. The first is the implementation of a competition control regime as already outlined above that potentially bars digital conglomerates from access. In this case, however, the conflict between the envisaged access regimes and the control regime of digital conglomerates needs to be resolved. To this end, the general competition law control regime needs to be applicable in sector-specific access regimes and needs to prevail. Moreover, the administrative responsibilities and collaboration between the NCAs and the specific supervisory agencies need to be adjusted. The second option would be to formulate asymmetric sector-specific access rights that bar already data-rich incumbents from relying on the access rights unless they can prove efficiency. This solution may also depend on the adjustment of the relationship between horizontal and sector-specific access regimes and may make the balancing of different regulatory goals necessary. The third option would entail an asymmetric reciprocity clause that makes the reciprocal sharing of data mandatory.[113]

C. *Evaluation of the data access regimes for digital payment services*

The access regimes enshrined in the PSD2 relate to both the public interest of further increasing competition and innovation in the payments market and the private interests of customers to make use of certain innovative payment services. This is important when assessing to what extent the sector-specific access regimes of the PSD2 considered the regulatory principles for enhancing data-driven innovation outlined above. This may not only make both a public and/or private law regulatory approach possible, it also may cause certain tensions when a right of the payment service user to make use of certain innovative payment services – enshrined in contract laws - is contradictory to a necessary data governance approach that safeguards innovation. This contribution outlines that private interests need to be duly reconciled with the public interest of safeguarding competition and thus innovation in the payments markets. This will ultimately increase consumer welfare and thus better benefit the customers in the long run.

113 Fabiana Di Porto and Gustavo Ghidini, 'I access your data, you access mine: Requiring data reciprocity in payment services' (2020) 51 International Review of Intellectual Property and Competition Law 307, 319–27.

There are two different innovation capacities in the payments sector. Increasing innovation in financial technology (FinTech) or payments technology (PayTech) and the evolution of retail banking prompted by Open Banking.

As one of the key concepts of new digital business models builds upon customer-centricity that is particularly demand side-driven by the generation of millennials, the role of market forces to foster demand side-driven innovation seems to already serve as an incentive for traditional incumbents to further innovate.[114] A look at the global FinTech investments as early as 2015 and the FinTech-specific IPOs, with companies such as PayPal, Square, WorldPay and First Data achieving multi-billion-dollar market capitalisations – larger than many traditional incumbent financial institutions, seems to support this assumption. Therefore the question inevitably arising is what role the legislature should (have) play(ed) in further accelerating the surge of FinTech companies in the increasingly data and technology-driven payments markets.[115] In the US, for example, the legislature abstained from direct innovation-enabling regulation and focused its regulatory interventions on specific consumer protection laws and financial supervisory laws.[116] In Europe, however, the disruptive market penetration of (independent) FinTech providers and the FinTech innovation capabilities of incumbents traditionally seemed to lag behind the global trends, particularly those in the US.[117] This led to a more industrial policy-driven, innovation-enabling regulatory approach in the EU that

114 Alex Lipton, David Shier and Alex Pentland, 'Digital Banking Manifesto: The end of banks?' (MIT 2016) 6 <www.getsmarter.com/blog/wp-content/uploads/2017/07/mit_digital_bank_manifesto_report.pdf> accessed 31 August 2020; PwC, 'Blurred Lines: How FinTech is shaping financial services – Global Fintech Report' (2016) 8 <www.pwc.de/de/newsletter/finanzdienstleistung/assets/insurance-inside-ausgabe-4-maerz-2016.pdf> accessed 31 August 2020. Though see for the issue of consumer inertia Amelia Fletcher, 'Disclosure as a tool for enhancing consumer engagement and competition' (2019) Behavioural Public Policy 4.

115 Accenture, 'Fintech and the evolving landscape: landing points for the industry (2016) 3 <www.accenture.com/t20161011T031409Z_w_/pl-en/_acnmedia/PDF-15/Accenture-Fintech-Evolving_landscape.pdf> accessed 31 August 2020.

116 Cf. Diana Milanesi, 'A new banking paradigm: the state of open banking in Europe, the United Kingdom and the United States' (2017) TTLF Working Paper No. 29, 26–30 <https://law.stanford.edu/publications/a-new-banking-paradigm-the-state-of-open-banking-in-europe-the-united-kingdom-and-the-united-states/> accessed 31 August 2020.

117 Gregor Dorfleitner and Lars Hornuf, 'Neue digitale Akteure und ihre Rolle in der Finanzwirtschaft – Eine Analyse des deutschen Marktes unter besonderer Berücksichtigung von Datenschutzaspekten' (abida 2018) 8 <www.abida.de/sites

should create more competition in a market with concentrations tendencies.

By introducing asymmetric regulation, the potential un-contestable competition advantages of already existent incumbents should be offset. By reducing the high regulatory entry barriers with a special licence for third-party payment providers (TPPs) and by introducing the access-to-account rules – strengthening consumer engagement by directly outlining the rights of payment services users and indirectly of TPPs – should force incumbents to enable data-driven FinTech services. The laws enshrined in the PSD2 aim to provide not only a level playing field in the payments market but also directly spur innovation.[118] The question remains, however, whether the PSD2 is not putting traditional incumbents at such a disadvantage that it will diminish innovation incentives and unduly infringe their right of freely conducting a business. This again leads back to the very question of whether a market failure existed and whether ex ante market regulation or a more flexible competition law solution would have been the right response for tackling foreclosure scenarios by factual (data) exclusivities in the payments market.

I. Payment initiation services

1. Overview

With regard to new front-end payment services or products, payment initiation services (PISs) proved to be efficient, not only reducing transaction costs for consumers but also enabling e-commerce for consumers without payment cards or other digital forms of payment.[119] PIS providers (PISPs) are FinTech companies that offer low-cost solutions for consumers to pay instantly for their online transactions. These online services enter a user's payment account to initiate the transfer of funds between the user's account and the merchant's account with the user's consent, and inform the merchant once the transaction has been initiated and funds are on their way. This is done by establishing a software bridge between the website of the merchant and the online banking platform of the payer's account at

/default/files/Gutachten_ABIDA_Neue_Digitale_Akteure_Finanzwirtschaft.pdf> accessed 31 August 2020.

118 Emphasis added by the author. See Recitals 4, 33 PSD2 (n. 10).

119 See Recital 27 PSD2 (n. 10).

the account servicing payment service provider (ASPSP) via application programming interfaces (APIs). What is crucial to note is that access to the user's payment account, and thus typically cooperation between ASPSPs and the PISP, is needed.

At this point, the PSD2 sets out the obligation for ASPSPs to grant access by executing payment orders initiated through PISPs on the condition that the customer has given explicit consent and that the account is accessible online.[120] Such obligation does not depend on any existing contractual relationship between the ASPSPs and the PISPs and is not dependent on typical competition law thresholds. Moreover, ASPSPs must treat all the payment orders transmitted through the services of a PISP 'without any discrimination other than for objective reasons, in particular in terms of timing, priority or charges vis-à-vis payment orders transmitted directly by the payer'.[121] Accordingly, the intermediation service conducted by PISPs should not be dealt with differently with regard to charges for directly transmitted payment orders. Indeed, this means that unless there are any objective reasons, no additional charges should be collected from the accounts holder.[122] Therefore, the PIS is not free stricto sensu, but it is only part of the fixed amount that is already regularly charged by the bank vis-à-vis the account holder.[123] Nevertheless the legal wording is unclear with regard to whether banks can charge an additional fee from the PISPs. 'Without any discrimination vis-à-vis payment orders transmitted directly by the payer' could be interpreted in two ways – no additional charges at all or merely no additional charges vis-à-vis the customers. The wording only refers to the legal relationship between the customer and the ASPSP. It does not refer to any legal relationship between an intermediary and the ASPSPs. From a legal systematic and dogmatic point of view, the implementation of the access obligation in private or public laws may further clarify this point.

In a first line of thought, – within a private law solution – the non-discriminatory access obligation that defines the scope of duties under the framework contract between banks and their customers may also define the obligations of the ASPSs in relation to the PISPs. This obligation is

120 Arts 66(1), (4), 64(1) PSD2 (n. 10).

121 Art. 66(4) lit. c) PSD2 (n. 10).

122 Art. 66(4) lit. c) PSD2 (n. 10).

123 See Dutch Authority for Consumers & Markets, 'Fintechs in the payment system: the risk of foreclosure – Report' (2017) 35 <www.acm.nl/sites/default/files/documents/2018-02/acm-study-fintechs-in-the-market-the-risk-of-foreclosure.pdf> accessed 31 August 2020.

bonam partem and thus it would still be in line with privity-of-contract principle. The same modalities as for payment orders transmitted directly by the account holder should apply, which means that the ASPSPs should grant access to PISPs without additional charges, unless objectively justified.

The second interpretation – under a public law approach – resembles a traditional compulsory licence obligation known in refusal-to-deal cases. This would restrict the non-discrimination obligation to the fee scheme between bank and costumers, without having any effect on the legal relationship between ASPSPs and PISPs. Accordingly, the PSD2[124] may be implemented by merely setting out an obligation to enter into a licensing contract and the modalities of access could be freely negotiated within the general limitations of excessive pricing under antitrust laws and the data governance provisions – laid down in the financial supervisory laws – applicable in this context. Yet, it has to be noted that the PSD2 does not explicitly set out a right for PISPs. Article 36 PSD2, which outlines a POND (proportionate, objective and non-discriminatory) access regime to payment account services of credit institutes, does not refer to the opening up of account interfaces in PIS cases.

Although not explicitly addressing the legal relationship between the ASPSP and the PISP, the current scholarly debate puts forth arguments for both interpretations.[125] Looking at the implementation of the PSD2, the German legislature implemented the access obligations outlined in the PSD2 in both private and public laws. It outlined the right of the customer (consumer and merchant) to make use of PIS within Germany's special law of obligations pertaining to payment services without the need for ASPSPs and PISPs to enter into a contract.[126] The legislature further out-

124 Art. 66(1) PSD2 (n. 10).

125 See Giuseppe Colangelo and Oscar Borgogno, 'Data, Innovation and Transatlantic Competition in Finance: The Case of the Access to Account Rule' (2019) European Union Law Working Papers No. 35, 16–17 <https://papers.ssrn.com/sol3/papers.cfm?abstract_id=3251584> accessed 31 August 2020; Inge Graef, Martin Husovec and Jasper van den Boom, 'Spill-overs in data governance: the relationship between the GDPR's right to data portability and EU sector-specific data access regimes' (2020) 9(1) Journal of European Consumer and Market Law 3, 12; de la Mano and Padilla (n. 106) 504; Di Porto and Ghidini (n. 113). Colangelo and Borgogno as well as Graef, Husovec and van den Boom argue in favour of possible charges for TPPs. Di Porto and Ghidini as well as de la Mano and Padilla interpret the access provisions as granting free access for TPPs and criticise the lack of remuneration for incumbent banks.

126 Sec. 675f(3) German Civil Code (*BGB*).

lines the duties of ASPSPs and PSPs in the Payments Services Supervision Act, which then refers to the Delegated Regulation concerning Regulatory Technical Standards (RTS Delegated Regulation) that orders the opening up of account interfaces.[127] By implementing the obligations of the different parties involved into both public and private statutory laws, the legislature fails to provide a coherent solution that sufficiently addresses the legal relationship between the ASPSP and PISP. The questions whether the PISP has a right vis-á-vis the ASPSs or whether remuneration can be granted for ASPSPs by the TPPs remain unclear and need further clarification. Yet it should be kept in mind that remuneration should be possible in order to safeguard innovation incentives for incumbent banks.

2. *Non-market-driven FinTech innovation regulation and structural disadvantages of incumbent banks*

Against the backdrop of the role of data exclusivity for incentivising undertakings to further invest in data-driven innovation it firstly has to be acknowledged that payment initiation services build on access to data on two different grounds. First, the PISP needs the information whether the credit transfer has been successfully conducted. Second, this information has to be transmitted in real time, as instant processing of the payment services is one of the key innovation parameters of the offered services. In this sense PIS constitutes a rather technology-driven innovation that needs only a very limited amount of data. The data are essential for the PISPs though, as without immediate confirmation of the credit transfer the e-commerce sale transaction cannot be conducted quickly.

With regard to the investments made, it is not the production or analysis of data but rather the transmission of data that is costly, as the PSD2 together with the RTS Delegated Regulation provide for a data governance regime that should guarantee secure communication via access interfaces.[128] This requires additional investment in in-house IT-infrastructure

127 See Secs 48, 49 German Payment Services Supervision Act (*Zahlungsdiensteaufsichtsgesetz, ZAG*), Art. 36 Commission Delegated Regulation (EU) 2018/389 of 27 November 2017 supplementing Directive (EU) 2015/2366 of the European Parliament and of the Council with regard to regulatory technical standards for strong customer authentication and common and secure open standards of communication [2017] OJ L69/23 (RTS Delegated Regulation).

128 In this context, application programming interfaces (APIs) have been deemed the most reliable and tested technology to facilitate secure and reliable access to

and/or demands closer cooperation with financial technology developers, which eventually may even change the entire value chains of the incumbents.[129] Moreover, the new regulatory framework on payment systems also creates certain risks, which cause costs that traditional banks as incumbents have to address unilaterally. This includes increased operational risk, due to the necessity to allow access to customer payment account (information) and the threat of losing the direct customer interaction on the front end. Incumbent banks will therefore potentially end up as deposit holders for customers ('dump pipes') as they may lose the possibility to fully capture the margins that stem from value-added services within direct customer relations.[130] There are also increased ICT-related, data protection, security and fraud risks as data are shared with third parties, which – although authentication is needed – cannot be freely chosen by banks anymore. The risks stemming from TPPs therefore have to be borne mainly unilaterally by the incumbent banks.[131] These aspects place the banks at an additional disadvantage relative to the TPPs, which are freed from most of the risk and compliance considerations mentioned above and are thus free-riding on the expenses of market incumbents. Moreover, they also do not need to bear the minimum cost of a regulated entity in terms of compliance and capital requirements. Asymmetric regulation with regard to financial supervisory laws further enables the entry of PISPs by establishing a special licence and thus leaves the market incumbents with higher operational costs. This becomes particularly relevant in light of the fact that the PISPs offer a functionally equivalent service that renders the bank and the PISPs competitors aiming for the direct customer relationship and operat-

customers' accounts, even though the technology is not directly mentioned in the directive or the RTS Delegated Regulation. See also Marcos Zachariadis and Pinar Ozcan, 'The API economy and digital transformation in financial services: the case of open banking' (2016) SWIFT Institute Working Paper No. 2016–001, 4 <https://papers.ssrn.com/sol3/papers.cfm?abstract_id=2975199> accessed 31 August 2020.

129 Ibid. 15.

130 See Simonetta Vezzoso, 'Fintech, access to data, and the role of competition policy' in Vicente Bagnoli (ed.) *Competition and Innovation* (Scortecci 2018) 35.

131 See on the risks of Open Banking and the mitigating measures enshrined in the PSD2, Brad Carr, Pablo Urbiola and Adrian Delle-Case, 'Liability and Consumer Protection in Open Banking' (Institute of International Finance 2018) 5 <www.iif.com/portals/0/Files/private/32370132_liability_and_consumer_protection_in_open_banking_091818.pdf> accessed 31 August 2020.

ing on the same market – and not on another (after) market.[132] As the choice to include this asymmetric access regulation in the PSD2 also enables digital conglomerates to enter the market, this puts the market incumbents at a further competitive disadvantage. As outlined above, digital conglomerates have established ecosystems on which to build their businesses. Together with their data superiority, they may end up re-shaping traditional retail banking and payment markets with the risk of further monopolisation in the long run.[133] This in turn would negatively affect one of the regulatory goals of the PSD2, namely the spurring of further innovation to create more competition and thus more financial stability.

The access regulation for PIS deviates from the economic criteria outlined above, whereby welfare-enhancing effects should be achieved through more exclusivity, rather than through open access as the default rule. Although the retail banking and payment sector has always been characterised by lock-in problems, a low elasticity of demand and a general lack of competition, it should also be considered that in the payments market, there have been disruptions despite the lack of access to the customers' accounts. Distributed ledger technology led early on to the creation of virtual currencies, and as already outlined above, other payment providers such as PayPal, Wirecard, Venmo and Klarna were also already existent in the payments markets in Europe before the PSD2 entered into force.[134] Thus it is questionable whether the market really failed due to a lack of competition or whether the reasons for less successful implementation of FinTech services in the European payments markets rather stem from a lack of demand, i.e. the unwillingness of consumers to share their data and to use new payment technologies.[135] In the latter case however, ordering

132 This ultimately depends on the relevant market definition. It seems that customers do not make any difference between third-party payment providers and other means of payment and thus are both operating on the same relevant market.

133 De la Mano and Padilla (n. 106), Eisenmann, Parker and Van Alstyne (n. 106).

134 PwC (n. 114) 12; Joint Committee of the European Supervisory Authorities, 'Joint Committee Discussion Paper on the Use of Big Data by Financial Institutions' (2016) 6 <www.esma.europa.eu/system/files_force/library/jc-2016-86_discussion_paper_big_data.pdf?download=1> accessed 31 August 2020; Emilios Avgouleas, 'Regulating Financial Innovation' in Niamh Moloney, Eilis Ferran and Jennifer Payne (eds), *The Oxford Handbook on Financial Regulation* (OUP 2015) 610.

135 In already existing private initiatives, consumers have shown reluctance to share their data with third parties due to concerns about security and privacy as well as

further data access rights might still not efficiently remedy the informational and behavioural market failure of consumer inertia.

From a legal competition policy perspective, it is also questionable whether a denial of access for PIS would have met the legal requirements of Article 102 lit. b) TFEU and the exceptional circumstances test outlined by the CJEU in refusal-to-deal cases. There has been already considerable competition within the retail banking market that makes both exploitative abuse and exclusionary abuse of market dominance under essential facility considerations unlikely. Indeed the terms and conditions regarding the opening up of bank accounts were standards already set by the bank incumbents and the lack of consumer engagement may have led to a lack of choice on exactly this service attribute. Yet, TPPs were already present in the market and there were other means of payment without having access to the customer's account. These competition-specific considerations build on market dominance, which depends on the vague concept of the relevant market and indeed could be assessed differently. Nonetheless, it is doubtful whether denying third parties access to the customers' bank accounts was indispensable, whether it actually illegally excluded other competitors and thus constituted an exclusionary abuse, and whether this in fact caused harm to competition and limited innovation. Unlike the *Microsoft* case, where Microsoft's exclusionary conduct and incontestable dominant market power justified the sharing of interoperability information in order to disseminate a technical standard that enables interoperability as well as competition and innovation, the case in payments markets is different. Payment services are highly regulated. This may confine market force-driven efficiencies. Price competition in relation to the already existent payment methods is limited, as rules on pricing schemes of other means of payment exist.[136] Also with regard to other modalities of the payment services that could be positively influenced by competition in

uncertainty and a lack of trust. See Optimisa, 'Informing the development of communication tools designed to increase consideration of switching among PCA and SME customers – Research Report prepared for the Competition and Markets Authority' (2016) <https://assets.publishing.service.gov.uk/media/56dd710ded915d0376000008/Qualitative_report_of_findings_prepared_by_Optimisa.pdf> accessed: 31 August 2020.

136 See for example Regulation (EU) 751/2015 of the European Parliament and of the Council of 29 April 2015 on interchange fees for card-based payment transactions [2015] OJ L123/1 or further regulation in the PSD2, which established a maximum multilateral interchange fee level per card transaction and banned retailers from imposing surcharges on customers for the use of these types of cards. Also, Art. 62 PSD2 regulates the fee scheme.

the payments market, the PSD, the PSD2, the RTS Delegated Regulation and other payments regulations set a high level of data governance rules under which data protection, data security and both syntactic[137] and semantic interoperability[138] should be established. Under these circumstances, an even more competitive market brought about by enabling entry to PISPs might not have necessarily led to the creation of better or more innovative services and thus more static and dynamic efficiencies. This holds particularly true as incumbent banks were already streamlining value-added solutions by incorporating (open) APIs and collaborating with FinTech providers.[139] This – ipso facto – also casts doubt upon the causality of a lack of universal entry of PISPs to all bank accounts of customers and less innovation capacities in the payments market. It is further important to notice that the purpose limitation embodied in the PIS access regime already further limits innovation that goes beyond the provision of PIS. Thus, it is the legislature that not only defines how the innovative payment service should look, it further orders their universal dissemination in the markets.

On the other hand, it is arguable whether the universal access regime may negatively influence innovation of payment services in the long run as incentives for incumbent banks to invest and innovate are reduced. As the regulatory framework pertaining to PIS creates a data governance frame-

137 Here it has to be noted that the new RTS Delegated Regulation (n. 127) does not entirely standardise the transmission of data via interfaces. Both APIs and direct customer interfaces (i.e. Homebanking Computer Interface (HBCI), or Financial Transaction Services (FinTS)) are still allowed in order to maintain technical neutrality. The Euro Retail Payments Board, SWIFT and the API evaluation group are currently working on standardised 'plug and play' APIs and standardised forms of communication under the SWIFT ISO 20022 standard. Yet, there are still private, proprietary APIs within the 4000 retail banks that cause enormous practical impediments and different data models used that do not fully offer full interoperability. See on this Clemens Jestaedt, 'Kontoinformationsdienste – neue Online-Services unter Regulierung' (2018) Zeitschrift für Banken- und Kapitalmarktrecht 445, 447; Zachariadis and Ozcan (n. 128) 6.

138 With regard to the question of sufficient funds, Art. 36(1) lit. c) RTS Delegated Regulation (n. 127), and with regard to personal credentials, the IBAN rules already standardise semantic interoperability under Art. 5(1) lit. a) Regulation (EU) No. 260/2012 of the European Parliament and of the Council of 14 March 2012 establishing technical and business requirements for credit transfers and direct debits in euro and amending Regulation (EC) No. 924/2009 [2012] OJ L 94/22 (SEPA Regulation).

139 PwC (n. 114) 10.

work, which ambition is to already establish high-quality services,[140] the potential negative effects of overly broad access regimes seem to be outweighed at first sight. Yet it has to be noted that there is still no de facto standard with regard to communication in the payments sector.[141] Moreover, the widely used SWIFT ISO 20022 standard does not fully offer (semantic) interoperability and a higher degree of data granularity that is needed for efficient use of ML.[142] Moreover, the entrance of digital conglomerates certainly creates strong incentives for incumbent banks to further invest and build value-added solutions for customers. Nevertheless, incumbent banks might fail to build up their own ecosystems, which would be ultimately necessary to compete with the digital conglomerates.[143] Thus, from both the perspective of maintaining the competition process per se and Article 16 CFR, it is questionable whether such a regime may eventually safeguard competition in the payments market in the long run and whether it really appropriately confines the incumbent banks' right to freely conduct a business.

Thus it would have been advisable to apply a more competition-centric approach that would align both the public interest in spurring innovation and private interests involved. Instead, it must be acknowledged that the PIS regulation still seems to be yet another industrial policy-driven attempt

140 The goal of interoperable communication solutions that should be achieved by following communication standards of international or European standardisation organisations is one example. Cf. Art. 30(3) and Recitals 21, 22 RTS Delegated Regulation (n. 127). The SWIFT ISO 20022 standard for instance already establishes a certain granularity of data by defining data model and communication standards in order to harmonise communication in the international finance and payments sectors. The same applies to private standardisation endeavours with regard to APIs. Cf. SWIFT, 'SWIFT ISO 20022 Migration Study – Consultation Paper' (2018) <https://buyerscredit.files.wordpress.com/2019/04/swift_standards_iso20022_migration_study_consultation_paper.pdf> accessed 31 August 2020; Berlin Group, 'Joint Initiative on a PSD2 Compliant XS2A Interface – Next GenPSD2 XS2A Framework, Operational Rules Version 1.3' (21 December 2018) <https://77cb457b-3353-4bdc-8ab6-ff6bb2ccdc98.filesusr.com/ugd/c2914b_2cf4db130e4d4aa9a5547acd342865e2.pdf> accessed 31 August 2020.

141 There are multiple communication standards in the payments sector that are still not interoperable, e.g. EDIFACT, IFX, OAGi, TWIST. Cf. Bankenverband, 'ISO 20022 im Überblick' <https://bankenverband.de/media/files/ISO-20022_im-ueberblick.pdf> accessed 31 August 2020.

142 Cf. 'ISO 20022 White paper', 5 <www.iso20022.de/white-paper/> accessed 31 August 2020); SWIFT (n. 140) 23. There is no possibility of bijective display of information once different standards are used, i.e. MX-to-MT conversions do not work properly.

143 Cf. de la Mano and Padilla (n. 106) 504–505; Di Porto and Ghidini (n. 113) 9.

to directly shape innovation[144] instead of merely safeguarding competition, which would have led to market force-driven innovation that not only responded to the sovereign will of market actors but also guaranteed more innovation in the long run.

This observation is attenuated when one broadens the regulatory perspective and looks at the role of consumers' data sovereignty, which led the legislature to introduce a data portability regime in Article 20(2), (1) GDPR. The same considerations may also justify a broader access regime in PIS cases. The horizontally applicable data portability regime set out in Article 20(2), (1) GDPR for instance has a Janus-faced character, being set in between competition law and data protection law. Particularly data protection-specific considerations give rise to an interpretation of the data portability right as a right to information, which has to be granted for free – as long as such right is not abusively used by the data subject.[145] Such interpretation does not resemble an ownership-like right of the data subject. It rather strengthens the sovereignty of the data subject by merely strengthening control over the personal data and tackling data lock-ins.[146] However, in contrast to the GDPR, the PSD2 does not refer to data subjects' right of data portability in order to strengthen their control over personal data. The wording simply refers to a right of the consumer to make use of a specific third-party payment service – which was already possible in some cases prior to the PSD2 but not valued by customers.[147] The remedial function of the access-to-account rule and the data portabili-

---

144 This also led to the creation of FinTech-specific innovation hubs and regulatory sandboxes. For an overview of the regulatory endeavours to further boost innovation in FinTech in the UK and the EU see Milanesi (n. 116) 23.

145 Art. 12(5) GDPR.

146 See Recital 68 of the GDPR. In this line of interpretation of the data portability regime see Kai von Lewinski, in Heinrich Wolff and Stefan Brink (eds) *Beck'scher Online-Kommentar Datenschutz-Grundverordnung* (2020) Art. 20 para 7. Data protection law is also one of the core determinants of further data-driven business models that depend on the portability of data in order to avoid data-induced lock-ins that may have negative effect on competition. Therefore, the right of data portability also remedies a market failure that stems from competition specific considerations. See on this Heike Schweitzer and Martin Peitz, 'Datenmärkte in der digitalisierten Wirtschaft: Funktionsdefizite und Regelungsbedarf?' (2017) ZEW Discussion Paper No. 17–043, 45 <http://ftp.zew.de/pub/zew-docs/dp/dp17043.pdf> accessed 31 August 2020.

147 See the wording of Art. 66(1) and the correlating Recitals 29–32 PSD2 (n. 10). Contrary to Recital 68 of the GDPR where the legislature explicitly refers to the data portability right in order to ensure consumers' data sovereignty, the PSD2 is more neutral and solely addresses the need for harmonising regulation, filling

ty regime under Article 20(2), (1) GDPR are different. Although both in fact tackle consumer lock-ins, the lock-in addressed under the PSD2 access-to-account rule does not stem from a privacy law-induced market failure, as the portability regime under Article 20 GDPR does.[148] It is not only the personal information held by the ASPSs that is needed in order to make use of PIS. The decision of the BKartA pertaining to the general terms and conditions used by some retail banks that banned the use of personal security credentials (PIN and TAN) on e-commerce platforms in order to make use of certain PIS also shows this. Here, the BKartA held that this constituted inter alia a breach of Article 101(1) TFEU. The chosen terms and conditions were not essential for establishing a coherent security and data protection concept for their offered services. According to the BKartA these retail banks rather tried to foreclose other innovative market entrants offering payment initiation services by introducing this duty with a correlating exemption from liability where PISs were used.[149] Moreover, as already outlined above it is the real-time direct access to the account that is needed in order to effectively enable PIS, and not further usage of personal information provided by the retail banks, which could just as well have been brought before the court under the control of terms and conditions and private law enforcement. This is also the reason why the fallback option of providing access via the already existing customer ASPSPs interface as opposed to direct access via APIs was criticised as not completely eliminating the perceived competition issues.[150] This is not only the reason why the access-to-account rule could not be substituted with the data portabili-

---

regulatory gaps and addressing competition and data protection issues with regard to newly arising third-party payment services.

148 See on the market failure behind the data portability right enshrined in Art. 20 GDPR, Schweitzer and Peitz (n. 146) 50.

149 See *Deutsche Kreditwirtschaft, Bundesverband der Deutschen Volksbanken und Raiffeisenbanken e.V., Deutscher Sparkassen- und Giroverband e.V., Bundesverband Deutscher Banken e.V., Sofort GmbH, giropay GmbH*, Bundeskartellamt, 29 June 2016, Case 4 – 71/10, 4 <www.bundeskartellamt.de/SharedDocs/Entscheidung/DE/Entscheidungen/Kartellverbot/2016/B4-71-10.pdf?_blob=publicationFile&v=4> accessed 31 August 2020.

150 See on the issue of direct and indirect access via already existing interfaces, position statement of the BKartA, 'Stellungnahme des Bundeskartellamts zu dem Gesetzesentwurf der Bundesregierung – Entwurf eines Gesetzes zur Umsetzung der zweiten Zahlungsdiensterichtlinie – BT-Drucksache-18/11495' (21 April 2017) <www.bundestag.de/resource/blob/503786/d5ae19e200f8d617a2ae0797d23ba0cb/03-data.pdf> accessed 31 August 2020.

ty right under Article 20(2), (1) GDPR,[151] it also makes clear that the PSD2 access-to-account rule goes beyond the GDPR's data portability scope of transmitting personal data in order to increase consumers' data sovereignty.

3. Adverse effects on privacy, competition and innovation – the need for new asymmetric regulation

Considering the information that PISPs can obtain and use under the access-to-account rule, namely the confirmation of payment execution, adverse effects on consumer sovereignty and choice seem unlikely. Even though the payment executions provided by PISPs may give insights into the purchasing behaviour of customers, the information gathered from the PIS does not have the same potential for algorithmic governance that account information does, for instance. Moreover, there are certain limitations enshrined in the PIS data governance regime that not only limit the actual available information but also restrict the options for possible use of this information in other data value chains.[152] New technical innovations with regard to cryptographic measures can also guarantee that data are actually not used for any other purpose, e.g. ML-enabled profiling and algorithmic governance.[153] As the available information together with such us-

151 The two regimes are applicable in parallel, though the scopes of their provisions are not identical. See Article 29 Working Group, 'Guidelines to the right of data portability' (5 April 2017) 7 <http://ec.europa.eu/newsroom/document.cfm?doc_id=44099> accessed 31 August 2020. It is questionable though whether the information needed falls under provided information within the meaning of Art. 20(1) GDPR and the condition of technical feasibility set out in Art. 20(2) GDPR together with the potential IP protection pertaining to APIs Art. 20(4) would exempt the banks from their duty. Here potential software copyright protection for APIs becomes not relevant as Art. 20(1), (2) GDPR does not refer to the direct access via APIs – contrary to the PSD2.

152 See Sec. 49(4) of the German Payment Services Supervision Act (*ZAG*), implementing Art. 66(3) lit. e), f), g) PSD2.

153 This is not embodied in the Regulatory Technical Measures and certainly one aspect that can hardly be efficiently enforced. Nonetheless, particularly the current discussion pertaining to Personal Information Management Systems are already taking such new technical measures into account. See, for instance, Bundesamt für Sicherheit und Informationstechnik, 'Technische Richtlinie für Kryptographische Verfahren: Empfehlungen und Schlüssellängen' (2020) BSI TR-02102–1 <www.bsi.bund.de/DE/Publikationen/TechnischeRichtlinien/tr02102/tr02102_node.html> accessed 31 August 2020.

age restriction also seems to restrict the competitive advantages that stem from increased data access in PIS cases – particularly with regard to the use of AI in order to offer a fully integrated customer experience and thus better digital ecosystems – the likelihood of data-induced distortions of competition also seems to be low.

Yet the access-to-account rule gives PISPs the possibility to enter into a direct customer relationship, which enables digital conglomerates to implement the customer into their existing platform business models and to gather valuable insights into their purchasing behaviour. As this is a new source of information, it may provide knowledge that goes beyond that already gained from their data value chains.[154] Customers' purchasing information is logically intertwined with available information about customer preferences, habits and conduct and is thus a valuable input for further data-driven innovation in the context of AI and inferred data in ML applications.

This however may not only give rise to further algorithmic governance, but it is also likely to reduce competition in the long run. Through the combination of payments data with the other customer profile data, digital conglomerates gain further market power and can play out their competitive advantages. This holds particularly true as not only the data in terms of scope and scale but also increasing technological advancements in AI, computing power and cryptography are predominantly aggregated by digital conglomerates and can hardly be achieved by anyone else.[155] The value of combined data together with their financial strength and strong portfolio effects may deter others from entering digital markets where the digital conglomerates are already active or are likely to become active. In these markets business would not only require ex ante investments for achieving the same customer insights through ML applications, but also the lack of a digital ecosystem and strong network effects may make business for other competitors hardly lucrative anymore. These structural market entry barri-

154 This is exactly the reason why undertakings are currently changing their business strategies towards platform business models.

155 This could also be compared to a ring fencing strategy, where innovations are secured by blocking other competitors via extensive IP protection. In this context it is interesting to see who has filed the most AI specific patent applications WIPO (n. 27). On the relevancy of strategic market entry barriers and the role of ring fencing see for instance John Vickers and Donald Hay (eds) *The Economics of Market Dominance* (Basic Blackwell 1987) 24.

ers together with strategic foreclosure behaviour of digital conglomerates,[156] i.e. enveloping strategies and customer lock-ins, may distort competition in the long run. This is likely in the case of 'Big Tech' banking.[157] Once consumers stop multi-homing and instead concentrate their business on the digital conglomerate's single platform it will be more convenient for customers to stay within the same ecosystem and to also concentrate their banking system on this platform. This will likely affect most retail banking markets, for instance customer and SME lending markets, where borrowers will most likely act via the platform and not an incumbent bank's online or offline distribution channel.[158] This lock-in effect is even exacerbated by the fact that the platforms dominate the front-end customer relationship and serve as an information intermediary, which enables them to favour their own or 'pay for display' services. Even though in *Google Search (Shopping)*[159] and *Google AdSense*[160] the European Commission found that Google's conduct of favouring the display of its own services or blocking other service providers from providing the same service infringed Article 102 lit. b) TFEU, it is unclear to what extent self-preferencing – if there is a dominant firm – really constitutes an abuse of dominance.[161] Yet experience has already shown that digital conglomerates apply enveloping strategies, which lead to an increasing monopolisation of the Asian payments and retail banking market, for instance, where players take advantage of high network effects.[162]

156 Cf. Jay P. Choi, 'Tying in two-sided markets with multi-homing' (2010) 58 Journal of Industrial Economics 607.

157 Cf. de la Mano and Padilla (n. 106) 507.

158 Cf. Matthew Quint, David Rogers and Rick Ferguson, 'Showrooming and the rise of the mobile assisted shopper' (2013) 11 <https://www8.gsb.columbia.edu/globalbrands/sites/globalbrands/files/images/Showrooming_Rise_Mobile_Assisted_Shopper_Columbi-Aimia_Sept2013.pdf> accessed 31 August 2020.

159 *Google Search (Shopping)* (Case AT.39740) Commission decision of 27 June 2017 [2017] OJ C9/11.

160 European Commission Press Release, 'Commission fines Google €1.49 billion for abusive practices in online advertising' (20 March 2019) <https://ec.europa.eu/commission/presscorner/detail/en/IP_19_1770> accessed 31 August 2020.

161 Google appealed the decisions and pled to the General Court. Cf. on a critical side Bo Vesterdorf, 'Theories of Self-Preferencing and Duty to Deal – Two Sides of the Same Coin' (2015) 1(1) Competition Law and Policy Debate 4; in favour of an abuse see Nicolas Petit, 'Theories of Self-Preferencing Under Article 102 TFEU: A Reply to Bo Vesterdorf' (2015) Competition Law and Policy Debate 1.

162 It can already be seen in Asia and the rise of Ant Finance how digital conglomerates impact the retail-banking sector. It also has to be noted that in Europe digital conglomerates already entered certain markets in the financial sector. Google

Even though there are defensive strategies in theory, they will most likely not be successful in the case of Big Tech banking. If these conglomerates' competitors were to increase their cooperation with other third parties, transforming their business models into shared open platforms in order to benefit from co-investments and data sharing among all platform participants, this may not only raise concerns under Article 101 TFEU,[163] the shared platform will most likely not scale up and be able to assemble a comparable bundle of services that could compete with the digital ecosystem of the digital conglomerate. Moreover, the matching of the digital conglomerates' bundling strategy with the strategic use of customer insights is unlikely, as the competitive advantages of digital conglomerates seem unassailable.[164]

Indeed, the rise of FinTech has positioned the bank as an intermediary for account holders and TPPs thereby including digital conglomerates. Thus, it is rather the digital conglomerate being integrated in the platform business model of the retail bank and not the other way around. This may not hinder the digital conglomerate from bundling its own platform's functionality with that of the retail banks so as to leverage shared user relationships and increase its enormous data-specific competition advantages.[165] This might not prevent entry in markets with high regulatory entry barriers[166] and markets that are still lacking customer demand for digital financial services. And yet the aggregated information may strengthen their digital ecosystem to such an extent that other digital markets with strong network effects may tip in favour of the digital conglomerate. Due to their gained knowledge, they may eventually provide better services,

already allows customers to make online payments via e-mail (Google Wallet), Amazon is offering loans within its platform (Amazon lending) and Apple Pay has begun to integrate payments in its touch authentication device. Also, Facebook has tried to launch its cryptocurrency 'libra', which still lacks authentication from European Financial Supervisory Authorities.

163 Cf. Case C-238/05 *Asnef-Equifax* ECLI:EU:C:2006:734.

164 De la Mano and Padilla (n. 106) 509; Eisenmann, Parker and Van Alstyne (n. 106).

165 See Joint Committee of the European Supervisory Authority (n. 134) 6; Milanesi (n. 116) 22. For a dissenting opinion see Anja Lambrecht and Catherine E. Tucker, 'Can big data protect a firm from competition?' (2017) Competition Policy International <www.competitionpolicyinternational.com/can-big-data-protect-a-firm-from-competition/> accessed 31 August 2020.

166 Credit institutes for example have more additional fiduciary duties and liabilities and need another, more costly licence, which requires high credit deposits and insurances.

which will attract more users, leading to both direct and indirect network effects on both sides of the platform.[167] It is thus important to assess the negative competition effects of further granting access on a strictly reciprocal basis.

Therefore, access regimes for PIS must be limited and the access right asymmetrically restricted. Even though the solution of cross licensing data may tackle the competitive disadvantages vis-à-vis digital conglomerates, the question inevitably arising is whether data protection laws may eventually render this solution impractical.

This might make a special preventive restriction of access for digital conglomerates together with an amendment of the financial supervisory laws (the data governance provisions) necessary. Access should be excluded for 'undertakings of paramount importance for competition across markets'.[168] Such preventive ban with an authorisation option would make a case-by-case decision possible. This would then guarantee a better balancing of interests, i.e. the undertaking's right to freely conduct a business and to enter into the payments market and the general interest of safeguarding competition against the backdrop of sector-specific peculiarities (particularly data governance rules) and potential productivity efficiencies. With regard to the latter, the onus of proof would lie with the undertaking seeking access. The supervisory laws should therefore be adapted accordingly. This also requires further intra-agency collaboration between the Federal Financial Supervisory Authority and the BKartA. As some of these undertakings already operate in the market, the question ultimately arising is whether such undertakings should be banned. Either way, such considerations could also provide guidance with regard to new sector-specific data governance regulation that may justify different outcomes.

---

167 Cf. *Facebook*, BKartA, 15 February 2019, Case B6–22/16 <www.bundeskartellamt.de/SharedDocs/Entscheidung/DE/Entscheidungen/Missbrauchsaufsicht/2019/B6-22-16pdf?_blob=publicationFile&v=8> accessed 31 August 2020.

168 As stated in Sec. 19a *GWB*.

II. Account information services

1. Overview

Under the notion of 'open banking',[169] retail banking is increasingly focusing on sharing data in order to increase transparency, efficiency of incumbent businesses, competition and innovation in the banking and financial services industry. Moreover, the use of data is intended to create a more personalised customer experience and more compelling customer engagement, as well as greater control of customers over their data.[170] Though financial players have always used data to make business decisions and reduce operational costs, the use of consumer financial data and account information, including for innovative complementary products and services, is constantly growing. The variety of data-driven services and products is immense and the advancements in AI that come with increased data from related sources, computing power and data scientists' know-how has further spurred data-driven innovation in the retail-banking sector.[171]

---

169 See Competition and Markets Authority (CMA), 'What Is Open Banking? Competition and Markets Authority Retail Banking Market Investigation: Infographic' (2016) <https://assets.publishing.service.gov.uk/government/uploads/system/uploads/attachment-data/file/908412/what-is-open-banking.pdf> accessed 31 August 2020, stating that open banking means reliable, personalised financial advice, precisely tailored to a customer's particular circumstances and delivered securely and confidentially. Cf European Banking Association (EBA) – Open Banking Working Group, 'Open Banking: Advancing Customer Centricity – Analysis and Overview' (2017) 16 <www.abe-eba.eu/media/azure/production/1474/euro-banking-association-analysis-focuses-on-open-banking-advancing-customer-centricity-1.pdf> accessed 31 August 2020.

170 For instance, some of these products and services enable the provision of real-time information, which helps consumers make better-informed and more efficient decisions about spending, saving and borrowing. Others enable consumers to view and manage their financial account information on a consolidated basis across multiple accounts and financial institutions, thus giving them the convenience of a holistic overview of their financial activities. Some leverage automation and insight to help consumers achieve their savings or budgeting goals or to profile consumers and develop behavioural-based services or provide for better strategic decision making; others facilitate more targeted investment, financial planning and portfolio management solutions or simply support compliance with regulatory requirements by firms or back-test software solutions.

171 See Open Data Institute, 'Introducing the Open Banking Standard. Helping Customers, Banks and Regulators Take Banking into a Truly 21st Century, Connected Digital Economy' (2016) 2 <https://dgen.net/1/Introducing-the-Open-Banking

In the past a lot of data-driven services have been conducted through data access via screen scraping.[172] Such technology raised challenges and risks for consumers and the incumbent banks that led to further regulation.[173] These challenges were related not only to cyber security issues, as authentication credentials were passed over the internet and no secure communication could be guaranteed. The trend also created certain qualitative shortcomings with regard to the offered services, as data might be out-dated. Moreover, it posed the threat for incumbent banks that access to data may be abused – as typically banks were not aware of third parties entering the customers' online accounts.[174] This in turn also caused data protection issues with regard to the excessive use of personal data of consumers.

To respond to this development, the EU decided to pave the way for secure Open Banking via the PSD2 and established a data governance regime with regard to account information services in order to provide consumers with adequate protection of their payment and account data.[175] Therein, TPPs are first of all obliged to authenticate themselves before accessing data and secondly obliged to communicate solely via banks' communication interfaces.[176] This in turn led to a ban of the screen scraping technology and actually as a result created factual data exclusivity with regard to the account information. The legislature further introduced a data access right

---

-Standard.pdf> accessed 31 August 2020; Joint Committee of the European Supervisory Authority (n. 134) 10.

172 Screen Scraping is a practice of collecting ('scraping') data from the consumer's account information environment. There are two forms of screen scraping, server-based screen scraping and client-based screen scraping. In both scenarios, consumers shares their bank authentication credentials with a FinTech company, which passes them on to a data aggregator and then deletes them from its own records. The data aggregator stores the consumer's bank authentication credentials and creates an associated UID. In the server-based screen scraping scenario the data aggregator enters the credentials (UID) into the bank's website and scrapes the required consumer data. In the client-based scenario, the data aggregator passes the bank authentication credentials to a small application on the consumer's local computer, which then redirects the bank authentication credentials to the bank's website.

173 See on the challenges and risks associated with screen scraping Milanesi (n. 116) 34.

174 Here the banks typically have tried to exclude screen-scraping technologies via individual contract clauses or terms and conditions. As already mentioned above (n. 149) this was deemed to infringe Art. 101(1) TFEU.

175 Recital 28 PSD2 (n. 10). It has to be further noted that the legislative process of the PSD2 took place before the European Parliament adopted the GDPR.

176 Art. 67(2) lit. b), c) PSD2 (n. 10).

for account information service providers. According to this right, payment service users can make use of services enabling access to account information, i.e. account information services (AISs), once the account is accessible online.[177] This is again not dependent on any contractual relationship between the ASPSPs and AISPs.[178]

In contrast to PIS, inferred data from account information is typically part of the value chain of AIS. However, it is not clear what services fall under the term 'account information services' and whether this term really only covers services that build on inferred knowledge from the analysis of the account information.[179] As already outlined above, AIS can only be considered data-driven innovation once data are actually used and not only aggregated.[180] The question arising is therefore whether account information services ought to be narrowly interpreted and should only cover such services that provide additional knowledge to the payment service users – similar to the new-product rule – or whether it may also encompass functionally equivalent information services that may not build on inferred data. Here, the PSD2 further elaborates in its recitals that the user should be 'provided [...] with aggregated online information' in order to be 'able to have an overall view of its financial situation immediately at any given moment'.[181] The German legislature actually defines account service provider as an online service that provides 'consolidated' – instead of 'aggregated' – information.[182] By this deviation from the PSD2 it may favour a more narrow interpretation of 'account information service'.

2. *Lack of investment incentives and the need for maintaining market options for incumbent banks*

A narrow interpretation is justified against the backdrop of the innovation incentive function of factual exclusivity and the incumbents' right to freely conduct a business. As AISs build on the data and the embedded account

177 Art. 67 PSD2 in conjunction with Annex I (8) PSD2.

178 Art. 67(4) PSD2 (n. 10).

179 Arts 4(10), 67(1) PSD2 (n. 10) only refer to Annex I (8) PSD2 that clarifies that account information services are considered payment services in the meaning of Art. 4(3) PSD2.

180 Cf. OECD (n. 21).

181 Recital 28 PSD2 (n. 10).

182 Sec. 1(34) German Payment Services Supervision Act (*ZAG*) defines account information service as '*Onlinedienst zur Mitteilung konsolidierter Informationen*'.

information, the quality of data is the key value-adding factor of the service. Data quality has various dimensions and quality indicators.[183] Particularly with regard to AIS it is important that data are timely, credible, accurate, consistent and complete. Even though the RTS Delegated Regulation set out an obligation for AIPSPs to keep their communication interfaces interoperable and thus declares the sharing of interoperability information at no charge as a mandatory prerequisite for enabling AIS,[184] they do not regulate data standards. Therefore, particular data semantics and thus the subject of the mandated access regimes can still be freely determined by the ASPSPs and are not unequivocally defined by the access regime. Even though private ordering has already led to the implementation of certain data standards, semantic interoperability is still not thoroughly addressed in the current data standardisation framework with regard to account information. This may eventually de facto hinder data integration and the efficient provisioning of AIS – despite the access-to-information rules outlined in the PSD2 and the RTS Delegated Regulation that do not explicitly define a direct access right of competitors.[185] As the mandated access regime eliminates the ASPSPs' market options with regard to potentially monetising account information, this may not only reduce market and competition-driven data quality in this context, it may also negatively impact further data-driven innovation that is conducted by the incumbents. Input aggregation and factual data exclusivity is particularly important with regard to further data-driven innovation enabled by AI.[186] As there exists legal uncertainty to what extent IP laws may still be applicable to AI as a tool and AI generated output, input aggregation may be one of the key factors of firm's innovation strategies.[187] Once data may be shared with others – and data-rich digital conglomerates in particular – this may leave the incumbents with fewer incentives to generate high-quality data. As regulation is not remedying such loss of incentives by establish-

183 See for an overview of different data quality categories and the existing standards under the ISO-8000 data standard Cai and Zhu (Fn. 28) 5.

184 See Art. 30(3) RTS Delegated Regulation (n. 127). This becomes particularly interesting as the software copyright protection outlined in Article 6 Directive 2009/24/EC of the European Parliament and of the Council of 23 April 2009 on the legal protection of computer programs (Codified version) [2009] OJ L111/16 and Sec. 69e of the German Copyright Act pertaining to APIs or other communication interfaces is, as of now, not clear.

185 Art. 36(1), (4) RTS Delegated Regulation (n. 127) set out both obligations, the duty to provide information and the duty to let AISPs access information.

186 See Hilty, Hoffmann and Scheuerer (n. 20) 21.

187 Ibid.

ing the same data-quality standards, too broad data access should not be mandated. In this context, however, it must be noted that before the AIS data governance regime entered into force, banks were already exposed to third-party access to the customer accounts via screen scraping.

Moreover, the AIS access regime sets out further restrictions with the same purpose limitation as for PIS and thus also limits the multipurpose use of the data. Yet the account information service itself may already provide the undertaking seeking access with such knowledge that might lead to a competitive disadvantage for the ASPSPs vis-à-vis the AISPs. Similar to PISs, most of the operational risks and costs associated with such access are still unilaterally borne by the ASPSPs. Therefore, a narrow interpretation of the term 'account information services' is needed. To this end, functionally equivalent information services should not fall under the definition of account information services. As already outlined above, assessing whether information services are a functional equivalent may be a hard task to fulfil – particularly when AI is involved. Here, it should only be assessed whether the information service provided obviously offers the same information service.[188] This should also be borne in mind when defining consolidated information in the German access provision.

With regard to possible remuneration for granting access, the same explanations as outlined above can be applied *mutatis mutandis*. If access is mandated and the factual data exclusivity eliminated, it is necessary to maintain the right to exploit the granting of access via potential remuneration options. This will not only safeguard some market and competition-driven incentives for generating better quality data, it will also appropriately confine the undertakings' right to freely conduct a business. Here, it is questionable whether FRAND licensing regimes are needed or whether simply mechanisms to control excessive pricing under general competition law can be sufficient.

With regard to the role of direct innovation-enabling regulation on data-driven innovations, it has to be noted that before the PSD2 entered into force banks and other account providers already used to provide account information services to their customers. Third parties either directly collaborated with banks and other account providers or entered into a chain of contract with aggregators that again have a contract with the respective bank or account provider. Ultimately, third parties could also operate through data access via screen scraping. Only by introducing the authorisa-

188 This could be similar to the inventive step four-step approach regarding the non-obviousness of the invention applicable in the UK.

tion duty, they actually create factual exclusivity of the account information, which then makes an access regime necessary. In this light, the AIS data governance regime could also be seen as only mitigating the risks that were associated with the screen scraping techniques and establishing a secure way of communication but in principle maintaining the market situation as it was. However, with the introduction of the access-to-account rule and the portability right applicable to AISs, the legislature also imposed mandatory access that eliminated any market option for the ASPSPs. The access-to-account rule restricts the ASPSPs' right to freedom of contract that should be typically safeguarded by competition laws and not destroyed by ex ante regulation, which abstains from a competition policy approach. As already outlined above, however, this ultimately depends on the relevant market with regard to the account information needed. If account information cannot be substituted and are indispensable, there are exceptional circumstances that justify the mandatory granting of access under certain conditions. Otherwise factual data exclusivity would result in monopolisation over account information that would lead to a bargaining power asymmetry, making effective decentralised decision-making between parties impossible. This point always depends on the existent market structure – as unlike Art. 20 GWB that follows the rationale of unfair competition laws – relative market power still does not constitute an abuse of dominance under Art. 102 TFEU. As long as there is enough system competition within the retail payments market there should be enough possibilities to enter –freely- into licensing contracts. Only if this is not the case, the legal intervention and a more centralised decision-making – as in the PSD2 access-to-account regulation on AIS – is justified. It must be noted though that legislative intervention should be kept to a minimum and should not inappropriately infringe the ASPSPs' right of to freely conduct a business. This not only requires a narrow interpretation of what constitutes account information services and the entire modalities of access, it further makes the remuneration possibility for ASPSPs necessary.

The conflicting data protection dimension behind data access regulation again may attenuate these considerations. As the data portability right enshrined in Article 20(2) and (1) GDPR establishes a right that aims at safeguarding data sovereignty with a limited remuneration option,[189] these two regimes may be conflicting if personal data of data subjects are involved and thus may need to be aligned. Both legal regimes are deemed

189 Data should be provided for free as long as no excessive use of the right is made: Art. 12(5) GDPR.

to be applicable in parallel.[190] Both regimes provide consumers –the PSD2 also merchants – with a right to data portability.[191] The scope of the rights, however, varies, as the modalities of data portability and access are differently outlined. The PSD2 access regime for AIS goes beyond the GDPR's data portability regime as it further creates an access-to-account option for AISPs and it does not restrict the data access and portability right to cases where it is technically feasible, as does Article 20(2) GDPR.[192] The narrow interpretation of the access-to-account rule for AIS under the PSD2 together with an option of remuneration is therefore justified.

3. *Tackling BigTech banking by introducing new asymmetric regulation*

Unlike the information in PIS, account information is relevant when it comes to gauging potential adverse effects of a too-broad data access regime with regard to algorithmic governance and data-induced distortions of competition. Transaction history and payments information may not only allow for conclusions about customers' purchasing behaviour, it also indirectly provides multiple other behavioural insights, e.g. into customers' personal life and emotions or risk affinity. This in turn provides exactly the source of information on which further algorithmic governance can build on and thus is also the reason why such information can be considered highly relevant for competition.

There are two legal restrictions regarding the further use of data, though that need to be considered. The PSD2 itself has already restricted further usage options. Moreover, account information is personal information, which makes data protection rules relevant.[193] Both restrictions already

---

190 See Article 29 Working Group (n. 151).

191 It is unclear whether according to the data portability right enshrined in Art. 20(2) and (1) GDPR competitors can also invoke the right directly or it can only be invoked by the consumers.

192 Technically feasible requires less in order to perform than factual impossibility would require. The latter is typically needed for the performing party to be exculpated.

193 Art. 94(1) and (2) PSD2 (n. 10) and Sec. 59(3) German Payment Services Supervision Act (*ZAG*) explicitly refer to the applicability of data protection rules. Even though the PSD2 only refers to Data Protection Directive 95/46/EC, the GDPR is still applicable in parallel.

prevent anti-competitive effects – at least to some extent – as data can only be further used to the extent outlined in both legal regimes.[194]

Both the PSD2 and the German legislature have implemented usage restrictions pertaining to account information limiting the use of information to the respective account information service explicitly requested by the payment service user.[195] The narrow usage restriction only evolved in the course of the law-making process. The European Commission's first draft of the PSD2[196] did not mention any such limitation. At an intermediate stage further use was made dependent only on the explicit will of the customer, and then, in its final version, the usage restriction was drafted even more narrowly, as outlined above.[197] Here it is not clear whether such restriction should only give rise to data protection considerations and might thus be overridden by the contrary explicit consent of the payment service user. In light of the above-mentioned considerations, this should not be possible, as the adverse effects of such broad interpretation would likely occur. This also makes any contractual exclusion of the usage restriction impossible.

Such restriction of use however could potentially be in conflict with the GDPR's data portability regime, as the portability regime may further en-

194 This was already acknowledged by the European Commission in *Verizon/Yahoo* (Case COMP/M8180) Commission decision of 21 December 2016 C(2016) 8978 final. In this case both Verizon and Yahoo used certain data generated by user activity on their websites, apps and other services such as their ad networks to improve their online advertising services (e.g. sold to advertisers and publishers) and better target advertising on websites and apps. The EC saw two issues concerning these online advertising services as a result of the combination of the two datasets previously held independently by Verizon and Yahoo: (i) the increased market power of the merged entity; and (ii) the elimination of competition based on the data that existed between Verizon and Yahoo prior to the merger. See also *Sanofi/Google/DMI JV* (Case COMP/M.7813) Commission decision of 23 February 2016 C(2016) 1223 final.

195 Art. 67(2) lit. f) PSD2 (n. 10), Sec. 51(1) German Payment Services Supervision Act (*ZAG*) both state that the information should not be used, accessed or stored for any other purpose than for performing the account information service explicitly requested by the payment service user.

196 See Art. 58(2) lit. d) Proposal for a Directive on payment services in the internal market COM(2013) 547 final.

197 The first draft of the PSD2 lacking usage restriction was already criticised by the European Data Protection Supervisor and the European Central Bank for being not compliant with data protection and IT security standards. Almost one year after the first adaption of the first usage restriction amendment, the Committee on Economic and Monetary affairs further amended the usage restriction to its final version.

able the transmission of data to digital conglomerates that are already subject to the special competition control regime. This is another tension where the consumers' data sovereignty and individual interest conflict with the goal of protecting competition and innovation. This needs to be reconciled by limiting the portability regime and addressing this issue on a supranational level.

Moreover, the AIS itself could already have the same effects as potential further use of the account information. The subject of the service may already constitute what is considered algorithmic governance or another step for further consolidating digital ecosystems. Therefore, one should also consider asymmetric regulation vis-à-vis digital conglomerates and thus apply the abovementioned considerations pertaining to PIS *mutatis mutandis* in the case of AIS.

D. Conclusion

Although enhanced access to data has positive welfare effects and further spurs data-driven innovation, there are five points that must be considered.

First of all, any regulatory approach pertaining to data access on a B2B level needs to build on a regulatory theory that takes the multi-purpose functions of data as its starting point. Only such comprehensiveness may enable the legislature to fully grasp the multi-dimensional implications of data and the regulation of compulsory access and their potential adverse effects.

Second, the notion of data-driven innovation – particularly in the context of AI – should not be too heavily relied on as a blanket justification for overly broad access regulation. It must be considered, under both innovation incentives and the undertakings' fundamental right of freely conducting a business, that the openness of data should not be considered as the default rule. In this context, both the economic and the legal analysis show that access should and has generally only been granted under exceptional circumstances. Therefore, it is important to align any sector-specific data access regulation with the general competition-law thresholds – also with regard to remuneration options. Moreover, investment incentive considerations may require a restriction of data access to services that are not a functional equivalent to the data or data-driven service already provided. Too broad access regimes might also have negative effects on the levels of quality of the data. This ultimately depends on sector-specific data governance regimes that provide some basic guarantee of a certain level of data quality. In this context, however, the role of (semantic) interoperability is a key factor for welfare-enhancing data spill-overs that has not been considered sufficiently.

Third, under the orthodoxy of a free market economy one has to abstain from too heavy-handed ex ante access regulation and choose a more competition policy specific regulatory approach. Innovation should be market force-driven and not subject to mere industrial policy considerations. Competition still leads to market equilibria in which dynamic efficiencies are typically inherent in the coordination process of market actors. Better engaging customers in order to tackle the inertia of customers to value specific digital services and enable competition on certain non-salient products or certain product parameters is key. This potential behavioural market failure, however, cannot be remedied by mandating overly broad access to data.

Fourth, once there are personal data involved, data protection considerations become intertwined with the factual exclusivity of data and the role of – indirectly – granting access to competitors. Empirical studies have shown that a consent-based data protection solution still gives undertakings the chance to analyse data and eventually create such knowledge that may not only unconsciously influence consumers but also generate enormous competition advantages. Even though paternalistic approaches are currently being discussed that would tackle the bounded rationality of consumers who seem not to value privacy, not granting access or specific data use restrictions may be a more efficient solution for preventing further algorithmic governance – that may also negatively affect both competition and innovation.

Fifth, enhanced access to data – particularly for already data-rich undertakings – has to be assessed against the backdrop of potential disruptions of competition even across markets, and it thus reinvigorates the role of ex ante market regulation. Potential ways forward may be asymmetric regulation, restricting the parties entitled to access data, or a specific preventive competition control regime for 'undertakings of paramount importance for competition across markets' – as outlined in the 10th amendment of the GWB and in the Digital Markets Act. In this context the (enormous) productivity efficiencies, the thin line between competition on the merits, safeguarding the competition process per se and establishing non-competition specific market regulation detached from market concentrations considerations need to be thoroughly assessed and cautiously defined.

When it comes to the access regimes applying to PIS and AIS it is important to note that both regimes have to be differently assessed as the role of data within these services varies tremendously. The PIS regime provides a direct access right for customers and fails to sufficiently address the legal relationship between ASPSPs and PISPs. Yet, any direct access right of costumers together with the obligation of the ASPSPs to grant access provides indirect access for competitors. It remains questionable though how competitors can enforce such indirect access possibility. The implementation of the PSD2 in Germany in both public and private laws not only unveils the tensions between private and public interests in these cases, it further creates legal uncertainty regarding the different rights and obligations of all the parties involved. A more dogmatically consistent implementation of the PSD2 into German law would have been desirable. The access to account for PIS is granted below the competition specific thresholds outlined above and is thus another policy-driven attempt of direct market intervention to shape certain markets for FinTech-driven innovation. The negative consequences on the quality of services, however, seem to be rather low as the data governance regime outweighs a potential lack of incentives. This should not divert attention from the fact that asymmetric financial supervisory regulation and the access-to-account rule together provide new entrants with so great an advantage that it makes negative effects on competition even across markets likely, with a possible impact on dynamic efficiencies and financial stability. Therefore, a remuneration option for ASPSPs vis-à-vis TPPs should be possible and asymmetric regulation regarding 'undertakings of paramount importance for competition across markets' considered. This may make an alignment of the two regimes and the data portability regime under Article 20(2), (1) GDPR necessary. With regard to AIS, the same considerations regarding the lack of directly addressing the legal relationship between ASPSPs and AISPs apply *mutatis mutandis*. Moreover, it is crucial that the economic and legal competition considerations pertaining to refusal-to-deal cases should be reflected in the interpretation of AIS. This may even require – contrary to the Microsoft case – under economic considerations a limitation of the access regime to non-functional equivalent account information services. This has been partly foreseen by the German legislature. However, also in this case, a remuneration option and the asymmetric regulation for digital conglomerates should be guaranteed.

The PSD2's regulatory model of sector-specific access and governance regimes can serve as a good starting point for defining a legal framework that safeguards data-driven innovation. It already entails a data governance regime that correctly restricts further data usage options and has the ambition to establish secure communication standards. However, there are shortcomings. (Semantic) interoperability is still not sufficiently addressed, APIs are not standardised and are not the sole means of secure communication. Moreover, as already shown above, the PIS regime not only resembles a policy-driven approach of direct market intervention, both regimes – for PIS and AIS – do not properly reconcile the different interests involved and do not take the various dimensions of data in this context into account, and thus need further regulatory adjustments.

The European Commission's envisioned data strategy for the future,[198] in which the role of the European legislature in further boosting the data economy entails refraining from *fiat* and focusing on promoting private ordering and private incentives for sharing data, should be supported. The European Commission rightly foresees the role of the EU as facilitating voluntary data sharing and abstaining from overly detailed, heavy-handed ex ante regulation. The latter ought to only be the case if it is doubtful that competition law can solve the identified market failure, and only if exceptional circumstances dictate compulsory access to data. Nevertheless, sector-specific data governance rules may require sector-specific solutions. This should not mean that sector-specific market regulation should deviate from a competition policy based regulatory approach. A competition policy approach does not only better reconcile the different interests involved it also safeguards innovation in the long run. Here – again – it should be added that any data access regulation must reflect the different relevant dimensions of data and assess the regime in light of all potential adverse effects outlined above. This approach should be combined with a broader industrial strategy for a data-agile economy. The European Commission thereby rightly envisions investments in standards, tools and new infrastructures – like data trusteeship models or GaiaX. In particular, the standardisation of data models and APIs need to be on the agenda.

198 See Commission, 'A European strategy for data' (n. 4).

Data access rights – A comparative perspective

Louisa Specht-Riemenschneider

A. Introduction

I. From data ownership to data access

Discussion about data access rights has replaced discussion of data ownership, at least among German academics. For quite a long time, experts debated whether there could be data ownership or other exclusive rights to data.[1] Most importantly, some scholars emphasised the legal uncertainty that could arise in that if the existence of such rights is rejected. Based on this argument one can reason that exclusive rights in data are necessary. Nevertheless, the introduction of such exclusive rights could lead to a strengthening of technically established power over data if the person technically controlling the data becomes the data owner. On the other hand, if an exclusive right to data is established to overcome technical control over data, e.g. by granting data ownership to the party suffering detriment from technical control by another party, data ownership may not be the correct description of the legal instrument that needs to be introduced. If a party other than the technical data controller is to be allowed to access data and use it, that party would be granted a "data access right".

II. Functional taxonomy of data access rights

Data access rights exist to varying degrees in different legal systems. These rights differ with regard to their function. Data access can be granted in two ways: Firstly, data access can be granted by virtue of disclosure obliga-

1 Fundamental: Herbert Zech, *Information als Schutzgegenstand* (Mohr Siebeck 2012). See also Louisa Specht, 'Ausschließlichkeitsrechte an Daten – Notwendigkeit Schutzbereich, Alternativen' (2016) Computer und Recht 288; Wolfgang Kerber and Louisa Specht-Riemenschneider, 'Datenrechte – Eine rechts- und sozialwissenschaftliche Analyse im Vergleich Deutschland-USA' (ABIDA 2017) <www.abida.de/en/node/426> accessed 31 August 2020.

tions without the requirement of filing a request, such as pursuant to Sections 3 and 12a of the German E-Government Act (*E-Government-Gesetz*) and the transparency laws of certain German federal states.[2] These disclosure obligations are intended to create transparency on the part of the government and the administration with regard to basic information. Secondly, data access can be granted upon request. These data access rights encompass more and other data than the data available pursuant to disclosure obligations, and requests may be declined for certain reasons, for example if third-party rights may be infringed if data access is provided. In this paper, the current debate on data access is primarily of interest with regard to how data access rights pursuant to a request can overcome technical power over data (i.e. 'genuine access rights').

Sub-categories of genuine access rights can be recognised regarding the functioning of the access rights. Genuine data access rights exist under contract law, where they are recognised because of information asymmetries, on the one hand, and also under antitrust law, where their purpose is to curb abuse of market power. The function of the third type of data access right is to overcome technical power over data without requiring constraint of market power, and without affecting contracts between the applicant and the data controller. This type of data access right is the focus of this paper.

Genuine data access rights that serve to overcome technical power over data without regard to contract law and antitrust law can in turn be subcategorised according to function. Rights can be directed against the state, as guaranteed for example under the Public Sector Information Directive, or directed against private individuals. Data access rights directed against private individuals are the sole concern here, as data access rights directed against the state are the subject of a different chapter of this volume. Lastly, claims for information regarding the infringement of intellectual property rights and personality rights are also excluded because these have a special function, the regulation of which is not within the scope of this paper.

In some jurisdictions, such as France, there are also data access rights which accrue to governments and administrations and are directed against

---

2 An overview can be found at Josef Drexl, 'Designing Competitive Markets for Industrial Data – Between Propertisation and Access' (2017) 8 Journal of Intellectual Property, Information Technology and E-Commerce Law 257; Josef Drexl and others, 'Data Ownership and Access to Data', Max Planck Institute for Innovation and Competition (2016) <www.ip.mpg.de/fileadmin/ipmpg/content/stellungnahmen/positionspaper-data-eng-2016_08_16-def.pdf> accessed 31 August 2020.

private individuals. These data access rights of governments and administrations will be examined in another chapter of the conference proceedings, too.

Fig. 1 – Functional taxonomy of data access rights

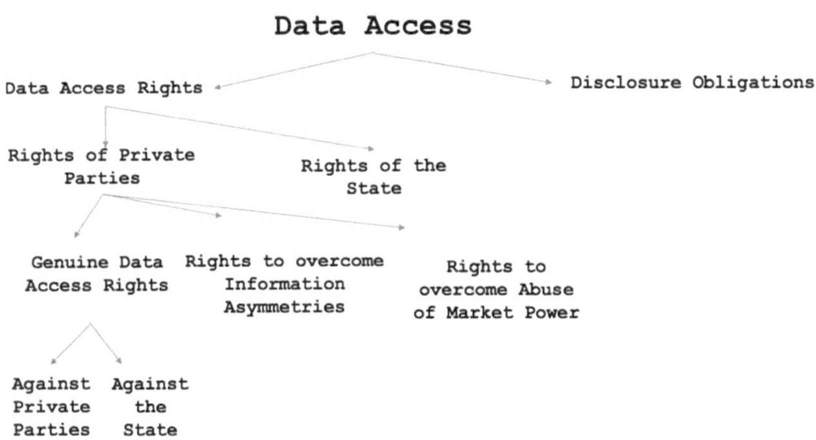

The question to be discussed in the context of comparative law is therefore: How are data access rights in relationships between private individuals – apart from contractual information asymmetries, infringements of intellectual property rights and personality rights and abuse of market power – guaranteed in the various legal systems?

B. Course of investigation

This question is to be examined in steps, following the elaboration of the specific question to be discussed. The first step in the comparative law method is to look at how the defined problem is solved in national law. I will not go into detail concerning national law, as the other papers in this volume will shed light on national law and its various guarantees of data access rights. I will therefore only briefly describe the instruments with which data access rights against private individuals are guaranteed, apart from contractual information asymmetries and the abuse of market power, before categorising these particular instruments.

Within this taxonomy, I will group the relevant foreign laws to point out the countries that guarantee data access rights in a manner similar to German law and which countries have chosen to recognise different data access rights. I will present these different data access rights and explain which similar foreign data access rights, in my opinion, have advantages over the data access rights existing under German law. I will also explain why certain other legal systems have chosen to recognise different data access rights than Germany has, and finally I will summarise my findings and derive policy recommendations from my research.

C. *National law: Taxonomy of data access rights*

The law in Germany grants data access rights in two ways, essentially: 'sole access' to data, which is processed by the controller, pursuant for example to Article 15 GDPR[3], and by way of a right to data portability, which covers the right to receive the data in a structured, commonly used and machine-readable format, as per Article 20 GDPR, for example. This is the primary finding. The second relevant finding regarding the categorisation taxonomy of data access rights under national law is that data access rights are guaranteed either for a specific sector or for a specific type of data. Conversely, there are no data access rights that are guaranteed across sectors or data types. Sector-specific data access rights can be found, for example, in Article 6 of Regulation (EC) 715/2007 which grants access to vehicle repair and maintenance information.[4]

The PSD2 Directive[5] also provides for a data access right in the banking sector. According to Article 67 of this directive, banks in the EU are required to open customer interfaces for third-party providers and grant these providers access to bank accounts. One difference versus data porta-

3 Regulation (EU) No. 2016/679 of the European Parliament and of the Council of 27 April 2016 on the protection of natural persons with regard to the processing of personal data and on the free movement of such data, and repealing Directive 95/46/EC, [2016] OJ L119/1.

4 Regulation (EC) No. 715/2007 of the European Parliament and of the Council of 20 June 2007 on type approval of motor vehicles with respect to emissions form light passenger and commercial vehicles (Euro 5 and Euro 6) and on access to vehicle repair and maintenance information [2007] OJ L171/1.

5 Directive (EU) 2015/2366 of the European Parliament and the Council of 25 November 2015 on payment services in the internal market, amending Directives 2002/65/EC, 2009/110/EC and 2013/36/EU and Regulation (EU) 1093/2010, and repealing Directive 2007/64/EC [2015] OJ L335/36.

bility under the GDPR is that PSD2 regulates access to interfaces which are to be connected with each other at all times. The right to data portability, in contrast, concerns a single release of data only.

Another sector-specific data access right is provided for in Article 16(4) of the Digital Content Directive, which is to be transposed into national law. It reads:

> Except in the situations referred to in point (a), (b) or (c) of paragraph 3, the trader shall, at the request of the consumer, make available to the consumer any content other than personal data, which was provided or created by the consumer when using the digital content or digital service supplied by the trader.
> The consumer shall be entitled to retrieve that digital content free of charge, without hindrance from the trader, within a reasonable time and in a commonly used and machine-readable format.

For the healthcare sector a sector-specific right of access to data is provided for in Section 630g of the German Civil Code (BGB), according to which the right holder has the right to access his or her patient file. In requiring mobile number portability, Section 46(3) of Germany's Telecommunications Act (*Telekommunikationsgesetz*) contains a right to data portability too, whereas Article 20 GDPR grants a cross-sector right to data portability. The data access rights provided for under Article 15 GDPR and Section 34 of Germany's Federal Data Protection Act (BDSG) also apply on a non-sector-specific basis. The rights cited here do not represent an exhaustive list of all existing data access rights, being intended rather to illustrate that data access rights may apply in specific sectors or be guaranteed across sectors.

Beyond classifying data access rights as sector-specific or non-sector-specific, data access rights can also be categorised as concerning specific data, such as personal data only, or concerning both personal and non-personal data. It is important to note that Germany's cross-sectoral data access rights are limited to personal data, while sector-specific rights are partly guaranteed for both personal and non-personal data. Thus there is no cross-sectoral, non-type-specific data access right, and there is no sector-specific right of access to personal data. However, German and European law do not require a sector-specific solution concerning personal data, because the GDPR exhaustively permits the processing of personal data across all sectors.

Fig. 2 – Classification of data access legislation

	sector-specific regulation	cross-sectoral regulation
data-specific regulation		Art. 15, 20 DSGVO, § 34 BDSG; Art. 16 (4) Digital Content Directive
cross-type of data regulation	Art. 6 VO 715/2007 Art. 67 PSD2 Directive § 46 (3) TKG	

D. *Foreign legal systems: Taxonomy of data access rights, comparison with German law*

There are three aspects of foreign data access rights of primary interest:

1. Does a foreign law system provide for data access rights that are guaranteed across sectors and data types?
2. If a foreign law system provides for sector-specific data access rights, what do these look like? What sectors are concerned? Who enjoys the right guaranteed? What requirements have to be met to obtain data access? What legal consequences are provided for if data access is unlawfully denied? Is the data right transferable, and does compensation have to be paid? What limitations apply?
3. If there are cross-sectoral regulations in foreign legal systems similar to the GDPR, in what points do the envisaged data access rights differ from the provisions of the GDPR, and why? What ideas from foreign legal systems could be incorporated into the GDPR, which is currently under evaluation?

The legal systems of the following states are taken into consideration, as they provide for substantial genuine data access rights:

- USA and California separately
- Brazil
- Australia
- Japan
- India
- New Zealand
- The Philippines
- Singapore
- Switzerland
- France
- Post-Brexit UK

Examining these different jurisdictions, it turns out that most of them provide for data access rights similar to the GDPR, which means they provide for cross-sectoral data access rights that are limited to personal data. I will thus provide an overview of the deviations from the GDPR in the various legal systems, taking a special look at New Zealand and the Philippines, whose regulations could possibly serve as a model.

The US provides for data protection in specific sectors only, primarily healthcare and banking, and the UK, as the Furman Report shows, is looking to follow a similar path. The UK's Personal Data Mobility Act would in any case limit the right to data portability to individual sectors, but it has not yet been enacted.[6]

Much in contrast, France has established very far-reaching data access rights that are designed to apply across sectors and data types. Australia guarantees a data access right across data types in the banking sector only, but this is to be extended to other sectors.

The article was written in December 2019 and is therefore on the status of the legislation at that time. However, Australian law has changed so fundamentally since then, and at the same time it contains such important new provisions that could be considered as model provisions for European law, that Australian law has been brought up to date to January 2021, the date of the final corrections.

6 Jason Furman and others, 'Unlocking digital competition – Report of the Digital Competition Expert Panel' (2019) 66 <https://assets.publishing.service.gov.uk/government/uploads/system/uploads/attachment_data/file/785547/unlocking_digital_competition_furman_review_web.pdf> accessed 31 August 2020.

I. Sectoral data protection regulation

The United States has established specific data access rights for the healthcare and banking sectors in the Health Insurance Portability and Accountability Act (HIPAA) and the Consumer Protection Principles (CPP) and for minors in the Children Online Privacy Protection Act (COPPA).

1. HIPAA

Section 164.524 HIPAA provides for a right to access protected health information:

> (1) Right of *access*. Except as otherwise provided [...], an individual has a right of access to inspect and obtain a copy of protected health information about the individual in a designated record set, for as long as the protected health information is maintained in the designated record set, except for:
> (i) Psychotherapy notes; and
> (ii) Information compiled in reasonable anticipation of, or for use in, a civil, criminal, or administrative action or proceeding; and
> (iii) Protected health information maintained by a covered entity [...][7]

This right basically corresponds to the right to information per Section 630g German Civil Code (*Bürgerliches Gesetzbuch*), and with the exception of the limited circle of addressees and certain other details, also corresponds essentially to Article 15 GDPR. There are reviewable and unreviewable grounds for denial, and the covered entity may impose a reasonable cost-based fee.

2. COPPA

The Children Online Privacy Protection Act (COPPA) provides for a very basic right to information for minors. In Section 1303(b) it states that

> (1) In General.–Not later than 1 year after the date of the enactment of this Act, the Commission shall promulgate [...] regulations that

7 Emphasis added.

(B) require the operator to *provide*, upon request of a parent under this subparagraph whose child has provided personal information to that website or online service, upon proper identification of that parent, to such parent –
(i) a description of the specific types of personal information collected from the child by that operator;
(ii) the opportunity at any time to refuse to permit the operator's further use or maintenance in retrievable form, or future online collection, of personal information from that child; and
(iii) notwithstanding any other provision of law, a means that is reasonable under the circumstances for the parent to obtain any personal information collected from that child.[8]

According to COPPA, the website operator neither has a duty to inform the child about the personal data gathered, in detail, nor is the operator obliged to act within a defined period. However, children can of course exercise the comprehensive information rights under the CCPA, which will be discussed in detail later on.

3. CPP

The Consumer Protection Principles are intended to reiterate the importance of consumer interests in the developing market for consumer-authorised use of financial data. The Principles are designed to ensure that markets for consumer financial products and services are fair, transparent and competitive. Consumers are to be afforded protection, utility and value.[9] The CPPs are implemented and enforced by the Consumer Finance Protection Bureau as its mission, defined by the US Congress in the Dodd-Frank Act.[10]

8 Emphasis added.
9 Consumer Financial Protection Bureau, 'Consumer Protection Principles: Consumer-Authorized Financial Data Sharing and Aggregation' (2017) <https://files.consumerfinance.gov/f/documents/cfpb_consumer-protection-principles_data-aggregation.pdf> accessed 31 March 2020.
10 Dodd-Frank Wall Street Reform and Consumer Protection Act <https://legcounsel.house.gov/Comps/Dodd-Frank%20Wall%20Street%20Reform%20and%20Consumer%20Protection%20Act.pdf> accessed 21 March 2020; Consumer Financial Protection Bureau, 'Consumer Protection Principles: Consumer-Authorized Financial Data Sharing and Aggregation' (2017) <https://files.consumerfinance.gov/

Principles 1 and 2 provide for:

1) Access
   Consumers are able, upon *request*, to *obtain information* about their ownership or use of a financial product or service from their product or service provider. Such information is made available in a timely manner. Consumers are generally able to authorize trusted third parties to obtain such information from account providers to use on behalf of consumers, for consumer benefit, and in a safe manner.
   Financial account agreements and terms support safe, consumer-authorized access, promote consumer interests, and do not seek to deter consumers from accessing or granting access to their account information. Access does not require consumers to share their account credentials with third parties.
2) Data Scope and Usability
   Financial data subject to consumer and consumer-authorized access may include any transaction, series of transactions, or other aspect of consumer usage; the terms of any account, such as a fee schedule; realized consumer costs, such as fees or interest paid; and realized consumer benefits, such as interest earned or rewards. Information is made available in forms that are readily usable by consumers and consumer-authorized third parties. Third parties with authorized access only access the data necessary to provide the product(s) or service(s) selected by the consumer and only maintain such data as long as necessary.

The main difference between the data access rights per the GDPR and per Principles 1 and 2 of the CPP is the possibility for third parties to exercise the right. With regard to Article 20 GDPR this has been much discussed.[11]

---

f/documents/cfpb_consumer-protection-principles_data-aggregation.pdf> accessed 31 March 2020.

11 Tim Jülicher, Charlotte Röttgen and Max von Schönfeld, 'Das Recht auf Datenübertragbarkeit' (2016) Zeitschrift für Datenschutz 358, 360; Carlo Piltz, 'Die Datenschutz-Grundverordnung' (2016) Kommunikation & Recht 629, 634; Moritz Hennemann, 'Datenportabilität' (2017) Privacy in Germany 5, 6; Sebastian Brüggemann, 'Das Recht auf Datenportabilität' (2018) Kommunikation und Recht 1; Tim Sperlich, 'Das Recht auf Datenübertragbarkeit' (2017) Datenschutz und Datensicherheit 377; Michael Strubel, 'Anwendungsbereich des Rechts auf Datenübertragbarkeit' (2017) Zeitschrift für Datenschutz 355, 356; Tobias Herbst, in Jürgen Kühling and Benedikt Buchner (eds), *Datenschutz-Grundverordnung/Bundesdatanschutzgesetz* (2nd edn, C.H. Beck 2018) Art. 20 DS-GVO para. 1, 19; Wulf Kamlah, in Kai-Uwe Plath (ed.), *DSGVO/BDSG* (3rd edn, Otto Schmidt 2018) Art. 20 DS-GVO paras 2–3; Matthias Rudolph, in Rolf Schwartmann and

II. Cross-sectoral data protection regulation

1. California

California takes a leading role in protecting privacy in the US. Although data protection and privacy protection are not exactly the same, as data protection is an aspect of privacy as interpreted in relation to Article 8 of the European Convention on Human Rights (ECHR),[12] the California privacy protection regime also focuses on prohibitions of data processing and on the rights of data subjects, including data access and data portability rights in particular. As the most detailed privacy regime within the US, another reason for its major importance is that most prominent tech companies are located in Silicon Valley and thus are subject to these quite stringent laws. Enacted in January 2020, the California Consumer Privacy Act (CCPA) has set even higher privacy protection standards than under previous laws.[13] Pursuant to California Civil Code Section 1798.145(a)(6) and Section 1798.140(c)(1), companies doing business in California have to comply with the CCPA. An exemption only applies if a company has an annual revenue of less than US$ 25 million, collects data from fewer than 50,000 Californians annually and earns less than 50 % of its income from data commerce.[14] The Assembly Bills 25 and 1355 exempt certain data, such as employee data and business communication data, from the scope of application of the CCPA until the first of January 2021.[15] Assembly Bill 874 clarifies that 'personal information' includes information that reasonably identifies, relates to, describes or can reasonably be associated with a

---

others (ed.), *DS-GVO/BDSG* (C.F. Müller 2018) Art. 20 DSGVO para. 24; Louisa Specht-Riemenschneider and Linda Bienemann, 'Datenübertragbarkeit anleger- und anlagerelevanter Daten' in Dimitrios Linardatos (ed.), *Rechtshandbuch Robo Advice* (Vahlen 2020) § 11 Rn. 7; Kai von Lewinski, in Heinrich A. Wolff und Stefan Brink (eds), *Beck'scher Online-Kommentar Datenschutzrecht* (31st edn, C.H. Beck 2020) Art. 20 DSGVO para. 7, 113–114; Article 29 Working Party, 'Guidelines on the right to data portability' (5 April 2017) 3 <http://ec.europa.eu/newsroom/document.cfm?doc_id=44095> accessed 31 August 2020.

12 Christoph Grabenwarter and Katharina Pabel, *Europäische Menschenrechtskonvention* (6th edn, C.H. Beck 2016) § 22 Rn. 9–10; Christina-Maria Leeb and Johannes Liebhaber, 'Grundlagen des Datenschutzrechts' (2018) Juristische Schulung 534, 535.

13 Lothar Determann, 'Kalifornisches Gesetz gegen Datenhandel' (2018) Zeitschrift für Datenschutz 443, 444.

14 Ibid.

15 Axel Spies, 'Änderungen und Klarstellungen zum California Consumer Privacy Act (CCPA) beschlossen' (2019) Zeitschrift für Datenschutz-Aktuell 06781.

particular consumer or household, or could reasonably be associated, directly or indirectly, with a particular consumer or household.[16] Thus the concept of personal information is largely identical with the concept of personal data under the GDPR.

The CCPA is quite similar to the GDPR, although there are some differences.[17] With regard to data access rights these differences are elaborated here in detail:

California Civil Code Section 1798.100 provides that

> (a) A consumer shall have the right to request that a business that collects a consumer's personal information disclose to that consumer the categories and specific pieces of personal information the business has collected.
> (b) A business that collects a consumer's personal information shall, at or before the point of collection, inform consumers as to the categories of personal information to be collected and the purposes for which the categories of personal information shall be used. A business shall not collect additional categories of personal information or use personal information collected for additional purposes without providing the consumer with notice consistent with this section.
> (c) A business shall provide the information specified in subdivision (a) to a consumer only upon receipt of a verifiable consumer request.
> (d) A business that receives a verifiable consumer request from a consumer to access personal information shall promptly take steps to disclose and deliver, free of charge to the consumer, the personal information required by this section. The information may be delivered by mail or electronically, and if provided electronically, the information shall be in a portable and, to the extent technically feasible, in a readily useable format that allows the consumer to transmit this information to another entity without hindrance. A business may provide personal information to a consumer at any time, but shall not be required to provide personal information to a consumer more than twice in a 12-month period.
> (e) This section shall not require a business to retain any personal information collected for a single, one-time transaction, if such information is not sold or retained by the business or to reidentify or otherwise link information that is not maintained in a manner that would be considered personal information.

16 Ibid.

17 Regarding these differences see Determann (n. 13) 446.

(1) Retain any personal information collected for a single, one-time transaction, if the information is not sold or retained by the business.
(2) Reidentify or otherwise link any data that, in the ordinary course of business, is not maintained in a manner that would be considered personal information.

Section 1798.100 is specified by Section 1798.110, which gives detailed information about what data has to be disclosed to the consumer, such as the categories of personal data collected about the consumer, the categories of sources from which personal data are collected, the business or commercial purpose for collecting or selling personal data, the categories of third parties with whom the business shares personal data, and, most importantly, the specific personal data the business has collected about a given consumer.

Section 1798.100 is furthermore specified by Section 1798.130, which states, highly significantly, that a business has to disclose and deliver the mandatory data to the consumer free of charge within 45 days of receiving a verifiable request from the consumer. The GDPR requires the data subject to be informed without delay, within one month at the latest, which means that the GDPR is much stricter in its details. According to the CCPA, the disclosure must cover the 12-month period prior to receipt of the verifiable request by the business, whereas under the GDPR the data controller is required to disclose all personal data received to date.

Section 1798.100 in conjunction with Section 1798.110 is to be qualified as a cross-sectoral right to disclose personal data, but it also provides for a right to data portability in Section 1798.100 item d. in conjunction with Section 1798.130 (2). The section refers to all personal data collected, collection being defined as 'buying, renting, gathering, obtaining, receiving or accessing any personal information pertaining to a consumer by any means. This includes receiving information from the consumer, either actively or passively, or by observing the consumer's behavior' – see Section 1798.140 item e.

The right does not only cover information being given by the consumer but also the information being gathered without the consumer recognising the data collection.[18] The wording could also be interpreted to cover derived data if derived data are interpreted as being part of observation data. This remains unclear. Section 1798.100. in conjunction with Sections 1798.110 and 1798.130 requires a verified request, whereas Article 15

18 Thomas Hoeren and Stefan Pinelli, 'Das neue kalifornische Datenschutzrecht am Maßstab der DS-GVO' (2018) Multimedia und Recht 711, 714.

GDPR only requires a verified request in case of doubt; see Article 12(1) and (6) GDPR. Section 1798.100 does not require a business to retain any personal data collected for a single, one-time transaction if 'such data is not sold or retained by the business, or to reidentify or otherwise link to information that is not maintained in a manner allowing it to be considered personal information'. A similar exception is provided for in Art. 11 (1) GDPR. Lastly, it must be mentioned that a business is not required to provide personal information to a consumer more than twice within a 12-month period. Article 12(5) GDPR only provides that excessive requests may be rejected, the question of what is excessive being decided on a case-by-case basis. Section 1798.115 provides for another right to disclose data in cases where data are sold. More importantly, Section 1798.125 provides for a right to non-discrimination against consumers exercising consumer rights, such as by withholding products.[19] The GDPR does not provide for such a right. The following provision, which could serve as a model for Europe, is worth quoting in its entirety:

> 1798.125.
> (a) (1) A business shall not discriminate against a consumer because the consumer exercised any of the consumer's rights under this title, including, but not limited to, by:
> (A) Denying goods or services to the consumer.
> (B) Charging different prices or rates for goods or services, including through the use of discounts or other benefits or imposing penalties.
> (C) Providing a different level or quality of goods or services to the consumer.
> (D) Suggesting that the consumer will receive a different price or rate for goods or services or a different level or quality of goods or services.
> (2) Nothing in this subdivision prohibits a business from charging a consumer a different price or rate, or from providing a different level or quality of goods or services to the consumer, if that difference is reasonably related to the value provided to the business by the consumer's data.
> (b) (1) A business may offer financial incentives, including payments to consumers as compensation, for the collection of personal information, the sale of personal information, or the deletion of personal information. A business may also offer a different price, rate, level, or quality of goods or services to the consumer if that price or difference

19 Determann (n. 13) 445.

is directly related to the value provided to the business by the consumer's data.
(2) A business that offers any financial incentives pursuant to this subdivision shall notify consumers of the financial incentives pursuant to Section 1798.130.
(3) A business may enter a consumer into a financial incentive program only if the consumer gives the business prior opt-in consent pursuant to Section 1798.130 that clearly describes the material terms of the financial incentive program, and which may be revoked by the consumer at any time.
(4) A business shall not use financial incentive practices that are unjust, unreasonable, coercive, or usurious in nature.

Enforcement of the CCPA is the responsibility of the Office of the Attorney General of California.

2. New Zealand

New Zealand's privacy regime is principle-based, in contrast to the more prescriptive nature of the GDPR. The Privacy Bill is to repeal and replace the Privacy Act of 1993, as was recommended in the Law Commission's 2011 review of the Act, but it has not yet been adopted.[20] The Bill outlines 13 privacy principles, one of which is 'access to personal information'. This Privacy Principle 6 is to be qualified as a cross-sectoral right to information on personal data retained, similar to Article 15 GDPR. The Privacy Bill does not provide for a right to data portability. Such a right to data portability was proposed by the Privacy Commissioner in 2017,[21] and is considered by the majority of New Zealanders[22] to be important, though it was not included in the latest draft of the Privacy Bill dated March 2019.

---

20 Privacy Bill 2018 (34–2) <www.parliament.nz/en/pb/bills-and-laws/bills-proposed-laws/document/BILL_77618/tab/digest> accessed 31 August 2020.

21 Privacy Commissioner/Te Mana Matapono Matatapu, 'Report to the Minister of Justice under Section 26 of the Privacy Act, Six Recommendations for Privacy Act Reform', para. 8 <www.privacy.org.nz/assets/Files/Reports-to-ParlGovt/OPC-report-to-the-Minister-of-Justice-under-Section-26-of-the-Privacy-Act.pdf> accessed 31 August 2020.

22 Ibid. para. 10.

Principle 6 of the Privacy Act 1993 reads:

> (1) Where an agency holds personal information in such a way that it can readily be retrieved, the individual concerned shall be
> (a) To obtain from the agency confirmation of whether or not the agency holds such personal information about them; and
> (b) To have *access* to that information. [...][23]

In Part 4 of the Privacy Bill, several details concerning Privacy Principle 6 are outlined, including chiefly the following:

> (46) A requestor may ask that an IPP 6 request be treated as urgent [...]
> (47) An agency must give reasonable assistance to an individual [...]
> (48) (1) This section applies if an agency that receives an IPP 6 request
> (a) does not hold the information to which the request relates, but believes that the information is held by another agency; or
> (b) believes that the information to which the request relates is more closely connected with the functions or activities of another agency.
> (2) The agency must promptly, and in any case not later than 10 working days after the day on which the IPP 6 request is received, transfer the request to the other agency and inform the requestor accordingly.
> (3) However, subsection (2) does not apply if the agency has good cause to believe that the requestor does not want the request transferred to another agency.
> (50A) (1) If an agency grants access [it] must state
> (a) the way the information is made available;
> (b) the charge (if any) payable [...];
> (c) the requestor's right to complaint to the Commissioner about the charge that is payable (if any).
> (50B) (1) An agency may refuse access to the personal information requested, only if the agency is able to rely on any of sections 52 to 57 [...].
> (2) The notice given [...] must state
> (a) the reason for the refusal; and
> (b) the requestor's right to make a complaint [...].
> (50C) (1) An agency may neither confirm nor deny that it holds the personal information, [if it]

23 Emphasis added.

(a) is able to rely on section 52(1)(a)(i) or [...]; and
(b) is satisfied that the interest protected by any of those provisions would be likely to be prejudiced by the agency confirming whether or not it holds the information about the requestor.
(52) (1) An agency may refuse access to any personal information requested if
(a) the disclosure of the information would—
(i) be likely to pose a serious threat to the life, health, or safety of any individual, or to public health or public safety; or
(ii) create a significant likelihood of serious harassment of an individual; or
(iii) include disclosure of information about another person who—
(A) is the victim of an offence or alleged offence; and
(B) would be caused significant distress, loss of dignity, or injury to feelings by the disclosure of the information; or [...]
(53) (1) An agency may refuse access [...] if—
(a) the information is evaluative material and the disclosure of that information or of the information identifying the person who supplied it would breach an express or implied promise—
(i) that was made to the person who supplied the information; and
(ii) that was to the effect that the information or the identity of the person who supplied it, or both, would be held in confidence; or [...]
(54) Security, defence, international relations as reason for refusing access to personal information [...]
(55) Trade secret as reason for refusing access to personal information [...]
(57) Other reasons for refusing access to personal information [...]
(58) (2) Instead of refusing access to the personal information requested, the agency may grant access to the information, but may impose *conditions* relating to either or both of the following:[24]
(a) the requestor's use of the information:
(b) the requestor's disclosure of the information to any other person.
(61) (1) If the personal information requested is contained in a document and there is good reason under any of sections 52 to 57 for withholding some of that information, the agency may decide to grant the requestor access to a copy of that document under section 50(2) with any deletions or alterations in respect of the information that could be withheld that it considers necessary.

24 Emphasis added.

> (72) (1) In relation to an IPP 6 request,—
> (a) a public sector agency may, if authorised under section 73, impose a charge for making information available in compliance, in whole or in part, with the request:
> (b) a private sector agency may, subject to the provisions of any applicable code of practice, impose a charge for—
> (i) providing assistance under section 47, but only if the agency makes information available in compliance, in whole or in part, with the request:
> (ii) making information available in compliance, in whole or in part, with the request.
> (4) A charge [...] must be reasonable and, [...] may be had to—
> (a) the cost of the labour and materials involved in making the information available; and
> (b) any costs involved in making the information available urgently [...].
> (5) An agency may require all or part of a charge to be paid in advance.

Information Privacy Principle 6 has two chief advantages over Article 15 GDPR, the first of which is that the requestor may ask that an IPP 6 request be treated as urgent. If a request is designated as urgent, it must be treated as such by the controller. The second advantage over Article 15 GDPR is that IPP6 offers the possibility of providing data under terms and conditions instead of refusing access to the personal data requested. The possibility to erase and correct data before it is provided to the data subject is offered in Article 15 GDPR as well, following from a teleological interpretation of this provision, as it aims to provide comprehensive protection for the data subject, and it is more suitable for the data subject to receive abridged data than no data at all.

There are two other details which may be seen as advantageous or disadvantageous depending on one's point of view. IPP6 provides for an extensive and detailed catalogue of reasons for refusing to provide information on data, whereas Article 15(4) GDPR only states that the information provided must not infringe the rights of third parties. Any third-party rights qualify; Recital 63 cites trade secrets and intellectual property rights by way of example only, including particularly software copyrights. Article 15(4) GDPR requires that the rights and interests concerned be weighed in each individual case, therefore allowing for greater case-by-case justice, while IPP6 creates greater legal certainty due to the explicit enumeration of reasons for exclusion.

The possibility of imposing a charge for making information available in full or partial compliance with a request may dissuade the data subject from exercising his or her rights, and therefore should not be provided for in the GDPR, except in the cases already envisaged in Article 15(3) no. 2 and Article 12(5) no. 2 GDPR.

3. Brazil

The Brazilian Lei Geral de Proteção de Dados (LGPD) is a cross-sector regulation to protect personal data, which will enter into force in August 2020. Heretofore, the 'Marco Civil da Internet' has afforded data protection for specific data processing instances on the internet only. According to Article 18(2) LGPD, the data subject has a right to access to his or her data being processed, which represents a right to be informed about such data, while Article 18(5) LGPD grants a right to data portability.

Article 18 LGPD provides that

> The personal data subject has the right to obtain the following from the controller, regarding the data subject's data being processed by the controller, at any time and by means of request: [...]
> II. *access* to the data; [...]
> V. *portability* of the data to another service or product provider, by means of an express request and subject to commercial and industrial secrecy, pursuant to the regulation of the controlling agency; [...].[25]

The LGPD is based on the GDPR, hence Article 18 LGDP largely corresponds to Articles 15 and 20 GDPR. The right to data portability is seen as one of the biggest innovations in Brazilian data protection law. The right applies to data being provided by the data subject and to generated data. Whether Article 20 GDPR has to be interpreted in the same way is subject to much discussion. The right to data portability is subject to commercial and industrial secrecy, which is also true for Article 20 GDPR. Article 20(4) GDPR even provides that the right to data portability may not adversely affect the rights and freedoms of other persons.

25 Emphasis added.

4. Japan

In Japan, The Act on the Protection of Personal Information (APPI) provides for cross-sector protection of personal data. Further data protection regulations can be enacted by each ministry for its specific area of competence, and the individual prefectures (federal states) make their own data protection law, some of which applies to the public sector only.

The APPI provides for a right to data access and the right to obtain a copy of the processed personal data under Article 28 APPI. The right to data portability is not provided for in Japan, but discussion of whether it should be introduced, especially with regard to the medical, finance and electricity sectors, is expected in 2020.

> Article 28 (Disclosure)
> (1) The person may request the business operator handling personal information to disclose the retained personal data that can be used to identify the person.
> (2) When the business operator handling personal information is requested under the provision of the preceding paragraph, the business operator must disclose the retained personal data without delay using the means that Cabinet Order provides for. However, in case falling under one of the following items, the business operator may choose not to disclose all or part of the retained personal data:
> (i) if disclosure is likely to harm the life, body, property, or other rights or interests of the person or a third party;
> (ii) if disclosure is likely to seriously interfere with the proper implementation of the business of the business operator handling personal information;
> (iii) if disclosure would violate any other law or regulation.
> (3) If a business operator handling personal information decides not to disclose all or part of the retained personal data as requested pursuant to the provision of the preceding paragraph (1), or there is no retained personal data, the business operator must notify the person of this without delay.
> (4) If, pursuant to the provisions of any other law and regulation, all or part of the retained personal data that can be used to identify a person is to be disclosed to the person by a means equivalent to what is prescribed in the main clause of paragraph (2), the provisions of paragraph (1) and (2) do not apply to either the whole or the relevant part of the retained personal data.

Article 28 APPI provides for a right of access to data as well as a right to obtain a copy, though the latter is not stated explicitly. The cabinet decides on the methods of disclosure but has not yet decided that access must be offered in an easy and precise way. No particular form is required, either. The request filed by the data subject also has to be precise. Exceptions of the duty to disclose data apply according to Article 28(2) APPI.

A crucial difference between the APPI and the GDPR is that under Article 33 APPI, disclosure of data can be made subject to payment of a fee. Apart from that, the provisions of the GDPR and the APPI are very similar.

5. India

Until recently, data protection obligations have only been imposed on companies, and have only been legislated in specific sectors (including telecommunications and finance) in India. These obligations are provided for in the Aadhaar (Targeted Delivery of Financial and other Subsidies Benefits and Services) Act, which dates from 2016. On 11 December 2019, India's Minister for Electronics and Information Technology introduced an updated draft of the Personal Data Protection Bill (PDPB) in the Lok Sabha, India's lower house of parliament. The Bill was referred to a Joint Select Committee consisting of parliamentarians from the lower and upper houses for examination and reporting.[26] The Committee is due to report back to the Lok Sabha by the second week of the 2020 monsoon session of parliament, which is about to run from September 14 to October 1.[27]

The new PDPB applies across sectors but to personal data only. General conditions for the exercise of the data subjects' rights are set forth in Section 21 PDPB, which mainly corresponds to Articles 13 and 14 GDPR.

26 Kurt Wimmer and Gabe Maldoff, 'India Proposes Updated Personal Data Protection Bill' (Inside Privacy 2019) <www.insideprivacy.com/india/india-proposes-updated-personal-data-protection-bill> accessed 31 August 2020; Hunton Privacy Blog, 'India's Draft Data Privacy Bill Introduced in Parliament' (2019) <www.huntonprivacyblog.com/2019/12/19/indias-draft-data-privacy-bill-introduced-in-parliament> accessed 31 August 2020.

27 Surabhi Agarwal, 'Joint parliamentary committee wants more time to submit data bill note' (The Economic Times) <https://economictimes.indiatimes.com/tech/internet/jpc-wants-more-time-to-submit-data-bill-note/articleshow/74800912.cms> accessed 31 August 2020.

While Section 17 of the PDPB provides for a right to access to data, Section 19 PDPB introduces a right to data portability. Another right to customer data portability is currently in discussion for the insurance sector.[28] Whether it will actually be introduced is not yet clear. The PBPD partly uses misleading terminology. For example, it refers to the 'data principal' and not to the 'data subject' as other laws do, and to the 'data fiduciary' instead of the 'controller'. However, Section 3(13) and 3(14) clarify that there is no difference in meaning between 'data principal' and "data subject' or between 'data fiduciary' and 'controller'. According to Section 3(13), a 'data principal' is the natural person to whom the personal data relates. Section 3(14) provides that a 'data fiduciary' is any person, including the state or any company, juristic entity or individual who alone or in conjunction with others determines the purpose and means of processing of personal data.

Sections 17 and 19 PDPB read as follows:

> Section 17 PDPB – Right to confirmation and access.
> (1) The data principal shall have the right to obtain from the data fiduciary—
> (a) confirmation whether the data fiduciary is processing or has processed
> personal data of the data principal;
> (b) the personal data of the data principal being processed or that has been processed by the data fiduciary, or any summary thereof;
> (c) a brief summary of processing activities undertaken by the data fiduciary with respect to the personal data of the data principal, including any information provided in the notice under section 7 in relation to such processing.
> (2) The data fiduciary shall *provide* the information under sub-section (1) to the data principal in a clear and concise manner that is easily comprehensible to a reasonable person.[29]
> (3) The data principal shall have the right to access in one place the identities of the data fiduciaries with whom his personal data has been shared by any data fiduciary together with the categories of personal

---

28 G. Naga Sridhar, 'Customer data portability to be introduced in insurance sector' (The Hindu Business Line 2018) <www.thehindubusinessline.com/money-and-banking/customer-data-portability-to-be-introduced-in-insurance-sector/article24584413.ece> accessed 31 August 2020.

29 Emphasis added.

data shared with them, in such manner as may be specified by regulations.

Section 19 PDPB – Right to data portability.
(1) Where the processing has been carried out through automated means, the data principal shall have the right to—
(a) *receive* the following personal data in a structured, commonly used and machine-readable format—
(i) the personal data provided to the data fiduciary;
(ii) the data which has been generated in the course of provision of services
or use of goods by the data fiduciary; or
(iii) the data which forms part of any profile on the data principal, or which the data fiduciary has otherwise obtained; and
(b) have the personal data referred to in clause (a) *transferred* to any other data fiduciary in the format referred to in that clause.[30]
(2) The provisions of sub-section (1) shall not apply where—
(a) processing is necessary for functions of the State or in compliance of law or order of a court under section 12;
(b) compliance with the request in sub-section (1) would reveal a trade secret of any data fiduciary or would not be technically feasible.

Although the PDPB is based on the GDPR, there are some small differences. One of these is that Section 17 PDPB provides for data subjects' right to receive a summary of the data processing activities conducted. As under Brazilian data protection law, the right to data portability under Indian data protection law applies to data which is provided by the data subject, generated data, data which forms part of any profile of the data principal and data which the data fiduciary has obtained otherwise. It does not apply if processing is necessary for functions of the state or to comply with a law or court order. Nor does it apply if compliance with the request would reveal a trade secret of any data fiduciary, or is not technically feasible. The data fiduciary is not obliged to comply with requests under Sections 17 and 19 PDPB where such compliance infringes the rights of any other data principal under this Act, pursuant to Section 21(5) PDPB. According to Section 21(2) PDPB, the data fiduciary may charge a fee for complying with requests per Sections 17 and 19 PDPB, whereas this is only possible in exceptional cases under Article 12(5) GDPR.

30 Emphasis added.

6. Philippines

The Philippines Data Privacy Act (DPA), which dates from 2012, is a cross-sectoral regulation on personal data. Section 16 DPA grants the data subject a right of access to data, and a right to data portability is established in Section 18 DPA.

The relevant sections read as follows:

> Section 16. Rights of the Data Subject.
> The data subject is entitled to: [...]
> (c) Reasonable *access* to, upon demand, the following:[31]
> (1) Contents of his or her personal information that were processed;
> (2) Sources from which personal information were obtained;
> (3) Names and addresses of recipients of the personal information;
> (4) Manner by which such data were processed;
> (5) Reasons for the disclosure of the personal information to recipients;
> (6) Information on automated processes where the data will or likely to be made as the sole basis for any decision significantly affecting or will affect the data subject;
> (7) Date when his or her personal information concerning the data subject were last accessed and modified; and
> (8) The designation, or name or identity and address of the personal information controller; [...]
>
> Section 17. Transmissibility of Rights of the Data Subject.
> The lawful heirs and assigns of the data subject may invoke the rights of the data subject for which he or she is an heir or assignee at any time after the death of the data subject or when the data subject is incapacitated or incapable of exercising the rights as enumerated in the immediately preceding section.
> Section 18. Right to Data Portability.
> The data subject shall have the right, where personal information is processed by electronic means and in a structured and commonly used format, to obtain from the personal information controller a *copy* of data undergoing processing in an electronic or structured format, which is commonly used and allows for further use by the data subject. The Commission may specify the electronic format referred to

31 Emphasis added.

> above, as well as the technical standards, modalities and procedures for their transfer.[32]
> Section 19. Non-Applicability.
> The immediately preceding sections are not applicable if the processed personal information is used only for the needs of scientific and statistical research and [...] for the purpose of investigations in relation to any criminal, administrative or tax liabilities of a data subject.

Apart from differences in details between Philippine data protection law and the GDPR, it is striking that under Section 17 DPA these rights are specifically transmissible, and may be invoked at any time after the death of the data subject, or when the data subject is incapacitated or rendered incapable of exercising the rights as enumerated in the immediately preceding section. Transmissibility is the subject of much discussion in relation to Article 20 GDPR.[33] The order of sequence of Section 17 DPA leaves ambiguity as to whether it refers only to Section 16 or to Section 18 as well. Since it concerns the rights of the data subject, it is to be assumed that despite its following after Section 16 it also refers to the right to data portability per Section 18 DPA.

Sections 16 and 18 are not applicable if the processed personal data are used only for scientific and statistical research, no activities are carried out on the basis of such nor decisions made regarding the data subject and the personal data are held under strict confidentiality and only used for the declared purpose. Nor are Sections 16 and 18 applicable to the processing of personal data gathered for investigation purposes regarding potential criminal, administrative or tax offences on the part of a data subject. Comparing the DPA with the GDPR, it is particularly striking that under the DPA data subjects' rights do not apply if the data is used for scientific research. Such an exception is missing in the GDPR. Although Article 89 GDPR provides that national law may allow exceptions to Article 15 for the purposes of scientific research and for exceptions to Article 20 if data is provided for public or archival purposes. Germany has not made use of this exception.

32 Emphasis added.

33 Jülicher and others (n. 11) 358, 360; Piltz (n. 11) 634; Strubel (n. 11) 356; Sperlich (n. 11) 377; Hennemann (n. 11) 6; Brüggemann (n. 11) 1; Herbst (n. 11) paras 1, 19; Kamlah (n. 11) Art. 20 DS-GVO paras 2–3; Rudolph (n. 11) Art. 20 DS-GVO para. 24; von Lewinski (n. 11) Art. 20 DSGVO paras 7, 113–114; Specht-Riemenschneider and Bienemann (n. 11) § 11 Rn. 7; Article 29 Working Party (n. 11) 3.

7. Singapore

The Singapore Personal Data Protection Act (PDPA) is a cross-sectoral regulation on personal data. Section 21 PDPA does not provide for a right to portability by law, but does grant data subjects a right of access to data. It is not applicable for the reasons listed in Section 21(2), (3) and (4).

Singapore is currently considering introducing data portability rights, as indicated by the government's latest discussion paper, but the country has not yet introduced such a right.[34]

> Access to personal data
> 21.
> (1) Subject to subsections (2), (3) and (4), on request of an individual, an organisation shall, as soon as reasonably possible, *provide* the individual with —[35]
> (a) personal data about the individual that is in the possession or under the control of the organisation; and
> (b) information about the ways in which the personal data referred to in paragraph (a) has been or may have been used or disclosed by the organisation within a year before the date of the request.
> (2) An organisation is not required to provide an individual with the individual's personal data or other information under subsection (1) in respect of the matters specified in the Fifth Schedule.
> (3) An organisation shall not provide an individual with the individual's personal data or other information under subsection (1) if the provision of that personal data or other information, as the case may be, could reasonably be expected to –
> (a) threaten the safety or physical or mental health of an individual other than the individual who made the request;
> (b) cause immediate or grave harm to the safety or to the physical or mental health of the individual who made the request;
> (c) reveal personal data about another individual;
> (d) reveal the identity of an individual who has provided personal data about another individual and the individual providing the personal data does not consent to the disclosure of his identity; or

34 The Personal Data Protection Commission Singapore, 'Discussion Paper on Data Portability' (2019) <www.pdpc.gov.sg/-/media/Files/PDPC/PDF-Files/Resource-for-Organisation/Data-Portability/PDPC-CCCS-Data-Portability-Discussion-Paper---250219.pdf> accessed 31 August 2020.

35 Emphasis added.

(e) be contrary to the national interest.
(4) An organisation shall not inform any individual under subsection (1) that it has disclosed personal data to a prescribed law enforcement agency if the disclosure was made without the consent of the individual pursuant [...] or under any other written law.
(5) If an organisation is able to provide the individual with the individual's personal data and other information requested under subsection (1) without the personal data or other information excluded under subsections (2), (3) and (4), the organisation shall provide the individual with access to the personal data and other information without the personal data or other information excluded under subsections (2), (3) and (4).

According to Section 21 PDPA and upon request, the data subject has a right to access the personal data used and to information on how the personal data has been or may have been used within the period of one year prior to the request date. The GDPR does not provide for such a temporal limitation. This right to access per Section 21 PDPA is subject to many exceptions. According to Section 21(2) PDPA, an organisation is not required to provide an individual with the individual's personal data or other information per subsection (1) in respect of the matters specified in the Fifth Schedule to the PDPA.[36]

Other reasons requiring compliance with Section 21(1) are stated in Subsection (3) PDPA. These include safety, health and privacy-related reasons, among others. In summary, Section 21 is subject to many more defined exceptions than is Article 15 GDPR.

36 The matters specified in the Fifth Schedule include opinion data, educational institutions, beneficiaries, private trusts, arbitral institutions and mediation centres, prosecution, protection of confidential commercial information and protection of trial, the prohibition of data processing by other special law, repetitious or systematic requests, unreasonable expenses, information that does not exist or cannot be found and trivial information (this can be compared to the purpose of protection per Art. 15(5) GDPR, which regulates that a request cannot be refused but that a fee may be charged). Thus Sec. 21(2) PDPA only offers a small opening clause for requests that are frivolous or vexatious, not a broad opening clause.

8. Switzerland

In Switzerland, the revised Data Protection Act is intended to replace the existing Swiss Federal Act on Data Protection (FADP). The FADP applies to personal data across sectors.

The revised version of the FADP provides for a right of access to data under Article 23, while a right to data portability is not provided for. However, a right to data portability is the subject of much current discussion. The Federal Council assumes that its introduction would be costly and its implementation difficult, which is why it has rejected a right to data portability.[37] Switzerland believes that not introducing such a right will not affect the attestation of equivalence within the meaning of the GDPR. The country thus favours sector-specific, voluntary agreements over a data portability right.

According to an expert from the University of Zurich, not having a right to data portability is not detrimental because companies could have the entitled person authorise them to exercise the right to information, thereby largely achieving the purposes of data portability via the current right to information.[38] It would be necessary however to amend the existing right to information in certain ways, and to exclude specific sectors which would be affected too negatively by such a right.[39]

Article 23 FADP (revised version) is scheduled to replace Article 8 FADP, and Article 24 FADP (revised version) will provide for exceptions to the right of access as provided for in Article 9 FADP today. Article 25 will provide for a right of refusal of information for the media, e.g. for the protection of informants as Article 10 FADP does currently. Articles 23, 24 and 25 essentially serve to implement Article 15 GDPR and contain only minor changes to the current legal situation. Information must be provided free of charge, but exceptions may be provided for by the Swiss Federal Council. Apart from details, Articles 8–10 FADP are very similar to the

37 Economie suisse, 'Gesetzliche Datenportabilität – kein Wundermittel' (2019) #05, 8 Dossier Politik <www.economiesuisse.ch/de/dossier-politik/gesetzliche-datenportabilitaet-kein-wundermittel> accessed 31 August 2020.

38 Rolf H. Weber and Florent Thouvenin, 'Gutachten zur Möglichkeit der Einführung eines Datenportabilitätsrechts im schweizerischen Recht und zur Rechtslage bei Personal Information Management Systems (PIMS)' (University of Zurich Center for Information Technology, Society, and Law 2017) <www.bakom.admin.ch/dam/bakom/de/dokumente/informationsgesellschaft/datenpolitik/180321%20BJ-Gutachten_final.pdf.download.pdf/180321%20BJ-Gutachten_final.pdf> accessed 31 August 2020.

39 Ibid.

provisions of the GDPR. There are no significant advantages which need to be discussed here.

The current legal provisions read as follows:

Article 8 – Right to information
(1) Any person may request information from the controller of a data file as to whether data concerning them is being processed.
(2) The controller of a data file must notify the data subject:
a. of all available data concerning the subject in the data file, including the available information on the source of the data;
b. the purpose of and if applicable the legal basis for the processing as well as the categories of the personal data processed, the other parties involved with the file and the data recipient.
(3) The controller of a data file may arrange for data on the health of the data subject to be communicated by a doctor designated by the subject.
(4) If the controller of a data file has personal data processed by a third party, the controller remains under an obligation to provide information. The third party is under an obligation to provide information if he does not disclose the identity of the controller or if the controller is not domiciled in Switzerland.
(5) The information must normally be provided in writing, in the form of a printout or a photocopy, and is free of charge. The Federal Council regulates exceptions.
(6) No one may waive the right to information in advance.
Article 9 – Limitation of the duty to provide information
(1) The controller of a data file may refuse, restrict or defer the provision of information where:
a. a formal enactment so provides;
b. this is required to protect the overriding interests of third parties.
(2) A federal body may further refuse, restrict or defer the provision of information where:
a. this is required to protect overriding public interests, and in particular the internal or external security of the Confederation;
b. the information would jeopardise the outcome of a criminal investigation or any other investigation proceedings.
(3) As soon as the reason for refusing, restricting or deferring the provision of information ceases to apply, the federal body must provide the information unless this is impossible or only possible with disproportionate inconvenience or expense.

(4) The private controller of a data file may further refuse, restrict or defer the provision of information where his own overriding interests so require and he does not disclose the personal data to third parties.
(5) The controller of a data file must indicate the reason why he has refused, restricted or deferred access to information.
Article 10 – Limitations of the right to information for journalists
(1) The controller of a data file that is used exclusively for publication in the edited section of a periodically published medium may refuse to provide information, limit the information or defer its provision provided:
a. the personal data reveals the sources of the information;
b. access to the drafts of publications would have to be given;
c. the freedom of the public to form its opinion would be prejudiced.
(2) Journalists may also refuse restrict or defer information if the data file is being used exclusively as a personal work aid.

III. Sector specific cross-type of data regulation

On 1 August 2019, Australia amended the Consumer and Competition Act (CCA)[40]2010 by introducing the so-called Consumer Data Right (CDR)[41] which is the basis for a sector-specific but cross-data type regulation. The CDR regime intends to give consumers extensive access to "their" data and should lead to a growth in (consumer) welfare.[42] For the purpose of such consumer welfare the CDR grants the consumer, among others, a right to data portability.[43] The purpose of Art. 20 GDPR, on the contrary, [44] is

40 Treasury Laws Amendment (Consumer Data Right) Bill 2019 (*As passed by both houses*) <https://parlinfo.aph.gov.au/parlInfo/download/legislation/bills/r6370_aspassed/toc_pdf/19126b01.pdf;fileType=application%2Fpdf> accessed 15 January 2020.

41 Consumer and Competition Act 2010 < https://www.legislation.gov.au/Details/C2017C00369> accessed 15 January 2020.

42 Explanatory Memorandum to Treasury Laws Amendment (Consumer Data Right) Bill 2019, part 1.3 et sey. <https://parlinfo.aph.gov.au/parlInfo/download/legislation/ems/r6370_ems_ce513d68-7222-49f4-a2fe-67e1c2b32fed/upload_pdf/712911.pdf;fileType=application%2Fpdf> accessed 15 January 2021.

43 Only a right is granted, but no corresponding, judicially enforceable claim. Judicial enforcement takes place at most indirectly through so-called civil penalties.

44 In addition to the portability right under the CDR, there is a cross-sectoral right of access comparable to that under Art. 15 GDPR. This is set out in the twelfth Australian Privacy Principle of the Privacy Act 1988 and relates to the storage and

mainly to address a data protection-related market failure in data markets.[45]

The CDR regime must be declared applicable to a specific sector and the legislator needs to work out specific regulations for that sector before they apply. Hence, the CDR regime can be described as a horizontal guideline for the legislator which gives orientation for specific regulation in certain sectors. Such specific regulation has yet only been implemented in the banking sector. Moreover, similar regulation is being prepared for the energy sector, and will follow for the telecommunications sector. [46]

According to Section 56AA CCA the object of the CDR is:

> (a) to enable consumers in certain sectors of the Australian economy to require information relating to themselves in those sectors to be disclosed safely, efficiently and conveniently:
> (i) to themselves for use as they see fit; or
> (ii) to accredited persons for use subject to privacy safeguards; and
> (b) to enable any person to efficiently and conveniently access information in those sectors that:
> (i) is about goods (such as products) or services; and
> (ii) does not relate to any identifiable, or reasonably identifiable, consumers; and
> (c) as a result of paragraphs (a) and (b), to create more choice and competition, or to otherwise promote the public interest.

1. CDR Data

Data (classes) which fall under the CDR regime can only be data that the legislature explicitly addresses or data which can be derived from such explicitly addressed data. CDR data can be both consumer and product related data.

---

control of personal information. Privacy Act 1988 <https://www.legislation.gov.au/Details/C2014C00076> accessed 15 January 2021.

45 Heike Schweitzer and Martin Peitz, `Data markets in the digital economy: functional deficits and regulatory needs' (2017) Discussion Paper No.17-043, 50 < http://ftp.zew.de/pub/zew-docs/dp/dp17043.pdf> accessed 15 January 2021.

46 For an overview of the implementation status <www.accc.gov.au/focus-areas/consumer-data-right-cdr-0> accessed 15 January 2021.

Section 56AI Meanings of CDR data, directly or indirectly derived and CDR consumer
CDR data is information that:
(a) is within a class of information specified, as described in paragraph 56AC(2)(a), in an instrument designating a sector under subsection 56AC(2); or
(b) is not covered by paragraph (a) of this subsection, but is wholly or partly derived from information covered by:
(i) paragraph (a) of this subsection; or
(ii) a previous application of this paragraph.
(2) CDR data is directly or indirectly derived from other CDR data if the first-mentioned CDR data is wholly or partly derived from the other CDR data after one or more applications of paragraph (1)(b).
(3) A person is a CDR consumer for CDR data if:
(a) the CDR data relates to the person because:
(i) of the supply of a good or service to the person or to one or more of the person's associates (within the meaning of section 318 of the Income Tax Assessment Act 1936); or
(ii) of circumstances of a kind prescribed by the regulations; and
[...]
(c) the person is identifiable, or reasonably identifiable, from:
(i) the CDR data; or
(ii) other information held by the other person referred to in paragraph (b); and
[...]

a) Consumer Data

Unlike the GDPR, the CDR does not intend to protect the informational self-determination but the data itself. Hence, legal entities can also be holders of the CDR data portability right if consumers have transferred the exercise of this right to them. However, whether data concerns the consumer and the consumer can therefore exercise or transfer the CDR rights depends on the identifiability of the consumer derived from European data protection law, see also 1.102 et seq. of the Explanatory Memorandum.

Speaking of derived data and the question whether the CDR rights apply to such derived data it needs to be pointed out that the meaning of 'derived data' in the GDPR differs from the meaning in the CDR regime. While the GDPR speaks of derived data as data being derived from data which has been entered by the data subject, the CDR regime means data being derived from the data which was explicitly addressed in the sector specific regulation by the legislature, see subsection 56BD(1) Note 1 CCA. The CDR rights do not apply to derived data in the latter sense but data being derived from data which the data subject has entered could be explicitly addressed in the sector specific regulation and therefore the CDR data rights could apply to derived data in this sense.

Whether and to what extent a fee can be charged for the disclosure of data or for their subsequent use depends on whether the legislator has declared the data (classes) as being subject to a fee.

The relevant sections for the CDR consumer rights read as follows:

> 56BC Rules about disclosure, collection, use, accuracy, storage, security or deletion of CDR data for which there are CDR consumers
> *Required disclosures in response to valid requests*
> (1) Without limiting paragraph 56BB(a), the consumer data rules may include the following rules:
> (a) requirements on a CDR participant for CDR data to disclose all or part of the CDR data, in response to a valid request by a CDR consumer for the CDR data, to:
> (i) the CDR consumer for use as the CDR consumer sees fit; or
> (ii) an accredited person for use subject to the privacy safeguards; (...)
>
> 56BD Limitations for rules about CDR data for which there are CDR consumers
> *Only designated CDR data can be required to be disclosed*
> [...]
> *No fee when fee-free CDR data is required to be disclosed*
> (2) The consumer data rules cannot allow a fee to be charged for:
> (a) the disclosure of fee-free CDR data under rules like those described in paragraph 56BC(1)(a) or 56BG(1)(a); or
> (b) the use of fee-free CDR data received as the result of such a disclosure.
> [...]

b) Product Data

Product data, in contrast, is data that does not relate to any particular identifiable consumer. It includes information about terms and conditions, eligibility criteria, product pricing and so on. A product data request may be for required product data, voluntary product data or both. Subsection 56BF CCA identifies the data which needs to be disclosed upon request.

While a fee cannot be charged for the disclosure of required product data, a fee can be charged for disclosing voluntary product data. Under European law, in business-consumer relations product information must be provided in accordance with certain EU directives. These include directives on consumer rights and the distance marketing of consumer financial services, the provisions of which are implemented in the national law of the Member States (such as Articles 246 et seq. of the Introductory Act to the Civil Code, EGBGB, and Sections 312 et seq. of the Civil Code, BGB, in Germany). These information obligations apply without regard to a request filed by the consumer. It is therefore unnecessary to introduce a data access right to product data.

The relevant sections for product data in the CDR regime read as follows:

> 56BE Rules about disclosure, collection, use, accuracy, storage, security or deletion of product data
> Without limiting paragraph 56BB(b), the consumer data rules may include the following rules for CDR data for which there are no CDR consumers:
> (a) requirements on a CDR participant for the CDR data to disclose all or part of the CDR data to a person in response to a valid request by the person;
> [...]
>
> 56BF Limitations for rules about product data
> *Only certain kinds of product data can be required to be disclosed*
> (1) The consumer data rules can only require a disclosure of CDR data for which there are no CDR consumers if:
> (a) the CDR data is about the eligibility criteria, terms and conditions, price, availability or performance of:
> (i) a product or other kind of good; or
> (ii) a service; and
> (b) in the case where the CDR data is about availability or performance-the CDR data is publicly available.
> *No fee when this CDR data is required to be disclosed*
> (2) The consumer data rules cannot allow a fee to be charged for:
> (a) the disclosure of CDR data under rules like those described in paragraph 56BE(a) or 56BG(2)(a); or
> (b) the use of CDR data received as the result of such a disclosure.
> [...]

2. *A hybrid approach to Data Governance*

The CDR regime does not only grant data access rights, but also determines the cornerstones of data governance, especially regarding the handling of these access rights. For example, a central body, the Data Standards Chair, should define technical standards for data transmission, which will then be binding. Such standards could also help to make Article 20 GDPR more effective.[47] Special attention should be paid to other actors described in the CDR regime who can and/or must be involved in handling data access:

a) Accredited persons

A difference between CDR and Article 20 GDPR is the possibility under the former that accredited persons may file consumer data requests on behalf of a consumer. In such situations the accredited person is authorized to receive or access the data directly. To be allowed to do so, the accredited person must pass a certification process , which means that several accreditation requirements must be met. These accreditation requirements may vary depending on the risk associated with the access to the data, i.e. in particular the type and manner of access and the sensitivity of the data in question – see 1.176 of the Explanatory Memorandum. In the banking sector, only one level of accreditation is provided for so far, which sets high standards for accreditation (for instance, an accredited person must take specific steps which relate to protecting CDR data from misuse, interference and loss - see subsection 5.2.3 of the Competition and Consumer (Consumer Data Right) Rules 2020).[48]

The GDPR does not provide for such a possibility for accredited person to receive or access data directly without the request of the data subject. Especially where markets are characterised by data-induced lock-ins, such a right could be helpful. By way of setting high standards for accreditation

47 See also Communication from the Commission to the European Parliament and the Council, 'Data protection as a pillar of citizens' empowerment and the EU's approach to the digital transition – two years of application of the General Data Protection Regulation' COM(2020) 264 final, 10 et seq.

48 See also the further discussion: Consultation Paper 'CDR rules expansion amendments' (2020) <www.accc.gov.au/system/files/CDR%20rules%20expansion%20amendments%20-%20consultation%20paper%20-%2030%20September%202020.pdf> accessed 15 January 2021.

the risk for the data subject in terms of a possible loss of control over their data could be minimized. Such high standards could even raise the level of data protection (market-based approach to data privacy).

b) Gateways

Gateways are intended to enable more efficient and secure data transfer where necessary – see 1.95 and 1.180 of the Explanatory Memorandum. According to subsection 56BG(1), gateways can be intermediaries, i.e. a mediating authority for the purpose of data access. According to the CDR regime they could have different tasks, which could be specified as follows: Gateways can (i) manage data access and transfer by acting as an intermediary for the transmission of data and/or (ii) take over the management of access requests prior to data access. If possible, gateways should be under effective state control – see 1.97 of the Explanatory Memorandum. Such gateways under Australian law show certain parallels to the data intermediaries currently discussed in European law under the catchword 'data trustees'. The CDR regime could therefore also inspire European law in this respect

IV. Cross-sectoral and cross-type of data regulation

Even before the GDPR came into force, France had already implemented a very comprehensive data access and data portability right.[49] This covered both personal and non-personal data and applied to all data which a consumer placed online, which was otherwise generated or was in any way connected with his or her account. However, Article 48 of the Law for a Digital Republic was repealed in the course of the implementation of the GDPR. Today the French regulations correspond to those of the GDPR.

49 Art. 48 *Loi n° 2016–1321 du 7 octobre 2016 pour une République numérique* (Law for a Digital Republic), implementing such right as Arts. L 224–42–1 to L 224–42–3 *Code de consummation* (Consumer Law Code).

E. Findings and recommendations

The results can be summarised as follows:

1. Sector-specific regulation
   Sector-specific regulation mainly takes place in the telecommunications, energy, banking and mobility sectors. Occasionally there are also regulations for the health sector. These appear to be the most relevant sectors from a consumer perspective. However, further sectors may be added when a need arises. The advantage of sector-specific regulation is that the rights and interests of the actors concerned can be assessed much more accurately than under 'one size fits all' regulation. Sector-specific regulation thus affords more appropriate differentiation.
2. Cross-sector regulation
   The different legal systems which provide for data access rights across sectors but only regarding personal data essentially contain regulations that correspond, basically, to those of the GDPR. There are only a few differences concerning details, the most important of which are the following:
   a) Some jurisdictions provide that fees may be charged for granting access to personal data. This may prevent the data subject from exercising his or her rights, and is therefore not recommended.
   b) In some jurisdictions, the right to information is limited to data processing operations during a certain period, e.g. the previous 12-month period. This also falls short of the provisions of the GDPR, and is in any case not advisable from the perspective of the data subject.
   c) The same applies to rules requiring only a summary of the data processed to be given to the data subject.
   d) Some jurisdictions provide for more detailed lists of reasons for exclusion of data access rights than the GDPR entails. This creates more legal certainty than an open-ended general clause such as Article 15(4) GDPR, but affords less case-by-case justice.
   e) California, as well as Brazil, India and Australia, has legislated data portability rights with regard to generated data. If this were to be clarified in Article 20 GDPR, legislators could look to those jurisdictions as models.
   f) Some jurisdictions provide for an exception to data subjects' rights regarding data processing for scientific purposes. Such a regulation would be possible on the basis of Article 89 GDPR in national law, and could be needed in particular for medical research.

g) New Zealand permits the disclosure of personal data under terms and conditions. This is likely to mean restrictions on use of the data obtained. This might serve as an alternative to a refusal to provide personal data, also in the GDPR.
h) Some laws provide for the transferability of data subjects' rights. Apart from the USA (CPP), this concerns mainly the Philippines. Australia limits this possibility to accredited persons. Provided that high standards like those Australia has implemented for the accreditation process and that sanctions for data protection violations are in place, this would be a compromise that poses less of a threat to data subjects' interests than would be the case with full transferability.
i) The introduction of a right to non-discrimination for the exercising of data subjects' rights as in California's CCPA is highly recommended. The upholding of this right would essentially have to be monitored by data protection authorities, but consumer associations could be given the same powers they already have to prosecute other forms of discrimination.

Paving the way for future reforms

From (horizontal and sectoral) data access solutions towards data governance systems

Wolfgang Kerber[*]

A. *Introduction*

The emerging data economy has triggered a broad and fast-evolving discussion about the governance of data. Whereas personal data are subject to the EU General Data Protection Regulation (GDPR), no clear legal framework exists for the increasing amount of other (non-personal or industrial) data that are collected and produced in the digital economy, e.g. sensor data in Internet of Things (IoT) contexts, anonymised data sets, or inferred data. After a brief debate about the need for a new exclusive right on those data, the discussion has shifted very fast to concerns that the huge amount of collected and produced data is not being used sufficiently to drive innovation and competition. This has led to a broad policy discussion about more data access and data-sharing.[1] From an economic perspective this is driven by the insights that (a) data are non-rivalrous in use, i.e. the same

* I thank the participants of the conference 'Verbraucherrechtstage 2019: Datenzugang, Verbraucherinteressen und Gemeinwohl' (12–13 December 2019 in Berlin) for valuable feedback. The author declares no conflict of interest.

1 See Herbert Zech, 'A Legal Framework for a Data Economy in the European Digital Single Market: Rights to Use Data' (2016) 11 Journal of Intellectual Property Law & Practice 460; Wolfgang Kerber, 'A New (Intellectual) Property Right for Non-Personal Data? An Economic Analysis' (2016) Gewerblicher Rechtsschutz und Urheberrecht Internationaler Teil 989; Wolfgang Kerber, 'Rights on Data: The EU Communication "Building a European Data Economy" from an Economic Perspective' in Sebastian Lohsse, Reiner Schulze and Dirk Staudenmayer (eds), *Trading Data in the Digital Economy: Legal Concepts and Tools* (Hart and Nomos 2017) 109; Josef Drexl, 'Designing Competitive Markets for Industrial Data – Between Propertization and Access' (2017) 8 Journal of Intellectual Property, Information Technology and ECommerce 257; Josef Drexl, 'Neue Regeln für die Europäische Datenwirtschaft? Ein Plädoyer für einen wettbewerbspolitischen Ansatz' (2017) 5 Neue Zeitschrift für Kartellrecht 339 (part 1) and 415 (part 2); Communication from the European Commission of 10 January 2017 to the European Parliament, the Council, the European Economic and Social Committee and the Committee of Regions – Building a European Data Economy, COM(2017) 2 final; Heike Schweitzer and Martin Peitz, 'Ein neuer Ordnungsrahmen für Datenmärkte?'

data can be used by many firms, (b) data are a key input for innovation, and (c) the lack of access to data can have negative effects on competition and innovation. In the meantime, there is a broad consensus that – in addition to facilitating voluntary data-sharing between firms and opening public sector data – it might be necessary also to have mandatory solutions for access to (or sharing of) data sets that are held by private firms. Most prominent in that respect are the current discussions (and legislative proposals) about facilitating access to data, either directly through competition law or indirectly through improving data portability.[2]

In this general discussion about mandatory solutions for the access to privately held data sets, two basic questions can be distinguished: (1) Under what conditions should data-holding firms have obligations to grant access to these data? (2) What legal instruments should be used for implementing and enforcing those obligations? It is the first question which so far has been at the centre of the policy discussion. Despite a general heated discussion about the justification of mandatory data access solutions, in the meantime, a basic consensus seems to be emerging about the most important criteria that are relevant for deciding under what conditions data-holding firms might have such data access obligations. Benefits through more innovation and competition, incentives for the production of data, protection of business secrets and privacy (compliance with GDPR), whether data claimants have participated in the production of data (co-generated data, e.g. in value chains) or bargaining power imbalances between firms are important criteria that can be included in a comprehensive

(2018) Neue Juristische Wochenschrift 275; Communication from the European Commission of 25 April 2018 to the European Parliament, the Council, the European Economic and Social Committee and the Committee of Regions – 'Towards a common European data space' COM(2018) 232 final; Heike Schweitzer, 'Datenzugang in der Datenökonomie: Eckpfeiler einer neuen Informationsordnung' (2019) Gewerblicher Rechtsschutz und Urheberrecht 569; OECD, *Enhancing Access to and Sharing of Data: Reconciling Risks and Benefits for Data Re-use across Societies* (OECD 2019); Communication from the Commission of 19 February 2020 to the European Parliament, the Council, the European Economic and Social Committee and the Committee of Regions – A European strategy for data, COM(2020) 66 final.

2 See for competition policy Heike Schweitzer, Justus Haucap, Wolfgang Kerber and Robert Welker, *Modernisierung der Missbrauchsaufsicht für marktmächtige Unternehmen* (Nomos 2018); Jacques Crémer, Yves-Alexandre de Montjoye, Heike Schweitzer, 'Competition Policy for the Digital Era' (2019) 91–107 <http://ec.europa.eu/competition/publications/reports/kd0419345enn.pdf> accessed 31 August 2020; Heike Schweitzer and Robert Welker, 'A legal framework for access to data – A competition policy perspective', in this volume.

balancing of the positive and negative effects of obligations for data access and data-sharing.[3] An important result of the discussion is that depending on the specific technological and economic conditions and the type of data a wide range of results is possible with regard to the extent that obligations for data access and data sharing can be recommended.

This article focusses on the second basic question: Assuming that certain obligations for data access and data-sharing can be recommended, how should these mandatory data access solutions be implemented? Therefore this article presents an analysis of the legal and regulatory instruments for solving data access problems in the data economy. Part B, which follows, gives an overview of the broad range of policy options that are under discussion (competition law, the data portability right of Article 20 GDPR,[4] contract law or unfair trading law). Data access claims against private firms can therefore be based upon general legal rules that apply to all sectors (horizontal data access solutions). However, they can also be the result of sector-specific regulations, as, e.g., the sectoral regulation for the access to bank account data in the Second Payment Services Directive (PSD2).[5] Such sector-specific solutions are also discussed for the data in connected cars or for data in energy markets. One of the main questions in this discussion is whether horizontal or sectoral access solutions might lead to better results. Therefore part B will also entail an analysis of the most important advantages and problems of both types of data access solutions.

The main thesis of this article, however, is that a narrow focus on the question whether data-holding firms might have an obligation to grant other firms access to data might not be sufficient for solving the problems for innovation and competition, and that therefore a broader approach for

3 See, for example, Schweitzer and others (n. 2) 158–162; Crémer and others (n. 2) 74; Schweitzer (n. 1); Wolfgang Kerber, 'Data-sharing in IoT Ecosystems and Competition Law: The Example of Connected Cars' (2019) 15(4) Journal of Competition Law & Economics 381, 400–402; and from a more general perspective Datenethikkommission, 'Gutachten der Datenethikkommission' (2019) 90–91, 145–147 <www.bmi.bund.de/SharedDocs/downloads/DE/publikationen/themen/it-digitalpolitik/gutachten-datenethikkommission.pdf;jsessionid=427D953199879513E7B9E0C2544E921E.2_cid364?__blob=publicationFile&v=6> accessed 31 August 2020.

4 Regulation (EU) No. 2016/679 of the European Parliament and of the Council of 27 April 2016 on the protection of natural persons with regard to the processing of personal data and on the free movement of such data, and repealing Directive 95/46/EC, [2016] OJ L119/1.

5 Directive (EU) 2015/2366 of the European Parliament and of the Council of 25 November 2015 on payment services in the Internal Market [2015] OJ L337/35.

finding proper data governance solutions is necessary. Particularly the analysis of the sector-specific data access solutions shows (1) the need for a more comprehensive analysis of data governance problems which takes into account the working of entire sectors or ecosystems, as well as (2) the importance of additional regulations, eg on interoperability (and standardisation), and safety and security, for ensuring the effectiveness of data governance solutions (part C). The main part D offers a more systematic framework for the analysis and design of entire data governance systems, which at an abstract level refer to all rights and legal rules that are relevant for data in a certain system. After section I distinguishes between the general data governance system of the entire economy and specific data governance systems for certain sectors or parts of the economy, section II emphasises the need for a deep analysis of the working of (often interrelated) markets and entire ecosystems in the digital economy. Here the analysis should particularly focus on the effects of (sometimes multiple) market failures and the question which data governance solutions and additional regulations might be suitable and necessary for solving the problems. The final section III of this part offers an overview of instruments that can be very helpful in general and specific data governance systems. This encompasses consumer data rights, data trustee solutions, and complementary regulatory solutions for interoperability and standardisation as well as for safety, security, and privacy problems. The final brief part E on further perspectives emphasises the need for a more anticipatory approach to data governance solutions and discusses open institutional questions.

B. Horizontal vs. sectoral data access solutions

I. Horizontal data access solutions

Horizontal solutions for facilitating data access and data sharing refer to legal rules that apply to the general economy and not only to specific sectors. Proposals that intend to facilitate generally voluntary data-sharing and the development of well-functioning data markets, eg by reducing transaction costs, can also be seen as such horizontal solutions, but here our analysis will be limited to mandatory solutions for data access to data that are held by private parties, usually firms.[6] In the general debate about data access a broad range of different horizontal solutions have been discussed. It cannot be the task of this chapter to analyse all of these solutions or even compare them with respect to their suitability, effectiveness, and specific problems. Instead we focus on the most important ones, i.e. on solutions based upon competition law, data portability rights, and some other solutions including, e.g., contract law. After a brief overview of these solutions, the general advantages and problems of horizontal solutions will be discussed.[7]

The most prominently discussed solutions are based upon competition law,[8] because the well-established 'essential facility' doctrine (EFD) seems already to offer a direct way in which firms might obtain access to data sets of dominant firms if they are essential for entering markets and/or for innovation. Despite a broad consensus that data sets can under certain conditions be such an essential facility, there has been broad scepticism in the literature concerning to what extent the EFD, which, e.g., in the EU (according to Article 102 TFEU) has been traditionally applied in a very restrictive way, can be used for solving competition problems that are caused by lack of access to exclusively held data of private firms. However, there are a number of proposals on making this approach, that the refusal to grant access to data can be seen as an abusive behaviour of a firm with market power, more effective. They range from proposing to apply the EFD more flexibly with regard to data (which can be justified from an economic perspective),[9] to develop a reasoning for such an abusive behaviour outside of the EFD (based, e.g., upon a leverage-of-market-power and foreclosure-of-competitors argument),[10] or to base such data access claims on the prohibition of abusive behaviour of firms with relative market power

6 See for ways to facilitate voluntary solutions, including through model contracts, Commission COM(2017) 9 final (n. 1); and most recently Bertin Martens and others, 'Business-to-Business Data Sharing: An Economic and Legal Analysis' (2020) JRC Digital Economy Working Paper 2020–05 <https://ec.europa.eu/jrc/sites/jrcsh/files/jrc121336.pdf> accessed 31 August 2020; and for the problem of opening public sector data Heiko Richter, 'The law and policy of government access to private sector data ("B2G data sharing")', in this volume.

7 For this analysis we will assume that under certain conditions granting access to data can be recommended from a policy perspective according to a set of criteria that have to be applied for justifying the access to these data in particular cases.

8 See for the following Kerber (n. 3) 395–422; see, in particular, also Schweitzer and Welker (n. 2).

9 See Schweitzer and others (n. 2) 171.

10 See Crémer and others (n. 2) 98.

(dependency concept), which implies that the data-holding company does not need to be a dominant firm (according to Article 102 TFEU). In the current draft proposal of the 10th amendment of German competition law new provisions can be found for facilitating the access to data from firms with market power.[11] Despite general broad support for facilitating more data access through competition law, it is so far unclear to what extent these efforts will be successful and able to lead to effective solutions for the data access problems.[12]

In the recent discussion the data portability right according to Article 20 GDPR is viewed as a potentially very promising option for solving data access problems. The basic idea is that the consumers can exert their right to the portability of their personal data to give access to such data that are held by one firm (e.g. a social media platform) to other firms, either for easier switching of services or for allowing the offering of additional complementary services that require access to these personal data. It is important that this data portability right of the GDPR has always been seen as a potential vehicle for facilitating competition (through reducing lock-ins caused by high switching costs). However, there is also a broad consensus that so far this right has not led to effective solutions, because of an unclear (and also insufficient) scope of this right, large technical and other feasibility problems, and too high transaction costs for consumers. The data portability right encompasses neither the right to the portability of data in real time nor does it contain interoperability requirements for ensuring the technical feasibility of data portability. Therefore it is not surprising that the discussion is shifting to the question of how this data portability right in the GDPR can be made more effective.[13] However data portability rights can also play a role independent of Article 20 GDPR (and therefore

11 Bundesregierung, 'Entwurf eines Gesetzes zur Änderung des Gesetzes gegen Wettbewerbsbeschränkungen für ein fokussiertes, proaktives und digitales Wettbewerbsrecht 4.0' (8 September 2020) <www.bmwi.de/Redaktion/DE/Downloads/Gesetz/gesetzentwurf-gwb-digitalisierungsgesetz.pdf?__blob=publicationFile&v=4> accessed 11 September 2020; see also Kerber (n. 3); Wolfgang Kerber, 'Datenzugangsansprüche im Referentenentwurf zur 10. GWB-Novelle aus ökonomischer Perspektive' (2020) 05 Wirtschaft und Wettbewerb 249.

12 See for the problems in competition law Kerber (n. 3) 403–407, 412–413, arguing that competition law solutions (even after legislative amendments like that in German competition law) can help, but only to a certain extent.

13 See for the discussion about the data portability right of the GDPR Article 29 Data Protection Working Party, 'Guidelines on the Right to Data Portability as last revised and adopted on 5 April 2017' (16 EN, WP 242 rev.01) <https://ec.europa.eu/newsroom/article29/item-detail.cfm?item_id=611233> accessed 31 August 2020;

outside of privacy laws), as is shown in the new discussion about consumer data rights.[14] It focusses on the question of what rights (especially with respect to access and portability) consumers should have regarding data that are collected as part of their role as consumers. Since the concept of consumer data can be independently (and more broadly) defined than the legal concept of 'personal data' in privacy laws, the consumer data rights approach allows for a much broader and open discussion on which of 'their' data consumers can make accessible in what form to other firms through exerting these rights against firms that hold their consumer data. Since however legislation on consumer data rights is still in its earliest stages, it is too early to make assessments about the effectiveness of such solutions.[15]

Commission Communication COM(2020) 66 final (n. 1) 10, 21 (about enhancing the data portability right under Art. 20 GDPR); for recent discussions see Inge Graef, Martin Husovec and Nadezhda Purtova, 'Data Portability and Data Control: Lessons for an Emerging Concept in EU Law' (2018) 19 German Law Journal 1356; Kommission Wettbewerbsrecht 4.0, 'Ein neuer Wettbewerbsrahmen für die Digitalwirtschaft' (2019) 39–44 <www.bmwi.de/Redaktion/DE/Publikationen/Wirtschaft/bericht-der-kommission-wettbewerbsrecht-4-0.pdf?__blob=publicationFile&v=12> 31 August 2020; Jan Krämer, Pierre Senellart and Alexandre de Streel, 'Making Data Portability more effective for the Digital Economy – Report' (Centre on Regulation in Europe 2020) <https://cerre.eu/publications/report-making-data-portability-more-effective-digital-economy/> accessed 31 August 2020; and in particular Ruth Janal, 'Data portability under the GDPR: A blueprint for access rights?', in this volume, who is very sceptical that the data portability right according to Art. 20 GDPR can be a model for B2B data access solutions.

14 See for the discussion about consumer data rights OECD, 'Consumer Data Rights and Competition – Background Note' (OECD 2020) DAF/COMP(2020)1 <https://one.oecd.org/document/DAF/COMP(2020)1/en/pdf> accessed 31 August 2020, which was triggered much by their introduction through legislation in Australia (see Louisa Specht-Riemenschneider, 'Data access rights – A comparative perspective', in this volume). Interesting in the Australian case is that it primarily adopts a horizontal approach that is however implemented step-by-step in a sector-specific way (hybrid of a horizontal and sectoral solution).

15 The consumer data rights approach is also very close to the proposal of Josef Drexl of nonwaivable data access rights for consumers with regard to data of connected devices. See Josef Drexl, 'Data Access and Control in the Era of Connected Devices' (2018) and Josef Drexl, 'Connected devices – An unfair competition law approach to data access rights of users', in this volume; see also Josef Drexl and others, 'Position Statement of the Max Planck Institute for Innovation and Competition of 26 April 2017 on the European Commission's "Public Consultation on Building the European Data Economy"' (2017) <www.ip.mpg.de/fileadmin/ipmpg/content/stellungnahmen/MPI_Statement_Public_consultation_on_Building_the_EU_Data_Eco_28042017.pdf> accessed 31 August 2020.

Beyond these two most discussed solutions a number of other options can also be found which might be applicable under specific conditions. For example, under certain conditions contract law might be capable of offering firms access to data as part of their contractual relationships with other firms, especially if the data claimant has participated in the generation of these data (co-generated data).[16] Also discussed is the option that data access claims might also be based upon unfair trading laws, especially in cases of unequal bargaining power between the data claimant and the data holder, i.e. the refusal to grant access to certain data sets might be seen as an unfair trade practice. However both solutions can only be applied in certain situations and are so far not developed. It is particularly unclear what the criteria are in these fields of the law, but it is important that such data claims might be based upon already existing laws. This is different for other data access/sharing proposals, such as, e.g., the opening of large sets of anonymised data for AI applications and the training of algorithms. Such a proposal can also be seen as a horizontal solution if it is applied to data from all sectors.[17] Particularly interesting are also proposals that combine different horizontal solutions, especially combinations between competition law and data portability rights. The idea of prohibiting the impediment of data portability as an abusive behaviour of firms with market power is a proposal that has emerged repeatedly and in different ways in the competition policy discussion about how to solve data access problems.[18]

---

16 See Schweitzer and others (n. 2) 181–183; Commission Communication COM(2018) 232 final (n. 1) 9–11 (key principles of B2B data-sharing that should be respected in contractual agreements); Datenethikkommission (n. 3) 28–30 (on unfair/inefficient B2B contracts about data and a legislative proposal for changing German contract law in that respect); for an analysis of data access solutions in general contract law see Axel Metzger, 'Access to and porting of data under contract law: Consumer protection rules and market-based principles', in this volume, who is sceptical about such mandatory access solutions in B2B contexts outside of competition law; see also Michael Grünberger, 'Data access rules: The role of contractual unfairness control of (consumer) contracts', in this volume, about data access through contractual unfair control of consumer contracts.

17 The approach of the European Commission in its strategy for data focusses on a cross-sectoral governance framework. See Commission Communication COM(2020) 66 final (n. 1) 11–25.

18 See, e.g., the proposal of the German Kommission Wettbewerbsrecht 4.0 (n. 13) 6, 54–55 for an EU regulation for dominant platforms that would also entail an obligation of these platforms to enable the portability of user and use data in real time and to ensure interoperability with complementary services.

What are the general advantages and problems of horizontal solutions for data access? There is overall a broad consensus that general rules that can be applied to the entire economy are theoretically preferable over sector-specific rules, due especially to the manifold costs and distortions that can arise through establishing different data access solutions for different parts of the economy. However the academic discussion about data access and data-sharing issues has shown that it is not easy to identify and apply general criteria for granting access to data. Although a general set of relevant criteria is now emerging in the discussion, decisions on whether to grant access to data depend very much on the specific economic and technological context. It has always been one of the counterarguments against general data access rules that their application might not be capable of distinguishing precisely enough between cases in which data access should be granted, and other cases where this is not advisable. Wrong decisions would lead to welfare losses through type 1 and type 2 errors. However, theoretically a differentiated application to the specific conditions of cases is also possible with general rules if a clear set of criteria exists that can be applied to specific cases. Through a process of developing groups and subgroups of cases, the law can develop a differentiated approach with solutions that are sufficiently adapted to the different conditions of different sectors, markets, and technologies. But such a process might take a long time, and depend very much also on who the driving force is behind such a differentiation. Is it a competition authority, which also can make decisions on enforcement priorities and issue guidelines, or is it the result of a process that relies mostly on private litigation and the courts? This implies that also the institutional design of the enforcement of the horizontal rules for granting access to data can be important for the finding of proper solutions and their effectiveness.[19]

There are however a number of additional problems. One important problem that so far has not been discussed much is the question what ac-

19 From an economic perspective the same balancing problem between benefits and problems of data access exists independent of the question which horizontal solution is applied from a legal perspective. Due to the different dogmatic approaches of these different laws and the different enforcement systems, certain horizontal solutions might be better capable of leading to good decisions than others. Therefore, competition law, which is much more familiar with the application of economic reasonings and is primarily enforced by a competition authority, might have relative advantages over unfair trading law or the data portability right of the GDPR. However, different horizontal solutions might also specialise with regard to different kinds of data access problems.

cess to data really means. Does it imply that data are transmitted to other firms (and they are free to use them in any way, or only for specific purposes) or do they only receive access to a server, where their use of the data is monitored (perhaps at a neutral institution)? Depending on the specific conditions of how access to data is given (and what can be done with the data), the benefits and problems of data access can be very different, which implies that horizontal solutions should also be capable of finding suitable solutions for this question. Particularly important is also that data access often only works if (1) data are also made available in a common data format, (2) easy-to-use technical interfaces (such as APIs) are available for transmitting the data, (3) the problem of fees and other conditions for data access is solved, (4) safety/security issues and the compliance with privacy laws (in the EU: GDPR) are dealt with, and (5) the problem of too high (transaction) costs of using these horizontal solutions for the data claimants and/or the consumers (in case of data portability rights) is solved. In a number of important cases, such as in IoT contexts (including connected cars), also (6) additional interoperability problems (due to technically closed systems) might have to be solved. Although this cannot be discussed here in detail, it is very unclear whether horizontal data access solutions as general competition law, the data portability right (Article 20 GDPR), unfair trading law or contract law can solve these additional problems. Very often this will be not possible. Therefore it is right now an open question to what extent the discussed horizontal solutions will be capable of solving the data access problems in an effective way in the foreseeable future.

II. Sectoral data access solutions

Sectoral data access solutions are usually regulatory solutions that try to solve problems of access to data or the sharing of data in a targeted way for specific sectors. In the general discussion about data access solutions, the option of sector-specific regulation has often been seen as a possibly superior solution at least in certain sectors.[20] Before discussing the general advantages and problems of sector-specific regulatory solutions, we will analyse briefly two examples of sector-specific solutions. One example is the data

20 Particularly in the discussion of data access solutions in competition law, it was always acknowledged that in certain sectors a sector-specific regulatory solution can lead to better solutions. See, e.g., Crémer and others (n. 2) 107.

access regime to bank account data that has been established in the banking sector by the PSD2. The other example refers to the current discussion about access to the data of connected cars, in which also a sector-specific regulatory solution is currently on the political agenda and the topic of heated discussion.

1. Opening of bank account data (PSD2)

The basic idea of the opening of bank accounts through the regulatory regime of the PSD2 is to enable new innovative financial services for the customers of banks for their online bank accounts, especially through new Fintech companies.[21] It is about the access of two different types of independent financial service providers, namely payment service providers who offer payment services via the bank accounts of the customers (PIS: payment initiation services), and other providers of financial services who based upon the data from bank accounts can offer additional financial services (AIS: account information services) to the bank account owners. The regulatory regime tries to solve a market failure problem due to insufficient innovation competition between banks regarding new digital financial services and a lock-in problem of customers of traditional banks. Since Fintech companies have problems offering their new innovative services to consumers, because banks can refuse them access to the bank accounts of their customers, a sector-specific regulatory regime obliging banks to give access to the bank accounts has been viewed as necessary for triggering more innovation with regard to these financial services. The decisive problem is that banks have the exclusive control over both the bank account data and the possibility to initiate payments from these bank accounts. Independent financial service providers, who offer services in competition with the banks, are therefore not capable of offering the bank customers their services without the permission of the banks. Therefore this sectoral access

---

21 See Directive (EU) 2015/2366 (n. 4); for an overview see Heike Mai, 'PSD 2, Open Banking und der Wert personenbezogener Daten' (2018) Deutsche Bank Research <www.dbresearch.de/PROD/RPS_DE-PROD/PROD0000000000470556/PSD_2%2C_Open_Banking_und_der_Wert_personenbezogener.PDF> accessed 31 August 2020; Simonetta Vezzoso, 'Fintech, access to data, and the role of competition policy' in Vicente Bagnoli (ed.), *Competition and Innovation* (Scortecci 2018) 30–41; see also, in particular, Jörg Hoffmann, 'Safeguarding innovation in the framework of sector-specific data access regimes: The case of digital payment services', in this volume.

regime encompasses an obligation of the banks to grant independent financial service providers (with the permission of the bank account holders) access to bank account data as well as the possibility to directly initiate payments from the bank account of the customers. This implies that banks no longer have the right to refuse such access to these data and the bank account by these independent service providers. The basic ideas of the PSD2 are much influenced by the Open Banking initiative of the UK competition authority CMA,[22] and can be interpreted from an economic perspective primarily as an innovation policy measure.

Particularly important for our analysis here is that the PSD2 regulation goes far beyond a pure regulation of data access. It is rather a package of regulatory solutions that consists of a number of important elements:[23]

(1) The account information service providers (AISP) have a right to access the bank account data, and can use them for offering additional financial services.
(2) The payment initiation service providers (PISP) have the right to access the bank account of a customer and directly initiate payments from this account.
(3) Since both forms of access require direct technical access to the bank account, the banks must provide open interoperable interfaces for these service providers. Here some form of standardisation (eg APIs) is required.[24]
(4) The banks are not allowed to demand fees for the access of these financial service providers.
(5) For increasing the security of the bank customers (as part of consumer protection) the regulation also includes additional requirements: (a) strong authentification of the bank customers (double authentification), (b) licensing of the financial service providers, and (c) liability of the bank (for mistakes and fraud).

---

22 UK Competition & Markets Authority, 'Retail banking market investigation – Provisional decision on remedies' (2016) <https://assets.publishing.service.gov.uk/media/573a377240f0b6155900000c/retail_banking_market_pdr.pdf> accessed 31 August 2020; Open Banking <www.openbanking.org.uk/> accessed 31 August 2020.

23 See European Commission Fact Sheet, 'Payment Services Directive (PSD2): Regulatory Technical Standards (RTS) Enabling Consumers to Benefit from Safer and more Innovative Electronic Payments' (2017) <https://ec.europa.eu/commission/presscorner/api/files/document/print/en/memo_17_4961/MEMO_17_4961_EN.pdf> accessed 31 August 2020.

24 There are still considerable problems regarding its practical implementation.

(6) The European Banking Authority has the regulatory oversight for this regulatory regime.

Since this Directive had to be transposed into national law, it is currently in different stages of implementation in the Member States. The pros and cons of this regulation for opening bank accounts in order to stimulate innovative financial services cannot be discussed here. But what is important is that it is widely seen as a regulatory model for supporting data-driven innovation through opening data. However there is also considerable criticism with respect to the details of the regulation and the question to what extent the regulation can achieve its objectives.[25]

2. Access to data in connected cars

The technological transition to connected cars (as an example of an IoT device), in which huge amounts of data are collected and produced in the car and directly transmitted to proprietary servers of the car manufacturers, has triggered a new regulatory discussion about 'access to in-vehicle data and resources'.[26] Independent service providers that want to offer aftermar-

25 See for a positive view and emphasis on its model character, e.g., Jason Furman and others, 'Unlocking digital competition – Report of the Digital Competition Expert Panel' (2019) 69 <https://assets.publishing.service.gov.uk/government/uploads/system/uploads/attachment_data/file/785547/unlocking_digital_competition_furman_review_web.pdf> accessed 31 August 2020. One of the important critical concerns is with the danger that large digital tech firms (e.g. Apple, Google) can use this data access for entering the market with potentially negative effects in the long term: See Miguel de la Mano and Jorge Padilla, 'Big Tech Banking' (2018) 14 Journal of Competition Law & Economics 494. Since these large platform firms do not have to open their data, demands for reciprocity of data access have emerged: See Fabiana Di Porto and Gustavo Ghidini, '"I Access Your Data, You Access Mine" – Requiring Data Reciprocity in Payment Services' (2020) 51 International Review of Intellectual Property and Competition Law 307; see also the critical analysis of Jörg Hoffmann, 'Safeguarding innovation in the framework of sector-specific data access regimes: The case of digital payment services', in this volume.

26 See as an overview: C-ITS Platform, 'Final Report' (2016) <https://ec.europa.eu/transport/sites/transport/files/themes/its/doc/c-its-platform-final-report-january-2016.pdf> accessed 31 August 2020; TRL, 'Access to In-Vehicle Data and Resources – Final Report' (2017) <https://ec.europa.eu/transport/sites/transport/files/2017-05-access-to-in-vehicle-data-and-resources.pdf> accessed 31 August 2020; Commission Communication COM(2018) 232 final (n. 1); Wolfgang Kerber, 'Data Governance in Connected Cars: The Problem of Access to In-Vehicle Data' (2018) 9

ket and other new innovative complementary services in this new ecosystem of connected cars to the car users are very concerned that the car manufacturers can use their monopolistic gatekeeper position to the data and to the car for controlling all markets for aftermarket and other complementary services that need access to these data and/or access to the car (e.g. providing remote repair and maintenance services). This can lead to the foreclosure of independent service providers and the leveraging of market power to these secondary markets in this new digital ecosystem of connected cars. This gatekeeper position is the consequence of the application of the 'extended vehicle concept' by the car manufacturers, which implies that they have exclusive de facto control of (1) all data produced in the car and (2) the technical access to the car, ie without the permission of the car manufacturer no access is possible to these data or the car. An economic analysis of this situation comes to the clear result that the concerns of the independent service providers are justified, and that therefore this gatekeeper position can lead to serious problems for competition, innovation, and consumer choice on these secondary markets.[27] Since 2016, the independent service providers have been demanding a regulatory solution for this problem. The European Commission has acknowledged this problem but has not yet made proposals for solving it.[28]

Journal of Intellectual Property Information Technology and E-Commerce Law 310.

27 See for an economic analysis of this access problem Kerber (ibid), which is based upon a systematic analysis of market failures in the ecosystems of connected cars; see also from an economic perspective Bertin Martens and Frank Mueller-Langer, 'Access to Digital Car data and competition in aftermarket maintenance services' (2020) 16(1) Journal of Competition Law & Economics 116.

28 See for contributions to this policy discussion C-ITS platform (n. 26); TRL (n. 26); Kerber (n. 3, n. 26); Wolfgang Kerber and Daniel Gill, 'Access to Data in Connected Cars and the Recent Reform of the Motor Vehicle Type Approval Regulation' (2019) 10 Journal of Intellectual Property Information Technology and E-Commerce Law 244. See for position papers of stakeholders ACEA, 'Access to Vehicle Data for Third-Party Services – Position Paper' (2016) <www.acea.be/uploads/publications/ACEA_Position_Paper_Access_to_vehicle_data_for_third-party_services.pdf> accessed 31 August 2020, BEUC, 'Protecting European Consumers with Connected and Automated Cars – Position Paper' (2017) <www.beuc.eu/publications/beuc-x-2017-138_dve_beuc_connected_autonomous_cars.pdf> accessed 31 August 2020, FIGIEFA, 'Commission Communication on "Free Flow of Data." Input from the Independent Automotive Aftermarket' (2016) <www.figiefa.eu/wp-content/uploads/Free-Flow-of-Data-FIGIEFA-Input-2016_12_23.pdf> accessed 31 August 2020; FIA, 'Policy Position on Car Connectivity' (2016) <www.fiaregion1.com/wp-content/uploads/2017/05/20160412fia_policy_brief_on_car_connectivity_fin.pdf> accessed 31 August 2020. After the acknowledgment

It is important to note that in the motor vehicle industry competition policy had to deal for decades with attempts of car manufacturers to foreclose independent repair and maintenance service providers from the lucrative markets for repair and maintenance services.[29] Therefore a long time ago EU competition policy already introduced a regulatory access regime for protecting competition on the automobile aftermarkets. This regime has granted independent service providers access to essential repair and maintenance service information for protecting competition between the authorised dealers of the car manufacturers and the independent providers of repair and maintenance services (including independent spare part producers). Since 2007 this access regime was included in the motor vehicle type approval regulation, which was reformed in 2018.[30] This current access regime to essential repair and maintenance information entails a FRAND-like obligation of the car manufacturers to make this information available in a non-discriminatory way, with 'reasonable and proportionate' fees, and in a standardised format. This regulation also includes standardisation of technical specifications for the access to this information (e.g., via websites and an obligatory on-board diagnostics (OBD) adapter in the car for diagnostic data). Also safety and security concerns are addressed in this regulatory regime, because repair and maintenance service providers need certification and approval for getting access to security-relevant information. However this current type approval regulation (even after its reform in 2018) has not been adapted to the new technological conditions of connected cars, and therefore cannot solve the competition problems caused by the new gatekeeper position of the car manufacturers with their exclusive control over access to the in-vehicle data and the car.[31]

---

of this competition problem in 2018 – see Communication from the Commission of 17 May 2018 to the European Parliament, the Council, the European Economic and Social Committee and the Committee of the Regions – on the road to automated mobility: An EU strategy for mobility of the future COM(2018) 283 final, 14 – the Commission has announced a further review of the type approval legislation in its European data strategy; see Commission Communication COM(2020) 66 final (n. 1) 28.

29 See for the following in more detail Kerber and Gill (n. 28).

30 Regulation (EC) No. 715/2007 of the European Parliament and of the Council of 20 June 2007 on type approval of motor vehicles with respect to emissions from light passenger and commercial vehicles (Euro 5 and Euro 6) and on access to vehicle repair and maintenance information, [2007] OJ L171/1.

31 See for an in-depth critique of the 2018 reform of the type approval regulation Kerber and Gill (n. 28).

What are the most important policy options that have been discussed for solving this problem?[32] The problem of 'access to in-vehicle data and resources' has always been seen as a problem that might be solved best through a sector-specific regulatory approach. One solution is the 'shared server'.[33] Technically it would, like the extended vehicle concept, also imply the transmission of all data to an external server but this server would be under the governance of a neutral institution for making these data available to all stakeholders in the ecosystem of connected cars (with certain principles, such as, e.g., non-discrimination) for enabling competition and innovation in the entire ecosystem of connected cars. This could be seen as a data trustee solution and would eliminate the gatekeeper position of the car manufacturers with respect to the data, but it would not solve the problem of lacking interoperability with the car. Therefore independent service providers would in the medium and long term prefer the transition to open interoperable telematic platforms (on-board application platforms), which would allow the storage of the data in the car and enable the owners of the car to decide whom they give access to the data and access to the car. For such open interoperable telematic platforms standardised technical interfaces would be necessary, as well as a sophisticated safety and security architecture, which would allow independent service providers to directly access the car, e.g. for performing remote services, without compromising the safety and security of the car. The car manufacturers have always argued that only their exclusive control of the technical access can ensure a high level of safety and security, but studies have shown that the safety and security problems can also be solved with open interoperable telematic platforms.[34] One relatively easy regulatory short-term solution, based upon the current technological design of connected cars, would be a comprehensive reform of the type approval regulation by (a) extending the mandatory access regulation to a much broader set of data, namely all data that are necessary for other service providers in the ecosystem of connected cars (and also beyond aftermarket services), (b) requiring standardised technical interfaces (for solving the interoperability problem), and (c) introducing a sophisticated safety and security solution to enable independent service providers to directly access the car in order

32 In Kerber (n. 3) it is analysed to what extent data access claims based upon competition law can be used for solving this problem of access to data in connected cars (as an alternative horizontal solution).

33 See for an overview and comparison of different technological options for access to data TRL (n. 26) 32–49.

34 See TRL (n. 26) 77.

to perform their services.[35] However, a transition to open interoperable telematics platforms, which would require a far-reaching standardisation of technical interfaces, would offer a much better perspective for good solutions.[36]

What are the general advantages and problems of sector-specific data access solutions? The most important advantage might be that with rules that are tailored to the specific economic and technological conditions of a sector, a much better balancing of the many trade-offs with regard to an optimal governance of data is possible. It can allow for better differentiation between different groups of stakeholders within the systems, such as, e.g., the traditional banks, the new innovative financial service providers, and the consumers (as bank account holders). Therefore it can be specifically regulated who should get access to what kinds of data, and under what conditions (e.g. with regard to fees). Additionally, it can be better decided what specific technological, safety/security, and privacy protection requirements have to be fulfilled, and how this should be implemented in this specific sector. This is directly linked to the possibility that such a sector-specific data governance solution often has an explicit regulatory character, which allows for setting ex ante rules (instead of ex-post control as, e.g., in competition law) and the use of a regulatory authority that can monitor and enforce the sector-specific regulation, and might also have some rule-

35 See Kerber and Gill (n. 28) 254–56. This solution would be technically based upon the 'extended vehicle concept' but the extended type approval regulation would give the independent service providers both broad access to the car data and access to the car for remote services. Since the European Commission has announced a review of the current EU type approval legislation to open it up to more car-data-based services, it might use this policy option of extending this already existing regulatory access regime to enable more competition and innovation in the ecosystem of connected cars. See Commission Communication COM(2020) 66 final (n. 1) 28.

36 This is also the recommendation of the TRL study (n. 26) 160. For an analysis that this wrong technological choice by car manufacturers can be the result of a market failure about choosing a too low level of interoperability (and not enough standardisation) see Kerber (n. 26) 322. For the economics of interoperability and standardisation that support the possibility of such a market failure due to wrong incentives to choose too-closed systems see Joseph Farrell and Timothy Simcoe, 'Four Paths to Compatibility', in Martin Peitz and Joel Waldfogel (eds), *The Oxford Handbook of the Digital Economy* (2012) 34, and Wolfgang Kerber and Heike Schweitzer, 'Interoperability in the Digital Economy' (2017) 8(1) Journal of Intellectual Property Information Technology and E-Commerce Law 39, 41–48.

making powers for adapting the rules over time.[37] Recently, it was the Furman report that emphasised the potentially large advantages of setting ex ante rules for a faster clarification of rules, particularly also with respect to opening data sets and open standards.[38]

However, sector-specific regulatory data access solutions also face a number of difficult problems. First and foremost, all the well-known general problems of regulatory solutions have to be taken into account. Do the rule-makers (legislature, regulatory authority) have sufficient knowledge for designing a well-adapted and effective regulatory regime? Can we rely on a regulatory authority to effectively enforce the regulations? Particularly critical regarding sector-specific regulations is the problem of 'regulatory capture', ie that important stakeholders in the sector might use their closeness to policy-makers to influence the regulation in favour of their own interests (rent-seeking behaviour), leading to wrong regulations that do not achieve (sufficiently) the intended policy objectives of more competition and innovation (regulatory failure).[39] Particularly important is also the problem of how a specific regulatory data access regime with ex ante rules can be adapted to the fast-changing economic and technological conditions due to the rapid technological change through innovations. This implies both the problem that an existing regulatory regime should not impede innovations and, vice versa, that innovations can render an old regulatory regime outdated and ineffective. In the fast-changing digital economy this is a huge challenge for sector-specific data access regulations. An additional important problem is that sector-specific regulatory access solutions will only be possible for a limited number of sectors, i.e. it is not possible to develop them for all parts of the economy. This implies that it will always be necessary to have horizontal data access solutions in addition to these sector-specific solutions. The resulting patchwork of different data access solutions can also lead to numerous problems, such as, e.g., problems with the proper delineation of the scope of these specific solutions and problems of asymmetric regulation.

---

37 Theoretically it is not necessary that sector-specific data access rules must be in the form of a regulatory regime with ex ante rules.

38 See in detail Furman and others (n. 25) 54–83. The Furman report also emphasised that these ex ante rules should primarily be developed in collaboration with the stakeholders.

39 See George J. Stigler, 'The Theory of Economic Regulation' (1971) 2 Bell Journal of Economics and Management 3.

C. *From data access solutions to data governance systems*

The results of part B have shown that both horizontal and sectoral data access solutions have advantages and problems, and it depends therefore on the type of data access problems and the specific technological and economic conditions, whether using a horizontal or a sectoral data access solution might be more advisable. One option for continuing this analysis would be to analyse more deeply the types of data access problems and the conditions for which (what kind of) horizontal solutions or sectoral solutions should be chosen, and how the specific design of these solutions should look. This would also include a discussion of the proper design of the enforcement system for these data access solutions. However, for this article a different path of inquiry has been chosen. The main thesis is that for a proper understanding of data access problems and finding effective solutions we have to use a broader approach that goes beyond the direct solution of the data access problem itself. Instead we have to think in terms of data governance systems. Before discussing in a more general way the basic architecture and building blocks of such data governance systems in part D, three important lessons can be learnt about the need for such a broader approach from our analysis of sector-specific data access solutions in part B.

(1) We cannot understand data access problems and their solutions if we only look at the bilateral relation between a data holder and a data claimant, and are trying to balance the benefits and costs of data access. This is a serious problem for all horizontal solutions, especially in combination with private litigation, in which the data claimant has to sue the data holder for access to data. Instead, the discussion of sector-specific solutions (PSD2 and connected cars) shows clearly that it might be necessary to analyse the working of an entire sector (or ecosystem) in order to understand the effects of the exclusive control of data by a data holder on a number of different (and often interrelated) markets, and the benefits and costs of different governance solutions for data for achieving the objectives of more competition and innovation. From an economic perspective this requires a careful analysis of the market failures in these sectors, which in addition to competition and innovation problems can also encompass informational and behavioural problems of consumers or wrong technological

decisions of firms with respect to standardisation and interoperability.[40] For example, in the case of the governance of data in connected cars, it is very important to understand the far-reaching effects of the monopolistic gatekeeper position of the car manufacturers on all secondary markets for aftermarket and complementary markets, and its implications for foreclosing independent service providers and leveraging market power. This does not mean that such a deep analysis into the markets should (always) be done in the application of horizontal solutions (which would not be feasible), but in choosing the specific criteria that are applied in horizontal solutions for data access (or data portability) one should consider this problem of the broader effects of granting or denying data access in the wider market context on competition and innovation.

(2) Data access discussions nearly always implicitly assume that the de facto control of a certain set of data by a firm is legitimate (in a similar way as we assume the legitimacy of the ownership of a physical 'essential facility'), and the relevant question is only whether other firms should also gain access to these data of this firm. However the discussion in our two examples shows that it might also be necessary to ask who should be in control of these data in the first place, ie we might also have to ask about the proper initial allocation of the de facto control of (or the rights in) these data. The data governance regime established by the PSD2 can also be interpreted as the definition and assignment of a new right to the owner of an online bank account to make the data of her bank account available to independent financial service providers as well as allowing payment service providers to initiate payments directly from this bank account without the permission of the bank. Therefore this regulatory regime not only defines and assigns an access right to independent service providers (with the consent of the bank account owners), but also reassigns the rights in the bank account data from a de facto exclusive control of the bank to the owner of the bank account (in the form of an additional right to data portability and interoperability).[41] Also, the policy discussion in the case of the data of the connected car is directly linked to this aspect of the initial allocation of the

40 Regarding the problem of the governance of data in connected cars, it could be possible to identify all of these market failure problems, see Kerber (n. 26) 316–25.

41 Very important in this respect is that the regulation does not allow the waiving of this additional right in the contractual relationship between the bank and the consumers as bank account owners. Otherwise the entire regulation might not work in the intended way. Emphasising the importance of the nonwaivability of data access rights see Josef Drexl and others (n. 14).

de facto control of (or rights in) the car data and the technical access to the car. The car manufacturers with their technological decision in favour of the 'extended vehicle' concept have allocated the exclusive de facto control of the data and access to the car to themselves (leading to a de facto 'appropriation' of the data). The alternative policy option of introducing the different technological solution of an open interoperable telematics platform would allow an initial allocation of the de facto control of the data and access to the car to the car owners. This also shows clearly that different technological solutions can lead to very different data governance solutions.[42]

(3) The third lesson to be learnt from sector-specific data access solutions refers to the problem that in many cases additional regulatory solutions are needed for making data access solutions effective, i.e. to achieve the intended effects of protecting or enabling competition and innovation. Therefore data access rules might have to be complemented by additional regulatory solutions. For example, the PSD2 data access regime addresses not only access to the bank account data but also stipulates that independent payment service providers can directly initiate payments from the bank account of the consumers, which requires that the banks offer a standardised technical interface (e.g. APIs) for enabling the interoperability of this complementary service with the bank account. A regulatory solution for interoperability might also be necessary in the example of connected cars, because certain complementary services of independent providers (e.g. remote repair and maintenance services) are only possible if the car manufacturers offer a standardised technical interface to enable the performing of such services. Also, safety and security concerns play an important role in both examples. Giving independent service providers access to data and enabling them to directly perform services can lead to additional risks for safety and security that require sophisticated solutions, such as mandatory certification of the independent service providers. Other regulations to help make these access regimes effective include the regulation of access fees and other access conditions such as non-discriminatory access.

The important insight from these three different lessons from sector-specific data access regulations is that it is often not enough to focus only on the direct data access problem itself, but it is necessary to use a broader analytical framework that allows for a more systematic analysis of data governance problems and a potentially broad set of legal and regulatory solu-

42 See Kerber (n. 26) 317 and also generally Datenethikkommission (n. 3) 15, emphasising that technology and its design can be used as a governance instrument.

tions for dealing in an effective way with data access problems. In the following part D, such a broader approach to analyse and design data governance systems for solving data access/sharing problems will be presented.

D. Data governance systems: Basic approach and instruments

I. General and specific data governance systems

One of the important results of the discussions about data rights in recent years is that the initial approaches of either introducing exclusive property-like rights on data or focussing primarily on simple access to data does not reflect enough the complex and context-dependent effects of the role and impact of data in the digital economy. There are no simple general 'one size fits all' solutions as to what data rights should look like. Rather, depending on the type of data and specific conditions, very different data governance solutions might be optimal. This can range from open data (public domain), through a multitude of different intermediate solutions, which might assign different rights in a set of data to different groups of stakeholders, to the other extreme solution of strict exclusive rights. From an economic perspective a 'bundle of rights' approach might be best suited for describing and analysing the vast scope of possible solutions concerning who should have what rights for what purposes in certain sets of data (or data streams). In the PSD2 example we have seen how the bundle of rights in online bank account data are defined and assigned to the different stakeholders, banks, bank account owners, and financial service providers. The 'bundle of rights' approach is a very flexible instrument that has the additional advantage of not being biased in favour of either the property (exclusionary) aspect or the access (sharing) aspect of data.[43] The same is true for using the broad and open concept of 'governance' of data.

---

43 The 'bundle of rights' approach goes back to the economic theory of property rights, which deconstructed 'property' as consisting of a bundle of rights with regard to an object, and asked for the economically efficient definition of such a bundle of rights. See for the property rights theory Armen A. Alchian and Harold Demsetz, 'The Property Right Paradigm' (1973) 33(1) The Journal of Economic History 16. For a focus on the analysis of 'rights in data' instead of an exclusive property-like right in data with the idea that in a multi-stakeholder situation as in the case of data of connected cars different stakeholders can have (different) rights in the same data see Kerber (2017) (n. 1) 127–31.

A data governance system refers to the entire set of rights and legal rules (and regulations) that are relevant for collecting, processing, analysing, using, sharing, and selling data in a certain system.[44] One can distinguish between the general data governance system of an entire economy and specific data governance systems for particular sectors, ecosystems, or other clearly delineated domains within an economy. The general data governance system of an entire economy encompasses all general rules that are relevant for data. In the EU this entails, in particular, the GDPR with the entire set of rights that are granted to persons with regard to their personal data, but also the many different rights and legal rules that are relevant for other data as well, such as civil law, IP law, competition law, consumer law, etc. All legally defined general rights in data and general legal rules and regulations that influence and shape the bundles of rights on collecting, processing, analysing, sharing, using and selling data can therefore be seen as part of the general data governance system of an economy. Therefore the horizontal data access solutions (using competition law, the data portability right of Article 20 GDPR, unfair trading law etc., as discussed in section B.I.) are part of this general data governance system. The current policy discussions about facilitating horizontal data access solutions (e.g. through an amendment of German competition law or enhancing the data portability right of Article 20 GDPR) intend to improve the general data governance system.[45]

Specific data governance systems refer to the specific sets of rights and legal rules that are relevant for data in a specific part of the economy. This can be a traditional industry or sector (or part of a sector), a digital ecosystem or platform, or an otherwise clearly delineable part of the economy, for which specific legal rights or rules for data exist that differ from the general rules about data. Sector-specific data access solutions, as have been discussed in part B, can therefore be seen as specific data governance sys-

44 The set of rights and legal rules of a data governance system can also be called a data governance regime. See Wolfgang Kerber and Severin Frank, 'Data Governance Regimes in the Digital Economy: The Example of Connected Cars' (2017) <https://ssrn.com/abstract=3064794> accessed 31 August 2020.

45 The set of rights and rules of the general data governance system can therefore also be seen as part of the general legal framework of the market economy, or, in the German ordoliberal approach, the so-called *Ordnungsrahmen* (economic order). Therefore the general data governance system can also be called *Datenordnung* and policies for improving this general set of rights and rules on data can be interpreted as *Ordnungspolitik*. See for this ordoliberal approach Viktor J. Vanberg, 'Freiburg School of Law and Economics', in Peter Newman (ed.), *The New Palgrave Dictionary of Economics and the Law*, Vol. 2 (MacMillan 1998) 172.

tems. The discussion about horizontal vs. sectoral data access solutions can then be reframed as a discussion about the question whether data governance problems should be solved through the rules of the general data governance system or by introducing a specific data governance system that leads to a different bundle of rights on data in this delineated part of the economy. The data-relevant rights and legal rules in a specific data governance system are usually a combination of (a) a set of system-specific rights and rules and (b) the rules of the general data governance system. For example, in the PSD2 regulation the additional rights on access to bank accounts and bank account data for bank account owners and financial service providers only apply to online bank accounts, and only with regard to a limited number of financial services, such as payment services and account information services. For all other data of bank customers, other bank accounts, or other services the general rules and not this specific set of rights and rules apply. One of the difficult questions in introducing specific data governance systems is therefore not only whether such a specific data governance system should be implemented and how to design the respective specific rights and rules. It is also necessary to delineate the scope of the specific data governance system, i.e. one must carve out for what part of the banking sector such a specific data governance system should be implemented, and which parts should remain under the rules of the general data governance system.

II. Market failures and policy objectives

What methodological approach should be used for analysing and designing data governance systems? In the discussion about granting access to data or sharing data, a number of criteria have emerged that are seen as relevant for deciding whether a claim for data access or data-sharing should be granted or not. As already mentioned in the introduction, these are: the benefits through more competition and innovation, incentives for the production of data, whether data claimants have participated in the production of these data, protection of business secrets and privacy (GDPR), bargaining power asymmetries between firms, and also public interests.[46] However, for the application of such a list of criteria it is necessary to analyse the effects of data access problems and data governance solutions with regard to these criteria. The problem is that all the relevant effects of differ-

46 See again the references (n. 3).

ent data governance solutions, ie whether we accept the exclusive control of data by data holders or grant access to other firms (via competition law or regulation), or introduce (or improve the effectiveness of) data portability rights can have many different effects on different markets, especially if opening data also leads to new innovations and the creation of new markets. Particularly the new economic and technological characteristics of the digital economy, in which markets can be interrelated in complex ways, such as in digital ecosystems with primary and secondary markets, and potentially large economies of scope between products and services within the ecosystems, might make deep economic analyses of the effects of different data governance solutions necessary.[47] Since in the digital economy the markets are much more linked with each other than before the digital transformation, the analysis of such effects as well as the delineation of separate sectors for introducing specific data governance systems has become much more difficult.

From an economic perspective the analyses should focus primarily on market failures and how to remedy them by using data governance solutions and other policies such as competition law, consumer law, data protection (privacy) law, standardisation policy, or direct regulatory solutions.[48] The most important market failure problems that are relevant with regard to data issues are competition problems (foreclosing competitors and leveraging market power through gatekeeper positions through exclusive control of data, lock-in problems, or quasi-monopolistic platform markets), information and behavioural problems of consumers (through intransparency about the collection and use of data by data-collecting firms, high transaction costs of self-managing privacy, etc.), externalities (eg with regard to the provision of data but also to harms caused by data breaches

---

47 See e.g. Crémer and others (n. 2) 19–38, Marc Bourreau and Alexandre de Streel, 'Digital Conglomerates and EU Competition Policy' (Center on Regulation in Europe 2019) 5–24 <https://cerre.eu/news/digital-conglomerates-and-eu-competition-policy/> accessed 31 August 2020. In our example of access to data in connected cars it is, e.g., a necessary precondition for proving the above-described competition problem with regard to the secondary markets that system competition between car manufacturers does not work sufficiently. This requires a deeper economic analysis, e.g. of lock-in effects and the behaviour of car buyers. See Kerber (n. 26) 387.

48 For an analysis of market failure with regard to data see, in particular, also Bertin Martens 'Data access, consumer interests and social welfare: An economic perspective of data', in this volume. Without the existence of market failures we could rely on the contractual relationships regarding data between firms or firms and consumers.

and cybersecurity risks), too low levels of interoperability and standardisation (due to biased incentives of firms with regard to interoperability and standardisation), and innovation problems (due to not enough use and sharing of data for data-driven innovation, data analytics, AI, and training of algorithms). Also of particular importance is that several market failures can exist simultaneously, which can make it necessary to analyse the interplay between these different market failures as well. This might lead to the need of a combination of different regulatory solutions in a specific data governance system. Our examples PSD2 and data in connected cars have shown both the existence of more than one market failure and the need for such a coordinated policy approach for solving competition, interoperability, and safety and security problems.

Since the economic market failure theory is based upon the concept of economic welfare, it cannot take into account additional policy objectives such as the protection of privacy as a fundamental value or distributional objectives, eg, the protection of vulnerable consumers or fairness considerations about the extent to which consumers can get a fair share of the value of their personal (or consumer) data. These and other additional policy objectives, which might be seen as relevant from a normative perspective, e.g. in specific contexts and sectors, have to be included in the analysis of the effects of different data governance solutions.[49] Based upon such analyses conclusions can be drawn about policy recommendations on the proper set of rights and rules with regard to data and additional necessary regulations for solving the problems.

III. Some instruments for data governance systems

This chapter has the task of providing a brief overview about specific instruments that can be used as basic elements of such data governance systems. All of these instruments can be found in the current discussion, and many of them can be used in combination with both general (horizontal) data access and (sector-)specific data governance solutions. Some of these instruments refer directly to the data themselves, and help to shape the definition and assignment of the 'bundle of rights' on data, whereas others

49 Such a broad economic policy approach that allows for including values and policy objectives beyond economic welfare can also lead to the need to deal with trade off-problems between economic welfare and these other values and policy objectives. One important example is the trade-off between privacy as a fundamental value and the effects of access to more personal data on economic welfare.

focus more on the additional regulatory solutions that might be necessary for making the data governance solutions effective.

1. *Consumer data rights and data portability*

A very interesting new instrument for defining and assigning rights on data is the already mentioned 'consumer data rights'.[50] Since data about consumers can be very valuable and consumers produce an increasing amount of data by using smart connected devices (IoT), the question has emerged whether consumers should have more control over these data and also participate more in the value of these data. This is also part of the discussion about data in connected cars, which according to a wide-spread opinion should be 'owned' by the car owners, and not by the car manufacturers (or by the manufacturers of smart devices in other IoT applications).[51] The consumer data rights approach asks what rights consumers should have with regard to the access, control and portability of their consumer data. An important objective of the consumer data rights approach is the empowerment of consumers to better control their consumer data, decide themselves whom they give access to these data, as well as participate in their value. Since most consumer data are also personal data as defined by privacy laws, such a control might also be exerted through the rights on personal data that are granted by privacy laws (such as, in particular, the GDPR in the EU). However, the advantage of the consumer data rights approach is that consumer data rights can be applied much more flexibly and in a more targeted form than rights in personal data provided for by privacy laws. For example, the scope of consumer data that are subject to these consumer data rights can be broader than what is defined as personal data in privacy laws, and might also encompass, e.g., observed or derived data.[52] It might therefore be an advantage to define and assign consumer data rights outside of privacy laws, because this allows for a much more sophis-

50 See as an overview OECD (n. 14).

51 That the owner of a smart device should be also the 'owner' of the data that are produced with this device was also the basic idea of the 'data producer right' proposed in Commission Communication COM(2017) 9 final (n. 1) 13.

52 See for this discussion, e.g., OECD (n. 14) 7–21; see also the concept of data mobility in Furman and others (n. 25) 65–71 that goes beyond the data portability right of the GDPR.

ticated and targeted fine-tuning of these rights to the specific problems of different sectors and ecosystems.[53]

This is also directly linked to the current critical discussion about the ineffectiveness of the data portability right of the Article 20 GDPR.[54] Here the solution of the PSD2, which defines data portability rights of the consumers outside of the GDPR and complements it with additional regulations, is superior to the application of Article 20 GDPR, which would have not been sufficient for opening bank accounts. In the same way the data portability right is also not capable of solving the data access problems in the data of the connected car example.[55] In its data strategy the European Commission wants to 'explore enhancing the data portability for individuals under Article 20 of the GDPR giving them more control over who can access and use machine-generated data'.[56] It might be important for this reform discussion to focus also on more data portability solutions outside of the GDPR, and the consumer data rights approach might be helpful in that respect.

2. *Data trustee solutions*

Data trustee solutions are another group of very promising data governance instruments that can be used in manifold ways for solving a wide range of problems in different contexts. Here only two main types of data trustee solutions will be distinguished. One discussion refers to the problems of consumers to manage their personal data and protect their privacy, the insight that they are often overwhelmed with the task of reading, understanding and managing long, intransparent privacy policies, and that therefore the currently applied 'notice and consent' solutions suffer from

53 Therefore the approach of the Australian government of introducing a general data consumer right, which is then implemented in sector-specific variants, reflects this flexibility. See Louisa Specht-Riemenschneider, 'Data access rights – A comparative perspective', in this volume.

54 See, e.g., Graef and others (n. 13), Krämer, Senellart and de Streel (n. 13).

55 See Daniel Gill and Wolfgang Kerber, 'Data Portability Rights: Limits, Opportunities, and the Need for Going Beyond the Portability of Personal Data' (2020), 2(2) CPI Antitrust Chronicle, 54.

56 Commission Communication COM(2020) 66 final (n. 1) 21; see also European Union, 'Consumer Data Rights and Competition – Note by the European Union' (2020) OECD Doc. DAF/COMP/WD(2020)40. See for other proposals Krämer, Senellart and de Streel (n. 14) 75–84.

serious market failure problems.[57] One possible solution might be new intermediaries acting in the interests of these consumers, and helping them to protect their privacy, especially through managing the rights in their personal data, ie whether and to whom they give consent for processing them and for what purposes according to their specific privacy preferences. These new intermediaries can also play an important role for making more data available for the data economy for innovation, research, and improving public policies, e.g. through donating or selling (or, more precisely, licensing) them. Such data trustee solutions as personal information management systems (PIMS) have been discussed for a long time,[58] but so far the attempts to develop profitable market solutions, e.g. by specialised start-ups, have not been successful. Recently a new discussion has started about the need to develop new data trustee solutions as one promising instrument for solving the privacy management problems of consumers, and what such solutions might look like.[59] Since experience has shown that pure market solutions do not seem to be successful, the future discussion might have to focus on the question of how the development of such intermediaries with a data trustee role for consumers can be supported by addi-

57 Despite a contentious discussion about the 'privacy paradox' there is an increasing consensus that here a serious market failure exists due to information asymmetries and behavioural problems of consumers that is aggravated by misleading strategies of data-collecting firms. See Patricia. A. Norberg, Daniel R. Horne and David A. Horne, 'The Privacy Paradox: Personal Information Disclosure Intentions Versus Behaviors' (2007) 41(1) Journal of Consumer Affairs 100; Daniel J. Solove, 'Privacy Self-Management and the Consent Dilemma' (2013) 126 Harvard Law Review 1880; Alessandro Acquisti, Laura Brandimarte and George Loewenstein, 'Privacy and Human Behavior in the Age of Information' (2015) 347(6221) Science 509; Katharine Kemp, 'Concealed Data Practices and Competition Law: Why Privacy Matters' (2019) University of New South Wales Research Series 19–53 <https://papers.ssrn.com/sol3/papers.cfm?abstract_id=3432769> accessed 31 August 2020.

58 Article 29 Data Protection Working Party (n. 13).

59 See Kommission Wettbewerbsrecht 4.0 (n. 13) 43, Datenethikkommission (n. 3) 133–136; Commission Communication COM(2020) 66 final (n. 1) 10; for a broad recent overview see Aline Blankertz, 'Designing Data Trusts. Why We Need to Test Consumer Data Trusts Now' (Stiftung Neue Verantwortung e.V. 2020) <www.stiftung-nv.de/sites/default/files/designing_data_trusts_e.pdf> accessed 31 August 2020; Aline Blankertz and others 'Datentreuhandmodelle' (2020) 66–73 <www.stiftung-nv.de/sites/default/files/20200428-datentreuhandmodelle.pdf> accessed 31 August 2020; and Krämer, Sennellart and de Streel (n. 14).

tional regulatory solutions.[60] For our discussion here is important that such data trustee solutions for helping to protect the privacy and manage the rights in personal data of consumers can be seen as an important building-block of the general data governance system (with regard to all personal data of the consumers). However, also specific data trustee solutions for a limited set of personal data, eg mobility data or energy consumption data, might be possible, which then can be integrated into a comprehensive specific data governance system.

The second type of data trustee solutions focusses mainly on the manifold problems that can emerge regarding data in B2B contexts. Data trustees can fulfil the function of providing a trustworthy neutral entity for managing problems between firms that can reduce transaction costs (through increasing trust), ensure compliance with data protection rules or IP protection, help to solve competition problems by making data available in a non-discriminatory way, or help to open data by providing access to large data sets according to certain principles.[61] One of the proposed policy solutions in the data in connected car example, the 'shared server', can be interpreted as a data trustee solution. It implies that all car data would be transmitted to an external server (outside of the car), which however is governed by a neutral entity that makes the data available to the stakeholders of the ecosystem of connected cars in a non-discriminatory way under certain general principles. In the same way other data sets (or data streams) which should be made available to (a certain group of) firms for enabling competition and innovation can also be administered by an entity which fulfils the role as a data trustee. In that respect data trustees might also play a role in the EU strategy of developing common European data spaces, in which for different sectors large data sets of, e.g. anonymised, data are made available for AI applications or the training of algorithms.[62] Data trustees might also play a role in all these cases where firms have to grant access to data due to competition law provisions (e.g.,

60 This need for additional regulatory support can refer to solving conflicts of interest between consumers and these data trustees but might also refer to the question whether there should be an obligation of data-collecting firms to negotiate with these intermediaries. One of the problems of such data trustee intermediaries is their lack of bargaining power vis-à-vis powerful data-collecting firms and platforms. See Blankertz (n. 59) 18–22, who despite preferring market solutions also discusses regulatory solutions which, e.g., can also mandate the use of such data trustees.

61 See for these and other objectives, e.g., Blankertz and others (n. 59) 2.

62 See Commission Communication COM(2020) 66 final (n. 1) 11–23.

the EFD according to Article 102 TFEU), but also where serious concerns emerge that a direct transmission of data to data claimants might lead to the danger of losing any control over the use of these data. In such cases neutral and trustworthy data trustees might offer solutions enabling other firms to access and use these data (for the purposes intended with this data access), but ensuring that the monitoring of this use by the data trustee helps to prevent any misuse (and therefore protects the interests of the data holders).[63] These different ways data trustee solutions can be used in B2B contexts show that they can play manifold roles both in the general data governance system and in specific data governance systems.

3. *Interoperability and standardisation*

Solving problems of interoperability and standardisation is an important issue with regard to many data governance problems, as we also have seen in our examples of PSD2 and connected cars. However, it is important to distinguish three different problems: (1) One problem concerns the well-known issue of 'common data formats' as a precondition for data access, data-sharing and data portability, which can be supplemented by the often additional need for data standardisation (clear definition of data sets and their quality). (2) Beyond these conditions for the data sets themselves, it is additionally necessary to have clear standardised technical interfaces for the access to or transmission of data. This might require regulation on a technological level, e.g. by requiring standardised APIs. It might be more challenging if independent service providers also need real-time access to data for providing their services. (3) It is necessary to distinguish an additional separate problem of providing technical interfaces that allow independent service providers to interoperate with a system, as, e.g., when initiating payments in bank accounts or remotely uploading software updates on the IT system of the connected car (for providing remote maintenance services). Here the problem is not primarily about transmission of (or access to) data but about performing complementary services, which can necessitate much higher requirements for interoperability and therefore the technical interface.[64] Depending on the technological and economic con-

63 This is also linked to the discussion about data sandboxes, in which innovators can experiment with consumer data, e.g. under the supervision of an agency, see Furman and others (n. 25) 71.

64 The last two distinctions correspond to the concepts 'data interoperability' and 'full protocol interoperability' in Crémer and others (n. 2) 83–86.

ditions of the data governance problems, only one, two, or all three of these problems have to be solved so as to enable competition and innovation in these data governance solutions. All three problems can be very relevant in both general and specific data governance systems. What is important from an economic perspective is that, on the one hand, there might be serious market failure problems due to biased incentives that lead to not enough interoperability and standardisation; on the other hand, however, it also has to be taken into account that more interoperability and standardisation does not always have positive effects on competition and innovation. This has to be considered with regard to general standardisation policy as well as with regard to interoperability and technological standardisation in specific data governance systems.[65]

4. *Minimum standards for safety, security, and privacy*

Another key issue for data governance systems in the digital economy with its new and huge problems of cybersecurity is the problem of how to deal with safety and security risks. These risks can encompass identity theft, data breaches, misuse of data, fraud, and the damaging of entire technical systems with potentially huge risks regarding accidents and loss of lives. So far the policy solutions for dealing with these risks, e.g. through liability and/or minimum standards for safety and security (especially regarding the many new IoT applications), are still very insufficient.[66] As far as data governance systems entail solutions for data access/portability and/or interoperability, it is necessary to also develop solutions for the safety and security problems that might be linked to these data governance solutions. Therefore (high) minimum standards for safety and security (as well as 'security by design' and sophisticated liability solutions) might be necessary. This refers also to the already discussed issue of more interoperability and stan-

65 For the economics of interoperability and standardisation (with the ensuing market failure problems) see John Palfrey and Urs Gasser, *Interop: The Promise and Perils of Highly Interconnected Systems* (Basic Books 2012); Farrell and Simcoe (n. 36), and as a brief overview Kerber and Schweitzer (n. 36).

66 See, e.g., for cybersecurity risks of smart home applications Sara E. Kettner and Christian Thorun, 'Big Data im Bereich Heim und Freizeit' (2018) <www.abida.de/sites/default/files/Gutachten_HeimUndFreizeit.pdf> accessed 31 August 2020. See generally for the economics of cybersecurity Tyler Moore, 'The Economics of Cybersecurity: Principles and Policy Options' (2010) 3(3–4) International Journal of Critical Infrastructure Protection 103.

dardisation, which might also have to itself include safety and security standards. But other solutions, such as the licensing or certification of independent service providers, might also be very helpful policy solutions that can be part of integrated specific data governance systems (as we have seen in the PSD2 and the current motor vehicle type approval regulation).

The policy measures for dealing with cybersecurity risks can also contribute to the protection of privacy for making the storage and processing of personal data more secure. However, as we have seen in our discussion of intermediaries that might help consumers to manage their data (PIMS), privacy risks also exist with respect to the collection of data due to intransparency (and misleading practices of data-collecting firms) regarding the extent of the collection and use of personal data and behavioural problems of consumers. Since so far the market solution of privacy-protecting data trustee solutions does not exist (and might also work only to a limited extent in future), it might be necessary to use more regulatory solutions for implementing additional minimum standards for the privacy policies of data-collecting firms. This might be done by either using more the current provisions in the GDPR (e.g. on consent or privacy-by-design/default) and in consumer law, or by introducing new additional regulations, e.g. also in certain sectors as part of specific data governance systems. These specific regulatory solutions can refer to the requirements for consent (opt-in, opt-out, etc.) or minimum rules for transparency regarding the collection and use of personal data, but might also encompass substantive minimum standards on limits for the collection and use of personal data.[67] Another important field of quasi-regulatory solutions that can constitute important elements of general and specific data governance systems is that of labelling and certification of firms regarding their compliance with the GDPR, or, additionally, on their level of data protection.[68] It can also be particularly

67 See, e.g., European Data Protection Supervisor 'Privacy and Competitiveness in the Age of Big Data: The Interplay between Data Protection, Competition Law and Consumer Protection in the Digital Economy, Preliminary Opinion 2014' (EDPS 2014) 24–25 <https://edps.europa.eu/sites/edp/files/publication/14-03-26_compettitition_law_big_data_en.pdf> accessed 31 August 2020.

68 For a critical analysis of the provisions on data protection certification in the GDPR see Eric Lachaud, 'Why the Certification Process Defined in the General Data Protection Regulation Cannot Be Successful' (2016) 32 Computer Law & Security Review 814; Irene Kamara and others, 'Data Protection Certification Mechanisms: Study on Articles 42 and 43 of the Regulation (EU) 2016/679 – Final Report' (2019) <https://ec.europa.eu/info/sites/info/files/data_protection_certification_mechanisms_study_final.pdf> accessed 31 August 2020. Also, industry-specific codes of conduct on compliance with the GDPR are possible.

important for the data economy to have clear rules on the standards for anonymisation of personal data, because anonymised data sets are not subject to EU data protection law. Sector-specific standards for anonymisation of personal data that take into account the sector-specific risks of reidentification can therefore be a very valuable element of specific data governance systems that can help to increase legal certainty in the context of both the privacy of consumers and the data economy.[69]

E. Perspectives

The most important results of this article are the following:

(1) Both horizontal and sectoral solutions for access to (or sharing of) data have advantages and problems, and it can be expected that depending on the specific technological and economic conditions in different parts of the economy either general data access rules or sector-specific data access rules are more suitable for solving the problems.
(2) Focussing only on the problem of whether one firm should get access to data that another firm holds will often be too narrow an approach for solving problems of insufficient access to data for competition and innovation. It is often necessary to use a broader analytical approach that, on the one hand, analyses a broader set of data governance solutions, including for example the use of data trustees or technological solutions that change the initial allocation of de facto control of data, and, on the other hand, might also allow for a broader set of remedies, including additional regulatory solutions like requiring interoperability and standardisation or minimum standards for safety, security, and privacy, for ensuring the effectiveness of the data governance solutions. This is the broader approach of analysing entire data governance systems, especially with respect to the effects of existing market failures on welfare and other policy objectives.
(3) In the last part we have briefly analysed a number of instruments that can be used as building-blocks in such data governance systems, both for the general and for specific data governance systems. Particularly interesting new instruments might be based upon the new approach of consumer data rights (especially with regard to data portability), the

69 See for the problem of data anonymisation and the difficulties in defining the precise requirements for a data set that qualifies as anonymous according to the GDPR Crémer and others (n. 2) 85–87.

manifold types of data trustee solutions (both for privacy management and in B2B contexts), interoperability and standardisation policies, as well as necessary regulatory policies with respect to safety and (cyber)security, as well as privacy. Whereas in the general data governance system these different policies will have to be applied independently of each other, they can be directly aligned through an integrated regulatory regime in specific data governance systems that try to address all market failure problems in a coordinated way.

In this article we have not addressed one key question about data governance solutions, namely the institutional question who should decide on data governance solutions. Although the ultimate decision-maker is always the legislature, the question emerges who should decide whether a specific data governance system should be implemented and how the specific rights and rules in both general and specific data governance systems should be designed. Should the courts be the de facto rule-makers and/or enforcement agencies (like competition authorities) who can publish guidelines and pursue enforcement priorities? Or should we have regulatory authorities with broader regulatory powers that also have the authority to decide on specific data governance systems with their specific rights and rules with respect to data? The 'digital market unit' proposal in the Furman Report suggests such an institutional solution, because it would confer on this new regulatory authority broad powers, (1) for designating which platform firms have a 'strategic market status' and should be subject to ex ante regulation, eg concerning 'codes of conduct', but (2) also for making decisions about enabling more data mobility, open standards and interoperability as well as opening data. Therefore the Furman proposal is primarily also an institutional proposal that a new regulatory authority should have the powers to introduce, change and shape important parts of data governance systems with regard to data access, data sharing and interoperability.[70] It is not possible here to discuss the merits and problems of such an institutional solution. However, the Furman proposal emphasises

70 What is important is that the regulatory powers with regard to data governance solutions in the Furman proposal are not limited to data access or interoperability problems caused by platform firms with a 'strategic market status.' They can also be applied to other firms, see Furman and others (n. 25) 70, 73. See also the proposal of a 'digital authority' with similar powers in the Stigler Report: Committee for the Study of Digital Platforms, 'Market Structure and Antitrust Subcommittee – Report' (1 July 2019), 9, 83–87 <https://research.chicagobooth.edu/-/media/research/stigler/pdfs/market-structure-report.pdf?la=en&hash=E08C7C9AA7367F2D612DE24F814074BA43CAED8C> accessed 31 August 2020.

the need for also finding proper institutional solutions for how the data governance solutions (including their necessary complementary regulations) can evolve and be adapted in a timely way to the ever-changing economic and technological conditions of the digital economy.[71] This is particularly important, because there is an urgent need for a more forward-looking perspective on data governance policy, eg to identify early new data governance problems that might threaten competition, innovation, and privacy, and to develop solutions that prevent the problems. This refers, among other things, to the emergence of new bottleneck and gatekeeper positions based upon the exclusive control of data. So far data governance policies tend only to react to already existing gatekeeper positions instead of more actively trying to prevent them.[72]

71 Another institutional proposal has been made by the German Kommission Wettbewerbsrecht 4.0 (n. 13) 6. It recommends the introduction of a new EU Framework Directive that would give the European Commission the powers to enact sector-specific regulations granting users the right to make their internet accounts accessible to third-party providers.

72 See also for an emphasis on a forward-looking approach Datenethikkommission (n. 3) 84.

Connected devices – An unfair competition law approach to data access rights of users

Josef Drexl

A. *Introduction*

The digital economy is no longer limited to the business models of Internet platform operators, the use of personal computers and smartphones. Through embedded sensors, artificial intelligence and advanced mobile telecommunications technology, connected devices collect data, analyse them automatically, communicate with multiple other devices and act autonomously. Through the advent of these devices, digitisation penetrates many sectors of the physical economy. Connected devices significantly contribute to the explosion of data in the digital era and thereby support the European Commission's recent observation that 'data will reshape the way we produce, consume and live'.[1]

The economic and social implications of the advent of connected devices are manifold. They often mark disruptive innovation with the power of completely replacing the previous generations of products. They fundamentally transform existing business models and markets. Connected devices also change the role of users and consumers. We no longer only buy and use a physical product. We also become data providers who actively contribute to the generation of data, including personal data, while it is typically the device manufacturer who remains in control of these data.

Data collected and generated by connected devices may be of great utility for a large group of players. First of all, these data serve the very interest of the users, since they are needed to guarantee the well-functioning of the connected device, especially in terms of utility, safety and convenience. The well-functioning of the device may also require data sharing with other devices, such as in the case of automated and autonomous driving where vehicles have to communicate with traffic lights and signs as well as other vehicles, including those produced and operated by competing manufac-

---

1 Communication from the Commission of 19 February 2020 to the European Parliament, the Council, the European Economic and Social Committee and the Committee of Regions – A European strategy for data, COM(2020) 66 final, 2.

turers. Beyond this, firms active in secondary markets also depend on data access. An example are independent providers of repair services of cars who are in need of access to the on-board data of these vehicles. Even the state may have a huge interest in access to especially aggregated data, such as anonymised health data collected through fitness trackers, mobile health devices and connected drugs, to pursue public interest goals.

In sum, this explains why there is general agreement that data sharing and access is of essence for the development of the digital economy.[2] This insight drives the debate on what kind of regulatory framework the digital economy needs. As regards the measures and approaches that ought to be taken, policymakers not least on the European level have progressed quite considerably in the past years. In 2017, in its Communication on 'Building a European Data Economy', which focused particularly on machine-generated data, the Commission still seemed prepared to consider a potential data producer's right for the owners or long-term users of connected devices for the purpose of enhancing the free flow of data.[3] Meanwhile, however, the perspective has changed. In its more recent Communication on the European Strategy for Data, the Commission announces the proposal of a Data Act, which is supposed to regulate the relationship between the different actors in the data economy.[4] This project seems to mark a final shift to data access legislation.[5] Indeed, the Commission states that the Act is intended to make 'access to data … compulsory, where appropriate under fair, transparent, reasonable, proportionate and/or non-discriminatory conditions'.[6] The focus on data access is also mirrored by the other new project of the Commission, a review of the existing intellectual property framework, including the Database Directive in particular,[7] with the objec-

---

2 See the early study of OECD, 'Data-Driven Innovation: Big Data for Growth and Well-Being' (OECD 2015), hinting at the importance of data access for promoting multiple public interest goals.

3 Communication from the European Commission of 10 January 2017 – Building a European Data Economy, COM(2017) 2 final, 13.

4 European Commission, 'A European strategy for data' (n. 1) 13.

5 Such policy shift has also been advocated by the author of this chapter. See, in particular, Josef Drexl, 'Data Access and Control in the Era of Connected Devices – Study on behalf of the European Consumer Organisation BEUC' (BEUC 2018) <www.beuc.eu/publications/beuc-x-2018-121_data_access_and_control_in_the_area_of_connected_devices.pdf> accessed 31 August 2020. This chapter builds on, and further develops, the analysis of this study.

6 European Commission, 'A European strategy for data' (n. 1) 13.

7 Directive 96/9/EC of the European Parliament and of the Council of 11 March1996 on the legal protection of databases, [1996] OJ L77/20.

tive of enhancing data access and use.[8] This additional initiative shows that legal exclusivity regarding data is now considered a potential impediment to the free flow of data rather than a tool to promote data access.

Data access rights are not a completely new legal tool. They have especially been in use in sector-specific regulation for quite some time. There, data access rights are typically vested in competitors.[9] An obligation to provide data access to competitors may also result from competition law provided that the refusal to grant access constitutes an abuse of market dominance in the sense of Article 102 TFEU.[10] In the competition law context, the terminology of compulsory licensing is often used, especially where the refusal relates to the use of intellectual property rights. Indeed, this terminology would better indicate that data access may also often require an additional (licensing) contract between the data holder and the person entitled to claim data access, whereby this contract fixes the terms and conditions of access, including the question of whether the data holder is entitled to remuneration.[11] Yet the concept of data access rights may still be unusual for experts of intellectual property rights and general private law

---

8 European Commission, 'A European strategy for data' (n. 1) 13. On the potentially negative impact of the protection of databases, not least due to the sui generis database right, see Drexl (n. 5) 67–85; P. Bernt Hugenholtz, 'Data Property in the System of Intellectual Property Law' in Sebastian Lohsse, Reiner Schulze and Dirk Staudenmayer (eds), *Trading Data in the Digital Economy: Legal Concepts and Tools* (Nomos 2017) 75; Matthias Leistner, 'Big Data and the EU Database Directive 96/9/EC: Current Law and Potential for Reform' in Sebastian Lohsse, Reiner Schulze and Dirk Staudenmayer (eds), *Trading Data in the Digital Economy: Legal Concepts and Tools* (Nomos 2017) 27; Matthias Leistner, 'The existing European IP rights system and the data economy – An overview with particular focus on data access and portability', in this volume.

9 See, for instance, on the right of independent providers of repair services to the on-board data of motor vehicles, Recital 8 and Arts 6–9 Regulation 715/2007 of 20 June 2007 on type approval of motor vehicles with respect to emissions from light passenger and commercial vehicles (Euro 5 and Euro 6) and on access to vehicle repair and maintenance information, [2007] OJ L171/1, as last amended by Regulation (EU) No 459/2012 of 29 May 2012, [2012] OJ L142/16.

10 See Joined Cases C-241/91 and C-242/91 *RTE and ITP v Commission* ('*Magill*') [1995] ECR I-743 = ECLI:EU:C:1995:98 (on the duty of TV broadcasters to license the copyright protecting the programming information to independent TV guide publishers); Case T-201/04 *Microsoft v Commission* [2007] ECR II-3601 = ECLI:EU:T:2007:367 (on the duty of Microsoft to grant access to interoperability information to allow competitors to program competing work-group server operating systems in a way to be compatible with Windows).

11 This is why, in the *Microsoft* case, the General Court (GC) was also requested to decide on principles for calculating 'reasonable and non-discriminatory' royalty

who are more used to thinking in terms of exclusive rights and contractual obligations. However, the Draft Principles for the Data Economy of the American Law Institute (ALI) and the European Law Institute (ELI) now acknowledge a large variety of legal tools and list data access rights as one sub-category of data rights.[12]

Yet introduction of data access rights should only be considered with caution. Obliging private actors to grant access to data constitutes a form of market regulation and intervention. From a constitutional perspective, data access rights, restricting the fundamental right of the data holder to conduct a business,[13] are therefore in need of a justification. Following the principles of sound economic regulation, data access regimes should only be adopted where they respond to a market failure. The Commission acknowledges such restrictions, noting that access to data should only become a legal obligation 'where specific circumstances so dictate'.[14] The Commission further indicates that data access rights should only be adopted in the framework of sector-specific regulation and under the condition that a market failure is identified that competition law cannot solve.[15]

In line with these considerations, this chapter seeks to explore under which conditions an access right to machine-generated data should be granted to the users of connected devices. Thereby, the scope of the following research goes beyond a strict sector-specific approach, as connected devices appear in a great variety of different sectors of the economy. However, it can be assumed that neither the underlying market failure nor the public and private interests involved will largely vary depending on the sector of the economy that now experiences the advent of connected devices. Therefore, the following analysis seeks to develop a common legal framework for data access rights in the context of such devices. This framework could be implemented either in the form of general cross-sectoral legislation or sector-specific legislation building on a set of general princi-

---

rates for access to interoperability data. See T-167/08 *Microsoft v Commission* ECLI:EU:T:2012:323.

12 These Principles are not final and therefore not yet publicly available. See, however, Christiane Wendehorst (Project Reporter representing the ELI), 'The ALI-ELI Principles for a Data Economy' in Alberto De Franceschi and Reiner Schulze (eds), *Digital Revolution – New Challenges for Law* (C.H. Beck and Nomos 2019) 42, paras 37–42.

13 Art. 16 EU Charter of Fundamental Rights. In general, on the constitutional framework for data access, see Thomas Fetzer, 'The constitutional framework of data access rights', in this volume.

14 European Commission, A European strategy for data' (n. 1) 13.

15 Ibid. 13 note 39.

ples. Yet the one does not exclude the other. Sector-specific and cross-sectoral legislation may co-exist, whereby the latter constitutes a form of framework legislation that applies where sector-specific legislation is missing.

In the following, this chapter will first define some general concepts that are used throughout the analysis (at B. below). It will then identify access rights as just one legal element of broader regulatory systems of data governance (at C. below). After describing how connected devices transform markets and business models (at D. below), the chapter will identify data lock-in as the underlying market failure (at E. below). However, data access rights will only be advisable and justified to the extent that existing remedies are not available or insufficient and that access rights are actually needed to remedy a market failure. Therefore, this chapter furthermore explores alternative regimes for data access rights (at F. below). Thereby, it will in particular show that contractual rights and competition law are not sufficient to provide data access. This is why the chapter ultimately proposes an additional unfair competition law approach to data access rights of the user of connected devices (at G. below).

B. General concepts

This research is in need of using uniform terminology. Yet the following definitions do not only serve the purpose of identifying the object of research of this chapter. They are also designed to prepare the design of the ultimately recommended data access right in the light of the underlying market failure.

I. Connected devices

This chapter uses the term 'connected devices' in a broad sense, namely, as all devices that (1) are connected with other things and persons through wired or wireless communication[16] and (2) generate data.

16 Connected devices are often understood as a feature of the Internet of Things, which relies on most modern, even 5G mobile telecommunications technologies. Yet the latter is not necessary condition. For instance, kitchen devices may easily communicate with each other based on Wi-Fi and the kitchen computer may order food through wired communication.

Such devices do not need to be 'intelligent' or 'smart' in the sense that artificial intelligence systems are embedded in the device. Nor does the term presuppose that the device can make autonomous decisions or act as an autonomous agent. The broader definition has the advantage of also capturing larger networks of devices in which specific functions are allocated across a network of units. For instance, as part of a monitoring system of medication, a drug may be equipped with a sensor that sends the information that the patient has taken the drug from the patient's stomach to a connected wearable, from where the information is further communicated to the central server of the pharmaceutical company; there, the information may be analysed, and, ultimately, either a human being or an autonomous digital agent takes further measures.

Hence, the term is to be understood in a technologically neutral sense. Even application of sensor technology, such as in cars, farming machines or smart wearables, is just one form of generating data. The concept also includes devices without sensors, such as smart meters, that collect data and transmit those data through wireless or wired communication. Furthermore, connected devices are not limited to those that communicate autonomously through the Internet of Things. Devices used by humans for the purpose of communication, such as PCs, tablets or smartphones, are equally covered, because it is not relevant to what extent the device stores and processes data without being influenced by the decisions of a natural person. This is because most data collection through connected devices is influenced by human decisions to some extent. For instance, in the above-mentioned example of a drug in which a sensor is embedded, the patient has to take the drug first and thereby starts the data collection and communication process. The extent of human influence on such data generation and processing will not matter for answering the question of whether there should be a data access right or not. Furthermore, the relevant data generated through a connected device do not have to be stored in the same device. Connected devices are also those that communicate and share dynamic data in larger networks in real time, even without storing data at all. Connected devices do not only function by using data they autonomously generate; they may also rely on data they receive through wired or non-wireless means from other sources, including other devices.

II. Data

In 2017, when the Commission for the first time was considering the future legal framework for 'Building the European Data Economy', it focused on machine-generated data as unstructured raw data.[17] This focus can only be explained by the intent to define the subject-matter of the data producer's right that should be allocated to the owner or long-term user of a connected device. Indeed, these raw data constitute the first level of digital data that the use of a connected device generates. In addition, the Commission was probably influenced by earlier legal writing that, at a time when connected devices and machine-generated data were still quite unknown, tried to design an ownership right in data.[18] There, the argument in favour of a data ownership right was predominantly that the act that ultimately leads to the digital encoding is the one that should be considered the act of 'producing data'. Since the focus at that time was on the recognition of a property right in 'digital' data, this approach attempted to restrict protection of data on the syntactic level, hence, without taking the semantic level, as the information that can be taken from the data or the function of the data (as in the case of software or music), into account.[19]

This approach had to face critique. Above all, it failed to explain why the recognition of such data producer's rights was needed from the perspective of an incentive theory. Indeed, it was not argued that such right was needed as an economic incentive to generate the data in the first place.[20] The objective of the scholarly proposal for recognising data ownership was a different one, namely, to enhance the tradability of data. The data producer's right was expected to create transparency as regards property rights in data as a basis for functioning data markets.[21]

Yet, in 2017, the Commission was tempted to pick up this proposal in substance, albeit with a different policy objective. The Commission considered using the economic interests of the owner or long-term user of a connected device to overcome a data lock-in. While the Commission may thereby have identified the underlying market failure correctly, it over-

17 European Commission, 'Building a European data economy' (n. 3) 8–10.

18 See, in particular, Herbert Zech, 'Daten als Wirtschaftsgut – Überlegungen zu einem "Recht des Datenerzeugers"' (2015) Computer und Recht 137. Yet, already at that time, other authors were opposed to the introduction of data ownership rights; see, for instance, Thomas Heymann, 'Rechte an Daten – Warum Daten keiner eigentumsrechtlichen Logik folgen' (2016) Computer und Recht 650 (in direct response to Zech).

19 Zech (n. 18) 138.

20 See Zech (n. 18) 144–45 (rejecting the incentive theory as a basis for the data producer's right).

21 See, in general, Herbert Zech, 'Information as a Tradable Commodity' in Alberto de Franceshi (ed.), *European Contract Law and the Digital Single Market* (Insentia 2016) 51.

looked important arguments against data ownership. In particular, it did not take into account that, in many instances, the machine-generated digital raw data will immediately go through additional stages of analysis and processing for the very purpose of guaranteeing the functioning of the device. In this regard, the Commission did not explain the relationship of the unstructured raw data with derived[22] or inferred data.[23] Even more importantly, the attempt to reduce the data producer's right to the syntactic level was destined to be futile. In the data economy, the economic value of data derives from the utility of the data in terms of their informational content or functionality. Hence, it is the semantic level that provides the data with value. Data in the digital context should not simply be defined as digital data in the form of bits and bytes but as 'digitally encoded information (or function)'.

Yet, already back in 2017, the Commission realised that – on the semantic level – raw machine-generated data could include personal information. To avoid a conflict with the right to data protection, the Commission therefore tried to limit the debate to 'non-personal' machine-generated data.[24] However, to identify the subject-matter of protection of the data producer's right in this sense, the semantic level of the data, in other words, the meaning or function of the data needs to be taken into account.

To focus on the utility of data on the semantic level is equally important for the object of a data access right. To decide for which data the user of a digital device should have such a right, it is necessary to identify the conflicting interests of this user and the data holder (typically the device manufacturer). This is confirmed by already existing sector-specific access rights of competitors. In these cases, the kind of data the law obliges data holders to grant access to is defined by the specific interest of the competitor claiming data access. In particular, it is the dependence on certain data for remaining in or entering a specific market that justifies access to data. This can be generalised: data access rights in this context serve a particular economic function. This function defines the concrete data that constitute the

22 The term 'derived data' denotes data derived from other data elements using a mathematical, logical or other type of transformation. In this sense, aggregated anonymised health data can be considered as derived data in relation to the original personal health data.

23 Inferred data are generated from statistical correlations, often resulting from big data analyses. Inferred data are probabilistic by nature. An example would be the credit scoring of individual consumers through analysis of large customer-related datasets.

24 European Commission, 'Building a European data economy' (n. 3) 9.

subject-matter of the access right on the semantic level. Accordingly, the law grants independent providers of motor vehicle repair services access to on-board data that these providers need in order to provide their repair and maintenance services.[25]

Equally, if the data access right of the user of the connected device serves the purpose of overcoming a data lock-in, the relevant data should be defined in the light of this purpose. Such interest is not necessarily limited to the first level raw data, which of course also contain certain information, but will often require access to derived or inferred data as information arising from subsequent steps of data processing and analyses.

Conversely, this purpose-oriented understanding of data for designing data access rights also limits the scope of the data access right. This does not rule out that other data access rights may serve different or additional, even non-economic, objectives. This is especially the case for the portability right regarding personal data in Article 20 General Data Protection Regulation (GDPR).[26] While this right may also apply with regard to data collected by connected devices[27] and also serves the purpose of helping the data subject (often a consumer) to switch suppliers,[28] the data portability right applies to any personal data that the data subject has 'provided' to a data controller. Here, beyond the goal of enhancing competition by facilitating the switching of suppliers, this data portability right is justified by the additional goal of guaranteeing data autonomy of the data subject based on fundamental rights considerations.

III. The user of connected devices

With the particular focus on the user of connected devices, this chapter makes a choice as regards the potential holder of the data access right. This choice does not preclude the legislature from also, or alternatively, considering vesting data access rights in competitors in particular.

This chapter uses the term of 'user' in a rather unspecific way. The 'user' does not need to use the device physically. What matters more is the partic-

---

25 See Arts 6–9 Regulation 715/2007 (n. 9).

26 Regulation (EU) No. 2016/679 of the European Parliament and of the Council of 27 April 2016 on the protection of natural persons with regard to the processing of personal data and on the free movement of such data, and repealing Directive 95/46/EC, [2016] OJ L119/1.

27 See the analysis by Drexl (n. 5) 151–153.

28 Ibid. 152.

ular interest a person has in the data generated by the device that justifies access. In this context, both the operator of a car rental service and the customer renting the car could qualify as users of the car, while only the former owns the car and the latter physically uses the car. The same holds true for farming machines that independent service providers physically operate on the land of farmers as their customers. Here, in addition to the service provider – who may typically own the machine – the individual farmer should also be considered a 'user' of the machine to the extent the machine collects data from the farmer's land. Hence, for the question of whether the farmer has a right of access to the data connected machines collect from the farmer's land, it should not matter whether the farmer also owns or physically operates the machine.

In contrast to access rights of competitors, this chapter focuses on the vertical dimension and specifically asks whether the user should have data access rights against the device manufacturer as the de facto data holder. Depending on the specific connected device and the concrete purpose of the use, the holder of the data right will often be a consumer in the sense of European consumer law. Thus, this chapter is also designed as a contribution to the development of European consumer law in the digital era. But it is not limited to consumer law, since connected devices, such as a connected car, smart farming machines or even manufacturing robots used in factories, can equally or will exclusively be used for commercial or other professional purposes.

IV. Data access

Moreover, this chapter uses the term 'data access' in a broad and flexible sense. Upfront, data access is not limited to a right of being informed of what information is contained in a dataset. Nor is it limited to 'portability' in the sense of the data portability right of Article 20 GDPR as a right to 'receive' the data or have the data 'transmitted' at a given point in time. What data access actually requires will depend on the interest that justifies the right. This can also mean that data access requires real-time data sharing.

C. *Data access rights as an element of data governance*

Data access and sharing will keep markets open and maintain incentives for digital innovation.[29] Yet data access rights should be seen as only one element of a broader, more holistic approach to data governance.[30]

Data governance has to take into account the interests of multiple stakeholders and multiple policy goals. Whatever measure is taken or recommended, including data access rights, these measures need to be devised and coordinated in the framework of such data governance systems. As regards the policy goals, promoting data access and data sharing should not be considered as the final goal. Rather, rights to data access and data sharing are to be advocated as measures that ultimately promote efficient and competitive markets as well as innovation.

Data governance requires a balancing of the interest in data access and sharing with conflicting interests. Most importantly, in a world where connected devices penetrate the private life of individuals, the constitutional right to data protection[31] needs to be taken account of. Since in many cases connected devices will collect both personal and non-personal data, data access rights must not ignore data protection rules. Yet personal data is not the only group of 'sensitive data'. Machine-generated data may also constitute trade secrets of the device manufacturer who has a legitimate interest in being protected against the making available of such data to competitors. This does not necessarily have to exclude data access rights of the users. Yet the nature of data as trade secrets of the data holder may argue for confidentiality obligations of the user to whom access to the data is granted.

Moreover, it is important to understand that the recognition of a right to data access is not sufficient to guarantee data access. Data governance has to include various kinds of measures, whereby legal measures only constitute one set of measures. In general terms, data governance has three – (1) technical, (2) regulatory and (3) organisational – dimensions.

From a technical perspective, data governance and, as part of it, data access and data sharing depend on the availability of many technologies, such as powerful mobile telecommunications technologies. Data access

29 European Commission, 'A European strategy for data' (n. 1) 2–3 (specifically referring to the dependence of innovative start-ups and SMEs on access to data and the role of access to data as training data for artificial intelligence).

30 See, in particular, Wolfgang Kerber, 'From (horizontal and sectoral) data access solutions – Towards data governance systems', in this volume.

31 Art. 8(1) EU Charter of Fundamental Rights; Art. 16(1) TFEU.

and data sharing requires data interoperability, standardisation of data formats and access to the use of application programming interfaces (APIs). As regards data protection, data governance has to rely on anonymisation technologies and technologies that prevent deanonymisation. Cutting-edge technologies, such as blockchain technology, may also enhance data autonomy and sovereignty of data subjects as regards their personal data.[32] The lack of such technologies constitutes obstacles to the application and enforcement of data access rights that also respect data protection rules.[33]

As regards the legal dimension, data access rights are part of the legal framework that defines the rights and obligations of the different actors in the data economy. The data governance approach requires the legislatures to take into account the rights and interests of the multiple stakeholders as well as other public interest grounds.[34]

It is on this level where data access rights have to be coordinated with other legal measures including data protection rights and intellectual property rights. As regards the latter, data governance should not blindly give priority to intellectual property protection over data access rights, as seems to be the case under Article 20(4) GDPR.[35] Therefore, it has to be considered a step in the right direction that the European legislature has now given priority to the right to re-use public sector information over government-held intellectual property rights in the framework of the recently revised Directive on Open Data and PSI.[36] Even more, it has to be welcomed

32 See Shraddha Kulhari, *Building-Blocks of a Data Protection Revolution – The Uneasy Case for Blockchain Technology to Secure Privacy and Identity* (Nomos 2017).

33 Data access rights have to take into account such technical obstacles. See, for instance, Art. 20(1) GDPR, which provides that a data subject can claim the transfer of the data in a 'structured, commonly used and machine-readable form'. Accordingly, the data subject depends on the existence of technology that fulfils these requirements.

34 The author of this chapter has proposed a comprehensive theory for regulation in earlier writing. See Drexl (n. 5) 49–59; Josef Drexl, 'Legal Challenges of the Changing Role of Personal and Non-Personal Data in the Data Economy' in Alberto De Franceschi and Reiner Schulze (eds), *Digital Revolution – New Challenges for Law* (C.H. Beck and Nomos 2019) 19, paras 7–41.

35 Rather opaquely, Art. 20(4) GDPR states that data portability 'shall not affect the rights and personal freedom of others'. In favour of a narrow interpretation according to which intellectual property rights of the data controller should not be considered rights of others, Drexl (n. 5) 83–85.

36 Accordingly, only documents in which third parties hold intellectual property rights remain excluded from commercial re-use. See Art. 1(2)(c) and Art. 3(2) Directive (EU) 2019/1024 of the European Parliament and of the Council of 20 June 2019 on open data and the re-use of public sector information, [2019] OJ L172/56.

that the European Commission now announces its intent to review EU intellectual property legislation in view of promoting data access and use.[37] In addition, nothing would prevent the EU legislature from adopting regimes on access rights that legally prevail over privately held intellectual property rights. Similar to competition law, such rules could be viewed as 'external' exemptions and limitations that apply horizontally to various intellectual property rights. Such rules would not collide with international treaty obligations in the field of intellectual property to the extent that legislation on access rights is compliant with the three-step test.[38] From a perspective of sound economic regulation, coordinating access rights with intellectual property would require the legislature to balance the diverse positive and negative effects on the incentives for innovation of both intellectual property protection and access rights. As part of this balancing, the legislation would have to take into account that the person seeking, or indirectly benefitting from, data access will often be a follow-on innovator. Moreover, intellectual property rights may prove particularly detrimental where they foreclose use of technologies that need to be used for data sharing. This is why courts should be cautious as regards recognition of copyright protection for APIs.[39]

From an organisational perspective, data access will depend on institutional arrangements concerning standard-setting mechanisms and bodies as well as platforms for the sharing of data. New types of actors can play an important role in enabling data access and sharing, such as independent data trustees, and therefore should be promoted. In particular, data trustees as intermediaries could enhance commercial transactions by assessing the utility of the data for the purposes of the person seeking data access, thereby helping overcome the economic problem of the information paradox. The information paradox is caused by an information asymmetry

37 European Commission, 'A European strategy for data' (n. 1) 13.

38 See Arts 13, 17, 26(2) and 30 Agreement on Trade-Related Aspects of Intellectual Property (TRIPS).

39 This matter is largely unaddressed or unresolved in the different jurisdictions. See, however, the US case *Oracle America, Inc v Google, Inc*, 886 F.3d 1179 (Fed Cir 2018), where the US Court of Appeals for the Federal Circuit held that Google infringed Oracle's copyright by integrating the Java programming language API in its Android operating system (also holding that Google is not able to rely on the US fair use exemption). On Google's request, the US Supreme Court has however granted certiorari and is expected to hear any time soon.

concerning the quality, provenance and value of data.[40] It describes the problem that the person seeking access to information cannot assess the value of the information without getting access to it. However, once somebody has access to the information, this person will no longer be willing to pay a price for access. However, this problem can be solved by intermediaries. A data analytics trustee could be appointed to run sample tests on the quality and utility of the dataset concerned and describe the utility of the dataset for the purposes of the person seeking access in general terms.[41] Furthermore, independent trustees can work as mediators or arbitrators for assessing the reasonableness of royalty rates for access to data.[42] Therefore, they could also play a role for enhancing the effectiveness of data access regimes.

D. Transformation of the markets

The advent of connected devices, building on sensor technology, mobile communication, data analytics and artificial intelligence, fundamentally transforms both the manufacturing process and the markets.

I. Competition-driven innovation

Connected devices are products with increased utility, higher quality and safety as well as convenience. Accordingly, connected devices can be con-

---

40 As coined by Kenneth J. Arrow, 'Economic welfare and the allocation of resources for invention' in National Bureau of Economic Research (NBER) (ed.), *The Rate and Direction of Inventive Activity* (Princeton University Press 1962) 609.

41 Such market solutions are nowadays considered an option to the claim that exclusive data ownership rights are needed to create workable markets for data. See, in general, Nestor Duch-Brown, Bertin Martens and Frank Mueller-Langer, 'The economics of ownership, access and trade in digital data', JRC Digital Economy Working Paper 2017–01 (European Commission 2017) 36. Wolfgang Kerber, 'A New (Intellectual) Property Right for Non-Personal Data? An Economic Analysis' (2016) Gewerblicher Rechtsschutz und Urheberrecht Internationaler Teil 989, 994, even assumes that the problem could be solved through the data holder by informing the prospective customer in general terms about the data. See also Drexl (n. 5) 136.

42 In the *Microsoft* case, based on EU competition law, the European Commission has ordered the appointment of an independent trustee to play such a role. See, in particular, Case T-167/08 *Microsoft v Commission* ECLI:EU:T:2012:323, para. 102.

sidered as innovation.[43] The most important driver of this innovation seems to be competition. In many instances, connected devices lead to disruptive innovation. Firms understand that if they do not 'digitise' their products, they may well have to leave the market soon.

In particular, pro-competitive advantages explain the success of digitisation of machines in the industrial context, often described as a Fourth Industrial Revolution ('industry 4.0'). For industrial customers, 'smart manufacturing' constitutes both process and product innovation. In terms of process innovation, smart machines allow for predictive maintenance and, hence, avoid down times, thus creating enormous potential for cost savings. This enhances the ability of manufacturers to compete on price even if they produce non-connected traditional goods. In terms of product innovation, smart manufacturing increases the quality of products, preventing technical failures and human mistakes that may otherwise result in the distribution of defective goods.

Connected devices are also sold to consumers. In this regard, increased utility, safety and convenience will typically be among the primary selling points. Yet consumers who are particularly sensitive to data protection may hesitate to buy connected devices that could 'spy' on their private life. Therefore, high standards of data protection should not only be considered as a potential obstacle to digitisation. Data protection rules and their effective enforcement can build trust as a basis for the success of connected devices in consumer markets.

II. Transformation of business models and markets

Connected devices do not only constitute disruptive innovation that has the power to replace the former generation of non-connected devices. Often, they are also disruptive for the business models and the markets in which they are sold.

This transformation is characterised by 'servicisation'. In the case of connected devices, the purchase of a physical device typically comes with a ser-

43 Relying on the notion that innovation requires implementation in goods and services that satisfy consumer demand. See OECD, Oslo Manual 2018 – Guidelines for Collecting, Reporting and Using Data for Innovation (4th edn, OECD 2018) 20, where 'innovation' is defined as follows: 'An innovation is a new or improved product or process (or combination thereof) that differs significantly from the unit's previous products or processes and that has been made available to potential users (product) or brought into use by the unit (process).'.

vice. In an industry 4.0 environment, the manufacturer of a smart machine will also provide predictive maintenance to the customer. At times of automated and autonomous driving, the manufacturer of a car also provides attached digital services that may gradually progress in the future from guaranteeing safe and convenient driving to the full provision of a transport service to 'passengers'. Producers of household devices that also sell a kitchen computer may develop into providers of comprehensive household management systems. Energy providers can use connected devices to become operators of facility management systems. And pharmaceutical companies no longer simply sell drugs; digitisation of drugs and smart wearables allow them to become health care providers. In many instances, the manufacturer or the downstream provider of a service may decide to retain the ownership of the device, which then only plays the role of a tool to provide a service.[44]

From a legal perspective, servicisation fundamentally changes the relationship between the end-consumer and the manufacturer. While in the past, end-consumers often bought devices from retailers, without direct contractual contact with the manufacturer, customers are nowadays required to sign additional contracts with the manufacturer of connected devices concerning the use of the embedded software or other digital services. In addition, where a device collects personal data from the end-user and the manufacturer seeks control of these data as the data controller, the manufacturer will additionally have to request consent pursuant to the data protection rules of the GDPR.

Depending on the concrete connected device and the business model chosen, this creates a complex relationship, which is characterised by three features: (1) bundling of multiple transactions regarding different subject matter (sale of the device, provision of digital services, processing and use of personal data);[45] (2) establishment of a long-term relationship with the manufacturer; and (3) triangulation of the relationship between manufac-

---

44 This is more likely to happen where, as in the case of a connected smoke detector, the connected device is of a lower value or requires constant monitoring. But the same may happen where a user is not in permanent need of the device, such as a farmer regarding certain farming machines or consumers regarding the use of cars.

45 Raising, for instance, the question of whether the provision of personal data could or should be considered a counter-performance for receiving a digital service especially in cases in which the service provider does not claim any monetary remuneration. The debate was especially driven by the use of the term 'counter-performance' in the proposal of the Commission for the Digital Content Directive to extend the scope of application of the Directive to contracts where con-

turer, retailer and final customer across the distribution chain. Triangulation creates legal challenges regarding, in particular, allocation of liability for non-conformity of the goods and services with the contract. In the context of the most recent reform of consumer law, the European legislature decided to allocate contractual liability as regards digital content or digital services that are incorporated in or inter-connected with consumer goods – so-called 'embedded software' and 'embedded services' – in the person of the seller of the device even if another person, such as the manufacturer in particular, supplies the digital content or the digital service.[46] Here, triangulation convinced the European legislature to set aside the fundamental private law principle of privity of contract. The choice to impose liability on the direct trader was not at all obvious and mostly due to the objective to simplify the claiming of rights for consumers.[47]

E. Data access rights as a means to overcome data lock-ins

As mentioned, already in 2017, the Commission, in attempt to launch a debate on the future legal framework of the European data economy, correctly noted that the data collected and generated in an IoT context often constitutes a key input for other innovative services and that access to such data for innovative firms could therefore enhance the data economy.[48] In

---

sumers provide personal data as a 'counter-performance' without undertaking to pay a price. On the private law implications of such concept, see Axel Metzger, 'Data as a Counter-Performance: What Rights and Duties Do Parties Have?' (2017) 8 Journal of Intellectual Property, Information Technology and E-Commerce Law 2. The final text of the Directive ultimately avoids the use of the term 'counter-performance'. On the reasons for giving up mentioning the term 'counter-performance'. See Art. 3(1)(2) Directive (EU) 2019/770 of the European Parliament and of the Council of 20 May 2019 on certain aspects concerning contracts for the supply of digital content and digital services, [2019] OJ L136/1. Even under the final version authors argue that consumers 'pay' with data to get a digital service. See Dirk Staudenmayer, 'The Directives on Digital Contracts: First Stepts Towards the Private Law of the Digital Economy' (2020) 2 European Review of Private Law 219, 225–26.

46 Art. 3(3) Directive (EU) 2019/771 of the European Parliament and of the Council of 20 May 2019 on certain aspects concerning contracts for the sale of goods, amending Regulation (EU) 2017/2394 and Directive 2009/22/EC, and repealing Directive 1999/44/EC, [2019] OJ L136/28. See in more detail Staudenmayer (n. 45) 231.

47 Staudenmayer (n. 45) 231.

48 European Commission, 'Building a European data economy' (n. 3) 8.

particular, the Commission was concerned that the 'generators of data', obviously referring to the manufacturers of connected devices, could keep these data to themselves to analyse them in 'silos',[49] thereby foreclosing access of innovative firms to downstream markets for data-related services.[50]

As regards the datasets that can be used in downstream markets, a distinction has to be made between aggregated data and individual-level data. On the one hand, the manufacturers use the connected devices to collect, analyse and aggregate data. These aggregated data can be of interest for firms, for instance for the purpose of training artificial intelligence systems, but also for the state or researchers to pursue public interest goals. Yet, in 2017, the Commission focused more on the individual-level data as the data collected by a single device. Indeed, withholding these data would foreclose market access for innovative firms that intend to provide data-related services to the user of such a device. An example would be a service that optimises harvesting by using the data collected by farming machines on the land of a given farmer. Such service could either be offered by the manufacturer of the farming machine or an independent digital service provider.

In general, control over machine-generated data enables the manufacturer of connected devices to bundle other goods and services to the sale of the device. Thus, the provider of a digital household assistant could in principle also tie manifold other household devices, such as the washing machine and the refrigerator, to the sale of the digital assistant. Since, in times of artificial intelligence and autonomous agents, such a household assistant could also take over consumer decisions on the purchasing of secondary goods needed in a household, including food or cleaning materials, such bundling could also extend to many more markets for consumer goods and retailing.

These examples show that, without legal guarantees of access to data, the decision to purchase a particular connected device may lead to a lock-in of the user with regard to many other goods and services. Such data lock-ins raise concerns from the perspective of innovation as well as consumer and competition policy. In particular, the objective of overcoming such data lock-ins should move to the centre of competition policy, to

49 Ibid.

50 Ibid. 9.

keep markets open, to maintain consumer choice and to safeguard incentives for innovation in the digital sector.[51]

As regards the means to overcome such data lock-ins, in 2017, the Commission was considering potential adoption of legislation on a new data producer's right to be vested in the owner or long-term user of a connected device.[52] At that time, the argument was that such right would 'open the possibility for users to utilise their data and thereby contribute to unlocking machine-generated data'.[53] From a consumer policy perspective in particular, it was quite appropriate to rely on the interests of the 'users' of connected devices as potential purchasers of additional connected devices and recipients of secondary digital services to 'un-lock' machine-generated data. However, creating a new exclusive data ownership right would have been the wrong instrument to remedy the market failure of the data lock-in for various reasons.[54] First, the Commission overlooked the fact that a data lock-in can only be expected where the manufacturer enjoys superior bargaining power. Yet property rights are not a suitable means to solve a problem of unequal distribution of bargaining power. A device manufacturer could easily include a clause in its standard contract terms requiring the users of the devices to transfer or license the data producer's right for free.[55] Rather than 'un-locking' data, a data producer's right could thus even strengthen the anyhow existing de facto exclusivity position of manufacturers. Secondly, the data producer's right could considerably distort the working of secondary markets for aggregated data, since a person seeking access to the aggregated data could no longer simply assume that the manufacturer, despite being the de facto data holder, holds all the legal

51 On the competition law dimension, see also Heike Schweitzer and Robert Welker, 'A legal framework for access to data – A competition policy perspective', in this volume.

52 European Commission, 'Building a European data economy' (n. 3) 13.

53 Ibid.

54 For a full evaluation of the data producer's right in this regard see Drexl (n. 5) 132–50.

55 See Josef Drexl and others, 'Position Statement of the Max Planck Institute for Innovation and Competition of 26 April 2017 on the European Commission's "Public Consultation on Building a European Data Economy"' (2017) para. 18, <www.ip.mpg.de/fileadmin/ipmpg/content/stellungnahmen/MPI_Statement_Public_consultation_on_Building_the_EU_Data_Eco_28042017.pdf> accessed 31 August 2020; Josef Drexl, 'On the Future EU Legal Framework for the Digital Economy: A Competition-based Response to the "Ownership and Access" Debate' in Sebastian Lohsse, Reiner Schulze and Dirk Staudenmayer (eds), *Trading Data in the Digital Economy: Legal Concepts and Tools* (Nomos 2018) 223, 235.

rights needed to provide data access. In any instance, adoption of exclusive data producer's rights for machine-generated data for the owner or long-term user of connected devices would create the need for rights clearance where third persons seek access to the aggregated data held by the device manufacturer.[56] In sum, rather than solving the problem of data lock-ins, a data producer's right would lead to legal uncertainty and, therefore, impede the development of the digital economy.

This shows that the appropriate legal instrument has to be tailor-made for the specific market failure it is supposed to remedy.[57] Hence, where purchasers or users of connected devices suffer from a lack of data access, the appropriate remedy has to be a data access right. This is not a new insight. Such data access rights, albeit for competitors in secondary markets, are known from sector-specific regulation.[58]

F. *Alternative legal instruments*

Yet adoption of a data access right of the users of connected devices should also take into account the availability of alternative legal regimes for access. Already today, the data portability right pursuant to Article 20 GDPR provides the owner or long-term user of a connected device with access to personal machine-generated data. However, this right is limited in many regards (at I. below).[59] More importantly, this following section will show that the two legal instruments essential for a functioning market economy, namely, contract law (at II. below) and competition law (at III. below), are insufficient to provide access to machine-generated data. This is not only the case as regards existing rules. Due to the inbuilt limitations of the contract and competition law systems, even potential future reforms would

56 Drexl and others (n. 55) para. 19; Drexl in Lohsse, Schulze and Staudenmayer (n. 55) 235–36.

57 See also Drexl and others (n. 55) para. 21.

58 As in the case of access of independent providers of repair and maintenance services to the on-board data of motor vehicles (see at n. 9, above) or in the case of access of providers of digital payment services to the bank account data of their customers. On the latter, see Art. 36 Second Digital Payment Services (DPS2) Directive (EU) 2015/2366 of the European Parliament and of the Council of 25 November 2015 on payment services in the internal market, amending Directives 2002/65/EC, 2009/110/EC and 2013/36/EU and Regulation (EU) No 1093/2010, and repealing Directive 2007/64/EC, [2015] OJ L337/35.

59 On the limitations of this right as regards machine-generated data see Drexl (n. 5) 150–54.

not achieve the goal of providing sufficient data access to the users of connected devices. In addition, the suitability of data access rights of users of connected devices need to be compared with data access rights of competitors (at IV. below). Finally, this following section seeks to clarify the relationship with exceptions and limitations of existing systems of intellectual property protection that may foreclose access to machine-generated data (at V. below).

I. The right to portability of personal data pursuant to Article 20 GDPR

As regards access to data generated by connected devices, the data portability right pursuant to Article 20 GDPR can already provide a data access right in certain instances. Yet this right is not sufficient to achieve the goal of providing data access to the extent that this is needed.[60]

On the one hand, the scope of application of Article 20 GDPR seems to be broader than needed, since it is not limited to data generated by connected devices. Yet the provision is limited to personal data. This will prove insufficient in many instances where the user of a connected device is required to get access to the machine-generated data for receiving a service from a third business operator. For instance, a farmer may be in need of access to the data generated by farming machines to contract with the provider of a digital farm management system. Here, the availability of a data access right should not depend on the debatable question of whether the data related to the soil of the land of an individual farmer makes these data personal data in the sense of the GDPR. It is more important to note that the objective to overcome a data lock-in in such circumstances should not depend on whether the data qualifies as personal data.

Furthermore, Article 20(1) GDPR only applies to personal data the data subject has 'provided' to the controller. Therefore, the major discussion regarding the application of this data portability right in an IoT context mostly concentrates on the extent to which personal machine-generated data can be considered as provided by the data subject. Indeed, the provision seems flexible enough to give it a broad meaning so as to include 'observed' data too. This would guarantee that the data portability right also covers the geolocation data generated by a smartphone or the data on the

60 See in general Drexl (n. 5) 108–10.

bodily functions of a person collected by a fitness tracker.[61] In all such instances, while the data subject is not acting with the intent to provide specific data to the data controller, the data subject fulfils an active element that results in data collection as part of the functionalities of the device and the service provided to the data subject. The extension to such 'observed' data is also needed to realise the full pro-competitive benefits of the data portability right. Thus, the holder of a car registering the driving habits of the driver could rely on the data portability right to benefit from a lower insurance premium when switching the car insurer. Yet the wording of Article 20(1) GDPR can no longer be considered as fulfilled in the case of 'derived' and 'inferred' data, which are generated through additional data processing and data analyses.[62] Such conclusion is supported by a comparison of Article 20(1) GDPR with the data access right in Article 15 GDPR, which, in contrast to Article 20(1) GDPR, does not include a right to claim the transfer of the data. Not limited to 'provided data', this data access right covers all personal data held by the data controller, including derived and inferred data.

In contrast, the data portability right provides a good template for an additional right of access to data generated by connected devices to the extent that Article 20(2) includes a right to claim the direct transfer to another data controller and that the data subject can claim the transfer at any time. Yet the wording of Article 20(1) and (2) GDPR seems to indicate that the right to data portability is limited to the 'transfer' of data, while in the interest of the users of connected devices, it would be important to also include a right to real-time data sharing. Thus, the user of a connected device

---

61 See Article 29 Data Protection Working Party, 'Guidelines on the right to data portability' (13 December 2016, revised 5 April 2017) 9–10, <https://ec.europa.eu/newsroom/article29/item-detail.cfm?item_id=611233> accessed 31 August 2020; Ruth Janal, 'Data Portability – A Tale of Two Concepts' (2017) 8 Journal of Intellectual Property, Information Technology and E-Commerce Law 59, para. 4.

62 Article 29 Data Protection Working Party, 'Guidelines on the right to data portability' (n. 61) 10. This interpretation is broadly accepted in legal writing. See, for instance, Paul De Hert, Vagelis Papakonstaninou, Gianclaudio Malgieri and others, 'The right to data portability in the GDPR: Towards user-centric interoperability of digital services' (2018) 34 Computer Law & Security Review 193, 200; Lucio Scudiero, 'Bringing Your Data Everywhere: A Legal Reading of the Right to Portability' (2017) 3 European Data Protection Law Review 119, 122–23; Lachlan Urquhart, Neelima Sailaja and Derek McAuley, 'Realising the right to data portability for the domestic Internet of things' (2018) 22 Personal & Ubiquitous Computing 317, 319.

could claim that a third service provider have permanent access to data continuously generated by the device.

II. Contract law

Contract law is an obvious candidate for addressing the issue of access to machine-generated data. Users of connected devices are typically direct or indirect purchasers of such devices.

Given the fact that especially consumers suffering from inferior bargaining power could easily contract away their right to data access, such right should be recognised as a part of mandatory European contract law. Beyond the portability right regarding personal data pursuant to Article 20 GDPR, European consumer contract law also provides for a data access right in Article 16(4) Digital Content and Services Directive (DCSD) as regards non-personal data.[63] Yet this right equally fails to provide sufficient access to data generated by connected devices.

Article 16(4) requires a trader to make available certain non-personal data, namely, 'content ... which was provided or created by the consumer when using the digital content or digital service supplied by the trader'.[64] This provision complements the portability right concerning personal data pursuant to Article 20 GDPR and will especially apply in cases where a consumer uploads content, such as pictures, music and other audiovisual content that does not necessarily qualify as personal data in the sense of the GDPR.

Yet the application of the provision is considerably restricted in several regards.[65] Most importantly, it does not apply to data collected through so-called 'embedded' software or services. The provision requires a contract on the 'supply of digital content or digital service'. According to Article 3(4) DCSD, this does not cover the case where digital content or services are 'incorporated in or inter-connected with' a tangible item in such a way that absence of the digital content or digital service would prevent the item from performing its function. The purpose of the provision is to delegate consumer protection as regards connected devices to the regime of the

63 Directive (EU) 2019/770 (n. 45).

64 On the interpretation of Art. 16(4) DCSD, see Axel Metzger, 'Access to and porting of data under contract law: Consumer protection rules and market-based principles', in this volume, Part B.

65 See Metzger (n. 64) Part B.II.

Sale of Goods Directive (SGD).[66] The two Directives are therefore meant to be complementary.[67] According to Article 16 SGD, in case of a malfunctioning of the device, which may also arise from the digital elements of the good,[68] the consumer has a right to terminate the contract according to Article 16 SGD. But unlike Article 16(4) DCSD, this provision does not include a right of access to the data,[69] which may not prevent the Member Stats to provide for a right to claim tranfer of the data under national law.[70]

This shortcoming does not rule out that future reform of EU consumer contract law will create additional access rights for consumers. Yet extending the model of Article 16(4) DCSD to data generated by connected devices would still remain insufficient. First, the right is limited to data that is 'provided and created' by the consumer. As in the context of the data portability right of Article 20(1) GDPR, 'provided data' could be understood in a broad sense, namely, to include 'observed' data that a connected device automatically registers as the result of the use of the device by the consumer.[71] Yet 'derived' or 'inferred' data generated through additional stages of data processing and data analyses could hardly be conceived as data 'provided or created' by the consumer.[72] Secondly, the access right is excluded under the conditions as provided by Article 16(3) lit. a), b) and c) DCSD. In particular, this excludes access to data that 'has no utility outside the context of the digital content or the service'.[73] Since, in the case of con-

---

66 See, on the scope of application, Art. 3(3) SGD (n. 46).

67 See Staudenmayer (n. 45) 230. This does not exclude that the rights even in case of lack of conformity for embedded software or services under the SGD differ from those granted under the DSCD. On this, see Jozefien Vanherpe, 'White Smoke, but Smoke Nonetheless: Some (Burning) Questions Regarding the Directives on Sale of Goods and Supply of Digital Content' (2020) European Review of Private Law 251, 261.

68 Art. 10(2) SGD.

69 See also the criticism of Metzger (n. 65) Part B.II. However, national law may provide for a right of the purchaser to claim transfer of the data. See Vanherpe (n. 67) 268 (hinting at Art. 3(6) SGD, leaving it to the Member States to define the consequences of termination of the contract).

70 See Vanherpe (n. 67) 268 (hinting at Art. 3(6) SGD, leaving it to the Member States to define the consequences of termination of the contract).

71 Janal (n. 61) paras 7–9; Ruth Janal, 'Data portability under the GDPR: A blueprint for access to rights?', in this volume; Drexl (n. 5) 152.

72 On the interpretation of Art. 20(1) GDPR in this regard, see Article 29 Data Protection Working Party, 'Guidelines on the right to data portability' (n. 60) 10 (regarding the personal customer profile generated through data analyses).

73 Art. 16(3) lit. a) DCSD.

nected devices, data are primarily generated to guarantee the functioning of the device, such rule would have the potential of practically excluding data access to machine-generated data. Thirdly, Article 16(4) DCSD only applies as of the moment of termination of the contract, while in the case of connected devices, the user of the device may well depend on data access especially for the purpose of receiving a data-related service from a third person at any time of the contract execution regarding the connected device.

Accordingly, a contractual access right requires much broader scope of application. Within consumer contract law, the reform should not only be limited to a reform of the Consumer Sales Directive by implementing a right of access to data generated by connected devices without a limitation to personal data and the limitations known from the DCSD. Since connected devices do not reach consumers exclusively through sales contracts, such data access right would need to be enacted for any kind of consumer contract to include any rental or other kind of service contract.[74]

In addition, the abovementioned imbalance of bargaining power resulting in a data lock-in is not limited to B2C relationships. Hence, there is also a need for an access right to data generated by connected devices in B2B contracts. Ideally, such right would have to be mandatory to be effective. This explains why, already in 2017, the Commission started a discussion on the introduction of default contract rules to promote access to data and extend fairness control of contract terms to B2B relations.[75] While Germany in particular has a lot of experience controlling the fairness of B2B contracts, the idea of the Commission did not find sufficient support in the public consultation following the Communication on Building a European Data Economy in 2017.[76] It seems that the Commission has meanwhile moved away from this idea. At least, in 2018, it proposed a reform of the Directive on Consumer Contract Terms that did not include

74 This is another short-coming of the SGD as compared to the DSCD. The latter refrained on purpose to limit the concept of contracts on digital services and content to certain types of contracts, such as sales contracts. See Staudenmayer (n. 45) 224.

75 European Commission, 'Building a European data economy' (n. 3) 12.

76 See European Commission, 'Synopsis Report – Consultation on the "Building a European Data Economy" Initiative' (2017) 5–6 <https://ec.europa.eu/information_society/newsroom/image/document/2017-36/synopsis_report_-_data_economy_A0EFA8E0-AED3-1E29-C8DE049035581517_46646.pdf> accessed 31 August 2020.

an extension of fairness control to B2B contracts.[77] Stakeholders participating in the consultation, inter alia, expressed the concern that the situation differs widely between sectors and that therefore fairness control of B2B contracts could harm the development of innovative business models.[78] In sum, for the time being, it cannot reasonably be expected that the EU legislature would implement protection of businesses against contracting away a right of access to data generated by connected devices any time soon.

But even if contractual protection was created, such rules would only apply where there is a contractual relationship between the user of the device and the de facto data holder. Of course, the legislature could take inspiration from the concentration of the contractual rights against the direct trader selling the devices with regard to contractual liability for defects arising from embedded software or services as implemented in the Consumer Sales Directive.[79] Thus, the trader would be legally obliged to grant data access even where the manufacturer holds the data. Such rule would force the manufacturer to design its distribution systems in such a way as to make its connected devices commercially viable. However, contractual data access claims against retailers are not necessarily a sufficient substitute for direct data access claims against the manufacturer, not least in case of insolvency of the retailer.

Moreover, limiting access rights against the direct trader (retailer) would not sufficiently work in many other instances. The chain of contracts between the manufacturer and the user may be too long to guarantee uncomplicated enforcement of the data access right and may include diverse kinds of – sales and service – contracts, such as in the case of a farming machine where the machine is not owned by the farmer but a service provider. In particular, access rights limited against the direct trader would hardly work where connected devices are resold as used goods by end-users.

---

77 See Art. 3 Proposal of Commission of 11 April 2018 for a Directive of the European Parliament and of the Council amending Council Directive 93/13/EEC of 5 April 1993, Directive 98/6/EC of the European Parliament and of the Council, Directive 2005/29/EC of the European Parliament and of the Council and Directive 2011/83/EU of the European Parliament and of the Council as regards better enforcement and modernisation of EU consumer protection rules, COM(2018) 185 final.

78 European Commission, Annex to the Synopsis Report (2017) 21 <https://ec.europa.eu/information_society/newsroom/image/document/2017-36/annex_to_the_synopsis_report_-_data_economy_A45A375F-ADFF-3778-E8DD2021E5CC883B_46670.pdf> accessed 31 August 2020.

79 See Art. 3(3) SGD.

The better solution in all those cases are direct data access rights against the manufacturer as the de facto holder of the relevant data. This solution would also be preferable in B2B relationships. Such claims would be possible without entering into a fundamental debate on extending mandatory contract law or unfairness control of contract terms to B2B relations, which would raise many additional issues regarding the fundamental principles of European contract law.

III. Competition law

While data access rights are a new issue for contract law, competition law appears a more appropriate and experienced legal basis for data access rights. Upfront, competition law seems to have several advantages. First, it provides framework regulation that applies horizontally across all sectors of the economy. Secondly, based on the prohibition of abuse of market dominance pursuant to Article 102 TFEU, competition law provides claims outside contractual relations, especially in cases of unilateral refusals to deal. Thirdly, competition law has already acquired relevant experience applying Article 102 TFEU to cases where undertakings refused to grant access to data.[80] And finally, given the underlying market failure of a data lock-in, which excludes market access for other undertakings, the competition law approach seems to be most appropriate concerning the market failure that is in need of being addressed. Therefore, is should not come as a surprise that some commentators have argued that competition law provides sufficient remedies and that, therefore, additional access rights are not needed to provide data access in the IoT context.[81]

However, closer scrutiny argues against this conclusion. As the following analysis will show, application of Article 102 TFEU to a refusal to grant access to data in the modern data economy in general and as regards connected devices in particular comes with many uncertainties and limitations that make competition law in its current form a rather unfit instrument

80 See, in particular, Joined Cases C-241/91 P and C-242/91 P *RTE and ITP v Commission* (*'Magill'*) [1995] ECR I-743 = ECLI:EU:C:1995:98; T-201/04 *Microsoft* [2007] ECR II-3601 = ECLI:EU:T:2007:289.

81 See Jürgen Kühling and Florian Sackmann, 'Rechte an Daten – Regulierungsbedarf aus der Sicht des Verbraucherschutzes?', Rechtsgutachten im Auftrag des Bundesverband Verbraucherzentrale (20 November 2018) 22 <www.vzbv.de/sites/default/files/downloads/2018/11/26/18-11-01_gutachten_kuehling-sackmann-rechte-an-daten.pdf> accessed 31 August 2020.

for enforcing data access.[82] However, this does not exclude a future reform of competition law. Indeed, the conviction has by now widely spread that digitisation and digital business models present major challenges for competition law. Following several recent studies conducted on behalf of the European Commission[83] and national governments,[84] there is now growing consensus that competition law is in need of a fundamental reform. This debate has also reached the political level in several jurisdictions. In Germany, in September 2020, the Federal Government submitted a bill for reforming the national competition law, based on the Act against Restraints of Competition,[85] with the major objective of safeguarding competition in the digital age.[86] The European Commission pursues the same ob-

82 This has already been argued by Max Planck Institute for Innovation and Competition, Position Statement on Data Ownership and Access to Data (16 August 2016), paras 32–38 <https://papers.ssrn.com/sol3/papers.cfm?abstract_id=2833165> accessed 31 August 2020; Josef Drexl, 'Designing Competitive Markets for Industrial Data – Between Propertization and Access' (2017) 8 Journal of Intellectual Property, Information Technology and E-Commerce Law 257, paras 123–51. A similar conclusion was reached in the more recent analysis of the independent Special Advisors to the EU Competition Commissioner. See Jacques Crémer, Yves-Alexandre de Montjoye and Heike Schweitzer, 'Competition Policy for the Digital Era – Final Report' (2019) 8–9 and 98–107 <https://ec.europa.eu/competition/publications/reports/kd0419345enn.pdf> accessed 31 August 2020.

83 Crémer, de Montjoye and Schweitzer (n. 82).

84 See, for Germany, Heike Schweitzer, Justus Haucap, Wolfgang Kerber and Robert Welke, 'Modernisierung der Missbrauchsaufsicht für marktmächtige Unternehmen' (29 August 2018) <www.bmwi.de/Redaktion/DE/Publikationen/Wirtschaft/modernisierung-der-missbrauchsaufsicht-fuer-marktmaechtige-unternehmen.pdf?__blob=publicationFile&v=15> accessed 31 August 2020; for the UK, Jason Furman, Diane Coyle, Amelia Fletcher, Derek McAuley and Philip Marsden, 'Unlocking Digital Competition – Report of the Digital Competition Expert Panel' (March 2019) <https://assets.publishing.service.gov.uk/government/uploads/system/uploads/attachment_data/file/785547/unlocking_digital_competition_furman_review_web.pdf> accessed 31 August 2020 (so-called 'Furman Report'). See also the Australian Competition & Consumer Commission (ACCC), 'Digital Platform Inquiry – Final Report' (June 2019) <www.accc.gov.au/system/files/Digital%20platforms%20inquiry%20-%20final%20report.pdf> accessed 31 August 2020.

85 *Gesetz gegen Wettbewerbsbeschränkungen* (*GWB*).

86 See the Bill of the Federal Government for the reform of the German Act against Restraints of Competition: Gesetzentwurf der Bundesregierung – Entwurf eines Gesetzes zur Änderung des Gesetzes gegen Wettbewerbsbeschränkungen für ein fokussiertes, proaktives und digitales Wettbewerbsrecht 4.0 und anderer wettbewerbsrechtlicher Bestimmungen (GWB-Digitalisierungsgesetz) (9 September 2020) <www.bmwi.de/Redaktion/DE/Downloads/Gesetz/gesetzentwurf-gwb-digitalisierungsgesetz.pdf?__blob=publicationFile&v=6> accessed 15 September 2020.

jective by making first steps for preparing legislation on a 'New Competition Tool' ('NCT').[87]

After analysis of the current EU framework for data access based on Article 102 TFEU, the following analysis will show that the envisaged reforms of German and EU competition law indeed have the potential of enhancing the availability of access claims as regards data generated by connected devices. Yet these reforms would still fail to provide for sufficient data access for users of connected devices because of inbuilt limitations of the competition law framework.

1. *Limitations of current EU competition law*

Article 102 TFEU provides for a duty to provide access to data under the condition that such a refusal to grant access to data constitutes an abuse of market dominance. Against the backdrop of existing case law, the benchmark for showing that there is dominance of a data holder as well as an abuse in such case is particularly high and fraught with uncertainties.

As regards the first requirement, European courts have confirmed dominance based on the control of information, especially in *Magill*.[88] In this case, complainant Magill sought access to the programming information of the three broadcasting organisations active in the Republic of Ireland and Northern Ireland (RTP, BBC and ITV), which was indispensable for Magill, an independent publisher, to enter the market with comprehensive TV guides. In this situation, it was not possible to consider the programming information held by the different broadcasting organisations as substitutes, as Magill was in need of the programming information of all channels to enter the market. Hence, the correct market analysis has to lead to assuming the existence of three separate upstream markets for complementary programming information in which all three broadcasting organisations individually held monopoly positions.

In other cases of the modern digital economy, however, the situation may be much more complex. In a world of big data, data analytics and artificial intelligence, data are often multi-functional. Therefore, control over

87 European Commission, Inception Impact Assessment – New Competition Tool (NCT) (4 June 2020), <https://ec.europa.eu/competition/consultations/2020_new_comp_tool/new_comp_tool_inception_impact_assessment.pdf> accessed 31 August 2020.

88 Joined Cases C-241/91 P and C-242/91 P *RTE and ITP v Commission* (*'Magill'*) [1995] ECR I-743 = ECLI:EU:C:1995:98, para. 47.

large datasets can provide great economic power in multiple markets. Conversely, extending economic activity to multiple markets increases the ability of digital businesses to predict customer preferences with much higher precision. This explains why especially the Internet platform economy is characterised by conglomerate firm structures. This is also relevant in the IoT context. To sell connected devices is just an additional strategy for the large Internet platform operators, such as Google or Amazon, to increase their knowledge about customer preferences. Due to the potentials of data to provide economic power across very different markets, the focus of the traditional competition law assessment on relevant markets and, subsequently, on market dominance is increasingly being called into question.[89]

Moreover, in the modern data economy, not all cases where an undertaking seeks data access are as clear as in the case of *Magill*, where the complainant depended on access to very specific programming information held by the broadcasting organisations. In the modern data economy, finding out about the utility of large datasets is often of essence for the undertaking seeking data access. In such an environment, where the utility of the data is not that clear, proving market dominance based on data control has to become more difficult.

In an IoT environment, where connected devices collect data through sensors, the petitioner for data access also needs to show that the same data cannot be collected from alternative sources. This leads to the question of how to understand the concept of sole-source data in an IoT context. While it is true that, for instance, connected vehicles of various manufacturers could in principle collect the same information by 'observing' the outside world, the situation of the user of a connected device is very different and resembles more the scenario in *Magill*. For overcoming the data lock-in, the user of a connected device depends on access to the first-level data collected by the concrete device. Yet this does not necessarily suffice to consider the de facto holder of these data a data monopolist. The problem is that the market for connected devices can still be quite competitive. This raises the question of how the relevant upstream market should be defined, as the device market or as a much narrower market for individual-level data linked to a concrete device. Accordingly, to confirm market dominance, the petitioner for data access would have to convince the law enforcer of the latter and, hence, an atomised market structure, where se-

89 This is also confirmed by the reform debate in Germany and on the EU level, as will be shown further below.

parate aftermarkets for the machine-generated data for each and every connected device need to be distinguished.

Secondly, EU case law on refusal to deal establishes a high threshold for abuse. Refusal to grant access to data have to be understood as a sub-category of refusal-to-deal cases. EU courts developed the requirements for an abuse in this regard mostly in cases on refusals to license intellectual property rights, including the *Magill* case, where UK and Irish courts, at least at the time of the refusal, considered the programming information to be protected under national copyright law. The *Magill* judgment hence became essential for guiding the development of a European essential facilities doctrine in intellectual property cases. In the more recent case of *IMS Health* of 2004, which has since remained the lead case of the CJEU, the Court stated four requirements for an abuse: (1) access to the subject-matter of intellectual property is indispensable for the petitioner to operate a particular business. (2) The refusal to license the intellectual property results in an exclusion of competition in a secondary market. (3) The refusal prevents the emergence of a new product for which there is potential consumer demand; and (4) there is no objective justification for the refusal.[90]

Already the first requirement of indispensability creates particular challenges in the context of connected devices. In *Bronner*, the CJEU clarified that access to a resource of a competitor cannot be considered indispensable if there are no 'technical, legal or even economic obstacles capable of making it impossible, or even unreasonably difficult' to duplicate the resource.[91] Thereby, the Court demonstrated considerable reluctance to accept the argument of lack of economic viability too easily. The Court stressed that it is not enough to show that duplication of the resource would not be economically viable against the benchmark of the petitioner's scope of business in the secondary market.[92] Rather, the question is whether it is economically viable to create the resource 'for production on a scale comparable to that of the undertaking which controls the existing product or service'.[93] This seems to indicate a standard for indispensability that does not depend on the size of the petitioner's business and that imposes on the petitioner the burden to make the same investment as that made by the dominant undertaking. Whether such test should also be applied with regard to data generated by connected devices remains unex-

90 Case C-418/01 *IMS Health* [2004] ECR I-5039 = ECLI:EU:C:2004:257, para. 38.

91 Case C-7/97 *Bronner* ECLI:EU:C:1998: 569, para. 44.

92 Ibid. para. 45.

93 Case C-418/01 *IMS Health* [2004] ECR I-5039 = ECLI:EU:C:2004:257, para. 28, with reference to Case C-7/97 *Bronner* ECLI:EU:C:1998: 569, para. 46.

plored for the time being. However, it does not make much sense to require an innovative start-up that specialises in data-related services to also enter the market for connected devices to generate its own data to be able to compete in the downstream service market. The *Bronner* test may make sense for the underlying case where a newspaper publisher sought access to the home delivery system of a competitor. Where access to data generated by connected devices is sought, the courts should also take into account the lock-in situation of customers, which excludes market access of competitors.

The second requirement of exclusion of competition in a secondary market identifies the European essential facilities doctrine as one on exclusionary conduct, whereby the dominant firm excludes competitors from a secondary market by refusing access to the indispensable input.[94] Accordingly, both the data holder and the petitioner for data access have to be active in the secondary (service) market. This creates considerable limitations to the application of Article 102 TFEU. On the side of the petitioner, Article 102 TFEU can be considered as a rule for access rights of competitors on which the legislature could further build for legislation on sector-specific data access rights. But Article 102 TFEU does not provide claims for users – private or commercial ones – of connected devices that are not active in a secondary data-related service market.

On the side of the data holder, the *IMS Health* test also fails if the data holder (manufacturer) is not active in the downstream service market. Whether there can be alternative theories of harm for arguing abuse is unclear and even unlikely for the time being. In *IMS Health*, the CJEU held that it 'suffices' for an abuse that said requirements are fulfilled cumulatively.[95] While this could be understood in the sense that the Court would not accept other sets of requirements for an abuse, it has to be noted that the *IMS Health* cumulative test explicitly refers to cases of a refusal to license an intellectual property right, for which the CJEU generally requires the existence of 'exceptional circumstances' to justify a competition law duty to license.[96] Hence, this standard may not apply where no intellectual property rights are at stake. Moreover, in *Huawei*, the CJEU has meanwhile clarified that there can be other 'exceptional circumstances' than those in *IMS Health* that can equally justify a duty to license.[97] In *Huawei*, the CJEU

94 See also Drexl (n. 82) para. 136.

95 Case C-418/01 *IMS Health* [2004] ECR I-5039 = ECLI:EU:C:2004:257, para. 38.

96 Ibid. paras 35–38.

97 Case C-170/13 *Huawei* ECLI:EU:C:2015:477, paras 47–48.

held that there are also exceptional circumstances in the case of (1) a patent which is essential to a standard fixed by a standardisation body, 'rendering its use indispensable to all competitors which envisage manufacturing products that comply with the standard'[98] and where (2) the patent holder has irrevocably committed to the standardisation body to license on fair, reasonable and non-discriminatory (FRAND) terms.[99] It is quite surprising that the CJEU, in *Huawei*, did not transfer the requirement of exclusion of competition to this new set of exceptional circumstances. However, it would go too far to take it for granted that the CJEU would also apply Article 102 TFEU to cases where the holder of a standard-essential patent (SEP), without being active in the downstream device markets, seeks injunctions against an implementer.[100] In formulating the first element of the *Huawei* exceptional circumstances, the CJEU has at least indicated that only implementers that are 'competitors' of the patent holder can rely on these circumstances. Moreover, at least as part of the reasoning, the CJEU identified competitive harm in terms of exclusion, stating 'the fact that the patent has obtained SEP status means that its proprietor can prevent products manufactured by competitors from appearing or remaining on the market and, thereby, reserve to itself the manufacture of the products in question'.[101]

Against the backdrop of the current case-law, this would mean that also refusals to grant access to data where the de facto data holder and the claimant for data access are not competing in any downstream market, a violation of Article 102 TFEU could only be argued in terms of exploitative abuse. However, such claims are equally unlikely to be successful given the problems of assessing the value of data as a benchmark for the appropriate price for granting data access.[102]

As regards the third requirement of the prevention of a new product (so-called 'new product rule'), the General Court clarified in its *Microsoft* judgment that it only applies where the refusal relates to the licensing of

98 Ibid. para. 49.

99 Ibid. para. 51.

100 However, such extension is to be advocated especially for the use of SEPs on mobile telecommunications standards in an IoT context where it becomes increasingly less likely that the holders of such SEPs will also be manufacturers of all kinds of connected devices in which the standard is implemented. See Beatriz Conde Gallego and Josef Drexl, 'IoT Connectivity Standards: How Adaptive is the Current SEP Regulatory Framework?' (2019) 50 International Journal for Intellectual Property and Competition Law 135, 147–51.

101 Case C-170/13 *Huawei* ECLI:EU:C:2015:477, para. 52.

102 See also Drexl (n. 82) para. 138.

an intellectual property right.[103] Hence, the benchmark for a competition law intervention will be higher where use of data by another person requires the licensing of intellectual property rights. Still European courts have so far left open whether a refusal to grant access to data that are protected as trade secrets also requires the application of the new product rule. Therefore, also from a competition law perspective, it is important that the Commission has now announced a review of the intellectual property systems as regards their impact on data access and use.[104]

Finally, the competition law framework does not necessarily provide the best institutional framework for the enforcement of data access rights. Where the law is enforced by competition agencies, enforcement of Article 102 TFEU only works retroactively by reacting to infringements in the past. In addition, competition law investigations and proceedings on unilateral conduct often take many years, even more so where decisions are subsequently appealed to the courts. In addition, lack of access to data generated by connected devices has the potential of becoming a mass phenomenon that can hardly be addressed effectively by competition agencies. Therefore, especially sector-specific enforcement, which can provide for ex ante regulation, and private enforcement should be the preferred options. Of course, the prohibition of abuse of market dominance under Article 102 TFEU is directly applicable and, therefore, can in principle be enforced by private law courts in the Member States. However, as the analysis shows, application of Article 102 TFEU requires a complex economic assessment of the relevant market and dominance and is fraught with many limitations and uncertainties that could easily deter private parties from going to court.

2. *Proposals for reform of German competition law*

The process of legal reform of competition law in view of the digital economy is most advanced in Germany. There the Federal Ministry for Economic Affairs and Energy published a Ministerial Draft Reform Bill in January 2020.[105] Subsequently, in September 2020, the Federal Government

103 T-201/04 *Microsoft* [2007] ECR II-3601 = ECLI:EU:T:2007:289, para. 334.

104 European Commission, 'A European strategy for data' (n. 1) 13.

105 Referentenentwurf des Bundesministeriums für Wirtschaft und Energie – Entwurf eines Zehnten Gesetzes zur Änderung des Gesetzes gegen Wettbewerbsbeschränkungen für ein fokussiertes, proaktives und digitales Wettbewerbsrecht 4.0 (GWB-Digitalisierungsgesetz) (24 January 2020), <https://www.bmwi.de/Red

adopted the Bill on the 10th reform of the Act against Restraints of Competition to be submitted to the German legislature.[106] Several elements of the Bill, though more broadly reacting to the challenges presented by the digital economy, are capable of promoting data access with regard to connected devices.

The least revolutionary proposal relates to the prohibition of abuse of market dominance and the German essential facilities doctrine as enacted in Section 19(2) No. 4 Act against Restraints of Competition.[107] While the current provision is limited to a refusal to grant access to a dominant undertaking's network or infrastructure facility, the proposal would expressly extend this clause to a refusal to grant access to data. Yet such reform would only amount to a clarification of the already existing legal framework, according to which a refusal to grant access to data could already be considered to be illegal under the general prohibition of abuse of market dominance, of which Section 19(2) No. 4 only provides one example.[108] Nonetheless, it is important to note that the explanatory memorandum of the Bill explicitly refers to the situation of a provider of secondary services relating to the use of a device, such as maintenance or repair services, where the service provider cannot enter the secondary market because the dominant undertaking refuses to provide access to data.[109] However, in conformity with the current application of Article 102 TFEU to such cases, the application of Section 19(2) No. 4 of the Act is and remains restricted to cases of exclusionary abuse, i.e. cases where the undertaking seeking data access is a (potential) competitor of the data-controlling dominant firm. The provision does and will not provide a claim in favour of undertakings as mere users of connected devices.

In addition, Section 19(2) No. 4 of the Act would continue to require a showing of market dominance of the de facto data holder. Yet, based on Section 20(1) of the Act, German law has a long tradition of also protecting the competitive process in cases of mere 'relative market power' ('*rela-*

aktion/DE/Downloads/G/gwb-digitalisierungsgesetz-referentenentwurf.pdf?__blob=publicationFile&v=10> accessed 31 August 2020. An unofficial English translation is available at <www.d-kart.de/wp-content/uploads/2020/02/GWB10-Engl-Translation-2020-02-21.pdf> accessed 31 August 2020.

106 Gesetzentwurf der Bundesregierung (n. 86).

107 English translation of the current Act available at <www.gesetze-im-internet.de/englisch_gwb/englisch_gwb.pdf> accessed 31 August 2020.

108 This clarifying function of the proposal is also highlighted in the explanatory memorandum of the Bill; see Gesetzentwurf der Bundesregierung (n. 86) 79.

109 Gesetzentwurf der Bundesregierung (n. 86) 83.

tive Marktmacht') below the threshold of market dominance. This puts German law in a much better position to use competition law as a legal basis for data access rights, where a showing of market dominance can be particularly burdensome. In addition, Section 20(1) is traditionally mostly enforced by private law courts. Another particularity of Section 20(1) is that it is not limited to protecting competitors. Rather, the provision specifically pursues protection in the vertical dimension, i.e. in favour of suppliers and purchasers. Therefore, in contrast to Section 19(2) No. 4 of the Act, Section 20(1) can in principle also be relied upon by undertakings as mere users of connected devices that seek access to data where the refusal to grant access results in unfair impediment to conducting a business or discrimination in the sense of Section 19(2) No. 1.[110]

The Reform Bill seeks to clarify the application of Section 20(1) of the Act as regards data access and, moreover, to extend its scope of protection beyond SMEs. Section 20(1) of the Act defines 'relative market power' as dependence 'in such a way that sufficient and reasonable possibilities of switching to other undertakings do not exist'. Already from this wording it should be clear that the concept of 'relative market power' should also be applicable in cases of data lock-ins. To confirm this explicitly, the Reform Bill proposes the introduction of a new paragraph 1a stating that dependence also exists where an undertaking depends on access to data to conduct its business. The explanatory memorandum of the Reform Bill distinguishes two scenarios of refusals to grant access to data where the rule could apply. The first scenario relates to the relationship between undertakings along the value chain where imbalances of bargaining power prevent sufficient access to data.[111] In this context, the explanatory memorandum explicitly mentions that a refusal to grant access may especially prevent an undertaking from switching to competitors in downstream service markets.[112] This shows that paragraph 1a could particularly be used by the users of connected devices to switch providers of secondary services. The second scenario regards the horizontal cases of data dependence of competitors that so far have not entertained a commercial relationship with the data holder. While not excluding intervention, the Bill states that assessment of the unfairness of the refusal to grant access requires particular scrutiny in these cases. The reason is that German case-law has been very

110 Legally, Sec. 20(1) extends the application of Sec. 19(2)(a), providing for an example of abuse, beyond market dominance to undertakings with relative market power.

111 Gesetzentwurf der Bundesregierung (n. 86) 93–94.

112 Ibid. 94.

reluctant to apply Section 20(1) in cases where the parties have so far not entertained any commercial relationship. In contrast, paragraph 1a would at least go further by explicitly confirming that a refusal to grant access to data can in principle also constitute an unfair impediment to conducting a business where the parties have no prior commercial relationship.[113]

As regards the personal scope of protection, the Draft Reform Act proposes to delete the general limitation of the application of Section 20(1) to SMEs. Thereby, the Bill acknowledges the modern view that the provision addresses a general problem for the competitive process and should therefore not be devised as a remedy that is only available to smaller undertakings.[114] Equally, the explanatory memorandum to the Reform Bill argues that even larger undertakings may depend on smaller operators of platforms that act as gatekeepers in the digital economy.[115] Still, the provision is planned to maintain an explicit requirement of a 'significant imbalance' ('*deutliches Ungleichgewicht*') of power between the parties as part of the concept of relative market power.

The most revolutionary and certainly contentious proposal of the Draft Reform Act concerning the digital economy relates to an additional prohibition in the area of unilateral conduct that addresses abuses of a new category of undertakings, namely, 'undertakings of paramount significance for competition across markets'.[116] The proposal seeks nothing less than to prevent undertakings in the digital economy from tipping markets in such a way that competition is gone for ever. In particular, control over large bulks of data can help digital firms to leverage market power in multiple markets. To preserve competition in such an economy, the newly proposed Section 19a of the Act is specifically designed and most likely to be applied to the operators of Internet platforms rather than to traditional device manufacturers that produce and sell connected devices.

However, it has to be taken into account that platform operators such as Apple, Google and Amazon are also active in IoT-related device markets (Apple's mobile devices, Amazon's home assistant Alexa) or reach out to control data collected by connected devices (such as Google's Android op-

113 Sentence 2 of proposed Sec. 20(1a).

114 Regierungsentwurf des Bundesministeriums (n. 86) 81. Explicitly taking up the arguments of Schweitzer and others (n. 82) 57.

115 Ibid.

116 In German: '*Unternehmen mit marktübergreifender Bedeutung für den Wettbewerb*'.

eration system and Google apps).[117] For these undertakings, connected devices are yet another means for collecting and controlling even more data that can be used for strengthening their position in multiple markets. While Section 19a is not specifically providing for data access rights, the provision contains several aspects that are directly related to data access. On the one hand, access to data is proposed as a criterion for the *Bundeskartellamt*, the German competition agency, to assess whether an undertaking can be qualified as one of paramount significance for competition across markets.[118] On the other hand, Section 19a is also proposed to vest the agency with the power to prohibit conduct that impedes access to data. More specifically, the provision empowers the agency to prohibit the undertaking from 'making the interoperability of products or services or data portability more difficult and thereby impeding competition'.[119]

3. *Discussion on the EU level*

While the German reform can inspire many other jurisdictions, there can be no doubt that the digital economy regarding connected devices is particularly in need of a coherent regulatory framework on the EU level. Indeed, following the Report of the independent Special Advisers on competition law in the digital economy,[120] the Commission now seems ready to reform EU competition law. Taking up the initiative for a 'New Competition Tool' (NCT), which pursues the goal of addressing gaps in the EU competition rules as regards their application in digital and other markets, the Commission has now made a first step towards the adoption of a new competition law instrument – most likely in the form of a new regulation – by publishing an Inception Impact Assessment.[121]

This Inception Impact Assessment provides a first impression of what can be expected from future legislation. Although it broadly addresses

117 Google is also collecting health-related data in IoT environments through cooperation with pharmaceutical companies. See the merger Decision of the European Commission of 23 February 2018, Case M.7813 – *Sanofi/Google/DMI JV*.

118 Sec. 19a(1) No. 4 Draft Reform Act.

119 Sec. 19a(2) No. 4 Draft Reform Act.

120 Crémer, de Montjoye and Schweitzer (n. 82).

121 European Commission, Inception Impact Assessment – New Competition Tool (NCT) (4 June 2020), <https://ec.europa.eu/competition/consultations/2020_new_comp_tool/new_comp_tool_inception_impact_assessment.pdf> accessed 31 August 2020.

competition problems in the digital sector, the Assessment also touches upon issues related to connected devices and access to machine-generated data. As regards the analysis of existing competition problems, the Commission highlights a structural lack of competition caused, inter alia, by consumer lock-in and lack of access to data.[122] In addition, the Commission justifies the need for the adoption of the NCT on the EU level with the cross-border nature of 'digitally enabled products and services', concluding that intervention on the national level would not effectively address the competition-related problems.[123]

On substance, the Inception Impact Assessment sketches four options.[124] However, at least two of these options are not likely to address the problem of lock-ins regarding the data generated by connected devices effectively. The reason is that both options – Option 1 with horizontal scope of application, Option 2 by adopting a sector-specific approach – are dominance-based and thereby linked with the prohibition of abuse of market dominance pursuant to Article 102 TFEU. Yet they go beyond this prohibition by allowing for intervention against a dominant firm prior to the infringement of Article 102 TFEU.

Option 3 and 4 – again the one following a horizontal, the other one a sector-specific approach – are designed to address market structure-based competition problems that cannot be addressed effectively so far. The common feature of these two options is that they are related to unilateral conduct without being limited to dominant undertakings. Thus, these options seem to acknowledge the insight that the structure of competition can also be negatively affected by unilateral conduct of firms below the level of dominance. This may open the door to legislation similar to Section 20(1) and future paragraph (1a) German Act against Restraints of Competition relying on the concept of relative market power.[125]

As regards the forms of intervention, the Commission envisages behavioural and structural remedies designed to improve the functioning of markets. Indeed, Options 3 and 4 could therefore provide the framework for legislation that allows for intervention where undertakings refuse to grant access to data, especially if one takes into account that the Commission explicitly identifies lack of access to data as a particular form of structural lack of competition. Given the fact that rules allowing for interven-

122 Ibid. 2.

123 Ibid.

124 Ibid. 3.

125 See at sub-section 2 above.

tion below the level of market dominance are very much alien to the European competition law tradition, such legislation would appear as truly revolutionary. Yet it is too early to judge whether and to what extent the European competition law reform will take inspiration from German law. Yet it should be noted that the independent Special Advisors have recommended the Commission adopting specific competition law-related rules to promote access of users to the data collected by machines to protect competition in aftermarkets.[126]

4. Remaining gaps

The analysis shows that there is a clear need and tendency to extend the reach of competition law below the threshold of market dominance to promote data access for the purpose of overcoming data lock-ins. Therefore, the current reform plans and proposals both on the national (German) and on the EU level should be welcomed. Especially the German reform proposal shows that competition law can also be used vertically in cases of refusal to grant data access to undertakings that are not competing in any market with the de facto data holder. This is part of the German tradition to also address impediments of the ability of suppliers and purchasers to conduct their business where such impediments may produce market foreclosure effects. This tradition is especially suited to promoting data access of users of connected devices to machine-generated data controlled by the manufacturer where the latter refuses data access along the value chain by relying on superior bargaining power.

Yet even the abovementioned reforms would not suffice to provide sufficient data access. This is because competition law remains limited to claims of undertakings, while connected devices are also purchased and used by non-commercial players. Most importantly, this includes consumers, but also non-commercial entities, such as the state. It goes without mentioning that the state in particular is among the most important purchasers and users of connected devices, such as in the context of traffic regulation or systems of smart cities. Of course, as part of its purchasing activity, the state can rely on tenders to guarantee sufficient data access. However, data access rights of the state may also be needed where connected devices are integrated in larger infrastructure networks, such as in the context of smart cities, and the state is not the purchaser of such devices.

126 Crémer, de Montjoye and Schweitzer (n. 82) 10.

In sum, there remains a considerable gap between contract law, including mandatory consumer contract law, and the competition law framework that can only be closed by additional data access rights.

IV. Sector-specific data access rights of competitors

Sector-specific regulation can play a particularly useful role to overcome data lock-ins. As regards machine-generated data, the primary example is the regulation of the repair and maintenance market for motor vehicles. For entering and staying in the market, independent service providers depend on access to the on-board data controlled by the manufacturers. In this case, the access right is not given to the final customer – or user of the vehicle – but directly to the independent service provider.[127] More recent EU legislation provides other examples where data access rights are directly vested in providers of secondary data-related services who would otherwise not be able to provide such services to customers. This includes the right of the providers of digital payment services against banks to claim access to the account data of customers.[128] In a similar vein, European legislation obliges the transport operators to make travel and traffic data available through central access points and establishes a right of providers of (multimodal) travel information services to re-use these data.[129]

Indeed, access rights of (potential) competitors in secondary service markets have particular advantages for consumers and other end-users. For them it suffices that access rights granted to competitors, as well as additional measures promoting the pooling and sharing of data such as in the case of travel and traffic data, will indirectly result in innovative data-based services, more choice and alternative offers. Thus, consumers benefit from more competition in secondary markets without having to enforce access rights before the courts.

Yet sector-specific access rights of competitors also have certain shortcomings: first, while they are useful tools to open up markets for secondary services, they do not help where the user personally wants to connect data

127 See Arts 6–9 Regulation 715/2007 (n. 9).

128 Art. 36 Second Digital Payment Services (DPS2) Directive (EU) 2015/2366 (n. 59).

129 See Art. 8 Commission Delegated Regulation (EU) 2017/1926 of 31 May 2017 supplementing Directive 2010/40/EU of the European Parliament and of the Council with regard to the provision of EU-wide multimodal travel information services, [2017] OJ L272/1.

from different devices and sources in its own organisational sphere without relying on a third-party service. This can be an industrial end-user of machines, a farmer, a city authority or also a consumer regarding the digitisation of a private home. Secondly, even where the user may wishes to rely on services by other firms, these services are less likely to be covered by sector-specific regulation. Finally, from a perspective of economic regulation, data access rights to users are less problematic than access rights of competitors. The reason is that 'vertical' data access rights only increase the utility of the connective devices in the interest of users, while data access rights of competitors necessarily come with the risk of unjustified free-riding on the investment of the data holder. Therefore, access rights of competitors, deviating from the general principle that undertakings should not be forced to deal with competitors in downstream markets, are in need of a particular pro-competitive justification.

The latter concern is also hinted at in the current proposal for a reform of Section 20(1) German Act of Restraints of Competition where the Draft Bill proposes to extend the prohibition of unfair impediment of conducting a business, relying on the concept of relative market power, to data dependence. While the Draft Bill explicitly states that the rule can in principle also lead to data access rights of competitors in secondary markets that so far have not entertained any commercial relationship with the data holder,[130] the explanatory memorandum to the Bill clearly expresses that an unfair impediment should only be confirmed cautiously. Thereby it mentions two possible scenarios for application: first, where the dependent competitor, based on the use of the data, generates significant economic value, and, secondly, where access will prevent excessive concentration in the secondary market.[131] This shows that in principle sector-specific regulation is the better approach to data access rights of competitors, since sector specific regulation is better placed to take into account the conflicting interests of data holders and their competitors in the given markets and to devise more targeted and pro-competitive solutions. In contrast, vesting data access rights in the users of connected devices is another way of safeguarding a pro-competitive outcome, even where the end-user will claim transfer of the data to a provider in a downstream service market. Data access will only be claimed where provision of the service by a competitor increases consumer welfare.

---

130 See at sub-section III.2. above.

131 Entwurf der Bundesregierung (n. 86) 94.

V. Data access and intellectual property

Data access and use has also moved to the forefront of the intellectual property debate. The reason is that re-use of data can potentially infringe intellectual property rights. This explains why intellectual property regimes need to be adjusted in such a way that they will not unduly restrict access and re-use of data. The major debate has so far concentrated on the introduction of additional exceptions and limitations to copyright protection in the case of text and data-mining.[132]

Yet, even if (new) exceptions and limitations apply, intellectual property law will not be an appropriate tool to provide access to data. The reason for this is that data holders can prevent third parties from gaining access, especially by using technological protection measures even where they cannot claim intellectual property protection. This shows that de facto control over data, combined with contract law allowing for controlled sharing of data with others, can in substance produce very similar results as intellectual property.

Likewise, the assertion that intellectual property regimes can serve the third-party interests in data access better since they provide a legal framework for exceptions and limitations, including compulsory licensing systems, is not convincing either. This argument overlooks the fact that access rights can promote data access against de facto data holders without the need of prior recognition of exclusive data ownership rights.

G. Proposal for an unfair competition law approach to data access

The preceding analysis shows that there is the need for a legal framework that provides a right of access of the users of connected devices to the data generated by these devices. This section will first explain this right as part of the unfair competition law (at I. below). In addition, unfair competition law principles can help structure the legal rules governing such data access rights (at II. below).

---

132 See Arts 3 and 4 Directive (EU) 2019/790 of the European Parliament and of the Council of 17 April 2019 on copyright and related rights in the Digital Single Market and amending Directives 96/9/EC and 2001/29/EC, [2019] OJ L130/92.

I. Why unfair competition law?

The preceding analysis has shown that both contract law and competition law can contribute to enhancing access of the users of connected devices to machine-generated data. Yet both systems have their inbuilt limitations. Data access rights are needed to overcome a problem of data lock-in that occurs due to an imbalance of bargaining power. In the EU tradition, mandatory contract law and unfairness control of contract terms is only available in the case of B2C relationships, while the imbalance of bargaining power can also affect users that are not consumers. Moreover, users of connected devices cannot necessarily rely on a direct or at least an indirect contractual relationship with the manufacturer as the de facto data holder. While not requiring a contractual relationship, competition law fixes particularly high thresholds for intervention especially on the EU level. Whether future reforms can lower such thresholds still remains uncertain. More importantly, competition law can only support data access of undertakings, excluding claims of consumers and other non-commercial entities.

The unfair competition law approach avoids these limitations. The core of European unfair competition law consists in rules of fair trading that apply outside the realm of contract law and seek to protect consumers in particular.[133] Yet European fair trading law has never been limited to protecting consumers. Already in 1984, at the beginning of European harmonisation in the field, the European legislature adopted rules on misleading advertising that were also designed to apply in B2B relationships.[134] More recently, the EU legislature adopted the Directive on fair trading practices in

133 See Directive 2005/29/EC of the European Parliament and of the Council of 11 May 2005 concerning unfair business-to-consumer commercial practices in the internal market, [2005] OJ L149/22.

134 Council Directive 84/450/EEC of 10 September 1984 concerning misleading advertising, [1984] OJ L250/17. In 1997, the European legislature added rules on comparative advertising. See Directive 97/55/EC of the European Parliament and of the Council of 6 October 1997 amending Directive 84/45/EEC concerning misleading advertising so as to include comparative advertising, [1997] OJ L290/18. After the adoption of the Unfair Trade Practices Directive (n. 133), the scope of the Directive on misleading and comparative advertising was limited to the protection of 'traders'. See Art. 1 Directive 2006/114/EC of the European Parliament and of the Council of 12 December 2006 concerning misleading and comparative advertising (codified version), [2006] OJ L376/21.

B2B relationships in the agricultural and food supply chain.[135] In general, this shows that EU fair trading rules seek to protect any other trading party, whether this is a consumer or a trader, albeit with partially diverging sets of rules.

In addition, application of EU fair trading law is not limited to the pre-sale advertising stage. Already the Unfair Trade Practices Directive of 2005 extended its scope of application beyond practices concerning promotion to also include the sale and supply of products.[136] For data access rights related to connected devices, the new Unfair Trading Practices Directive in B2B relationships in the agricultural and food supply confirms this approach. While the focus of the Directive is on protecting (upstream) suppliers – including agricultural suppliers in particular – and not (downstream) purchasers (as in the case of the users of connected devices), the Directive is informative for rights of access to machine-generated data because of its particular objective. The Directive is specifically designed to address imbalances of bargaining power in the supply chain that result in practices, including contractual arrangements, that are to the advantage of the trader.[137] In other terms, the Directive seems to respond to situations of 'relative market power' as known from Section 20(1) German Act against Restraints of Competition.[138] Therefore, to define its personal scope of application, the Directive fixes maximum turnover thresholds for the suppliers and minimum turnovers for traders as a proxy for the existence of such imbalance of power.[139] This shows that, while in the German tradition, protection against an imbalance of bargaining power in the supply chain can be located within the competition law framework, unfair trading law may provide the better framework in the EU tradition. The latter has the advantage of protecting consumers too.

Integrating data access rights within the realm of EU unfair trading law, as part of larger unfair competition law, is equally convincing on substance. On the one hand, it is for the manufacturer to decide whether and under what technical and legal conditions the users of connected devices will have access to the machine-generated data. The manufacturer is in

135 Directive (EU) 2019/633 of the European Parliament and of the Council of 17 April 2019 on unfair trading practices in business-to-business relationships in the agricultural and food supply chain, [2019] OJ L111/59.

136 See the definition of 'business-to-consumers commercial practices' in Art. 3 lit. d) Directive 2005/29/EC (n. 133).

137 Recital 1 Directive (EU) 2019/633 (n. 135). (Emphasis added.).

138 See at F. III. 2., above.

139 Art. 1(2) Directive (EU) 2019/633 (n. 135).

control of the product design, including the data formats and the digital interfaces, which are key for enabling data access. From a legal perspective, the manufacturer as the de facto data holder can decide on the terms and conditions of data access and use. Conversely, downstream users of connected devices have an interest in making full use of the device, including the use of the data generated by the device. Against the backdrop of the data lock-in, triggered by an imbalance of bargaining power, it is most convincing to regulate the terms and conditions of access and use relying on a fairness standard the application of which will be based on a balancing of the interests involved.

Integrating data access rights of users of connected devices in the legal framework of fair trading law also corresponds to the most recent claim of the European Commission to create additional access rights only 'where appropriate under *fair*, transparent, reasonable, proportionate and/or non-discriminatory conditions'[140] and where such rights respond to a 'market failure … which competition cannot solve'.[141] In this sense, legislation on data access rights of the users of connected devices within the realm of EU unfair trade practices law can be identified as competition-based legislation.[142]

As a side note, integrating data access rights of users of connected devices as part of the law against unfair trading practices and, hence, unfair competition is also important from the perspective of applicable law. Connected devices are sold and used in international markets. Characterisation of such access rights as unfair competition law, pursuant to Article 6(1) Rome II Regulation,[143] leads to the application of the law of the 'country where the competitive relations or the collective interests of consumers are, or are likely to be, affected'. Here, where the allegedly unfair trading practice relates to the sale and supply of a data-generating connected device, the applicable law should be considered the law of the country where the connected device first enters the end-user market under the control of the manufacturer (law of the country of first distribution). Accordingly, where the connected device is resold to another country by a user, the applicable law will not change. This makes the applicable law predictable for the manufacturer and still protects users appropriately.

140 European Commission, 'A European strategy for data' (n. 1) 13.

141 Ibid. 13 note 39.

142 See also the claim for such legislation at Drexl (n. 82) para. 122.

143 Regulation (EC) No. 864/2007 of the European Parliament and of the Council of 11 July 2007 on the law applicable to non-contractual obligations (Rome II), [2007] OJ L199/40.

II. Legal design of the data access right

Beyond what has just been explained, the unfair trading (unfair competition) law approach also influences the concrete legal design of the right of access to data generated by connected devices. The following principles confirm the use of the concepts as defined at the beginning of this chapter,[144] which is not a surprise since those concepts were defined in the light of the interests involved.[145]

(1) The access right should be designed as a legal and non-waivable claim. Since the access right is supposed to react to an imbalance of bargaining power, waivability or assignability would run counter to the objective of this right.

(2) The access right should cover both non-personal and personal data, since the scope of the right is defined by the end-users' interest to make full use of the connected device and the data it generates. Of course, the data protection rules need to be respected. Where data protection rights of third persons are at stake, the holder of the access right can at best claim access to anonymised data. Whether there is an obligation of the manufacturer to anonymise data and whether the manufacturer can claim compensation for the costs should be considered as part of the fairness assessment of the terms and conditions of data access.

(3) Yet the user should not be entitled to claim access to all, or just any, data generated by the connected device. The user can only claim access to data to the extent that the interest in making full use of the device, including the machine-generated data, justifies such access. This includes the use of the data for maintenance and repair purposes, for connecting the device with other devices or for receiving secondary data-based services from third-party service providers. In the light of such purposes, the data access right should not be limited to 'provided' or 'observed' data; it should also extend to derived and inferred data if justified by the concrete legitimate access interest. In addition, the data do not have to be stored in the device. It is the obligation of the manufacturer, albeit in the light of a balancing of interests, to organise data access in such a way that access is also possible to data stored in other places of a larger digital network, such as on a cloud server.

---

144 At section B. above.

145 The following legal design was initially produced, and explained in more detail than here, in Drexl (n. 6) 154–65.

(4) Flexibility is needed as regards the definition of the 'user' as the holder of the data access right. As already explained above,[146] this concept should also be defined in terms of the legitimate access interest. This will typically include the owner and user of the device. Yet physical use should not be required. It should suffice that the connected device collects and generates data connected with the person, such as personal data or data related to an asset owned or controlled by this person. The latter would capture the case of a farmer's access to the data generated by a farming machine used on the land of this farmer where the latter neither owns nor actively operates the machine.

(5) The data access right should be directed against the manufacturer, who is able to design the device in such a way that users can access the data. In this sense, the manufacturer can also be considered a de facto data holder. This does not exclude access to data stored on servers and devices of other parties as long as the manufacturer has a legal claim to access the data.

(6) In the light of the access interest and purpose, 'data access' should be understood broadly, as already indicated above.[147] Where the holder of the access right seeks a service to be provided by another person, the holder should also be allowed to claim the direct transfer of data to such service provider according to the model of the data portability right of Article 20(2) GDPR. The law should also allow the user as the holder of the access right to mandate the third-party service provider to seek data access on behalf of the user, which would additionally enhance the effectiveness of the data access right. Depending on the purpose, access can hence mean different things: access to the information purely on the semantic level, portability of the encoded data or even data sharing, which would extend the data access claim to real-time data.

(7) In many instances, implementation of the data access right will require conclusion of a contract – in the form of a data licensing agreement – that specifies the terms and conditions of data access and data use according to the fairness principle. In this context, a major question will be whether the manufacturer should be allowed to claim compensation of the costs of making the data available. This issue can be decided in terms of a general provision stating that access to and use of the data has to be grant-

146 At B. III., above.
147 At B. III., above.

ed on fair, reasonable and non-discriminatory (FRAND) terms.[148] In the context of connected devices, however, remuneration for the use of the data is not necessarily justified since the user of the device has contributed to the generation of the data (as so-called 'co-generated data') and, directly and indirectly, will usually pay a price for the purchase or use of the device. Conversely, the manufacturer is in principle able to factor in the costs for making the data available in the price it charges for the sale (or rental) of the device. Hence, a claim for remuneration or compensation should be considered the exception rather than the rule. This does not have to exclude compensation for specific costs, such as costs for anonymisation of personal data. Another complex issue regards the interest of the manufacturer in protecting its trade secrets. In particular, the access claim may relate to technical information regarding the connected device the secrecy of which the manufacturer has a legitimate interest in preserving. Since trade secrets protection in the EU equally follows standards of fairness as part of the larger law against unfair competition,[149] the integration of the data access right in unfair competition law is additionally suitable to coordinate the conflicting interests.

(8) Finally, there is the need to coordinate the access regime with other fields of the law. This is not only the case as regards systems protecting sensitive – personal and (secret) commercial – data, as already covered above. The most important and still open question is the relationship with intellectual property rights. As explained in earlier writing, potential sui generis database rights could especially undermine the working of the data access regime.[150] While Article 20(4) GDPR gives precedence to the rights of others, not sufficiently making clear whether this also relates to intellectual property rights of even the data controller, over the data portability rights concerning personal data, it is suggested here to provide that the data access right should prevail over such sui generis database rights.

148 Examples can be found in sector-specific legislation on data access rights. See, for instance, Art. 8(4) and (5) Delegated Regulation 2017/1926 (EU) on multimodal travel information services (n. 129). These provisions also allow for a charging of 'reasonable and proportionate compensation'.

149 See Directive (EU) 2016/943 of the European Parliament and of the Council of 8 June 2016 on the protection of undisclosed know-how and business information (trade secrets) against their unlawful acquisition, use and disclosure, [2016] OJ L157/1.

150 Drexl (n. 5) 67–85.

H. Conclusion

Users often have a legitimate interest in gaining access to the data that are collected and generated by these devices. Connected devices are technically designed to operate in larger digital networks. Therefore, to enable users to benefit fully from connected devices, access to the data is essential. Users should be allowed to integrate connected devices in 'their' digital networks and to choose freely among providers of data-based services in secondary markets. Yet the market does not necessarily guarantee that the manufacturers of the devices, who decide on the technical design of their products and terms and conditions of their marketing and use, will voluntarily allow access to the data. They may be tempted to remain in control of 'their' data, which they often consider as business secrets, and they may try to tie additional products and secondary data-based services to the sale of their connected devices. To protect the interest of users and to promote competition and innovation in secondary markets, data access rights are therefore needed where users of connected devices suffer from a potential data lock-in.

The analysis of this chapter shows that the law can make use of various means to promote access to data generated by connected devices. Access rights of competitors in secondary data-based service markets can most appropriately be used in the framework of competition-based sector-specific regulation. In addition, contract law and competition law can also enhance data access of users. In the European context, mandatory contract law and/or fairness control of contract terms constitutes the primary instrument to respond to imbalances of bargaining power. Therefore, contractual access rights appear as an appropriate means for data access, where consumers could rely on a direct, or at least indirect, contractual link with the manufacturers as the de facto data holders. Outside the realm of contract law, competition law can in principle provide for a duty to grant access to data. But the traditional focus of competition law on market dominance and exclusion of competitors as harm to competition considerably limits the availability of competition law remedies in case of refusals of access to data generated by connected devices. While reforms of competition law are now being debated and prepared in this regard, consumers and non-commercial entities will not likely to be able to rely on competition law even in the future. This is why this chapter proposes a third horizontally applicable access regime as part of fair trading law. This additional regime is not proposed as the better alternative to contract and competition law. Rather, these three regimes should be considered as complementary, partially overlapping regimes that can be applied for the same purpose of overcoming potential imbalances of bargaining power resulting in data lock-ins.

Data access rights of users as part of fair trading and the broader unfair competition law should build on a balancing of the legitimate interests of both the users and the manufacturers of connected devices and the fairness principle. Equally, legislation on these rights needs to be embedded in a larger data governance framework, whereby from a regulatory perspective, the privacy interest of data subjects in the protection of personal data and the innovation objective of the intellectual property systems also need to be taken into account. The principles of data access rights presented in this chapter could be implemented in different ways. Horizontal legislation – applicable across different sectors of the economy – could be considered, possibly in the form of another European fair trading directive for the digital economy. Such legislation would provide a generally applicable framework that may prove especially important outside of the realm of sector-specific regulation and help policy makers identify the sectors where data access is particularly difficult.

At the same time, the general principles set out in this chapter could also be taken into account in the framework of sector-specific legislation. It has to be noted that individual sectors are characterised by the use of very different connected devices, such as cars in the mobility sector or smart meters in the energy sector. Different connected devices may justify different rules concerning the terms and conditions of access against the backdrop of the fairness principle. In addition, access to the data of different kinds of connected devices will often be embedded in a different technological context as regards the existence of standards for data formats and APIs as technical preconditions of data access.

The law and policy of government access to private sector data ('B2G data sharing')

Heiko Richter

A. Issue

How can policymakers and legislatures improve the state's access to data held by private undertakings? Data are the basis for harvesting new insights, creating knowledge and providing innovative goods and services. Therefore, access to data can benefit the public welfare and serve society at large. Asking to what extent and by what means the state should be entitled to access private undertakings' datasets on behalf of the public interest lies at the core of the general discourse on the state's role in a data-based society. This chapter contributes to this debate and aims to advance regulatory approaches to data access.

The creation of rights for the state to access data held by private companies has been increasingly discussed in recent years. While the OECD has focused on fostering voluntary public-private cooperation,[1] France has introduced the notion of 'public interest data', which it implemented in its *Loi Lemaire* in 2016 after a comprehensive stakeholder consultation.[2] The EU followed the French initiative and became active in the field of B2G

1 For the OECD policies see Charlotte van Ooijen, Barbara Ubaldi, and Benjamin Welby, 'A data-driven public sector: Enabling the strategic use of data for productive, inclusive and trustworthy governance' (2019) OECD Working Papers on Public Governance No. 33 <www.oecd-ilibrary.org/docserver/09ab162c-en.pdf?expires=1605081692&id=id&accname=guest&checksum=54003ECF6F8210640E34FE63267EB459> accessed 31 August 2020; Alberto Alemanno, 'Big Data for Good: Unlocking Privately-Held Data to the Benefit of the Many' (2018) 9 European Journal of Risk Regulation 183, 187.

2 See provisions on data of general interest ('*données d'intérêt général*') under Arts 17–24 Loi n° 2016–1321 pour une République numérique of 7 October 2016 ('Loi Lemaire').

data sharing in 2017.[3] After delivering its 'data package' of 2018,[4] the Commission appointed an expert group on B2G data sharing, which issued its final report in February 2020. The expert group recommended that the Commission should further 'explore the creation of a regulatory framework enabling the development of fast, responsible and sustainable B2G data sharing for public-interest purposes'.[5] In Germany, in contrast, the debate is just getting started.[6] The country's Data Ethics Commission has considered the creation of an obligation to grant access to a defined subset of data for specific public authorities or purposes of general interest.[7] Moreover, the federal government's data strategy aims to better exploit the potential of using data to improve policy implementation and evaluation and to fulfil the tasks of state institutions in a more efficient and citizen-friendly way.[8] In any case, these developments underline the increasing initiative to address government access to data held by private undertak-

3 European Commission, 'DG CONNECT Draft report: 26 June 2017 workshop on access to privately-held data for public bodies' (European Commission 2017) <https://ec.europa.eu/information_society/newsroom/image/document/2017-28/final_-_report_from_reverse_psi_workshop_B7FA94EE-FA15-1929-8BBA2754D0D2FBE9_45916.pdf> accessed 31 August 2020.

4 See Communication from the Commission of 25 April 2018 to the European Parliament, the Council, the European Economic and Social Committee and the Committee of the Regions – 'Towards a common European data space' COM(2018) 232 final, 1–2.

5 European Commission, 'Towards a European strategy on business-to-government data sharing for public interest – Final report prepared by the High-Level Expert Group on Business-to-Government Data Sharing' (2020) 28 <www.euractiv.com/wp-content/uploads/sites/2/2020/02/B2GDataSharingExpertGroupReport-1.pdf> accessed 31 August 2020.

6 Only briefly dealing with the topic the German Data Ethics Commission, 'Report of the Data Ethics Commission of the Federal Government (2019) 154 <www.bmjv.de/SharedDocs/Downloads/DE/Themen/Fokusthemen/Gutachten_DEK_EN_lang.pdf?__blob=publicationFile&v=3> accessed 31 August 2020. See also Bundesministerium für Wirtschaft und Energie (German Federal Ministry for Economic Affairs and Energy), 'Ein neuer Wettbewerbsrahmen für die Digitalwirtschaft: Bericht der Kommission Wettbewerbsrecht 4.0' (2019) 46–47 <www.bmwi.de/Redaktion/DE/Publikationen/Wirtschaft/bericht-der-kommission-wettbewerbsrecht-4-0.pdf?__blob=publicationFile&v=12> accessed 31 August 2020, but only on companies which are linked to the fulfilment of public tasks.

7 See Data Ethics Commission (n. 6) 154.

8 Bundesregierung, 'Eckpunkte einer Datenstrategie der Bundesregierung' (2019) <www.bundesregierung.de/resource/blob/975226/1693626/60b196d5861f71cdefb9e254f5382a62/2019-11-18-pdf-datenstrategie-data.pdf> accessed 30 April 2020.

ings, including mandatory rules which regulate such access in the EU and the Member States.

However, the research on systematic approaches to laws and policies is underdeveloped.[9] This chapter will close this gap by inquiring into the justification, design and implementation of rules which mandate the state's access to data held by private undertakings (i.e. 'government access' or 'B2G data sharing'[10]). For this purpose, Section B outlines the broader context and the objectives of government access. Section C delineates the research focus, which lies on mandatory access rules that address private undertakings without any public link as well as on horizontal issues with regard to non-personal data. Section D elaborates on the key questions such access rules should address. Section E develops principles for designing and implementing access rules. Section F reflects on the opportunities and limitations of implementing horizontal B2G access frameworks. Finally, Section G highlights the implications for concrete legislative reforms, and Section H concludes this chapter.

B. Context and objectives of government access

I. Development context

To understand the objectives of government access to privately held data, it is helpful to grasp the broader technological and societal context of the debate. Some relevant developments highlight the growing significance of data: the disruptive technological innovations which led to the 'data revolution'[11] mark the starting point. New technology has enabled the advent of a decentralised, market-driven system of data collection that is unprecedented in scope. Moreover, cloud and high-performance computing has fa-

---

9 But see for research on specific aspects or fields of application Teresa Scassa, 'Sharing Data in the Platform Economy: A Public Interest Argument For Access to Platform Data' (2017) 50 UBC Law Review 1017; Niva Elkin-Koren and Michal Gal, 'The Chilling Effect of Governance-by-Data on Data Markets' (2019) 86 University of Chicago Law Review 403; Alfred Früh, 'Datenzugangsrechte: Rechtsrahmen für einen neuen Interessenausgleich in der Datenwirtschaft' (2018) sic! Zeitschrift für Immaterialgüter-, Informations- und Wettbewerbsrecht 521; rather general Alemanno (n. 1).

10 The term 'sharing' might be misleading as it connotes voluntary data exchange. Yet in practice it is often used as a synonym.

11 For the background Robert Kitchin, *The Data Revolution* (Sage 2014).

cilitated new techniques of data evaluation[12] while new means of data transmission have allowed for the immediate, worldwide transfer of large data streams.

These technological advancements and the corresponding cost reductions have enabled many private companies to collect data in vastly greater amounts,[13] of better quality and on new issues and circumstances. Airbnb's housing occupancy data[14] and Uber's data on trips[15] are prime examples. The public sector has benefited from this development as well – however, the scope of the state's legitimate, data-related activities is strictly disciplined in democracies which abide by the rule of law. As a consequence, the flourishing of data-driven markets has shifted the balance: public sector data stocks are no longer larger and better than those of private companies. In fact, the opposite is often the case.[16] Big private platforms collect and hold more data than many governments.[17] Therefore, states have become interested in accessing such privately held data to improve decision-making and public services.

The shift of balance from public to private has two implications on which this chapter will *not* elaborate, but which set the broader societal context and should therefore be borne in mind when discussing the policy and law of B2G data sharing. First, considering that 'knowledge is power', a data shift implies a shift of power.[18] In this light, government access to private data could reconfigure 'power imbalances'. Such power-related motives are often not made explicit,[19] even though they considerably affect the policy debate on B2G data sharing behind the scenes. Second, ethical considerations and perceptions of justice play an important role. Data-driven innovation raises general ethical concerns. When it comes to B2G data

12 For example, big data analytics, machine learning etc.

13 Bertin Martens and Néstor Duch-Brown, 'The economics of Business-to-Government data sharing' (2020) JRC Digital Economy Working Paper 2020–04, 5 <https://papers.ssrn.com/sol3/papers.cfm?abstract_id=3540122> accessed 31 August 2020.

14 See in detail Scassa (n. 9).

15 See <https://movement.uber.com> accessed 30 April 2020.

16 See Früh (n. 9) 524.

17 Jennifer Shkabatur, 'The Global Commons of Data' (2019) 22 Stanford Technology Law Review 354, 357.

18 For details on this conceptualisation Heiko Richter, 'The Power Paradigm in Private Law' in Mor Bakhoum and others (eds), *Personal Data in Competition, Consumer Protection and Intellectual Property Law* (Springer 2018) 527.

19 An illustrative example is the wording of Alemanno (n. 1) 185: 'private data remains the prerogative of a few big corporations who jealously guard it'.

sharing in particular, there continues to be widespread scepticism in the aftermath of the PRISM scandal. Edward Snowden revealed that an extensive, in-depth surveillance programme was being facilitated by government access to vast amounts of personal live communication and information which had been stored by private operators.[20] Policy and legislation can address such concerns e.g. by discussing restrictions to access that would protect privacy.[21] Yet the societal sensitivity of the debate on government access to data must always be taken into account, even if the focus of this chapter is on non-personal data.[22]

Concrete trends regarding data access emerge within this broader societal context. There is a clear political belief on the EU level in fostering data sharing between various actors in order to realise the full economic and societal value of data.[23] However, this is understood to go along with the increased practice of selective sharing. While 'open data', i.e. data for everyone for unrestricted purposes, was an ideal of the 2010s, the 2020s will reveal considerably more nuanced approaches to data sharing unlocked by new technologies.[24] Furthermore, the emphasis has begun to shift away from data quantity towards data quality. The recent recast PSI Directive[25] reflects this insofar as it defines high-value data sets and addresses real-time data and further quality characteristics in detail. Finally, combining the quality aspect with the fact that technology continues to become more

---

20 See Adam Florek, 'The Problems with PRISM: How A Modern Definition of Privacy Necessarily Protects Privacy Interests in Digital Communications' (2014) 30 John Marshall, Information, Technology & Privacy Law 571. In particular, the U.S. government could access data from Google, YouTube, Facebook, Microsoft, Skype, PalTalk, AOL, Yahoo, Apple etc.; see *James Ball and Dominic Rushe*, 'NSA Prism program taps in to user data of Apple, Google and others' (*The Guardian*, 6 June 2013) <www.theguardian.com/world/2013/jun/06/us-tech-giants-nsa-data> accessed 31 August 2020.

21 See proposals of Data Ethics Commission (n. 6).

22 See section C.V. below.

23 See Communication from the Commission of 19 February 2020 to the European Parliament, the Council, the European Economic and Social Committee and the Committee of Regions – A European strategy for data, COM(2020) 66 final.

24 Teresa Scassa, 'Keynote Address from Go Open Data 2019 Conference' (6 May 2019) <www.teresascassa.ca/index.php?option=com_k2&view=item&id=307:keynote-address-from-go-open-data-2019-conference> accessed 31 August 2020. Therefore, the idea of data commons is not restricted to its origin of research data; see Shkabatur (n. 17) 384.

25 Parliament and Council Directive (EU) 2019/1024/EU of the European Parliament and the Council of 20 June 2019 on open data and the re-use of public sector information [2019] OJ L172/56.

complex, higher investments are needed. This has implications for financing and compensation regimes.[26]

II. Objectives of government access

Making more and better[27] privately held data accessible to the state can serve various purposes. In any case, data access is a means to an end, its overall goal being social welfare enhancement.[28] But what exactly is the novelty of this discussion? One could argue that states' rights to access the information of private companies constitute a longstanding practice, e.g. when thinking about companies' taxation duties, business reporting obligations or legal compliance. However, the game-changing element lies in the new types and improved quality of datasets and the new analytical methods to harvest insights. In addition, new means of data transmission and cloud computing allow real-time data sharing and analysis and enable public authorities to 'tap into the data flow' of private companies.[29]

This technological advancement opens up numerous opportunities for the public sector to ultimately create social benefits and foster the common good.[30] Data access can increase the efficiency of the public sector, e.g. by reducing costs and effort if some data do not have to be collected again.[31] Moreover, data access can improve the internal performance of the administration on the basis of the accessed data.[32] Data access can also enable public sector bodies to innovate their policies and services, which is in line with the Commission's goal of unleashing the potential of data management and data-driven innovation.[33]

---

26 See sections D.VI., F.IV. and G.III. below.

27 As regards data quality, see van Ooijen, Ubaldi and Welby (n. 1) 30.

28 See Martens and Duch-Brown (n. 13) 9, who also point to methodological problems of determining and quantifying welfare gains.

29 Bram Klievink and others, 'Regulatory Compliance and Over-Compliant Information Sharing – Changes in the B2G Landscape' in Peter Parycek and others (eds), *Electronic Government* (Springer 2018) 249, 252.

30 See Martens and Duch-Brown (n. 13) 7.

31 European Commission (n. 5) 17; Martens and Duch-Brown (n. 13) 5.

32 See van Ooijen, Ubaldi and Welby (n. 1) 22–24.

33 European Commission Communication COM(2018) 232 final (n. 4) 1–3; European Commission (n. 5) 17; Stefaan G. Verhulst and Andrew Young, 'How the Data That Internet Companies Collect Can Be Used for the Public Good' (23 January 2018) Harvard Business Review <https://hbr.org/2018/01/how-the-data-that-i

For which purposes can the state legitimately use the data of private undertakings? One can identify three rather abstract categories. First, the data can deliver insights that guide decision-making and the design and evaluation of public policies.[34] A better basis of information may therefore improve policies ex ante and ex post.[35] Second, data can be directly or indirectly used in providing public services to citizens.[36] Such 'better public service delivery' addresses both the development and the performance[37] of the service. Third, the promotion of economic development and competition may be seen as another category.[38] This category is somewhat debatable, however, as it presumes that the state passes on the data to third parties. It will be seen that this case lies at the borderline of B2G sharing because it also covers the re-use of data which the state has obtained from private undertakings on the basis of mandatory access rules.[39]

III. Public task and examples

The above-mentioned categories of general objectives crosscut many concrete purposes and areas of application for government access to privately held data. The public task is the starting point for determining such purposes. Government access to data must serve a public task which reflects

---

nternet-companies-collect-can-be-used-for-the-public-good> accessed 31 August 2020.

34 See van Ooijen, Ubaldi and Welby (n. 1) 18–20; Martens and Duch-Brown (n. 13) 5; European Commission (n. 5) 17; European Commission Communication COM(2018) 232 final (n. 4) 12.

35 Laurent Cytermann and others, *Rapport relatif aux données d'intérêt général* (2015) 2 <www.economie.gouv.fr/files/files/PDF/DIG-Rapport-final2015-09.pdf> accessed 31 August 2020; Alemanno (n. 1) on the role to prove or falsify the effectiveness of regulatory measures.

36 See Martens and Duch-Brown (n. 13) 5. For the distinction and convergence of the concept 'consumer' vs. 'citizen' Sofia Ranchordás, 'Citizens as Consumers in the Data Economy: The Case of Smart Cities' (2018) Journal of European Consumer and Market Law 154.

37 See van Ooijen, Ubaldi and Welby (n. 1) 20–22; European Commission Communication COM (2018) 232 final (n. 4) 12; European Commission (n. 5) 17. See on personalisation of the services Ricard Munné, 'Big Data in the Public Sector' in Jose M. Cavanillas, Edward Curry and Wolgang Wahlster (eds), *New Horizons for a Data-Driven Economy* (Springer 2016) 195.

38 Cytermann and others (n. 35) 2.

39 See sections E.III. and G.IV. below.

the public interest.[40] The Member States are free to define the public interest and designate public tasks accordingly.[41] Thus, the public task is a dynamic concept. At the same time, technology determines possible tasks and the means of their fulfilment. Government access to data can therefore serve to improve the fulfilment of *existing* public tasks – e.g. protecting public health by gaining insights into the spread of pandemics on the basis of phone operators' movement data or improving urban housing planning by using rental data from rental platforms.[42] But beyond such improvements, the state can take on completely *new* public tasks. This can include the production of innovative outputs based on the data.[43] One emerging field regards strengthening state oversight of scoring algorithms.[44]

There are a countless number of examples of how the state may optimise the performance of existing tasks or fulfil new tasks on the basis of privately held datasets. This concerns e.g. environmental protection, official statistics, public health, natural hazard and disaster management, public safety, urban planning, transport, energy supply, smart cities in general, consumer protection, research and market monitoring.[45] Yet there is no particular order or taxonomy when it comes to public tasks and data access. The reason for this conceptual shortcoming lies in the multiple purposes which a single dataset can serve. Also, policy discussions have

40 On the different concepts of the 'public tasks' across the EU see Heiko Richter, 'Open Science and Public Sector Information' (2018) 9 Journal of Intellectual Property, Information Technology and E-Commerce Law 51, 65–66.

41 See on the problem of definition European Commission (n. 5) 17; in the EU context, the CJEU jurisprudence on 'determining services of general public interest' can give some guidance: see Case T-289/03 *BUPA and Others v. Commission* EU:T:2008:29, paras 165–70; Case T-17/02 *Olsen v. Commission* EU:T:2005:218, para. 216; Case T-106/95 *FFSA and Others v. Commission* EU:T:1997:23, para. 99; Case 127/73 *BRT v. SABAM* EU:C:1974:25, para. 23.

42 See Früh (n. 9) 526 on Airbnb.

43 See Martens and Duch-Brown (n. 13) 5.

44 In this direction Shkabatur (n. 17) 360.

45 For examples see European Commission Communication COM (2018) 232 final (n. 4) 14; Communication from the Commission of 10 January 2010 to the European Parliament, the Council, the European Economic and Social Committee and the Committee of the Regions – 'Building a European data economy' COM(2017) 9 final, 14; European Commission (n. 5) 19; Früh (n. 9) 527; Alemanno (n. 1) 184; Shkabatur (n. 17) 359; Data Ethics Commission (n. 6) 154; Bundesministerium für Wirtschaft und Energie (n. 6) 46.

evolved on the basis of use cases[46] in various areas. The evidence at hand is therefore anecdotal and not empirically reliable.

C. *Research focuses*

I. *Overview*

There are many potential ways for policymakers to improve governmental access to privately held data. However, 'B2G data sharing' is not clearly defined – the discourse is still at an early stage. This chapter does not aim to put forward a universal definition, but it must at least determine its focus by delineating the scope of research. As will be shown in the following, this chapter focuses on mandatory access rules which concern data held by private undertakings without public links. Furthermore, the chapter concentrates on overarching aspects and addresses neither sector-specific particularities nor personal data.

II. *Mandatory access rules*

Mandatory access rules – meaning binding laws, in contrast to non-binding guidelines[47] – predominantly concern statutory access rules. Yet one should keep in mind that mandatory access rules lie at one extreme of a spectrum. There are other, less interventionist instruments to foster data access (e.g. incentives, reduction of transaction costs or soft law approaches).[48] Mandatory access rules restrict the freedom of enterprises vis-à-vis the state. Therefore, they need substantive justification in the face of fundamental rights. As a consequence, the legislature has to master challenges of a different kind compared to the much-discussed issue of data access be-

46 Illustrative examples in European Commission (n. 3) 5; European Commission Communication COM (2018)232 final (n. 4) 12; Shkabatur (n. 17) 361; see also case studies in European Commission (n. 5) Annex II.

47 The Commission outlined such principles in its Communication COM (2018) 232 final (n. 4) 12–14 and revised them in European Commission (n. 5) 79–86. See also European Commission Staff Working Document, 'Guidance on sharing private sector data in the European data economy' SWD(2018) 125 final.

48 See Shkabatur (n. 17) 402–404 on 'carrots'; Martens and Duch-Brown (n. 13) 21.

tween private parties.[49] Mandatory access rules must be seen as a last resort within the range of measures to foster data access.

With this in mind, the EU has started to consider mandated sharing (alongside other instruments[50]) as a potential building block for a new regulatory framework.[51] But what is the relevance and value of focusing on mandatory access rules from a substantive point of view? The move towards mandatory rules aims to compensate for the actual deficiency of data shared on a voluntary basis despite its vast economic and societal potential.[52] In fact, the B2G data sharing debate originates from 'data philanthropy' initiatives in the humanitarian aid sector.[53] Voluntary sharing increasingly takes place. Accordingly, contractual agreements are the main legal tool.[54] There are various examples of 'data collaboratives',[55] among others in the transport[56] and utility[57] sectors and regarding mobile phone data.[58] However, so far cooperation appears sector- and context-dependent, selective, sporadic and rather experimental, and markets for data sharing are said to be nascent and small.[59] Reports on voluntary B2G data sharing between the state and private undertakings are generally pessimistic, forecasting a slow development and expressing doubt that pilot projects will

49 See the European Commission Communications COM(2017) 9 final (n. 45) and COM(2018) 232 final (n. 4). In detail Josef Drexl, 'Designing Competitive Markets for Industrial Data – Between Propertization and Access' (2017) 8 Journal of Intellectual Property, Information Technology and E-Commerce Law 257; Heiko Richter and Peter Slowinski 'The Data Sharing Economy: On the emergence of New Intermediaries' (2019) 50 International Review of Intellectual Property and Competition Law 4.

50 For the wide range of measures to be considered see European Commission (n. 5).

51 European Commission (n. 5) 75; Martens and Duch-Brown (n. 13) 21.

52 See Martens and Duch-Brown (n. 13) 11.

53 See UN Global Pulse <www.unglobalpulse.org/mapping-corporate-data-sharing> accessed 31 August 2020. See also Früh (n. 9) 529; Alemanno (n. 1) 186.

54 See European Commission (n. 5) 31.

55 See Alemanno (n. 1) 186; for a taxonomy see Verhulst and Young (n. 33).

56 See e.g. iSHARE Data Sharing Scheme in the Dutch logistics sector <www.ishareworks.org> accessed 31 August 2020.

57 See Shkabatur (n. 17) 392 on the 'California Data Collaborative' for water management, <http://californiadatacollaborative.org/> accessed 31 August 2020.

58 See Früh (n. 9) 529; according to Ramón Muñoz and Pablo Cantó, 'El INE arranca el rastreo de millones de móviles pero hay formas de esquivarlo' (*El País*, 17 November 2019) <https://elpais.com/economia/2019/11/17/actualidad/1574008445_307680.html> the Spanish National Institute of Statistics will pay half a million EUR to Telefónica, Vodafone and Orange.

59 Martens and Duch-Brown (n. 13) 11; Shkabatur (n. 17) 398; Alemanno (n. 1) 187.

evolve into sustainable initiatives.[60] However, the lack of empirical evidence forbids a generalisable conclusion. So far the B2G discussion has tended to follow anecdotal evidence and implicit assumptions.[61]

Still, it appears sensible to follow some theoretical, incentive-related arguments which appear to support the call for mandatory access. Their core premise is that the private party must somehow benefit from data sharing if it voluntarily decides to participate. In contrast, the abstinence from voluntary data sharing that we observe in reality can be explained by various disincentives: the cost associated with the processing and provision of the data; a loss of control over the data and especially the risk of data leaks to unauthorised third parties; the fear of infringing rights, especially in the areas of personal data, trade secrets, IP and competition law; strategic disadvantages in competition; and the concern that government might use the data against the company, e.g. by enacting market regulation or taking enforcement measures.[62]

Therefore, when considering mandatory access rules, one may not overlook specific market developments and their respective disincentives to share data. There may be public interest reasons to intervene, but mandatory access regulation remains the ultima ratio from a market standpoint. In any case, access rules have to account for their possible effects on voluntary data provision and the incentives for affected actors. This implies that access rules must also contain the safeguards that are necessary to keep mandatory rules from causing dysfunction.

III. Data of private undertakings without a public link

The focus on private *undertakings* concerns commercial entities that are not individuals. These entities have to be *entirely private*, meaning that they

60 European Commission (n. 5) 32; Martens and Duch-Brown (n. 13) 11; Alemanno (n. 1) 187.

61 Martens and Duch-Brown (n. 13) 5, 12, 13. Früh (n. 9) 529 says that private individuals are 'often' willing to disclose data on a voluntary basis, however, it does not appear clear what 'often' means from an empirical point of view. See Bertrand Pailhès, 'How to define and regulate "data of general interest"?' (2018) 1(2) Enjeux numériques <www.annales.org/enjeux-numeriques/2018/resumes/juin/09-en-resum-FR-AN-juin-2018.html> accessed 31 August 2020, who assumes that development does not progress without legal intervention.

62 See Martens and Duch-Brown (n. 13) 19; Alemanno (n. 1) 185; Früh (n. 9) 524, 528; European Commission (n. 5) 27.

are not at all linked to a public person.[63] This not only excludes *public* undertakings[64] but also privately controlled undertakings linked to public authorities on the basis of their involvement in the performance of public tasks[65] or their public financing. France addressed such 'para publics' in its legislation by adding a mandatory access clause to the rules on the award of service concessions in 2016.[66] The EU also discussed the introduction of such rules when revising the PSI Directive, but ended up merely recommending the Member States to enact such legislation.[67] In Germany, the *Kommission Wettbewerbsrecht 4.0* suggested that private companies entrusted with tasks of general interest should be obliged to make data generated in the course of this activity available to public authorities.[68] Such data should not only be made available to the public sector (for public purposes) but also to market participants.[69] The German legislature, however, has not taken up this issue yet.

The data of private undertakings with public links are left out because they have distinct functional features and pose different legal challenges. If there is already a link to the state, intervention seems less critical because its reason lies precisely in the planned involvement of the private undertaking in the fulfilment of public tasks. The undertaking's obligations are then coupled with privileges. There is usually a contractual relationship between the state and the private undertaking in such cases. Respective reform discussions therefore revolve around the effectiveness of agreements and the methodological challenge lies in getting evidence about the data provision as set out in these agreements. An important reason why the law imposes mandatory contract law is to correct government failure due to

63 See European Commission (n. 5) 35.

64 See Art. 2(1) PSI Directive (n. 25): '"public sector body" means the State, regional or local authorities, bodies governed by public law or associations formed by one or more such authorities or one or more such bodies governed by public law'.

65 See European Commission (n. 5) 20, particularly referring to 'data-sharing obligations as part of subcontracted services' and respective examples.

66 According to Art. L-3131 Code de la commande publique, the state should receive data from the concessionaire which 'have been collected or produced during the operation of the public service covered by the contract and are essential for its fulfilment'. For background see Ralf Schnieders, 'Die neue Open-(Government)-Data-Gesetzgebung in Frankreich und in Deutschland' (2018) Die Öffentliche Verwaltung 175.

67 See Recital 19 PSI Directive (n. 25); the basic idea is not at all new; see already European Commission, 'Amended proposal for a Council Directive on the Legal Protection of Databases' COM(93) 464 final, Art. 11(2)(b), 7.

68 Bundesministerium für Wirtschaft und Energie (n. 6) 46.

69 Ibid. 47.

asymmetries: when it comes to awarding contracts that include data clauses, municipalities often appear inferior to the private sector in terms of negotiating power and skills.[70]

IV. Horizontal aspects

Another focus of this chapter lies on overarching considerations for regulation. Therefore, sector-specific peculiarities are not addressed. This may come as a surprise since the B2G data-sharing debate has so far supported the sectoral (vertical) advancement of rules[71] instead of cross-sectoral (horizontal) regulation. In fact, sector-specific access rules already exist. From a policy point of view, there are good reasons for sector-specific advancement[72] because different interests – depending on the purpose[73] – and distinct competencies are involved. From a legal standpoint, access obligations may also account for different constitutional requirements that correspond with specific sectors and purposes.[74] Finally, sector-specific access obligations may better account for the practical circumstances of specific sectors: it may be easier to define concrete objectives and what data they require; furthermore, formats, compensation and technical interoperability differ across sectors.[75]

This chapter, however, takes another angle. It asks which aspects are to be addressed in general, regardless of the sector. Exposing the common denominator and drawing general principles can inform the further development of sector-specific rules. At the same time, the focus on overarching aspects can inform the issue in terms of gauging the benefits of establish-

---

70 For detailed background, see Cytermann and others (n. 35). Regarding problems in the smart city context (Amsterdam and Hamburg) see Früh (n. 9) 529–30, where the right to sell the solutions to other cities was reserved to private partners.

71 See Data Ethics Commission (n. 6) 154; Bundesministerium für Wirtschaft und Energie (n. 6) 47.

72 See Josef Drexl, 'Neue Regeln für die Europäische Datenwirtschaft? Ein Plädoyer für einen wettbewerbspolitischen Ansatz – Teil 2' (2017) 5 Neue Zeitschrift für Kartellrecht 415, 419; Data Ethics Commission (n. 6) 154 with particular emphasis on the sectors health, mobility and energy.

73 See Drexl (n. 49) 289, who stresses that security interests of the state would require other approaches than the prevention of epidemics, environmental protection or the functioning of 'smart cities'.

74 See Data Ethics Commission (n. 6) 154.

75 Drexl (n. 72) 419; Data Ethics Commission (n. 6) 154; Pailhès (n. 61) 5.

ing a horizontal B2G data access framework. This concrete question will be addressed later on.[76]

V. Non-personal data

Finally, this chapter does not elaborate on problems of privacy. Rather, it assumes that data access rules comply with given data protection rules. To avoid their violation, only derived, aggregated and processed data are shared in many cases.[77] This focus does not ignore the immense challenge B2G data access poses for data protection law, which becomes evident e.g. in the recent debate on accessing the data of mobile phone operators to fight the spread of the Sars-CoV-2 pandemic.[78] However, a thorough discussion of the data protection conformity of mandatory access rules lies beyond the scope of this paper and is reserved to further research.

D. Key questions that access rules should address

I. Overview

When thinking about the issues that mandatory access rules should address, it is helpful to ask five key questions: what for (purpose), for whom (beneficiaries), against whom (obliged parties), to what (relevant data) and how (modalities of access)?

II. Purpose (what for?)

The government's purpose in accessing the data (*what for?*) is the question to start with. The purpose reflects the public interest[79] and forms the reference point for all the subsequent questions that access rules should address. This means that the conditions for access largely depend on the pur-

---

76 See section G. below.

77 See Martens and Duch-Brown (n. 13) 18.

78 On the controversy regarding planned legislative amendments in Germany, Thomas Rudl, 'Jens Spahn lässt Testballon steigen' (*Netzpolitik.org*, 23 March 2020) <https://netzpolitik.org/2020/jens-spahn-laesst-testballon-steigen/> accessed 31 August 2020.

79 See also Commission Staff Working Document SWD(2018) 125 final (n. 47) 14.

pose that the data should serve. Usually, the purpose lies in solving a problem (e.g. optimising urban traffic) or serving a goal (e.g. fostering transparency). It therefore focuses on ends (outputs like knowledge and insights) rather than means (inputs, data).[80] Moreover, the purpose is context-specific because the concept of 'public interest' is a dynamic one.[81] Accordingly, access rules can address the purpose either in a specific and explicit or in a more general and implicit manner.[82] The regulatory challenge is to clearly define the purpose in correspondence with the public interest and to set up a transparent process that helps to identify the concrete public interest. Practices in the Member States largely differ.

Access rules which entitle the state vis-à-vis private undertakings naturally concern fundamental rights. Therefore, such rules encroach on legal positions, especially the freedom of business and (potentially) property protection.[83] While purpose limitation is an established data protection principle,[84] there is no general principle of purpose limitation outside the area of personal data. Nevertheless, the principle of purpose limitation[85] puts the rule of law in concrete terms – otherwise, the proportionality of concrete measures could not be assessed in relation to the legislative goal.[86] Considering that the same dataset can be used for various purposes, its 'general purpose nature' stands in natural tension with the principle of purpose limitation. This problem will be further discussed when examining the relationship between access rules and re-usability.[87]

---

80 This hints to the distinct focus of Martens and Duch-Brown (n. 13), who generally tackle the supply/input side by elaborating on different measures to generally increase data sharing and respective transactions by overcoming barriers to sharing.

81 See European Commission (n. 5) 16.

82 E.g. the definition of data itself can imply the purpose of access.

83 On the relevance of fundamental rights and data access regulation see Fabian Michl, 'Datenbesitz – ein grundrechtliches Schutzgut?' (2019) Neue Juristische Wochenschrift 2729; Andreas Wiebe and Nico Schur, 'Ein Recht an industriellen Daten im verfassungsrechtlichen Spannungsverhältnis zwischen Eigentumsschutz, Wettbewerbs- und Informationsfreiheit' (2017) Zeitschrift für Urheber- und Medienrecht 461.

84 See Paul M. Schwartz, 'Systematic government access to private-sector data in Germany' (2012) 2 International Data Privacy Law 289.

85 See European Commission Communication COM (2018) 232 final (n. 4) 13.

86 See Gertrude Lübbe-Wolff, 'The Principle of Proportionality in the Case-Law of the German Federal Constitutional Court' (2014) 34 Human Rights Law Journal 12.

87 See sections E.III. and G. IV. below.

III. *Beneficiaries (for whom?)*

As a next step, the entitled actor needs to be designated as a beneficiary (*for whom?*). The right to access the data of private undertakings is granted to 'the state', meaning public sector bodies. This includes public authorities but excludes public undertakings.[88] In any case, the principle of proportionality may require precisely specifying the entity that is authorised to access the data. As the focus lies on privileged access for the state, the state is not seen as one of many 'external stakeholders' but as an actor sui generis. Cases in which the state receives data in parallel to third parties[89] are therefore not considered as government data access cases.

Besides direct access between the state and private undertakings, some cases can also be considered as government data access but in modified forms adapted to the complexity of data ecosystems. This covers scenarios of 'mandated intermediaries', where the law empowers the state to mandate private data holders to make their data directly accessible to a private intermediary so that it can analyse the data and ultimately provide processed data or insights to the state. Such scenarios occur where the state lacks the capacity to perform the data analysis itself.[90] One regulatory challenge concerns how to deal with benefits that the private intermediary might gain from accessing the data. Such 'data advantages' are often a better incentive for firms to get involved than financial incentives.[91] Cases of 'mandated intermediaries' are distinct from scenarios where a third party gains access to the data but then provides the data or insights to the state

88 In fact, one could theoretically think of access rules which specifically entitle *public* undertakings to access *private* undertakings' data for the purpose of fulfilling their public interest mission. However, such constellations raise mostly sector-specific challenges and concerns.

89 E.g. through private open data obligations or policies of 'data for everyone', see proposal on progressive data sharing by Viktor Mayer-Schönberger and Thomas Ramge, *Das Digital – Markt, Wertschöpfung und Gerechtigkeit im Datenkapitalismus* (Econ 2017) 194.

90 This scenario resembles a portability right (e.g. Art. 20 GDPR); see for the general concept Inge Graef, Martin Husovec and Nadezhda Purtova, 'Data Portability and Data Control: Lessons for an Emerging Concept in EU Law' (2018) 19 German Law Journal 1359; Drexl (n. 49) 286.

91 This is for example reflected in the new rules on de facto exclusivity on data in public private partnerships according to Recital 50 and Art. 12(4) PSI Directive (n. 25); see also Richter and Slowinski (n. 49) 16, on sharing platforms.

and private providers.[92] An example is 'Copenhagen City Data Exchange', a data trading platform set up in cooperation with Hitachi.[93]

Another distinct scenario is one in which the state directly receives datasets from the private data holder but then passes them on[94] to third parties (which, however, cannot claim direct access against the original data holder). This is only to be considered a case of B2G data sharing (the state being the 'mandated intermediary') if the state's provision of the data to third parties is attached to a purpose limitation in accordance with the public task. Usually, this concerns the provision to selected parties (e.g. researchers, journalists or participants in a smart city network). The German 'Market Transparency Unit for Fuels' will be discussed later on as another illustrative example.[95]

An extension of this scenario is that the state passes on the datasets to everyone. This is the case when the accessed datasets fall under open data obligations.[96] Technically, the mandated B2G data access would extend the data holdings of the state, which would then be available for wide re-use. An example is the French *Loi Lemaire*, which (at least in theory) also allows the state to make the data of concessionaries further available for re-use.[97] Such unlimited re-use stands in evident conflict with the principle of purpose limitations. One could, however, frame 'open data' itself as a public task, e.g. by aiming to foster competition and innovation, economic welfare and transparency.[98] Especially the transparency aspect appears manifold since the B2G data sharing debate itself has raised calls for transparency obligations according to which public authorities should disclose their data sources.

---

92 Geoffrey Delcroix, 'Smart Cities and Innovative Uses for Personal Data: Scenarios for Using Data to Restore the Balance between Public and Private Spheres', (2017) Special Issue 17 Field Actions Science Reports 75, 79 <http://journals.openedition.org/factsreports/4489> accessed 31 August 2020.

93 See Früh (n. 9) 529.

94 This only considers the datasets accessed and not insights, otherwise the mere provision of information would fall under this scenario.

95 See section E.VI. below.

96 E.g. according to the rules of the PSI Directive (n. 25).

97 Art. L-3131–4 Code de la commande publique states that 'the licensing authority or a third party designated by it may freely extract and exploit all or part of such data and databases, in particular with a view to making them available for re-use free of charge or against payment'. In practice, this is highly contested.

98 See Recital 13 PSI Directive (n. 25).

IV. *Obliged parties (against whom?)*

Private companies, meaning commercial entities and not individuals, are to be defined as the obliged party (*against whom?*). There are different points of reference for further delineation. A common approach is to address the sector of the data holders, e.g. telecommunications operators, mobility providers, car manufacturers, retailers or social media providers.[99] Another way is to refer to economic or rather functional characteristics, e.g. access to data of online platforms.[100] A third possibility is to generally refer to 'holders' or 'creators' of the particular dataset needed. This is relevant when the desired insights can only be derived from combining datasets of different sources and a hold-up problem should be avoided.[101] The effectiveness of such an output-centred definition then fully depends on the data to be defined.

V. *Relevant data (what?)*

In any case, it is necessary to specifically define the affected data (*what?*). The definition of data as the subject matter of access rules corresponds to the public purpose to be fulfilled. Various data taxonomies exist for classifying the processing degree of data in the information value chain.[102] Among other things, access rules can address raw data, processed information or data-driven insights.[103] The access rules must also determine the degree of granularity and update frequency (static or dynamic) of the data

99 For examples see European Commission Communication COM (2018) 232 final (n. 4) 12; Alemanno (n. 1) 183; Verhulst and Young (n. 33).

100 E.g. when referring to 'online platforms'; see European Commission Communication COM (2018) 232 final (n. 4) 12. See also Art. 9 Regulation (EU) 2019/1150 of the European Parliament and the Council of 20 June 2019 on promoting fairness and transparency for business users of online intermediation services [2019] OJ L186/57 (P2B Regulation), which defines and regulates 'online intermediation services' and 'online search engines' and contains transparency obligations on the accessibility of their data.

101 See European Commission (n. 5) 21.

102 In general Kitchin (n. 11); Martens and Duch-Brown (n. 13) 17 distinguish between direct data delivery, indirect data trade (intermediate inputs) and data-based services.

103 See also European Commission (n. 5) 22–23. For a legal definition of 'raw data' see Sec. 12a German Act on digital administration (*Gesetz zur Förderung der elektronischen Verwaltung*).

and other quality parameters.[104] At the same time, definitions explicitly exclude certain data in order to protect private or public interests or because it would simply be too costly to make them available and would therefore pose an undue burden on the companies.[105] If personal data are at stake, data protection law applies and access rules must be designed in conformity with data protection regimes. The legislature has much less leeway as compared to access regimes which do not touch upon personal data.

Access rules can also address the issue of 'information about the data', which resembles Arrow's information paradox[106] in a data-driven context: How does the state find out about the datasets that private undertakings actually hold? And how can the state assess whether access to these datasets effectively provides the desired insights? One way to tackle these challenges is to include disclosure/transparency obligations on companies with regard to the types of data they hold. In addition, access rules could mandate support of the businesses to assess the quality.[107] Access rules can therefore be designed as a right that follows a three-step logic: 1. access to information about the datasets, 2. access to (sample) datasets for assessing their usefulness with regard to the public purpose, 3. access to datasets for using them in accordance with the purpose.

VI. Modalities of access (how?)

Finally, the modalities (*how?*) of data access must be defined. There is no clear delineation of what can be categorised as a modality, but it may help

---

104 See European Commission (n. 5) 73; European Commission Staff Working Document SWD(2018) 125 (n. 47) 14. For a legal definition of 'dynamic data' see Art. 2(8) PSI Directive (n. 25); for a sectoral approach to specify these parameters, see Commission Delegated Regulation (EU) 2017/1926 of 31 May 2017 supplementing Directive 2010/40/EU of the European Parliament and of the Council with regard to the provision of EU-wide multimodal travel information services [2017] OJ L272/1 (Multimodal Travel Information Regulation).

105 On the theoretical background Friedrich Schoch, *Informationsfreiheitsgesetz* (2nd edn, C.H. Beck 2016) Vor §§ 3–6, regarding the rights of access to information of public authorities; furthermore Heiko Richter, *Informationsweiterverwendungsgesetz* (C.H. Beck 2018) § 1 paras 23–32.

106 Kenneth J. Arrow, 'Economic Welfare and the Allocation of Resources for Invention' in NBER (ed.), *The Rate and Direction of Inventive Activity: Economic and Social Factors* (Princeton University Press 1962) 609–26.

107 See European Commission Staff Working Document SWD(2018) 125 final (n. 47) 15.

to think in terms of technical, economic and legal modalities. In general, all modalities need to serve the fulfilment of the purpose of mandated access.

Technical modalities relate to the technical infrastructure and solutions which enable data access. The regulator can base access rules on existing technical infrastructure or mandate the establishment of new infrastructure.[108] In this regard, access means the transfer or exchange of data. Direct state access to private databases is usually ruled out for security reasons. Rather, the law obliges companies to transmit data (e.g. via API), share them via trusted intermediaries, put them into a data pool[109] etc. Where suitable, it can be less intrusive or more effective to mandate the sharing of insights as compared to raw data. There are also technical solutions which allow the state to draw conclusions from data without having to transfer the data to it.[110] Further technical modalities concern standards for data exchange[111] and formats[112] as well as the access duration. Such time limits can satisfy the principle of proportionality or data protection rules.[113]

An important and vividly discussed condition is compensation.[114] Data access may incur significant costs and the regulator must decide who will bear them.[115] Access rules that address compensation can be regarded as

---

108 See for examples of legislation which led to the establishment of new data infrastructure Directive 2007/2/EC of the European Parliament and the Council of 14 March 2007 establishing an Infrastructure for Spatial Information in the European Community (INSPIRE) [2007] OJ L108/1; Directive 2010/40/EU of the European Parliament and of the Council of 7 July 2010 on the framework for the deployment of Intelligent Transport Systems in the field of road transport and for interfaces with other modes of transport [2010] OJ L207/1.

109 See Martens and Duch-Brown (n. 13) 18; Shkabatur (n. 17) 362; for data pools in particular see Björn Lundqvist, 'Competition and Data Pools' (2018) Journal of European Consumer and Market Law 146.

110 See European Commission (n. 5) 62; Martens and Duch-Brown (n. 13) 18; see e.g. the OPAL project <www.opalproject.org/> accessed 31 August 2020.

111 See the recommendation of the European Commission (n. 5) 72 to invest in the development of common standards for data, metadata, representation and standardised transfer protocols.

112 For a legislative approach see Art. 5 PSI Directive (n. 25).

113 See Commission Staff Working Document SWD(2018) 125 final (n. 47) 15.

114 See European Commission (n. 5) 39; Commission Staff Working Document SWD(2018) 125 final (n. 47) 15.

115 See Cédric Villani, *For a Meaningful Artificial Intelligence: Towards a French and European Strategy* (2018) 28; Shkabatur (n. 17) 398. If companies carry the cost, one has to ask whether they can pass them on to the consumers and what the effect on demand is.

'price regulation', which affects the private undertakings' incentives.[116] Constitutional requirements may demand compensation, but usually the principle of proportionality gives some leeway for the regulator to decide whether to introduce compensation,[117] so that it largely amounts to a policy decision.[118] Yet the sui generis database right could mandate compensation.[119] When it comes to determining compensation, different cost-based approaches exist: free of charge, marginal cost, full cost recovery or market price.[120] In any case, charging provisions should not negatively affect the company's ability to collect/create the data[121] or create negative incentives regarding the development of markets and competition. It is therefore important to understand that lower compensation may be necessary when accounting for market structure (monopolistic pricing for single source datasets),[122] while higher compensation may be appropriate to ensure a suitable level of data quality. But benefit-based approaches are also discussed. The type and amount of compensation would then depend on the benefits associated with the use or purpose of mandated data access. Cost-based compensation seems the more reasonable option from an economic standpoint because benefit-based compensation runs the risk of conflating distributional aspects and faces the general challenge of accurately estimating the benefits of data access for public purposes ex ante.[123]

Access rules should also address other legal issues in order to create legal certainty and system-wide trust. This concerns the handling of legally pro-

---

116 See Martens and Duch-Brown (n. 13) 13.

117 Under German law, this holds true as long as mandated access does not interfere with property positions protected by Art. 14 of the Basic Law (if there is intellectual property protection, the rationale of the judgment of the Federal Constitutional Court, 7 July 1971, Case 1 BvR 765/66 (1971) Neue Juristische Wochenschrift 2163 – *Schulbuchprivileg* applies; if there is no intellectual property protection, Federal Constitutional Court, 14 July 1981, Case 1 BvL 24/78 (1982) Neue Juristische Wochenschrift 633 – *Pflichtexemplare* becomes relevant).

118 According to Cytermann and others (n. 35) 3, there should be compensation in France if access goes *beyond* 'data of general interest with public link'.

119 See section G.III. below.

120 See European Commission (n. 5) 39. There is a significant body of literature about cost-based pricing of public sector information, see e.g. Marco Ricolfi and others, 'Principles governing charging for re-use of public sector information', (2011) XX/1–2 Informatica e diritto 105; Rufus Pollock, 'The Economics of Public Sector Information' (2008) University of Cambridge <https://rufuspollock.com/papers/economics_of_psi.pdf> accessed 31 August 2020.

121 See European Commission Communication COM(2018) 232 final (n. 4) 13.

122 See Martens and Duch-Brown (n. 13) 13.

123 See on the quality of data as 'experience goods' European Commission (n. 5) 21.

tected data (e.g. data protection, IP and trade secrets). The law should be clear on the interfaces. Furthermore, well-defined liability rules[124] can clarify the risks and remedies. Another important yet underdeveloped issue is the relationship between mandated access and the voluntary conclusion of data-sharing contracts. Regulation[125] should clearly address to what extent contracts between the state and private partners should take precedence over legal obligations.[126] Mandatory rules do not necessarily exclude voluntary measures.

A general issue concerns *preferential* conditions for the public sector regarding data access in the context of mandatory access rules.[127] This covers situations in which both the state and private actors can claim access, yet where the rules ensure better conditions for the state. Such preferential treatment can be reflected in lower prices, higher quality, earlier delivery etc.[128] It is important to distinguish between different grounds for such preferential treatment. Reasons can be found in the benefits enjoyed by the public if the state obtains the data (e.g. due to high positive externalities the state can effectuate or the high importance or urgency of the task to be fulfilled), in justice considerations and in social values underpinning the perception that it is unfair if the community has to 'buy back data or data-based services from private individuals at considerable cost'.[129] Preferential treatment can also be based on cost-related grounds and fiscal considerations. Regardless of the concrete motivation to include preferential treatment, such rules should always consider the effects on markets and potential distortions of competition.

---

124 See European Commission Staff Working Document SWD(2018) 125 final (n. 47) 16. The European Commission (n. 5) 26 identified the applicable liability regime as one of the major uncertainties to be tackled.

125 For a regulatory approach, see e.g. Art. 7(1) Directive (EU) 2019/790 of the European Parliament and of the Council of 17 April 2019 on copyright and related rights in the Digital Single Market and amending Directives 96/9/EC and 2001/29/EC [2019] OJ L130/92.

126 See Pailhès (n. 61) 5, arguing that contracts should override intervention.

127 Preferential conditions have so far only been considered in contractual arrangements, e.g. European Commission Communication COM(2018) 232 final (n. 4) 13.

128 Ibid.

129 See Früh (n. 9) 525.

E. Principles for developing access rules

I. Function of principles

The key questions above clarify what issues need to be addressed when formulating mandatory access rules and outline options for their design. However, they do not give any normative guidance on whether mandatory access rules should be introduced and according to which measures they should be developed. This section aims to give such normative guidance and develops four principles for designing access rules. These principles are based on economic theory, constitutional requirements and real-world observations. While the principles take the functioning of data-driven markets and innovation into particular consideration, they do not explicitly distinguish between horizontal and sectoral approaches.[130] Moreover, they do not address the policy concern of setting priorities between different purposes and concrete areas for which mandatory access is considered desirable.

II. Principle of justifying statehood

According to the *principle of justifying statehood*, legitimate reasons must be provided if a mandatory access right for the state vis-à-vis private undertakings is to be established. This principle addresses the justification for intervention as such (*'if'*), while the remaining three principles concern the means of intervention (*'how'*).[131] The principle of justifying statehood has a legal and an economic/political dimension. While fundamental rights can require a justification for state intervention, economic and political considerations inform whether mandatory access actually makes sense.

When reflecting on the justification for state intervention, much depends on the perception of the role of the state. Here, this long-standing debate is reflected in data policies: What does the principle of subsidiarity mean in a data-driven economy? For determining the intervention threshold, a liberal view would consider economics-based theory, which frames

130 This will be addressed in section F. below.

131 If there is, however, no feasible way to design them, this can lead to the conclusion that there should be no intervention at all.

justification for intervention on the grounds of market failure.[132] Mandatory access rules would correct this failure and enhance the general welfare of society (which would thus deem them legitimate).[133] However, the law (especially of the Member States) does not require market failure as a necessary condition for intervention. Instead, interventions on the basis of the public interest are legitimate as long as constitutional requirements – especially the purpose limitation and the principle of proportionality – are met.

The suggested principle of justifying statehood finds some middle ground. On the one hand, purely economic reasoning may not suffice, as it runs the risk of squeezing problems into the straightjacket of the market such that they cannot be adequately conceptualised. Also, such an emphasis raises methodological problems[134] which throw its applicability into question and run the risk of overlooking the public interest and democratic will at large. On the other hand, mere public interest-based reasoning[135] may be legitimate but not reasonable because it poses the risk of turning invocations of the 'common good' into a commonplace. Such a perspective fails to answer in which cases mandatory data access is reasonable and effective. It would also ignore the functional particularities of data as the concerned subject matter. Therefore, the following three characteristics of data access should be considered when justifying access rights for the state.

Firstly, the distinct feature of the state is its monopoly on the use of force. Mandatory access for the state would therefore require that only applying public force (meaning access against the will of the private undertaking) can guarantee that the data fulfil certain beneficial characteristics (e.g, completeness, punctuality and quality). Mandatory access rules can also address scenarios where reaching the goal is highly important or urgent, e.g. for the protection of public health. A conceptual problem is

132 See for this approach Martens and Duch-Brown (n. 13) 5; however, they (ibid. 12, n. 10) acknowledge other reasons for intervention by referring to the Commission's better regulation toolbox: regulatory failure, equity concerns and behavioural bias. On the methodology of creating data ownership and access rights Heiko Richter and Reto M. Hilty, 'Die Hydra des Dateneigentums – eine methodische Betrachtung' in Stiftung Datenschutz (ed.), *Dateneigentum und Datenhandel* (Erich Schmidt Verlag 2018) 241, <https://papers.ssrn.com/sol3/papers.cfm?abstract_id=3263404> accessed 31 August 2020.

133 See Martens and Duch-Brown (n. 13) 12–20.

134 Ibid. 9.

135 This could almost blindly refer to the fulfilment of public tasks and the (presumed) will of the majority, as long as fundamental rights – which protect the will of the minority – are obeyed.

whether the data must be an indispensable input for reaching the concrete purpose.[136] The requirement of indispensability should be generally upheld, though there can be problems when applying it to cases that concern the 'mere improvement' of existing services or if the data are available on the market but at too high costs. These issues are well known in competition law (*essential facilities doctrine*), which can inform the further development of access rules in this regard.[137]

Secondly, the economic features of data – especially economies of scale and scope – may lead to centralisation advantages, which the state (and not private actors) might be able to effectuate for the benefit of all by harvesting insights based on private data sources. This can correspond to the matter of completeness, especially if market forces lead to hold-up problems. To a certain extent, one can draw the analogy of a state as a powerful data platform. However, the state is obviously subject to different logics of function and control than the private sector.

Thirdly, the extent to which the state is trusted more than private individuals is relevant. Trust not only strengthens incentives for voluntary cooperation; it may also increase the social acceptance of legal obligations. As stated above, B2G data access is framed by the debate of trust in democratic decision-making vs. trust in the functioning of markets.[138] Depending on the political leadership, the public sector in particular may be regarded as a trustworthy partner, making companies more willing to provide data to it.[139]

III. Principle of holistic rules

According to the *principle of holistic rules*, it is elementary to consider the incentives of all actors who are involved or potentially affected. It requires an understanding of the relationship between causes and effects in their

136 See Früh (n. 9) 531.

137 See e.g. Inge Graef, *EU Competition Law, Data Protection and Online Platforms: Data as Essential Facility* (Wolters Kluwer 2016); Jacques Crémer, Yves-Alexandre Montjoye and Heike Schweitzer, 'Competition Policy for the digital era' (European Commission 2019) 98–107 <http://ec.europa.eu/competition/publications/reports/kd0419345enn.pdf> accessed 31 August 2020; Thomas Tombal, 'Economic Dependence and Data Access' (2020) 51 International Review of Intellectual Property and Competition Law 70.

138 See section B. I. above.

139 See Shkabatur (n. 17) 393.

entirety. By that means, the legislature can avoid the emergence of unintended side-effects (e.g. evoking new market failures through the introduction of dysfunctional rules). When designing mandatory access rules, it is therefore important to consider where the data come from (how did the private undertakings themselves get the data?) and what the state does with them (does the state further distribute the data to third parties or even to the public at large?).[140]

One should not overlook a natural tension which is inherent to the incentives of data sharing: on the one hand, the widest possible dissemination of data maximises the societal benefits; on the other hand, this opening up of data can reduce the willingness of a company to generate or collect data and to share them with the state. To take this a step further, it could reduce the willingness of third parties to provide data to the companies for their part if they know that the state will further distribute these data.[141] The constitutional assessment echoes this ambiguity: on the one hand, the further dissemination of data by the state increases the benefits for the common good and may thus justify legislative intervention; on the other hand, such data dissemination can also intensify the intervention into constitutionally protected positions of the company. These opposing effects are to be taken into account when assessing the proportionality of legal intervention.

Regulation could address this 'opening dilemma' by providing selective disclosure. This means that the state would only pass on data to third parties who would not harm the incentives for the generation or sourcing of these data. Appropriate legal and technical arrangements can safeguard these interests. What can be seen is that rules on the re-use of data can impact the incentives to provide data and may therefore undermine the design of access rules. Legal clarity on re-use is therefore an important prerequisite for effective and legitimate rights of government access to privately held data.

140 See also Martens and Duch-Brown (n. 13) 13, who rightly emphasise that one must look at the upstream data market and downstream services markets as an integrated entity.

141 On this hypothesis regarding personalised law Elkin-Koren and Gal (n. 9) 414–29.

IV. *Principle of responsibility*

When designing access rules, new rights correspond with new obligations. A state that accesses datasets of private undertakings must therefore be responsible to individuals, the undertaking and the public at large. Under this *principle of responsibility*, the state should protect private interests and safeguard the legitimate interests of companies.[142] This claim is reflected in the constitutional principles of purpose-relatedness and proportionality of interventions.[143] Mandatory access appears delicate, particularly regarding datasets that are critical for the competitiveness of the company and where their analysis by the state and disclosure to third persons could undermine the company's business model.[144] There is also the more general concern that different degrees of openness may lead to distortions of competition. Conflicts of objectives must be identified and addressed. It is therefore important that access rules refer to the protection of business secrets, privacy and competition as such and clarify the relationship between them.

Looking at society at large, mandatory access for the state can create an informational advantage and therefore increase arcane knowledge. To hold the state accountable and trustworthy, transparency obligations[145] should force the state to plausibly account for its access to and use of the privately held data.

V. *Principle of proximity*

Finally, the *principle of proximity* can inform the decision on where and how to introduce mandatory access rules. This principle acts as a rule of thumb which may increase the effectiveness of such access rules. The principle of proximity is very general – it means that thinking in terms of the proximity of relationships can be beneficial for the development of access rules. Close relationships may exist on many different grounds. For example, a legal obligation to provide information or transfer data between the state and the affected entities may already exist. Also, existing technical in-

142 See European Commission Communication COM(2018) 232 final (n. 4) 13; European Commission (n. 5) 46.

143 However, the exact delineation with regard to property protection remains unsettled; see with regard to Art. 17 EU Charter of Fundamental Rights Fabian Michl (n. 83).

144 See Martens and Duch-Brown (n. 13) 21.

145 See European Commission (n. 5) 46.

frastructure or know-how can constitute such proximity. Moreover, de facto close relationships can often be observed in the smart city context, where different actors share a common public space. To put it in other words: the proximity principle means that introducing mandatory access rules should follow a step-by-step approach with strategic foresight.

VI. Example: German 'Market Transparency Unit for Fuels'

A successful example of a 'new regulatory approach'[146] to mandatory access rules can illustrate these principles. In 2013, the 'Market Transparency Unit for Fuels' (MTS-K) was set up at the German competition authority *Bundeskartellamt* (BKartA). Its original purpose was to monitor fuel price formation and thereby facilitate the detection of cartel violations (*principle of justifying statehood*).[147] To this end, a mandatory access law[148] expanded the state's information base: it obliges all 14,500 petrol stations in Germany to report price changes for three types of fuel in real time to the BKartA.[149] This obligation is subject to a fine and is without compensation. The BKartA evaluates these data.[150] In addition, the law authorises the BKartA to pass on the real-time data to private consumer information services. To prevent abuse, these services need to register (*principle of responsibility*). Their 'fuel price apps' are intended to increase consumer sovereignty and to discipline the fuel market. Such apps existed before, but they were mostly based on user-generated data and were by far not as comprehensive, precise and up to date (*principle of justifying statehood*).

146 See also Matthias Knauff, 'Staatliche Benzinpreiskontrolle' (2012) Neue Juristische Wochenschrift 2408, 2412.

147 Bundesregierung, 'Entwurf eines Gesetzes zur Einrichtung einer Markttransparenzstelle für den Großhandel mit Strom und Gas' (21 June 2020) Bundestages-Drucksache 17/10060, 2 <https://dip21.bundestag.de/dip21/btd/17/100/1710060.pdf> accessed 31 August 2020.

148 More precisely, the model follows multi-level regulation: law, ordinance and general administrative ruling (which contains more detailed provisions on the technical design of data transmission).

149 Cf. Sec. 47k German Act against Restraints of Competition (GWB).

150 On the genesis see Bundesregierung, 'Bericht über die Ergebnisse der Arbeit der Markttransparenzstelle für Kraftstoffe und die hieraus gewonnenen Erfahrungen' (3 August 2018) Bundestags-Drucksache 19/3693, 3 <https://archive.org/details/ger-bt-drucksache-19-3693> accessed 31 August 2020.

To a considerable extent, the success of the MTS-K can be explained by its reliance on existing technical infrastructure.[151] It could therefore efficiently utilise already existing expertise and infrastructure (*principle of proximity*). Moreover, informing the consumer about the prices was deliberately left to private companies (*principle of holistic rules*) and thus to market forces.[152] There are currently about 50 private providers, some of them with innovative business models.[153] In fact, a market of service providers who have developed solutions for price reporting has also emerged.[154]

There is, however, a strict purpose limitation for re-using the data. The law only allows disclosure of the data to the Monopolies Commission and the Ministry of Economics (*principle of holistic rules*).[155] So far, third parties do not have a right to access these data, even though there have been further requests.[156] Yet in some cases the consumer information services have apparently passed on some data to third parties, which the MTS-K does not regard as objectionable as long as the data are used in accordance with the regulatory objectives.[157] It is currently debated whether at least statistical offices should be given access upon request.[158] In any case, the MTS-K has to regularly evaluate and report on the data collected and the effectiveness of the measure (*principle of responsibility*).

151 Costs could be significantly reduced by cooperating with the *Bundesanstalt für Straßenwesen*, where an IT system ('Mobilitäts Daten Marktplatz') already existed.

152 See Bundesregierung (n. 150) 25.

153 Ibid. 10.

154 Ibid. 7.

155 Sec. 47k(4) GWB.

156 See Bundesregierung (n. 150) 11–14, 24: all of them were rejected.

157 Ibid. 12.

158 See ibid. 24. However, see Gesetzentwurf der Bundesregierung – Entwurf eines Gesetzes zur Änderung des Gesetzes gegen Wettbewerbsbeschränkungen für ein fokussiertes, proaktives und digitales Wettbewerbsrecht 4.0 und anderer wettbewerbsrechtlicher Bestimmungen (GWB-Digitalisierungsgesetz) (9 September 2020) 15 <www.bmwi.de/Redaktion/DE/Downloads/Gesetz/gesetzentwurf-gwb-digitalisierungsgesetz.pdf?__blob=publicationFile&v=6> accessed 15 September 2020, which proposes to include an extension, according to which the MTS-K 'can also pass on location information, aggregated or older data to other authorities and offices of the direct federal and state administration for their legal tasks, but quantity data must always be highly aggregated'.

F. *Towards a horizontal B2G access framework?*

I. *Overview*

As outlined above,[159] this analysis has focused on overarching regulatory aspects without addressing sector-specific peculiarities. Yet the chapter has reflected on substantive common denominators by raising key questions and developing general principles which could inform the development of both sector-specific rules and horizontal rules. However, questions remain as to whether a horizontal access framework can indeed be beneficial and what its regulatory focus could be. This section explores whether and how legislatures should introduce a horizontal B2G data access framework. It focuses on mandatory rules; voluntary guidelines are not discussed.[160]

The policy debate on introducing a mandatory horizontal framework is just beginning. One can observe a certain reluctance because B2G data access is a sensitive issue. Even in France, where a horizontal framework has been considered since early on, such a general legal regime for 'data of general interest' was held to be 'neither desirable nor legally possible', taking the diversity of the sectors and data concerned into account.[161] Rather, a sectoral, case-by-case approach was recommended and followed.[162] However, the European Commission explicitly inquired into the need for a horizontal approach, and the B2G expert group has reinforced this concern by recommending the Commission to further 'explore the creation of an EU regulatory framework to enable and facilitate B2G data sharing for public interest purposes'.[163] The expert group considers mandatory rules, as it addresses cases in which 'private companies would be required to share the necessary data' and argues for obligations with regard to data that are scarce, unique, needed to ensure compliance or part of cross-border datasets.[164] Compared to the Member States, however, the Commission has a slightly different perspective that emphasises the internal market. The need for and potential design of a horizontal framework therefore depends on its supposed purpose.

159 See section C.IV. above.
160 See on the activity already (n. 47).
161 See Cytermann and others (n. 35) 2.
162 See Villani (n. 115) 28.
163 See European Commission (n. 5) 41.
164 Ibid. 43.

II. Purpose of a horizontal framework

Whether it is sensible to introduce mandatory horizontal rules on B2G data sharing and how to design such rules depends on the purpose of choosing a *horizontal* approach. A horizontal framework should amount to more than just a common denominator of sectoral rules – it should offer some additional advantages that stem from its horizontal nature. One should therefore be cautious about pleading for simply turning existing non-binding B2G access principles[165] into mandatory law without clarifying the actual purpose and extra benefit of introducing horizontal mandatory rules.

The European Commission sees the benefits of an EU-wide framework in the potential for cross-border harmonisation to ensure a consistent approach between the Member States and to decrease fragmentation.[166] However, one can argue that increasing coherency is a means rather than an end in itself. Given the different concepts and preferences for defining public interest, there is also no doubt that frameworks must provide a certain flexibility for the Member States,[167] a major issue being the scope of application: French law could not authorise French authorities to claim access to data of companies in Spain, even if the datasets could be of use for the French authorities. Only overarching, EU-wide rules could reasonably address such issues, but it remains doubtful whether the EU's competence reaches this far. The EU must either base its laws on special designated policy competences or on the general internal market competence.[168] To justify the latter, economic and market reasoning shift to the centre of attention.

Another purpose of a horizontal framework is cross-sectoral harmonisation. A minimum level of harmonisation could lead to more consistency in the development of sectoral rules and prevent fragmentation between sectors.[169] Again, consistency in itself seems rather a means than an end. It would be desirable for cross-sectoral harmonisation to serve substantive forms of improvement, such as decreased costs and higher efficiencies for B2G data sharing or more legal certainty. Cross-sectoral harmonisation

---

165 See n. 47.

166 See European Commission (n. 5) 36, also identifying an 'uncoordinated approach'.

167 Ibid. 41.

168 See for a debate of the scope of the internal market competence Annegret Engel, *The Choice of Legal Basis for Acts of the European Union* (Springer 2018) 20–27.

169 See European Commission (n. 5) 36, 41.

could also effectuate synergies, e.g. regarding the findability of the data needed.

Ultimately, a binding horizontal framework can serve the achievement of substantive goals. These goals are reflected in the substantive issues the framework would address (e.g. pricing, formats etc.). Therefore, the key question concerns which additional benefits a codification of horizontal obligations would provide. One can distinguish between market-related and non-market-related goals. Thus, substantive rules need to be tested against the question of why their horizontally binding quality would improve the status quo. While possible substantive issues will be further discussed in detail below,[170] some general characteristics of a potential horizontal framework are examined in the following.

III. Possible functions of a horizontal framework

Which functions can a horizontal B2G data access framework perform? Depending on its purpose, such a framework can fulfil different functions which are reflected in its design.

First, the framework can fulfil an enabling function. This means that it provides a minimum standard of rules, which should enable Member States to 'make data sharing mandatory for purposes that are particularly relevant to their national or local priorities'.[171] However, it is already the case that the Member States can themselves introduce mandatory rules on sharing if they prefer to. The above-mentioned cross-border cases are an exception. Also, enabling frameworks appear relevant for EU sectoral policies and for the Member States themselves with regard to any national access rules. The enabling function of frameworks is also relevant in terms of the hierarchy of rules. In practice, access regimes often stretch over several regulatory levels. Especially technical details are mostly found in sub-legal regulations.[172]

---

170 See section F.IV. below.

171 European Commission (n. 5) 44.

172 See INSPIRE Directive and ITS Directive for examples, where details are addressed in delegated acts and implementing decisions. The same applies to financial data (see Directive (EU) 2015/2366 of the European Parliament and of the Council of 25 November 2015 on payment services in the internal market [2015] OJ L337/35) and vehicle repair information (see Directive (EC) 715/2007 of the European Parliament and of the Council of 20 June 2007 on type approval of motor vehicles with respect to emissions from light passenger and commercial

Second, a horizontal framework could harmonise procedures rather than substance. For example, France discussed drawing up a common framework which included procedural rules that were not meant to be necessarily binding for the sectors.[173] One could also think about setting up binding procedures to ensure transparency and broad engagement for the further development of rules. This is particularly relevant for procedures which define the public interest and designate the respective purposes and datasets.

Third, a horizontal framework could address interfaces with other legal regimes. Alternatively, the legislature could amend other horizontal regimes by systematically including or modifying rules on B2G data sharing. For example, competition law could include indemnity or safe harbour[174] provisions for violations without creating generic access rights. Furthermore, the platform regulation[175] could accommodate respective issues of B2G data sharing.

Fourth, an important function of an EU horizontal framework lies in the provision of default rules from which Member States can deviate. Actually, such optional regulation is inherent to any EU rules that pose minimum and not full harmonisation.[176] Rather, default rules can provide 'harmonised flexibility' by specifying a bundle of concrete regulatory options.[177] If Member States must 'opt in' to these rules, the rules serve mere standardisation purposes and can provide legal certainty and lower transaction costs. 'Opt out' rules may provide additional benefits because they could – depending on the procedure[178] – pressure Member States to justify their deviation from the default. Should the horizontal framework require

---

vehicles (Euro 5 and Euro 6) and on access to vehicle repair and maintenance information [2007] OJ L171/1).

173 See Cytermann and others (n. 35) 3.

174 See Früh (n. 9) 528.

175 See already the EU P2B Regulation (n. 100); see also Communication from the Commission of 19 February 2020 to the European Parliament, the Council, the European Economic and Social Committee and the Committee of the Regions – Shaping Europe's digital future (Communication) COM (2020) 67 final, 10 on plans for a 'Digital Services Act' to address large platforms with ex ante regulation.

176 See e.g. Art. 1 PSI Directive (n. 25), according to which the 'Directive establishes a set of minimum rules'.

177 See Art. 4 Multimodal Travel Information Regulation (n. 104), which mandates access to static travel and traffic data, while Art. 5 standardises modalities only '[w]here the Member States decide to provide the dynamic travel and traffic data'.

178 One could consider a 'comply or explain' mechanism.

that substantive requirements must be met for opting out, such rules can be mandatory in effect. In any case, a horizontal framework would have to clearly name the criteria and procedures according to which Member States can exercise the provided options. Such 'harmonised flexibility' can also concern the (co-)existence of sector-specific measures. Depending on which substantive issues the horizontal framework addresses, it would also need to explicitly clarify its relationship to sector-specific regimes.[179]

IV. Substantive issues for a horizontal framework

When it comes to substantive matters that a horizontal framework could address, one can think of the horizontal commonalities of all sectors and overarching issues.[180] Considering the legislative competence of the EU, a meta question is how these issues relate to the internal market. Not all issues can be directly framed as a market problem, but a wider perspective can include consequences for competition, at least if the framework addresses its core parameters (like price and quality).

One substantive issue that a horizontal framework could address concerns the point of reference for defining the accessible data.[181] Here, the horizontal framework would not address datasets regarding their particular information content but would outline rather general criteria as reference points for defining the data which are subject to mandatory access. The regulatory approach can follow three different, more abstract rationales. First, the framework could specify ways of determining and defining the public interest that would justify access.[182] Obviously, 'social benefit' would provide an overly broad category that would call for refinement. An example is the recast PSI Directive, which outlines more concrete criteria to assess 'high-value datasets'.[183] The framework could specify measures for assessment, e.g. the likelihood and amount of benefits and costs, the urgency, the harm of not using the data and other possibilities of accessing

179 Particularly to eliminate any ambiguity about the relationships of lex specialis and lex posterior.

180 See Cytermann and others (n. 35) 3.

181 This implies that datasets themselves are not enumerated, which could then be done in delegated or implementing acts of the EU or left to the Member States.

182 See European Commission (n. 5) 44, mentioning relevant criteria for assessing whether data sharing should be required for a given use case.

183 See Arts 13–16 PSI Directive (n. 25).

the needed data.[184] Second, the framework could refer to the competitive relevance for defining the data concerned. This approach would emphasise the bottleneck function of particular datasets (single-source data). One would have to further define requirements for access to such data, e.g. whether their indispensability is decisive. Much can be borrowed from competition analysis.[185] Third, horizontal reference points can be of a rather technical nature. This is the case if the framework addresses data that are 'stored in databases'[186] or if it refers to the modalities of their creation (e.g. when collection takes place in public space or when using state infrastructure[187]).

Another major issue that horizontal rules could address is compensation (i.e. pricing).[188] Horizontal rules can set out under which circumstances no compensation is required. In any case, they must take the incentives of the private undertakings into account. The framework could also outline pricing standards, means of calculating cost and transparency rules. Making a choice between the concrete available approaches to compensation (as mentioned above)[189] depends on the goals and the balancing of interests: competition-oriented approaches will take the market structure into account and address the problem of excessive (monopoly) pricing.[190] At the same time, the benefits of introducing a marginal cost principle can lie in imposing a duty to justify pricing in general and to bring pricing practices under legal scrutiny before the courts. An additional issue is price discrimination, which a horizontal framework could address through a general provision that undertakings must grant access to the state on preferential conditions.[191]

The horizontal framework can address further issues, such as formats, technical issues and findability (i.e. 'information about the information'[192]). Furthermore, a horizontal framework can be used to absorb negative consequences, e.g. by harmonising liability rules which address the risk of reducing incentives to collect data, which can lead to an undersup-

184 See European Commission (n. 5) 44.
185 See n. 137.
186 Under the meaning of Directive 96/9/EC of the European Parliament and of the Council of 11 March 1996 on the legal protection of databases [1996] OJ L77/20.
187 See Früh (n. 9) 526.
188 See the focus of Martens and Duch-Brown (n. 13) 12–16.
189 See section D.VI.
190 See Martens and Duch-Brown (n. 13) 13.
191 See European Commission (n. 5) 39.
192 This resembles Art. 9 PSI Directive (n. 25) on practical arrangements which aim to improve findability of the information.

ply.[193] The horizontal framework could also clarify the relationship between statutory access rules and contracts. In fact, studies have revealed that some markets for B2G data sharing are about to evolve.[194] When following a strict principle of subsidiarity, the horizontal framework could even reverse the logic and define in which cases access to datasets may *not* be mandated.

V. PSI Directive as a model?

The potential need for EU-wide horizontal rules that address B2G sharing calls to mind the PSI Directive. Can the PSI Directive serve as a model for designing horizontal B2G access rules?[195] The PSI Directive of 2003, amended in 2013 and recast in 2019,[196] was the first horizontal framework that regulated data re-use. Based on the notion that everyone should benefit from collectively financed goods,[197] the Directive regulates the re-use of public sector information (e.g. weather data, registries, court decisions etc.).[198] The Directive aims to stimulate the development of digital innovation and to foster transparency.[199] At the same time, it seeks to prevent the distortion of competition in the internal market.[200] For this purpose, the PSI Directive contains rules (e.g. on charging, formats, conditions and exclusivity) that apply to the re-use of information of public sector bodies

193 See Früh (n. 9) 525.

194 See Martens and Duch-Brown (n. 13) 10–11.

195 This question is different from the issue of whether the PSI Directive applies to data that originally came into the domain of the state via the B2G access right (see principle of holistic rules, section E.III. above).

196 After its recast, the PSI Directive is often also referred to as 'Open Data Directive'.

197 While some of their creation is financed by fees or charges, most of them are tax-funded.

198 The recast of 2019 includes public undertakings within the scope of the PSI Directive; see in detail Heiko Richter, 'Exposing the public interest dimension of the digital single market: Public undertakings as a model for regulating data sharing' (2020) Max Planck Institute for Innovation and Competition Research Paper No. 20–03 <https://papers.ssrn.com/sol3/papers.cfm?abstract_id=3565762> accessed 31 August 2020.

199 See Recital 3, 13 PSI Directive (n. 25).

200 See Recital 7 PSI Directive (n. 25). On this issue, see Björn Lundqvist, 'Turning Government Data Into Gold: The Interface Between EU Competition Law and the Public Sector Information Directive' (2013) 44 International Review of Intellectual Property and Competition Law 79.

across the board. It provides a minimum level of harmonisation: national, re-use-friendlier rules prevail.[201]

However, framing the issue of B2G government access as 'PSI in reverse' appears misleading and should be avoided because there are major functional and conceptual differences between the subject matter of the PSI Directive and the challenges facing B2G data access. The PSI Directive concerns individual rights against the state, while B2G data access refers to the opposite situation of the state claiming access against private undertakings. From a legal point of view, many more restrictions apply due to the impairment of fundamental rights. This is reflected in the significance of purpose limitation, which is a seminal principle and a starting point for the constitutionality of B2G data access. In contrast, the PSI Directive aims at the opposite goal of unrestricted re-use of data.[202] Moreover, the PSI Directive follows competition reasoning and aims to foster the development of markets, which justifies its reliance on the internal market competence. Finally (and related to the issue of legislative competence[203]), the PSI Directive only regulates re-use of, not access to data. In contrast, the discussion about B2G data sharing concerns mandatory access rights and the corresponding regulatory design. Given all these differences, the PSI Directive cannot serve as a blueprint for an EU-wide mandatory framework for B2G data sharing.

This does not imply, however, that the PSI Directive lacks any informative value. In fact, the Directive can serve as inspiration for the design of rules, as it contains established definitions e.g. on the bodies concerned and on formats.[204] Especially with regard to pricing, the PSI has a well-refined set of rules, the product of long-standing discussions on different pricing models.[205] This can inform B2G access as well.[206] Yet one has to acknowledge the diverging rationale on which the pricing rules of the PSI Directive are based. Either they presume tax-financed information or –

201 E.g. lower charges and less restrictive licensing terms; see Recital 18 PSI Directive (n. 25).

202 This reflects the very idea of 'open data', which is echoed in Arts 3, 8 PSI Directive (n. 25): purpose limitations are deemed restrictions of re-use which need justification.

203 In detail Richter (n. 198).

204 E.g. public sector bodies according to Art. 2(1) and formats according to Art. 2(13), (14), (15) PSI Directive (n. 25).

205 See Art. 6 PSI Directive (n. 25).

206 Especially when it comes to pricing regulation, Martens and Duch-Brown (n. 13) 14 draw analogies to the PSI Directive; see also European Commission (n. 5) 39, which refers to the pricing models of the PSI Directive.

even if they allow for full cost-recovery – refer to the financing of the public sector body from a purely fiscal perspective, but do not account for the incentives to create the information.[207] In contrast, pricing rules for B2G access must take the incentives of *private* actors to innovate into account. Therefore, one should be careful about transplanting PSI rules on charging into the B2G data access context without thorough reflection.

An innovative part of the recast PSI Directive of 2019 concerns the special rules on high-value datasets.[208] The model character of the procedure and the general criteria according to which datasets and sharing conditions are to be determined were already highlighted above.[209] Another important implication of the PSI Directive's focus on re-use relates to the potential chilling effects of access rights. This means that overly strict re-use rules (i.e. a standardisation regime) can hamper data access if the entities which hold the data or the national legislature can choose whether to submit particular information to this horizontal standardisation regime.[210] The legislature must consider this lesson if it intends to standardise only the conditions for B2G data without mandating access as such. Finally, the PSI Directive points to the relevance of the intersection with database law,[211] an important interface that runs the risk of being overlooked. This, among other things, will be further discussed in the following.

VI. Conclusion

In conclusion, this analysis abstains from making a concrete proposal for EU-wide mandatory B2G access regulation. It rather points to the challenge of concisely identifying the purpose of horizontal mandatory frameworks while emphasising the functions of such frameworks and how to shape the rules appropriately. The analysis has highlighted the difficulties and challenges that face the concrete design of legitimate and effective hor-

207 Recital 36 PSI Directive (n. 25) justifies the exemptions with 'the necessity of not hindering the normal running of public sector bodies'.

208 See Arts 13–16 PSI Directive (n. 25).

209 See sections D.V. and D.VI. above.

210 Further discussed in Richter (n. 198).

211 See Art. 1(6) PSI Directive (n. 25). For background see Estelle Derclaye, 'Does the Directive on the Re-use of Public Sector Information affect the State's database sui generis right?' in Jens Gaster, Erich Schweighofer and Peter Sint (eds), *Knowledge rights – Legal, societal and related technological aspects* (Österreichische Computer Gesellschaft 2008) 137.

izontal rules. While the PSI Directive cannot serve as a blueprint, it does offer some lessons. Its implications not only concern EU-wide regulation but can also inform national horizontal B2G access rules, which the Member States themselves are free to introduce in future.

G. *Recommendations for concrete reforms*

I. *Reaching beyond access rules*

In the following, some recommendations for concrete legislative reforms are made which concern government access to the data of private undertakings. These recommendations reach beyond the concrete design of access rules. Rather, they address existing legal regimes which are seen as crucial in further developing mandatory access rules. By addressing them, legislatures can set the course for an effective implementation of access rules in future – whether of a horizontal or sector-specific nature.

II. *Reform laws on official statistics*

Reforms regarding government access to data are desirable in official statistics laws. Statistical obligations concern the transfer of information to the state by their very nature, and there is a long-standing tradition for such obligations in the Member States. Statistical offices appear well positioned to implement new forms of data access and can serve as a model: they already have infrastructure and high competence in data analysis and are particularly experienced in handling personal data. In addition, statistical offices are experienced in further distributing information and can therefore be seen as 'key information providers'[212] in a big-data world. The policy discussion regarding access to new data sources for statistical offices has advanced further than in other domains.[213] In future, this area may be perceived and developed as an 'experimental ground' for B2G data access.

What are the relevant areas of application? One can think of a wide range, e.g. statistics on population movements, price development, the in-

212 Peter Struijs, Barteld Braaksma and Piet J.H. Daas, 'Official statistics and Big Data' (2014) 1(1) Big Data & Society 1; on trust in statistical offices Shkabatur (n. 17) 394.

213 See European Commission Communication COM (2018) 232 final 12 (n. 4) 14.

ternet economy, energy, transport etc. The creation of such statistics can be enabled and improved by access to privately held data sources, e.g. to mobile phone data, satellite images, social media data, cash register scanners, traffic sensors and smart electricity meters.[214] Expectations for the social benefits are high[215] because access to privately held data promises to foster efficiency. It can reduce costs for the statistical offices – e.g. if they can use data from telecommunications providers to quantify commuter movements instead of conducting complex individual surveys.[216] It can also reduce costs on the side of businesses – e.g. when fulfilling their reporting obligations.[217] Moreover, data access can improve the generic quality of official statistics – e.g. through quicker delivery, up-to-dateness, higher reliability, data quality and granularity and through gathering new insights when combining new datasets with administrative data.[218]

About a decade ago, a discussion developed on voluntary cooperation between statistical offices and private data providers.[219] Yet the authorities

---

214 For examples see UN Statistics Division, 'Supplementing the United Nations Fundamental Principles of Official Statistics: Implementation Guidelines' (Background Document of 5–8 March 2019) <https://unstats.un.org/unsd/statcom/50th-session/documents/BG-Item3b-FPOS-Implementation-guidelines-E.pdf> accessed 31 August 2020, 22–25; Lara Wiengarten and Markus Zwick, 'Neue digitale Daten in der amtlichen Statistik' (2017) 5 WISTA 19, 26; Bund-Länder-Arbeitsgruppe zur Reduzierung von Statistikpflichten, 'Abschlussbericht der ressortübergreifenden Bund-Länder-Arbeitsgruppe zur Reduzierung von Statistikpflichten' (2019) 16 <www.bmwi.de/Redaktion/DE/Downloads/A/abschlussbericht-reduzierung-von-statistikpflichten.html> accessed 31 August 2020.

215 UN Statistics Division (n. 214) 18.

216 See Statistisches Bundesamt, 'Digitale Agenda des Statistischen Bundesamts' (Destatis 2019) 16 <www.destatis.de/DE/Service/OpenData/Publikationen/digitale-agenda.pdf?_blob=publicationFile> accessed 31 August 2020; on questionnaires see European Commission Communication COM (2018) 232 final (n. 4) 12.

217 See European Commission Communication COM(2017) 9 final (n. 45) 14; Statistischer Beirat, 'Fortentwicklung der amtlichen Statistik: Empfehlungen des Statistischen Beirats für die Jahre 2018 bis 2022' (Destatis 2018) 9 <www.destatis.de/DE/Ueber-uns/Leitung-Organisation/Statistischer-Beirat/fortentwicklung-nov-2018-2022-teil3.pdf> accessed 30 April 2020.

218 Statistischer Beirat (n. 217) 9–10; National Academies of Sciences, Engineering, and Medicine, *Innovations in Federal Statistics: Combining Data Sources While Protecting Privacy* (The National Academies Press 2017) 64; Wiengarten and Zwick (n. 214) 27; Früh (n. 9) 526; European Commission Communication COM (2018) 232 final (n. 4) 12.

219 On the background UN Statistics Division (n. 214); Wiengarten and Zwick (n. 214) 22; Struijs, Braaksma and Daas (n. 212) 3–4; on different forms of cooperation National Academies of Sciences, Engineering, and Medicine (n. 218) 65–66.

lacked a legal basis for mandatory access.[220] Therefore, the trend towards legal standardisation of access rights does not come as a surprise.[221] In 2016, France enacted a general clause allowing access for the government.[222] Details must be regulated on the basis of a decision by the minister, a consultation of the National Council for Statistical Information and a feasibility study.[223] One year later, the UK enacted a law which authorises statistical offices to instruct private companies to submit data for statistical purposes.[224] In contrast, such developments are largely on hold in Germany,[225] where so far only price statistics have been addressed by new rules on access to scanner data from supermarket checkouts.[226]

In future, more legislation can be expected. Yet policymakers and legislators face some challenges, for instance in providing high quality and accurateness of statistical data while protecting private interests, namely personal data and business secrets.[227] Another issue is compensation for the associated costs for private businesses. Traditionally, statistics laws do not grant compensation – the French and U.K. legislation are in line with that. Finally, the laws on statistics could also be revised to introduce provisions through which statistical offices could further share the data provided to them (e.g. with the scientific community).[228]

---

220 See UN Statistics Division (n. 214) 18.

221 For a plea see European Statistical System, 'Position paper on privately held data which are of public interest' (European Commission 2017) <https://ec.europa.eu/eurostat/documents/7330775/8463599/ESS+Position+Paper+on+Access+to+privately+held+data+final+-+Nov+2017.pdf> accessed 31 August 2020.

222 See Art. 19 of LOI n° 2016–1321 pour une République numérique of 7 October 2016.

223 Ibid.

224 See Sec. 80 Digital Economy Act (2017), which modified Sec. 45D Statistics and Registration Service Act 2007.

225 See Statistisches Bundesamt (n. 216) 24 point B10.

226 See Act amending the Act on price statistics of 10 December 2019, Art. 1, Nos 7–8. See also Früh (n. 9) 528 on similar projects in France, Italy, the Netherlands and Poland. See for the harmonisation on the EU level Parliament and Council Regulation (EU) 2016/792 of 11 May 2016 on harmonised indices of consumer prices and the house price index, and repealing Council Regulation (EC) No 2494/95 [2016] OJ L135/11.

227 See UN Statistics Division (n. 214) 18; National Academies of Sciences, Engineering, and Medicine (n. 218) 67; Statistischer Beirat (n. 217) 10.

228 See Statistischer Beirat (n. 217) 11.

III. Modify database protection

The sui generis protection for databases (Articles 7–11 Directive 96/9/EC) may set an – often overlooked – barrier to the future introduction and design of B2G access rules.[229] It is unclear which (technical) forms of data access affect database protection and what the scope of protection is.[230] Therefore, it appears likely that companies that own databases will claim more protection if the state gets mandatory access but does not provide compensation.[231] Even if national legislatures want to provide compensation (e.g. by including respective provisions on compulsory licensing in an access law), there are good reasons to argue that the Database Directive does not allow this, because its exhaustive list of limitations does not cover this case. Especially the limitations for 'public security or for the purposes of an administrative or judicial procedure'[232] often do not help the state in this respect.

In fact, compensation is an issue that the access rules themselves should cover.[233] To enable this, the EU legislature should introduce an opening clause into the EU Database Directive according to which special access rules of the Member States could take precedence over database protection.[234] Otherwise, due to its major uncertainties, the sui generis database right runs the risk of blocking mandatory rules on government access to the data held by private undertakings.

---

229 See general remarks in Cytermann and others (n. 35) 74–75.

230 This concerns definitions, the threshold for substantiality, protected investments etc.; see Josef Drexl, 'Data Access and Control in the Era of Connected Devices – Study on behalf of BEUC' (BEUC 2018) 67–85 <www.beuc.eu/publications/beuc-x-2018-121_data_access_and_control_in_the_area_of_connected_devices.pdf> accessed 31 August 2020; Matthias Leistner, 'Big Data and the EU Database Directive 96/9/EC: Current Law and Potential for Reform' in Sebastian Lohsse, Reiner Schulze and Dirk Staudenmayer (eds), *Trading Data in the Digital Economy* (Hart and Nomos 2017) 27. See also European Commission Staff Working Document, 'Evaluation report of the European Commission on the Database Directive 96/9/EC of 25 April 2018' SWD(2018) 147 final.

231 In general Drexl (n. 230) 82, but not referring to the state in particular.

232 See Art. 9(c) Database Directive (n. 186).

233 Drexl (n. 230) 82.

234 See in general Drexl (n. 230) 83.

IV. Coordinate advancement of re-use law

The principle of holistic rules has highlighted the significance of the relationship between B2G access rules and rules on data re-use. In many instances, fundamental rights prevent the state from further disseminating the data for re-use. However, in other cases wide re-use is legitimate and welfare-enhancing. In order to provide legal certainty and regulatory effectiveness, the interface between access and re-use regimes must therefore be clearly defined.[235] For this purpose, re-use regulation could be further developed in a forward-looking manner and made compatible with data access regimes.

In particular, re-use rules (i.e. the PSI Directive and respective national implementing acts) could regulate 'standard scenarios' which address different degrees of re-usability. Access regimes – whether on the EU level or national – could then explicitly refer to the adequate re-use scenario. Such reforms can currently be observed in Australia,[236] where a legislative proposal distinguishes between three scenarios: 'closed data', 'shared data' and 'open data release'.[237] Moreover, the proposal diligently combines procedures and technical infrastructure. Such an approach could be further refined and adapted in the frame of the next reform of the PSI Directive.[238]

V. Strengthen subjective access rights

Finally, one should keep in mind that B2G data access concerns a politically highly sensitive area. It can never be ruled out that the state will misuse data to wield its power over society. New technical possibilities enable selective (i.e. manipulative) data provision practices by the state.[239] Access

235 Further discussed in Richter (n. 198).

236 See on the current project the discussion paper of the Australian Government, 'Data Sharing and Release – Legislative Reforms' (Data Commissioner 2019) <www.datacommissioner.gov.au/sites/default/files/2019-09/Data%20Sharing%20and%20Release%20Legislative%20Reforms%20Discussion%20Paper%20-%20Accessibility.pdf> accessed 31 August 2020.

237 Ibid. 3.

238 According to Art. 18 PSI Directive (n. 25), the Commission shall carry out its evaluation not sooner than 17 July 2025.

239 See Heiko Richter, 'Informationen der öffentlichen Hand als Rohstoff für den Datenjournalismus: Rechtliche Gestaltungsprinzipien zum Erhalt der Meinungsvielfalt' (2019) 83 UFITA – Archiv für Medienrecht und Medienwissenschaft 196.

rules in favour of the state generally expand its data stock, but it is always uncertain who is going to rule over them in future. Therefore, it is paramount to equally empower society as a counterbalance. This can be achieved by strengthening citizens' subjective rights to access information of the state.[240] This is the aim of the Tromsø Convention,[241] which should therefore be signed, ratified and implemented in all Member States. The significance of freedom of information acts may have been stressed early on,[242] but in view of the advancement of technical and societal development, this claim takes on much greater significance nowadays.

H. Outlook

This chapter has pointed out that a systematic establishment of rights for government access to the data of private companies is still in its infancy. It gives guidance on how to deepen the discussion and design regulatory concepts. While the further development of access rules will mainly take place on a sectoral basis, horizontal frameworks may provide benefits if they are conceptualised and designed thoroughly. This chapter makes suggestions for concrete reforms. It discusses how a targeted and coherent bundle of measures taken by the EU and its Member States can ensure that laws and policies on data access will effectuate and combine the common good and the development of individual freedom in the best way possible.

This chapter's introduction stated that the data access debate lies at the core of a general discussion on the state's role in a data-based society. When looking at further initiatives, one should therefore keep in mind that EU policies on B2G data access affect much more than just data flows across the internal market. They rebalance public and private powers. For this very reason, the state must not neglect its active role in protecting the functional conditions for a democratic society under the rule of law.

---

240 On the significance of subjective rights, see ibid. 214 (n. 116 with further references), 223.

241 Council of Europe Convention on Access to Official Documents of 18 June 2009, Tromsø, Council of Europe Treaty Series (CETS), No. 205.

242 For background see Dacian C. Dragos, Polonca Kovač and Albert T. Marseille (eds), *The Laws of Transparency in Action* (Palgrave Macmillan 2019); on initiatives in Germany Schoch (n. 105) Einleitung paras 295–97.

Contributors

Josef Drexl
Professor, Dr. jur., LL.M. (UC Berkeley), Director of the Max Planck Institute for Innovation and Competition in Munich, Honorary Professor of the Faculty of Law of the University of Munich.

Thomas Fetzer
Prof. Dr. jur., LL.M. (Vanderbilt), Professor at the University of Mannheim, Chair of Public Law, Regulatory Law and Tax Law.

Michael Grünberger
Prof. Dr. jur., LL.M. (NYU), University of Bayreuth.

Jörg Hoffmann
Research Fellow, Max Planck Institute for Innovation and Competition, Munich.

Ruth Janal
Prof. Dr. jur. Ruth, LL.M. (New South Wales), Professor of Civil Law, IP Law and Economic Law at the University of Bayreuth.

Wolfgang Kerber
Professor of Economics, Dr. rer. pol., Marburg Centre for Institutional Economics (MACIE), School of Business & Economics, University of Marburg, Germany.

Christine Lambrecht
Federal Minister of Justice and Consumer Protection, Member of the german Bundestag.

Matthias Leistner
Prof. Dr. iur., LL.M. (Cambridge), Chair of Private Law and Intellectual Property Law, with Information and IT Law (GRUR Chair), LMU Munich.

Bertin Martens
Ph.D. (Economics), Senior Economist, Digital Economy Unit at the Joint Research Centre (Seville) of the European Commission.

Axel Metzger
Prof. Dr., LL.M. (Harvard), Professor at the Humboldt-Universität zu Berlin, Chair for Private Law and Intellectual Property.

Christian Reimsbach-Kounatze
Dipl.-Inform.Wirt, Information Economist and Policy Analyst at the Directorate for Science, Technology and Innovation (DSTI) of the Organisation for Economic Co-operation and Development (OECD).

Heiko Richter
Dr. iur., LL.M. (Columbia), Senior Research Fellow, Max Planck Institute for Innovation and Competition, Munich.

Heike Schweitzer
Prof. Dr. jur., LL.M. (Yale), Professor at the Humboldt-Universität zu Berlin, Chair for Private Law and Competition Law and Economics.

Louisa Specht-Riemenschneider
Prof. Dr., Professor of law at the University of Bonn, Chair for Civil Law, Information and Data Law.

Indra Spiecker genannt Doehmann
Prof. Dr. jur., LL.M. (Georgetown), Professor at Goethe University in Frankfurt/Main, Chair in Administrative and Constitutional Law, Information Law, Environmental Law and Legal Theory; Director Data Protection Research Institute.

Robert Welker
Research fellow at the faculty of law at Humboldt Universität zu Berlin.